GENEALOGICAL RESOURCES

IN THE

NEW YORK METROPOLITAN AREA

Edited by Estelle M. Guzik

Compiled and published by the

Jewish Genealogical Society, Inc.

P.O. Box 6398

New York, NY 10128

1989

Printed in the United States of America

Second Printing

The paper used in this publication meets the minimum requirements
of American National Standard for Information Sciences--
Permanence of Paper for Printed Library Materials, ANSI Z39.48-1984.

The text was prepared using Bitstream® Dutch typeface.

Library of Congress Cataloging-in-Publication Data

Genealogical resources in the New York metropolitan area /
edited by Estelle M. Guzik.
　　　　　　　p.　　　　　cm.
Includes index.
ISBN 0-9621863-0-9
　　1. New York Metropolitan Area--Genealogy--
Archival resources--New York Metropolitan Area--
Directories. 2. Jews--Genealogy--Archival resources--
New York Metropolitan area--Directories. I. Guzik,
Estelle M. II. Jewish Genealogical Society (New York,
N.Y.)
Z5313.U6.N523   1989
[F128.25]
929'.37471--dc19　　　　　　　　　　89-1729
　　　　　　　　　　　　　　　　　CIP

CONTENTS

NATIONAL ARCHIVES AND RECORDS ADMINISTRATION

FOREWORD

The Jewish Genealogical Society (JGS) was founded in 1977 and has grown into an organization of more than 500 members. Thirty-five similar groups have been established in other cities around the world.

Based in New York City, the JGS offers monthly programs of interest to beginners and experts; publishes a quarterly newsletter, *Dorot*; sponsors an annual Beginners' Workshop; arranges visits to local repositories; and maintains the computerized Jewish Genealogical Family Finder.

The first summer conference for Jewish genealogists in 1981 was sponsored by the JGS in New York. Following this precedent, there have been seven national summer seminars and two international seminars on Jewish genealogy.

The JGS is an activist organization. In addition to contributing funds enabling several repositories to purchase genealogical materials, the JGS was instrumental in the transfer of historic Health Department marriage records to the New York City Municipal Archives -- thereby making them accessible to all researchers.

The JGS is open to people of all backgrounds. Membership includes a subscription to *Dorot*. For information, write to Jewish Genealogical Society, Inc., P. O. Box 6398, New York, NY 10128.

The JGS is proud to publish this new, comprehensive guide to research facilities in and around New York. *Genealogical Resources in the New York Metropolitan Area* serves not only Jewish genealogists, but anyone doing research in the metropolitan area. This book would not exist without the remarkable contribution of its editor, Estelle M. Guzik.

Estelle, a longtime JGS member and officer, edited *Resources for Jewish Genealogy in the New York Area* for the Fifth Summer Seminar on Jewish Genealogy in 1985. We are pleased that she agreed to prepare for publication a revised and enlarged book that could be distributed widely.

She began work on her own family history in 1970, when she realized she did not know the names of aunts, uncles and cousins lost in the Holocaust. Estelle has a B.A. in political science from Brooklyn College and a master's degree in urban planning from Hunter College. She currently works for the U.S. Department of Housing and Urban Development as director of compliance, and was formerly staff director to the Federal Regional Council in New York.

In addition to her fulltime career responsibilities, Estelle's commitment to seeing this project through to completion meant two years and thousands of hours of writing and editing the material through several drafts, as well as hundreds of phone calls and visits to the facilities described in this book. She was assisted by many JGS members who helped make possible the publication of this volume, *Genealogical Resources in the New York Metropolitan Area*.

The Jewish Genealogical Society and researchers everywhere owe an enormous debt of gratitude to Estelle. On behalf of all of these people: Thank you, Estelle.

Steven W. Siegel
President
Jewish Genealogical Society

INTRODUCTION

Genealogical Resources in the New York Metropolitan Area had its genesis as a looseleaf book, *Resources for Jewish Genealogy in the New York Area,* compiled for participants in the Fifth Summer Seminar of the Jewish Genealogical Society (JGS) in 1985. That document, based on the collective knowledge of 25 members of the JGS, and describing 50 facilities, received great attention from the genealogical community. The copies not distributed at the Seminar were in great demand, and it was clear that the material was of interest to libraries, archives and genealogists nationwide.

In the process of preparing the current book, the 1985 manuscript has more than doubled in size to include 104 facilities including archives, libraries and agencies in the New York metropolitan area. With the help of 56 JGS members, we uncovered new resources and finding aids never before used by genealogists. Our discussions with facility directors helped many of them focus on how they can better serve genealogical researchers.

GEOGRAPHIC AREAS COVERED: The majority of the facilities covered are in New York City. Six suburban counties in New York State and New Jersey are included: Nassau, Suffolk and Westchester in New York, and Bergen, Essex and Hudson in New Jersey. Readers will find that a knowledge of the basic records maintained by public agencies in these counties of New York and New Jersey will help them in locating records in other counties as well.

Because of the highly centralized nature of recordkeeping in New Jersey, key agencies in Trenton, the State's capital, are included. Also included are the New York State Archives, Library and Health Department located in Albany, each of which has significant records concerning New York metropolitan area residents.

Historical differences in county/borough boundaries are noted throughout the text. These can affect the location of records. For example, Nassau County was part of Queens until 1899. Thus, a search for pre-1899 marriage or property records must be made in Queens County records for residents of what later became Nassau County.

Counties are subdivisions of the State in New York and New Jersey. Boroughs are subdivisions of New York City. Within New York City, county and borough boundaries are identical but three have different county/borough names: New York/Manhattan, Kings/Brooklyn and Richmond/Staten Island. These differences are noted in the text. To reduce confusion, both names are used.

ORGANIZATION: The material is organized geographically so that researchers can coordinate their visits to facilities within a particular area. Borough or county offices in New York City are grouped with other public and private institutions by borough, rather than by offices having similar functions. For example, the City Clerk's Office has five borough offices--in Manhattan, Bronx, Brooklyn, Queens and Staten Island. Each office is found under the county/borough subheading.

There are two exceptions to this format: The Family History Centers (LDS) in New York and New Jersey are grouped together in one section. Each has the same indexes and has access to the same material in Salt Lake City. Furthermore, many records described throughout this book have been microfilmed by the Family History Library and are available at Family History Centers around the world.

The second exception is the National Archives, Northeast Region, which is planning to move to lower Manhattan from its current location in Bayonne (Hudson County), New Jersey. The final site has not been selected.

INFORMATION PROVIDED: For each facility we provide the name and title of the facility director, address (and mail address when different), telephone number, cross streets, closest public transportation, travel directions, hours of operation, description of resources, finding aids, description of facility, fees/copies and restrictions on use.

Generally, the first subway (or train) listed under "Closest Public Transportation" is closest to the facility. Directions are given for transportation requiring the shortest walk from the subway/train station or bus stop.

Under "Description of Resources," we have attempted to include the geographic scope and time span of each record group. Records relating to all ethnic/religious groups are included. In a given repository, unique collections of Jewish records as well as collections of other ethnic/racial groups are listed.

A detailed description of the available indexes is included under "Finding Aids." Where a record group or finding aid also is available at other facilities, this is noted. If this other facility is covered in the book, its name is in small capital letters.

Under "Description of Facility," readers will learn the number of seats, staff, microfilm readers/printers, photocopy machines, etc. and whether researchers have direct access to records and books. "Fees/Copies" describes the cost of using the facility and of copying materials.

Limitations on the use of records or advance order requirements are noted under "Restrictions of Use." Where telephone orders are taken, it is so noted.

Appendix A provides the most complete listing to date of Yizkor books memorializing communities destroyed in the Holocaust. Appendix B consists of sample forms to order birth, marriage and death records from New York City, New York State and New Jersey agencies covered in the book. These forms can be photocopied for ready use. Other appendixes include Soundex code systems, detailed lists of directories and newspapers at the New York Public Library, and a listing and map of Jewish cemeteries.

INDEXES: There are name, place and subject indexes. The name index includes names of authors, names in collections and names that appear in the title of a collection. It does *not* include names of facility directors.

The place index includes all localities -- countries, cities, villages and neighborhoods that are mentioned under "Description of Resources." It includes the name of a locality when it is mentioned in the title of a book and, if relevant to the contents of a book, where the book is published. Generally, the latter are *not* included in this index. Place names are spelled as they appear in the text with minor exceptions, e.g. Apter (the adjectival form) is listed under Apt.

The subject index includes every type of record that appears in the book. In addition, it includes names of organizations and agencies whose records are covered. Where a type of record is available in many places, e.g. the five boroughs and six suburban counties, the place name is cross-referenced in the subject index.

IS THIS BOOK MEANT FOR JEWISH GENEALOGISTS ONLY? No! One hundred four libraries, archives and public agencies are covered in the book. Of these, 86 hold records or books on all groups (mostly non-Jewish). Only 18 (17%) are specifically Jewish in character. Some of these repositories have records of interest to non-Jewish researchers. For example, Yizkor books often contain photographs and maps of small towns and villages of eastern Europe which may be the only published sources of information on these localities.

IS THIS EVERYTHING? We hope not! Archives and libraries are constantly acquiring additional materials. 1988 was a year of major acquisitions and losses. The National Archives acquired the Naturalization records of the U.S. District Court of New Jersey (Camden and Newark Offices); the Bergen County Historical Archives opened; the Municipal Archives in New York City accessioned marriage records, 1866-1937, and death records, 1920-1929.

On the negative side, the Municipal Archives accessioned and was then required to return birth records, 1898-1909. One archives had a major fire (Agudath Israel) and one closed (St. Francis College, The James A. Kelly Institute). The St. Francis College collection has been transferred to the Municipal Archives.

Three facilities are planning to move in 1989: the National Archives and the Manhattan Borough and Staten Island Borough Offices of the Board of Elections.

A Living Memorial to the Holocaust--Museum of Jewish Heritage, sponsored by the New York Holocaust Memorial Commission, is scheduled to open in lower Manhattan (Battery Park City) in the future. In addition to historical artifacts and fine art, the museum will include personal memorabilia, documents, manuscripts and photographs.

The Ellis Island Restoration Commission, a private non-profit group, is planning a Family History Center to be located next to the Great Hall in the Main Building on Ellis Island. The Center plans to open in 1992 and will have a computerized data bank on 17 million immigrants who passed through Ellis Island.

Instead of waiting for all these changes to occur, we decided to make this book available now. We think you will agree that this was the right decision.

ACKNOWLEDGEMENTS: A book of this magnitude could not have been written by one individual. It took painstaking field work, interviews with facility staff, examination of finding aids and writing up the results. Without the tireless leg work of members and friends of the Jewish Genealogical Society, this book could not have been completed. Contributors, in alphabetical order, were:

Larry Adler	Blanche Fingeroth	Rhea Plottel
Nathan Altman	Karen S. Franklin	Eileen Polakoff
Zachary Baker	Alex E. Friedlander	Pauline Reich
Arye Barkai	Gary Gelber	Steven E. Rauch
David Blumengarten	Esta Gildwarg	Lana Rosenfeld
Michael Brenner	Ira Goldberg	Lawrence Rubin
Edith Brensel-Tuber	Jacqueline Graf	Rochelle Schneider
Jeanne Chimes	Naomi Schubin Greenberg	Judy Seed
Sandra Cohen	Lucille Gudis	Robert Selden
Jeffrey K. Cymbler	Valerie Josephson	Steven W. Siegel
Shirley Davidson	Jerome Katcher	Paul Silverstone
Marsha Saron Dennis	Lynn Kaye	Rabbi Malcolm H. Stern
Nancy Deutsch-Sinderbrand	Sheila B. Kieval	Evan Stolbach
Louis Diamantstein	Sol Krongelb	Jeanne Tell
Howard Dreises	Shelley Lantheaume	Yitz Twersky
Ilene Eagle	Gary Mokotoff	Sheppard Wahnon
Carol Eiseman	B-Ann Moorhouse	Ira Wolfman
Naomi Bard Feller	Rochelle Morse	Gwynn Russler Zatz
Joseph Fibel Jr.	Diane Perry	

Special mention must be made of those who were always available to double-check facts or investigate one more facility. These included Michael Brenner, Marsha Dennis, Nancy Deutsch-Sinderbrand, Alex Friedlander, Naomi Greenberg, Lucille Gudis, Rochelle Schneider, Rabbi Malcolm Stern and Gwynn Zatz.

We thank Zachary M. Baker, Head Librarian at YIVO Institute for Jewish Research, for updating his Bibliography of Eastern European Memorial (Yizkor) Books, which is the basis for Appendix A.

Steve Rauch took on the grueling task of typing the Yizkor book appendix. Jeff Cymbler and Sheila Kieval also helped with typing parts of the book. Computer assistance and final set-up for printing were provided by Rob Selden. Gary Mokotoff spearheaded advertising, publication and distribution.

In addition, the efforts of the following JGS members (not listed above) to the 1985 book served as a basis for this book:

Donna Balopole	Lillian Faffer	Helene Schwartz Kenvin
David H. Blum	Roslyn Freiman Samuelson	David M. Kleiman
Jeannette Blumengarten	Raymond M. Goldberg	Miriam Weiner
Matt Darrish	David J. Priever	

Key staff in each of the agencies and repositories described in *Genealogical Resources in the New York Metropolitan Area* helped tremendously in putting this material together. Directors and/or staff of every facility included in the book reviewed the material or provided detailed answers to our questions. Some were outstanding in their assistance and demonstrated tremendous patience. They deserve special mention:

Bruce Abrams, New York County Clerk's Office, Division of Old Records
Thomas Bourke, New York Public Library, Microforms Division
David Carmicheal, Westchester County Archives

Kenneth Cobb, New York City Municipal Archives
Carl Falowczany, Westchester County Archives
Anthony Fantozzi, National Archives, Northeast Region
David Gardner, City Register's Office, New York County
Barbara Lebovitch, Suffolk County Clerk's Office
Sandy Palermo, Bergen County Clerk's Office
Joseph Sanfedele, City Clerk's Office
Frank Torres, Richmond County Clerk's Office
Joseph Van Nostrand, New York County Clerk's Office, Division of Old Records
Marek Web, YIVO Institute for Jewish Research, Archives
Devra Zetlan, New York City Municipal Reference and Research Center

We thank the Sprung Monument Corporation for permission to use the map of Jewish Cemeteries and the Regional Plan Association for the Tri-State Urban Region map.

There is one person whose persistence and insight helped shape *Genealogical Resources in the New York Metropolitan Area.* JGS President Steven W. Siegel read, re-read, commented and re-commented on the manuscript in addition to contributing written material. Steve gave us guidance in gathering the facts and assisted by reviewing the manuscript for accuracy and completeness. He raised questions that led to new resources and finding aids. Steve is known nationwide as *the* expert on New York City resources and he has been selfless in his willingness to share this knowledge with us.

Finally, I would like to thank my family, in particular my parents, David and Helen Guzik, who put up with my midnight hours and noncommunication for the last 18 months while I worked on this book. They inspired me with their caring for family. In truth, they have been my best genealogical resource!

Estelle M. Guzik
Editor

New York, January 1989

MANHATTAN

AGUDATH ISRAEL OF AMERICA
ORTHODOX JEWISH ARCHIVES

Facility Director:	Rabbi Moshe Kolodny, Archivist
Address:	84 William Street New York, NY 10038
	(Cross Street: Corner of Maiden Lane)
Phone Number:	(212) 797-9000

Hours of Operation:

Monday to Thursday: 10:00 am to 5:00 pm
Friday: 10:00 am to 12:00 noon

Closed Friday afternoon, Saturday, Sunday, Jewish and legal holidays.
NOTE: Access is by appointment only.

Closest Public Transportation:

Subway: 2, 3, 4 or 5 to Wall Street
J, M or Z to Broad Street
A or C to Broadway/Nassau Street

Bus: M15 to Maiden Lane and Water Street
M1 or M6 to Maiden Lane (Courtlandt Street) and Broadway

Directions:

Take the #2 or #3 train to the Wall Street station. Use the exit at the <u>north</u> end of the platform. Exit up the stairs to "Pine Street/Cedar Street." Turn right to the "Cedar Street/William Street" exit in the Chase building. Go up the next stairs and exit the building. Walk south on William Street to #84. The Archives is located on the 11th floor.

Description of Resources:

(This facility suffered severe damage as a result of a fire at the building on May 6, 1988. It is unknown as we go to press whether the records described below have been damaged.)

The Archives has a 15-page booklet, *Checklist of Jewish Materials in Archives of Agudath Israel of America*, which describes the 40 collections in its holdings. The following information was extracted in part from this booklet.

The collections cover Jewish immigration from the turn of the century to the present; the work of the Vaad Hatzala (Orthodox Jewish Rescue Committee) in providing relief and rescue to Jews trapped in Nazi Europe; Jewish educational activities; children's camps; employment and social welfare programs.

Collections which may be of interest to genealogists include:

1. <u>David Kranzler Collection</u>: Yearbooks and journals from students of orthodox yeshivot in the New York area, 1910 to present; and bills of divorcement from northeast USA rabbinical courts, 1910-1948.

2. <u>West Side Institutional Synagogue Collection</u> (Manhattan), 1935-1959: Lists of students and Jewish schools in Poland and Lithuania, 1937-1939.

3. <u>Nathan Baruch Collection</u>, 1947-1948: Data on Displaced Persons (DPs) and Jewish survivors after the Holocaust.

4. <u>Harry Fischel Papers</u>: Includes his autobiography.

5. <u>Joan Fredericks Collection</u>: Research material on the train of 1,200 inmates rescued from Theresienstadt Concentration Camp including interviews and correspondence with survivors.

6. <u>Harry Goodman Collection</u>, 1936-1960: Includes the *Jewish Weekly* (*Yiddishe Vochenzeitung*) and the *Jewish Post* published in London, England.

7. <u>Herman Landau Collection</u>: Two minute books of Orthodox youth groups in Fuerth, Germany, 1919-1936.

8. <u>Yeshiva Torah Vodaath, Community Service and Public Relations Collection</u> (Brooklyn), 1948-1980: Placement records and solicitation letters for the school throughout the U.S. and Canada.

9. <u>Rabbi Michael Munk Collection</u>: Biographical material on his father, Rabbi Ezra Munk of Berlin, and letters to the Rabbi from individuals. In addition, the collection includes documents on the Jews of Prague in the late 1700s.

10. <u>Otto Schiff Collection</u>: Includes 34 boxes containing immigration files of individuals assisted by the Refugee Immigration Division of Agudath Israel, 1946-1970s. The files include draft copies of Petitions for Naturalization and sometimes affidavits of support, visa applications, tax returns, marriage and birth certificates and personal correspondence.

11. <u>Jacob Oppenheim Diary</u>: Records his observations of the Holocaust beginning with Kristallnacht, November, 1938.

12. <u>Moreinu Yaakov Rosenheim Collection</u>: Correspondence of the Orthodox Jewish rescue efforts for Jews trapped in the Holocaust includes letters on behalf of Jews in Czechoslovakia, Sweden, France, Germany, Rumania, Italy, Poland and China (Tienstin).

13. <u>Periodicals</u>: The Archives has a collection of current Orthodox journals and newspapers from the USA, Israel and Great Britain, as well as:

Beth Jacob and *Agudath Israel,* Poland, 1930s (Hebrew/Yiddish)
Dos Vort, Vilna, 1925-1937 (microfilm)
Kol Yisrael, Jerusalem, 1923-1949 (weekly)
Heijnt, Riga, Latvia, 1938-1939 (single copies)
Juedische Presse, Vienna, 1922-1923 and 1931-1938
Ha Modia, Poltowa, Russia, 1912-1914 (xerox copy)

The Archives also has extensive photographic holdings of European and American religious personalities. In addition, it has c.200 relief and refugee photos from World War II, DP camps and Israel.

Finding Aids:

A copy of the *Checklist of Materials* can be obtained for a nominal fee ($2 for mailing to individuals) or free to institutions.

Description of Facility:

This is a small office which also serves as a research facility. Records can be obtained immediately. Space can be made available to serve up to 3 people at a time. There is one staff member to assist researchers. The Archives has one microfilm reader.

Fees/Copies:

A photocopy machine is available at $.15 per page. Copies from microfilm cost $.25 per page.

Restrictions on Use:

The collections are subject to the privacy privileges of living individuals or family members and general copyright laws where applicable. All records of Agudath Israel created after 1960 require the consent of the Board of Directors before being used.

AMERICAN GATHERING OF JEWISH HOLOCAUST SURVIVORS

Facility Director: Benjamin Meed, President

Address: 122 West 30th Street, Suite 205
New York, NY 10001

(Cross Streets: 6th and 7th Avenues)

Phone Number: (212) 239-4230

Hours of Operation:

Monday to Friday: 9:00 am to 5:00 pm
Closed Saturday, Sunday, Jewish and legal holidays.

NOTE: Researchers may submit mail requests or come to the office during these hours to drop off the Search Form.

Closest Public Transportation:

Subway: 1 to 28th Street

Bus: M5, M6 or M7 to Avenue of the Americas (6th Avenue) and West 30th Street (northbound)
M10 to 7th Avenue and West 30th Street (southbound)

Directions:

Take the #1 train to the 28th Street station. Exit the station and walk north on 7th Avenue to 30th Street. Turn east on West 30th Street to #122. Take the elevator to the 2nd floor.

Description of Resources:

The American Gathering maintains the National Registry of Jewish Holocaust Survivors. This is a computerized data base of over 65,000 survivors and their children in the U.S. and Canada. The Registry includes current name, address, places of residence before the War, places of internment or residence during the War, occupation, name before and during the War, maiden name, date and place of birth, spouse's name and information on the spouse and other family members. The Registry may be able to provide information on whether an oral history of a particular survivor was recorded and, if so, the year recorded and place in which the oral history can be found. The aim of the Gathering is to have all survivors recorded in this historical archive.

The Registry was created in 1981 by the American Gathering in Jerusalem and developed further at its Washington Gathering in 1983. It is being continuously updated.

Finding Aids:

In order to have a search made, the researcher must complete a Search Form which can be obtained from the American Gathering. If the correct spelling of the name is unknown, a special soundex system can be utilized for the search.

Fees/Copies:

Although there is no charge for a search, a contribution (tax-deductible) is appreciated. Send a self-addressed stamped envelope with your inquiry.

Restrictions on Use:

Because of confidentiality restrictions, searches are limited to persons identified at least by surname and town. Searches cannot be made for all persons with a particular surname or for all persons from a particular town.

AMERICAN JEWISH JOINT DISTRIBUTION COMMITTEE ARCHIVES

Facility Director:	Denise Gluck, Archivist
Address:	711 Third Avenue, 10th Floor New York, NY 10017 (Cross Streets: East 44th and 45th Streets)
Phone Number:	(212) 687-6200

Hours of Operation:

Monday to Friday: 9:00 am to 4:30 pm (by appointment only)

Friday closing hours vary during the winter months. Closed Saturday, Sunday, Jewish and legal holidays.

Closest Public Transportation:

Subway: 4, 5, 6 or 7 to Grand Central/42nd Street

Bus: M101 or M102 to Lexington Avenue and 44th/45th Street (southbound)
         M101 or M102 to 3rd Avenue and 44th/45th Street (northbound)

Directions:

Take the #4 or #5 (express) train to the Grand Central/42nd Street station. Exit the train and walk east one block to Third Avenue. Walk north on Third Avenue to #711.

Description of Resources:

The American Jewish Joint Distribution Committee (JDC) was established in 1914 by three American Jewish organizations -- the American Jewish Relief Committee, the Central Relief Committee and the People's Relief Committee -- in response to the devastation of European Jewry. During WWI and postwar its functions included the distribution of food, clothing and medical supplies; the reconstruction of decimated areas and resettlement of refugees. The Holocaust era included efforts to rescue Jews from Nazi-occupied lands and negotiations with the American and foreign governments. Post-WWII activities included the administration of displaced persons camps, relocation of refugees and migration to Israel.

Because of the extensive nature of this collection, only a sampling of the files are noted below. Researchers should consult the finding aids for additional subjects and place names mentioned. File numbers are in brackets.

1. <u>Photographic Archives</u>: Beginning with the portrait of the very first members of the JDC Executive Committee in 1918, photographs are available that illustrate the JDC's work. See "Restrictions on Use."

2. <u>Records, 1914-1918</u>: Files of particular interest to genealogists are organized under the following sub-headings:

   <u>Organizational Structure of JDC</u>: Includes records of relief funds sent by the Transmission Bureau to individual families in Europe from relatives in America. Names and addresses are often included.

   <u>Subject Matter</u>: Includes files on the following subjects: refugees in Russia (from Poland and Lithuania), refugees in Salonika (from Monastir, Serbia [now Bitola, Yugoslavia]); rabbis (refugees) in Alexandria and in Austria; prisoners of war by location, e.g. Austria and Germany (from Russia), Bulgaria (from Rumania); American citizens deported from Palestine; relatives and friends, information service, 1915-1916 (arranged alphabetically); students in Switzerland (from Russia); and writers in Copenhagen and Switzerland (from Russia).

Geographical Areas: Includes files on the following places in Lithuania: Kovno, Lida, Pren (Prienai), Schaulen (Shavli or Siauliai), Skaudvile, Suwalki, Vilna and Wladyslawow.

3. Records, 1919-1921: This collection of 800 files includes documentary material on prevailing conditions in Eastern Europe such as pogroms (eye-witness accounts, diaries, memoirs and lists of victims); Prisoners of War in Siberia (hand-written messages, photographs and minute books of POW camps). Materials are arranged under the following sample sub-headings:

JDC Administration, NY [1-60]: Executive staff [7-15]; personnel [28-43]; transmission of funds (includes lists of names of remitters) [55-60].

Overseas Administration [61-71]: Overseas personnel [68].

Subject Matter [88-108]: Child care [88-89]; emigration and immigration [91]; pogroms and persecution [94]; POWS; refugees [99]; relatives and friends [100-100a]. These latter files include, by city, lists of persons in Europe seeking relatives in New York. The names and European addresses of the searchers are included.

Localities [109-290]: These files are grouped by country.

4. Records, 1921-1932, 1933-1944 and 1945-1964: These collections are arranged in a similar manner to those above. The 1933-1944 collection includes 1,141 folders which span the Nazi and Holocaust eras. The majority of these files are arranged by country and region, although similar Subject Matter files as those described above are also included.

Finding Aids:

In order to locate specific information of interest, the researcher should consult the catalogs at the Archives. There are five catalogs arranged in groups of years: 1914-1918, 1919-July 1921, August 1921-December 1932, 1933-1944, and 1945-1964. A sixth catalog is a guide to the papers of Saly Mayer, JDC's representative in Switzerland, 1940-1949. The seventh catalog lists the records of the Dominican Republic Settlement Association (DORSA), the governing body of a unique experiment in Jewish farming in the Dominican Republic, 1939-1977.

Each catalog corresponds to a Record Group (RG). Within each RG/catalog are details of the holdings, with the file number noted in front of the description of the file. Use this file number plus any other key information that is contained in the description to order the file.

The 1919-1921 catalog includes three appendices arranged alphabetically: Index of Localities; Reference List of Individuals; List of Landsmanshaftn.

The catalogs are being microfilmed. The first catalog and part of the second have already been filmed.

The Archives is currently cataloging its photograph collection.

Description of Facility:

This is a working office. Researchers must check in and wait at the reception desk upon arrival. The Archivist will escort visitors into the office. There is a conference room area adjacent to the Archives where 1-3 researchers can work. This is also where the microfilm reader/printer is located.

Fees/Copies:

Photocopy services are provided at a cost of $.15 per page. Copies of microfilm are $.25 per page.

Restrictions on Use:

Access to the photo collection is currently restricted because of overriding preservation needs.

BOARD OF ELECTIONS
MANHATTAN BOROUGH OFFICE

Facility Director: Bartholomew M. Regazzi, Chief Clerk
Adam Corti, Chief Warehouse Technician

Address: 131 Varick Street, 9th Floor
New York, NY 10013

(Cross Streets: Spring and Dominick Streets)

NOTE: The Manhattan Borough Office is planning to move in 1989. Call in advance.

Phone Number: (212) 924-8557
(212) 675-2260 (Warehouse)

Hours of Operation:

Monday to Friday: 9:00 am to 5:00 pm
Closed Saturday, Sunday and legal holidays.

NOTE: Researchers should arrive no later than 4:00 pm. Persons wishing to view records at the warehouse should call in advance for an appointment. A prior appointment is also recommended to view records at the Varick Street office (especially around elections).

Closest Public Transportation:

Subway: C or E to Spring Street
1 to Houston Street

Bus: M10 or M21 to Spring and Varick Streets

Directions:

Take the C or E train to the Spring Street station. Exit at the <u>south</u> end of the station. Walk one block <u>west</u> on Spring Street to Varick Street and cross Varick to #131. The office is on the 9th floor.

Description of Resources:

This office has voter registration records for voters residing in Manhattan from 1916-1920 (gaps) and 1923 to the present. The forms, in many cases, include the date of naturalization and the court in which naturalized. Records (microfilm), 1957-1978, and records (hard copy) from 1979 to the present are on-site. These records are arranged by Assembly/Election District (AD/ED) and then alphabetized by surname. Records, 1916-1956, are located in the Board's warehouse at 448 West 16th Street (between 9th and 10th Avenues).

The office has AD/ED maps going back to 1905.

Registers of Voters, 1872-1922 (gaps), were transferred to the MUNICIPAL ARCHIVES. See "NEW YORK CITY DEPARTMENT OF RECORDS AND INFORMATION SERVICES, MUNICIPAL ARCHIVES."

Finding Aids:

Current registrations are in computer printouts arranged alphabetically by surname. These printouts list the AD/ED of the voter. With the AD/ED information, a researcher can locate the current records which are arranged in binders by AD/ED and then alphabetically by surname.

Records of voters who did not vote after 1978 are in file cabinets arranged by AD/ED. Earlier files of inactive voters are arranged by year, AD/ED and address. The address of the individual is essential. The staff can help find the address on the AD/ED map for a given year.

Description of Facility:

This is a NYC government office. Five to six persons can be assisted at one time. There is one microfilm reader available at the Board's office on Varick Street.

Fees/Copies:

There is no charge for viewing (or hand copying) these records. Mail requests are accepted for a $3 fee (certified check or money order payable to the Board of Elections, City of New York). This covers a search for one name in one year. Each additional name and/or year is $3. No refund is made if the record is not found. Provide the full name at registration, address where residing at the time of registration, and date of birth or age. Use the address in a Presidential election year when the individual was more likely to have voted.

Restrictions on Use:

Active records are not available for examination ten business days before or after primary and general elections.

Only red pencil may be used in copying records. The office has a supply.

BUND ARCHIVES OF THE JEWISH LABOR MOVEMENT

Facility Director: Dr. Benjamin Nadel, Director

Address: Atran Center
25 East 21st Street, Room 303
New York, NY 10010

(Cross Streets: Broadway and Park Avenue South)

Phone Number: (212) 473-5101

Hours of Operation:

Monday to Friday: 10:00 am to 4:00 pm
Closed Saturday, Sunday and all major Jewish and legal holidays.

NOTE: A preliminary appointment by phone or letter is required.

Closest Public Transportation:

Subway: 6, N or R to 23rd Street

Bus: M1, M2, M3 to 20th Street and Park Avenue South (northbound)
M2, M3 or M5 to 21st Street and 5th Avenue (southbound)
M26 (23rd Street crosstown) to Broadway and 23rd Street

Directions:

Take the #6, N or R train to the 23rd Street station. From the #6, walk south on Park Avenue South to 21st Street and turn west to the building. From the N or R, exit on Fifth Avenue and 23rd Street. Walk south to 21st Street and turn east to the building. Take the elevator to the 3rd floor. Turn right through an unmarked door and then turn left down a corridor. The Archives is in Room 303.

Description of Resources:

The Jewish Labor Bund began as an underground political movement in Tsarist Russia in 1897. Two years later, the Bund Archives was established in Switzerland. It specializes in materials relating to the history of the Jewish labor and socialist movements, particularly in Eastern Europe and the Americas.

For the genealogist whose relatives were active in the labor movement, the Archives offers a wealth of biographical and historical material. The Archives' socialist and labor holdings (1,247 linear feet) date from the 1870s to the present.

The collection includes rare manuscripts, letters, minutes, newspapers, books, pamphlets, photographs and personal documents (passports, birth and death certificates and diplomas). A large percentage of the collection is unique and not available elsewhere. In addition to materials on the Bund, the Archives has important materials on Russian Social-Democrats, the Socialist Revolutionary Party (SR), Poale Zionists, Anarchists, Jewish Communists and Trade Unions. The following describes a small portion of what is available here. This summary is based, in part, upon the guide, *Bund Archives of the Jewish Labor Movement*, 1987, edited by Dr. Benjamin Nadel and Eleanora Golobic:

1.   The Jewish Labor Bund

    The collection includes newspapers, correspondence, minutes and documents of hundreds of local Bund organizations, such as:

    Newspapers: the Bund's underground and legally permitted press in Russia, 1897-1921, Poland, 1918-1948, Galicia, 1905-1920, and the complete collections of Bund press in the U.S., Israel, Argentina, Australia, England, France, Latvia, Mexico, Rumania and South Africa. (The underground press generally did not use the real names of members, except to report trials or executions.)

Congresses and conferences: delegates lists, 1897-1920 and 1947-1985 (gaps).

Bundist print shop mailing lists, pre-1917, and Bund in Poland, Central Committee mailing list, 1931.

Correspondence: the letters of Nahmanson, Abramovitch and Koigen, 1912; and correspondence of other leading Socialists and Bundists: Caindet, Cohen, Ditkowsky, Dunant, Ephrus, Feinberg, Filippov, Fraenkel, Goldberg, Idelsohn, Kilimnik, Koigen, Koltsov, Kopelson, Kosovsky, Kursky, Lerey, Levidi, Lewin, Maknovets, Mazover, Perenoud, Polinkovsky, Rakov, Rein, Reibalka, Rosen, Scharenberg, Smovsinovsky, Stschupak, Synchniker, Teplov, Terman, Trachtenberg, Tsetlina, Ziegel.

Tsarist indictments and verdicts, 1900-1912, against Bundists: Freinkel, Furman, Itelson, Katz, Lifszyc, Lutenberg, Lurie, Rudkovskii, Slutskaia, Trelin, Zakon; and against agent-provocateurs: Kaplinskii, Rabinovich, Vilbushevich-Shochat.

Latvian documents, 1918-1939: the fascist coup of 1935 and arrest of Bundists; the trial of Braun (Riger), 1921; and files on Charlash, Maisel and Levin-Schatzkes.

Rumanian documents: correspondence of Kissman and Kaswan.

Polish Bundists arrested in Soviet Russia, lists, 1939-1941: Bundists deported in Soviet Russia, post-war questionnaire; aid for Bundists in Russia, telegrams and addresses, 1941-1945; Jewish refugees in Vilna, 1940; lists and correspondence concerning packages sent to Bundists; and documents on Bundist victims of Soviet terror: Erlich, Alter, Pizyc, Rosenthal and Zeleznikov.

Polish Bundists in Shanghai, lists; and letters from Bundists in Japan.

Holocaust documents: Auschwitz prisoners register book, 1943-1944; manuscripts, letters and testimony of surviving Bundists in the ghettos of Bialystok, Gombin and Vilna; letters from the Bund's London delegation and Bund representatives in the Polish Parliament in Exile (Zygelboim, Scherer, Blit, Oler), 1940-1945; and a collection of documents and letters from Jews in the Polish Army.

American representatives of the Bund in Poland: a list of visas, documents on lobbying efforts for emigration papers and relief for Bundists stranded in Soviet Russia and Western Europe.

Post-World War II documents: lists of Bund refugees in Austria, 1947-1948; France, individual files on Abragam, Shchupak and Schrager; lists of Bundists in Germany in displaced person camps such as Feldafing, Foehrenwald, Neu-Freimann, 1945-1954; correspondence on Bundist refugees in Italy, 1945-1949; and the Kissman collection of letters from people trying to find relatives in Rumania, 1945 to mid-1950s.

Bundist questionnaires from various countries, 1957-1987, provide: age, place of birth, parents' names, occupation, education, if ever used an alias, history of arrest, imprisonment and/or exile, if applicable, interesting events in the worker's life, and often includes a personal photograph.

Biographies: *Doires Bundistes* [Bundist biographies], 3 volumes, 1956-1967; and some 750 biographical files of Bundists in Russia, Poland, Bukowina-Rumania, Latvia, France, England, Denmark, Israel and the U.S. The following is a sample of the surnames included in these files:

Russia: Abramovitch, Aronson, Berenstein, Blond-Michalewicz, Eisenstadt (Yudin), Gozhanskii (Lonu), Grosser, Gurevitch, Hersch, Kahan (Virgili), Kaplinskii (agent-provocateur), Koigen, Kosovsky, Kopelson, Kremer, Kursky, Lekert, Levit, Liber, Litvak, Medem, Mill, Michalewicz, Mutnik (Gleb), Portnoy, Rosenthal, Teplov, Vinaver.

Poland: Aleksandrowicz, Alter, Berman, Bernstein, Blit, Blum, Celemenski, Dubnowa-Erlich, Einaugler, Feiner, Frydrych, Gliksman, Goldstein, Gutgold, Hodes, Honigwil, Himmelfarb, Iwinska, Kazdan, Klepfisz, Leszczynski (Chmurner), Lifszyc, Mendelson, Milgroim, Milman, Muszkat, Nowogrudsky, Nowogrudzka, Oler, Orzech, Pat, Scherer, Schneidmil, Schwartz, Shulman, Szafran, Szweber, Tabaczynski, Trunk, Wapner, Wasser, Zelmanowicz, Zybert, Zygelboim (Artur).

2. Jewish Political Trends Other than the Bund

Membership list (no date) of the Jewish Folk Party in Poland and biographical information on 69 personalities in Europe/Israel (54) and America (15) including:

Jewish Folk Party: Dubnow, Shabad, Prilutsky

Religious Jewish Labor Movement: Friedman

Eastern European Socialists and Territorialists: Ben Adir (A. Rosin), Czernichow (Danieli), Doeblin, Latzki-Bertoldi, Lestchinski, Levin, Shatz-Anin, Syrkin, Steinberg, Zangwill, Zilberfarb.

3. <u>International Socialist Movement</u>

Election ballots to the Ekaterinoslav Duma (Ukraine), March 1917 Revolution, with names of 358 candidates of the following left-wing parties: Poale-Zion, Ukrainian Social Democrats, Bolsheviks, Polish Democratic Club, National Socialist Labor Party, United Mensheviks, Bund, Polish and Latvian Social Democrats.

Political prisoners in Kiev, lists, 1901 (Bund, Foreign Committee collection); and original letters from Russian prisons, 1904-1916.

Biographical material on some 80 personalities in Europe and Israel including Populists, Russian Social-Democratic Worker's Party (RSDRP), Menshevik, Bolshevik, Socialist Revolutionary, Socialist Revolutionary Left and other Socialist and Ukrainian Socialist (Jewish and non-Jewish) members.

Documents on the 1923 trial of Boleslaw Drobner and the 1930 Brzesc trial, and letters from political prisoners in Poland, 1913-1951.

4. <u>International Anarchism and Jewish Anarchists</u>

Biographical material, correspondence and clippings on Berkman, Edelshtat, Gedalyahu (Palmer), Goldman, Cohen and Pesotta.

5. <u>International Communism and Jewish Communists</u>

A list of vanished members of the Central Committee CPSU, 1934, from *Pravda;* and biographical material on 85 European/Israeli and 24 American personalities.

6. <u>Holocaust</u>

German DP Camps (Admont, Foehrenwald, Feldafing, Landsberg), 1945-1950, bulletins, posters and leaflets providing information on survivors in these camps.

Survivors after World War II, lists; letters and testimony of survivors of concentration camps.

Yizkor books, material for the memorial volumes of Minsk, Vitebsk and Czestochowa.

Polish Jews who perished (Hannover-Bathfeld, Germany) and whose names were commemorated in the local cemetery of Ravensbruck, Weimar.

Dachau - Jews executed, Jewish Labor Committee published list, 2 vols., 1947.

Jewish children, accounts of their survival and fate under the Nazis, no date (typed manuscripts).

7. <u>The Jewish Labor Movement and Jewish Socialists in North America</u>

Amalgamated Clothing Workers of America: documents and publications from its founding in 1914; membership list of its Aid Committee for Bund.

Dress Pressers' Club: trade bulletins, 1934, 1940 and 1947.

International Ladies Garment Workers Union: publications and documents from its founding in 1886, such as the *Ladies Garment Worker,* 1915-1951; periodicals, 1910-1919; souvenir journal published in 1902 by the ILGWU; membership book, Local 9.

Hebrew Butchers Union: questionnaires, 1943.

Hebrew Typographical Union: anniversary publications, 1933, 1938 and 1948.

Mineral (Seltzer) Water Workers Union: minutes, 1922-1956 (gaps), lists of members and correspondence, 1943-1965 (gaps).

United Hebrew Trades: handwritten membership cards, 1910-1966; list of participants at its 1948 convention.

Workmen's Circle: correspondence, photographs and documents from the Circle's 240 branches in the U.S. and Canada, from its founding as a national organization c.1900. Many of the branches were organized as landsmanshaftn. A sampling of files from the NYC division includes:

Bialystoker #88
Bobroisk #118, 1923-1958
Dvinsk #101, 1909-1950s
Grodno #100, 1920s
Kielce #139, 1939 pamphlet
Lodzer #324
Lomza #124, 1919-1948
Lubliner Young Mens #392
Novi Dvor-Grodner #637
Vilna #167, 1929-1960s and Vilner #367
Vitebsk #126, 1912-1960s

This collection also includes a published biographical lexicon of Builders of the Workmen's Circle, prepared in 1966 with 1,000 names of active members, dates of birth and arrival in the U.S., other personal data and some photos; and souvenir journals, 1935, 1940, 1948-1985.

Biographies of 57 personalities in the Jewish labor movement in America; and personal files of such Jewish Labor Committee leaders as Vladeck, Epstein, Held, Pat, Schwartz and Tabaczynski.

8. Yizkor Books

The Archives has over 400 books on Jewish community history including 150 Yizkor books. See Appendix A.

9. Jewish History from 1880s

Material related to Jewish history that does not fall into any of the above categories but which may be of interest to genealogists includes:

Bialystok: report of the Fund for the Orphans' Society includes benefactors, amounts contributed, a short biographical description of the orphans (including their place of origin, state of health and the present location of any living parents), and photographs of the children. [M-14/File #17]

Jewish Library "Kadima" (Australia): annual report, 1950, lists members. [M-14/File #1a]

Ostrower Relief Committee: banquet journals (English, Yiddish). [M-14/File #7]

Landsmanshaft Nusach Vilna: yearly bulletins of this group since its founding in 1959, membership cards and obituaries. The bulletins include material about searches for survivors, maps (pre-WWII) and photographs. In the September 1961-December 1962 bulletin, there is a list of Jews killed in Schoenberg, Germany, that gives dates of birth and death.

Finding Aids:

There is a comprehensive card catalog for the book collection and other printed materials.

A new 108-page guide to the Archives, *Bund Archives of the Jewish Labor Movement,* edited by Dr. Benjamin Nadel and Eleanora Golobic, has been completed and will be published when funds become available. A more detailed internal finding aid exists for archival materials.

Researchers should maximize their use of the facility by studying the guide first or reading other printed material about its holdings before actually visiting the Archives. These include:

Directory of Jewish Archival Institutions, edited by Philip P. Mason, Detroit, 1975, pp 39-47.

Bulletin of the Bund Archives of the Jewish Labor Movement, New York. Published annually, 1960-1967 and 1979 to the present.

Yizkor books are cataloged in Yiddish and Hebrew by the name of the locality. The full collection is now shelved. See Appendix A.

Description of Facility:

Space is limited in the Archives for only two researchers at a time. There are two or three staff members and two qualified volunteers available to provide assistance. The Archives has one microfilm reader.

(CYCO Bookstore, which specializes in Yizkor books and other books in and about Yiddish, is located across the hall.)

Fees/Copies:

There is no fee for using the Archives but contributions are most welcome. Only staff may use the one photocopy machine. Copies cost $.10 per page.

Restrictions on Use:

Because of a shortage of storage space, about 25%-30% of the Archives' books and other printed material are being stored in cartons in Brooklyn and are not presently accessible. All archival material is on-site and accessible.

A reading knowledge of Yiddish and/or Polish and Russian is necessary to use much of the Archives' holdings.

Permission from the Director must be obtained to photocopy rare and/or fragile material. Only five percent of a given file may be photocopied but any amount of material may be copied by hand.

Access to some material is restricted to protect personal privacy and legitimate proprietary rights of living persons.

No filming or microfilming of the collection is allowed without written permission of the Director.

Visitors are discouraged from bringing their own printed material (books, pamphlets, newspapers) into the Reading Room of the Archives.

CITY CLERK'S OFFICE - MANHATTAN
MARRIAGE LICENSE BUREAU

Facility Director:	Charles Cuevas, City Clerk
	Joseph Sanfedele, Assistant to the City Clerk
Address:	Municipal Building
	1 Centre Street, Room 252
	New York, NY 10007

(Cross Streets: Brooklyn Bridge and Chambers Street. Chambers Street runs through the center of the building.)

Mail Address:	Add "Attention: Marriage Record Unit" to lower left corner of the envelope.
Phone Number:	(212) 669-8170

Hours of Operation:

Monday to Friday: 9:00 am to 4:00 pm
Closed Saturday, Sunday and legal holidays.

Closest Public Transportation:

Subway: 4, 5 or 6 to Brooklyn Bridge
J, M or Z to Chambers Street
N or R to City Hall
A or C to Chambers Street (north end)
2 or 3 to Park Place

Bus: M1 or M6 to Broadway and Chambers Street
M15 or M22 to Centre and Chambers Streets

Directions:

Take the #4 or #5 (express) or #6 (local) train to the Brooklyn Bridge station. Go up the staircase at the <u>center</u> of the platform. Turn at the top of the stairs and go straight ahead to the exit. Go up the wide staircase. You will emerge on the street level of the Municipal Building. Turn right, around the staircase, to the entrance to the building. The office is on the 2nd floor. Be sure to enter at the <u>south</u> end of the building, i.e. near the subway entrance. The 2nd floor of the north end does not connect.

Description of Resources:

Manhattan City Clerk's Office marriage records are available from 1908 to the present. The records of this Office include all of the Bronx, 1908-1913.

Note: Two independent sets of records exist for the years 1908-1937 when both the Department of Health and the City Clerk's Office maintained marriage records. The Health Department records, 1866-1937, are being accessioned by the MUNICIPAL ARCHIVES. See "NEW YORK CITY DEPARTMENT OF RECORDS AND INFORMATION SERVICES, MUNICIPAL ARCHIVES" for these and earlier Manhattan marriage records.

The City Clerk's records, 1908 to the present, consist of the application (affidavit) filed by the couple <u>before</u> the wedding, a summary of the application (for applications filed from 1908-1943) and the marriage license filed <u>after</u> the wedding by the officiating person (e.g. rabbi) certifying that the wedding actually occurred, showing the date, place and witnesses. This information then was added to the summary. This Office also has copies of applications for marriages that never took place.

Marriage certifications, 1908 to May 1943, were required to be filed in the borough in which the <u>bride resided</u>. For out-of-city brides, the record was filed in the borough where the license was obtained. After May 1943, all marriage certifications were filed in the borough in which the <u>couple obtained their license</u>.

Finding Aids:

Finding aids on-site are not open to researchers. Each borough office has indexes for licenses filed in its office. For the years, 1908-1971, the City Clerk's Office has alphabetical ledger indexes for brides and grooms. The ledgers are arranged by the first 2 letters of the surname, chronologically by date of application (not date of marriage). There are computerized indexes for brides and grooms from 1972 to the present. The computerized indexes show both bride's and groom's names, the date they filed their application and, after 1973, the brides's birth date.

NOTE: The NYC Health Department index books for marriages for Manhattan and the Bronx, August 1888 to 1937, and for Brooklyn, Queens and Staten Island, 1898-1937, are available in the NEW YORK PUBLIC LIBRARY, U.S. HISTORY, LOCAL HISTORY AND GENEALOGY DIVISION (315N) or in the MICROFORMS DIVISION (315M) and in the NEW YORK CITY DEPARTMENT OF RECORDS AND INFORMATION SERVICES, MUNICIPAL ARCHIVES. The MUNICIPAL ARCHIVES also has a microfilm copy of the Health Department's card index, 1866-1937 for brides and 1866-1910 for grooms. Published indexes, 1904-1933, are also available in the NEW YORK GENEALOGICAL AND BIOGRAPHICAL SOCIETY LIBRARY.

The published indexes include only those who were actually married and for whom Health Department marriage returns were submitted. Further, they are alphabetical listings by the name of the groom only.

Description of Facility:

This government office has a waiting area with table and chairs. The clerk behind the counter will do the search which can take an hour. The originals of the City Clerk's Office marriage records for Manhattan are in storage. The summaries (in ledgers) are available in the office for the period 1908-1943. The City Clerk's Office records from 1930 to the present are on microfilm (on-site).

Fees/Copies:

Go to the counter to obtain an application (see Appendix B-1) or to submit your completed application for processing. You will be assigned a number which will be called when the search for your record is completed. Only then will you be asked to pay the fee.

The City Clerk's Office uses the summary of the marriage record, 1908-1930, to prepare a typed transcript. For marriages which occurred in 1930 or later, copies are made from microfilm. If the microfilm is damaged (or not available) the copy will be a typed transcript from the City Clerk's Office summary. If the record is on microfilm, you may be able to obtain the copy in person. Typed transcripts are mailed.

The fee is $5 for the transcript or photocopy plus $5 for a one-year search, $1 for the second year and $.50 for each additional year. The total fee for a one-year search is $10. If you apply in person, you will be expected to pay in cash. If you apply by mail, do not send cash or stamps. While the application form states that payment should be by certified check, money order, etc., the office will accept personal checks by mail.

If the search for a marriage record by the Manhattan City Clerk's Office is unsuccessful, application may be made to other boroughs or to the MUNICIPAL ARCHIVES. The MUNICIPAL ARCHIVES will conduct a search and provide a copy of the Health Department certificate, if found. Submit a copy of the City Clerk's "not found" statement along with payment of the MUNICIPAL ARCHIVES' fee and request for a search.

Restrictions on Use:

Records are provided to the couple or their authorized representative. Genealogists should indicate their relationship to the couple. Generally, this will be sufficient for records pre-1930. For later records, a statement providing dates of death or authorization from the parties or their next-of-kin may be necessary to obtain the record.

CITY REGISTER'S OFFICE
MANHATTAN

Facility Director: John Lariviere, Deputy City Register

Address: 31 Chambers Street
New York, NY 10007

(Cross Streets: Centre and Elk Streets)

Phone Number: (212) 566-3734 (City Register)
(212) 669-4392 (Real Property Assessment Bureau)

Hours of Operation:

Monday to Friday: 9:00 am to 4:00 pm
Closed Saturday, Sunday and legal holidays.

Closest Public Transportation:

Subway: 4, 5 or 6 to Brooklyn Bridge
J, M or Z to Chambers Street
N or R to City Hall
A or C to Chambers Street (north end)
2 or 3 to Park Place

Bus: M1 or M6 to Broadway and Chambers Street
M15 or M22 to Centre and Chambers Streets

Directions:

Take the #4 or #5 (express) or #6 (local) train to the Brooklyn Bridge station. Exit to "City Hall/Park Row/Chambers Street." The exit is at the <u>south</u> end of the platform. Go up the stairs, turn right and exit the gate. After the gate, go up the stairs to the right. You will emerge at the corner of City Hall Park on Chambers and Centre Streets. 31 Chambers Street is the Surrogate's Court building, located across Chambers Street.

Description of Resources:

New York County (Manhattan only) deeds, mortgages, maps, satisfactions and miscellaneous real estate items are maintained here. Miscellaneous real estate items may include wills, transfer of dowager rights, etc. The earliest records date back to 1654.

The records for sections of the Bronx that were annexed to New York County at the end of the 19th century are located in the City Register's Office in the Bronx. However, the Manhattan grantor/grantee and mortgagor/mortgagee indexes, 1874-1891, include western Bronx properties.

All records and indexes in this office are on microfilm reels or in microfilm jackets (except Torrens properties, described below), arranged chronologically by date recorded. Paper copies of some records in libers are still available. (These are being moved off-site.) Starting in 1968 for the convenience of researchers, copies of microfilm frames have been cut and placed in plastic jackets arranged by block and lot. These block/lot jackets look like microfiche. NOTE: Block/lot jackets may not include all recorded instruments.

Finding Aids:

Records in this office may be searched either by name of property owner or by property location.

To identify all records for a particular person or corporate body, there are indexes for grantor, grantee, mortgagor and mortgagee, for various time periods from the 17th century to the present. Alphabetical indexes for the years 1680-1981 (microfilm) and 1982 to the present (microfiche) are in Room 205. They are not easy to use since the names are indexed only by the first two letters of the last name, in chronological sequence. (Name indexes, 1949-1982, are also available in libers in Room 203). For deeds recorded up to 1856, there is also a published set of volumes, *Index of Conveyances* (separate grantor and grantee books), located on the wall of Room 204 nearest to Room 205.

NOTE: Grantor (seller), grantee (buyer) and mortgagor (borrower) indexes include names of property owners. Mortgagee indexes include primarily lending institutions.

To trace the ownership of a particular piece of property, the street address or location must be converted into a block and lot number. Every parcel of land has a unique block and lot number. There are several ways to obtain these numbers:

1. If the building still exists, use the computer in Room 204 or Room 205. To search by address, type the word "FIND" (in capital letters). Fill in the borough and address as indicated on the screen to obtain the block and lot number; or,

2. The Office has copies of the *Real Estate Owner's Directory of Manhattan* issued by Real Estate Data Incorporated (REDI). Locating block and lot numbers is very easy if this volume is used. It is arranged by address and shows block and lot numbers, as well as other information such as name, address and telephone number of the current owner of each parcel. Unfortunately the book is accessible only to clerks of the City Register's Office and representatives of title search firms. It is not available for use by the general public in this office. However, both the New York Public Library, Economic and Public Affairs Division (Room 228) and the BROOKLYN BUSINESS LIBRARY, Reference Desk, have copies of this Manhattan directory; or,

3. Room 204 has an atlas of block and lot numbers on a standing carousel of sectional maps. The maps show block and lot numbers for each parcel, along with other recent information about each property; or,

4. If the building no longer exists or if the street name and/or numbering has changed, consult the Real Property Assessment Bureau across the street at One Centre Street (Municipal Building), 9th floor. That office can look up information on any property in Manhattan and advise of physical changes to the buildings, streets and/or numbering sequences. If they are not busy, current block and lot number may be provided by telephone (see above).

Once the block and lot numbers are known, for the years 1891-1917 the researcher must determine the (land) section number. A chart listing block and lot numbers in each section is posted on the inside of the main door to Room 205. Once section, block and lot number (for 1891-1917) or block and lot numbers (for all other years) are known, consult the several different indexes in Rooms 203, 204 and 205 described below to obtain the liber and page numbers (or reel and page numbers if recorded after 1968) for deeds, mortgages and other instruments on file for a particular parcel. The liber and page numbers are necessary in order to find instruments recorded <u>before</u> 1968. (Reel and page information are not needed for instruments recorded <u>after</u> 1968 if the block/lot jacket is used.)

1. Indexes by block (on microfilm) are in Room 205. The original index volumes (paper copy) are available in Room 203 for some years. For the 1654-1965 series, within groups of years there are separate libers (or reels) for each type of instrument (deed or mortgage). The libers (or reels) are arranged by block number and date recorded. The series for deeds, 1654-1916, has block maps and historical information on farm ownership displayed at the start of each block's pages.

   Comprehensive liber indexes (Block/Lot Tickler Indexes), which include all types of instruments in one index, are available from 1966 to January 1982. These libers (or reels) are arranged in groups of years, by block number and date recorded.

   For records after 1982 except Torrens properties (described below), researchers should use one of the two computer terminals located in Room 204 or Room 205. The computer can access information for <u>all</u> NYC boroughs except Staten Island. A search can be made four ways: by borough and surname; borough, block and lot number; borough, reel and page number; or borough and address. Instructions on how to conduct a computer search are posted behind both computers. Indexes to documents recorded from 1945 to the present will be computerized and accessible for all boroughs (except Staten Island) from each borough office in the future. The Bronx indexes from 1945 will be

accessible shortly. Manhattan indexes, 1945-1981, will be computerized next, followed by Queens and Brooklyn. The actual copies of the documents can be found only in the borough office where the property is located.

2. In Room 204 is another useful index for deeds and mortgages created originally by the Works Progress Administration (WPA). These WPA indexes (green-covered books) are arranged by block and lot and list all deeds and mortgages recorded for a particular lot, from the late 19th century to about 1966. At the start of each block (most blocks take up more than one volume), there are maps of the block, with street numbers as well as lot numbers marked. Different instruments are on color-coded pages. These WPA indexes are not considered "official" records although the City Register's Office did continue to maintain them after the WPA project was completed.

3. Researchers should be aware that some properties are not filed by block and lot number and are not included in the computer index. These are recorded under the Torrens Land Title Registration System. They include large tracts of land which, for example, may have been owned by the same family through several generations. Transfers are made by Memorial Certificates rather than by deed. Fewer than 25 Torrens properties exist in Manhattan. The Block index may indicate "Torrens" or "Land Title Registration" instead of liber/page numbers.

To examine an instrument recorded for a particular parcel (except Torrens properties), proceed to Room 205. The documents are on microfilm reels or microfilm jackets.

For pre-1968 records, indicate whether you seek a deed or mortgage and provide the liber and page numbers obtained from the index (either the name index or one of the block and lot indexes). Section number is also required for 1891-1917. Records in block/lot jackets (1968 to the present) may be requested by stating only the block and lot number on the request form. For records on microfilm 1968 or later, provide the reel and page number.

For Torrens properties, proceed to Room 201 to examine the file. There is no index to these records. The Office has a (red) ledger on top of the file cabinet in the anteroom to Room 201 listing Torrens properties by certificate number. Files are arranged by certificate number.

Room 205 also has on film all maps filed with the City Register's Office. There is an index to filed maps in Room 202.

Tax maps, available at the Real Property Assessment Bureau, may also be useful in identifying information about a particular property.

Description of Facility:

The City Register's Office is a large, busy government office occupying most of the 2nd floor of 31 Chambers Street. Enter Rooms 203 or 204 through Room 205.

All index libers are on open shelves. The block and lot atlas is on a standing carousel in Room 204. Long tables provide standup reading space for referencing the volumes. All of the records are immediately available. There are 6 microfilm readers, 2 microfilm reader/printers, 33 fiche readers and 2 fiche reader/printers. The Office has 2 computer terminals, one in Room 204 and one in Room 205. Both are supported by printers.

There are approximately 12 staff on duty throughout the facility. Any of them will answer short questions but they will not conduct searches for the public.

Fees/Copies:

There is no cost for computer printouts of the index. Paper copies of the microform records can be made at $.25 per page. The cashier in Room 202 can make change. If you provide the clerks with block and lot, liber (or reel) and page numbers, certified copies of records can be made by the Office. Certified copies take 72 hours (less in emergencies) or copies can be mailed. There is a fee of $4 per page.

Quick copies of the block/lot microfilm jackets can be made on microfiche at a cost of $.50 per fiche. This office will accept cash, certified checks or money orders. No personal checks are accepted.

Restrictions on Use:

Copies of records can be made from microfilm or microfiche. Photocopy machines in this office are for Uniform Commercial Code records.

No mail requests for searches will be honored. A form letter is sent in response to such requests which suggests the inquirer contact the New York State Land Title Association, 17 Battery Place, New York, NY 10004, (212) 635-9100. This organization of underwriting companies, abstracters and title insurance agents will provide a listing of all of its members who operate within a particular County. These firms are not inexpensive. Contact them for their fee schedule prior to requesting a search.

However, the Office will supply certified copies of real property instruments by mail when sufficient document location data is supplied (document type, date, liber/reel and page numbers) and a check for the proper amount ($4 per page) is enclosed.

No pens may be used when working with the index libers.

CIVIL COURT OF THE CITY OF NEW YORK
MANHATTAN (NEW YORK COUNTY)

Facility Director: Myles McKenna, Clerk of the County

Address: 111 Centre Street
New York, NY 10013

(Cross Streets: Franklin, White and Lafayette Streets)

Phone Number: (212) 374-8174, 8443 (Clerk of the County)
(212) 374-8410 (Record Room)

Hours of Operation:

Monday to Friday: 9:00 am to 5:00 pm
Closed Saturday, Sunday and legal holidays.

Closest Public Transportation:

Subway: 4, 5 or 6 to Brooklyn Bridge
J, M or Z to Chambers Street
N or R to City Hall
A or C to Chambers Street (north end)

Bus: M1 or M6 to Broadway and Chambers Street
M15 to Worth and Centre Streets
M22 to Lafayette and Reade Streets

Directions:

Take the #4 or #5 (express) or #6 (local) train to the Brooklyn Bridge station. Go down the staircase at the <u>north</u> end of the platform. Turn right at the bottom of the stairway, then left and follow the signs to "BMT & Pearl Street." Go up the stairs at the end of the long corridor, exit through the gate and go up the next flight of stairs ahead to the far right. Walk north on Centre Street to the New York City Civil Court building at 111 Centre (or walk north on Lafayette Street to #75).

Description of Resources:

The Court has change of name records from May 1887 to the present. Records, 1887-1962, were those filed in the City Court. After 1962, this became the Civil Court of the City of New York.

For the period 1887 to June 13, 1906, the case records explaining why the name change was requested and the Court's decision on the case are in bound volumes in groups of years. From June 14, 1906 to 1936, the bound volumes include only the Court's decision. The June 14, 1906 to December 31, 1931 case files, including the explanation of why the name change was requested, appear to have been lost or were destroyed. From 1932 to the present, separate file folders are available on each case.

Finding Aids:

From May 1887 to 1936, indexes in the front of each record book are arranged alphabetically by the first letter of the surname. From 1937 to the present, the bound volumes include only the index (arranged the same way).

The indexes include both the old and new names but are alphabetized only under the old name pre-1938 and from 1958 to the present. From 1938 to 1957, the old and new surnames are alphabetized by the first letter of the name. Each volume, 1887-1916 and 1938 to the present, covers a group of years. There are annual volumes covering the period 1917-1937.

Description of Facility:

The records and indexes, 1887-1931, and indexes, 1932-1969, are located in Room 214 (second floor) in a large cabinet facing the entrance. The indexes after 1969 are located in Room 488 (fourth floor) at the left end of the counter.

All records can be obtained in Room 214. Case files from 1932 to the present must be requested from the clerk on duty. Files prior to 1957 are located in Room 225, section 6, but requests for these files should be made to the clerk in Room 214. A request form may be required for each file.

There is one clerk on duty in Room 214. Counter space (standing room) is available for about 3-4 researchers.

Fees/Copies:

While there is no photocopy machine in Room 214, two are available in Room 225. The clerk in Room 214 may accompany researchers who wish to make copies to Room 225. Copies cost $.10 per page. The clerk can provide a certified copy at $4 per page.

Restrictions on Use:

None.

COUNTY CLERK'S OFFICE - STATE SUPREME COURT
NEW YORK COUNTY (MANHATTAN)

Facility Director:	Norman Goodman, County Clerk
	Alturo Hassell, Chief Clerk
Address:	60 Centre Street, Room 103B
	New York, NY 10007
	(Cross Streets: Worth Street and Foley Square)
Phone Number:	(212) 374-8587

Hours of Operation:

Monday to Friday: 9:00 am to 5:00 pm
Closed Saturday, Sunday and legal holidays.

Closest Public Transportation and Directions:

See "CIVIL COURT OF THE CITY OF NEW YORK, MANHATTAN (NEW YORK COUNTY)." The U.S. Court House will be to the right and the State Supreme Court building to the north of it, also on the right as you emerge from the subway. Go up the main stairs to the rotunda and take an elevator down one flight to the first floor.

Description of Resources:

The following records for New York County (Manhattan) are available in the State Supreme Court building. For earlier Court records, see "COUNTY CLERK'S OFFICE - STATE SUPREME COURT - NEW YORK COUNTY (MANHATTAN), DIVISION OF OLD RECORDS."

1. New York State Census 1905, 1915 and 1925 - original copies of the NYS Census books for New York County (Manhattan). The Bronx is included in the 1905 census. Data included in these censuses are: address, surname, first name (or initial), relationship to head of household, race, sex, age, nativity, years in the U.S., citizen or alien and occupation. The 1925 census also asked, for naturalized citizens, the date and court of naturalization. See "Restrictions on Use."

2. Naturalizations - pre-1907 naturalization records for New York County filed in:

    New York County Court of Common Pleas, 1792-1895
    New York State Supreme Court in New York County, 1868, 1896-1906
    Superior Court of New York City, 1828-1895

    Copies of these records are also available in the NATIONAL ARCHIVES, NORTHEAST REGION.

3. Business Names include:

    Certificates of Incorporation, 1939 to the present (includes incorporation records for synagogues and
        landsmanshaftn societies)
    Limited Partnerships, 1923 to the present
    Trade Names "Doing business as...," 1925 to the present

4. Military Discharge Records are filed on a voluntary basis by veterans after the first and second World Wars. See "Restrictions on Use."

5. Name Changes filed in Supreme Court, New York County, 1935 to the present.

6. Court Cases filed in Supreme Court, New York County, 1941 to the present. Includes all records of cases filed in New York County during this period.

7. Matrimonial Records - divorces, separations and annulments brought in New York County, 1941 to the present. See "Restrictions on Use."

8. Incompetency Records and Conservatorships involving persons who could not handle their own affairs or persons committed. Incompetency Records are available from 1941 to the present, and Conservatorships from 1977 to the present.

9. Surrenders of Children filed from 1927 to the present. See "Restrictions on Use."

Finding Aids:

1. For Census records, the street address is necessary for a search. The card index that matches street address to Assembly/Election District is not open to the public.

2. Researchers do not have access to the index of Naturalizations pre-1907 in this building. However, this index is available in two other locations. See "COUNTY CLERK'S OFFICE - STATE SUPREME COURT - NEW YORK COUNTY (MANHATTAN), DIVISION OF OLD RECORDS" and "NATIONAL ARCHIVES, NORTHEAST REGION."

3. A computer index (printout) is available for Business Names registered in New York County. This index is arranged alphabetically by company name and covers all records from 1812 to the present.

4. Military Discharge Records are indexed in an alphabetical card file. See "Restrictions on Use."

5. Liber indexes for Name Change records are available for 1911-1923, 1942-1946, 1947-1969 and 1970 to the present. For 1911-1923 and 1947 to the present, these are arranged alphabetically by the first letter of the old surname only. For 1942-1946, the index is arranged by the first letter of the old and new surnames. Liber indexes pre-1947 include name changes of corporations as well as individuals. Indexes from 1947 to the present include only individuals. Two volumes, 1924-1933 and 1934-1941, can not be located.

   In addition to these libers, researchers can use the annual case liber index, Index to Clerk's Minutes - Individual (in Room 103B). However, this is a much more tedious process since several libers will have to be examined instead of one if the exact year is unknown. If the name change occurred before 1935, researchers should use the index cards (alphabetical) available in the COUNTY CLERK'S OFFICE - STATE SUPREME COURT - NEW YORK COUNTY (MANHATTAN), DIVISION OF OLD RECORDS.

6. Matrimonials, Incompetency Records and all other Court Cases involving individuals are indexed by surname of the plaintiff in the annual Index to Clerk's Minutes - Individual. From 1941 to May 1971, indexes are in libers arranged by year and then by first initial of the surname. From May 1971 to the present, court cases are identified in computer lists, 1971-1986 and 1987 to the present, in alphabetical order of the name of the plaintiff.

Description of Facility:

These offices are located on the first floor of the New York State Supreme Court Building. Researchers are not permitted behind the counters. There is no seating available in most rooms. The exception is the Business Section (Room 117B) where there is seating for 8 researchers at two long tables and the Record Room (Room 103B) which can seat 24 researchers. There are 1-2 staff persons in each room who take record requests.

Records and indexes can be found in the following rooms:

1. Census Records and Naturalizations are at the notary desk to the far left in Room 141B.

2. Business Names: The computer index and records are in Room 117B.

3. Military Discharge Records: Indexes and records are located in Room 109B (to the far right) behind the counter.

4. Name Changes: Liber indexes pre-1947 and records, 1935-1946, are in Room 117B. The old libers are not arranged in any particular order. First search the shelves in the second liber book case to the left of the entrance to this room.

   Name Change liber indexes from 1947 to the present are at the far right in Room 141B (near the entrance to the Record Room). Name Change records from 1947 to the present are in the Record Room (Room 103B).

5. Matrimonials, Incompetencies and other Court Cases: The computer index from May 1971 to the present is in Room 141B near the entrance to the Record Room. Liber indexes from 1941 to May 1971 and case files from 1941 to the present can be obtained in the Record Room (Room 103B).

6. Surrenders of Children: Records of surrenders are maintained in a vault in Room 109B. See "Restrictions on Use."

Fees/Copies:

A certified copy (extract) of the Census data is $1 per address per surname and census year. Allow one week for the extract to be mailed. Searches are not conducted on the spot.

Copies of Naturalizations are provided upon request. The person's name (spelled as it was on the Naturalization), date of arrival, name of ship and port of entry are to be provided to assure a thorough search. If the date of Naturalization and/or the certificate number are provided, the search will be easier. No Naturalizations are provided on the day of request. Allow 3-6 weeks for response.

Business records and Name Change records may be examined by researchers. Copies may be made at $.10 per page. Copy machines are available at the entrance to each room.

Most case files are open and may be copied. See "Restrictions on Use" for limitations. For older records on microfiche, a free copy of the microfiche will be provided to the researcher.

Restrictions on Use:

The County Clerk's staff conducts all Census and Naturalization searches. No public access is allowed. NOTE: The NEW YORK STATE EDUCATION DEPARTMENT, OFFICE OF CULTURAL EDUCATION, NEW YORK STATE LIBRARY in Albany has a duplicate copy of the 1915 and 1925 New York State census which is accessible to researchers.

Access to Military Discharge Records is restricted to the concerned individual or his/her immediate family.

Matrimonial cases are closed except to the involved parties or their attorneys. Indexes are open.

Surrenders of Children (indexes and records) are closed except by court order.

Use of pencils only is allowed.

COUNTY CLERK'S OFFICE - STATE SUPREME COURT
NEW YORK COUNTY (MANHATTAN)
DIVISION OF OLD RECORDS

Facility Director:	Joseph Van Nostrand, Archivist/Principal Court Analyst
	Bruce Abrams, Archivist/Senior Court Analyst
Address:	31 Chambers Street, 7th Floor
	New York, NY
	(Cross Streets: Centre and Elk Streets)
Mail Address:	New York County Clerk's Office
	60 Centre Street, Room 161
	New York, NY 10007
Phone Number:	(212) 374-4376, 4781

Hours of Operation:

Tuesday, Thursday: 9:00 am to 5:00 pm
Monday, Wednesday,
  Friday: by appointment only
Closed Saturday, Sunday and legal holidays.

Closest Public Transportation and Directions:

See "CITY REGISTER'S OFFICE, MANHATTAN."

Description of Resources:

This Division of the County Clerk's Office is the custodian of old records of the State Supreme Court in New York County and its predecessor courts, as well as other materials which fall within the jurisdiction of the County Clerk. For more recent business, matrimonial, military and court records, see "COUNTY CLERK'S OFFICE - STATE SUPREME COURT, NEW YORK COUNTY (MANHATTAN)." The following records are located at this office:

1. Census Records

    NY State Census, New York County (Manhattan), 1855 (originals), 1905, 1915, 1925 (on microfilm). See "Restrictions on Use."

    NOTE: The NEW YORK PUBLIC LIBRARY, MICROFORMS DIVISION has the 1855 Census on microfilm for many counties including New York County; and the NEW YORK STATE EDUCATION DEPARTMENT, OFFICE OF CULTURAL EDUCATION, NEW YORK STATE LIBRARY has the 1915 and 1925 Census on microfilm.

    U.S. Census, New York County (Manhattan), 1870 - The New York County (Manhattan) enumeration of the 1870 Census was done twice. The first enumeration is available here.

2. Naturalizations

    Petitions for Naturalization filed in NYS Supreme Court, 1907-1924 (originals and microfilmed copies). Declarations of Intention, 1828-1924. See "Restrictions on Use."

    Microfilm index to pre-1907 Naturalizations in all NYC courts. (A microfilm copy of the index cards and photostatic copies of the records are also available at the "NATIONAL ARCHIVES, NORTHEAST REGION.")

3. City Directories

Manhattan/Bronx* City Directories (paper copies) for 1850-1868, 1870-1902, 1909, 1911-1913, 1916-1918, 1920-1922/23, and 1933/34. The Division also has damaged Directories for 1905/6 and 1908-1910. Use may be restricted because of condition.

*NOTE: Parts of the Bronx are included from 1875 to 1895 and all of the Bronx from 1896 to 1933/34.

The Directories alphabetically list head of household by surname (male adults primarily; women usually are included only if widowed), occupation, home address and/or business address. Entries for businesses (except for 1931) are also included. The Directories make excellent finding aids for the 1890 Police Census, the NYS Census and the U.S. Census.

4. Business Names

Certificates of Incorporation, 1812-1938 (includes incorporation records for synagogues and landsmanshaftn societies)
Limited Partnerships, 1822-1922
Trade Names "Doing business as...," 1900-1924

5. Maps

Enumeration and Assembly Districts for 1855 and 1870, New York County (Manhattan)
Maps/Condemned Areas (contained in condemnation case files, as well as individual maps), 1797 to the present
Maps of Manhattan, 1893-1894

6. Matrimonial Records

Divorce, separation and annulment cases brought in New York County, 1784-1940. See "Restrictions on Use."

7. Military Records

State Militia Enrollment, 1917 (includes name, address, age, birthdate, occupation and prior military service of men ages 18 to 45 liable for service)

8. Name Changes

Individuals whose names were legally changed, 1847-1934

9. Other Court Records

Attorneys admitted to practice in NY, 1754-1895. (After 1895, these records were filed with the Appellate Division of NY Supreme Court.)
Court of Chancery, 1765-1848 (85% of these records are after 1820). See also "NEW YORK STATE EDUCATION DEPARTMENT, OFFICE OF CULTURAL EDUCATION, NEW YORK STATE ARCHIVES."
Mayor's Court (after 1821, became Court of Common Pleas), 1674-1895
Supreme Court of Judicature, Parchments, 1685-1848. (Most of the records date from 1780-1800.)
Supreme Court, Pleadings, 1754-1910
Superior Court Cases, 1828-1895
Supreme Court Common Law Judgments, 1799-1940. (After 1910, case folders include all papers filed in the case in addition to the final judgment.)
Supreme Court Equity Cases, 1848-1910. (After 1910, equity cases were filed together with Supreme Court Common Law Judgments.)

10. Marriage Records

Marriages performed by the Mayors of New York, 1830-1850 (2 volumes)

11. Adoptions

Adoptions arranged through New York County SURROGATE'S COURT, 1874-1934. (These are duplicate orders filed with the County Clerk. The actual case files are on file in the SURROGATE'S COURT.)

Finding Aids:

There are two <u>Naturalization</u> indexes for 1907-1924: A card index arranged alphabetically by surname, 1907-1925; and liber indexes, grouped by years and indexed by the first letter of the last name. Experienced genealogists are now permitted access to the index cards. Declarations of Intention, 1907-1924, are indexed in each volume. See "Restrictions on Use."

Indexes to <u>Court Records</u> are arranged by the name of the plaintiff. Separate alphabetical card indexes are available for each of the following record groups:

Court of Chancery	1765-1848
Mayor's Court/Court of Common Pleas	1683-1895
Supreme Court of Judicature, Parchments	1685-1848
Supreme Court, Pleadings	1754-1910
Superior Court Cases	1828-1895
Supreme Court Common Law Judgments	1799-1910
Supreme Court Cases	1911-1940

The following records are indexed in a combined alphabetical card index, the Miscellaneous Records Index:

Name Changes	1847-1934
Marriage Records	1830-1850

Liber Indexes, arranged by year or groups of years and then alphabetically or by the first letters of the surname, are available for:

Attorneys Admitted (three volumes)	1754-1895
Limited Partnerships	1822-1922
Chancery and Supreme Court Equity Cases	1804-1910
Matrimonials (divorces and annulments)	1784-1910

A computer index (printout) is available for <u>Business Names</u> registered in New York County. This index is arranged alphabetically by company name and covers all records from 1812 to the present.

Description of Facility:

The Old Records Division occupies the 7th and 8th floors of 31 Chambers Street. The office and Reading Room are located on the 7th floor to the right of the elevator lobby.

Seats are available for 8 researchers at two sloped tables in the Reading Room, Room 703. There are three staff members on duty on open days who can provide assistance. There is one microfilm reader and one reader/printer.

Census volumes, 1855 and 1870, Naturalization Petitions, 1907-1924, City Directories, and all indexes described above are on open shelves or in cabinets on the 7th floor.

Declarations of Intention are located on the 8th floor. Microfilms are located on the 7th floor and accessed through the Reading Room.

Fees/Copies:

A photocopy machine is available at $.15 per page. Bring change or go to the CITY REGISTER'S OFFICE cashier on the 2nd floor. Mail requests for Census searches are $1 per name, per address and year. State-mandated fees for photocopies of any other record are $4 per page. Payment by certified check or postal money order, payable to the New York County Clerk, must accompany the order. Allow 2-3 weeks for a return reply. At the present time, there is no charge for copies of Naturalization records.

Restrictions on Use:

<u>Microfilm</u>: The Division has one (old) microfilm reader and one reader/printer. In order to assure access to microfilmed records, researchers are requested to call in advance to make an appointment.

Census: At the present time, the Division does not have a copy of the 1905, 1915, 1925 index to convert addresses to Assembly/Election District (AD/ED) nor does it have the AD/ED maps for the 1905, 1915 or 1925 census.

Declarations of Intention pre-1907 are not very accessible. Each of the 393 volumes is indexed separately. Further, separate volumes exist for each year or for parts of a year, by country of origin and also by court. Only three major country groupings were used: Germany, Great Britain/Ireland and Italy. Declarations by immigrants of such countries as Poland, Russia or Austria are usually located in the volumes for Germany. Researchers must know approximately in what year and court the Declaration was filed.

Direct access to these volumes is currently limited since they are located on the 8th floor which is off-limits to the public. (NOTE: Declarations, 1907-1924, are being microfilmed by the Genealogical Society of Utah. See "FAMILY HISTORY CENTERS (LDS)." It is anticipated that copies of the microfilms will be made available to this Office.)

Adoption indexes and records are sealed and cannot be viewed except by court order.

Matrimonial cases are only available if more than 100 years old. Indexes are open.

Some materials are accessed by the staff only and can be used only under staff supervision, e.g. fragile parchments or books.

HADASSAH - THE WOMEN'S ZIONIST ORGANIZATION OF AMERICA ARCHIVES

Facility Director: Ira Daly, Archivist

Address: 50 West 58th Street
New York, NY 10019

(Cross Streets: 5th and 6th Avenues)

Phone Number: (212) 355-7900

Hours of Operation:

Monday to Friday: 9:00 am to 12:00 noon; 1:00 pm to 5:00 pm
Closed Saturday, Sunday, Jewish and legal holidays. Call for an appointment. The Archivist is not available to assist researchers between 12:00 noon and 1:00 pm (lunch hour).

Closest Public Transportation:

Subway: N or R to 5th Avenue
           4, 5 or 6 to 59th Street/Lexington Avenue
           E or F to 5th Avenue
           Q to 57th Street/6th Avenue

Bus: M1, M2, M3, M4, M5, M30 or M32 to 5th Avenue and 59th Street (southbound)
           M5, M6, M7 to 6th Avenue and 57/58th Street (northbound)
           M103 to 59th Street and 5th Avenue (crosstown)
           M28 to 57th Street and 5th Avenue (crosstown)

Directions:

Take the N or R train to the 5th Avenue station. Walk one block south on 5th Avenue to 58th Street. Turn west to #50. The Archives is in the basement of the building.

Description of Resources:

The Archives has the records of Hadassah, its chapters and departments and related organizations such as the Hadassah Medical Organization. Items of interest to genealogists include:

1.   <u>Hadassah Publications</u>

    Hadassah Monthly Bulletin, 1914-1918
    Hadassah Monthly Newsletter, 1920-1960
    Hadassah Magazine, 1961-1981
    Hadassah Headlines, 1938-1969
    Young Judean Magazine, 1933-1939
    Junior Hadassah Yearbook, 1924-25, 1927, 1928, 1930-31, 1935, 1940, 1941, 1949-50

2.   <u>Photographs</u>

    There are approximately 55,000 photographs including those of Hadassah presidents, Zionist leaders, immigrants to Israel, and Israeli ambassadors. The collection also includes photos of kibbutzim and cities and towns in Israel, Hadassah Medical Organization, Youth Aliyah, Young Judea, Junior Hadassah, Hadassah conventions and Hadassah vocational education programs in Israel.

3.   <u>Papers of Hadassah Leaders</u>

    Brandeis Collection, 1915-1942. Correspondence with Louis Brandeis by Hadassah leaders, articles by and about Brandeis, and a copy of Brandeis' will.

Jacobs, Rose G., 1910-1960. Correspondence, reports, diaries and other material concerning the American Zionist Medical Unit, Hadassah Medical Organization and Hadassah Training School for Nurses as well as correspondence with other Jewish leaders. The collection includes autobiographical material, correspondence concerning the Jacobs family, 1932-1933 and 1946, and the memoirs of her husband Edward delineating his wife's Hadassah connections. Also included are biographical material, intimate accounts and memoriam essays on others associated with Hadassah.

Elyachar, Anna Tulin. Correspondence and other material concerning the Isakower estate, 1976-1984; Siegfried Ullman's will, 1964-1976; petition of Emanuel Neumann to the NY Court of Appeals, 1932; and clippings concerning Henrietta Szold and other subjects, 1960-1983.

Seligsberg, Alice L., 1917-1942. Correspondence, notes and reports about work with orphans in Palestine, including the Palestine War Orphans Commission, 1920-1923, and the Palestine Orphans Committee of the American Jewish Joint Distribution Committee, as well as correspondence with other Jewish leaders. The collection includes personal correspondence with Nellie Straus Mochenson, 1919-1923.

Szold, Henrietta, 1860-1945. Szold family correspondence, 1889-1942, documents relating to the life of her father, her own life and Szold genealogical materials, 1888-1964. The collection includes material on her activities in Zionist and Jewish affairs as well as correspondence with prominent Jewish leaders.

Ezekiel, Denise Tourover, 1935-1981. Correspondence and cables concerning transport of Polish Jewish refugee children from Teheran to Palestine, 1942-1943, correspondence with other Jewish leaders and biographical material on Ezekiel.

The Archives also has the following collections:

David Ben Gurion Papers, 1947-1973
Tamar de Sola Pool Papers, 1925-1979
Rose Halprin Papers, 1930-1964
Jessie Zel Lurie Papers, 1947-1978
Miriam Freund Rosenthal Papers
Bernice Salpeter Tannenbaum Papers, 1962-1985

4.   Hadassah Projects

Annual Conventions Archives, 1914-1971. These files include speeches made by various individuals for all years, correspondence related to the conventions and delegates' lists for 1939-1955, 1958-1960, 1964-1967 and 1971-1975. The 1943 files also include a membership list.

Hadassah Medical Organization (HMO) Archives, 1918-1984. Of particular interest to genealogists are the records, correspondence and minutes related to personnel. These include discussions of the qualifications of medical staff for positions and promotions, as recorded in the Medical Advisory Council minutes, 1948-1959 and the minutes (microfilm) of the Board of the Hebrew University Medical School, 1950-1963, and Dental School, 1958-1969. Files include resumes, credentials, biographical sketches, obituaries and correspondence about doctors and nurses; and a list of the Hebrew University Medical School staff, 1950-1958. In addition, there is correspondence on cases of disabled soldiers treated by the Occupational Therapy Department, 1948-1949.

Youth Aliyah Archives, 1933-1960. Includes Szold's analysis of the individuals who were connected with the Youth Aliyah movement from the early days; biographical material on the London Youth Aliyah Executive Committee and correspondence on the shortcomings of leading candidates for the Director's position in Palestine, c.1947. The collection includes case files on former Youth Aliyah leaders and students whom Hadassah chose to help after they completed their service or graduated; case histories of Youth Aliyah children in 1938, as well as those who arrived in Palestine from Transdniestria, 1944, and Teheran, pre-1944. Also included are lists of children by country c.1945; the bulletins of the Jewish Agency for Palestine, which contained eyewitness accounts of the slaughter of Jews in Eastern Galicia, Pinsk, Polish White Russia, Transdniestria,

Salonika, Crete and various camps; and lists of Hadassah delegates to the Youth Aliyah conference in Amsterdam, c.1939.

Zionist Political History Archives, 1894-1985. Includes such items as the Gertrude Rosenblatt diaries, 1911-1914; Shulamit Cantor and Helena Kagan, M.D. autobiographies; biographical sketch of Bertha Landsman, 1937, and family correspondence, 1921-1924; Hadassah membership lists, 1920-1960; World Zionist Congress-Hadassah delegate lists, 1946; and the Dorothy Bar Adon case histories of concentration camp survivors, 1944-1945.

Hadassah Vocational Education Archives, 1940-1962.

5. Membership Lists

The Archives has membership lists on microfilm, 1969-1975. The records are grouped by city, i.e. Atlanta, Miami, etc. but do not appear to be in any particular order. The names appear on individual cards which list also address and contribution.

Finding Aids:

In addition to *A Guide to the Hadassah Archives,* 1986, there are booklets for each collection which describe each record group. Each finding aid includes an introduction, chronology or biographical sketch, scope and content note, series listing and descriptions, and box and folder lists. Eight finding aids have been published:

The Hadassah Medical Organization Papers, 1918-1981.
The Hadassah Medical Organization Archives, 1947-1984: A Guide to the Microfilms.
The Archives of Youth Aliyah, 1933-1960.
Zionist Political History in the Hadassah Archives, 1894-1985. (2 vols.)
The Alice L. Seligsberg and Rose G. Jacobs Papers, 1918-1957.
The Papers of Denise Tourover Ezekiel, 1936-1981.
The Henrietta Szold Papers, 1875-1965.

Description of Facility:

The Archives is located in a separate room within the Mail Department in the basement. It is a small narrow area with an aisle through the stacks. There is a desk and sitting area that can accommodate one person. The Archives has one microfilm reader.

Fees/Copies:

Photocopies can be made at $.10 per page. Copies of photographs can be made at $12.50. There may be extra copies available of stock photos. These cost $1.

Copies of *A Guide to the Hadassah Archives* are free. Printed finding aids are $3.50 each.

Restrictions on Use:

No items can be removed from the room.

HEBREW UNION COLLEGE - JEWISH INSTITUTE OF RELIGION
THE KLAU LIBRARY

Facility Director: Dr. Philip E. Miller, Librarian

Address: One West Fourth Street
New York, NY 10012

(Cross Streets: Broadway and Mercer Street)

Phone Number: (212) 674-5300

Hours of Operation:

Monday to Thursday: 9:00 am to 5:00 pm
Friday: 9:00 am to 4:00 pm

Closed Saturday, Sunday, Jewish and legal holidays. (Between September and May, may be open occasional evenings; telephone to inquire.)

Closest Public Transportation:

Subway: N or R to 8th Street
        6 to Astor Place
        A, B, C, D, E, F or Q to West 4th Street/Washington Square

Bus: M1 (South Ferry), M5 or M6 to Waverly Place and Broadway (southbound)
        M1, M2 or M3 to 8th Street and Broadway (southbound)
        M1 to Lafayette and East 4th Street (northbound)
        M5 or M6 to Avenue of the Americas and West 4th Street (northbound)

Directions:

Take the N or R train to the 8th Street station. Exit the station and walk south on Broadway to West 4th Street. Turn west on West 4th Street to the entrance.

Description of Resources:

The following is a bibliographical sampling of available works useful for genealogical research at the HUC-JIR Library. Call numbers are in brackets:

CEMETERY RECORDS

Algiers. Bloch, Isaac. *Algiers Cemeteries.* Paris, 1888. [HS/210]

Austria. Eisenstadt, Mattersdorf, Zielheim, Kobersdorf, Lackenbach, Frauenkirchen, Kittsee. Goldstein, Moshe. *Maamar sheva kehilot* [Command of seven communities]. Tel Aviv, 1956. [HS/189]

Austria. Graz. Herzog, David. *Die juedischen Friedhofe in Graz.* Graz, 1937. [HS/609.2]

Barbados. Shilstone, E. M. *Jewish Monumental Inscriptions in Barbados.* New York, 1956. [HS/1260]

Curacao. Emmanuel, I. S. *Precious Stones of the Jews of Curacao: Curacaon Jewry, 1656-1957.* New York, 1957. [HS/1257]

Czechoslovakia. Prague. Jerabek, L. *Der alte prager Judenfriedhof* [The old Jewish cemetery of Prague]. Prague, 1903. [HS/190]

    Prague. Lion, Jindrich. *Der alte prager Judenfriedhof* [The old Jewish cemetery of Prague]. Prague, 1960. [HS/191]

Prague. Lieben, Koppelman. *Grabensteininschriften des prager israelitischen alten Friedhofs* [Gravestone inscriptions of the Old Prague Israelite cemetery. Contains the most complete record of epitaphs - in German gothic type]. Prague, 1856. [HS/190]

Denmark. Copenhagen. Margolinsky, Julius. *Jodiske Dodsfald 1693-1976* [Jewish cemetery]. Copenhagen, 1978. [HS/1206]

Greece. Salonika. Emmanuel, I. S. *Gedole Saloniki le-dorotam* [Leaders of Salonika in their generations; 500 inscriptions, 1500-1660]. Tel Aviv, 1936. [HS/755]

Salonika. Emmanuel, I. S. *Matsevot Saloniki* [Epitaphs of Salonika]. 2 vols. Jerusalem, 1963. [HS/889]

Salonika. Molcho, Michael. *Bet ha-alamin shel yehude Saloniki* [The Jewish cemetery of Salonika]. Salonika, 1975. [HS/889.2]

Hungary. Scheiber, Sandor. *Jewish Inscriptions in Hungary from the 3rd century to 1686.* Leiden, 1983. [DS135 H9 S29 1983]

Budapest. Scheiber, Alexander. *Newly found Jewish tombstones at Buda.* Budapest, 1953. [HS/415]

Israel. Jerusalem. Cohen, Shear Yashub. *Har ha-zetim* [Mt. of Olives]. Jerusalem, 1969. [LB]

Lithuania. Vilna. Klausner, Israel. *Korot bet ha-olamin ha-yashan be-Vilna* [History of the old cemetery in Vilna]. 1935. [HS/928.2]

Netherlands. Amsterdam. de Castro, Henriques. *Keur van Grafsteenen op de Nederl. Portug. Israel. Begraafplaats te Oudekerk* [Record of epitaphs of the Dutch Portuguese-Jewish Cemetery at Oudekerk, the oldest Sephardic cemetery in the Netherlands]. Leiden, 1883. [HS/645.1]

Amsterdam. Vega, L. Alvares. *Het Beth Haim van Oudekerk...* [The cemetery at Oudekerk: images of a Portuguese Jewish cemetery in Holland]. Assen, 1975. (Dutch and English) [DS135 N5 0937 1975]

St. Thomas. Margolinsky, Julius. *299 Epitaphs from the Jewish Cemetery of St. Thomas, V.I., 1837-1916.* (mimeographed) Copenhagen, 1957. [HS/1229]

Spain. Cartera & Millas. *Las Inscripciones Hebraicas de Espana* [Hebrew inscriptions of Spain]. Madrid, 1956. [HS/756]

United States. Charleston, SC. Elzas, B.A. *The Old Jewish Cemeteries at Charleston, S.C..* Charleston, 1903. [F279 C4 E5 1903]

Galveston, TX. Dreyfus, A. Stanley. *Hebrew Cemetery No. 1 of Galveston, TX.* (mimeo-graphed) [ALU]

New York, NY. de Sola Pool, David. *Portraits Etched in Stone: Early Jewish Settlers, 1632-1831.* New York, 1952. [HS/1254]

Savannah, GA. Levy, B. H. *Savannah's Old Jewish Community Cemeteries.* Macon, 1983. [F294 S2 L47 1983]

West Germany. Frankfurt am Main. Hulsen, Julius. *Der alte Judenfriedhof in Frankfurt a.M.* [The old Jewish cemetery in Frankfurt am Main]. Frankfurt, 1932. [HI/472.3]

Rheinpfalz. Friedmann, Hugo. *Merischonim loachronim: Verstorbenlisten der juedischen Gemeinden der Mittelmosel von Wintrich bis Enkirch* [From first to last: Death lists of the Jewish communities of the central Mosel valley, from Wintrich to Enkirch]. (typescript) Berncastel-Cues, 1929. [HS/407]

Wuerttemberg. *Juedische Gotteshaeuser und Friedhofe in Wuerttemberg* [Jewish synagogues and cemeteries in Wuerttemberg]. Stuttgart, 1932. [HS/440]

VITAL RECORDS AND LISTS

England. London. Barnett, L.D. and G.H. Whitehill. *Bevis Marks Records* (Sephardic Congregation). v.1: Early history of the congregation; v. 2: Marriages, 1687-1837; v.3: Marriages, 1836-1901. London, 1940, 1973. [HS/337]

Portugal. Coimbra. Bivar Guerra, Luiz de. *Inventario dos Processos da Inquisicao de Coimbra (1541-1820)* [Catalog of the trials of the Inquisition of Coimbra, Portugal, 1541-1820. Names are indexed in vol. 2]. Paris, 1972. [HS/772]

GENEALOGIES

United States. Stern, Malcolm H. *First American Jewish Families; 600 Genealogies,* 1654-1977. Cincinnati and Waltham, 1978. [ALU (RBR)]

West Germany. Frankfurt am Main. Dietz, Alexander. *Stammbuch der Frankfurter Juden* [Genealogies of the Jews of Frankfurt am Main]. Frankfurt, 1907. [HS/605]

COMMUNAL HISTORIES AND YIZKOR BOOKS (Pre- and Post-World War II)

The following books are not included in Appendix A:

Bavaria. Weinberg, M. *Die Memorbuecher der juedischen Gemeinden in Bayern* [Memorial books of the Jewish communities in Bavaria]. Frankfurt, 1937-1938. [HS/323]

Salfeld, Sigmund. *Das Martyrologium des Nuernberger Memorbuch* [Martyrology of Jews in Bavarian towns]. Berlin, 1898. [HS/350]

Brest-Litovsk. *Brzesc nad Bugiem (Brisk) Ir Tehilah* [Brisk, City of Prayer]. Warsaw, 1886. (Hebrew) [HI/912]

Busk. *Toldot yehudim* [History of the Jews]. Tel Aviv, 1962. [HI/926.3]

France. Klarsfeld, Serge. *Memorial to the Jews Deported from France, 1942-1944* [Registers of the dead]. New York, 1983. [DS135 F83 K4313 1983]

Kalisz. *Toldot yehude Kalish* [History of the Jews of Kalisz]. Tel Aviv, 1961. [HI/909.3]

Krakow. Friedberg, B. *Luhot zikaron* [Tablets of Memory]. Frankfurt am Main, 1904. [HI/929.1]

Lithuania. *Da'at kedoshim* [Religion of the holy. 1658 pogrom. Mentions these families: Eisenstat, Bachrach, Ginzberg, Heilprin, Morwitz, Mintz, Friedland, Katzenelbogen, Rapoport and Rokeach]. St. Petersburg, 1897/98. [HI/921]

Dubnow, Simon. *Pinkas ha-medinah Lita* [Ledger of the province of Lithuania]. Berlin, 1925 (photocopy). [HI/917]

Lodz. *Kehilat Lodz* [The community of Lodz]. Jerusalem, 1948. [HI/905]

Ha-yehudim be-Lodz [The Jews in Lodz]. Warsaw, 1893. [HI/926.1]

Yasni, A. Wolf. *Die geshikhte fun yidn in Lodz* [The history of the Jews in Lodz]. Israel, 1960. [HI/922.3]

Lublin. Balaban, Majer. *Die Judenstadt von Lublin* [The ghetto of Lublin]. Berlin, 1919. [HI/907] and Hebrew edition [HI/907.2]

Lwow. *Zydzi Lwowscy* [Jews of Lwow]. Lwow, 1909. (Polish) [HI/903.2]

Anshe shem [Men of renown]. Krakow, 1895. (Hebrew) [HI/904]

Die Lemberger Juden Pogrom Nov. 1918-Jan. 1919. [HI/910]

Minsk. Eisenstadt, Ben Zion b. Moses. *Ravnei Minsk* [Chief Rabbis of Minsk]. Vilna, 1898. [HI/921.1]

Ostraha/Ostrov. *Mazkeret li-gedole Ostraha* [Memorandum of the Leaders of Ostraha]. 1907. [HI/906]

Pinsk. Aharoni, Avraham. *Maftehot shemot ha-ishim ve-ha-yishuvim shel sifre Pinsk* [Indexes of the names of the men and settlements of the records of Pinsk]. Haifa, 1982. [DS135 R93 P5433 1982]

Russia. *Juden Pogrome in Russland* [Jewish pogroms in Russia - giving the story of each community]. 2 vols. Koeln/Leipzig, 1910. [HP/100]

Ukraine. Revyuk, E. *Polish atrocities in the Ukraine.* 1931. [HP/73]

Vilna. Fein, Rabbi Samuel Joseph. *Kiryah Ne'emanah* [Faithful City]. Vilna, 1915. [HI/926]

Haivrit b'Vilna. *Toldot ha-kehilah* [History of the Community]. Vilna, 1935. [HI/923.2]

Zolkiew. *Sefer Zolkiew* [The book of Zolkiew]. 1843. [HI/905]

GAZETTEERS

Cohen, Chester G. *Shtetl Finder Gazetteer.* Los Angeles, 1980. [REF DS135 R9 C58]

Szajkowski, Z. *Analytical Franco-Jewish Gazetteer, 1939-45.* New York, 1966. [HP/166]

BIOGRAPHICAL DICTIONARIES

Who's Who in American Jewry. 1926, 1928, 1938-39, 1980.

Who's Who in World Jewry. 1955, 1965, 1972, 1978, 1980.

Whittemore, Henry. *Progressive, Patriotic, and Philanthropic Hebrews of the New World* [Biographies of leaders of the NYC community with a history of their philanthropic institutions]. New York, 1907.

PERIODICALS

Allgemeine Zeitung des Judenthums [General Newspaper of Jewry], 1837-1922.

American Jewish Historical Society: *Publications,* 1892-1947, *American Jewish Historical Quarterly,* 1947-1977, *American Jewish History,* 1977- .

American Jewish Archives, 1949- .

American Jewish Year Book, 1899- . Of interest to genealogists:
Lists of every Jewish organization in the US: 1900-01, 1907-08, 1919-20.
Biographical sketches of rabbis and cantors: 1903-04; 1904-05.
Biographical sketches of communal workers: 1905-06.
Necrologies - every volume.
Individual biographies of prominent Jews.

Canadian Jewish Year Book, 1939-1941.

Chicago Jewish Forum, 1942-1969.

The Jewish Forum, 1918-1960.

Jewish Times, 1869-1872.

The Occident (edited by Isaac Leeser), 1843-1868.

Western States Jewish Historical Quarterly, 1968- .

PERIODICALS ON MICROFILM

The American Hebrew, New York, 1879-1884, 1890-1900, 1926-1941.

The Reform Advocate (edited by Emil G. Hirsch), Chicago, 1891-1922.

The Israelite (edited by Isaac Mayer Wise, now *The American Israelite*), Cincinnati, 1854-1913.

AMERICAN JEWISH ARCHIVES (AJA) MICROFILMS

Portions of the holdings of the AJA in Cincinnati are on microfilm in the library. These include some congregational records, family histories and other data. The following are the records of genealogical interest. Film numbers are in brackets:

Amsterdam. Portuguese Congregation ketubot, 1690-1893. [833-840]

Barbados. Ledger books and burial records, 1696-1887. [822]

Efroymson-Feibleman-Kahn genealogy. [2764]

Hamburg, Germany. Sephardim, 1672-1682. [751]

Jamaica, West Indies. Wills, 1692-1798. [140]

Lisbon, Portugal. Inquisition records: New Christians, America to Lisbon. [606-650, 736-745, 842-847]; Mexico. [720-722]; Brazil to Lisbon. [783-794]

Mexico. Inquisition records, 1597-1718. [856-859]

St. Thomas, VI. Vital records, 1786-1956. [125]

Surinam. Portuguese Congregation records, 1754-1920. [67-67o]

Portuguese Community records. [176-198]

> Records of the Portuguese Jews. [527-527t]

United States. American Jewish Joint Distribution Committee, papers, 1918-1980. [2798]

> Atlanta, GA. Hebrew Benevolent Congregation (The Temple), vital records, etc., 1890-1950. [552]

> Charleston, SC. Congregation Beth Elohim, minutes, 1838-1850. [84]

> Cincinnati, OH. Judah Touro Cemetery, 1856-1970. [2160-61]

>> United Hebrew Cemetery, records, 1850-1951. [48]

>> United Hebrew Cemetery, burials, 1850-1930, 1951-1959. [439-439a]

> Erie, PA. Congregation Anshe Chesed, minutes, etc. 1875-1936; cemetery records, 1865-1920. [3066-3069]

> Nashville, TN. Vine Street Temple, marriages and deaths, 1881-1928. [592]

> New Orleans, LA. Touro Synagogue and Hebrew Rest Cemetery, 1846-1955. [221-222]

> New York, NY. Congregation B'nai Jeshurun, records (marriages, 1825-1930; deaths, 1853-1928). [493-493h]

>> Congregation Shearith Israel (Spanish & Portuguese), records, 1706-1949. [1-1g]

>> *New York Herald Tribune,* Index, 1875-1906. [3-3b]

> Philadelphia, PA. Association for the Protection of Jewish Immigrants, 1884-1921. [137-137d]

>> Reform Congregation Kneseth Israel, minutes, 1847-1880. [90]

> Piqua, OH. Anshe Emeth Congregation records, 1874-1956. [560]

> St. Louis, MO. Mt. Sinai Cemetery, 1859-1972. [861]

Finding Aids:

The Library has three card catalogs (adjacent to the library entrance):

1. The original (Kiev) catalog, created by former librarian Edward Kiev, includes author, subject, and title. Call numbers consist of letters, usually followed by numbers (e.g. HS/88). Note that Hebrew books are cataloged separately in drawers following A-Z.

2. The newer catalog is subdivided into author-title and subject catalogs using the Library of Congress system (e.g. DS135 R93 P5433).

3. A catalog of post-1964 acquisitions in the Cincinnati campus Klau Library.

In addition, the Library has the following large-sized, bound catalogs, located in the first bookcase beyond the desk:

4. *Catalog of the Klau Library of Hebrew Union College-Jewish Institute of Religion.* 32 vols. Cincinnati, 1964.

5. *Manuscript Catalog of the American Jewish Archives.* 4 vols. Cincinnati, 1971; supplement, 1 vol. 1975. A short description of each collection is included in the *Guide to the Holdings of the American Jewish Archives,* by J.W. Clasper and M.C. Dellenbach, Cincinnati, 1979.

6. *Catalog of the Jewish Collection, New York Public Library.* 14 vols., 1960; supplement 7 vols., 1975.

Description of Facility:

This is primarily a research library in a cheerful, spacious area on the second floor of the building, accessible only by elevator. There are individual carrels (working tables) with comfortable chairs. There is one microfilm reader. Two to four staff members are usually on duty to obtain materials and provide assistance.

Encyclopedias, many histories, bound periodicals and the finding aids described above are on open stacks in the reading room. Most of the works mentioned above are in the stacks and are available only on request at the desk at the hours specified below.

Fees/Copies:

A photocopy machine is available for use at $.10 per copy.

Restrictions on Use:

All visitors must secure an admission badge from the receptionist in the lobby, and must sign in at the library counter facing the elevator. Material is brought from the stacks only 3 times per day - 11:00 am, 2:00 pm and 4:00 pm. It is best to notify the Library in advance of the works you wish to consult. Return all books and materials to the cart at the desk. Five microfilm reels at a time may be requested. Only HUC-based personnel are permitted to borrow books.

HIAS (HEBREW IMMIGRANT AID SOCIETY)
LOCATION DEPARTMENT

Facility Director: Karl Zukerman, Executive Vice President

Mail Address: 200 Park Avenue South
New York, NY 10003

Phone Number: (212) 674-6800

Hours of Operation:

Monday to Friday: 9:00 am to 5:00 pm
Closed Saturday, Sunday, Jewish and legal holidays.

Closest Public Transportation, Directions and Description of Facility:

Not applicable. All inquiries must be made by mail.

Description of Resources:

HIAS is an important source for immigrant family information. A scattering of files for immigrant arrivals from the early 1950s and all case records, 1956-1978, are in HIAS' warehouse. Case files after 1978 are in HIAS' office. See "Restrictions on Use."

See "YIVO INSTITUTE FOR JEWISH RESEARCH - ARCHIVES" for earlier HIAS case files, office and organizational files and case files for families assisted by the Joint Distribution Committee (which merged with HIAS in 1954).

All case files pre-1937 have been destroyed.

Finding Aids:

Requests for information should include the individual's name (as spelled at the time of arrival) and, if known, the year of arrival, port of entry into the USA, and the names of other members of the household with whom the immigrant was travelling.

Additional information such as date of birth and last known address would be helpful in corroborating that the record is that of the individual sought. HIAS uses the following indexes to locate records:

1. Arrival Index Cards, 1909-1979 (1909-1964 on microfilm). Index cards, 1909-1949, are arranged by year of arrival and within each year alphabetically by the name of the head of the traveling party. Cards, 1950-1979, are arranged by HIAS' Case Name Indexing (Soundex) System (see Appendix C).

    Index cards include the case number, and may include dates/places of birth, names and family relationship of people travelling together, last place of residence, destination and details of arrival. (The actual files no longer exist for cases pre-1937. The index card is all that remains for these earlier years).

2. Master Card Index, 1950-1979. This is a cross-reference index identifying all members of the travelling party that appear on the Arrival Cards.

3. For 1980 to the present, HIAS has a computerized index of HIAS-assisted arrivals.

4. Index cards of arrivals, 1939-1950, of families assisted by the National Refugee Service and the United Service for New Americans, which merged into HIAS in 1954. These cards are organized by HIAS' Case Name Indexing (Soundex) System and are stored in HIAS' warehouse.

5. Joint Distribution Committee (JDC) index cards. The originals are in HIAS' warehouse but a microfilm copy is available at the office. This index is arranged alphabetically.

6. Record cards are also in HIAS' warehouse for children brought to the United States immediately following World War II by the European Jewish Children's Aid.

NOTE: HIAS is in the process of placing <u>all</u> index cards in one computerized system.

Fees/Copies:

There is no charge for a record search. Donations, however, are welcome. For a location search requiring advertisements, etc. to locate the person, HIAS requests a $25 contribution.

Restrictions on Use:

At the present time searches can only be conducted by mail. However, researchers can view the microfilm copy of the Arrival Index Cards, 1909-1979, the Master Index Cards, 1950-1979, and the JDC Index at the YIVO INSTITUTE FOR JEWISH RESEARCH, ARCHIVES. NOTE: Of the agencies that merged with HIAS, only the JDC index is available at YIVO.

For permission to view the actual case file, write to the Central Files Unit at HIAS. Individual case information can be shown only to a person whose family is documented in that material.

JEWISH THEOLOGICAL SEMINARY OF AMERICA
ARCHIVES OF CONSERVATIVE JUDAISM

Facility Director:	Jack Wertheimer, Director, Archives of Conservative Judaism
Address:	3080 Broadway New York, NY 10027
	(Cross Streets: West 122nd and 123rd Streets)
Phone Number:	(212) 678-8869

Hours of Operation:

Monday to Friday: by appointment only
Closed Saturday, Sunday, Jewish and legal holidays.

Closest Public Transportation:

Subway: 1 to 116th Street and Broadway
Bus: M4, M5 or M104 to 122nd Street and Broadway

Directions:

Take the #1 train to the 116th Street station. Exit at the center of the platform. Walk 6 blocks north on Broadway to 122nd Street. The entrance to the building is on the northeast corner. Enter the courtyard, turn right, walk down the right side of the quadrangle. Enter the building and go up to the 2nd floor to reach the Library.

Description of Resources:

These records of Conservative congregations and rabbis, although housed in the Rare Book Room, constitute a separate collection. It is currently being assembled and already has material of value to genealogists. These include:

1. <u>Congregation B'nai Jeshurun</u> (New York City): Marriage certificates (12 volumes), 1826-1973, and wedding book, 1897-1902; registers of deaths, including name, age, date, 1853-1928; cemetery burial permits, 1914-1934; perpetual care lists (index at 1972, 1975 and 1978); cemetery account ledgers, 1882-1926; minutes of the Joint Cemetery Committee (B'nai Jeshurun and Shaaray Tefila), 1857-1901; a "Book of Life" which includes yahrzeit dates of benefactors of B'nai Jeshurun, 1862-1965; eight files on estates and burial plots of congregants; correspondence concerning condolences, 1953-1954, and congratulatory correspondence, 1950-1952.

    Also available is the Religious School register, 1855-1919 (listing name, address, parent's name, and attendance of students), and 1946-1947 (listing names and addresses of students); a Bar Mitzvah Information Book (including name, parent's names and address), 1945-1953; and a copy of *The Clarion*, the B'nai Jeshurun Religious School Year Book, 1952.

    There are members' dues ledgers, 1904-1923; lists of congregation members (names and addresses), 1928-1931, 1935-1946, 1949-1951 and 1957; seat deeds, 1886-1958; contribution acknowledgements, 1947-1954; minute books of the congregation, 1825-1966 (gaps); correspondence of its rabbis, cantors and officers; and rabbis' letters and applications for a pulpit position, 1917.

2. <u>Baith Israel Anshei Emes - Kane Street Shul</u> (Brooklyn): A list of marriages, 1913-1917 (included in the financial records of the synagogue); seat books, 1908-1949 (gaps), 1975-1981; membership receipts, 1922-1923; membership lists and contributions, 1930; scrapbook, 1955-1956; souvenir journals, 1916-1986 (gaps); and centennial banquet book, 1956.

Includes the Baith Israel Sunday School Register of Pupils, 1889-1890; and Talmud Torah Anshei Emes tuition book, 1922-1924; records of plots in Beth El, Washington and Mt. Carmel cemeteries, c.1919, and Cemetery Board records, 1919-1930.

3. <u>Temple Beth Zion - Beth Israel</u> (Philadelphia, PA): Includes 8 volumes on the congregation's history; typed "History of 100 years of Temple Beth Israel, 1840-1940" (23 pp.); centennial celebration book, 1940; and five notebooks of names on memorial tablets.

   Includes records of donations, 1840-1895; a book of Board Managers, 1901-1960; account books, 1842-1900, showing seats, pew rents, offerings and/or membership; cemetery account book, 1934-1948; account book for receipts and disbursements, 1949-1963; minute books, 1873-1907 (annual general meetings) and 1926-1940 (Board of Managers meetings).

4. <u>Temple Shomrei Emunah</u> (Montclair, NJ): Includes minute books of general meetings, 1905-1955 (gaps); Sisterhood meetings, 1940-1948; Board of Trustees meetings, 1951-1969; congregational correspondence, 1929-1940; newsletter, 1936-1969; and fifth anniversary bulletin, 1955.

5. <u>Chisuk Emuna Bnai Russia Congregation</u> (Harrisburg, PA): Includes cemetery lot records, 1937-1968; cemetery correspondence, sale of lots, perpetual care and legal papers, 1879, 1884, 1904, 1931, 1949-1974; blueprint of plots, 1945; fiscal records of membership accounts, 1926-1949; holiday honors, 1935-1949; and congregational minutes, 1893-1897 and 1929-1970 (gaps).

6. <u>Other Collections</u> recently acquired and currently being organized include the Brooklyn Jewish Center, Anshe Chesed (New York) and Shaarey Zedek (New York).

7. <u>Rabbinical Records</u>: Include biographical material, sermons and correspondence of Rabbi Ben Zion Bokser, Rabbi Abraham Hurvitz, Rabbi Ario Hyams, Rabbi Nathan Kollin, Rabbi Israel H. Levinthal, Rabbi Louis Levitsky and 30 other rabbis.

   Rabbi Isaac Klein's collection includes also the Jewish divorces given or held by him; wedding sermons, Buffalo and Springfield; revised ketubah material (in which Rabbi Klein was involved); and eulogies.

Finding Aids:

There are typed or handwritten inventories for each collection.

Description of Facility:

The Archives of Conservative Judaism is housed in, but administratively separate from, the Rare Book Room. The finding aids for the Archives are in a file cabinet in a workroom on the 5th floor of the Jewish Theological Seminary Library building.

Fees/Copies:

Photocopies can be made at $.10 per page. Mail requests are charged $.25 per page plus postage and a $2 handling charge.

Restrictions on Use:

None.

JEWISH THEOLOGICAL SEMINARY OF AMERICA
LIBRARY, ARCHIVES AND RARE BOOK ROOM

Facility Director:	Dr. Mayer Rabinowitz, Librarian
	Rabbi Jerry Schwarzbard, Librarian, Rare Book Room
	Zofia Kubar, Archivist

Address:	3080 Broadway
	New York, NY 10027

(Cross Streets: West 122nd and 123rd Streets)

Phone Number:	(212) 678-8080 (Library)
	(212) 678-8076, 8973 (Rare Book Room and Archives)
	(212) 678-8081 (Circulation Desk)

Hours of Operation:

Library:	Winter/Summer Semesters	Academic Recess
Monday to Thursday:	8:00 am to 10:00 pm	8:30 am to 5:00 pm
Friday:	8:00 am to 5:00 pm*	8:30 am to 5:00 pm*
Sunday:	9:30 am to 10:00 pm	Closed
	* or earlier, i.e. Seminary closing time	

Rare Book Room and Archives:

Monday to Friday:	12:00 noon to 4:00 pm	12:00 noon to 4:00 pm

The Rare Book Room or Archives can be opened earlier, i.e. 10:00 am to 12:00 noon, by appointment made at least one day in advance. See "Restrictions on Use" concerning the Archives.

NOTE: Winter and summer semesters generally run from September to the end of July. Academic Recess hours generally apply to the month of August and any days between semesters.

The entire facility is closed Saturday, Jewish and legal holidays.

Closest Public Transportation and Directions:

See "JEWISH THEOLOGICAL SEMINARY OF AMERICA, ARCHIVES OF CONSERVATIVE JUDAISM."

Description of Resources:

(Adapted from *Toledot*, Spring 1979, "Genealogical Resources at the JTS" by Judith Endelman and from *Archives - Library of the JTSA: Preliminary Listings of Holdings,* February and May 1978)

1. Seminary Library

    The Library has a large collection of Yizkor books (See Appendix A) and rabbinic biographies. Its collection includes hundreds of histories of local Jewish communities throughout the world.

    The Periodical Collection includes local Jewish newspapers from communities in Europe, America, North Africa and the Near East. These include such diverse titles as:

    Ami d'Israél, Strasbourg, April, 1841 (microfilm), 1851-1858, 1862
    The Canadian Jewish Chronicle, 1914/15-1930, 1941-1948
    Davar Aher, Calcutta, 1918
    Emanu-el, San Francisco, 1903-1930
    Esra, Vienna, 1919-1920
    The Jewish Chronicle, London, 1841-1842, 1844-1899, 1900-1939 (gaps), 1956-1988; index, 1841-1880
        (on microfilm, except 1900-1939)
    Jewish Daily Bulletin, New York, 1924-1935
    Jewish Times, Baltimore, 1869-1951

Juedische Rundschau, Berlin, 1902-1906, 1924-1938 (microfilm), 1933, 1936

2. Rare Book Room

The bulk of the material in the Rare Book Room located on the 5th floor is of a literary-religious character. However the collection includes:

a. Communal record books (Pinkasim) from Europe and the U.S. such as the Pinkasim of the Chevra Kadisha of (call numbers are in brackets):

[3873]	Alsace	[9286]	Louisville, KY, 1892
[8537]	Askenaz, 1729-1782	[8499]	Madi, Hungary, 1793-1890
[3874]	Eisenstadt, 1775-1869	[3947]	Pesaro, Italy (Cemetery)
[4028]	Krotoschin	[8513]	Trinbach
[3872]	Lissa, 1833-1854	[8510]	Sultz
[8956]	Lithuania, 1828, some communities	[8601]	Sziget, Hungary, 1884-1922

The Rare Book Room has many other Pinkasim listed in the catalog (Hebrew). The subjects of these Pinkasim are not listed, e.g. Bamberg [8540], or are clearly not from the Chevra Kadisha. These books may still be of interest to genealogists, e.g. London, Beit Din [3584] or Venice, Pinkas of payments 1575-1734 [8593]. In addition, there are other Pinkasim in the collection still uncataloged and inaccessible to researchers.

b. Nearly 300 Ketubot (Jewish Marriage Contracts). Most are from Italy and the Levant (North Africa, Egypt, Russia and Syria) but there are some from America, Great Britain and Europe. The majority date from the 17th to 19th centuries. A few are from the 20th century.

c. A collection of approximately 100 genealogical charts (uncataloged) of European and American families including the Rothschilds, the Caro Rabbinic dynasty, the Oppenheimer family (Frankfurt), the Phillips family (London and America) and the Yehya family (Spain).

3. Archives

The Archives is located on the 5th floor with the Rare Book Room. The holdings include:

a. Personal papers of communal leaders and scholars including Cyrus Adler, Solomon Schechter, Israel Rosenberg, Moritz Steinschneider, Zadoc Kahn, the Adler family of London, Albert Bettelheim, Louis Levitsky and others.

b. Communal and organizational records (most uncataloged but retrievable) such as:

The American Jewish History Center, for
    Cleveland (Anshe Chesed minute books, 1907-1920)
    Milwaukee (several congregations, periodicals)
    Philadelphia (Congregation Beth Israel)
France. Consistoire records, 1808-1905
France. Jewish communities records 1669-1940s
Historical Documents, 15th-20th centuries (Jewish communal records -- German, French and
    Italian communities)
Morocco. Jewish community records, 20th century (Fez mostly, but also Meknès, Rabat, Safi, Salé,
    Sefrou and Tangier)
New York. Independent Slonimer Benevolent Association records, 1935-1936
Paris. Temple Israélite, minute books, 1851-1875

c. Print and Photograph Collections -- includes portraits of individuals, Jewish communities, synagogues, cemeteries and maps.

Finding Aids:

The Library's card catalog, located on the 2nd floor, is divided into five sections: General Catalog, Old Catalog, Subject Catalog, Hebrew Title Catalog and Periodical Title Index.

The General Catalog includes authors and titles in one alphabetical listing. This catalog should be used to locate books in the Library's 2nd and 3rd floor holdings. Some (but not all) of the books in the Rare Book Room are also in this catalog. These rare books can be identified by the year of publication indicated on the index card. Generally books published from 1600 to 1800 can be found in the Rare Book Room.

The Old Catalog should be used only to locate books published before 1600 which are in the Rare Book Room. These are indicated in this catalog by an asterisk (*) in the call number. The Old Catalog should not be used to find books in the general collection, since it includes many books that were destroyed in the fire of 1966.

The Library's Subject Catalog is arranged by topic or subject heading. It does not include the category "town name."

The Hebrew Title Catalog is arranged by title only. Not all editions of a work are listed. Check the General Catalog to locate all editions owned by the Library.

Yizkor books (memorial books) can be found by utilizing the call numbers in Appendix A or by looking up "Holocaust - place" and/or "Jews - place" in the Subject Catalog or the author's name in the General Catalog. Since JTS uses Library of Congress call numbers and all of its holdings are on open shelves (2nd and 3rd floors), one can find most of these books as well as books related to pre-WWII pogroms in the series beginning DS135 (3rd floor, right of elevator). For example, DS135 R93 includes books on communities in Russia; DS135 P62 in Poland; DS135 H92 in Hungary; and DS135 C96 in Czechoslovakia.

Genealogy books are arranged under the CS series, and rabbinic biographies primarily under BM750 (collective biographies) and BM755 (individual biographies). These are all on open shelves on the 3rd floor.

The Rare Book Room has other books and materials which are not included in the 2nd floor catalogs. Preliminary Catalogs for these collections are located in the Rare Book Room on the 5th floor. Manuscript materials such as Pinkasim and Ketubot fall within this category. To determine whether this Library has a Pinkas for a community, consult the catalog by name of community or by looking under "Pinkas" in the Hebrew Catalog. To locate a Ketubah, check the Preliminary Card Catalog for Non-Rabbinic Manuscripts in the Rare Book Room.

The *Preliminary Listings of Holdings* of the Archives can be found in the Rare Book Room. These describe both cataloged and uncataloged collections in the Archives. For the French records, use the unpublished book catalog, "JTS-Archives-French Documents" by Roger S. Kohn, which provides a box-by-box description of the holdings.

Description of Facility:

The library can seat 300 individuals. There are 3 microfilm readers available, one of which is a reader/printer. The microfilm center, reference collection, bound periodicals and Stack Books PJ-Z, are located on the 2nd floor. Stack Books A-PI, JTS dissertations and some duplicate bound periodicals are on the 3rd floor. All materials in the Library (except special collections) are on open shelves.

Records/documents in the Rare Book Room/Archives must be requested but can be obtained immediately. The Rare Book Room is located on the 5th floor.

Fees/Copies:

There are 3 photocopy machines available at $.10 per page. Mail requests are charged $.25 per page plus postage and a $2 handling charge.

Members of the library (annual membership fee $100) may borrow books up to four weeks.

Restrictions on Use:

There is a part-time Archivist available 2 days per week. While the Rare Book Room staff can locate a collection and bring the box of material to the researcher, they cannot provide further assistance. Call in advance to determine the Archivist's schedule or to request assistance.

LEO BAECK INSTITUTE
LIBRARY - ARCHIVES

Facility Director:	Dr. Fred Grubel, Director
	Ms. Evelyn Ehrlich, Librarian
	Dr. Diane Spielmann, Archivist
Address:	129 East 73rd Street
	New York, NY 10021
	(Cross Streets: Lexington and Park Avenues)
Phone Number:	(212) 744-6400

Hours of Operation:

	September to June	July
Monday to Thursday:	9:00 am to 5:00 pm	9:00 am to 4:00 pm
Friday:	9:00 am to 3:00 pm	9:00 am to 4:00 pm

Closed Saturday, Sunday, Jewish and legal holidays and the month of August.

Closest Public Transportation:

Subway: 6 (local) to 77th Street

Bus: M1, M2, M3 or M4 to 72nd or 73rd Street and Madison Avenue (northbound)
 M101 or M102 to 72nd Street and Lexington Avenue (southbound)
 M30 (72nd-57th Street crosstown) to 72nd and Lexington Avenue

Directions:

Take the #6 (local) train to the 77th Street station. Walk 4 blocks south on Lexington Avenue to 73rd Street. The Leo Baeck Institute is to the right on 73rd Street.

Description of Resources:

(Adapted from *Toledot*, Spring 1979, "German-Jewish Genealogical Research: Selected Resources at the Leo Baeck Institute, New York" by Sybil Milton)

The Archives and Library of the Leo Baeck Institute (LBI), founded in 1955 by the Council of Jews from Germany, offer the most comprehensive collection of documents, manuscripts and books dealing with the life and history of Jews in German-speaking lands available for research. The materials are mostly in German, with some other languages, including Hebrew, Yiddish, and - increasingly - English, represented. The Archives and Library of the LBI comprise one of the largest documentary collections in this field, containing over 2,000 linear feet of archives, a specialized library of 50,000 volumes, over 600 periodicals and newspapers, 500 memoirs, and an art collection.

LIBRARY:

The Library has an outstanding collection of German-Jewish communal histories, biographical dictionaries, and genealogical resources. Books and microfilm are available on interlibrary loan. In addition, the collection includes such general references as encyclopedias in English and German and German-English/English-German dictionaries.

The LBI Library holdings of newspapers are described at length in the LBI published catalog, volume I. The following is a sample of items of interest to genealogists. Call numbers are listed in brackets.

1. Biographical Dictionaries:

 Austria. *Osterreichisches Biographisches Lexicon, 1815-1950.* Graz-Koeln, 1957-date (A-R published so far). [CT913 035]

Bohemia/Czechoslovakia. *Biographisches Lexikon zur Geschichte der Boehmischen Laende.* Prag, 1979-date (A-O published so far). [DB202 B56]

Central Europe. *International Biographical Dictionary of Central European Emigres, 1933-1945.* 1980. Vols I & III (index) in German; Vol. II (pts. 1-2) in English. [CT1053 B56]

Prussia. *Juden in Preussen.* 1981. Biographical dictionary and numerous communal histories. [DS135 G34 L68]

Who's Who. *Wer ist's.* 1908, 1922, 1935. (Title changed to:) *Wer ist Wer*, 1951, 1958, 1965, 1967, 1974/5, 1983. [DD85 W3]

2. Holocaust:

Germany. *Gedenkbuch: Opfer der Verfolgung der Juden, 1933-1945.* Koblenz: Bundesarchiv, 1985. 2 vols. (With cooperation from Yad Vashem, Jerusalem, this book lists all Jews of Germany who perished, with birth place, how they died and where; appendix gives data on each concentration camp.) [Ref f DS135 G33 G38]

3. Genealogical Resources:

Czellitzer, Arthur. *Mein Stammbaum* [My Genealogy]. Berlin, 1934. [CS14 C99 M4]

Juedische Familien-Forschung. nos. 1-50. Berlin, 1924-1938. The journal of Jewish genealogy (microfilm). [Per/B184/film]

Heintze-Cascorbi. *Die deutschen Familiennamen.* 1925. [CS2541 H4 1925]

North America. Stern, Malcolm H. *First American Jewish Families: 600 Genealogies, 1654-1977.* 1978. [CS59 S76 1978]

Leipzig. Freudenthal, Max. *Leipziger Messgaeste, 1675-1764.* Frankfurt a/M, 1928. Genealogical data on Jews who attended the Leipzig fairs, 1675-1764. [DS135 G32 F74 L4]

4. Communal Histories:

Austria. Gold, Hugo. *Geschichte der Juden in Oesterreich; ein Gedenkbuch.* Tel Aviv, 1971. [f DS135 A9 G65]

Baden. Dreifuss, Erwin Manuel. *Die Familiennamen der Juden, unter besonderer Beruecksichtigung der Verhaeltnisse in Baden zu Anfang des 19 Jahrhunderts. Ein Beitrag zur Geschichte der Emanzipation.* Frankfurt am Main, 1927. [DS135 G4 B167 D74]

Baden. Sauer, Paul. *Dokumente ueber die Verfolgung der juedischen Buerger in Baden-Wuerttemberg durch das nationalsozialistische Regime 1933-1945.* Stuttgart, 1966. [Ref DS135 G37 S3 D6]

Berlin. Jacobson, Jacob. *Die Judenbuergerbuecher der Stadt Berlin, 1809-1851; mit Ergaenzungen fuer die Jahre 1791-1809.* Berlin, 1962. [DS135 G4 B4 J31]

Berlin. Jacobson, Jacob. *Juedische Trauungen in Berlin, 1723-1759.* Berlin, 1938. [DS135 G4 B4 J318]

Berlin. Jacobson, Jacob. *Juedische Trauungen in Berlin, 1759-1813; mit Ergaenzungen fuer die Jahre von 1723 bis 1759.* Berlin, 1968. [DS135 G4 B4 J32]

Bohemia. Gold, Hugo. *Die Juden und Judengemeinden Boehmens in Vergangenheit und Gegenwart.* Bruenn-Prag, 1934. [q DS135 C954 G63]

Bovenden. Busch, Ralf. *Die juedischen Einwohner Bovendens vom 17. bis 18. Jahrhundert.* Goettingen, 1971. [DS135 G4 B648 B81]

Breslau. Brilling, Bernhard. *Geschichte der Juden in Breslau von 1454-1702.* Stuttgart, 1960. [DS135 G4 B66 B711]

Chemnitz. Diamant, Adolf. *Chronik der Juden in Chemnitz, heute Karl-Marx-Stadt; Aufstieg und Untergang einer juedischen Gemeinde in Sachsen.* Frankfurt am Main, 1970. [DS135 G4 C52 D5]

Dresden. Diamant, Adolf. *Chronik der Juden in Dresden; von den ersten Juden bis zur Bluete der Gemeinde und deren Ausrottung.* Mit einem Geleitwort von Robert M.W. Kempner. Darmstadt, 1973. [DS135 G4 D74 D5]

Eschwege. Cohn, Joseph. *Das Eschweger Memorbuch; ein Beitrag zur Geschichte der juedischen Stadt- und Landgemeinden im Kreise Eschwege.* Hamburg, 1930. [DS135 G4 E82 C6]

Essen. Samuel, Salomon. *Geschichte der Juden in Stadt und Stift Essen bis zur Saekularisation des Stifts, von 1291-1802; mit urkundlichen Beilagen und einer Stammtafel.* Essen-Ruhr, 1905. [DS135 G4 E88 S24]

Frankfurt am Main. Arnsberg, Paul. *Die Geschichte der Frankfurter Juden seit der franzoesischen Revolution. Hrsg. vom Kuratorium fuer Juedische Geschichte, Frankfurt am Main.* Bearb. und vollendet durch Hans-Otto Schembs. Darmstadt, 1983. [Ref DS135 G4 F7 A7]

Frankfurt am Main. Dietz, Alexander. *Stammbuch der Frankfurter Juden. Geschichtliche Mitteilungen ueber die Frankfurter juedischen Familien von 1349-1849, nebst einem Plane der Judengasse.* Frankfurt am Main, 1907. [DS135 G4 F7 D54]

Freiburg. Lewin, Adolf. *Juden in Freiburg i. B.* Trier, 1890. [DS135 G4 F74 L48]

Fuerth. Barbeck, Hugo. *Geschichte der Juden in Nuernberg und Fuerth; auf Grund des vorhandenen gedruckten Materials, der in den koenigl. Archiven zu Nuernberg und Bamberg befindlichen Akten und Urkunden, der Archivalien im Cultusgemeindebesitz...herausgegeben und bis auf die Neuzeit ergaenzt.* Nuernberg, 1878. [DS135 G4 N8 B3]

Hannover. Wahl, Margret. *Der alte juedische Friedhof in Hannover.* Hannover, 1961. [DS135 G4 H38 W3]

Heilbronn. Franke, Hans. *Geschichte und Schicksal der Juden in Heilbronn; vom Mittelalter bis zur Zeit der nationalsozialistischen Verfolgungen (1050-1945).* Heilbronn, 1963. [DS135 G4 H44 F73]

Hesse. Arnsberg, Paul. *Die juedischen Gemeinden in Hessen; Anfang, Untergang, Neubeginn.* Frankfurt am Main, 1971. [Ref DS135 G4 H48 A75]

Mainz. Levi, Sali. *Beitraege zur Geschichte der aeltesten juedischen Grabsteine in Mainz; herausgegeben anlaesslich der Rueckfuehrung dieser Steine auf den alten "Judensand" Mainz.* [n.p.] 1926. [DS135 G4 M35 L4]

Munich. Cohen, Arthur. *Die Muenchener Judenschaft 1750-1861; eine bevoelkerungs- und wirtschaftsgeschichtliche Studie.* Berlin, 1931. [DS135 G4 M86 C64]

Oldenburg. Schieckel, Harald. *Die juedischen Wehrpflichtigen in Oldenburg von 1867-1918 und ihre Vorfahren.* Neustadt, 1971. [DS135 G4 O5 S3]

Palatinate. *Dokumentation zur Geschichte der juedischen Bevoelkerung in Rheinland-Pfalz und im Saarland von 1800 bis 1945, hrsg. von der Landesarchivverwaltung Rheinland-Pfalz in Verbindung mit dem Landesarchiv Saarbruecken.* Koblenz, 1972-82. [DS135 G4 P35 P3]

Tuebingen. Zapf, Lilli. *Die Tuebinger Juden; eine Dokumentation.* Tuebingen, 1974. [DS135 G4 T84 Z3]

Ulm. Brann, Marcus. Juedische Grabsteine in Ulm. Breslau, 1917. [DS135 G4 U44 B72]

Vienna. Bato, Ludwig. *Die Juden im alten Wien.* Wien, 1928. [DS135 A92 V5 B37]

Vienna. Frankl, Ludwig August. *Zur Geschichte der Juden in Wien. Der alte Freithof. Der Tempelhof.* Wien, 1853. [DS135 A92 V5 F66]

Westphalia. Brilling, Bernhard. *Familiennamen der Juden in Westphalen.* Bonn, 1958-59. [BM729 N3 B7]

Worms. *Zum 900 jaehrigen Bestehen der Synagoge zu Worms. Eine Erinnerungsgabe des Vorstands der Israelitischen Religionsgemeinde Worms.* Berlin, 1934. [DS135 G4 W6 Z8]

Wuerttemberg. Jeggle, Utz. *Judendoerfer in Wuerttemberg.* Tuebingen, 1969. [DS135 G37 J4 J8]

Wuerttemberg. Wuerttemberg Israelitische Religionsgemeinschaft. *Juedische Gotteshaeuser und Friedhoefe in Wuerttemberg.* Stuttgart, 1932. [q BM317 W84 J8]

ARCHIVES:

The Archives collection is so rich in source material that the following list is a sample of only some of the items of use to genealogists. See "Finding Aids" below to locate other materials.

1.   Adoption of German Surnames

Several collections at the LBI Archives help document the change from patronymics to surnames in early 19th-century Germany. These include the literary estates of Berthold Rosenthal (b.1875-d.1957) and Jacob Jacobson (b.1888-d.1968). The Jacobson estate includes substantial remnants of the Gesamtarchiv der deutschen Juden (Archives of German Jewry) established in Berlin in 1905 as the central depository for the records of German-Jewish communities and organizations. Information in brackets identifies the particular item in the collection; JJC refers to the Jacob Jacobson Collection [AR 7002]:

Baden - includes c.500 pages of detailed notes about the name changes and family names adopted by the Jews of Baden in 1809. Volumes are organized alphabetically by town name. The collection includes historical material about the history of Jews in Baden and the Palatinate as well as 70 family trees. [AR 649; also 207, 210, 652, B12, B15]

Berlin files contain lists of Jewish families living legally in Berlin on 24 March 1813, lists of family names taken in 1812, and a list of Jews who had taken family names and Christian first names before 1812 (379 entries). [JJC I:51, I:58, and I:82]

Lippe-Detmold, 1810, list of family names. [JJC III:50]

Marienwerder district, West Prussia (Jacobson estate), 1845, lists of family names. [JJC III:88 and VIII:61]

Posen, alphabetical register of Jews naturalized, copied by Isidor Hirschberg, Bromberg, 1836. [JJC III:32]

Individual family histories tell stories such as the Strauss family [AR 4492] and the Heilner family. [AR 4471]

2.   Circumcision and Birth Records

The following communities and years are represented by circumcision registers in the LBI Archives. Information in brackets identifies the particular item in the collections.

Aurich, 1758-1806. [JJC III:4]

Berlin, 1714-1840. [JJC I:1-4, I:19, I:55, I:75-76, and I:96] Also alphabetical birth registers, 1813-1840. [JJC I:42-43]

Filehne, Register, 1812-1850, of Rabbi A. Wreschner, containing 200 entries from Filehne and 32 entries from other places, and register, 1817-1864, of the Rabbinical Judge Aron Lazarus, containing 335 entries. [AR 2470/No. 1-2]

Frankfurt am Main, Register, 1698-1836, kept by the ancestors of Moritz Abraham Stern, 63 pages. [AR 380/No. 233]

Fuerth, Registers, 1761-1806, of Benjamin Berlin and Mordechai Jafe, handwritten copy in German. [JJC III:20]

Munich, Register, 1826-1874, of Rabbi Hirsch Aub, including entries for Prag, 1816, and Baiersdorf, 1819; registers, 1840-1878 and 1834-1885. [Ernst Kitzinger Collection, AR 3086/I:1-3]

Munich, Register, 1913-1938, by Jewish community official Heinrich Glaser, 300 entries. [AR 143/No.11-13]

Prague, Worms, Pfalz, 1782-1823. [JJC III:65]

Randegg/Baden, Register, 1828-1881, of Baruch Bloch, copy with explanations by Dr. S. Moos-Moore, 1972. [AR 2483/No. 9]

Schildberg/Posen, Register, 1866-1906, of Elkan Lewy, 376 entries. [Elkan Lewy Collection, AR 3126/No. 1]

Schildberg, 1838-1866, and Bunzlau, 1867-1887, photocopies of register of Abraham Unger. [JJC III:76]

Schleswig-Holstein, 1775-1817. [JJC III:77]

Wuerttemberg, 1882-1908. [AR 147/No. 18]

Among other community and family collections in the LBI Archives are numerous examples of individual birth certificates and announcements.

3. Marriage Records

The LBI Archives contain marriage registers of communities, contracts (ketubot), individual engagement and wedding announcements, as well as special newspapers issued for weddings. The following communities and years are represented by marriages registers in the LBI Archives:

Berlin, list of marriages (Trauungsliste), 1759-1813. [AR 7002, JJC I:12]

Berlin, register, 1813-1829, 1830-1837, 1837-1847, 1847-1851, photocopies made by the Reichsstelle fuer Sippenforschung. [JJC I:9-10, I:12, I:40-41, I:46-47, and I:63]

Breslau, 1789-1818. [JJC III:10]

Dresden, table of births, marriages, and deaths, 1786-1819/20. [JJC I:2 and I:55]

Nuernberg, 1872-1912, including four pages of marriages in Switzerland. [AR 1706/No. 3]

4. Death Records

It is important to remember that rights of domicile were not always synonymous with burial privileges. Thus, no Jew could be buried in Breslau until 1671. Jews from Breslau were buried in Krotoschin, Zulz, and other outlying communities; the death certificates are therefore filed with these towns rather than with Breslau records. The following communities and years are represented by death records in the LBI Archives:

Allersheim near Wuerzburg, list of deceased, 1799-1903, typed in German. [AR 7002, JJC III:1]

Altstrelitz, cemetery register, c.1740-1923. [JJC III:2]

Arnswalde, miscellaneous tombstone inscriptions and documents, earliest c.1780, mostly from 19th century. [JJC III:3]

Berlin, death registers, 1751-1813, 1818-1829, 1830-1837, 1847-1855. [JJC I:5-6, I:34, I:44]

Berlin, inscriptions from grave monuments in the old Jewish cemetery, Grosse Hamburgerstrasse 26, by L. Landshuth, 2767 entries, mainly in Hebrew, 13 volumes. [JJC I:20-32]

Bretten/Baden, Memorbuch, 1725-1884. [AR 2799/ No. 6-9]

Duesseldorf, Memorbuch, 1714. [JJC III:13]

Dyhernfurth, Chevra Kadisha records, 1782-1807. [JJC III:14]

Frankfurt am Main, death register, 1805-1808. [JJC III:17]

Gnesen, record book (Pinkas) of the Chevra Baalei Hamisakim Ubikur Cholim (burial society and society for visiting the sick), including list of deaths, 1841-1892. [JJC III:22]

Haigerloch, photographs of Jewish tombstones. [JJC VIII:57]

Hannover, Memorbuch. [JJC III:29]

Harburg, Memorbuch. [JJC III:30]

Koenigsberg (today Kaliningrad, USSR), requests for birth, marriage, and death certificates, 1847. [JJC III:39]

Krotoschin, Chevra Kadisha and death records, 1785. [JJC III:41a]

Potsdam, Jewish tombstone inscriptions, 1746-1836, typed list. [JJC I:54]

5. Other Collections with Regional Materials

The following collections at the LBI Archives contain material of particular interest to the genealogical researcher:

Michael Berolzheimer Collection: includes over 50 family trees for the families Mannlein, Berolzheim, Berolzheimer, Offenbacher, Rindskopf, Gosdorfer, Besels, Wertheimer, Brilin, and Simon Wolf Oppenheim (Oppenheimer). The papers include copies of Jewish community registries from 18th and 19th century Bavaria, copies of the Fuerth Testamentenbuch (register of wills, estates, and death dates of selected members of the community--translated by Rabbi Max Freudenthal), a Schutzgeldliste (tax list for rights of residence of protected Jews) from Fuerth for 1716-1718, and other valuable genealogical notes. [AR 4136]

Max Markreich Collection: includes extensive typed manuscripts about the Jewish communities in Aurich, Ostfriesland, and Bremen. Markreich was head of the Jewish community in Bremen and emigrated to the United States by way of Trinidad. His collection contains material as diverse as original documents on the Jewish community of Leer, 1748-1749; the Aurich Mohelbuch; items on Jewish life in Trinidad, 1939-1940; and records of Congregation Shaare Zedek of Astoria (New York City), 1942. [AR 7043]

Karl D. Darmstaedter Collection: unusually rich in materials about Jews from Mannheim and their fate in Nazi Germany. The documentation about Mannheim, Baden, and Worms includes photocopies and photographs of cemeteries in Prag and Neckarbischofsheim. [AR 2562-3; 3736-7, 3850, 3898-3999]

Vierfelder Family Collection: includes a six-generation history of the Vierfelder family from Buchau. The collection also includes 52 photographs of the Jewish community in Buchau and copious newspapers and historical clippings about Buchau. [AR 3599]

Rudolf Simonis Collection: contains several hundred family trees, family histories, and related correspondence for Berlin, northern Germany, and Sweden. There is also a copiously illustrated Simonis family tree. [AR 7018]

Arthur Czellitzer Collection: includes personal and family papers as well as information on the genealogical society he created, the Gesellschaft fuer Juedische Familienforschung [discussed in *Toledot*, Summer 1977 and in *Search*, Winter 1987]. A full set of this organization's periodical, *Juedische Familien-Forschung*, 1924-1938, is available in the LBI Library (see above).

The Berthold Rosenthal and Jacob Jacobson Collections referred to earlier are obviously rich in vital statistical and historical data for the genealogist.

Ele Toledot, compiled by Shlomo Ettlinger during the first half of this century. The work is in three parts (no part "A"): Part "C" (22 volumes) lists the Jews of Frankfurt a/M chronologically by date of death, 1241-1824. Part "B" (9 volumes) list male (Maenner) Frankfurt Jews alphabetically by surname; and (2 volumes) list women (Frauen) by their first name. Part "D" (2 volumes) lists the remainder (Reste) and converts (Judentaufen), 1241-1811. Biographies usually mention parents and children.

The Alsace and Lorraine collection [AR 2863] is divided into the following folios: Censuses [1-173]; Consistorial tax lists, 1816-1825 [226-592]; Notables [797-809]; Rabbis and cantors, 1841-1863, 1853-1864 [935-941, 1244-1253].

6. Deportation Lists

Baden: 11 Gestapo lists of Jews still resident in Baden on 1 February 1941, including full Jews and those living in mixed marriages, 840 names from 12 or more towns; Jews who moved to the East, Easter 1942, 78 names; Jews who moved to the East, Summer 1942, 45 names; Jews who "emigrated" from Baden to Theresienstadt, 22 August 1942, 139 names, and addenda, 90 names; Jews deported from Baden-Baden, Freiburg, Heidelberg, Mannheim, etc. on 22 August 1942; Jews expelled from Baden on 1 March 1943. [AR 2037/No. 1-11]

Koblenz: 4 Gestapo lists, 1942, of Jews deported from Koblenz and the region, especially Bendorf-Sayn (printed by the Jewish community, c.1947-1948). [AR 7085/No. 1]

Konstanz: names, dates of birth, and last residence of the Jews of Konstanz, deported to Gurs (Vichy France) in 1940 (photocopies of Nazi documents). [AR 2165/No.2]

Pfalz: 2 Gestapo lists, undated, 220 names; also a list for transports from Rheinpfalz, undated, 11 names. [AR 2039/No. 1-3]

Regensburg: deportees who arrived in Theresienstadt, 24 September 1942, 117 names. [AR 1425/No. 6]

Wuerzburg: transport II/26 of Jews who arrived in Theresienstadt, 24 September 1942, 610 names. [AR 3788/No. 1]

Several other lists of Jews deported to Gurs and Theresienstadt are located in the LBI Archives in the Bernhard Kolb, Karl D. Darmstaedter, and Max Plaut Collections. See also, under Library (above), *Gedenkbuch...*

Finding Aids:

Library: There are two card catalogs -- author/title and subject (with English headings). The subject index includes place names and family names. Communal histories are cataloged under "[Community], Jews in." Check the subject catalog also for sources listed under province name or town name.

Archives: The catalog, in German, is primarily by subject. Family trees and histories are indexed alphabetically under the subject "Stammbaum" (family tree). Communal records are filed under the heading "Gemeinde" (community).

There is an excellent finding aid for the manuscript collections in the alphabetically labeled, black binders in the first bookcase on the left as you enter the room. These binders record in detail the contents of each collection and give call numbers. Occasional miscellaneous lists are included; e.g. volume A has a typescript list of former German towns now in Poland, indicating both German and Polish town names and province. In addition, finding aids for archival collections, microfilms and memoirs are being placed on a data base to facilitate searching.

Many libraries have the 1968 publication, *Leo Baeck Institute, New York, Bibliothek und Archiv, Katalog,* vol. 1, listing pre-1968 holdings by title, place, and subject.

The LBI also publishes two newsletters periodically, the *LBI News* and the *LBI Library and Archives News* which detail new accessions.

Description of Facility:

The main reading room of the Library is on the second floor (front room). Reference works in the Library are on open shelves. Other items are in closed stacks and may be secured by call slips given to the librarian on duty. The Archives is located at the rear of the first floor.

The Library has two staff persons and the Archives has four to assist researchers. Eight researchers can be accommodated in each facility. The LBI has 2 microfilm readers (upstairs).

Fees/Copies:

Photocopying is done by staff at $.20 per page ($.40 for reducing a double-sized page). Requests for photocopies take 15 minutes in person, and 2-6 weeks by mail. A service charge is added for large orders. Personal checks are accepted but not traveler's checks.

Membership applications are available to anyone. Annual dues are $35 and $15 for students. Members are entitled to the newsletters, free lectures, and a 20% discount on publications. Higher-level contributors receive the annual *Yearbook,* containing articles and lectures, chiefly in English, and the *Bulletin,* with scholarly articles in German.

Restrictions on Use:

Difficulties may be encountered in reading German-Gothic or Judaeo-German (German in Hebrew letters) particularly in the communal records. Staff has a sample page of German-Gothic to help readers decipher the alphabets.

Staff is helpful with finding materials and quick translation or interpretation of German-Gothic script or print. They cannot do research.

A few collections are restricted by donors.

NEW YORK ACADEMY OF MEDICINE
LIBRARY

Facility Director: Brett Kirkpatrick, Librarian
Claudia Perry, Head of Reference Department

Address: 2 East 103rd Street
New York, NY 10029

(Cross Streets: Corner of Fifth Avenue)

Phone Number: (212) 876-8200

Hours of Operation:

Monday:	12:00 noon to 5:00 pm
Tuesday to Friday:	9:00 am to 5:00 pm
Saturday:	9:00 am to 5:00 pm (closed on **Saturday in the summer**)

NOTE: Paging and photocopying services cease at 4:00 pm.
Closed Sunday and legal holidays. The schedule for summer months may vary. Call beforehand.

Closest Public Transportation:

Bus: M1, M2, M3 or M4 bus to Madison Avenue and 103rd Street (northbound) and Fifth Avenue and 102nd Street (southbound)

Directions:

From midtown, take the M1, M2, M3 or M4 bus north on Madison Avenue to 103rd Street. Walk west on 103rd towards Fifth Avenue. The entrance is on 103rd Street.

Description of Resources:

The Library, which is second in size in the health field only to the National Library of Medicine, maintains a collection in excess of 680,000 cataloged works and 275,000 cataloged illustrations and portraits. It receives over 4,100 periodicals and journals annually.

The following are of particular interest to genealogists (call numbers are listed in brackets):

1.   National and International Medical Directories

American Medical Directory. 1906- . Published by the American Medical Association for the U.S. and Canada. The Directory is arranged alphabetically by state, locality and name. There is a cumulative index arranged alphabetically by name, state and locality. Entries include education, year of license, primary and secondary specialties, type of practice, awards and local address.

Directory of Medical Specialists. 1939- . [2AA]. This Directory lists physicians alphabetically by specialty, state, locality and name. There is a cumulative index arranged alphabetically by name, state, locality and specialty. The Directory gives biographical information about the physician which includes date and place of birth, education, career history, military record, awards, society memberships, office address and telephone number.

Holloway, Lisabeth M. *Medical Obituaries: American Physicians' Biographical Notices in Selected Medical Journals Before 1907.* New York, 1981. [3]

Examples of international biographical directories include the:

Akademiya Meditsinskiyh Nauk Soyuza Sovetskikh Sotssialisticheskikh Republik. 1947. (Reference data concerning the active members of the Academy of Medical Science of the USSR.) [Q11054]

Canadian Medical Directory. 1987 [2HA]

Medical Directory of Australia. 1980 [2HA]

The Medical Directory [Great Britain]. 1986 [2HA]

Examples of biographical information that is specifically Jewish include:

Levy, Mary L. *Some Jewish Physicians at the English Court (1102-1921).* 1966. [RB 145096]

Falstein, Louis, ed. *The Martyrdom of Jewish Physicians in Poland.* 1963, New York. (Includes biographies pp. 303-500) [.3]

The Library also has directories of psychologists, nurses, dentists, pharmacists and other scientists, although not as large a collection as that for physicians. Examples include:

Alumnae Association of Presbyterian Hospital of New York. *Alumnae Biographical Register, 1894-1942.* 1946. (Biographies of nurses). [146191]

Directory, American College of Hospital Administrators: A Biographical Directory of the Membership. 1938-1984 (gaps). [2AA]

Who's Who in Dentistry. 1916, 1925. (Biographical sketches of prominent dentists in the U.S. and Canada.) [s.3]

2. Biography (Obituary) File: This is a unique index created by the Academy Library c.1920 and continued until c.1978. Obituaries and biographies of physicians are either pasted directly on an index card or the source, date, volume/page of the obituary/biography are noted on the card. The earliest date noted for a source is 1877, but there may be earlier ones. The Library stopped entering data c.1978, but resumed clipping obituaries/biographies c.1985. These have not yet been entered into the file.

3. Portraits Catalog: Like the Biography (Obituary) File, this catalog is a unique tool created by the Academy Library. It is an index to photographs of physicians in books and periodicals acquired by the Library up to 1975. If a written biography is also available, the source, date, volume and page number are noted on the card. This catalog is arranged alphabetically by surname in 5 volumes to 1960, and in three supplementary volumes -- 1959-1965, 1966-1970 and 1971-1975. The *Portraits Catalog* and supplements have been published by G.K. Hall and may be available in other libraries.

4. *Index Medicus* and its predecessors have been published annually by the National Library of Medicine from 1879 to the present. This is an index to approximately 2,000 biomedical journals. Two sets of volumes exist for each year. One is an Author Index and one is a Subject Index. Not all the journals covered by the index are available in this Library.

Finding Aids:

In addition to the catalogs described above, the Library maintains a name and title catalog on index cards covering everything in its collection. The Library also has two subject catalogs. The *Subject Catalog of the Library* is a set of blue volumes which include photo duplicates of the Library's subject card file on all materials acquired prior to 1969. Items acquired after 1968 are in the subject catalog on index cards in the catalog room.

The Library also has a computerized catalog (Online Public Access Catalog) which includes books cataloged since 1976 and journals received since 1847. The catalog does not contain any citations to individual journal articles. See *Index Medicus* for such citations. Searches can be made by personal name, corporate/conference name, title, subject or key word.

To locate biographical directories on physicians in the *Subject Catalog of the Library,* look under "Biography, Medical" or "Biography, Medical, by localities." For nurses or dentists, look under "Biography, Nurses" or "Biography, Dentists," etc.

To obtain books from the stacks, a call slip must be submitted to the circulation desk. No more than 5 call skips may be submitted at one time.

Description of Facility:

The Library is on the third floor of the New York Academy of Medicine building. This is an old-fashioned, institutional building, erected in the 1920s, with meeting rooms, high ceilings, flowing spaces and a club atmosphere. The Library Lobby is a large gallery which houses the card and computer catalogs, the circulation desk and some biographical dictionaries. The Biography (Obituary) card file is located behind the reference desk in the Lobby.

The Library has one very spacious room, the Main Reading Room, and a smaller one, the Current Periodicals Room. The Main Reading Room has seating for about 100 researchers. The Current Periodicals Room seats 36. The *Index Medicus* volumes (1879-present), the *Subject Catalog of the Library,* and the *Portraits Catalog* are located in the Main Reading Room. The current volumes of the *Index Medicus* are located on a table to the far left of the entrance. The older volumes are on open shelves against the wall to the far left. The *Subject Catalog* and *Portraits Catalog* are located on a table near the center of the room.

Fees/Copies:

Photocopies are made by the staff. The order is placed at the circulation desk and the charge is $.25 per page. Copies of photographs or slides can be made from photographs in the Library's collection. These range in cost from $5 to $35. Ask for the Library's Photoduplication Price List. See "Restrictions on Use."

The Library will respond to mail requests for research. If the research takes 15 minutes or less, there is no charge. If more time is needed, the inquirer will be informed that a $50 per hour research fee is charged. Requests are usually responded to within 2 weeks but may take longer.

Restrictions on Use:

The Library is open to the public. However, it is necessary to make an appointment to use the Rare Book collection. Call numbers beginning with [RB] would be located here.

Only Fellows of the Library and Library Subscribers (usually firms heavily into medical research) have borrowing privileges. However, the Library does participate in the inter-library loan program and non-reference materials can be borrowed in this manner. Requests may be submitted through the individual's local public library.

No orders for photocopies are taken after 4:00 pm. On Saturday, there is only a skeleton staff for photocopying and it may not be possible to get copies made -- particularly around lunch hour.

When entering the New York Academy of Medicine building there is a checkroom to the left. Coats and bags must be checked. Only the minimum of notebooks, paper and writing implements may be brought into the Library.

Although the Library may be open on Saturdays, the switchboard is not. Callers on Saturday get a recording. During the week, the switchboard does not put calls through to the Library until 11:00 am.

NEW YORK CITY DEPARTMENT OF HEALTH
BUREAU OF VITAL RECORDS

Facility Director: Irene Scanlon, Director of Vital Records

Address: 125 Worth Street, Room 133
New York, NY 10013

(Cross Street: Centre and Lafayette Streets)

Phone Number: (212) 566-8193 or 8194
(212) 566-6404 (for credit card use)

Hours of Operation:

Monday to Friday: 8:00 am to 4:30 pm
Closed Saturday, Sunday and legal holidays.

Closest Public Transportation and Directions:

See "CIVIL COURT OF THE CITY OF NEW YORK, MANHATTAN (NEW YORK COUNTY)." The Health Department building is straight ahead when you emerge from the subway. Enter on the Worth Street side. Turn right at the information booth. The office is the last room on the right on the ground floor.

Description of Resources:

This office maintains for all five New York City boroughs, birth records, 1898 to the present and death records, 1930 to the present.

For older records see "NEW YORK CITY DEPARTMENT OF RECORDS AND INFORMATION SERVICES, MUNICIPAL ARCHIVES."

Finding Aids:

This office has book indexes for each year of record. The indexes are arranged by year, then alphabetically by surname. Some of the earlier indexes are arranged by year, borough and surname. For these years, consult all five sections for the relevant name.

In addition to these indexes, the office has Soundex indexes (see Appendix C) for births in all boroughs, 1898-1909, geographic indexes by street address for births in Manhattan, 1895-1909 and for the other four boroughs, 1898-1909, and a Manhattan hospital birth index, 1880-1904.

The indexes in this office are not open to the general public but researchers may view them on-site for a fee. See "Fees/Copies." The published indexes through 1982 and the Soundex indexes (but <u>not</u> the geographic or hospital indexes) are available for free viewing at the NEW YORK PUBLIC LIBRARY, U.S. HISTORY, LOCAL HISTORY AND GENEALOGY DIVISION AND MICROFORMS DIVISION.

Description of Facility:

This is a noisy, busy government office. The information desk in the building lobby has application forms and return envelopes. There are several tellers at the request windows in Room 133 who accept forms and payments. For questions, complaints or requests to use the birth and death indexes, go to the information window in Room 138.

Fees/Copies:

To obtain a copy of a birth or death record, complete the appropriate application (see Appendix B-2 or B-3) and fill out a self-addressed envelope (no stamp needed). Submit these with your payment to the teller at the appropriate window, or send in your request by mail. Certified copies of the original records are available at $5 per copy. Searches include any two consecutive years. Additional years are $1 per year/per name.

At least two pieces of information about a deceased person (other than information found in the indexes) should be included in the application for a death record. Items such as parents' names, occupation of the deceased or spouse's name qualify. Be sure to indicate your relationship to the deceased person on the application.

For birth records (other than your own) and death records, a copy will not be provided immediately even if you come in-person. Allow 6 to 8 weeks for a return reply by mail.

Birth records from 1920 to the present are available in shortened computer form. These short forms do not include parents' ages, place of birth, occupation or number of children previously born to the mother. The short forms cost the same $5. You must specifically ask for the long form if you wish this additional information for post-1920 records.

There is a fee of $5 per day for viewing the New York City Health Department birth and death indexes. Bring two pieces of identification.

Payments may be made by cash, personal check or money order for requests submitted in person. A credit card may be used only to order your own birth certificate by telephone. Do not send cash when requesting by mail. All checks should be made out to "New York City Department of Health" and must have your name and address imprinted on the check.

Restrictions on Use:

No records (except your own short form birth record) can be obtained immediately.

Birth records are only available to the individual of record and/or a direct descendant. If the individual is deceased, a copy of the death certificate must accompany the request. If the person of record is living, the request must be accompanied by a notarized letter of authorization from that individual, naming the person who may request a copy of the record.

NEW YORK CITY DEPARTMENT OF RECORDS AND INFORMATION SERVICES MUNICIPAL ARCHIVES

Facility Director:	Idilio Gracia-Pena, Director
	Kenneth Cobb, Deputy Director

Address:	31 Chambers Street, Room 103
	New York, NY 10007
	(Cross Streets: Centre and Elk Streets)

Phone Number:	(212) 566-5292

Hours of Operation:

Monday to Friday: 9:00 am to 4:30 pm
Closed Saturday, Sunday and legal holidays.

Closest Public Transportation and Directions:

See "CITY REGISTER'S OFFICE, MANHATTAN." The Municipal Archives is on the first floor of the Surrogate's Court building.

Description of Resources:

The Municipal Archives, a division of the NYC Department of Records and Information Services (DORIS), open to the public, was established to maintain, catalog and make available historic New York City government records. The following records are of particular genealogical use:

1. <u>New York City Vital Records</u>: Include the pre-1898 birth, pre-1930 death and pre-1938 marriage records (on microfilm) for New York City. Pre-1898 records are also available here for some of the localities which became part of NYC in 1898. Vital records are indexed and arranged according to the locality/borough in which they were originally filed. For Manhattan/Bronx* births, marriages and deaths, 1866-1887, and Brooklyn births and marriages, 1866-1879, and deaths, 1862-1879, the Archives has both liber records (registers) <u>and</u> certificates.

   NOTE: New York City, before 1898, consisted of Manhattan and parts of the Bronx. Manhattan records include the western area of the Bronx (Kingsbridge, West Farms and Morrisania), 1874-1897, and the eastern area of the Bronx, 1895-1897. These areas were annexed by New York City in 1874 and 1895 respectively. (The Bronx became a separate borough in 1898.) For vital records in these areas and years, a search of Manhattan records, as noted by *, should be made.

   At least two independent sets of marriage records were maintained for the period 1908-1937 in each borough. The records of the NYC Health Department are being accessioned by the Municipal Archives. The second set of records are those of the CITY CLERK'S OFFICE. For more information on these records, see the individual borough offices of the CITY CLERK'S OFFICE.

   A list of existing liber records and certificates (on microfilm) for each locality/borough follows. Unless otherwise noted, records are <u>liber records</u>. Records noted with ** may not be available yet due to accessioning and/or microfilming schedule. Call the Archives before visiting to assure that these records are accessible:

   <u>MANHATTAN (NEW YORK COUNTY)</u>*

Births:	Manhattan	Jun 1, 1847-Dec 31, 1848
	Manhattan/Bronx*	Jul 1, 1853-Dec 31, 1887
	Manhattan/Bronx*	Jan 1, 1866-Dec 31, 1897 (certificates)
Deaths:	Manhattan	Jul 26, 1795-Oct 25, 1795
	Manhattan	Jan 1, 1802-Jul 31, 1804
	Manhattan	May 1, 1808-Jul 31, 1808
	Manhattan/Bronx*	Jan 1, 1812-Dec 31, 1887
	Manhattan/Bronx*	Jan 1, 1866-Dec 31, 1937 (certificates)

Marriages:	Manhattan	Jun 1, 1847-Dec 31, 1848
	Manhattan/Bronx*	Jul 1, 1853-Dec 31, 1887
	Manhattan/Bronx*	Jan 1, 1866-Dec 31, 1937 (certificates)**
	Delayed and Imperfect Marriages*	1873-1916**
	Mayor's Office, Registry of Marriages*	1875-1897**
	Mayor's Office/City Court, Registry	
	of Marriages by Judge Ehrlich*	1886-1895*
	City Clerk Record of Certificates	
	or Contracts of Marriage*	1902-1908**

BRONX*

Births:	Morrisania (Town)	1872-1874
	S. Mt. Vernon (Village)	Aug 6, 1890-May 20, 1895
	Westchester (Town)	Jan 15, 1847-Dec 8, 1849,
		Feb 14, 1881-May 10, 1895
Deaths:	Bronx (Borough)	Jan 1, 1898-Dec 31, 1929 (certificates)
	S. Mt. Vernon (Village)	Aug 27, 1890-Jun 4, 1895
	Westchester (Town)	Jan 3, 1847-Dec 27, 1849,
		Dec 8, 1887-Apr 24, 1895
Marriages:	Bronx (Borough)	Jan 1, 1898-Dec 31, 1937 (certificates)**
	S. Mt. Vernon (Village)	Nov 23, 1890-May 22, 1895
	Westchester (Town)	Dec 18, 1847-Dec 19, 1849,
		1871-1873, 1876, 1881,
		Feb 1, 1882-Apr 24, 1894
	County Clerk, Marriage License	
	Religious Certificates	1914-1929 (certificates)**

BROOKLYN (KINGS COUNTY)

See St. Francis College Collection for additional Brooklyn vital records.

Births:	Brooklyn (City)	Jan 1, 1866-Dec 31, 1879
	Brooklyn (City/Borough)	Apr 3, 1866-Dec 31, 1897 (certificates)
	Flatbush (Town)	Jan 5, 1847-Dec 1, 1851,
		Dec 15, 1880-Apr 28, 1894
	Flatlands (Town)	Sep 4, 1880-Dec 30, 1895
	Gravesend (Town)	Nov 8, 1880-May 6, 1894
	New Lots (Town)	Mar 3, 1881-Jul 31, 1886
	New Utrecht (Town)	Nov 22, 1880-Jun 26, 1894
Deaths:	Brooklyn (City)	Jan 1, 1848-Dec 31, 1853,
		Jan 1, 1857-Dec 31, 1879
	Brooklyn (City/Borough)	Jan 1, 1862-Dec 31, 1929 (certificates)
	Flatbush (Town)	Feb 10, 1847-Nov 19, 1851,
		Dec 5, 1880-May 6, 1894
	Flatlands (Town)	Sep 5, 1880-Dec 31, 1895
	Gravesend (Town)	Aug 14, 1880-May 3, 1894
	New Lots (Town)	Jun 9, 1881-Jul 31, 1886
	New Utrecht (Town)	Dec 27, 1880-Jun 29, 1894
Marriages:	Brooklyn (City)	Jan 1, 1866-Dec 31, 1879
	Brooklyn (City/Borough)	Jan 1, 1866-Dec 31, 1937 (certificates)**
	Flatbush (Town)	Jan 11, 1847-Jul 16, 1851,
		Oct 1880-Apr 1894
	Flatlands (Town)	Dec 1880-Dec 1895
	New Utrecht (Town)	Dec 1880-Jun 1894
	New Lots (Town)	May 1881-Jul 1886
	Gravesend (Town)	Feb 1881-May 1894
	Delayed Registration	1875-1934**
	Special Marriages	1898-1937**
	Metropolitan Board of Health	
	Register of Marriages	1866-1879**

QUEENS

Births:	College Point (Village)	Nov 1, 1889-Jan 16, 1898
	Far Rockaway (Village)	Dec 3, 1889-Dec 11, 1897
	Flushing (Town)	Jan 2, 1847-Dec 27, 1849,
		Jan 1, 1881-Oct 12, 1897
	Flushing (Village)	Oct 14, 1889-Dec 29, 1897

	Jamaica (Town)	Jan 23, 1847-Dec 30, 1848,
		Jul 9, 1881-Dec 16, 1897
	Jamaica (Village)	Jul 23, 1889-Jan 12, 1898
	Long Island City	May 2, 1871-Dec 31, 1897
	Newtown (Town)	Jan 31, 1847-Dec 22, 1849,
		Jun 23, 1881-Jan 2, 1898
	Richmond Hill (Village)	Dec 14, 1895-Dec 7, 1897
	Rockaway (Village)	Jun 29, 1897-Jan 14, 1898
	Whitestone (Village)	Sep 1, 1889-Dec 28, 1897
Deaths:	Queens (Borough)	Jan 1, 1898-Dec 31, 1929 (certificates)
	College Point (Village)	Nov 12, 1889-Jan 18, 1898
	Far Rockaway (Village)	Dec 12, 1889-Dec 21, 1897
	Flushing (Town)	Jan 4, 1847-Dec 31, 1849,
		Jan 1, 1881-Jan 6, 1898
	Flushing (Village)	Oct 17, 1889-Jan 13, 1898
	Jamaica (Town)	Jan 14, 1847-Dec 30, 1848,
		Jul 3, 1881-Jan 15, 1898
	Jamaica (Village)	Jan 17, 1881-Jan 16, 1898
	Long Island City	May 26, 1871-Dec 31, 1897
	Newtown (Town)	Jan 31, 1847-Jan 8, 1849,
		Jul 1, 1881-Jan 8, 1898
	Richmond Hill (Village)	Sep 8, 1895-Dec 28, 1897
	Rockaway Beach (Village)	Jul 20, 1897-Jan 3, 1898
	Whitestone (Village)	Oct 22, 1889-Dec 8, 1897
Marriages:	Queens (Borough)	Jan 1, 1898-Dec 31, 1937 (certificates)**
	Flushing (Town)	Jan 10, 1847-Dec 30, 1849
	Jamaica (Town)	Jan 1, 1847-Feb 9, 1848
	Long Island City	May 7, 1871-Jul 28, 1890,
		1881-1897**
	Newtown (Town)	1881-1898**
	College Point, Far Rockaway, Flushing, Jamaica, Richmond Hill, Rockaway, Whitestone	1881-1898**

STATEN ISLAND (RICHMOND COUNTY)

Births:	Castleton (Town)	Jan 3, 1882-Dec 30, 1897
	Edgewater (Village)	Aug 25, 1885-Dec 22, 1897
	Middletown (Town)	May 3, 1882-Nov 23, 1897
	Northfield (Town)	Jan 25, 1882-Dec 11, 1897
	Port Richmond (Village)	Feb 10, 1888-Dec 24, 1897
	Southfield (Town)	Jul 9, 1882-Dec 29, 1897
	Tottenville (Village)	Jun 27, 1890-Dec 30, 1897
	Westfield (Town)	Apr 17, 1882-Dec 23, 1897
	Mixed Towns	Jan 4, 1847-Apr 28, 1852
Deaths:	Staten Island (Borough)	Jan 1, 1898-Dec 31, 1929 (certificates)
	Castleton (Town)/ New Brighton (Village)	Jan 2, 1881-Dec 30, 1897
	Edgewater	Sep 5, 1885-Dec 29, 1897
	Middletown (Town)	May 15, 1882-Dec 27, 1897
	Northfield (Town)	Jun 9, 1872-Feb 17, 1873,
		Nov 8, 1881-Dec 30, 1897
	Port Richmond (Village)	Feb 16, 1888-Dec 30, 1897
	Southfield (Town)	Jul 28, 1882-Dec 29, 1897
	Tottenville (Village)	Aug 19, 1890-Dec 31, 1897
	Westfield (Town)	Apr 26, 1882-Dec 29, 1897
	Mixed Towns	Jan 9, 1847-1850, 1852
Marriages:	Staten Island (Borough)	Jan 1, 1898-Dec 31, 1937 (certificates)**
	Castleton (Town)	Jan 5, 1848-Oct 31, 1849,
		Feb 21, 1882-Dec 30, 1897
	Edgewater (Village)	Jul 2, 1883-Dec 30, 1897
	Middletown (Town)	Apr 11, 1882-Nov 3, 1897
	Northfield (Town)	Jan 6, 1847-Dec 30, 1849,
		Feb 14, 1882-Aug 29, 1896
	Port Richmond (Village)	Feb 8, 1888-Dec 19, 1897
	Southfield (Town)	Feb 28, 1848-Dec 30, 1852,
		Oct 5, 1882-Sep 29, 1897

Tottenville (Village)		Apr 21, 1864-Mar 19, 1865, Jul 29, 1890-Sep 27, 1897
Westfield (Town)		Jan 2, 1882-Dec 31, 1897

MISCELLANEOUS

Deaths:	Bodies in Transit through Manhattan	1859-1894
	Daily Return of Deaths by Cholera	1866**
	Tenement House, 2nd District	1875**

NOTE: The birth, marriage and death records (certificates) for Queens and Richmond Counties, 1880-1898, the eastern portion of the Bronx (then part of Westchester County), 1880-1895, and Kings County towns prior to annexation to the City of Brooklyn, 1880-1896, are available also from the NEW YORK STATE HEALTH DEPARTMENT in Albany. The Municipal Archives has the liber records only for these communities and years.

2. 1890 New York City Police Census: This population census of Manhattan and the western Bronx is arranged by Assembly/Election District. It lists, by street address, the name of each resident, including children, their sex and age. The census is on microfilm.

3. Almshouse Records, 1758-1953, include admission, discharge, census and housekeeping records for municipal institutions (Almshouse, Workhouse, City Home and hospitals) located on Blackwell's (Welfare) Island.

4. Court Records, 1808-1935: The collection consists of case files, indictments, docket books and other records relating to criminal and civil actions. These include the Court of General Sessions, Marine Court (later City Court), Police Court, Municipal Court, Magistrate's Court and the Court of Oyer and Terminer. Most of these records are for New York County. Magistrate's Court records include other boroughs. The time periods covered by each court or set of records vary.

5. District Attorney Records: Indictments, case files, docket books and other records relating to criminal investigations and prosecutions for New York County, 1800-1951; Kings County (Brooklyn), 1940-1945.

6. Photographs depicting streets, highways, sewers, bridges and other public structures from the Manhattan Borough President's Office, 1915-1949, Brooklyn Borough President's Office, 1918-1956, Queens Borough President's Office, 1880-1940, and Department of Bridges/Plant and Structures, 1901-1938 (glass plate negatives). The Department of Taxes collection, 1938-1940, includes photographs of improved property for assessment purposes. Photographs from the Department of Docks and Ferries, 1901-1938, depict waterfront scenes. See also WPA Collection below.

Since December 1982, developers seeking permits to demolish existing structures have been required to submit photographs of the sites with their applications to the Buildings Department. Newly-filed photos are required to be sent immediately by the Buildings Department to the Municipal Archives. This is currently a very small collection of photos but it can be expected to grow substantially in the future. To date, the quality of these pictures has been very poor.

7. Works Progress Administration, Federal Writers' Project, NYC Unit, 1936-1943. Rough drafts, notes, research materials, original manuscripts and photographs assembled for the *New York City Guide* and other publications. The collection includes a partial survey of NYC synagogue records as part of the Historical Records Survey.

8. Voter Registrations: Includes 50,000 volumes from the Board of Elections:

New York County: records of naturalized voters, 1872-1878, and registers of voters, 1872-1922 (gaps). See "Restrictions on Use." Some volumes, 1916-1920, are at the warehouse of the BOARD OF ELECTIONS, MANHATTAN BOROUGH OFFICE.
Queens County: registers of voters, 1898-1948.
Richmond County (Staten Island): registers of voters, 1898-1956, and one volume for the Town of Castleton (Richmond County), 1897.

The voter registration information varies over time but generally includes name of registrant, country or state of birth, race, age, street address, length of residence in state, in county, in Assembly District and in Election District. Most important for the genealogist is the information showing native or naturalized voter, date of naturalization and court where naturalization occurred. In addition, the records may indicate the city and state where last registered to vote, whether registrant owned his/her residence, marital status, whether a citizen by marriage, occupation, location of business and party affiliation.

9. <u>Coroner's Records</u>: The records, including inquests and records of deaths, span the years 1823-1918, but are not available for all boroughs in each year.

10. <u>Richmond (Staten Island) County Clerk's Office Records</u>: The following records have been deposited with the Archives:

Appointment of City Officials, 1880-1900 and 1921-1929
Business records including Certificates of Incorporation, 1848-1897
Certificates of Notary Public, 1870-1929
Coroner's records including inquests, 1851-1897
Court records spanning the years 1706-1947. These include records of defunct courts on Staten Island, such as Sessions and General Sessions, Justice, Oyer and Terminer and County Court, as well as records of the Supreme Court, Richmond County. The records include Special Proceedings, 1840-1929, in which Name Change cases and Incompetency cases were filed, as well as Judgments, 1816-1934, Indictments, 1706-1931 and Actions, 1929-1947.
District Attorney Records, 1880-1910
Jury Lists, 1820-1890
Matrimonial records including Divorce Judgments, 1861-1933
Military records on service exemptions, 1917
Naturalization records including affidavits, 1820-1906; certificates, 1902-1921; petitions, 1920-1926; posted petitions, 1920-1930; military petitions, 1918-1921; Department of Labor reports, 1918-1938; and hearings, 1936-1945.
Orders of Filiation (child support), 1859-1897
Passport Applications, 1940-1953
Volunteer Firemen rolls and certificates of membership, 1900-1930

11. <u>Annual Record of Assessed Valuation of Real Estate</u>: These are ledger books compiled yearly which list owner or occupant, description and value of real estate, including buildings. The pre-1898 books are arranged by ward. After 1897, the books are arranged by block and lot numbers. The Archives has:

Manhattan	1789-1792, 1794-1795, 1799, 1802, 1806-1975/76
Bronx	1898-1961/62
Brooklyn	1866-1974/75
Queens	1899-1974/75
Staten Island	1899-1970/71

12. <u>St. Francis College, The James A. Kelly Institute for Local Historical Studies</u>, which closed in 1988, transferred to the Municipal Archives original records of the City of Brooklyn and Kings County. This collection will be integrated with other records of the Municipal Archives. The records include:

City of Brooklyn Common Council minutes, 1846-1897; Brooklyn Town meeting book, 1785-1823.
Bushwick Town records, deeds and births of slaves, 1660-1825.
Flatbush Town records, 1819-1851, 1888-1892; Supervisors annual reports, 1886-1893; School District 3 tax lists, 1877-1881; Board of Health minutes, 1874-1876; military records; chattel mortgages, 1883-1890; State Census (E.D. 1 and 2), 1845; assessment rolls, 1854-1894; Court of Common Pleas minutes, 1800-1833.
Flatlands Town minutes, 1783-1895; police blotter, 1893; Board of Health minutes, 1880-1895; road records, 1684-1719; military records, record of troops, 1861-1865; assessment rolls, 1849-1895; personal mortgages, 1886-1891; chattel mortgages, 1847-1895; school district records, 1844-1895; slave records, 1799-1838.
Gravesend Town records, minutes of meetings, deeds and leases, 1645-1895; school district records, 1857-1894; persons liable for military service and records of troops, 1861-1865; assessment rolls, 1859-1893; Board of Health minutes, 1880-1893; births of slaves, 1799-1819, 1830-1843.
New Lots Town assessment rolls, 1857-1885.

New Utrecht Town records, historic deeds, 1659-1831; school papers, 1827-1894; Town Meeting minutes, 1793-1894; records of troops, 1861-1865; assessment rolls, 1795-1822, 1830-1894; chattel mortgages, 1875-1894.

Williamsburg Town Clerk's Book, 1842-1855; Town records, 1832-1837; tax rolls, 1841-1853; City of Williamsburg Common Council minutes, 1852-1854.

Kings County Board of Supervisors, minutes, 1714-1893; proceedings, 1861-1895; lists of trial and grand jurors, 1897-1898; deeds, 1679-1909; mortgages, 1757-1811; chattel mortgages, 1873-1895; wills, 1658-1891; administrations, 1844-1865; religious incorporations, 1785-1875; court and road records, 1668-1825; physician's and surgeon's affidavits, 1908-1924; horseshoer's register, 1896-1904; military exemption claims, 1851; oaths of office, 1838-1846.

Maps and charts, c.1700s-1888: property lines, topographical and profile street maps, atlases and locality plats relating to Kings County, Brooklyn Town, the Towns of Gravesend, Flatbush, New Utrecht, Bushwick and the City of Williamsburg. Most are hand-drawn.

Vital records, including births, marriages and deaths (folder) for Bushwick, 1857, Flatbush, 1847-1848, 1851, Flatlands, 1847, Flatlands Almshouse, 1847 (indexed); deaths, Lunatic Asylum and Kings County Almshouse, 1848; marriages performed by mayors of Brooklyn, 1839-1887 (indexed); index to marriages, 1591-1831 (scattered years), includes Elsworth family tree (pp. 130-135); index to marriages, Kings County, June 1, 1864-May 31, 1865.

NOTE: Brooklyn Town became a City in 1834. In 1855 it absorbed the Town of Bushwick and the City of Williamsburg. In 1886 it annexed the Town of New Lots. The Towns of Gravesend, Flatbush and New Utrecht were annexed in 1894. The last Town, Flatlands, joined the City in 1896. In 1898 the City of Brooklyn became one of the five boroughs of New York City.

13. Town Records, 1663-1898, include records of cities, towns and villages in areas of the Bronx (formerly Westchester), Queens and Richmond Counties prior to consolidation with New York City. A sample of the records are:

Jamaica Town (Queens), Town records, 1660-1897; census of pupils, 1896-1897; overseer of the poor, record of applicants, 1879-1897.

Flushing Town (Queens), Town Clerk records, 1868-1885; school district records, 1860-1896; Town Board records, 1790-1893.

Newtown Town (Queens), Town Board minutes, 1700-1897; records of schools, 1888-1897; military records, 1865; criminal dockets, 1659-1688, 1895-1897.

Morrisania Town (Westchester County, now part of the Bronx), voter registration rolls, 1863-1867; assessment rolls, 1858-1869 (gaps).

Westchester Town (Westchester County, now part of the Bronx), births of slave children, 1800-1823; manumission of slaves, 1787-1816; military rolls, 1851, 1852, 1854, 1862.

Castleton Town (Richmond), mortgages, 1849-1879; school district minutes.

14. Department of Personnel, Bureau of Examinations records include eligible lists Brooklyn City, 1883-1898, and New York City, 1895-1971; promotion lists, 1908-1929, 1932-1938 and 1945-1954; registers of applications, 1925-1936 and 1938-1945.

15. City Directories

New York (Manhattan/Bronx): 1873-1913, 1915-1918, 1920, 1922, 1924, 1931, 1933/34.
Brooklyn: 1796, 1802/3, 1811/12, 1822-1826, 1829-1910, 1912/13, 1933/34.

16. Potters Field records of burials, 1881-1985 (gaps). Arranged by trench number and date of burial. Includes name, age, birthplace, how long in country, date and place of death, cause of death, date of burial.

Finding Aids:

Most of the collections in the Municipal Archives have some type of finding aid. These include:

1. New York City Vital Records: Indexes (microfilm) are arranged by locality or borough, year and surname. Researchers examining pre-1898 indexes should be aware that several indexes may exist for a particular year. Check with the staff to be sure that you have seen all the liber and published indexes for localities in a particular borough. For vital records in the Bronx, a search of Manhattan

records, as noted by *, should be made. Indexes noted with ** may not be available yet due to accessioning and/or microfilming schedule. Call the Archives before visiting to assure that these indexes are accessible.

<u>Births/Deaths</u> - The Archives has card, liber and published indexes (on microfilm) to birth/death <u>certificates</u> as follows:

		Card Indexes	Liber Indexes	Published Indexes
Births:	Manhattan/Bronx*	1866-1897	-	1881-1897 (Soundex)
	Brooklyn (City)	1866-1897	1880-1885, 1888-1894	1881-1897 (Soundex)
Deaths:	Manhattan/Bronx*	1868-1890	-	August 1888-1929
	Bronx	-	-	1898-1929
	Brooklyn (City/Borough)	1862-1897	1880, 1886-1894	1895-1929
	Queens	-	-	1898-1929
	Staten Island	-	-	1898-1929

The Archives also has the following indexes to <u>liber records</u>. NOTE: There are indexes for some years for which there are no records.

		Card Indexes	Liber Indexes	Published Indexes
Births:	Manhattan/Bronx*	1857-1865	1873-July 1888	-
Deaths:	Manhattan/Bronx*	-	1873-July 1888	-
	Brooklyn (City)	1848-1866	1848-1871	-

All card indexes and published death indexes are arranged alphabetically by name. Card indexes for births include the parents names. Published birth indexes, 1881-1897, are Soundex indexes. See Appendix C for a description of the Health Department's Soundex system. Liber indexes for Manhattan are arranged by the first letter of the surname and for Brooklyn by the first three letters of the surname.

NOTE: There are no indexes to Manhattan <u>liber records</u> for births, 1866-1872, or pre-1873 <u>liber records</u> for marriages and deaths. However, Manhattan <u>liber records</u> pre-1873 (births, deaths and marriages) are maintained by month/day/year of the registration of the event (not the event itself) and grouped by the first letter of the surname.

There are no indexes to Brooklyn <u>liber records</u> for births and marriages, 1866-1879, and deaths, 1872-1879. However, Brooklyn <u>liber records</u> for deaths, 1872-1879, are arranged alphabetically by the first letter of the surname.

In addition to these card, liber and published indexes for Manhattan/Bronx and Brooklyn, the Archives has liber indexes to all town/village liber records; and a geographic index by street address for Manhattan (including western Bronx) birth certificates, 1880-1894.

<u>Marriage Indexes</u> - The Archives has the following finding aids (on microfilm) for Health Department marriage <u>certificates</u>:

	Card Indexes		Liber Indexes	Published Indexes
	Brides	Grooms	Brides/Grooms	Grooms
Manhattan*	1866-1937	1866-1910	-	1888-1937
Bronx	1898-1937**	-	-	1898-1937
Brooklyn	1866-1910, 1930-1937	1866-1907**	1880-1893	1894-1937
Queens	1905-1938**	-	-	1898-1937
Staten Island	1898-1937**	1898-1932**	-	1898-1937

The Health Department published indexes (all boroughs) are arranged alphabetically by name of the groom only. Card indexes are arranged in two alphabetical series by names of the bride and groom. Brooklyn liber indexes are arranged by the first three letters of the surname of both brides and grooms in one alphabetical series.

In addition to the indexes to marriage certificates, there are also liber indexes to <u>liber records</u> for Manhattan/Bronx, 1873-1888**, arranged by the first letter of the groom's surname.

The Archives also has liber indexes to town/village marriage records pre-1898; the Health Department index to Delayed and Imperfect Marriages, 1874-1916**, for Manhattan (including parts of the Bronx); and an index to Special Marriages, Brooklyn, 1908-1934**.

Some of the published NYC Health Department index books for <u>certificates</u> of birth, marriage and death are also available in the NEW YORK PUBLIC LIBRARY, U.S. HISTORY, LOCAL HISTORY AND GENEALOGY DIVISION (315N) or in the MICROFORMS DIVISION (315M); the NEW YORK GENEALOGICAL AND BIOGRAPHICAL SOCIETY LIBRARY; and the NEW-YORK HISTORICAL SOCIETY.

2. <u>1890 NYC Police Census</u>: Use the City Directories to find an address, then locate the cross streets using the tables in the front of the City Directories. Look for the correct Assembly District (AD) and Election District (ED) by locating the cross streets on the AD/ED map. With the AD/ED numbers look up the census enumeration book number in the Census Book Reference Guide prior to requesting microfilm reels. It is advisable to request the book for the AD/ED on the opposite side of the street also. The addresses are arranged haphazardly within each census book. You may have to scan the entire book. NOTE: The Archives staff is currently preparing a geographic index to this census.

3. <u>Almshouse Records</u>: The Archives has a bound volume describing the holdings in this collection. For some institutions, records are arranged by date of admission or date of discharge. Others are arranged by date of death.

4. <u>Court Records</u>: Records are usually arranged chronologically. Some court cases are filed alphabetically by surname with no separate index available.

5. <u>District Attorney Records</u>: Pre-1896 records are arranged chronologically (no index). Closed cases, 1896-1965, are indexed by year of indictment and defendant's surname.

6. <u>Photographs</u>: There is a geographic card index to photographs from the Brooklyn Borough President's Office. Most other collections have captions listed. The Buildings Department photos are arranged by demolition application number. This number must be obtained from the Buildings Department.

7. <u>Works Progress Administration, Federal Writers' Project (and Historical Records Survey)</u>: Not indexed. The box list identifies material on Jews and synagogues.

8. <u>Voter Registrations</u>: The records are arranged by year, Assembly/Election District (AD/ED) and then alphabetized by surname or first letter of the surname. To locate records, the researcher must provide the Archives staff with the year and AD/ED. (Try to use a year in which there was a Presidential election.)

To determine the AD/ED, an address is required. Check the AD/ED maps in the DEPARTMENT OF RECORDS AND INFORMATION SERVICES, MUNICIPAL REFERENCE AND RESEARCH CENTER or at the BOARD OF ELECTIONS office in the appropriate borough. These maps are <u>not</u> available at the Archives. To verify that the person sought actually registered, consult the *List of Enrolled Voters* for that year and AD/ED. These lists are available at the MUNICIPAL REFERENCE AND RESEARCH CENTER and at the NEW YORK PUBLIC LIBRARY - CENTRAL RESEARCH LIBRARY, GENERAL RESEARCH DIVISION.

9. <u>Coroner's Records</u>: Not indexed. However, the records are arranged chronologically. Inquests were generally held shortly after the date of death.

10. <u>Richmond (Staten Island) County Clerk's Office Records</u>: The Archives has an inventory listing the subject, years and location/box number for each set of records. It does not have name indexes to these records. The indexes, where they exist, are in the COUNTY CLERK'S OFFICE - STATE SUPREME COURT, RICHMOND COUNTY (STATEN ISLAND).

The indexes in the COUNTY CLERK'S OFFICE include those for: Naturalization Petitions; Court Cases, 1930-1947 (includes Matrimonial records, 1930-1933, in the <u>Index to Rule Books</u>); Certificates of Incorporation, 1891-1897; and Special Proceedings (includes Name Change and Incompetency records), 1913-1929. These indexes cover only a small portion of the Staten Island material in the Archives' collection.

11. <u>Annual Record of Assessed Valuation of Real Estate</u>: The Archives has an atlas which can be used to convert addresses to block and lot numbers.

12. <u>St. Francis College, The James A. Kelly Institute for Local Historical Studies Collection</u>: There is no index to this collection. An inventory is being prepared by the Archives.

13. <u>Town Records</u>: The Archives has a bound volume, <u>Index to Old Records</u>, which is arranged alphabetically by Town/Village and subject. Entries include the type of record, years covered and file number.

14. <u>Department of Personnel, Bureau of Examinations</u>: Records in this collection are not indexed.

Description of Facility:

The Reference Room is quiet and can seat 20-25 researchers. Ten microfilm readers (four 16mm and six 16mm/35mm) are available. Two of these are reader/printers.

There are two staff members on duty behind the counter to assist researchers. Birth, marriage and death records (microfilm) are in self-service cabinets. The indexes to these records and all other materials must be requested from the staff.

Fees/Copies:

There is no charge for use of this facility <u>except</u> when using the <u>New York City Vital Records</u> (see below). Researchers can make copies of microfilm material (<u>except</u> New York City Vital Records) on the reader/printers at $.25 per page. A photocopy machine at $.15 per page is available. Copies 11" x 17" can be made at $.25 per page.

The Archives charges a $5 fee for use of the <u>New York City Vital Records</u> (microfilms of birth, marriage and death records) for a day or any part thereof. Researchers may hand copy records at no additional cost. Photocopies of vital records are made by staff only. The fee is $5 for a copy of a birth, marriage or death certificate (includes a one year/one borough search if the certificate number is not provided). $1 is charged for each additional year searched and $1 for each additional borough searched. A certified copy of the certificate or transcript of the record is supplied, if found. Complete the Municipal Archives' Application for a Copy of a Birth Record, Death Record or Marriage Record (see Appendix B-4, B-5 and B-6).

While Health Department marriage records are being microfilmed, the Archives will make copies (if the certificate number is provided) but will not conduct searches for 1908-1937 records. Researchers are advised to apply to the appropriate CITY CLERK'S OFFICE for a search and copy of a record. If the City Clerk's search is unsuccessful, send the "not found" statement along with payment of the fee and request for a search to the Municipal Archives.

The Archives will do searches of the <u>1890 NYC Police Census</u> when the address of an individual (or family) in 1890 is provided. The fee for the search and photocopy of the entry is $3. A search conducted by Archives staff for an entry in a <u>City Directory</u> costs $1 per name per year and a photocopy of the entry will be provided. Limit: 5 listings per mail request.

Prints (8" x 10") of photographs can be made from existing negatives at $10. For larger prints, see the posted price list. If there is no negative, an additional $5 is charged.

Send mail requests with a check or money order payable to the NYC Department of Records and a stamped, self-addressed envelope.

Restrictions on Use:

<u>Court Records</u>, <u>District Attorney Records</u>, <u>Voter Registrations</u>, <u>Assessed Valuation of Real Estate</u>, <u>Richmond County Clerk's Office</u>, <u>St. Francis College Collection</u> (part), <u>Town Records</u> and <u>Department of Personnel</u> records are not on site and must be requested in advance. Materials are retrieved from other storage locations. Researchers wishing to see these records should be sure to order them at least one week in advance. It can take from one to seven days to retrieve records depending on staff availability.

<u>Richmond County Clerk's Office</u> records cannot be accessed easily. The actual indexes are not available here. See "COUNTY CLERK'S OFFICE - STATE SUPREME COURT, RICHMOND COUNTY (STATEN ISLAND)."

Some Manhattan <u>Voter Registration</u> records were severely water damaged. Check with the Archives staff for the inventory of available records.

<u>Other</u>

Because of the limited number of microfilm readers, researchers are advised to arrive early.

Only materials needed for research are permitted at the reading tables. All other personal belongings must be left at the coat rack near the door. (This prohibition does not apply to users of microfilm machines.)

Smoking, eating and drinking are not permitted. All notes must be taken with pencil, typewriter or recorder. No pens or ink allowed when using original records.

Physical condition of the materials may limit reproduction and photocopies. Reproductions are for the researcher's personal use only. Written permission must be obtained from the Director of the Municipal Archives if the copied material is to be used for publication. There is a $15 publication use fee.

The Municipal Archives appreciates receiving copies of any research results.

NEW YORK CITY DEPARTMENT OF RECORDS AND INFORMATION SERVICES
MUNICIPAL REFERENCE AND RESEARCH CENTER

Facility Director: Anne Taylor, Director

Address: 31 Chambers Street, Room 112
New York, NY 10007

(Cross Streets: Centre and Elk Streets)

Phone Number: (212) 566-4284

Hours of Operation:

Monday to Friday: 9:00 am to 5:00 pm
Closed Saturday, Sunday and legal holidays.

Closest Public Transportation and Directions:

See "CITY REGISTER'S OFFICE, MANHATTAN."

Description of Resources:

The Municipal Reference and Research Center, established in 1913 as the Municipal Reference Library, is a depository for all official reports and studies issued by New York City government agencies. In addition to approximately 250,000 reports, books and other publications, the Center has an extensive collection of clippings and pamphlets on New York City matters. These include:

1. <u>Biographical Binders</u>: These contain mounted clippings, from local New York City newspapers and other sources, about people in or having an impact upon New York City government and political life. The biographical clippings are mounted in binders and date from the early 1950s to the present.

2. <u>Vertical Files</u>: Newspaper clippings that deal with individuals or groups of people in the City's government are located in vertical files under "Officials and Employees" or in specific subject or Department files. In addition, the "NYC Politics" file contains information on selected campaigns, primaries and elections from 1917 to the present. A person who campaigned for office but was not elected may show up here.

3. <u>New York City Neighborhood Files</u>: These include newspaper clippings, pamphlets and other material on neighborhoods within New York City.

4. <u>Street Name Historical File</u>: This card file contains references to street names and street name changes within the five boroughs of New York City. This index is updated annually to reflect name changes approved by the Mayor and City Council. In some years, park and playground names were included also. Each card shows the name, location, date of name change, background information on the name and history of the site. A high percentage of the name changes honor a person, usually a deceased person.

5. <u>Map Collection</u>: The Center has a microfiche collection of maps showing the boundaries of old Assembly Districts (AD) and Election Districts (ED) for Manhattan (1872-1956), the Bronx (1914-1954), Brooklyn (1914-1954) and Queens (1917-1954). Each AD is on a separate fiche. As a result, these maps may be difficult to use unless the researcher has a good idea of the location of the area being sought. Also, the Election Districts are color-coded and not easy to decipher because of poor color contrast.

   The Center has a complete set of AD/ED maps (paper copy), 1956-1973, and a scattering of earlier and later maps. Consult with the Research Librarian on other maps in the collection.

6. <u>Civil Service Lists ("Civil Lists")</u>: These are lists of New York City employees, including employees of the Board of Education, from 1883 to the present. The lists from 1952/1953 to 1969 are on

microfilm and those from 1969 to the present are on microfiche. Pre-1952/1953 lists are on paper copy stored off-site.

Pre-1969 lists include the Department in which employed, job title, surname, first name, date entered into service and salary.

1969 and 1970 include surname, first letter only of first name, home address, employee number, Department number, job title number and salary. (The Center has a complete set of job descriptions corresponding to these numbers.)

1971 to 1983 include the same data as above, except Social Security number and pension number replaced employee number.

1984 to present - As a result of Local Law 80, passed by the City Council on November 20, 1984, lists after 1983 do not include the employee's home address, pension number or Social Security number. These later lists include Department number, surname, first letter of first name, job title number and salary.

7. Biographical Publications: The Center has a small but varied collection including:

    Who's Who in New York. 1904, 1909, 1911, 1914, 1918, 1924, 1929, 1938, 1947 and 1952. [920 W62N]

    Old Merchants of New York. 1863, 1870, and 1968. [920.B27 omo]

    Spengler, Otto. *Das Deutsches Element der Stadt New York.* 1913. [920 Sp3]

    Architects in Practice, NYC, 1840-1900. Committee for the Preservation of Architectural Records.
    [82 F84 aipny]

8. New York City Histories: The collection includes books written about New York City, its neighborhoods, government and people.

9. Proceedings: The Center has a complete set of minutes of the Common Council, 1675-1831; proceedings of the Board of Aldermen, 1831-1937; and proceedings of the City Council, 1938 to the present. In addition, the collection includes proceedings of the Board of Estimate, 1871-1980; a complete set of the *City Record,* 1871 to the present; and annual reports, journals or minutes of such agencies as the Civil Service Commission, 1908-1954, Board of Education, City Planning Commission, and Department of Public Charities (mid-nineteenth century).

    Information on individuals, scattered in these proceedings, may be included in resolutions in memoriam to a former or current member of the Board, Council, Commission or Department, announcements of appointments, etc. Of particular interest to genealogists are Civil Service Commission proceedings and Board of Estimate actions on the New York City Employees Retirement System.

    Civil Service Commission proceedings include actions related to individuals who were NYC employees. Information in these items varies but generally include name, position title and salary.

    Board of Estimate proceedings list applications received from individuals for retirement benefits, disability benefits or the continuance of death benefits under the New York City Employee Retirement System. These lists are included in Board of Estimate proceedings, 1936-1969, and show employee name, job title, agency where last employed, current address (which may be the place to which the employee retired), years of service, date of membership (i.e. date of employment), date of retirement, details of the pension and Social Security number. Data on retirees appear in Board of Estimate proceedings prior to 1936 but are not organized in a manner that allows for convenient reference. See "Finding Aids.".

10. *List of Enrolled Voters* and *Registry of Voters:* The *List of Enrolled Voters* (known as *Enrollments,* 1899-1912) were published annually in the *City Record* or as a separate publication of the Board of Elections. They include name, address, political party in which registered, Assembly District and Election District. Since 1957, the lists include also the voter's number and the names of voters who did not appear on the previous year's list.

Registry of Voters was also published in the *City Record*. Similar data is included (name, address, Assembly District, Election District) but the lists are organized differently. See "Finding Aids."

List of Enrolled Voters is available for 1899-1912 *(Enrollments)*, 1939-1974/1975. *Registry of Voters* is available for 1883-1887, 1896, 1901-1902, 1904-1969. NOTE: There are gaps in these sets.

The NEW YORK PUBLIC LIBRARY has more complete sets of *List of Enrolled Voters* and *Registry of Voters*, 1881-1903, which are on-site and immediately accessible. See "NEW YORK PUBLIC LIBRARY, CENTRAL RESEARCH LIBRARY, GENERAL RESEARCH DIVISION."

Finding Aids:

1. Biographical Binders: These binders are arranged alphabetically by the name of the individual.

2. Files: The Vertical Files are arranged alphabetically. An article about an individual would be either under "Officials and Employees" or the Department in which the individual worked. The "Officials and Employees" files are broken out alphabetically, i.e. A-M, N-P, Q-Z. A complete listing of subject headings in the vertical files can be found in a blue binder (front section) on the librarian's desk in the City/State room.

   An index to the Neighborhood Files is in the back of the blue binder. The neighborhoods are arranged by borough and then alphabetically by name. Each neighborhood has been assigned a number. The file can be located once the number is known.

3. Street Name Historical File: These index cards are filed alphabetically and are cross-indexed by the current and old names of the street.

4. Map Collection: The Assembly District maps on microfiche are arranged by borough, year and Assembly District. The Assembly District maps (paper copy) are arranged by year and borough in drawers. The lowest drawer has the oldest maps (1956 and 1957).

5. Civil Service Lists ("Civil Lists"): These are annual lists. Those from 1969 to the present are on microfiche arranged alphabetically by surname. The pre-1969 lists are more difficult to use. They are arranged by Department, sub-divisions of the Department, job title and finally surname. Sub-divisions of the Board of Education include offices within the Board's headquarters as well as each individual school. To determine on which microfilm reel a particular Department can be found, use the annual master lists printed in the *City Record*. These lists are located near the microfilm cabinets.

6. Biographical Publications and New York City Histories can be found in the catalog in the main room under "N.Y.C. Biographies" and "N.Y.C. History." Most of these volumes can be found on open shelves under classification numbers that begin with 920 or 974.

7. Proceedings: Indexes to proceedings are generally available and are located in each volume or the last volume of the year. Board of Estimate proceedings indexes, 1955-1980, are in separate volumes. The NYC Employee Retirement System (NYCERS) applications index, 1937-1969, is an addenda at the back of the annual Board of Estimate index. A similar list exists for 1936, but it is included within the regular Board of Estimate index under "Estimate and Apportionment, New York City Employee Retirement System." In earlier years, there was no separate listing for actions related to the NYCERS.

8. *List of Enrolled Voters* and *Registry of Voters:* Lists, 1965-1975, are in bound books on open shelves in the City/State room. Earlier volumes are not on-site.

   Prior to 1957, Lists are organized by year, borough, Assembly District, Election District and the first letter of the surname. Lists, 1957-1960, are arranged in a similar manner except that voters who registered in the district for the first time are listed separately, in italics, after the printed listing of regular voters for each letter of the alphabet. Names are completely alphabetized beginning in 1957.

   Lists after 1960 are organized by year, borough, Assembly District, Election District, surname and first name. New voters are not separated out but are noted by an asterisk.

   Registry of Voters are organized by year, borough and Assembly District, Election District, street name, building number, name of voter. Names are not alphabetized. These volumes are not on-site.

The reference librarian can consult an inventory of *Registry of Voters* and pre-1966 *List of Enrolled Voters* located at the desk in the main reading room to determine if the volume for a particular year is available.

Description of Facility:

The Center is located on the ground floor of the Surrogate's Court building opposite the main entrance. It consists of two public rooms, the main room and the City/State room. The Biographical Binders, vertical and neighborhood files, *List of Enrolled Voters,* proceedings, most biographical publications and New York City histories are located in the City/State room.

The Civil Service lists on microfiche are located at the desk at the entrance to the main room. These must be requested from the staff person on duty. As security, a photo-identification card must be deposited with the person on duty while using these materials. The lists on microfilm are located in the microfilm cabinet near the desk.

The Assembly District maps (microfiche) and Street Name Index are located in the Technical Services room which is not open to researchers. These must be requested from the librarian. No identification is needed. The Assembly District maps (paper copy) are located in the map cabinet in the main room near the entrance to the Technical Services Room.

There is one microfilm reader and one microfiche reader. The library can accommodate 40 researchers. There are four reference librarians available to assist the public.

Fees/Copies:

Two photocopy machines are available. Photocopies are $.15 per page. The microfilm and microfiche readers are reader/copiers. Copies can be made at $.10 per page. The Center does not make change. Bring coins or go to the CITY REGISTER'S OFFICE cashier on the second floor (Room 202) for change.

Restrictions on Use:

Paper copies of Civil Service Lists (pre-1956), *List of Enrolled Voters* (pre-1966) and *Registry of Voters* (all) are not on-site and must be ordered in advance. At least two days (to be safe, make it three days) notice is required to obtained these lists. The Center will accept requests by telephone.

The Municipal Reference and Research Center collections are primarily for reference use within the Center. Limited categories of materials are allowed to be circulated for short periods of time to city government employees only.

NEW YORK GENEALOGICAL AND BIOGRAPHICAL SOCIETY LIBRARY

Facility Director:	Dr. Gunther Pohl, Librarian (for policy)
	Betty H. Payne, Associate Librarian (day-to-day operations)

Address:	122 East 58th Street
	New York, NY 10022-1939
	(Cross Streets: Park and Lexington Avenues)

Phone Number:	(212) 755-8532

Hours of Operation:

Monday to Saturday: 9:30 am to 5:00 pm (closed Saturdays, June to September)
Closed Sunday, legal holidays and the month of August.

Closest Public Transportation:

Subway: 4, 5 or 6 to 59th Street
         N or R to Lexington Avenue

Bus: M101 or M102 to East 59th Street and Lexington Avenue (southbound) and to 59th Street and 3rd Avenue (northbound)
         M1, M2, M3 or M4 to Madison Avenue and East 58th Street (northbound)
         M28 to Lexington Avenue and East 57th (crosstown)
         M32 (to Queens) or M103 (crosstown) to Lexington Avenue and East 59th Street

Directions:

Take the #4, #5 (express) or #6 (local) train to the 59th Street station. Exit to East 59th Street and Lexington Avenue. The exit is at the south end of the station. Walk one block south on Lexington Avenue to East 58th Street and turn west to the building. The Library is reached by elevator to the fourth floor.

Description of Resources:

The Society's collection includes over 65,000 volumes, 25,000 manuscripts and 3,000 microfilm and microfiche on genealogy, local history and biography. The emphasis is predominately early American with large segments devoted to New York and the northeast. See "Restrictions on Use" in regard to manuscripts and microform.

The collection is divided between reference works, accessible to non-members in an area at the entrance to the Library, and the bulk of the collection, beyond the railing in the larger members' reading room with balconies and other rooms

The following materials are in the collection. Call numbers are listed in brackets.

1. New York City Vital Records

    The following indexes are in book form and available to non-members:

    Births: 1911-1934 (all boroughs)
    Marriages: 1894, 1899, 1904-1933 (all boroughs)
    Deaths: 1904-1932 (all boroughs)

    Additional indexes on microfilm (restricted):
    Births: 1888-1898 (Manhattan/Bronx); 1899-1915 (all boroughs)

    The Library also has the following records on microfilm (restricted):
    Deaths: 1795-1865 (Manhattan); 1847-1853, 1858-1861 (Brooklyn)

See "Restrictions on Use." All of these indexes and some records (Deaths, 1798-1865, Manhattan) are available also at the NEW YORK PUBLIC LIBRARY, U.S. HISTORY, LOCAL HISTORY AND GENEALOGY DIVISION AND MICROFORMS DIVISION (no fee for viewing). Birth indexes to 1897, marriage indexes to 1937 and death indexes to 1929 are also available at the NEW YORK CITY DEPARTMENT OF RECORDS AND INFORMATION SERVICES, MUNICIPAL ARCHIVES.

2.   City Directories

The Library has the NYC Directories (Manhattan and parts of the Bronx), 1786-1934, and Brooklyn Directories, 1796-1934 (gaps). Most of the set is on microfilm (see "Restrictions on Use"), but the NYC Directories, 1786-1862 and Brooklyn Directories, 1841-1862, 1882, 1887/8-1892 are available on the shelf. The Library also has Buffalo City Directories, 1832-1869 (gaps), and many of other U.S. cities.

3.   Material on Other Localities

The Society has a comprehensive collection on New Jersey, upstate New York and all of the New England states, including published cemetery inscriptions, vital records and town and county histories. Some of the latter material is on microfilm. See "Restrictions on Use."

4.   Manuscript Collection

Holdings range from family bible records and family genealogies to church and cemetery records.

5.   Obituaries

New York Death Notices (clippings). Vol.1, 1870-1890, indexed; Vol. 2, 1890-1891. [NYC G-oversize]

6.   Wills and Letters of Administration

Manhattan:
Sawyer, Ray C. *Index of Wills for New York County, 1630-1850.*

Brooklyn:
Van Buren, D. *Abstracts of Wills of Kings County, Recorded at Brooklyn.* Libers 1-6, 1787-1843.
    (typescript) [K10]

Queens:
Sawyer, Ray C. *Abstracts of Wills for Queens County, NY.* 4 vols in 2. (typescript, 1936-1937). v.1: 1797-1813; v.2: 1813-1828; v.3: 1828-1843; v.4: 1843-1850; McCormack, L.J. v.5: 1848-1856. [Q5]

Staten Island:
Fast, F.S. *Richmond County, NY Index of Wills, 1787-1863; Index of Letters of Administration and Guardianship, 1787-1866.* (typescript) [R12]

The Society also has other indexes and abstracts of wills for Manhattan and Brooklyn. See listing under "NEW YORK PUBLIC LIBRARY, U.S. HISTORY, LOCAL HISTORY AND GENEALOGY DIVISION."

7.   Census

Census indexes, 1790-1850 or 1860, are available for most states. The Library has on microfilm the following (see "Restrictions on Use"):

Federal Census:

New York State, 1790-1870, 1880 Soundex index
New York City, 1890 (special schedule for soldiers, sailors, marines, and widows of veterans)
New York City, 1900 (all boroughs)

State Census:

New York State, 1855 (scattered counties)

8.   Genealogical Publications and Indexes

The Society has an extensive collection of reference materials such as "how to" books and pamphlets, lineage books, genealogical periodicals and indexes including:

New York Genealogical and Biographical Society Record. Indexes: Barber, G.A., *Surnames,* vols. 1-20, 21-40; *Subject,* vols. 39-76, 71-94. Worden, J.D. *Master index,* 1870-1982.

Combined Indexing to Genealogical Periodicals. Maryland, 1963-1975. [CS 42.11]

Crowther, G.R. *Surname Index to 65 Volumes of Colonial and Revolutionary Pedigrees.* [CS 42/N43]

DAR Patriot Index. 3 vols. [REF SOC 22]. Also: *Index to the rolls of honor (ancestors index) in the Lineage books of the National Society Daughters of the American Revolution.* 4 vols. [REF SOC 21]

Herbert, M. & B. McNeil. *Biography and Genealogy Master Index* [to biographical dictionaries and encyclopedias, Who's Who, etc]. 8 vols., 1980, and supplements, 1981-1985, 1986, 1987 and 1988. [CT 214/U5 B57]

Historical-Biographical Dictionaries Master Index. [CT 215/U5 H15]

Master index to New York State DAR Genealogical Records. [Collection at NYPL]. (At desk).

National Genealogical Society Quarterly and *Topical Index* vols. 1-50, 1912-1962. (Later volumes indexed separately.) [CS 42/N4]

Rider, F., ed. *American Genealogical-Biographical Index.* [CS 44/A57]

The American Genealogist. With indexes. [CS 42/A51]. Worden, J.D. *Subject Index to v.1-20.* 1986.

NOTE: Much of the material described above is available also in the NEW YORK PUBLIC LIBRARY, U.S. HISTORY, LOCAL HISTORY AND GENEALOGY DIVISION (Room 315N).

Finding Aids:

In addition to the above indexes, the Library has a card catalog alphabetically integrating author, title and subject.

The card catalog for the Manuscript Collection is subdivided by surnames, New York towns, New York counties, other states, other countries and Bible records (see "Restrictions on Use").

Description of Facility:

The NYG&BS Library occupies the 4th and 5th floors of the building. The Library has 3 microfilm readers, 2 microfiche readers and a microfilm/fiche-reader/printer available for use by members only. Seating in the non-member area is usually available for 10 persons. One librarian is always on duty.

Reference materials on open shelves include a complete set of the *New York Genealogical and Biographical Record* and a collection of genealogical how-to books. Assorted indexes to genealogical periodicals can be found on the table facing the coat rack.

Fees/Copies:

A minimum daily donation of $3 is requested of non-members. Society membership is $50 per calendar year. Membership includes full access to the Library collection, a subscription to the quarterly, *The New York Genealogical and Biographical Record,* and attendance at lectures and programs. Photocopy service is provided at $.35 per copy. Up to 10 pages will be furnished by staff if the material is not fragile.

Restrictions on Use:

Non-members do not have access to the manuscript or microform collections. Staff members will bring books to the non-member area and will check the manuscript catalog, but only members may examine the manuscripts. Non-members can, however, view NYC indexes to vital records in the member's area in which they are located.

NEW-YORK HISTORICAL SOCIETY
LIBRARY AND MANUSCRIPT ROOM

Facility Director: James E. Mooney, Librarian
                             Thomas Dunnings, Curator of Manuscripts

Address: 170 Central Park West
                           New York, NY 10024

                           (Cross Streets: West 76th and 77th Streets)

Phone Number: (212) 873-3400

Hours of Operation:

Tuesday to Saturday: 10:00 am to 5:00 pm
Closed Sunday, Monday and legal holidays.

NOTE: Open on Monday during the summer (Memorial Day to Labor Day).

Closest Public Transportation:

Subway: B or C to 81st Street
          1 to 79th Street

Bus: M10 to West 76th/77th Street and Central Park West
         M17 (79th Street Crosstown) to West 81 Street and Central Park West

Directions:

Take the B or C train to the 81st Street station. Exit at the <u>south</u> end of the station to Central Park West and 79th Street. Walk south on Central Park West to #170.

Description of Resources:

The Library has the following materials of interest to genealogists:

1.   <u>New York City Vital Records</u>

     Birth, death and marriage indexes, 1889-1905

     NOTE: Pre-1898 these indexes include only New York County (Manhattan and the Bronx). Brooklyn, Queens and Staten Island were not included in these indexes until 1898.

2.   <u>City Directories</u>

     New York (Manhattan/Bronx), 1787-1933
     Brooklyn, 1896-1904, 1912

3.   <u>Newspapers</u>

     The Society has an outstanding collection of New York City newspapers from the first NYC paper, *Bradford's New-York Gazette,* to present publications. It has the fourth largest collection in the country of original issues of newspapers published in the USA before 1820. The newspaper collection is on microfilm and microcards.

     Of note also, the Society has typed lists of announcements of deaths, and marriages, 1801-1890, from the *New York Post*.

4.   <u>Probate Records</u>

     Abstracts of Wills on File in the Surrogate's Office, City of New York, 1665-1800, 17 vols. plus index. Published by the New-York Historical Society.

5. Map Collection

The Society has some 30,000 maps and atlases (mostly American, some foreign) including real estate and street atlases of Manhattan and Long Island.

6. Family Histories/Genealogies

The collection includes some 15,000 genealogies and family histories as well as 120,000 works on local history. Many are in manuscript form. Some include naturalization records and passport applications. See the card catalog.

Special collection of manuscripts -- Jews in South Carolina 1783 to 1897 -- includes a list of Jewish cemeteries with lists of burials.

7. Military

This is the complete library of the Seventh Regiment, New York National Guard, c.1813-1949, which includes officers accounts, rosters, company minute books, scrapbooks, photographs, court martial records and muster rolls.

8. Photo Collection

The Print Room of the Library has an outstanding photograph collection. This is a useful resource in studying buildings and neighborhoods.

9. Business Collection

The Bella C. Landauer Collection includes such diverse items as advertising cards (popular in the late 19th and early 20th centuries) and many manufacturers' catalogs, including those of Jewish manufacturers. An appointment must be made in advance to use this collection which is located in the Print Room.

10. The Hendricks Family Collection

The Manuscript Room holds this collection of papers of a Jewish Sephardic family which dates back to before the Revolutionary War.

Finding Aids:

The Library card catalog is arranged by author, title and subject. There is a genealogical catalog arranged by family name and there are separate newspaper indexes. Special collections such as the Seventh Regiment are cataloged separately. The librarians are very helpful in locating uncataloged items.

The Manuscript Room has its own catalogs. There is also *A Guide to the Manuscript Collections of the New York Historical Society,* 1972, by Arthur J. Breton (2 vols).

At present, only the negatives in the Print Room are cataloged. A catalog of Print Room materials will be published within the next year.

Description of Facility:

The Library is located on the second floor. The Manuscript and Microfilm Rooms are adjacent to it. The Library has a seating capacity of 52, and the Manuscript Room seats 10. There are three or more staff persons available in the Library and two in the Manuscript Room to assist researchers. Materials can be obtained in 5-15 minutes; some are on open shelves, including biographical dictionaries, Historical Society publications, encyclopedias of history, indexes to New York newspapers, City Directories and guides to the manuscript collections.

The Microfilm Room has 4 microfilm, 2 microfiche and 2 microcard readers. In addition, there are 3 reader-printers.

The Print Room is located on the 3rd floor. Eight to nine people can be seated at 3 tables in this room.

Fees/Copies:

There is a $2 entrance fee for non-members to the building and $1 fee for use of the Library and/or Manuscript or Microfilm Rooms. Cash or personal checks are accepted. The fee is not in effect on Tuesdays. A contribution is required but the amount is left up to the user.

Photocopy service costs $.35 per page. Copies are made by Society personnel only. It can take from a few minutes to a few hours to obtain a copy in person. Copies are made twice a day (or more often if demand requires). There is a $1.50 additional charge for mailing. Some materials may not be photocopied because of the fragility but may be microfilmed or photographed. Requests for all services must be made before 4:30 pm.

Membership fees range from $20 for students to $35 for an individual ($20 non-resident; $25 senior).

Restrictions on Use:

Vital record indexes for New York City and City Directories are originals and the Society prefers that the microfilm copies in the NEW YORK PUBLIC LIBRARY be used by researchers.

Coats, bags, packages, briefcases and books must be checked. They are not allowed in the Library or Manuscript Room. Adults only may use the facility. Use of pencil is mandatory. Hand-held copiers may not be used.

Users wishing to use rare books and newspapers or the broadside collection are required to submit identification and are restricted to one item at a time.

NEW YORK PUBLIC LIBRARY
ANNEX

Facility Director: Richard Hill, Annex Supervisor

Address: 521 West 43rd Street
New York, NY 10036

(Cross Streets: 10th and 11th Avenues)

Phone Number: (212) 714-8520 (General Number)
(212) 714-8525 (Annex Supervisor)

Hours of Operation:

Monday to Saturday: 9:00 am to 5:00 pm
Closed Sunday and legal holidays.

Closest Public Transportation:

Subway: A, C or E to 42nd Street and 8th Avenue
1, 2 or 3 to 42nd Street/Times Square
7 to 42nd Street/Times Square (last stop)
N or R to 42nd Street/Times Square

Bus: M42 to 10th Avenue and 42nd Street (crosstown)
M11 to 42nd Street and 9th Avenue (southbound)
M11 to 42nd Street and 10th Avenue (northbound)

Directions:

Take any of the above subways to the 42nd Street station. Either walk or take the crosstown M42 bus (which runs along 42nd Street) to 10th Avenue. Walk north one block to West 43rd Street. Turn left to #521. Go up a short flight of steps. The entrance is on the left.

Description of Resources:

The Annex, one of the Research Libraries of the New York Public Library, houses its collection of back-dated telephone directories from all over the world (excluding New York City), City Directories from around the country and newspapers both foreign and local. In addition, *Lloyd's Register of Shipping* (Merchant Ship lists) from 1850 to the present and the Library's patent collection are available here. The following are of particular interest to genealogists:

1.   <u>Foreign Telephone Directories</u>

Original and microfilm copies of telephone directories from more than 50 foreign countries including some Canadian cities. (See Appendix D)

Current foreign phone directories are in the stacks in the NEW YORK PUBLIC LIBRARY - CENTRAL RESEARCH LIBRARY, GENERAL RESEARCH DIVISION.

2.   <u>U.S. and Canadian City Directories</u>

An extensive collection of U.S. City Directories from 1870 and Canadian City Directories from 1843 in paper copy. Paper copies of pre-1870 City Directories are at the GENEALOGY DIVISION. In addition, Directories for New York City and over 300 other U.S. Cities are on microfilm in the MICROFORMS DIVISION. See Appendix E and "NEW YORK PUBLIC LIBRARY, U.S. HISTORY, LOCAL HISTORY AND GENEALOGY DIVISION AND MICROFORMS DIVISION."

3. <u>U.S. Telephone Directories</u>

Paper copies of pre-1976 telephone directories for cities other than NYC. Later years are available for a few cities.

The latest U.S. telephone directories are in the Main Reading Room (Room 315) at the NEW YORK PUBLIC LIBRARY - CENTRAL RESEARCH LIBRARY, GENERAL RESEARCH DIVISION. See "NEW YORK PUBLIC LIBRARY, U.S. HISTORY, LOCAL HISTORY AND GENEALOGY DIVISION AND MICROFORMS DIVISION" for telephone directories available after 1975 on Phonefiche.

4. <u>Newspapers</u>

Some of the major NYC newspapers at the Annex include:

Brooklyn Evening Star	1846
Brooklyn Daily Union	1863-1871
Commercial Advertiser	1821-1904 (incomplete)
Evening Journal	1895-1937
Daily Mirror	1924-1963
Daily News	1855-1872, 1902-1905, 1919 to date
Herald-Tribune	1924-1966
Home News (Bronx-Harlem-Washington Heights)	1911-1916, 1917-1948 (incomplete)
New York Post	1801-1984
New York Times	1851 to date
New York Times Index	1851 to date (open shelf)
Telegram	1867-1931
The Sun	1833-1950 (incomplete)
Tribune	1841-1924
Tribune Index	1875-1906 (open shelf)
Worker (Socialist Weekly)	1901-1908
World	1860-1931
World Telegram	1931-1950
World Telegram and Sun	1950-1966

The Annex collection includes newspapers for many states in the U.S. and for foreign countries. In major states (e.g. California) or countries (e.g. Germany) there may be more than one. These are on microfilm and are current up to filming, i.e. 3 months behind. The Annex has the *London Times* and *Index* from 1785 to the present. Appendix F includes a selection of U.S. and foreign newspapers in the collection at the Annex. For other U.S. or foreign newspapers see the catalog.

Jewish and Hebrew newspapers published in NYC, other U.S. cities or foreign countries are located at the JEWISH DIVISION.

5. *The New York Sun* Morgue

The Annex has the morgue clipping files for the *New York Sun* from the late 19th century to the end of the 1940s. The files are arranged by name and by subject.

Finding Aids:

The Annex has the following catalogs and lists available:

Foreign Telephone Book list (copy reprinted in Appendix D)
Foreign Newspaper Card Catalog
New York City Newspapers List (complete list of holdings)
Newspaper Card Catalog
Newspaper List (at front desk) - not complete
Dictionary Catalog of the Research Libraries - See "NEW YORK PUBLIC LIBRARY - CENTRAL RESEARCH LIBRARY, GENERAL RESEARCH DIVISION" for a description of this catalog.

Description of Facility:

The Annex is located on the first floor. Seating is available for 48 researchers. In addition, there are 20 microfilm readers (behind the front desk). There are one to two librarians available to assist researchers. Indexes to the *London Times, New York Times* and selected other newspapers are on open shelves, to the left of the front desk. Catalogs are opposite the front desk. There is a short wait for microfilm and a 10-20 minute waiting period to receive printed materials.

Fees/Copies:

Self-service microfilm copiers are located opposite the Reprographic Services desk. Copies can be made at $.30 per page. Copies of paper pages are made by staff at the Reprographic Services desk.

Restrictions on Use:

None.

NEW YORK PUBLIC LIBRARY - CENTRAL RESEARCH LIBRARY
GENERAL RESEARCH DIVISION

Facility Director: Elizabeth Diefendorf, Chief

Address: Fifth Avenue at 42nd Street
New York, NY 10018

(Cross Streets: 40th and 42nd Streets; 5th and 6th Avenues)

Phone Number: (212) 930-0561 (general information)
(212) 661-7220 (library hours)
(212) 930-0830, 0831 (to locate a book)
(212) 340-0849 (telephone reference service)
(212) 930-0816 (Reprographic Services)

Hours of Operation:

Public Catalog, Current Periodicals and Main Reading Rooms:
Monday to Wednesday: 10:00 am to 9:00 pm
Thursday to Saturday: 10:00 am to 6:00 pm

Reprographic Services Division:
Monday to Wednesday: 10:00 am to 8:00 pm (no orders taken after 7:30 pm)
Thursday to Saturday: 10:00 am to 6:00 pm (no orders taken after 5:30 pm)
Closed Sunday and legal holidays

NOTE: Not all Divisions of NYPL are open these hours. Check the individual Division listings which follow. The complete schedule for the Research Libraries is available at any information desk.

Some Divisions will allow materials to be sent to the Main Reading Room Delivery Desk, in order to permit researchers to use them on days or evenings when the Division is closed. The policy differs for each Division. Check with the librarian of the appropriate Division, if not covered here.

Closest Public Transportation:

Subway: B, D, F or Q to 42nd Street/6th Avenue
7 to 5th Avenue/42nd Street
4, 5 or 6 to 42nd Street/Grand Central Station

Bus: M1, M2, M3, M4, M5 or M32 to 42nd Street and 5th Avenue (southbound) and to 42nd Street
and Madison Avenue (northbound)
M5, M6 or M7 to Avenue of the Americas (6th Avenue) and 42nd Street
M42 (crosstown) or M104 to 5th Avenue and 42nd Street

Directions:

Take the B, D, F or Q train to the 42nd Street station. Exit at 42nd Street and 6th Avenue (Avenue of the Americas). Walk <u>east</u> on 42nd Street. Or, take the #7 to the 5th Avenue/42nd Street station. Exit at 42nd Street and 5th Avenue. Walk about 100 feet <u>west</u>. Enter the Library through the 42nd Street entrance (between 5th and 6th Avenues).

Description of Resources:

The New York Public Library was created in 1895 and moved into its current location on 42nd Street in 1911. Today, the Library consists of the Central Research Library, the PERFORMING ARTS RESEARCH CENTER AT LINCOLN CENTER, the SCHOMBURG CENTER FOR RESEARCH IN BLACK CULTURE, and the ANNEX, as well as the branch libraries. The Central Research Library, housed at 42nd Street and 5th Avenue, includes eight Divisions and five special collections including the JEWISH DIVISION, the MAP DIVISION, the MIRIAM AND IRA WALLACH DIVISION OF ARTS, PRINTS AND PHOTOGRAPHS, the SLAVIC AND BALTIC DIVISION, the U.S. HISTORY, LOCAL HISTORY AND GENEALOGY DIVISION and the MICROFORMS DIVISION. The General Research Division, with over 2,000,000 volumes in the arts and humanities, administers the Public Catalog Room, the Main Reading Room, the DeWitt Wallace Periodical Room and the Astor Hall Information Desk of the Central Research Library.

The General Research Division is responsible for more than one-half the total book holdings of the Research Libraries. The Main Reading Room houses over 36,000 books on open shelves. Items of interest to genealogists include:

1. Biographies: The collection is rich in collective and individual biographies, as well as biographical dictionaries. These include:

   Biography and Genealogy Master Index. 17 vols., 1981-1988. [*R-AA; South Hall, east wall 7]

   Contemporary Authors. 123 vols., 1964-1988. [*R-AB; South Hall, east wall 11-12]

   Dictionary of Scientific Biography. 16 vols, 1970-1980. [*R-AB; South Hall, east wall 12-14]

   Dictionary of Literary Biography. 71 vols., 1978-1986. [*R-AA; South Hall, east wall 12-13]

   The New York Times Index. September 1851- . [*R-*A]. *Personal Name Index to the New York Times Index, 1851-1974* and supplement, *1975-1984.* [*R-*A 80-3601; North Hall, east wall 164-167]

2. Telephone Directories: Current phone directories for most United States cities are available in paper copy in the North Hall. Current foreign directories, such as Paris, Great Britain and Germany, may be ordered from the stacks.

3. *Cole Directory,* a reverse directory by address and by phone number, is available from 1970/1971 to the present for Suffolk County; from 1971 for Nassau County and for all NYC Counties; and from 1973 for Westchester and Putnam Counties. [Current year, South Hall, east wall 1; earlier years, Stack 7 (County)]

4. Foreign City Directories such as the *Berliner Address Book,* 1896-1939 [BAZ+]; *The Post Office London Directory,* 1799-1967 (gaps) and *Kelly's Post Office London Business Directory,* 1968-1984. [CO (London Post Office Directory)]

   See also "NEW YORK PUBLIC LIBRARY, U.S. HISTORY, LOCAL HISTORY AND GENEALOGY DIVISION AND MICROFORMS DIVISION" for additional London City Directories on microfilm. The current *Kelly's London Business Directory* is available in the Economic and Public Affairs Division of the Library.

5. Voter Registration Lists, New York City, include *List of Enrolled Voters,* 1899-1975 (missing: 1915, all boroughs; 1919-1922, Manhattan) [*SYA+]; and *Registry of Voters,* 1881-1903 [*SYA+]. These lists can be used to access the Voter Registration records in the MUNICIPAL ARCHIVES. This set is the only readily accessible collection in the City. See "NEW YORK CITY DEPARTMENT OF RECORDS AND INFORMATION SERVICES, MUNICIPAL ARCHIVES."

Finding Aids:

The NYPL public catalog is in two parts, a retrospective catalog closed in 1971 and a computerized system, Catalog of the New York Public Library (CATNYP). At the present time, only books cataloged beginning in 1972 can be accessed on the computer terminals located in the Public Catalog Room (Room 315). Classmarks (call numbers) are found at the bottom of each entry display. Books and periodicals can be searched under author, subject or title. Books with Hebrew/Yiddish titles cataloged since August 1981 also are included in CATNYP using ANSI romanization of the Hebrew alphabet. Manuscript materials are not included in CATNYP. CATNYP is easy to use. For instruction on how to proceed with a search, type "HELP."

Books in Roman characters cataloged up to the end of 1971 are listed in the 800-volume *Dictionary Catalog of the Research Libraries of the New York Public Library, 1911-1971.* Classmarks are located in the upper right hand corner of each entry. Sets are available for consultation in the Public Catalog Room, the Main Reading Room (Room 315) and at other locations throughout the building.

Prior to 1972, each Division of the Library also had its own card catalog. See the description of these catalogs under "Finding Aids" of the particular Division. Copies of some of these catalogs can also be found in the Main Reading Room.

The Library began publishing integrated book catalogs in 1972. There are three sets of book catalogs listing the holdings of all the Divisions. (These need be used only when the CATNYP system is down.) Each Division has copies of these books:

1. Blue Books (*Research Libraries Catalog, 1972-1980.* 64 vols.) - Cover the holdings of all the Research Libraries cataloged from 1972 to 1980. Authors, subjects and titles are integrated in one sequence. Works in Hebrew/Yiddish are also represented by an additional entry, arranged by title in Hebrew alphabetical order at the end of the "Z" volume.

2. Red Books (*Research Libraries Catalog, 1972-1980.* 12 vols.) - Supplement the Blue Books by including material left out of this catalog; and cover all materials cataloged to July 1981.

3. Green Books (*The NYPL, The Research Libraries, Interim List: Index Includes Titles Cataloged August 1981-March 1985.* 25 vols.) - These do not include books with Hebrew/Yiddish titles.

For recent acquisitions (not yet cataloged) ask a librarian for assistance. Librarians have access to a computer terminal which updates these catalogs and CATNYP.

Once the classmark is identified, fill out a blue-and-white call slip for each book or periodical being requested. Most Library materials are in closed book stacks and may be retrieved only by Library personnel. Materials may be housed in other Divisions or at one of the other Research Library buildings. Researchers may wish to consult with a librarian at the Information Desk in the Public Catalog Room in order to determine the location of an item before handing in a call slip at the west end of the Information Desk. A stub with a number will be provided by the clerk. Pick up the books requested at the Delivery Desk in the South Hall of the Main Reading Room when the number appears on the Indicator Board.

The Subject Guide to Reference Material on Open Shelves, in a loose-leaf binder at the main Information Desk, outlines the types of materials on the open shelves of the Main Reading Room and provides the classmark and location by wall section.

Description of Facility:

The Public Catalog Room (Room 315), a spacious room on the third floor, houses 29 on-line computer terminals (supported by printers that provide hard copy) to the right of the entrance. Bound catalogs line the shelves around the room. Four reference librarians can assist researchers in locating materials throughout the Research Libraries. There are 8 long tables at which the bound catalogs can be consulted. Some seats (stools) are available.

The Main Reading Room, a vast room two city-blocks long, is entered through the Public Catalog Room. The room is divided into a North Hall and a South Hall. The Delivery Desk is in the area between these two rooms. The Indicator Board (immediately to the right of the entrance to the South Hall) is over the Delivery Desk. In addition to the reference works on open shelves in this room, 88 miles of shelves (not accessible to the public) are located beneath the room, where more than 100 staff members with the aid of a computer-controlled dumbwaiter system provide requested items within 10 minutes. There are 18 tables seating 288 researchers in the South Hall, and 8 tables seating 128 researchers in the North Hall. The MICROFORMS DIVISION takes up part of the North Hall.

The Reprographic Services Division is also located in the North Hall. There are 9 self-service microform reader/printers in the Reprographic Division, and 40 microfilm and 8 microfiche readers in the MICROFORMS DIVISION.

Biographies and biographical dictionaries are located in the South Hall of the Main Reading Room along the east wall. Biographical dictionaries [classmark *R-AA and *R-AB] are in wall sections 6 to 15 and individual biographies [classmark *R-AN] are in sections 27-37.

The current editions of *Cole Directory* are in section 1 of the east wall of the South Hall behind an information desk. A call slip must be provided to the librarian at this information desk in order to use these directories. Past editions of *Cole Directory* and the *Lists of Enrolled Voters* are in the stacks.

Telephone directories are on one side of the book cases that run along the aisle parallel to the east wall of the North Hall. *The New York Times Index* and the *Personal Name Index to the New York Times Index* are also in the North Hall [east wall 164-167].

Fees/Copies:

Paper copies are made by Reprographic Services staff. These will be electrostatic copies at $.25 per sheet (8.5" x 11") or $.45 per sheet (11" x 17"). There is a $6 surcharge for mail or phone orders plus a $3 search fee.

Copies of maps or prints (matte finish) 11" x 17" cost $8 and 18" x 24" cost $11. Glossy finish prints 11.5" x 14" cost $5.50. In addition, there is a $6 service charge for each order. See the list of rates for other duplicating services.

Researchers can make copies themselves from microfilm (e.g. census record, passenger record). These cost $.30 per page. There are 9 microform reader/printers. Consult with the staff at the booth if the copy comes out too dark/light. Change can be obtained at the window marked "Quick Copy."

In order to make copies of materials located in other Divisions (outside the Main Reading Room), inform the librarian of that Division, get a pass to carry the material out of the room, and take it to Reprographic Services. A pass is not needed to take microfilm or microfiche from the MICROFORMS DIVISION to a reader/copier. The Division will mark on the pass whether the "reader must immediately return" the material after copying or whether it can be left at Reprographic Services for "regular return." All microfilm or microfiche from the MICROFORMS DIVISION must be returned there by the researcher.

Restrictions on Use:

There is a check room at the 42nd Street entrance for all personal books, bags and coats.

Bags and packages must be opened for inspection by the guard when leaving the Main Reading Room and when leaving the building.

Researchers are requested to sign the registration book at the desk of each Division. No sign-in is required to use the materials in the Main Reading Room.

No more than three items can be requested at a time in the Main Reading Room. No materials can be borrowed.

NEW YORK PUBLIC LIBRARY
JEWISH DIVISION

Facility Director: Leonard S. Gold, Dorot Chief, Jewish Division and Assistant Director for Jewish, Oriental and Slavonic Studies

Address: Fifth Avenue at 42nd Street, Room 84
New York, NY 10018

(Cross Streets: 40th and 42nd Streets; 5th and 6th Avenues)

Phone Number: (212) 930-0601

Hours of Operation:

Monday, Wednesday,
  Friday, Saturday: 10:00 am to 6:00 pm
Tuesday: 10:00 am to 9:00 pm

Closed Thursday, Sunday and legal holidays. Researchers wishing to view materials on Thursday or during Monday or Wednesday evening may do so in the Main Reading Room. Telephone requests are accepted by 5:30 pm the day before. In-person requests must be made by 5:30 pm the same day. Only materials in good condition will be transferred to the Main Reading Room.

Closest Public Transportation, Directions and Fees/Copies:

See "NEW YORK PUBLIC LIBRARY - CENTRAL RESEARCH LIBRARY, GENERAL RESEARCH DIVISION."

Description of Resources:

The Jewish Division has one of the great collections of Judaica in the world. It was established in 1897, just two years after the formation of the Library. Today, the Division contains some 227,000 books, microfilms, manuscripts, newspapers and periodicals from all over the world. The collection includes forty 15th-century works and over 1,500 16th-century works.

Items of interest to genealogists include (NYPL classmark indicated in brackets):

1. Census

   Jews in Alsace, 1784: *Dénombrement Générale des Juifs...* [*PXP+ 80-4713]

2. Rabbinic Responsa

   These books of answers provided by rabbis to questions on halakhic matters usually make some reference to the rabbi's lineage on the first page or may have an introduction that was added posthumously providing some biographical information.

3. Newspapers

   An extensive collection of newspapers and periodicals printed in Europe and America in the last two centuries, including:

   The Jewish Daily Forward (New York, Yiddish), 1897 to present (complete collection).
     [*ZAN-*P142]

   The Day (New York, Yiddish), 1914-1957. [*ZY-*P2]

   Freie Arbeiter Stimme [Free Voice of Labor], (New York, Yiddish) 1890-1892, 1899-1952, 1963-1977.
     [*ZAN-*P183]

4. Marriage Records

   20 Italian Ketubot from the 17th and 18th centuries.

5. Holocaust Resources

The second largest collection of Yizkor books in New York City (see Appendix A).

Yad Vashem Archives of the Destruction: A Photographic Record of the Holocaust.
[microfiche; *XMH-2067]

6. Community History

Books on Jewish communities around the world.

7. Gravestone Inscriptions

De Sola Pool, David. *Portraits Etched in Stone: Early Jewish Settlers 1682-1831.* New York, 1951.
[*PXY]

Hock, Simon. *Mishpahat K"K Prague.* Pressburg, 1892. [*PXT]

Klein, Samuel. *Juedisch-Palaestinisches Corpus Inscriptionum* [Tombstones in Palestine]. Hildesheim,
1974. [*PWN 72-1014]

Kober, Adolf. *Jewish Monuments of the Middle Ages in Germany* [110 tombstone inscriptions from
Speyer, Cologne, Nuremberg and Worms 1085-c.1428]. New York, 1944-1945. [*PBL - American
Academy for Jewish Research Proceedings, Vols. 14-15]

Molho, Michael. *Matsevot bet ha-olamim shel yehude Thessalonika* [Tombstones in Thessalonika].
Tel Aviv, 1974. [*PWN 78-5700]

Weiss, Izak. *Sefer avne bet ha-yotser* [Tombstones in Bratislava]. Jerusalem, 1970. [*PWN 75-759]

8. Biographies and Genealogies

An extensive collection of biographical texts and genealogies such as:

Azulai, Joseph D. *Shem ha-gedolim ha-shalem* [An encyclopedia of 1300 rabbis in the 18th century].
Jerusalem, 1905. [*PWR]

Bader, Gershon. *Medinah ve-hakhamehah* [Biographies of leading Jews in Galicia]. New York, 1934.
[*PWR]

Balaban, Majer. *Di yidn-shtot Lublin* [The Jews of Lublin]. Buenos Aires, 1947. [*PWZ]

Chones, Shimon. *Toldot ha-poskim* [Rabbinic authorities and their works]. Warsaw, 1921. [*PWR]

Cohen, Israel. *Vilna.* Philadelphia, 1943. [*PWZ]

Dembitzer, Chaim. *Kelilat yofi* [Rabbis of Cracow and Lwow]. Cracow, 1888. [*PWR]

Eisenstadt, Ben Zion. *Dor rabanav ve-sofrav* [Generations of Rabbis and Authors]. Warsaw,
1895-1905. [*PWR]

Eisenstadt, Ben Zion. *Dorot ha-aharonim* [Recent Generations]. New York, 1913, Brooklyn,
1936-1941. [*PWR]

Eisenstadt, Ben Zion. *Hakhme Yisrael be-Amerikah* [Israel's Scholars in America]. New York. 1903.
[*PWR]

Federbusch, Simon. *Hokhmat Yisrael be-ma'arav Eyropah* [Science of Judaism in Western Europe].
Jerusalem, 1958-1965. [*PWR]

Frumkin, Arieh L. *Sefer toldot hakhme Yerushalayim.* Jerusalem, 1910. [*PWR]

Ghirondi, Mordechai and Ch. Nepi. *Toldot gedole Yisrael u-geone Italyah* [History of the Scholars of
Israel and the Sages of Italy] and *Zekher tsadikim le-verakhah.* Trieste, 1853. [*PWR]

Halachmi, David. *Hakhme Yisrael* [Biographies from the 13th to 20th century]. Tel Aviv, 1958.
[*PWR]

Halperin, Raphael. *Atlas ets hayim* [Encyclopedia of rabbis and Jewish scholars]. 14 vols. published of 20 projected. Tel Aviv, 1978- . [uncataloged]

Horodetzky, Samuel. *Keren Shlomo* [Solomon Luria]. Drohobycz, 1896. [*PWZ]

Lifschutz, Arieh L. *Avot atarah le-banim* [Katzenellenbogen, Wahl, Lifschutz and related families]. Warsaw, 1927. [*PWZ 80-2207]

Schwartz, Sigmund. *Shem ha-gedolim le-gedole Hungaryah* [Encyclopedia of Hungarian Sages]. Brooklyn, 1959. [*PWR]

Stern, Abraham. *Sefer melitse esh* [2000 medieval and modern rabbis and scholars]. Jerusalem, 1974. [*PWR 77-3833]

Unger, Menashe. *Admorim she-nispu be-shoah* [Biographies of rabbis who perished in the Holocaust]. Jerusalem, 1969. (Hebrew) [*PWR]. Also in Yiddish as *Sefer Kedoshim.* New York, 1967. [*PWR]

Walden, Aaron. *Shem ha-gedolim he-hadash* [An encyclopedia of rabbis in the 19th centuries]. Warsaw, 1879. [*PWR]

Wininger, Salomon. *Grosse Juedische National-Biographie* [An international biographical dictionary of Jews from the Middle Ages to the 20th century]. Czernowitz, 1925-1936. [*PWR]

For a list of additional biographical books, many of which are in the collection of the Jewish Division, see *Toledot,* Vol. 4, No. 3, pp. 3-15, "Jewish Genealogical Materials in the Library of Congress" by Ellen Murphy; or David Einsiedler, "Rabbinic Genealogy Sources: A Bibliography by Type," printed for Jewish Genealogical Society Seminars, Israel and Los Angeles.

9. Name Indexes

Gorr, Shmuel, joint venture with Gary Mokotoff. *Palestine Gazette Name Changes, 1921-1948* [List of 27,000 Jews whose name changes were published in the *Palestine Gazette*]. 1984. [microfiche; uncataloged]

Kaganoff, Benzion. *A Dictionary of Jewish Names and their History.* New York, 1977. [*P-*PWP 79-67]

Kaufman, Isidore. *American Jews in World War II: The Story of 550,000 Fighters for Freedom* [Lists Jewish soldiers who died in their country's service or who received awards/recognition of valor]. 2 vols., New York, 1947. [*PXY]

Singerman, Robert. *Jewish and Hebrew Onomastics: A Bibliography.* New York, 1977. [*PCL 77-3586]

Zubatsky, David S. and Irwin M. Berent. *Jewish Genealogy: A Source Book of Family Histories and Genealogies.* New York, 1984. [*PWO 85-614]

Finding Aids:

For material of Jewish interest in any language and publications in Hebrew characters, cataloged before 1972, the Jewish Division's card catalogs should be consulted. There are two card catalogs unique to this Division:

1. Original Card Catalog includes the Jewish Division's holdings through 1960. Author and subject are integrated in one sequence. There is no title index for this period. In 1960, a set of bound volumes, *The NYPL Jewish Collection Catalog,* was created from this catalog.

2. Supplementary Card Catalog contains older cards altered between 1960 and 1971 and new cards added during the same period. It is an integrated author, subject and, for some books, title catalog.

After 1972, the Library began publishing integrated book catalogs. See "NEW YORK PUBLIC LIBRARY - CENTRAL RESEARCH LIBRARY, GENERAL RESEARCH DIVISION" for a detailed description. Books with Hebrew/Yiddish titles are not included in the book catalogs, 1981-1985 (green books).

Hebrew/Yiddish books cataloged since August 1981 are included in CATNYP, the computer catalog, using the ANSI romanization of the Hebrew alphabet. Under this system, one letter in the roman alphabet is assigned to one Hebrew letter, e.g. sefer = spr, in ANSI. There are two CATNYP terminals in this Division. Consult the librarian for Hebrew/Yiddish books not found in these catalogs. The librarian can check if it was acquired after the listing in the published catalogs. Librarians have access to a computer terminal which updates these catalogs, and to a Hebrew/Yiddish "in-process" file.

To find information about a particular community, see "Jews in ..." in the published and CATNYP catalogs or the place name in the card catalog. To find books on gravestone inscriptions, see "Epitaphs" in each catalog.

All classmarks (call numbers) starting with [*P] are located in the Jewish Division. Classmark groupings of interest to genealogists include: Epitaphs [*PWN], Genealogy [*PWO], Biographical Material [*PWP], Collective Biographies [*PWR] and Individual Biographies [*PWZ]. Information about Jewish Communities are grouped in classmarks by country: Orient [*PXL], Israel [*PXLB], Italy [*PXN], Spain/Portugal [*PXO], France [*PXP], Great Britain [*PXQ], Germany [*PXS], Austria-Hungary [*PXT], Poland [*PXV], Russia [*PXW], America [*PXX] and U.S. and Canada [*PXY]. These call numbers are not unique and must always be used together with the title and author of the book.

Description of Facility:

The Jewish Division is located in Room 84 on the ground floor to the right of the entrance on 42nd Street (between 5th and 6th Avenues). The room can seat 60 researchers. Four microfilm readers are available. There are 1-2 librarians available to provide assistance and one paging assistant. Indicate your seat number on the call slip and the page will bring materials directly to your table.

Reference books (encyclopedias, biographical dictionaries, etc.) are on open shelves around the room. All other books, except rare books, are in closed stacks but can be obtained immediately. See "Restrictions on Use."

Restrictions on Use:

Researchers are requested to sign the registration book at the desk.

No more than five items can be requested at a time. No materials can be borrowed.

Rare materials must be requested in advance. Readers are notified by mail when the material is available.

NEW YORK PUBLIC LIBRARY
MAP DIVISION

Facility Director: Alice Hudson, Chief

Address: Fifth Avenue at 42nd Street, Room 117
New York, NY 10018

(Cross Streets: 40th and 42nd Streets; 5th and 6th Avenues)

Phone Number: (212) 930-0587

Hours of Operation:

Monday & Wednesday: 10:00 am to 6:00 pm
Tuesday: 10:00 am to 9:00 pm
Friday & Saturday: 10:00 am to 6:00 pm

Closed Thursday, Sunday and legal holidays.

Closest Public Transportation and Directions:

See "NEW YORK PUBLIC LIBRARY - CENTRAL RESEARCH LIBRARY, GENERAL RESEARCH DIVISION."

Description of Resources:

The Map Division has the most extensive collection in New York City of gazetteers, maps, including pre-19th century maps and world atlases, produced in both the United States and Europe, dating from the 1800s through the present. The collection includes 375,000 maps and 14,000 atlases and books.

A.   GAZETTEERS

1.   *U.S. Board on Geographic Names Gazetteer*

Despite the post-WWII dates, these gazetteers are particularly useful for locating very small towns in Poland and the USSR that are thought not to exist since the war. They provide latitude and longitude for every place name and also indicate place name changes in such countries as:

Austria, 1962	Poland, 1955
Czechoslovakia, 1955	Rumania, 1960
East Germany, 1959	Syria, 1983
France, 1964	USSR, 1970
Hungary, 1961	West Germany, 1960
Italy, 1956	

2.   *Ritters Geographisch-Statistisches Lexikon*

1874 (1983 reprint), 1905, 1906 and 1910 (in German)

3.   *Columbia Lippincott Gazetteer of the World*

1880, 1898, 1906, 1952 and 1960

4.   Defense Mapping Agency/Army Map Service - *Index to Names on AMS 1:250,000 Map of Eastern Europe* (Series N501)

Provides latitude and longitude. (See #3 in the Map section below.)

5.   *Austria-Hungary 1913 Index*

A detailed place name index, based on *Stieler's Hand Atlas,* is kept at the reference desk. (See #5 and #6 in the Map section below). The accompanying map is available.

6. *Shtetl Finder Gazetteer*

A copy is found also in the JEWISH DIVISION.

7. *Rand McNally Commercial Atlas*

This has the most detailed place name index for the U.S. It lists all communities, even those with zero population. It is published annually, and the Map Division has back editions since the 1880s. While not all editions are available, there is at least one per decade, usually for the year of (or following) the census, in order to provide accurate population data.

8. *Bartholomew Gazetteer of the British Isles*

This place name index which describes each location is available for 1887, 1893, 1943, 1955 and 1970.

9. *The London Times Atlas of the World*

The latest edition of this classic British atlas, 1985, with its valuable A-to-Z gazetteer (with latitudes and longitudes) is available along with some back editions starting in 1895 (gaps).

10. Other Foreign Gazetteer Sources

In addition to the gazetteers in the Map Division, the SLAVIC AND BALTIC DIVISION (Room 217) has the 15-volume *Slownik Geograficzny* (geographical dictionary) which provides detailed late 19th-century information on most East European communities (in Polish); and the JEWISH DIVISION has resources in addition to the *Shtetl Finder*.

B. MAPS

1. Greater New York Area

Road maps, national atlases, NYC geographical maps from the 1600s to date and NYC property maps. These include maps such as Sanborn Fire Insurance, Sanborn Land Books, E. Belcher Hyde, Bromley or Perris for:

Bronx	1870s to 1959, 1969, 1987
Brooklyn	1855-1929, 1988
Manhattan	1850 to present
Queens	1901-1904, 1928-1973, 1988
Staten Island	1874-1917

Sanborn property maps for cities in Connecticut, New Jersey and New York are available on microfilm from the 1880s through the 1950s.

New York [City] Boroughs, tax maps and ownership information, indexed three ways - by street address, block and lot number, and alphabetically by owner's name, produced by Real Estate Data, Inc. (REDI), on microfiche for Brooklyn, the Bronx, Queens and Staten Island, 1987 and 1988. [*XLK 88-4531]

The New York Public Library, Economic and Public Affairs Division (Room 228) has a paper copy of the *Real Estate Owner's Directory of Manhattan* issued by REDI.

2. United States and Canada: Road maps, national atlases. The Map Division maintains an extensive historical file of maps of all 50 states going back to the 1700s as well as an extensive Canadian collection.

3. Military Surveys of Europe: Detailed surveys from the mid-19th century to the present include:

1:250,000 AMS (Army Map Service) for Eastern Europe (N501 Series) and Western Europe (M501 Series)
1:200,000 set for Central Europe
1:100,000 AMS series for Poland and Germany (nearly complete set)
1:75,000 AMS series for Austria-Hungary
Generally complete map sets for the Soviet Union on scales greater than 1:250,000

4. Country Map Files: The Division has extensive files of general maps for individual countries during different time frames. These are particularly good for reviewing a country's borders and assessing the geopolitics during particular historic eras.

5. *Stieler's Hand Atlas:* Several editions of this world atlas are available. It has good coverage of Europe, particularly in the 19th century. There is a detailed place name index. German spellings are used throughout.

6. Austria-Hungary 1913 Map: A large, very detailed map of this region has been reproduced from *Stieler's* and is kept at the reference desk. A place name index in book form is also available. (See #5 in the Gazetteer section above.)

Finding Aids:

The Map Division has book catalogs of its own holdings through 1971 and a CATNYP terminal for post-1971 holdings. The Division's Place Name Search Worksheet, which asks for all known pertinent information, aids the staff and the researcher in finding a desired location.

See "NEW YORK PUBLIC LIBRARY - CENTRAL RESEARCH LIBRARY, GENERAL RESEARCH DIVISION" for a description of the computerized catalog mentioned above.

The Map Division has a directory that lists many other map collections in the United States, such as the extensive holdings at Yale University and the University of California at Berkeley.

Description of Facility:

The Map Division is located on the first floor of the Library in Room 117. The room can seat 25 people at tables, and has one counter which serves as a work area for oversized maps. There is one staff member on duty at the reference desk. One microfilm and one microfiche reader are available. The catalogs are to the left of the entrance.

The staff will conduct short place name searches in response to telephone requests. Typically, time permitting, they will look at two or three sources located at the reference desk to provide a latitude and longitude or a nearby city, as well as any alternative spellings. Patrons must come in to conduct actual research.

Fees/Copies:

See "NEW YORK PUBLIC LIBRARY - CENTRAL RESEARCH LIBRARY, GENERAL RESEARCH DIVISION." All copying is done at the discretion of the staff, depending on the map's condition and age. No fragile or antique maps, nor any maps larger than 11" x 17", can be quick-copied. The staff will cooperate in finding alternative materials or ways of reproduction. For example, researchers with staff permission may photograph (preferably with a 35mm camera on a sunny day using no flash) or make a tracing (only with a Mylar sheet, supplied by the staff, to protect the map and only in pencil). As an alternative, the Library will reproduce the map using a non-damaging method which currently costs a minimum of $17 for an 18" x 24" image and takes 2-3 weeks. The Library also can prepare slides and photographs.

Restrictions on Use:

Researchers must sign in at the register. Materials can be obtained quickly unless a lot of material is ordered. Five items can be requested at a time (less if very busy). Researchers may be allowed to use a particular item for a limited time, if it is in high demand. See "Fees/Copies" for limitations on copying.

NEW YORK PUBLIC LIBRARY
MIRIAM AND IRA D. WALLACH DIVISION OF ART, PRINTS AND PHOTOGRAPHS

Facility Director: Robert Rainwater, Assistant Director, Miriam and Ira D. Wallach Division of Arts, Prints and Photographs
Paula Baxter, Head, Art and Architecture
Roberta Waddell, Curator, Print Collection
Julia Van Haaften, Curator, Photograph Collections

Address: Fifth Avenue at 42nd Street, Rooms 308 and 313
New York, NY 10018

(Cross Streets: 40th and 42nd Streets; 5th and 6th Avenues)

Phone Number: (212) 930-0834 (Art and Architecture)
(212) 930-0817 (Prints and Photographs)

Hours of Operation:

	Art and Architecture	Prints and Photographs
Monday & Wednesday:	10:00 am to 6:00 pm	1:00 pm to 6:00 pm
Tuesday:	10:00 am to 9:00 pm	1:00 pm to 6:00 pm
Friday & Saturday:	10:00 am to 6:00 pm	1:00 pm to 6:00 pm

Closed Thursday, Sunday and legal holidays.

Closest Public Transportation, Directions and Fees/Copies:

See "NEW YORK PUBLIC LIBRARY - CENTRAL RESEARCH LIBRARY, GENERAL RESEARCH DIVISION."

Description of Resources:

The Division's collections provide extensive biographical information on artists and artisans as well as samples of their work. There are pictorial and historical holdings covering places, both local and foreign, in the form of prints, photographs and original art. Pictures of eminent people are also available. Several specialties such as upholstering, goldsmithing and jewelry making are covered. Some aspects of life, such as costumes and religious attire, are covered from a historical and multinational perspective. The Division's holdings include:

A. The Art and Architecture Collection contains a reference collection of 200,000 volumes including periodicals, scrapbooks and clippings on subjects such as the fine arts, antiques, architecture, design, furniture and interior decoration. It covers all peoples and periods.

    1. Art - Several sources of information are available on artists:

      The Artists File (on microfiche), arranged alphabetically by the artist's name, provides biographical information and includes newspaper and magazine clippings, press releases, catalogs, manuscripts, original photographs and reproductions. It covers both American and foreign artists, architects, collectors, crafts people and art historians.

      The Division's Inside File (white-labeled drawers) is a cross-index by artist to books and periodicals in the Division's collection that have reproductions of a particular artist's work or biographical information. The Inside File was created during the 1930s as a WPA project. For later information, researchers should consult *The Art Index*, a published index to art periodicals from 1929 to the present, or the *RILA* volumes (*Répertoire International de la Littérature de L'Art*), an international index to art literature. NOTE: Not all periodicals or books listed in these indexes are in the Division's collections.

      The Division also has a collection of scrapbooks that cover various subjects. Information on a particular artist or architect may be found in these books. The Inside File (pink-labeled drawers) indexes the contents of these scrapbooks by name of artist as well as subject.

2. Architecture - The <u>Inside File</u> (blue-labeled drawers) contains sources on European and American buildings in the Library's holdings, such as pictures of clubs, hotels, public buildings, prominent family houses/mansions, department stores, synagogues and churches. Architect biographies and portraits are also indexed here.

B. The <u>Prints and Photographs Collections</u> have books and other pictorial resources. The <u>Prints Collection</u> has reference materials useful for studying the history of print making, individual print makers and print making processes, as well as original prints. It covers the areas of engraving, woodcuts and lithography as well. It includes some 175,000 prints and 12,000 books and pamphlets. The <u>Photographs Collection</u> has over 70,000 entries in the catalog, and includes single photographs by subject and biographical material on photographers.

1. The <u>Portraits File</u> contains clippings, photographs and engravings of eminent, although not necessarily famous, people. The file is arranged by sitter. These could be prominent business people, professionals, leaders of organizations, unions, etc. NOTE: The Division's card index to separately cataloged portraits is located to the right of the librarian's desk. An index to portraits in selected books which are <u>not</u> shelved in the Print Division, "Portraits (Not in Room 308)," is located in the back room

2. <u>I. N. Phelps Stokes Collection of American Historical Prints</u> covers historical events, cities, landscapes, maps and plans of American cities, 1497-1891. The collection includes 207 views and 30 maps of New York City. A book catalog of this collection is arranged by year and indexed by artist, engraver and subject (views).

3. <u>Eno Collection of New York City Views</u> is similar to the Stokes Collection but covers only New York City. A book catalog is available arranged by borough and year and indexed by artist and subject.

4. The <u>Print Makers File</u> (engravers, etchers, etc.) includes all sorts of ephemera, reproductions of works, exhibition notices, clippings, reviews and obituaries. It is arranged in envelopes by the name of the print maker.

There is a card index which includes all reference material on print makers in published volumes and periodicals located in the Print Collection. This index is arranged alphabetically by name of print maker.

5. <u>Book Illustrator's Index</u> is a card index arranged alphabetically by name of book illustrator. It includes illustrated books shelved elsewhere in the Research Libraries.

6. <u>Bookplate Index</u> is a card index arranged alphabetically by the name of owners of bookplates included in books throughout the Research Libraries.

7. <u>Photographer's File</u> is a vertical file including clippings which may have biographical information about photographers as well as the subjects photographed. A card index to these files is arranged alphabetically by name of photographer.

8. The <u>Photography Catalog</u> of all materials in the Division is a card index arranged by name of photographer and the subject photographed.

Finding Aids:

As noted above, many of the special collections have their own catalogs. This Division also has book catalogs of its own book holdings through 1971. For acquisitions after 1972, the Library began publishing integrated book catalogs. See "NEW YORK PUBLIC LIBRARY - CENTRAL RESEARCH LIBRARY, GENERAL RESEARCH DIVISION" for a detailed description. The Division also has a computer terminal in Room 313 for post-1971 holdings. Original prints are not part of these catalogs, and photographs are only partially covered. Card files supplement the main catalog.

Staff members will help direct researchers to the appropriate catalog. The staff will also conduct short searches in response to telephone requests. Time permitting, they will look at two or three sources located at the reference desk to verify that information on an artist is available. Patrons must come in to conduct actual research.

Description of Facility:

Both the Art and Architecture Collection (Room 313) and the Prints and Photographs Collections (Room 308) are located on the third floor of the Library. At least two staff members are on duty in each room. The Art and Architecture room can seat approximately 50 people at 5 tables, while the Prints and Photographs room can seat 12 to 15. The catalogs are located next to the reference desk in each room. There is one microfiche reader available in Room 313.

Restrictions on Use:

For research in the Prints and Photographs Collections, a Card of Admission is required. This room is always locked and only those with a card are admitted. Apply in person to the Office of Special Collections in Room 316. Proper identification and purpose of research must be stated. Normally, the card is issued immediately. A genealogical request, such as the need for information on a specific artist, or a print of a specific location, is considered sufficient.

Researchers must sign in at the reference desk. Materials can be obtained quickly unless many items are ordered. Depending on the category of material, five items may be requested at one time (fewer if very busy). Researchers may be allowed to use a particular item for a limited time, if it is in high demand.

All copying is done at the discretion of the staff depending on the material's condition and age. No original, fragile or rare materials, such as prints or photographs, can ever be quick-copied. The staff will assist in finding alternative materials or ways of reproduction. For example, staff permission may be granted to take a photograph (preferably with a 35mm camera using existing lights but no flash or special lights). Sometimes a negative may already exist in the file. A reproduction can then be made for about $8-$9.

None of the materials in this Division can be sent to the Main Reading Room for use when the Division is closed.

NEW YORK PUBLIC LIBRARY
SLAVIC AND BALTIC DIVISION

Facility Director: Edward Kasinec, Chief

Address: Fifth Avenue at 42nd Street, Room 217
New York, NY 10018

(Cross Streets: 40th and 42nd Streets; 5th and 6th Avenues)

Phone Number: (212) 930-0713, 0714

Hours of Operation:

Monday & Wednesday:	10:00 am to 6:00 pm
Tuesday:	10:00 am to 9:00 pm
Friday & Saturday:	10:00 am to 6:00 pm

Closed Thursday, Sunday and legal holidays. Researchers wishing to view materials on Thursday may do so in the Main Reading Room. A call slip must be submitted in person by 6:00 pm Wednesday evening.

Closest Public Transportation and Directions:

See "NEW YORK PUBLIC LIBRARY - CENTRAL RESEARCH LIBRARY, GENERAL RESEARCH DIVISION."

Description of Resources:

The Slavic and Baltic Division (formerly the Slavonic Division) has over 300,000 books and other materials in 12 Slavic and Baltic languages. No Estonian, Hungarian, Romanian or Albanian materials are kept here since these belong to other language groups. English- and German-language materials on Slavic and East European studies can be found in the General Division (Main Reading Room). Judaica in the Slavic languages are usually found in the JEWISH DIVISION. Books with classmarks (call numbers) beginning with [*R] can be found on open shelves. The following are some of the resources of interest to genealogists in this Division:

1.   <u>Guides to Archives/Libraries</u>

    Cracow Archiwum Aktow Dawnych Miasta Krakowa [Catalog of the Krakow Archive]. 1907-15. (Polish) [*QR]

    Grant, Steven and John H. Brown. *The Russian Empire and Soviet Union: A Guide to Manuscripts and Archival Material in the US.* 1981. [*R-Slav.Div. 83-43]

    Grimsted, Patricia. *Archives and Manuscript Repositories in the USSR.* 3 vols., 1976- . These volumes cover Moscow and Leningrad; and Estonia, Latvia, Lithuania and Byelorussia. The volume on the Ukraine and Moldavia is already in manuscript form and is due to be published shortly. These books provide geographic place names as well as listings of the holdings of various archives. [*R-Slav.Div. 82-829, 82-830, 82-1212]

    Grossman, Iu. *Spravochnik nauchnogo rabotnika* [Handbook for Scholars]. 1979. Lists the archives of the USSR with addresses. (Russian) [*R-Slav.Div. 84-2615]

    Lewanski, Richard C. *Guide to Polish Libraries and Archives.* 1974. [Desk-Slav.Div. 83-1169]

    Magocsi, Paul R. *Ucrainica at the University of Toronto Library: A Catalogue of Holdings.* 1983. 2 vols. A guide to Ukrainian material at the University of Toronto Library. [Desk-Slav.Div. 86-1866]

    Mehr, Kahile B. and Daniel M. Schlyter. *Sources for Genealogical Research in the Soviet Union.* 1983. [uncataloged]

    Moskva. 1962. Address book of Russian Institutions. (Russian) [*R-Slav.Div.]

    Odessa: Tzentral'na Naukova Biblioteka [Odessa Public Library Catalog]. 1927-29. [*QGAA]

Sturm, Rudolf. *Czechoslovakia, A Bibliographic Guide.* 1967. [F-11/5001]

2. Gazetteers and related works

Atlas, U.S.S.R., 1969. Includes maps from 1:1,500,000. [*R-Slav.Div.]

Horecky, Paul L. *East Central and Southeast Europe.* 1976. A guide to basic publications about each country. [Desk-Slav.Div. 78-139]

Akademie der Wissenschaften und der Literatur. *Russisches Geographisches Namenbuch.* 10 vols., 1962-78. A German-language gazetteer of the Russian Empire. Place names are in Cyrillic script. [*R-Slav.Div.]

Semionov-Tyan-Shanski, Piotr. *Geografichesko Statisticheskii Slovar' Rossiiskoi Imperii* [Geographic Dictionary]. 5 vols., 1863-1885. (Russian) [*R-Slav.Div.]

Slownik Geograficzny. 1900. A 16-volume geographical dictionary which provides detailed late 19th-century information on most East European communities. (Polish) [*R-Slav.Div. 78-445]

3. Newspapers

Karlowich, Robert. *Russian Language Periodical Press in New York City from 1880-1914.* 1981. (English) [Desk-Slav.Div.]

4. Census

Tzentralnyi Statisticheskii Komitet. *Obshchii svod, 1-2.* 2 vols., 1897. This is a statistical summary of the 1897 census of the Russian Empire by region/city. (Russian-French) [*QB (Russia)]. Of particular interest are the tables which provide by Oblast/City, the following:

    Table IV - religion of the population;
    Table XI - number of cemeteries by religion; and,
    Table XII - number of synagogues and churches.

5. Cemetery Lists

Nicholas, Grand Duke of Russia. *Moskovskii Nekropol* [Tombstone Lists Moscow Area]. Non-Jewish; Pre-Russian Revolution. 1907-1908. [*QE]

6. Name Indexes

Sack, Sallyann and Suzan F. Wynne. *The Russian Consular Records Index and Catalog.* 1987. [*R-Slav.Div. 87-4638]

Unbegaun, Boris O. *Russian Surnames.* 1972. [*R-Slav.Div. 85-4708].

7. Encyclopedias

Evreiskaia Entsiklopediia [Russian Jewish Encyclopedia]. 16 vols., St. Petersburg, 1906-1913. [*QAC].

Brockhaus, F.A. and I.A. Efron, eds. *Novyi Entsiklopedicheskii Slovar* [New Encyclopedia - lists cities and shtetlach, and, in some cases, the Jewish population as of the 1897 census]. 1904. (Russian) [*QAC]

8. City Directories

A sample of available Directories which list names of individuals are those for:

Ekaterinoslav, 1912	St. Petersburg/Leningrad, 1894-1935 (gaps)
Gomel, 1908	Saratov, 1911
Moscow, 1915, 1929	Siberia, 1924
Odessa Gubernia, 1926, 1927	Southwestern Region (Kiev, Podolsk
Omsk, 1911	and Volinsk Gubernia), 1913
Russia, 1899, 1903, 1911/12	

In addition, the Division has business and organization directories for various localities.

9. <u>Dictionaries</u> (On open shelf)

This Division has dictionaries of all Slavic and Baltic languages (Russian, Polish, Ukrainian, Bulgarian, Czech, Lithuanian and Latvian) to English.

Finding Aids:

The 44-volume *Dictionary Catalog of the Slavonic Collection* includes the pre-1972 holdings of the Division. Materials acquired and cataloged by the Division after 1972 are included in the Library's central cataloging system. See "NEW YORK PUBLIC LIBRARY - CENTRAL RESEARCH LIBRARY, GENERAL RESEARCH DIVISION" for a description of these catalogs. The Division has a full set of the published catalogs. Classmarks beginning with [*Q] can be found in the Slavic and Baltic Division.

Researchers should consult the general catalog for materials that are not written in a Slavic language.

For additional City Directories, check the catalogs under "Russia - Directories" or "Vsia Rossiia." All directories have the call number [*QCA].

Description of Facility:

The Slavic and Baltic Division is located on the second floor in Room 217. The room can seat 24 persons. There are one to two staff members on duty to assist researchers in finding materials. There are 2 microfilm and one microfiche readers in the room.

Fees/Copies:

See "NEW YORK PUBLIC LIBRARY - CENTRAL RESEARCH LIBRARY, GENERAL RESEARCH DIVISION." Researchers may leave materials photocopied at the Reprographic Services Division or bring them back to the Slavic and Baltic Division if they wish to continue using them.

Restrictions on Use:

No more than 5 books can be requested at one time.

Rare books (generally pre-1850) are provided to researchers at a designated table in the Slavic and Baltic Division. Researchers must show some identification when requesting these materials.

NEW YORK PUBLIC LIBRARY
U.S. HISTORY, LOCAL HISTORY AND GENEALOGY DIVISION AND MICROFORMS DIVISION

Facility Director: Ruth Carr, Chief, U.S. History, Local History, and Genealogy Division
Thomas Bourke, Chief, Microforms Division

Address: Fifth Avenue at 42nd Street, Rooms 315N and 315M
New York, NY 10018

(Cross Streets: 40th and 42nd Streets; 5th and 6th Avenues)

Phone Number: (212) 930-0828 (Genealogy)
(212) 930-0838 (Microforms)

Hours of Operation:

	Genealogy Division	Microforms Division
Monday & Wednesday:	10:00 am to 6:00 pm*	10:00 am to 9:00 pm
Tuesday:	10:00 am to 9:00 pm	10:00 am to 9:00 pm
Thursday to Saturday:	10:00 am to 6:00 pm	10:00 am to 6:00 pm

Closed Sunday and legal holidays.

*After 6:00 pm Monday and Wednesday, materials of the Genealogy Division (classmark beginning with [I]) can be requested at the west end of the Information Desk in the Public Catalog Room for use in the Main Reading Room. Materials with classmark beginning [AP] (except reference or desk books) being used in the Genealogy Division can be taken to the Main Reading Room at 6:00 pm with a librarian's permission.

NOTE: Researchers should request materials no later than 25 minutes before closing time, i.e. 5:35 pm or 8:35 pm. Microforms photocopying closes at 7:30 pm Monday-Wednesday and 5:30 pm Thursday-Saturday.

Closest Public Transportation, Directions and Fees/Copies:

See "NEW YORK PUBLIC LIBRARY - CENTRAL RESEARCH LIBRARY, GENERAL RESEARCH DIVISION."

Description of Resources:

The Genealogy Division has a vast collection of materials of interest to genealogists. Some of the materials, on microfilm or microfiche, are in the adjacent Microforms Division. The Information Desk in the Genealogy Division can advise researchers on these materials. The following listing includes key holdings of both Divisions. Materials on microfilm are so noted.

1.   U.S. Census (microfilm)

New York State, New Jersey and Connecticut, 1790 to 1880
New York State only, 1900 [*ZI-263] and 1910 [*ZI-349]

See "NEW YORK PUBLIC LIBRARY - SCHOMBURG CENTER" for U.S. Census of other states. Microfilms at SCHOMBURG can be ordered for viewing at the MICROFORMS DIVISION on 42nd Street. Make the request in person one week in advance at the Genealogy Division Information Desk.

2.   New York State Census (microfilm)

1855 census, 41 counties. Among those missing are Kings (Brooklyn), Queens, Westchester and Dutchess Counties. [*ZAN-G124]

3.   Canadian Census (microfilm)

1871 [*ZI-353]

4. <u>City Directories</u> - New York City (all on microfilm)

NYC Directories (generally Manhattan and parts of the Bronx), 1786-1933/4
Brooklyn City Directories, 1796, 1802/3, 1811/12, 1822-1826, 1829-1910, 1912/13, 1933/4
Trow's Directory for Queens, 1898, 1912
Polk's NYC Directory, Boroughs of Queens and Richmond, 1933/4
Webb's Consolidated Directory of the North and South Shores of Staten Island, 1886, 1888, 1890/1, 1892/3
Standard Directory of Richmond County, 1895/6
Trow's Business and Residential Directory of the Borough of Richmond, City of NY, 1898
Standard Directory of Richmond Borough, 1906

NOTE: There are two reverse NYC City Directories arranged by street addresses: 1812 (Reel A6) and 1851 (Reel A14).

5. <u>Other City Directories</u> (microfilm/microfiche)

The Microforms Division has City Directories for about 300 major U.S. cities, 1752-1860 [*XMG-156] and 1861-1935 [*ZAN-G67]; and London City Directories from the Guild Hall Library, 1677-1855 (gaps) [*ZAN-G68]. See Appendix D for a complete list of U.S. Directories.

See also "NEW YORK PUBLIC LIBRARY - CENTRAL RESEARCH LIBRARY, GENERAL RESEARCH DIVISION" for additional foreign City Directories and the ANNEX for additional U.S. and Canadian City Directories.

6. <u>Telephone Directories</u> (microfilm/microfiche)

	White Pages	Yellow Pages
Manhattan*	1878-1924	-
Manhattan (includes Bronx)	1924-1928	1928
Manhattan	1929-current	1929-1976/77
Bronx	1929-current	1931-1976/77
Brooklyn, Queens, SI	1924-1928/29	-
Brooklyn	1929-current	1944-1976/77
Queens	1927-current	1957-1976/77
Staten Island	1927/28-current	(combined with White Pages)
Rockaway (Queens)	1928-1976	(combined with White Pages)
Rockaway (Queens) and 5 Towns	1977	(combined with White Pages)
Nassau	1913-current	1957-1976/77
Suffolk	1928-current	1957-1976/77
Suffolk, Nassau, Queens	1910-1947	-

*The pre-1924 Manhattan telephone directories include other New York City boroughs and sometimes Nassau/Suffolk, Westchester and some New Jersey communities. Consult the <u>Index to NYC Telephone Directories</u>, 1958, located in a black binder at the Microforms Information Desk, to find out which localities are included.

The Microforms Division has a complete set of Phonefiche for telephone books around the country. Phonefiche copies start in 1976, but not all cities were included from the start. See "NEW YORK PUBLIC LIBRARY - CENTRAL RESEARCH LIBRARY, GENERAL RESEARCH DIVISION" for paper copies of current telephone directories.

The NEW YORK PUBLIC LIBRARY, ANNEX has pre-1976 telephone directories in paper copy for cities other than those in the NYC area

7. <u>Address Telephone Directories for NYC</u> (microfilm)

Bronx, Brooklyn, Manhattan, Queens 1929-1980, 1986
Staten Island 1952-1980, 1982, 1986

Westchester (Southern)   1956-1980, 1986

See "NEW YORK PUBLIC LIBRARY - CENTRAL RESEARCH LIBRARY, GENERAL RESEARCH DIVISION" for additional address directories (*Cole Directory*).

8.   New York City Vital Records

Records (microfilm):

Deaths (Manhattan only), 1798-1865 [*ZI-201]

Indexes:

The Library has the NYC Health Department indexes spanning the following years:

Births   August 1888 to 1982
Deaths   August 1888 to 1982
Marriages (grooms) August 1888 to 1937

Brooklyn, Queens and Staten Island (Richmond) are not included until 1898 in the birth, marriage and death indexes. Beginning in 1937 all boroughs of NYC are merged in one alphabetical listing. Prior to that year, separate listings (or volumes) were made for each borough. Marriage index volumes, 1911-1937, are on open shelves inside the entrance of the Genealogy Division.

Because of the aging condition of the indexes, the Library is in the process of microfilming them. The following are on microfilm or microfiche:

Births   August 1888-1915, 1922 [*ZI-328], 1898-1975 [Fiche, *XMG-1108]
Deaths   August 1888-1945 [*ZI-348]
Marriages   August 1888-1910, 1913-1914, 1921, 1928 [*ZI-329]

The birth indexes, 1898-1909 (microfiche), are arranged according to the NYC Health Department Soundex system. The copies on microfilm are arranged in alphabetical order. This Soundex system was used again from 1943 to 1945 in both the microfiche and paper copies of the birth indexes. See Appendix C for an explanation of this system.

The Library will withdraw paper indexes from circulation for microfilming as necessary. Researchers should check in advance on the availability of those volumes not yet microfilmed.

See "NEW YORK GENEALOGICAL AND BIOGRAPHICAL SOCIETY" and "NEW YORK CITY DEPARTMENT OF RECORDS AND INFORMATION SERVICES, MUNICIPAL ARCHIVES" for indexes not available in the NYPL. The MUNICIPAL ARCHIVES has microfilm copies of vital records in addition to the indexes.

9.   Marriage Announcements

Marriages Taken from the Brooklyn Eagle (Index), October 27, 1841 to December 31, 1880. [APRN]
    (On open shelf)
New York Evening Post Marriages (Index), November 16, 1801 to December 31, 1890. [APRN] (On
    open shelf)
New York Marriage Bonds 1753-1783, by Dr. Kenneth Scott, 1972. [APRN 78-3023]
Names of Persons for Whom Marriage Licenses Were Issued...Previous to 1784, New York State.
    [*R-APR New York State] (On open shelf)
Index to Marriages and Deaths in the New York Herald, 1835-1855, by James P. Maher, 1987. [APR]

10.   Obituaries

New York Evening Post, New York City, Deaths (Index), November 16, 1801 to December 31, 1890, by
    Gertrude A. Barber, 1933-1947. [APRN] (On open shelf)
Deaths Taken from the Brooklyn Eagle (Index), October 27, 1841 to December 31, 1880, by Gertrude
    A. Barber, 1936-1966. [APRN] (On open shelf)
The New York Times Obituaries Index: 1858-1978. 2 vols. (At the Information Desk)
Boston Evening Transcript. *The Index to Obituaries,* 1875-1899, 1900-1930 [APK+]
New York Tribune. *Obituaries 1875-1897* [APK+] (At the Information Desk)

11. Cemeteries

Fairchild Cemetery Manual, 1910 [*ZI-266]
Directory of United States Cemeteries, Volume I only, 1974 [APK 75-1060]
Local Cemeteries in New York [APM 84-92]

12. Wills and Administrations - Abstracts and Indexes

Manhattan:
New-York Historical Society. *Abstracts of Wills on File in the Surrogate's Office, City of New York, 1665-1800.* 17 vols. + index. [APRN (New York)]
Sawyer, Ray C. and G.A. Barber. *Abstracts of New York County Wills, 1801-1856.* 19 vols. [APRN (New York)]
Sawyer, Ray C. *Index of Wills for NY County, NY, from 1851-1875 inclusive.* NY, 1950-51. [APRN]
Barber, Gertrude A. *Index of the Letters of Administration filed in NY County from 1743-1875.* NY, 1950-51. [APRN]

Brooklyn:
Thomas, Milton H. and C. Shepard. *Index to the Wills, Administrations, Guardianships of Kings County, NY, 1650-1850.* Washington, DC, 1926. [APR (Kings County)]
Barber, G.A. *Index of Wills Probated in Kings County, NY Jan.1, 1850-Dec.31, 1890.* 3 vols. (typescript, 1949) [APR (Kings County)]

Queens:
Surrogate's Court Records in the Office of the County Clerk, Jamaica, Long Island, NY - 1680-1781. Wills and administrations, guardians, and inventories. Brooklyn, 1918. [APR (Queens County)]
Queens County, NY Surrogate Records at Jamaica, NY - 1787-1835. Brooklyn, 1905-1918. [APR (Queens County)]

See "NEW YORK GENEALOGICAL AND BIOGRAPHICAL SOCIETY" for additional Brooklyn, Queens and Staten Island abstracts not in the New York Public Library collection.

13. Passenger Records and Indexes

Passenger lists of vessels arriving at New York harbor from 1820 to April 5, 1906. These lists are arranged in order of arrival. [*ZI-131]
Indexes: 1820-1846 [*ZI-80]; June 16, 1897 to June 30, 1902 [*ZI-333]; and July 1902 to December 1943 [*ZI-333A]. There is no name index from 1846 to June 15, 1897.
German Immigrants: Lists of Passengers Bound from Bremen to New York, compiled by Gary J. Zimmerman and Marion Wolfert, 1985- . [Lists only passengers with places of origin.] Vol. 1, 1847-1854. [APK 85-3230] Vol. 2, 1855-1862 and vol. 3, 1863-1867 are on order.
Germans to America: Lists of Passengers Arriving at U.S. Ports, 1850-1855, edited by Ira A. Glazier and P. William Filby, 1988. [Passenger lists are derived from original ship manifest schedules and are published in their entirety in chronological order of arrival date at U.S. east coast ports. The determining factor for inclusion of a particular list is the presence of 80% or more passengers with German surnames.] Of the 10 volumes planned, vol. 1, Jan. 2, 1850-May 23,1851 and vol. 2, May 24, 1851-June, 1852, have been issued and are on order.

The Library has the following lists of vessels to assist the researcher in locating a passenger record:

Register of Vessels Arriving at the Port of New York from Foreign Ports, 1789-1919. (microfilm) [*ZI-391]

Morton Allan Directory of European Passenger Steamship Arrivals, for the years 1890-1930 for the Port of New York, and 1904-1926 for the Ports of Philadelphia, Boston and Baltimore. [79-906, 80-974] (At the Genealogy Division Information Desk)

14. Veterans (microfilm)

Revolutionary War Pension and Bounty Warrant files [*ZI-132]
1812 War Pension Index [*ZI-234]
Mexican War Pension Index [*ZI-388]

Civil War Veterans - index to the Compiled Service records of the Volunteer Union Soldiers who served in Organizations from the State of New York. [*ZI-411]

For additional resources, consult "Selected Military Sources for United States Genealogy: Rosters, Regimental Histories and Handbooks - Pre-World War II," a bibliography compiled by Asa Rubenstein. (At the Genealogy Division Information Desk)

15. Name Indexes

American Genealogical Biographical Index [name index to many genealogies, mostly non-Jewish]. [APG] (On open shelf)

British Biographical Archive. Biographical sketches in one alphabetical listing of 324 English-language biographical reference works published between 1601 and 1929. [Fiche, *XM-16,823]

Daughters of the American Revolution, New York Master Index - Genealogical Records [APR]. Most of the 600-volume set is available either in hard copy or microfilm.

Dau's NY Blue Book. 1907-1935 (gaps). Lists name, address and household members of "prominent" New Yorkers (includes many Jewish families). [Film, *ZAN-4605]

International Genealogical Index (IGI) published by the Genealogical Department of the Church of Jesus Christ of Latter-Day Saints, Salt Lake City, 1988. Available in paper copy [*XMG-1041+] or microfiche [*XMG-1041]

Family Registry - Index published by the Genealogical Department of the Church of Jesus Christ of Latter-Day Saints, Salt Lake City, 1984. [Fiche *XMG-1117]

The *International Genealogical Index* and *Family Registry* microfiche are located in file drawers near the three microfiche readers in the Genealogy Division.

16. Genealogy Guides

The Library has an extensive collection of "how to" books. Among those available on open shelves or at the Genealogy Division Information Desk are:

Bailey, Rosalie Fellows. *Guide to Genealogical and Biographical Sources for NYC (Manhattan) 1783-1898.* New York, 1954. [APRN]

Beard, Timothy F. and Denise Demong. *How to Find Your Family Roots.* New York, 1977. [APB 78-817]

Eakle, Arlene and Johni Cerny. *The Source: A Guidebook of American Genealogy.* Salt Lake City, 1984. [APB 84-1480]

Everton, George B. *The Handy Book for Genealogists, 1981.* [APB 82092]

Gnacinski, Jan and Len. *Polish and Proud: Your Polish Ancestry.* Wisconsin, 1979. [APB 80-1324]

Hoff, Henry B. "Research in New York Downstate," *Tree Talks,* March 1982. [APR New York]

Kronman, Barbara. *Guide to NYC Public Records.* New York, 1984 (3rd edition). [IRGV 84-2902]

Kurzweil, Arthur. *From Generation to Generation.* New York, 1980. [APB 80-3575]

Rottenberg, Dan. *Finding Our Fathers.* New York, 1977. [APB 77-1002]

Smith, Clifford N. and Anna P.C. Smith. *Encyclopedia of German-American Genealogical Research.* New York, 1976. [ATA 80-950]

Smith, Jessie C. *Ethnic Genealogy; A Research Guide.* Westport, CT, 1983. [APB 84-208]

United States Works Progress Administration. *Guide to Vital Statistics in the City of New York, Church records.* [Location of church records.] New York, 1942. [APRN]

Wellauer, Maralyn. *Tracing Your Polish Roots.* Wisconsin, 1979. [APB 80-800]

Wellauer, Maralyn. *Tracing Your German Roots.* Wisconsin, 1978. [APB 80-1696]

17. Photo Collections - NYC

Photographic Views of New York City 1870's to 1970's (microfiche). The collection had its origins in the 1920s and includes some 54,000 photos of streets and buildings in NYC. Each photo is accompanied by a description (street, cross street, date, direction of photo and name of building, if known). This collection is available both in the Genealogy Division and the Microforms Division. (See "Finding Aids" below.) It is also available at the QUEENS BOROUGH PUBLIC LIBRARY.

Lloyd Acker Collection -- Views of NYC buildings from 1935 to 1975 by Lloyd Acker, a commercial photographer who photographed specific buildings and indexed them by address. Photos are not dated. [*ZI-300]

Eugene Armbruster Collection of Long Island photographs, 1890s-1930s. (being organized)

Check with the librarian at the Genealogy Division Information Desk for a complete listing of photograph collections that may be of interest to genealogists.

18. Newspapers (microfilm)

New York Times	September 18, 1851 to present
New York Post	May 1967 to present
World Journal Tribune	September 1966 to May 1967

See "NEW YORK PUBLIC LIBRARY, ANNEX" for other newspapers.

19. Other: In addition to the above, the Genealogy Division has an extensive collection of genealogical periodicals, newsletters, family histories and published genealogies, and county, town and village histories.

Finding Aids:

1. Catalogs of materials in the Genealogy Division are in bound volumes to the left of the Information Desk in Room 315N. There are three sets of volumes. One is unique to the Genealogy Division:

Dictionary Catalog of the Local History and Genealogy Division (Green volumes) includes the collection as of 1972. Holdings are listed by author and subject, rarely by title.

For materials acquired after 1972, consult the computer terminals in the Public Catalog Room (Room 315). For a description of the Research Libraries' catalogs, see "NEW YORK PUBLIC LIBRARY - CENTRAL RESEARCH LIBRARY, GENERAL RESEARCH DIVISION."

The librarians in the Genealogy Division are the best "finding aids." They are familiar with the materials most frequently requested and often have this material at the desk.

NOTE: Classmarks (call numbers) beginning with [A] or [I] can be obtained in the Genealogy Division. Classmarks beginning with [*Z] or [*X] are in the Microforms Division.

2. Census Indexes: The Library holds published Census indexes, 1790-1850, for most states and for 1860 for some states. In addition, the Microforms Division has the Soundex for New York, New Jersey and Connecticut for 1880 [*ZI-50a] and for New York State for 1900 [*ZI-263a]. See Appendix C for an explanation of the National Archives Soundex system.

For 1910, a paper copy of the New York City (except Queens) street index to the Enumeration Districts (ED), *Guide to the Enumeration Districts, 1910 Census,* is available on open shelf inside the entrance of the Genealogy Division. With this index (by borough/street/house number) the researcher can identify the ED in which the house was located. The Microforms Division and Genealogy Division have a National Archives publication which converts these EDs into reel numbers.

Since there is no 1910 Queens index, the Library has microfilmed a copy of the 1910 *List of Enrolled Voters* for Queens. This list is arranged by Assembly/Election District and first letter of the surname. See also "NEW YORK PUBLIC LIBRARY - CENTRAL RESEARCH LIBRARY, GENERAL RESEARCH DIVISION" for the original copy of this list.

Specialized map indexes to U.S. Censuses for New York City are on the last table to the right inside the Genealogy Division.

3. Canadian Census: A book index covering parts of Ontario is available.

4. Photographs: The index for *Photographic Views of New York City* is in three bound volumes. Volume 1, *Street Index*, has entries by street name and includes the cross street, date of photo, direction of photo and fiche and row/photograph numbers. Volume 2, *Building Index*, has similar entries by building name. Volume 3, *Subject Index*, has general entries such as "Synagogues." It does not identify the name or street, just the fiche and row/photograph numbers.

One set of microfiche and index volumes is located on the last table to the right inside the Genealogy Division. The fiche are in 3 long boxes next to the fiche readers. They are arranged by fiche number and are in alphabetical order of street name. The set in the Microforms Division is not as easily accessible. The index volumes are behind the desk and no more than six sheets of fiche may be ordered at a time.

The original card index for the Lloyd Acker Collection can be requested in the Genealogy Division. The index is also on microfilm in the Microforms Division. It is a geographic index, arranged numerically for numbered streets and alphabetically for named streets.

Description of Facility:

The U.S. History, Local History and Genealogy Division, also known as the Genealogy Division, is in Room 315N at the north end (42nd Street) of the third floor. The room has a seating capacity of 50. Two to three staff persons are available to help researchers. Census indexes, major genealogical periodicals and marriage indexes are on open shelves around the room.

The Microforms Division is in the Main Reading Room (North Hall) and has 40 microfilm and 8 microfiche readers.

Call slips must be completed for each item (up to 4 on one slip, e.g. "NYC Health Department - Births, 1920, 1921, 1922, 1923"). However, call numbers are not always required where these volumes are in constant use. Consult the librarian on items of interest. In the Genealogy Division, indicate "seat number" on the call slip, since staff will bring the books directly to that seat.

Restrictions on Use:

Researchers must sign the register before requesting materials in the Genealogy Division or microfilms in the Microforms Division.

Only 4 bound volumes, 6 reels of microfilm or 6 fiche may be requested at a time.

No books or microfilms may be taken out of the room without a pass. Passes are needed to photocopy materials from the Genealogy Division. No passes are required to photocopy items from the Microforms Division.

Books must be returned to the table to the left of the Information Desk in Room 315N when no longer needed. Microfilms are returned to the counter to the left of the Microforms Information Desk (Room 315M).

NEW YORK PUBLIC LIBRARY
PERFORMING ARTS RESEARCH CENTER AT LINCOLN CENTER

Facility Director:	Donald McCormick, Curator, Rodgers and Hammerstein Archive of Recorded Sound
	Madeline Nichols, Curator, Dance Collection
	Dorothy Swerdlove, Curator, Billy Rose Theatre Collection
	Jean Bowen, Chief, Music Division

Address: 111 Amsterdam Avenue, 3rd Floor
New York, NY 10023

(Cross Street: Corner of 65th Street)

Phone Number: (212) 870-1663 (Recorded Sound)
(212) 870-1657 (Dance Collection)
(212) 870-1639 (Theatre Collection)
(212) 870-1650 (Music Division)

Hours of Operation:

	September to May	June to August
Monday & Thursday:	10:00 am to 8:00 pm	10:00 am to 6:00 pm
Tuesday, Wednesday, Friday, Saturday:	10:00 am to 6:00 pm	10:00 am to 6:00 pm

Closed Sunday and legal holidays.

Closest Public Transportation:

Subway: 1 to 66th Street

Bus: M104 to 66th Street and Broadway
M11 or M29 to Amsterdam Avenue and 66th Street

Directions:

Take the #1 (local) train to the 66th Street station. Exit at the downtown end of the station to the Lincoln Center Plaza. The Library is at the northwest corner of the Plaza (next to the Vivian Beaumont Theatre). NOTE: A second entrance is on Amsterdam Avenue at 65th Street.

Description of Resources:

There are four collections of interest to genealogists:

1. Rodgers and Hammerstein Archive of Recorded Sound: This repository houses over 460,000 recordings and music-related videotapes, including early operatic performances recorded on wax cylinders, poetry, popular music and historic broadcasts of famous personalities and statesmen.

    The Benedict Stambler Memorial Archives of Recorded Jewish Music is of particular interest to Jewish genealogists. The 78s in this collection date back to 1910 and the LPs to 1950. The "Vistas of Israel" radio program collection is also available here.

2. Dance Collection: This section of the Research Center contains 10,000 reels of film and videotape of live dance performances, as well as taped interviews with well-known choreographers. The collection also includes 565,000 manuscripts, 21,000 files of newspaper clippings, 500,000 photographs, 1,200 reels of microfilm, 1,800 original costume and set designs and 36,000 books as well as periodicals, diaries, notebooks and letters. Five centuries are spanned in the collection in all forms of dance including ballet, modern, social, ethnic and folk.

Of particular note are the Collected Papers of Fred Berk, who worked on a Bibliography of Jewish Dance during his lifetime. This incomplete project is documented here (on microfiche).

3. Billy Rose Theatre Collection: Every aspect of the entertainment world, including drama, film, radio, television, circus, vaudeville and magic is covered in this collection. The Yiddish theatre dating back to the 1920s is also documented.

    The collection includes clipping files from newspapers and periodicals organized under 25,000 headings with files on individual performers, designers, dramatists and directors. Obituaries of theatre personalities are included. There are thousands of photographs, playbills, prints, posters, programs and scripts in the collection.

    The Theatre Collection houses the Robinson Locke Collection of Dramatic Scrapbooks, some 900 bound volumes and over 2,300 portfolios which include loose clippings and photographs; the Hiram Stead Collection on the British Theatre, 1672 to 1932, which contains letters, autographs and portraits in 600 portfolios; and the Henin Collection which covers the Parisian stage during the 18th and 19th centuries. The Theatre on Film and Tape (TOFT) Collection includes film and videotape of live performances as well as informal dialogues with important theatrical personalities about their careers and techniques.

4. Music Division: The world of music is documented in this Division through composers' scores, an extensive clipping collection, programs, photographs, original scene designs, manuscripts and books.

    The Division has Biographical Index Cards which include biographical data, paste-on clippings or references to sources with biographical information on a particular musician or composer.

    Among the books in the Division of particular interest to Jewish genealogists are:

    Federation of Jewish Philanthropies. *In the Jewish Tradition: A Directory of Performing Artists* [A current directory of Jewish performing artists, including photographs and biographies]. Hazel Weinberger and Robin Mayers, eds., 1985. [JNC 87-4]

    Nulman, Macy. *The Concise Encyclopedia of Jewish Music.* 1975. [DE JME 75-181] (on open shelf)

Finding Aids:

1. Rodgers and Hammerstein Archive of Recorded Sound: The Archive has a card catalog arranged by name of composer or artist, subject and title of work for most acquisitions through 1977. The librarian also has access to a computerized index covering holdings acquired after 1977. A separate card index exists for recordings that are included in the WNEW collection (78 and 45 recordings played on WNEW radio). This index has a "Performers" section.

    There is a book index to the Stambler Archives, which lists the LP holdings by name of performer and numerically by shelf arrangement.

    For old recordings (mostly 78s), check the *Rigler-Deutsch Record Index* on microfiche. The microfiche are arranged by title, performer, composer and label. (This index also includes the record holdings of Syracuse, Yale and Stanford Universities and the Library of Congress.)

    For current recordings (after 1977), the Archive has the *Schwann Catalog* (U.S. recordings) and the *Gramophone* (English classical recordings).

2. Dance Collection: The *Dictionary Catalog of the Dance Collection* (pre-1974 holdings) is in books. The post-1974 index is on microfiche. All special collections and clipping files have been integrated into these catalogs which are arranged by author, title and subject. Names of performers and choreographers are included here.

3. Billy Rose Theatre Collection: The integrated card catalog for non-book materials (programs, clippings, photographs, etc.) in the reading room includes names of performers, subjects and titles of productions. Another catalog, similarly arranged, covers archival materials (correspondence, etc.) and is located in the adjacent Katharine Cornell-Guthrie McClintic Reading Room. A separate card catalog covers books and periodicals cataloged through 1971. Materials cataloged since 1972 are listed in the Library's published catalogs. See "NEW YORK PUBLIC LIBRARY - CENTRAL RESEARCH LIBRARY,

GENERAL RESEARCH DIVISION" for a description of these Red, Blue and Green catalogs. Items in these published catalogs are being added to the Library's CATNYP system. At present, the only computer terminals available on the 3rd floor are in the Music Division.

4. <u>Music Division</u>: Biographical Index Cards (file drawers with beige cards) are arranged alphabetically by name. The *Dictionary Catalog of the Music Division* catalogs books acquired pre-1972. Later acquisitions are computerized. The Division has four computer catalog terminals. Materials are arranged in both by author, subject and title. The Division has no index for its extensive clipping files which are arranged alphabetically by name. Submit a call slip requesting a file on a particular person or all files with a particular surname.

The Center will provide limited reference service by telephone and mail.

Description of Facility:

All of the special collections described above are located on the third floor of the Performing Arts Research Center. Three of the rooms are spacious and can provide seating for 50 to 75 researchers each. The exception is the Rodgers and Hammerstein Archive of Recorded Sound. This room has 20 carrels and seating for 7-9 additional persons at a table.

There is one librarian on duty in each room to assist the public, and an additional librarian in the Special Collections Reading Room of the Music Division. In addition, there are two to three staff persons who retrieve materials at the call windows of the Music Division and Billy Rose Theatre Collection.

The Rodgers and Hammerstein Archive of Recorded Sound is to the right of the elevators. The Archive has staff in the basement who play the requested music or video. The audio can be heard at the 20 individual Automated Recorded Sound Media Terminals and the video seen on the 3 available video terminals. The Archive also has 2 microfilm and 2 microfiche readers. A television screen on the librarian's desk allows researchers to see the jackets of the records they have requested.

The Billy Rose Theatre Collection is opposite the elevators. There are four microfilm and one microfiche readers in the back of this room. There are also three videotape monitors for viewing the Theatre on Film and Tape (TOFT) collection.

The Music Division is located down the corridor (left or right) from the elevators. There are 6 microfilm readers in this room and 6 additional readers and carrels for scholars in the Special Collections Reading Room.

The Dance Collection is located behind the Music Division. This room has 9 video machines, two 16mm film viewers, 2 microfilm readers, one movieola machine and 7 microfiche readers (for catalog only).

Fees/Copies:

The Office of Reprographic Services, in the corridor to the left of the elevators, provides quick copies and photographic reproductions of research materials, as permitted by Division librarians. This Office is open from 10:30 am to 5:30 pm, Monday through Saturday. On Saturday it is closed from 2:00 pm to 3:00 pm. Staff members make the copies. Quick copies cost $.25 or $.45 depending on the size. More than one item can be included on one page. Prices for photographs start at $8.75 (if a negative exists). Microfilm copies cost $.20 per frame and microfiche $1.25 per card. A complete price list is available.

Copies of LPs, 78 rpm recordings and other conventional formats cost $40 per hour of recording ($20 minimum). Cylinders, wire recordings and other non-standard formats cost $50 per hour (one hour minimum). Shipping/handling charges (in USA) cost $2.50. This does not include the tape costs (from $2 to $25) or pitching to score ($100 per hour). Payment should be by check or money order, payable to the NYPL/Rodgers and Hammerstein Archive. The curator must approve all requests.

Restrictions on Use:

Coats and briefcases must be checked on the first floor. The Center will provide a plastic bag to carry papers and other personal items.

None of the materials in the Performing Arts Research Center may be borrowed. They must be consulted in the appropriate reading room. Researchers wishing to copy material must obtain a pass from the librarian.

The call windows will not take call slips after 5:30 pm (or 7:30 pm Monday and Thursday).

Written permission from the union, the film company and/or the choreographer may be needed to view some films and videotapes in the Dance Collection. The librarian will advise of restrictions. Restrictions have been placed also on some manuscripts and on some oral histories.

A special appointment is needed to view the tapes in the TOFT Collection of the Billy Rose Theatre Collection. Various restrictions will be explained at the time the appointment is made.

NEW YORK PUBLIC LIBRARY
SCHOMBURG CENTER FOR RESEARCH IN BLACK CULTURE

Facility Director: Howard Dodson, Director

Address: 515 Lenox Avenue
New York, NY 10037

(Cross Street: Corner of 135th Street)

Phone Number: (212) 862-4000

Hours of Operation:

	June to September	October to May
Monday & Wednesday:	12:00 noon to 8:00 pm	12:00 noon to 8:00 pm
Tuesday:	10:00 am to 6:00 pm	12:00 noon to 8:00 pm
Thursday & Friday:	10:00 am to 6:00 pm	10:00 am to 6:00 pm
Saturday:	closed	10:00 am to 6:00 pm

Closed Sunday and legal holidays.

NOTE: The Archives closes at 5:00 pm. The art collection can be visited by appointment only.

Closest Public Transportation:

Subway: 2 or 3 to 135th Street
Bus: Bx33, M7 or M102 to Lenox Avenue and 135th Street

Directions:

Take the #2 or #3 train to the 135th Street station. Exit at the center of the platform to Lenox Avenue. The Library is on the corner.

Description of Resources:

The Schomburg Center specializes in Black history. Its primary interest for genealogists is in its Census holdings. It also has materials on Black Jews and on relations between Jews and Blacks.

The library has an almost complete collection of U.S. Census records, for all states from 1790 to 1880 and the fragmentary 1890 Census. The library does not have a complete set of the 1900 or 1910 Census. Twenty-nine states and the District of Columbia are available for 1900. These include all of the states in the New York metropolitan area. Only parts of six states (Georgia, North Carolina, South Carolina, Oklahoma, Tennessee and Virginia) are available here for the 1910 Census.

NOTE: The MICROFORMS DIVISION at the Central Research Library on 42nd Street has a complete collection for New York State only. The NATIONAL ARCHIVES, NORTHEAST REGION, has the U.S. Census for all years and all states.

Finding Aids:

The Center has the Soundex index for the 1880 and 1900 Census for all states. The indexes only for Georgia and Virginia are available here for the 1910 Census. In addition, the Center has the 1910 Soundex index for military installations. (However, it does not have the actual Census reels for these installations.) See Appendix C for a description of the National Archives Soundex system.

The *1900 Federal Population Census Catalog of Microfilm Copies of the Schedules,* 1978, is available to identify the appropriate reel number for a particular locality in 1900.

The Center's microfilms can be viewed at the NEW YORK PUBLIC LIBRARY at 42nd Street by completing a call slip and submitting it at the Information Desk in the NEW YORK PUBLIC LIBRARY, U.S. HISTORY, LOCAL HISTORY AND GENEALOGY DIVISION. Requests should be submitted at least one week in advance. For immediate viewing, visit the Schomburg Center.

Description of Facility:

The Schomburg Center is located in the heart of Harlem. Enter the facility from Lenox Avenue. The Census records are located on the Court level, one floor below the entrance. The Center has a seating capacity of about 200. There are 11 microfilm readers of which 6 are reader/copiers. Eight librarians are available to assist researchers. Encyclopedias, indexes, scrapbooks and the catalogs of other Black collections are on open shelves.

Fees/Copies:

Microfilm copies can be made at $.25 per page. Bring a roll of quarters. The library does not make change. The quality of the copy is usually good.

Restrictions on Use:

Researchers must request each reel by call slip. Only 5 reels can be requested at one time. There may be a wait of 15 minutes before reels are delivered.

NEW YORK UNIVERSITY, ELMER HOLMES BOBST LIBRARY
TAMIMENT INSTITUTE LIBRARY AND ROBERT F. WAGNER LABOR ARCHIVES

Facility Director: Peter Allison, Head Librarian
Dorothy Swanson, Tamiment Librarian

Address: 70 Washington Square South
New York, NY 10012

(Cross Streets: LaGuardia Place and Mercer Street)

Phone Number: (212) 998-2630

Hours of Operation:

Monday and Thursday: 10:45 am to 9:00 pm
Tuesday, Wednesday
  and Friday: 10:45 am to 5:00 pm
Saturday: 10:00 am to 5:00 pm

Closed Sunday and major legal holidays. The Library may be open on some holidays such as Election Day. During the summer and semester breaks, evening and weekend hours vary. Call in advance.

Closest Public Transportation:

Subway: N or R to 8th Street
        A, B, C, D, E, F or Q to West 4th Street
        6 to Astor Place or Bleecker Street

Bus: M5 or M6 to West 4th Street and Broadway (southbound) or West 4th Street and Avenue of the Americas (northbound)

Directions:

Take the N or R train to the 8th Street station. Exit the station and walk south on Broadway to West 4th Street. Turn west on West 4th Street and walk two blocks to Washington Square South (#70).

Description of Resources:

These collections cover labor history, socialism, communism, anarchism, utopian experiments, women's movements and other radical activities in the United States since 1865. Tamiment has a collection of 20,000 books and 500,000 pamphlets, leaflets, flyers and internal documents from labor and left organizations. It has 5,000 non-current periodicals, roughly 800 current periodicals and 3,000 oral histories and other sound recordings. There are over 200,000 photographic images, posters, video and raw film footage.

The extensive archival holdings often include minutes and, in a few instances, membership lists and case histories. While many of these collections deal more with the leadership than with rank-and-file members, some individual members may be mentioned.

The following list is a sampling of the holdings of possible interest to genealogists:

1.   <u>Socialist Collections</u>: There are over 35 collections, most of which are personal papers of different individuals including Mendel Halushka, Morris Hillquit, Sergius Ingerman, Harry Laidler, Meyer London, Jacob Panken, Morris Paris, Abraham Shiplacoff, B. Charney Vladeck, Art Young and Sam Zagat.

2.   <u>Communist Collections</u>: The 16 collections in this group include the personal papers of Israel and Sadie Amter, Alexander Bittleman, Sam Darcy, Edward Falkowski, David Gordon, Gil Green and Charlotte Stern.

3. Other Radical Collections: The more than 30 collections in this group include the personal papers of Max Bedacht, Alexander Berkman, Sam Dolgoff, Raya Dunayevskaya, David Fender, Albert Goldman, Emma Goldman, Max Nomad, Max Shachtman and Isadore Wisotsky.

4. Labor Collections: There are over 50 labor collections, many of them relating specifically to New York City. These consist mostly of written records: minutes of meetings, newsletters, newspapers, memoranda, correspondence, organizing leaflets, issue-oriented files and personal accounts of union activists.

The holdings document activities of a wide range of New York working people including painters, printers, professors, postal workers, teachers, tunnel workers, department store clerks, librarians, clerical workers, transit workers, social service employees, city engineers, fire fighters, flight attendants, actors, burlesque and vaudeville artists, dancers, musicians and scenic artists. They sometimes include individual grievances and membership lists.

There are seven groups of collections:

Entertainment Workers: Actors' Equity Association, 1913-1983; Actors' Fund, 1882-1980s; American Guild of Variety Artists, 1945-1980; American Federation of Musicians, Local 802, 1932-1978; Associated Actors & Artists of America, 1919-1982; Equity Library Theater, 1943-1964; The Labor Theater, 1979-1984.

Public Employees: District Council 37, AFSCME, 1947-1983; New York Metro Area Postal Union, APWU, 1907-1981; New York Public Library Guild, Local 1930, District Council 37, AFSCME, 1962-1979; Professional Staff Congress, CUNY, Local 2334 AFT & AAUP, 1938-1980; Social Service Employees Union, Local 371, 1940-1981 and Local 372, 1966-1973; Transport Workers Union, 1933-1980s; Union of State Employees, 1937-1983; United Federation of Teachers, Local 2, AFT, 1935-1980.

Craft Employees: Headwear Joint Board ACTWU, 1926-1980s; International Brotherhood of Electrical Workers, Local 3, 1902-1982; National Writers Union, NYC Chapter, 1980s; Paperhangers Local 490, 1884-1952; Tunnelworkers Union, Local 174, 1939-1975; Typographical Union No. 6, Benefit Board ITU, 1907-1966.

Wholesale and Retail Employees: District 65, UAW, 1933-1970; Department Store Workers' Union, Local 1S RWDSU, 1939-1979.

Engineering Employees: Engineering and Professional Guild, Local 66 IFPTE, 1936-1979; Civil Service Technical Guild, Local 374 AFSCME, 1937-1984; Engineers Association of ARMA, Local 418 IUE, 1953-1983.

Central Bodies/Coalitions: Jewish Labor Committee, 1933-1980 (include case files on WWII refugees and orphans placed by the union); NYC Central Labor Council, 1933-1982; New York Committee on Occupational Safety & Health, Campaign to Save OSHA, 1980-1981; New York State AFL-CIO Legislative Department, 1938-1983; Union Label & Service Trades Council of Greater NY, 1911-1980s.

Personal Papers: 7 collections.

5. New York City Labor Records Survey: Brief organizational histories and inventories of extant records for over 400 metropolitan labor organizations.

6. Pictorial and Non-Print Collections: There are over 60 videotapes on labor history and radical politics. The photograph and negative collection is of individuals and events connected with left-wing and labor history in NYC.

7. Oral History Collections: Each of the 10 collections has its own listing of the names of those interviewed. In some cases, abstracts are available. For example, there is a guide to the Oral History of the American Left which has over 750 interviews (see "Finding Aids"). The New York City Immigrant Labor History Collection, which has 285 interviews, may also be of interest to Jewish genealogists. The collection New Yorkers at Work: Oral Histories of Life, Labor and Industry is a radio program including 150 interviews.

8. Vertical Files: These contain leaflets, fliers, memoranda and periodicals, both current and non-current. The files are arranged by organization, author, subject and surname. The latter is the case for the biographical files included in this collection.

Finding Aids:

Most of the Library's collection is in the New York University, Bobst Library card catalog or in its computerized successor, BobCat. Records of over 100 collections are computer-cataloged. There are also several specialized archival card catalogs and vertical files which are well cross-referenced. In addition, finding aids with folder level control have been prepared for most of the archival collections.

The Library has a 4-page (free) bulletin, *Tamiment Institute Library & Robert F. Wagner Labor Archives, NYU Elmer Holmes Bobst Library, Information Bulletin 8*, which provides a brief overview of the scope of the entire collection. In addition, there are several published bibliographies including:

Swanson, Dorothy. *Guide to the Manuscript Collection of the Tamiment Library*. [This guide is outdated but it describes the core of the collection.] 1977.

Socialist Collections in the Tamiment Library, a Guide to the Microfilm Edition. [A guide to the purchased microfilm collections.] New York, 1979.

Guide to Oral History of the American Left. Tamiment, 1984.

Wechsler, Robert. *New York Labor Heritage: A Selected Bibliography of New York City Labor History*. [This bibliography of secondary sources is arranged by industry, ethnic group and time period.] 1981.

The staff will conduct short searches in response to telephone requests. Typically, time permitting, they will look at two to three sources and advise the researcher on the next steps. Patrons must come in to conduct actual research.

There is a specialized archivist for the Non-Print Collection who should be consulted by researchers who plan to use these materials.

Description of Facility:

The Library is located on the 10th floor of the Bobst Library between the elevator banks. The room can seat 40 people at tables. There is one staff member on duty at the reference desk. One microfiche and four microfilm readers are available. Some of the catalogs are to the left of the reference desk; the rest are behind the desk. Consult the staff.

Fees/Copies:

All non-archival materials (books, periodicals, etc.) can be copied by the researcher after the librarian gives him/her a pass. Archival materials are only copied by the Library staff, after the researcher fills out a special form. Up to 125 pages from any collection can be copied. Copies can be picked up or mailed in one week. The cost is $.20 per page plus postage (if mailed).

Restrictions on Use:

Researchers must present identification to receive pass and enter the Bobst Library. In the Tamiment room, researchers must sign in at the register. Five items may be requested at a time (less if very busy).

All photocopying is done at the discretion of the staff, depending on the material's condition and age. No fragile or antique materials can be photocopied. Appropriate copyright restrictions apply.

RESEARCH FOUNDATION FOR JEWISH IMMIGRATION
ARCHIVES

Facility Director:	Dennis Rohrbaugh, Archivist
Address:	570 Seventh Avenue, 16th Floor New York, NY 10018
	(Cross Street: Corner of 41st Street)
Phone Number:	(212) 921-3871

Hours of Operation:

Open to the public by appointment only. Call or write.

Closest Public Transportation:

Subway: 1, 2, 3, 7, N or R to Times Square/42nd Street

Bus: M10 (south) or M42 to 42nd Street and 7th Avenue
         M6, M7 or M104 to 42nd Street and Broadway

Directions:

Take any of the above trains to the Times Square/42nd Street station. Exit the station and turn south on 7th Avenue to 41st Street. The building is on the southwest corner.

Description of Resources:

The collection consists of material on 25,000 individuals gathered in preparation of a biographical dictionary on émigrés from Germany, Austria and German-speaking Czechoslovakia. It contains information on individuals -- regardless of religion, profession or place of resettlement -- who emigrated from these countries between 1933 and 1945.

There is information on the individual's personal and professional life and family both before and after emigration, including copies of published sources (e.g. *Who's Who,* newspapers, professional journals) and material from private sources (e.g. questionnaires compiled by the biographee, information from relatives). In addition, the Archives' Oral History Collection has 275 transcriptions of taped interviews with German-Jewish émigrés to the United States from the Nazi period on.

Published materials of the Archives also available include:

1. *International Biographical Dictionary of Central European Emigres, 1933-1945,* edited by Herbert A. Strauss. Includes 8,700 biographies. 3 vols., 1980.

2. *Jewish Immigrants of the Nazi Period in the USA,* edited by Herbert A. Strauss.

   Vol. 1: *Archival Resources,* by Steven W. Siegel, 1979.

   Vol. 2: *Classified and Annotated Bibliography of Books and Articles on the Immigration and Acculturation of Jews from Europe to the USA Since 1933,* by H. Friedlander, A. Gardner, K. Schwerin, H. Strauss and J. Wasserman, 1981.

   Vol. 3, Part 1: *Guide to the Oral History Collection of the Research Foundation for Jewish Immigration, New York,* by Joan Lessing, 1982

   Vol. 3, Part 2: *Classified List of Articles Concerning Emigration in German Jewish Periodicals, January 30, 1933 to November 9, 1938,* by Daniel Schwarz and Daniel Niederland, 1982.

   Vol. 4: *The Persecution and Emigration of German Jews, 1933-1945, An Annotated Source Book,* by Norbert Kampe, in translation.

Vol. 5: *The Individual and Collective Experience of German-Jewish Immigrants 1933-1984, An Oral History Record,* by Dennis Rohrbaugh, 1986.

Vol. 6: *Essays on the History, Persecution and Emigration of German Jews,* by Herbert A. Strauss, 1987.

Finding Aids:

1.   Complete card index by surname of individuals in the collection.

2.   Partial card index arranged by country of resettlement.

3.   Partial card index arranged by profession.

4.   Complete card index of émigrés to Israel (Palestine), arranged by profession.

Description of Facility:

The Archives, located on the 16th floor of an office building, can serve 3-4 researchers at a time. One staff person is available by appointment to assist researchers. Biographical files, typed interview transcripts and a small collection of books and papers are on open shelves. Records can be viewed immediately. Mail requests are responded to within 2 weeks, on average. Requests for information may also be made by telephone.

Fees/Copies:

Small numbers of photocopies can be made at $.10 per page.

Restrictions on Use:

A small amount of personal biographical material has not been released to the public by the biographee. Some material may not be photocopied.

SURROGATE'S COURT - NEW YORK COUNTY (MANHATTAN) RECORD ROOM

Facility Director: Robert M. Reeves, Chief Clerk, Surrogate's Court
Peter Tosto, Record Room Supervisor

Address: 31 Chambers Street, Room 402
New York, NY 10007

(Cross Streets: Centre and Elk Streets)

Phone Number: (212) 374-8286

Hours of Operation:

Monday to Friday: 9:00 am to 5:00 pm. (NOTE: Files are pulled until 4:45 pm.)
Closed Saturday, Sunday and legal holidays.

Closest Public Transportation and Directions:

See "CITY REGISTER'S OFFICE - MANHATTAN." The Record Room is on the 4th floor immediately in front of the elevator bay.

Description of Resources:

The County Surrogate's Court has wills and indexes, 1654 to the present; and all records of probate, letters of administration and estate taxes for New York County, 1830 to the present. Inventories of estates, 1783-1844, are at the QUEENS COLLEGE, HISTORICAL DOCUMENTS COLLECTION. In addition, the Court has guardianship cases from 1808 and adoptions and commitments from 1924 to the present. NOTE: Family Court also has jurisdiction for adoptions since 1961.

Some estate files include a copy of the death certificate and testimony from individuals identifying family members, i.e. potential heirs.

Copies of probated wills are also found in Records of Will libers in the Liber Room (Room 405). Documents in will libers give the names and addresses of the witnesses and executor to a probated will, as well as the names of heirs mentioned in the will (but not necessarily all the heirs). These libers can be used as a quick way to see part of a probated case if the full file does not exist, i.e. pre-1830, or if the file is not in the building. Letters of Administration, in the room adjacent to the Liber Room, can also be used as a preliminary source for date of death and the name of the Executor pending retrieval of a full file. Delegations of power of attorney and other assignments can be found in the Records of Conveyances and Mortgages of Interests of Decedent Estates and Powers of Attorney, 1904 to the present. These records often include a description of relationship to the deceased which may not be included in the case file.

The Surrogate's Court is in the process of placing all of its records on microfiche. Estate records (probate, letters of administration and estate taxes), 1964-1966, have already been filmed.

The Surrogate's Court records included records of residents of parts of the Bronx, 1874-1897, and all of the Bronx, 1898-1914.

Finding Aids:

Liber indexes for probate cases/wills, letters of administration, estate taxes and guardianships are arranged alphabetically by the first letter of the surname and then chronologically by date of filing. Each type of record, 1654-1949, is indexed for groups of years in different libers. Letters of administration prior to 1743 are recorded in the probate index libers. Separate liber indexes are available for Records of Conveyances and Mortgages...and Powers of Attorney.

All types of cases from 1950 to date are maintained in card indexes. The cards are arranged alphabetically by last name of the deceased/guardianship of record and chronologically within two groupings, 1950-1963 and 1964-present. Cards, 1950-1963, include the will liber number in addition to the case number. Cards, 1964-present, include the date of death, last address and case number.

Minutes to probate and administration records, 1924 to the present, are also available. This index includes will liber number and date of death.

Each probate, administration, guardianship and estate tax file is available on request. Request forms must be filled out and submitted in the Record Room.

Description of Facility:

The Record Room can seat 8 researchers. There are two staff members to assist researchers and pull files. Index libers for probate records, 1654-1949, and administration, 1654-1949, are on open shelves. The card indexes are found in catalog drawers by the work tables. Liber indexes for guardianships, 1808-1961, are in the Liber Room, Room 405.

Three microfiche readers and one reader/copier are located in Room 301A. However, this is not a public room. Go to the Record Room first for permission to view files on microfiche. The clerk will either provide the hard copy of the file for viewing or will call Room 301A for permission to use a microfiche reader. The Court plans to add at least three reader/copiers to service the public directly in Room 402.

The Liber Room (Room 405), open to the public, is located in the northwest corner of the 4th floor corridor. Open shelves with steep rolling ladders line the walls of the room. All of the will libers, administration libers and Records of Conveyances and Mortgages...and Powers of Attorney libers are maintained here. The room is dark, dusty and there is no place to sit. You must pull the libers yourself and replace them yourself. It is suggested that researchers dress accordingly.

Adoption records are in Room 508. See "Restrictions on Use."

Fees/Copies:

Certified copies of wills and letters of administration are available at $4 per page. Two photocopy machines ($.15 per page) are available for public use. The clerks cannot make change. Bring your own or go to the CITY REGISTER'S OFFICE cashier on the second floor in Room 202.

Mail requests cost $53 for a search of records over 25 years old and $20 for records under 25 years, plus $4 per page for a copy of the record. The search fee is not charged if the file number is provided by the researcher.

Restrictions on Use:

Only 3 files per researcher per day will be pulled if the staff is busy. Cases prior to 1964 are stored off-site and require one week to ten days for retrieval. However, the will libers, administration libers and Records of Conveyances and Mortgages...and Powers of Attorney libers for any case may be examined on the spot.

Commitments and adoptions are sealed records. Commitments may only be examined after obtaining a court affidavit from the NY County Surrogate's Court and a court order to open the files. Adoption records can never be examined although a court affidavit and court order may be obtained for specific information, i.e. birth certificate or health information.

Personal cameras may not be used to copy documents. It is preferred that pencils be used when handling original materials. No papers may leave the Record Room at any time.

U.S. DISTRICT COURT - SOUTHERN DISTRICT OF NEW YORK
NATURALIZATION DIVISION

Facility Director: Francine A. Madorma, Supervisory Naturalization Clerk

Address: Jacob K. Javits Federal Building
26 Federal Plaza, Room 7-120
New York, NY 10278

(Cross Streets: Broadway, Worth, Lafayette and Duane Streets)

Phone Number: (212) 264-5884

Hours of Operation:

Monday, Tuesday,
  Thursday, Friday: 8:30 am to 5:00 pm
Wednesday: 12:00 noon to 5:00 pm

Closed Saturday, Sunday and legal holidays. The office may be open Election Day. Check in advance.

Closest Public Transportation:

Subway: 4, 5 or 6 to Brooklyn Bridge
           J, M or Z to Chambers Street
           N or R to City Hall
           A or C to Chambers Street (north end)

Bus: M1 or M6 to Broadway between Chambers and Reade Streets
          M15 or M22 to Lafayette and Duane Streets

Directions:

Take the #4 or #5 (express) or #6 (local) train to the Brooklyn Bridge station. Go down the staircase at the <u>north</u> end of the platform. Turn left immediately and go out the Lafayette-Reade Street exit. Go up the right stairs (to Lafayette Street). The Federal Building is the checker-board building set back from Duane and Lafayette Streets. This office is on the seventh floor.

Description of Resources:

This office has Petitions for Naturalization filed in U.S. District Court, Southern District of New York, from December 19, 1940 to the present and Declarations of Intention filed from September 21, 1976 to the present. The bound Petitions books, arranged by petition number, may also contain a copy of the Declaration of Intention and the Certificate of Arrival.

NOTE: Southern District Naturalization records, 1824-1929 (indexes, 1824-1940) and Declarations, 1842-1940 (indexes, 1842-1954), are located at the NATIONAL ARCHIVES, NORTHEAST REGION. Naturalizations, 1929-December 19, 1940 and Declarations, 1967-1976, are in the custody of the Federal Records Center of the NATIONAL ARCHIVES AND RECORDS ADMINISTRATION (not in the NATIONAL ARCHIVES, NORTHEAST REGION).

The Southern District covers Manhattan, Bronx, Westchester, Dutchess, Orange, Putnam, Rockland and Sullivan counties in New York. However, residents of upstate counties were more likely to file for naturalization at the local Supreme Court in these counties. Few, if any, upstate residents were naturalized through the Southern District Court in New York. Persons living outside of the Southern District area of jurisdiction may also have filed their papers in this District Court. Residency was not a requirement for filing. Many Brooklyn residents who worked in Manhattan filed papers through this office.

Finding Aids:

To the right of the entrance are index card file drawers arranged in groups of years and alphabetically as follows: 1941-1950, 1950-1959, 1960-1971, 1972-1981, 1982-present. Each card includes the name and petition number.

NOTE: Index cards for Petitions dated between December 19, 1940 and December 31, 1940 are not here but are located at the NATIONAL ARCHIVES, NORTHEAST REGION. (This is because 272 Petitions from December 1940 are in the first bound book of the 1941 Petitions.)

The office also has index stubs for Naturalizations, March 1, 1926 to the present which include Petition number. Stubs, March 1926-June 1929, include name, age of petitioner and name, age and residence of wife and minor children. From July 1929 to November 1947, stubs include only name, age and address of petitioner. After November 1947, date of birth is included instead of age. The stubs are arranged chronologically by date of Naturalization and then alphabetically. As a result, they are difficult to use unless the researcher knows the exact date when Naturalization occurred.

There is no index to Declarations of Intention.

Description of Facility:

This is a government office located in Room 7-120 of the Federal Building. The four staff persons in this room do other work, but can answer questions. About 4-5 researchers can use the index file at a time. Since the records are on moveable shelves, only one person at a time can retrieve records. Records can be viewed immediately.

Fees/Copies:

Records may be copied by hand. No photocopy machine is available. To obtain a photocopy, write to the Immigration and Naturalization Service, 26 Federal Plaza, Room 7-130, New York, NY 10278 and request a copy under the Freedom of Information Act. It can take several months before a response is mailed out.

Restrictions on Use:

Books must be returned to their proper place. Index cards may not be removed from file drawers.

Declarations of Intention, 1941-1967 (except those bound with Naturalizations), are missing.

YESHIVA UNIVERSITY
ARCHIVES

Facility Director: Dr. Roger S. Kohn, Archivist

Address: 2520 Amsterdam Avenue, Room 405
New York, NY

(Cross Streets: West 185th and West 186th Streets)

Mail Address: 500 West 185th Street
New York, NY 10033

Phone Number: (212) 960-5451

Hours of Operation:

Monday to Thursday: 9:00 am to 5:00 pm (by appointment only)
Closed Friday, Saturday, Sunday, Jewish and legal holidays.

Closest Public Transportation:

Subway: 1 to 181st Street (and St. Nicholas Avenue)
           A to 181st Street (and Ft. Washington Avenue)

Bus: M101 to 185th Street and Amsterdam Avenue (stops opposite the Library)
        M3 to 186th Street and St. Nicholas Avenue
        M4 to 186th Street and Ft. Washington Avenue

Directions:

Take the #1 train to the 181st Street station. Walk north on St. Nicholas Avenue to 185th Street. Turn east on 185th and walk two blocks to Amsterdam Avenue. Turn north on Amsterdam. The entrance is near the corner of 185th Street.

Or,

Take the A train to the 181st Street station. Use the exit to 184th Street and Overlook Terrace. Walk four blocks east on 184th Street to Amsterdam Avenue. Turn north on Amsterdam to 185th Street.

Description of Resources:

The Archives consist of 540 linear feet of records comprising some 240 collections of mostly Orthodox Jewish institutions and individuals. These are primarily organizational records, letters, memoirs, newspaper clippings, genealogies and photographs. The major collections of interest to genealogists are described below. Researchers should consult with the Archivist to determine whether other collections have documents related to their family histories or genealogy:

1.   <u>The Central Relief Committee Collection (1914-1959)</u>: Records, 1914-1918, include information about yeshivot in inter-war Europe; correspondence concerning requests to locate missing relatives, 1914-1916 (Boxes 10, 14); correspondence requesting funds for transportation of relatives from Palestine to the U.S., 1916-1917 (Box 13); lists of Palestine (Boxes 15-19) and Russian remittances, 1916 (Box 25); and general correspondence with individuals (Boxes 30-40).

Records, 1919-1929, contain questionnaires filled out by yeshivot in Eastern and Central Europe. Most are from Poland but Austria, Czechoslovakia, Rumania, Germany, Hungary, Yugoslavia, the Baltic States and Soviet Union are also covered. The collection includes mostly institutional information. Some lists of students are included.

2.   <u>Mordechai Bernstein Collection, 1605-1965</u>: Includes original documents of 58 Jewish communities in Germany and photocopies of documents of 38 Jewish communities. The earliest original document

includes five records from the rabbinical court in Pappenheim, 1605-1619, on questions of heritage. Also included are a handful of marriage contracts, deeds of divorce and court records from such communities as Brakel, Castell, Darmstadt, Eppendorf, Luebeck, Petershagen, Muelhausen, Warburg and Zinnwald. The documents include general meetings of the Jewish community of Esslingen on the Neckar (in Judeo-German), 1816-1825; a 1819-1843 volume of the burial society of Laupheim; excerpts of records of charitable endowments to the Jewish community of Laupheim, 1869-1872 (in German); a volume containing handwritten entries of circumcisions performed in an unidentified city, 1772-1796, and in Koenigsberg, 1852-1875; an account book of a burial society in Altenmuhr, 1845-1870, and a list of the Jewish residents of Fulda before 1933, with their location after 1945; documents regarding the Jewish cemetery and Jews living in Schiltz, 1935-1947; and a list of the Jewish residents of Stuttgart, 1940-1941.

Includes photocopies of the Memorbuecher from Koblenz, 1610-1850, and from Ehrenbreitstein, 1703-1883; photocopies of community records from Mikulow (Nikolsburg) in Moravia, 18th century; the records of a burial society in Prague, 1785-1870; and photographs of buildings, cemeteries and tombstones in over 50 Jewish communities in Germany, Czechoslovakia, Italy and Poland. This subseries contains a folder of transcriptions of the Hebrew text of tombstones in the Jewish cemetery of Sinsheim, 1891-1938.

Of note, this collection includes 115 inventories of Jewish records in Staatsarchivs in the following German communities:

Amberg	Gunzenhausen	Neumarkt (Oberpfalz)
Amorbach	Hamburg	Neuwied
Ansbach	Hameln	Nuremberg
Assenheim	Hannover	Oberehrenbreitstein
Bamberg	Hesse	Pappenheim
Birsteien	Hildesheim	Regensburg
Braunschweig	Huettenbach	Reugland
Castel	Jebenhausen	Reutlingen
Coburg	Karlsruhe	Schweinfurt
Darmstadt	Koblenz (Coblenz)	Sigmaringen
Donaueschingen	Landshut	Speyer
Duesseldorf	Ludwigsburg	Stuttgart
Esslingen	Luebeck	Weikersheim
Floss	Marburg an der Lahn	Wertheim
Frankfurt	Memmingen	Wiesbaden
Friedberg	Munich	Wiesentheid
Fuerstenberg	Neuburg	Wolfenbuettel
Goettingen	Neuenstein	Wuerzburg

3. National Council of Jewish Women, Service to the Foreign Born: Includes an estimated 350,000 records on individuals and families who came through the port of New York and whom the National Council helped to become citizens. The records include the New York Section, 1939-1968, and Brooklyn Section, 1942-1955. See "Restrictions on Use."

4. Vaad Hatzala Collection (1939-1963): Includes information on the rescue efforts of the Union of Orthodox Rabbis of the U.S. and Canada (Agudath Ha Rabbonim). The files include correspondence, lists, visas and affidavits of support concerning rabbinical and student refugees, 1941-1948 (Boxes 4, 13-16, 19, 26-30, 38, 42-43); searches for missing relatives, 1944-1948 (Boxes 17, 40, 44); lists of non-quota immigrants, 1947, lists of sponsors, 1946, and lists of applicants for rabbinical positions, 1948 (Box 17); lists of refugees in concentration camps (Bergen-Belsen - Box 18; Dachau - Box 30), in Displaced Persons Camps (Box 18), in Camp Vittel, France (Box 26), and elsewhere (Boxes 18, 22, 31, 38, 39); identification papers (including photos) issued by the Vaad in Katowice, Poland (Box 18); list of students of the Windsheim Yeshiva transported from Frankfurt, Germany to Lyons, France, 1948 (Box 31); lists of Jews of various nationalities who arrived in Sweden, 1945 and n.d. (Boxes 34, 40); list of 1,200 persons who left Theresienstadt for Switzerland, n.d. (Box 35); lists of refugees to be transferred to Paris (Box 40); and lists of Jews authorized to enter Tangier.

5. Louis Rittenberg Collection: Includes biographical data on famous American Jews. This data was accumulated for the preparation of the *Universal Jewish Encyclopedia* (1939-1944). These papers also

include documentation of Jewish life in New York from the 1930s to 1960s, especially the rise of the Jewish community in Washington Heights.

6. Rescue Children, Inc. Collection (1946-1985): Includes files documenting the rescue of children who survived the Holocaust. RCI set up special centers in France, Belgium, Sweden and Germany. The organization supported 2,200 orphans between 1945 and 1948, and identified or located the families of more than two-thirds of the children. The bulk of the archival material is from information supplied by the children through interviews seeking biographical information and recollections of people in their home towns. See "Restrictions on Use."

7. Yeshiva University Records (1895-1970): Contains records of the University including biographical files on Presidents Bernard Revel, Samuel Belkin, Norman Lamm; on Deans Pinchos Churgin, Moses Issacs, 1930-1970 and personal (family) files of Dr. Shelley R. Saphire, 1914-1960; applications for faculty positions at Yeshiva University and the High School, 1926-1952; faculty files, 1926-1946; files on foreign faculty, 1939-1941; Teacher's Time Book (Talmudical Academy) English Department, 1915-1921; and lists of faculty members and administrators, 1947, 1954-1955, 1957.

Records on students include grades, Talmudical Academy, 1917-1919, and Yeshiva College, 1936-1937; applications for admission, withdrawn or rejected applicants, 1926-1942; student (registration) cards 1924-1949; applications for stipends, dormitory applications or dormitory residents, 1929, 1943-1944, 1946-1947; lists of students, 1949-1950, 1957; and graduate school mailing list, 1946. This record group also includes alumni questionnaire replies, 1935-1936; a file on Talmudical Academy Alumni, 1942-1954; questionnaires, B. Revel Graduate School, 1930-1946; and records of donations with names/addresses of donors, by year, 1909-1934. Access to some files is restricted.

8. Institutional Synagogue Records (1917-1967): Includes annual membership meetings, 1928, 1929, 1938 and 1941, regarding election of Board members; Fanny Henning will, 1937; and a bound volume of the synagogue's bulletin, *The Institutional,* 1933-1940 (with gaps).

9. Shelley Ray Saphire Collection (1890-1970): Includes personal correspondence with his future wife and other family members; applications for teaching positions at the Talmudical Academy, the High School Department of Yeshiva University, 1944-1950.

10. Henry S. Morais Collection (1860-1935): Contains biographical sketches of eight persons mentioned in his book, *The Jews of Philadelphia:* Col. Mayer Asch, Victor Caro, Joseph Chumaceiru, Col. Max Friedman, Dr. Samuel J. Gittleson, Abraham Jacob, Rev. Lee Reich, and one signed "S.S.C." Also, invitations to weddings and correspondence, mostly incoming, covering his years as a journalist and Rabbi in Philadelphia and New York.

11. Jamie Lehmann Memorial Collection: Records of the Jewish Community of Cairo (1886-1961): Contains the records of three major institutions: The Sephardic Jewish community, the Ashkenazi community and the B'nai B'rith Lodges (Cairo Lodge and Maimonides Lodge). The collection contains account books, case files, certificates, correspondence, minutes and photographs. Most of the original documents were created between 1920 and 1960.

The records of the Jewish Community Council include proceedings of meetings, 1925-1934 (Box 1); minutes of meetings of the B'nai B'rith Lodges, 1911-1928 (Box 11); and proceedings of meetings of the Administrative Committee supervising the Cairo synagogue which include letters from synagogue personnel and ritual slaughterers (Box 8). General correspondence, 1926-1957, includes a list of rabbis and employees of the Chancellerie, with their nationality (no date); correspondence regarding the Abraham Btesh school and its personnel; and correspondence on personal matters such as deeds of marriage and divorce, 1953 (Box 2).

Passport forms (in Arabic), are available for 1919, containing name, age, date and place of birth, father's citizenship, father's profession, date of arrival in Egypt and length of stay in Egypt, profession, address, previous country of residence, place of destination and reason for travel. Some contain photographs of individuals or families (Box 2).

The records of the Chief Rabbinate include general correspondence, 1941-1959 (Box 3). The correspondence deals with Palestinian Jewry regarding personal status and assistance to war prisoners. Correspondence with Alexandria, 1936-1946, include deeds of marriage and divorce and the status of foreign Jews.   Out-going letters, 1947-1950, include letters about Jewish political detainees and complaints about attacks against Jews (Box 5). A list of butchers in Alexandria, 1945, is in Box 4).

The Register of Deeds Regarding the Personal Status of Private Individuals, 1944-1946, includes birth, marriage and death certificates or affidavits (in Arabic). Each entry lists the name of the person involved in Arabic and French. The entries for Attestation of Personal Status, 1886, 1936-1937, 1947 (registration of requests for certificates) include the name of the person, date and a statement of purpose. The most frequent purposes attested to were birth, celibacy, betrothal, marriage, divorce, widowhood, death, notarization of judicial sentences and passport (Box 5).

Accounting documents of the Chancellerie, 1946, include salaries of the staffs of the Rabbinate and the Arikha; a (Hebrew) list of ritual slaughterers in Cairo; and for 1949-1950, a ledger containing accounts of individuals, associations and schools in Cairo (Box 6). Account books of contributions to the Ba'al Hanes Synagogue, 1890-1909 (Box 8); and of the Synagogue Al Ostaz al Amshati in al Mahalla al Kubra (no date), are also available. Records of the Ashkenazi Community of Cairo, 1933-1955, list funds distributed to indigent families, 1947; and include accounting records for 1950 (Box 10).

Identification records (5 booklets) include entries for date, name, date and place of birth, profession, address, name of father, destination, spouse's name and place of birth and names of children, 1946-1947. Most entries also have a photograph (Box 7).

The collection includes completed forms (in French) prepared by the Cairo Jewish Hospital on patients, 1959-1961; and forms (in Arabic and French) prepared by the Italian Hospital of Abbassieh, 1960-1961 (Box 9).

An unidentified register (may be assisted families) contains names of individuals living in Cairo neighborhoods. Each entry (in French) provides the name, number of persons in the family and address. An additional list, providing name, age and profession is scribbled on the back of a registration form of Yeshiva Ahaba Veahva in Cairo (Box 9).

12. French Consistorial Collection (1809-1939): Includes also records of the Consistories of Rome, Italy, 1809-1810, and Treves and Koblenz, Germany, 1810-1812. The latter include tax exemption requests from individual Jews; lists of young men serving in the army; the decision of the mayor of Treves to expel Isaac Levy from that City, 1810; and letters by Simon Samuel, a British prisoner of war to the Central Consistory, 1812 (Box 1).

Extracts from the census of Parisian Jews, 1809, list all Jewish professionals and soldiers. Includes proceedings of the first meetings of the Consistory of Paris, 1909 and the records of the welfare committee containing certificates for foreign Jews, 1811-1813 (Box 1).

The records of the Administrative Commission for the Synagogues in Paris contain lists of synagogues' seat owners, 1834-1835, 1851 and 1853; and a contract hiring Cantor Israel Loevy, 1823 (Box 2). Consistory of Paris, Central Administration records include lists of funeral processions in Paris, 1834-1839, 1884 and 1886, circumcisions and members of benevolent societies (Box 3).

The "Ritual Bath" folder contains the certificates of many converts to Judaism, 1880-1885. The "Rabbinical Seminary" folder contains certificates of Lazard Wogue, 1817-1897, and Lazard Isidore, 1814-1888 attesting that converts underwent the ritual immersion in a mikve. Correspondence of the Central Consistory includes a letter from Rabbi Emmanuel Deutz, Chief Rabbi of the Central Consistory to Rabbi Abraham Andrade of Bordeaux concerning the marriage of a Jew from Bordeaux, 1936. The records include complaints against rabbis, cantors and ritual slaughterers (Box 3 and 4).

The collection includes a list showing the Jewish population of the following communities: Auxerre, 1810, Dijon (n.d.), La Orleans, c.1810s, 1872, Reims, 1837, Tours (n.d.), Le Havre, c.1835, Reims, 1838, 1851 (Box 4).

Records of the Association Consistoriale Israélite de Paris include elections, 1908 and proceedings of meetings, 1924 and 1939 (Box 4). Records of the Departmental Consistories include a register of pupils at the Jewish vocational school in Marseilles, 1830; letters from Oran, Algiers regarding Moroccan refugees, 1859; Consistory of Strasbourg elections, 1835-1860 and Bordeaux elections, 1810-1812 (Box 5).

Finding Aids:

Published inventories are available for some of these collections. Nevertheless, the records may be difficult to use because name indexes are not available in most cases:

1. The Central Relief Committee: The published inventory available for 1914-1918 does not list names of individuals assisted but rather describes the type and subject of records included in each file. Only "Correspondence with individuals, 1914-17" is arranged alphabetically by surname.

   An inventory covering the 1919-1929 period is in preparation. Researchers must know the name of the yeshiva, period of attendance and the person's function in the yeshiva to find information on individuals in the responses to questionnaires.

2. Mordechai Bernstein Collection: Original documents, transcripts and some photographs in the collection are arranged alphabetically by city. A detailed list of the inventories of the Staatsarchivs and of microfilms of Jewish personal records is at the beginning of Box 17.

3. National Council of Jewish Women, Service for the Foreign Born: The records are arranged by code number. However, the collection includes several finding aids listing names in alphabetical order within a particular time period. Researchers must have name, birth date and birth place for access. See "Restrictions on Use."

4. Vaad Hatzala Collection: A published inventory is available. Names of individuals assisted are not listed in the inventory. Most of the files of interest to genealogists are categorized under the series "Foreign Activities" (Boxes 22-44). These are arranged primarily by country. Others are in the "Immigration and Rehabilitation" series (Boxes 15-21) and appear to be organized by correspondent. A description of the contents of each file is available which will allow researchers to narrow their search somewhat.

5. Louis Rittenberg Collection: A card catalog listing the contents of each box is available.

6. Rescue Children, Inc. Collection: A published inventory is available. Boxes 11-12 contain alphabetical index cards with the names of the children and biographical information prepared by the Stern College Rescue Children Inc. Project.

7. Yeshiva University Records: The preliminary published inventory has an index which allows relative ease in finding subject files. Some faculty members are listed under their own names. For others, see the "Faculty" listings. For records on students, see "Yeshiva College" or "Talmudical Academy" listings. For Alumni records, see "Alumni."

   NOTE: The published inventory includes the biographies of 10 former Administrators of Yeshiva University.

8. Institutional Synagogue Records: A published inventory is available. The Fanny Henning will is in folder 43.

9. Shelley Ray Saphire Collection: There is a published inventory for this collection. Personal correspondence is in folders 1-12. Applications for teaching positions at the Talmudical Academy are arranged by Department, e.g. Biology and Science, Business, Music, etc.

10. Henry S. Morais Collection: The published inventory to this collection has an alphabetical index to the correspondence in Morais' papers. Wedding invitations are not indexed but are arranged alphabetically by sender in folders 102 to 104. Biographical sketches are in folder 126.

11. Jamie Lehmann Memorial Collection: Records of the Jewish Community of Cairo: The published inventory provides a detailed description of the contents of each box and folder. General correspondence and correspondence with Alexandria are arranged alphabetically by the name of the correspondent.

12. French Consistorial Collection: The published inventory provides a brief history of the Consistories and outlines the contents of each box. The arrangement of the records reflects the history of the Consistorial institution, i.e., the Napoleonic era, 1809-1822 (Box 1), the Central Consistory in Paris and provincial Jewish communities under its aegis, 1822-1905 (Boxes 2-4); the records of the successor

organization, the Association Consistoriale Israelite de Paris (Box 4); and records of other departmental Consistories, including Bordeaux, Lyons, Marseilles, Metz, Nancy and Strasbourg (Box 5).

Description of Facility:

The Archives is located on the 4th floor in Room 405. An appointment is necessary. There are three staff persons who can assist researchers. Documents can be obtained immediately. The Archives has one microfilm reader.

Fees/Copies:

Copies can be made by Archives staff at $.50 per page. The published inventories can be purchased. They range in price from $3 to $10. The Inventories Order Form lists the cost of each.

In addition to those listed above, the Archives is currently preparing inventories for the following collections:

Peter Wiernik and Bertha Wiernik Collection, 1886-1950, Records of the American Jewish Joint Distribution Committee, 1916-1946

Records of the Central Relief Committee, 1919-1929

Restrictions on Use:

Researchers may view only one box at a time. Specific restrictions are imposed by donors on some collections. Materials must be handled with care.

The National Council of Jewish Women, Service to the Foreign Born case files and the Rescue Children, Inc. files are restricted to the individual concerned or his/her immediate family.

Access to Yeshiva University Records should be requested from Yeshiva University's Senior Vice-President.

YESHIVA UNIVERSITY
GOTTESMAN LIBRARY OF HEBRAICA-JUDAICA

Facility Director:	Leah Adler, Head Librarian Zalman Alpert, Reference Librarian
Address:	2520 Amsterdam Avenue, 5th Floor New York, NY (Cross Streets: West 185th and 186th Streets)
Mail Address:	500 West 185th Street New York, NY 10033
Phone Number:	(212) 960-5382, 5383, 5384

Hours of Operation:

	School Year	Summer
Monday to Wednesday:	9:00 am to 12:45 am	9:00 am to 5:00 pm
Thursday:	9:00 am to 11:45 pm	9:00 am to 5:00 pm
Friday:	9:00 am to 12:30 pm	9:00 am to 12:00 noon
Sunday:	12:00 noon to 10:45 pm	Closed

Closed Saturday, Jewish and legal holidays.

NOTE: School Year ends in mid-June. The Library is closed for 2 weeks in August.

Closest Public Transportation and Directions:

See "YESHIVA UNIVERSITY - ARCHIVES."

Description of Resources:

The Library includes the following in its holdings:

1. An extensive collection of rabbinic materials including rabbinical responsa and rabbinic lexicons.

2. Family histories, biographies and genealogies.

3. Jewish community histories including a collection of Yizkor books (see Appendix A).

4. Orthodox German weekly newspapers from the 1860s to the 1930s, such as *Der Israelit,* 1864-1937, and *Jeschurun,* 1854-1870.

5. Books with information on tombstones in Jewish cemeteries.

6. Hebrew periodicals from Eastern Europe that included news items as well as scholarly articles, such as *Ha-Meilits,* 1878-1899 and *Ha-Tzefirah,* 1874-1918, printed in Russia.

Finding Aids:

Most of the Library's books are on open shelves. There are four catalogs - Old English, New English, Old Hebrew and New Hebrew - which can be found on the 5th floor.

Researchers should use primarily the New English Catalog (based on the Library of Congress system), which is an integrated author/title/subject catalog. The New English Catalog has useful subject headings such as:

Responsa (grouped by years, e.g. 1800 to 1900)
Rabbis - biography
Jews - biography
Jews - [place name] - biography

The Old English Catalog (based on the Dewey Decimal system) is a title/author catalog. A small but separate subject catalog is available but it is not comprehensive. The Old Hebrew (Dewey Decimal) and New Hebrew (Library of Congress) are basically title catalogs only. Researchers looking for a specific book by title can use the Old English or Old and New Hebrew catalogs.

The Reference Desk has a loose-leaf folder listing periodicals in the Library's collection.

Rare books will be listed in the catalogs, but manuscripts are not. Most of these are uncataloged and inaccessible to researchers. The Library has published a list of rare books in its collection that were published pre-1500.

Description of Facility:

The Library is located on the fifth floor. Six staff persons are available to assist researchers. Seating is available for more than 150 persons. The Library has two microfilm reader/printers and one microfiche reader.

Fees/Copies:

Donations are accepted. Two photocopy machines are available at $.10 per page. Copies from microfilm are also $.10. Books in bad condition may not be copied. No mail research is conducted.

Restrictions on Use:

Manuscripts in the Rare Book Collection are uncataloged and inaccessible to researchers.

YIVO INSTITUTE FOR JEWISH RESEARCH
ARCHIVES

Facility Director:	Marek Web, Head Archivist
	Fruma Mohrer, Associate Archivist
	Daniel Soyer, Associate Archivist

Address: 1048 Fifth Avenue
New York, NY 10028

(Cross Street: Entrance is on East 86th Street)

Phone Number: (212) 535-6700

Hours of Operation:

Monday, Tuesday, Thursday, Friday: 9:30 am to 5:30 pm
Closed Wednesday, Saturday, Sunday, Jewish and legal holidays.

NOTE: YIVO closes during summer heat waves since it is not air-conditioned. It is advisable to call before going.

Closest Public Transportation:

Subway: 4 or 5 (express), or 6 (local) to 86th Street

Bus: M1, M2, M3 or M4 on Madison Avenue to East 86th Street
M18 to Fifth Avenue and East 86th Street (westbound) or East 84th Street (eastbound).

Directions:

Take the #4 or #5 (express) or #6 (local) train to the 86th Street station. Walk 3 blocks west to Fifth Avenue.

Description of Resources:

YIVO Archives has an extensive and fascinating collection of materials relating to Eastern European Jewry. The holdings include more than 1,100 collections of records from organizations and papers from individuals. For the most part, the individuals are people who were famous and/or published authors in Eastern Europe.

Researchers, please be aware that many of these materials are in Yiddish, Hebrew, Polish and/or Russian. In addition, there are many items that are hand-written in Hebrew or Cyrillic script, some of which are illegible even to the YIVO staff. Do not go to YIVO with unrealistic expectations. The degree of success in utilizing YIVO's collections is directly related to a researcher's reading ability in the above languages. Although titles and descriptions of materials may be given in English, assume that most of the items are in a foreign language. Members of YIVO's staff are available to help find materials (and their assistance is invaluable), but they cannot provide translations.

A sample of the collections of importance to students of genealogy and family history follows. Record Group numbers are in brackets.

1. The Landsmanshaftn Archive: YIVO has gathered material from more than 800 societies, arranged in 303 collections. According to *A Guide to YIVO's Landsmanshaftn Archive,* the Archive includes:

   "minutes...; financial records, including membership dues books; records of special committees (relief, burial, loan fund, old age...); membership records (application lists, cards, censuses); burial records (golden books listing names, dates of death, records of interments, endowments, cemetery maps, burial permits); anniversary celebration and banquet programs, menus, journals, photographs; correspondence, meeting announcements, and bulletins; honorary certificates and citations; memorial (yizkor) books, publications manuscripts and materials; ...personal immigration records and papers of society members."

Additional acquisitions since the publication of the *Guide* in 1986 include the records of:

Chevra Anshe Antipole, 1950-1980
Apter Workmen's Circle Branch #566, 1934-1957
Horodoker Benevolent Society, 1936, 1940-1953
Kolomear Friends Association, 1945-1947
Kurlander YMBA Society, 1938-1939
Molodetzner YMBA, 1914-1965
United Meseritzer Relief, 1948-1952
Independent Orler Benevolent Society, 1946
New First Sandez Society (Nowy Sacz)
Slutsker YMBA, 1925, 1954
Stoliner-Lubashover and Lulinetzer, Workmen's Circle Branch #531-231-481, 1961-1982
Tetiever Relief Fund, 1919

2. HIAS (Hebrew Immigrant Aid Society) Collection [RG 245]: Most of the HIAS records in YIVO's collection are administrative and are of historic rather than genealogical interest. See "HIAS (HEBREW IMMIGRANT AID SOCIETY), LOCATION DEPARTMENT" regarding records in HIAS' possession. There are, however, the following materials about which researchers should know:

    a. HIAS Ellis Island Bureau Records, 1905-1923 [RG 245.2], include troublesome cases involving deportation, illness, or detention requiring the services of the HIAS Ellis Island Bureau. These records consist of 26 rolls of microfilm, arranged alphabetically by name of person being detained or about to be deported.

    b. HIAS Office and Organizational Files: YIVO has many HIAS historical files, 1910-1950s, containing inter-office memos, correspondence, etc. They do not include individual case files. An individual might be mentioned in a letter or memo, but retrieving this information is extremely difficult and time-consuming, as the material is not indexed by name.

    c. HIAS Case Files After 1937: There are thousands of case files from 1937 to the 1960s. Most are from 1945 through 1950. These files are not on site and difficult to retrieve from the warehouse where they are kept in original order by agency that processed the files--e.g. National Refugee Service, German Jewish Children's Aid, New York Association for New Americans, European HIAS, etc. (These files are part of YIVO's HIAS collection because the other agencies were merged into the United Hias Service.) Permission to see a case file is usually needed from HIAS and is provided only for an individual's own file or for a very special reason.

    d. HIAS Index Cards, 1909-1979: HIAS index cards are available at YIVO in three series of films. See "HIAS (HEBREW IMMIGRANT AID SOCIETY), LOCATION DEPARTMENT" for a description of the information contained in these index cards.

        i.   Arrival index Cards (approx. 110 reels), 1909-1949
        ii. Master Index Cards (6 reels), 1950-1979
        iii. Joint Distribution Committee (JDC) Index (6 reels), post-WWII

    e. Photographs Relating to HIAS: These are mainly of the Ellis Island Bureau, HIAS offices, citizenship classes, etc. rather than of individuals. Individuals in photographs are not identified.

3. JDC (American Jewish Joint Distribution Committee) Records [RG 335]: Includes the records of the JDC Landsmanshaftn Department. Many of these societies were formed in response to a particular disaster (such as a pogrom) and worked closely with the JDC to provide disaster relief. The records are arranged by town in two series: (1) 1937-1939; (2) post-1945. See also "AMERICAN JEWISH JOINT DISTRIBUTION COMMITTEE."

4. Records of Vaad Hayeshivot [RG 25]: This was an office in Vilna, Lithuania, that arranged for financial support of 70 yeshivot and their students throughout Lithuania. It had contact with about 350 towns that sent students to the yeshivot. The correspondence, written in Yiddish script, is mainly from the 1920s and 1930s.

5. <u>Territorial Photo Collection</u>: YIVO's photographs of life in Eastern Europe include:

   a. <u>The Polish Collection</u>: For purposes of this collection, "Poland" is defined as those areas that were politically part of Poland between 1919 and 1939.

      i. "Poland" photographs between 1864 and 1939 are under the curatorship of Lucjan Dobroszycki. An appointment with Dr. Dobroszycki is necessary to research this collection.

      ii. "Poland" photographs taken after 1945 are available in the Archives.

   b. <u>The Russian/Soviet Union Collection</u>: YIVO has been adding photographs in this area as part of a special project. The collection is divided into two main parts with different Finding Aids (see below) but both are available in the Archives.

      i. "Russia I" includes all photographs that were in YIVO's collection prior to the inception of the special project.

      ii. "Russia II" are those photographs that were collected for the new project.

   c. There are also photographs of Jewish life in other European countries and the United States, e.g. Jewish agricultural settlements, immigration period, labor movement, etc.

   d. <u>The Videodisc Project</u>: YIVO has close to 100,000 photos, some 17,000 of which are original prints from pre-war Europe which are stored on videodisc. This project includes photos from the Polish and Russian Collections (described above), and the Baltic States, Hungary and Rumania. Catalog descriptions can be displayed following each frame.

   e. <u>The Slide Bank</u>: The Archives has a large slide collection of images of Eastern Europe, religious artifacts, synagogues, and scenes of towns.

6. <u>French Holocaust Archives</u>: Contains over 200,000 documents including the full records of the French Judenrat [RG 210]; the Kehiles Hahareydim [RG 340], the underground Lubavitch children's rescue project in France; and Rue Amelot [RG 343], another underground rescue agency. The records include lists of people in camps and people receiving assistance.

7. <u>Collection on Genealogy and Family History</u>: The following names, taken from the card catalog, represent genealogies and family histories in the Archives. Where available, the town, country or time period covered by the collection is shown:

Abramoff, Samuel (Vasilkov, Bialystok)
Albert, Ruth
Bendovid, Morton and Anna (Kremenchug, Brudne)
Buck, Miriam
Cantor, Max
Cohen, Abraham (1839)
Craig, Margrit L.
Dall (Yoniskas, Lithuania)
Dunkelman, David
Edelman, Hannah
Effron, Jacob (Kharkov)
Eisenberg, Samuel and Hershl
Fehl, Gertrude
Fichtner (Zloczow)
Fishman, Samuel (Kishinev)
Fried
Friederike, Meyer
Friedkas, Joseph (Vienna, Lwow, Pinsk, Czernowitz)
Getzel, Eliokum
Gildesgame, Leon L.
Goichberg-Greenberg (Russia, England, US, 1910/20)
Goldman, Moshe
Goldnadel, M. (Zivolen)
Gorbulov, Khayim

Greenberg, Jacob
Grenadier, Israel (Uman district, Kiev)
Grossgott, Sy
Hadra, Edmund/Josefa Rubin (1943)
Halevi (Olszanica)
Henigson, Abraham (Suwalki)
Herbst, Sydney (Sedziszow)
Herbstein, Regina
Herz, Rosel
Hoffman, Frances B.
Holtz, Zalmen (Skierniewice)
Kalnitsky, Mini (Russia)
Kagan, Khane, Ziml (Vilna, Lininetz, Slovetchne)
Kaplan, Moshe
Klein, Elaine (Zidok, Lithuania, 1920/30)
Kling, Henry
Krarastan, Abraham
Kussy and Abeles families
Kweskin, Sam (Vilkija)
Lager, Lafzitsky, Lagrzitski families
Leanid, Gan (Korsk)
Lederman
Levine, Benjamin
Lipshitz, B. (1886)
Lourie, Anton/Landau, Alfred

Lowensohn, Amalia
Mendelson, Herman/Tsvi (1906-1967)
Minkin, Yehuda (1920-1940)
Morgenstern, Moshe (Wlodawa, 1937)
Myslobodsky (Bialystok, Sluck)
Nagel/Nogelberg, Ivan (Rohatyn, Galicia)
Nelkin, Edna and Morton, Telechin family
Oshrin, Joyce Schneider, Szeynersnayer family
Ostroff, Shmuel and Leah
Poliakoff, Michael (Russia)
Porter, Max
Rabinowicz, M. (Brzostowice, 1888, 1892)
Rappaport, Sam
Rassas, Abraham (Konotop, Russia, 1885)
Reiser, Lea
Resnick, Moshe (1896)
Richter (Zbaraz, Poland, 1906)
Rabbiner, Lillian and Delatiner, Debra: photos of Moshe Cyna from Lodz and Mendel Cina of Glasgow; Ida Kapilow family (Minsk, 1928)

131

Ring, Jacob and Lovinsohn, Rosa
Rosler, Solomon & Bayla (1914-1947)
Rosenberg, Rywka (Minsk, 1936)
Safier, Israel and Ollda Serka Safier (1872)
Salamanov-Rabinov, Khayim (Mogilev, Stary)
Schuster, Wolf (Biala Podolska, 1933)
Segal, Phillip (Poland, 1913-1960)
Shapiro, Lillian (1895-1976)
Spivack
Spiwack, Miriam (Talin, Estonia, 1920s, 1930s)

Sutro, Samuel (The Hague, 1930-1941)
Taub/Terkeltaub (Poland, Hungary, 1901-1936)
Taussig, Harry
Taylor, Libby (Pinsk, 1930s)
Teitelbaum, Meyer (Nikolayev, Voznesink, Ukraine, 1872-1910)
Tzitlenk, Nochomov (Niezhin, Russia, 1901)
Uttal
Volarsky, A. (Mlava, 1920s, 1930s)
Vordren
Vulcan, P. and Finkelstein family (Otwock, Poland)

Wayman, Samuel (Warsaw Ghetto, Soberoa. Palestine, 1925-1947)
Weinshel, Shmuel-Pesach (Uscilvy, Wolhynia, 1900-1923)
Weinstock, Bennett
Wiesenfeld, Leon (Rzeszow, Poland, 1920s, 1930s)
Winik, Doris (Pinsk, Domatchevo, 1920s)
Witkin-Kaufman, Laura (Slutsk)
Yahuda, Abraham Shalom (Lisbon, 1904-1922)
Zalzman, Pinchask, Yechiel, and Chava
Zucker, Pinchas

8. Collection of Autobiographies [RG 102]: Includes 350 autobiographies (mostly in Yiddish) prepared by immigrants in response to a YIVO-sponsored contest in 1942. The contestants describe why they left Europe and what they accomplished in America. Family backgrounds are included.

9. National Desertion Bureau [RG 297]: This New York-based organization assisted Jewish families in which a parent had deserted, by attempting to locate the parent. The collection covers roughly 25,000 families from the 1920s to the 1950s. See "Restrictions on Use."

10. Records of Displaced Persons (DP) Camps and Centers [RG 294]: Some 300,000 pages including correspondence, minutes of meetings, leaflets and posters on Displaced Persons Camps have been placed on microfilm. The documents show how survivors of the war ran their daily affairs as they were relocated in dozens of DP camps in Germany, Austria and Italy. Lists of people are occasionally included. The collection includes material on those camps that were under the supervision of the American Army and agencies established by the United Nations.

11. Hebrew Technical Institute [RG 754]: Includes detailed alumni career records of the oldest vocational school for Jewish boys in New York City. The career of each individual student was recorded as he moved from position to position. The records include annual reports and catalogs (9 vols.); alumni career records, class years, 1886-1939 (13 vols.); class standing records, 1884-1939 (34 vols.); and roll books, mainly 1896-1939 (27 vols).

12. Records of the Jewish Community Council of Minsk, 1825-1921 [RG 12]: This collection contains fragmentary registers of births, marriages, and deaths. The records are hand-written in Cyrillic.

13. Records of Lithuanian Jewish Communities, 1844-1940 [RG 2]: These are mainly community records, 1919-1924, such as minutes of council meetings about tax collections or elections in those towns that were part of the independent Republic of Lithuania. Most of the material in the collection was generated by the Ministry of Jewish Affairs and is in Yiddish or Lithuanian.

14. Records of Jewish Communities of Ostrowo [RG 13], Krotoschin [RG 14], and Briesen [RG 15].

15. Borenstein-Eisenberg Collection on Early Jewish Migration [RG 406] has a few passenger lists from the late 1880s and early 1890s.

16. Tcherikower Archive [RG 80-89]: Contains miscellaneous records on Jewish life in the Ukraine and includes lists of victims of Ukrainian pogroms. Thorough knowledge of Yiddish and Russian script is required to use this collection.

17. Monika Krajewska Photo Collection [RG 1137]: Exhibit prints and contact sheets of photos, 1974-1986, taken in preparation for Monika Krajewska's book on Polish cemeteries, *Czas Kamieni* [Time of Stones], Warsaw, 1982 (available in the NEW YORK PUBLIC LIBRARY, JEWISH DIVISION in English. The collection includes photos of tombstones in almost 100 cemeteries; an article about the Jewish cemetery in Sieniawa written in September 1982 (Polish); and information and photographs of some synagogues.

Finding Aids:

General Archival Collections: Although the Archives staff is very helpful (and so knowledgeable that they often can tell what is available without resorting to finding aids), there is usually only one or, at most, two people on duty. While the finding aids are complicated, research will progress much faster if you understand them:

There are three levels of finding aids in the Archives:

Summary Guide, in Record Group (RG) sequence, lists all collections by title and inclusive dates.

RG Description Sheets: These are contained in black volumes on open shelves. The sheets are arranged by RG number. They contain further information about each collection and usually indicate whether it is inventoried.

Inventories: These are folder-by-folder descriptions of collections. Several hundred of the more than 1,100 collections have inventories. Not all collections have inventories.

These finding aids are not entirely up-to-date. YIVO is always acquiring new material and not all of it has been cataloged.

1. The Landsmanshaftn Archive: YIVO has a published volume, *A Guide to YIVO's Landsmanshaftn Archive,* to assist in locating these records. The *Guide* is arranged alphabetically by place name for locality-based societies and alphabetically by society name for non-locality-based societies (mutual aid societies based on occupation, family circles and synagogue benevolent societies).

2. HIAS Collection: The inventory for "The United HIAS Service Archive" is described in over 80 pages in a looseleaf notebook. There are also individual inventories to several subgroups of HIAS collections. The inventory to the HIAS Ellis Island Records indicates on which reel alphabet groups (e.g. "A to Br", "Li to NA") can be found. The index for HIAS Case Files is outlined above under HIAS Index Cards. See "HIAS (HEBREW IMMIGRANT AID SOCIETY), LOCATION DEPARTMENT" for a detailed description of these indexes. An explanation of the HIAS Case Name Indexing (Soundex) system is included in Appendix C. There is no name index for cases mentioned in HIAS Office and Organizational Files.

4. JDC Records: There is an inventory of files which is arranged by locality.

5. Records of Vaad Hayeshivot: The inventory is arranged by town.

6. Territorial Photo Collection: The inventory, which does not include Russia II, is arranged alphabetically by country and locality. Russia II can be accessed by name of donor only.

   It is anticipated that a cross-index will be available for the Videodisc Project arranged by primary geographic listing, the time the photo was taken, proper names, common nouns and every word in the description.

7. French Holocaust Archives: There are no name or locality indexes. There are, however, written inventories for these collections.

8. Collection on Genealogy and Family History: An index card file is available. The current entries are listed above under "Description of Resources."

9. Collection of Autobiographies: The collection is indexed alphabetically in a card file.

10. National Desertion Bureau: There is no finding aid to this collection at YIVO. The collection is not arranged alphabetically. Contact the Family Location and Legal Services Division, Jewish Board of Family and Children's Services, Inc., 235 Park Avenue South, New York, NY 10003, (212) 460-0900. This agency has an alphabetical card index to these records.

11. Records of DP Camps and Centers: In order to find anything useful about an individual, the researcher must know the name or location of the camp where the individual was. The collection is subdivided by country. (It is not arranged by surname.) The inventory reflects the administrative departments of the camp organizations.

12. <u>Hebrew Technical Institute</u>: There is an inventory which specifies the nature of the files and reflects the organizational structure of the school. There is no name index.

13. <u>Records of the Jewish Community Council of Minsk</u>: There is a written inventory (in Yiddish), arranged in chronological order.

14. <u>Records of Lithuanian Jewish Communities</u>: The inventory is arranged alphabetically by name of town.

15. <u>Records of Jewish Communities of Ostrowo, Krotoschin and Briesen</u>: The finding guide describes the nature of each file but does not include any names.

16. <u>Borenstein-Eisenberg Collection</u> (RG 406): There is a detailed inventory of the files and a description of the contents.

17. <u>Tcherikower Archive</u> (RG 80-89): The inventory is not arranged in any particular order. It is in handwritten Yiddish and sometimes Russian script.

18. <u>Monika Krajewska Photo Collection</u>: The collection is not indexed. The location of the cemetery is noted on the back of the photos.

Description of Facility:

The Archives Reading Room is located on the second floor. The Archives itself is in the basement. Seating is available for 10-12 researchers. All material must be requested. Two staff persons are available to assist researchers. There is one microfilm reader.

Fees/Copies:

There are two photocopy machines ($.15 per page), one in the Archives and one in the Library. Researchers can become members of YIVO by contributing $30 for individuals, $50 for families and up to $1,000 for Patrons. Members receive Newsletters, annual publications and free or discounted admission to events at YIVO. Copies of *A Guide to YIVO's Landsmanshaftn Archive* can be purchased at $7.95 for members and $9.95 for non-members.

YIVO will make copies of photographs, to be mailed to researchers, for $18 per photo. These copies will be made only for personal use. If the researcher intends to publish them, permission is necessary from YIVO and there is an additional publication charge of $25 per photo.

Restrictions on Use:

<u>Photo Archives</u>: In order to see the Polish photo collection, 1864-1939, an appointment is necessary with Dr. Lucjan Dobroszycki.

<u>National Desertion Bureau</u> records are for scholars who use them for random statistical purposes. Access to these files for other purposes can only be obtained through the donor, the Jewish Board of Family and Children's Services.

<u>HIAS Collection</u>: Since YIVO does not have a microfilm reader with printer capability, researchers can request a positive copy of an index card from HIAS.

Permission to view the HIAS case files must be obtained from HIAS.

<u>Monika Krajewska Photo Collection</u>: Photos can be reproduced but credits have to be given by anyone who plans to use them as source material in his/her own research.

<u>Other</u>: There may be some restrictions on materials permitted to be photocopied.

YIVO INSTITUTE FOR JEWISH RESEARCH
LIBRARY

Facility Director:	Zachary Baker, Head Librarian
	Stanley Bergman, Administrative Librarian (and genealogical specialist)
	Dina Abramowicz, Reference Librarian
Address:	1048 Fifth Avenue
	New York, NY 10028
	(Cross Street: Entrance is on East 86th Street)

Phone Number, Hours of Operation, Closest Public Transportation, Directions, Researchers, please be aware, and Fees/Copies:

See "YIVO INSTITUTE FOR JEWISH RESEARCH - ARCHIVES."

Description of Resources:

For the genealogical researcher, the following materials are of interest (call numbers are in brackets):

1. Memorial or Yizkor Books: YIVO has one of the most extensive collections in the world of memorial books. Included are both the better-known Yizkor books commemorating communities destroyed by the Nazis and the lesser-known books written after World War I, about towns desecrated by pogroms. Call numbers for YIVO's Yizkor books (post-WWII) are included in Appendix A. Most Yizkor books are in Hebrew and/or Yiddish. Some contain small sections in English. About 80% of the books do not have indexes.

2. Geographical material: YIVO has many items that will help locate small towns, verify the spelling of their names, and give descriptions of the towns or the areas in which they are located. Examples are:

   a. *Slownik Geograficzny* [Polish Gazetteer]. 1885-1891. (Polish). A 16-volume gazetteer that gives the name of the town, its population, what district it belongs to, etc. [DK403 S5]

   b. *Evreiskaia Entsiklopediia* [Jewish Encyclopedia]. St. Petersburg, 1906-1913. (Russian). Contains entries about cities and many small towns in Russia. [DS102.8 E7]

   c. *Yahadut Lita* [Lithuanian Jewry]. 4 vols., 1959-1984. (Hebrew). Volume 3 includes descriptions of these communities and, in some cases, photographs of them. [DS135 L5 Y3]

   d. *Pinkas Ha-kehillot* [An encyclopedia of communities]. 1969- . (Hebrew). There is a volume on each of the following: Rumania (2 vols.), Hungary, Bavaria, Poland (Lodz region), Poland (Eastern Galicia), Poland (Western Galicia) and Holland. (See Yizkor Book list, Appendix A.)

   e. Books on Synagogues, such as *Wooden Synagogues* by M. and K. Piechotka [12/51537], often contain both photographs of the synagogues and descriptions of the town they were in.

   f. Old Maps: YIVO has maps and atlases of Poland from the period between the two World Wars.

3. Rabbinic Material: These sources may be used both to trace rabbinic ancestors and to gather information about the religious heritage of the towns ancestors were from. Among these sources are:

   Wunder, Meir. *Meorei Galicia* [Encyclopedia of Galician Rabbis and Scholars]. 1978- . (Hebrew). Includes biographical sketches of rabbis and sometimes their family trees. Three volumes in this series have been published to date. [BM750 W8]

   Friedmann, Nathan Zebi. *Otzar Harabanim* [Rabbis' Encyclopedia]. 1975. (Hebrew). Contains about 20,000 entries, alphabetized by the rabbi's first name. Gives the rabbi's year of birth or death, father, son or son-in-law, a general description of who the rabbi was, and a list of his works. [BM750 F7]

Gottlieb, Samuel Noah. *Ohole-Shem*. 1912. (Hebrew). List of rabbis in Eastern Europe and the United States in 1912. [BM750 G6]

Alfasi, Yitshak. *He-hasidut*. 1974. (Hebrew). Contains information on Hasidic rabbis from the Ba'al Shem Tov to the present and has an index of towns and an index of rabbis (by their first names). [BM198 A5]

4. Holocaust Sources: YIVO's library contains an important collection of material relating to the Holocaust in addition to the Yizkor books noted above. For example:

Blackbook of Localities Whose Jewish Population Was Extinguished by the Nazis. 1965. Published by Yad Vashem. (English). Lists communities in the Soviet Union and Europe and gives the Jewish population for each town. The sections on Poland and Germany are arranged by province. [D810 J4 Y2]

Gedenkbuch: Opfer der Verfolgung der Juden, 1933-1945. Koblenz: Bundesarchiv, 1985. 2 vols. This book lists all Jews of Germany who perished, with birth place, how they died and where; appendix gives data on each concentration camp. [9/80818]

Guide to Unpublished Materials of the Holocaust Period. 1970- . (YIVO has vol. 1-5). A series of books that list, by town, original documents in the Yad Vashem archives. An entry might include documents relating to deportations, war criminals, refugees, orphanages, etc. Researchers can write to Yad Vashem to determine the cost of copying documents. [D810 J4 G8]

Klarsfeld, Serge. *Le Mémorial de la Déportation des Juifs de France*. 1978. (French). English ed.: *Memorial to the Jews Deported from France, 1942-1944*. 1983. Lists transports of Jews to concentration camps, including both those that originated in France and those that passed through France. Information relating to about 90 transports is given. The names of victims are listed alphabetically for each transport and, when known, the birth date and place of birth are included. Also given are the number of people who survived each transport and its destination. YIVO has similar books for other countries, such as Belgium and Germany. [9/76780-French; 9/79227-English]

Register of Jewish Survivors in Poland. 1945. Like Yad Vashem and the International Tracing Service, YIVO has a collection of lists giving the names of survivors, the places where they registered, and (when known) their ages. Among the lists in YIVO's collection, in addition to Poland, are those for Warsaw, Riga, Lublin, Italy, and Yugoslavia. [3/22766A]

5. Name Indexes

Lifschutz, Eziekiel, Compiler. *Bibliography of American and Canadian Jewish Memoirs and Autobiographies in Yiddish, Hebrew and English*. New York, 1970. [E36 L5]

Sack, Sallyann and Suzan F. Wynne. *The Russian Consular Records Index and Catalog*. 1987. [CS856 J4 S23]

Zubatsky, David S. and Irwin M. Berent. *Jewish Genealogy: A Source Book of Family Histories and Genealogies*. 1984. [Z6374 B5 Z79]

6. Miscellaneous Sources: Includes much material describing Jewish life in Eastern Europe. Among items of interest are memoirs, historical commentaries, histories of communities, and fiction that describes Jewish life and culture.

Finding Aids:

The Library's holdings are cataloged according to the language in which the material is written. As a result, there are separate catalogs for materials in the Latin alphabet, the Cyrillic alphabet, the Hebrew language, the Yiddish language and for a special collection of rabbinical books (mostly in Hebrew). The catalogs are arranged by author and title though titles are not always indexed. This makes it difficult to locate a book where the title is known but the author is not.

In addition, the Library has one numerically classified subject catalog which includes, in one sequence, works found in the four separate author-title catalogs. The Library has an innovative finding aid to the English (and Yiddish) catalogs which refers English-speaking researchers to the subject catalog: Green index cards have been added to both the English and Yiddish catalogs, directing readers to relevant classifications in the subject catalog.

The only materials not in the subject catalog are the holdings that were part of the original collection of rabbinica rescued from Vilna during WWII. To locate books in this collection, consult the librarian.

Description of Facility:

The Library is located on the second floor. Climb one flight up the staircase (or take the elevator). Turn left for the entrance to the Library. All reference works are on open shelves in the reading room. Most materials, however, are in closed stacks and must be requested. Seating is available for 8-10 researchers. There are 3 staff persons available to assist researchers. The Library has one microfilm reader.

Fees/Copies:

There is one photocopy machine in the Library. Copies cost $.15 per page ($.25 per page if copied by staff).

Restrictions on Use:

No materials can be borrowed. Only materials in good condition can be photocopied.

YOUNG MEN'S & YOUNG WOMEN'S HEBREW ASSOCIATION (92nd STREET "Y") ARCHIVES

Facility Director: Steven W. Siegel, Library Director and Archivist

Address: 1395 Lexington Avenue
New York, NY 10128

(Cross Streets: East 91st and 92nd Streets)

Phone Number: (212) 415-5542

Hours of Operation:

Sunday to Friday: by appointment only
Closed Saturday, Jewish and legal holidays.

Closest Public Transportation:

Subway: 4, 5 (express) or 6 (local) to 86th Street

Bus: M101 or M102 to Lexington Avenue and 92nd Street (southbound)
or 3rd Avenue and 91st Street (northbound)
M18 to 86th Street and Lexington Avenue (crosstown)
M19 to 96th Street and Lexington Avenue (crosstown)

Directions:

Take the #4, #5 (express) or #6 (local) train to the 86th Street station. Go up the staircase to the left as you exit the station. Walk north on Lexington Avenue to 92nd Street. The Archives is located on the 2nd floor in the Library.

Description of Resources:

The 92nd Street YM-YWHA is the oldest Jewish community center in North America in continuous existence. It was founded in 1874 as the Young Men's Hebrew Association. The Archives at the 92nd Street Y holds records of the following organizations:

    Young Men's Hebrew Association (YMHA), 1874-1945, and its successor,
    Young Men's and Young Women's Hebrew Association (YM-YWHA), 1945 to date
    Young Women's Hebrew Association (YWHA), 1902-1945
    Clara de Hirsch Home for Working Girls, 1897-1962
    Surprise Lake Camp of the Educational Alliance and YMHA, 1902-1976
    Holy Society of the City of New York, 1849-1968

The records are arranged in record groups and sub-groups according to their organizational and departmental provenance, and in part by physical type (oral histories and memoirs; printed materials; audiovisual materials; art, artifacts and memorabilia).

Of particular interest to genealogists are the following materials:

1.   <u>YMHA Employment Department</u>

    Employer's ledgers, 1905-1928, and applicants' registers, 1911-1930, documenting the placement of thousands of young men with employers in New York City. Includes data about the applicants' backgrounds and job histories. (Arranged chronologically; no name index.)

    Applicant registration forms, 1930-1934, for approximately 1,200 men with last names Babbit to Bixgorin, Haar to Hymowitz, Rosanes to Ryvicker and Smith (Irving) to Sussman. Includes detailed personal histories and usually a photograph. (Arranged alphabetically.)

2. YMHA Medical Department

Physical examination records, September 1904 to February 1905 for 198 men. Includes some family information. (Arranged chronologically; no name index.)

Medical record cards, 1930-1936, for approximately 3,800 men. Includes family and medical history. (Arranged alphabetically.)

3. YMHA and YM-YWHA Membership Department

Membership registers, 1882-1957. Includes name and address only. (Arranged chronologically; no name index.)

Published membership lists, 1886 and 1896-1916. Includes name and address only. (Arranged alphabetically by membership category.)

Membership record cards, 1900-1930, for approximately 24,000 men and boys. Includes name, address, other personal information and dates of membership. (Arranged alphabetically by category, i.e. older men, younger men, schoolboys.)

Membership record cards, 1930-1972, for tens of thousands of men and women. (Not completely arranged.)

4. YMHA Military and Veterans Activities

Personal information on, and photographs of, members in military service during World War II. (Arranged alphabetically.)

5. YMHA and YM-YWHA Residence Department (for young adults, 18 to 26)

Application cards, 1930-1958, for approximately 4,000 male residents, and 1930-1932, for approximately 500 men who applied for residence but did not move in.

Application cards, 1950-1958, for approximately 1,000 female residents (with last names Aaronson to Schwenkert).

Application forms, 1959-1968, for approximately 2,000 male and female residents.

Residents' registration cards, 1968-1980, for approximately 2,500 men and women.

NOTE: Each series of records is arranged alphabetically and contains personal and family information. Records since 1959 are restricted.

6. Young Women's Hebrew Association Residence

Residents' card files, 1920-1934, 1934-1942 and 1942-1950. Includes personal and family information. (Arranged alphabetically within each set of years.)

7. Clara de Hirsch Home for Working Girls

Record of applications, 1897-1900, and register of residents, 1897-1899. Includes personal information. (Arranged chronologically with name indexes.)

Residence applications, 1954-1960. Includes personal and family information. (Arranged by year of departure from the Home. No name index.)

8. Holy Society of the City of New York (one of the earliest non-synagogue Jewish benevolent societies to be incorporated in New York City. It was founded in 1846 and dissolved in 1968.)

Biographical data about members, c.1900-1930. (Arranged alphabetically).

Burial permits, 1872-1927, for members interred in the Society's plot in Washington Cemetery, Brooklyn. (Arranged chronologically. No name index.)

Cemetery maps for the Society's plot.

Finding Aids:

In addition to those described above, the Archives has inventories and descriptions of each record group.

Description of Facility:

Archival materials are consulted in the Library on the 2nd floor. Seating is available for 30 researchers.

Fees/Copies:

The Library has one photocopy machine. The cost of a copy is $.15 per page.

Restrictions on Use:

The bulk of the records in the Archives may be used without restriction, although certain record series have restrictions to protect the privacy of individuals.

THE BRONX

BOARD OF ELECTIONS
BRONX BOROUGH OFFICE

Facility Director:	Kay Amer, Chief Clerk
Address:	1780 Grand Concourse Bronx, NY 10457
	(Cross Street: Eastburn Avenue)
Phone Number:	(212) 299-9017

Hours of Operation:

Monday to Friday: 9:00 am to 5:00 pm
Closed Saturday, Sunday and legal holidays.

Closest Public Transportation:

Subway: C or D to 174th-175th Street

Bus: Bx1 or Bx2 to 175th Street and Grand Concourse
               Bx36 to Tremont Avenue and the east side of the Grand Concourse

Directions:

Take the C or D train to the 174th-175th Street station. Exit toward the <u>north</u> end (3rd car from front) of the station. Exit to the <u>east</u> side of the Grand Concourse (to the right as one faces the token booth).

Description of Resources:

The Bronx office has voter registration records from 1897 to the present. Records, 1957-1982, are on microfilm. Records from 1983 to the present, including cancelled records, are on "buff" cards. Many of these registration forms provide the date of naturalization and the court in which naturalized. See "Restrictions on Use."

Finding Aids:

Current registrations are in computer printouts arranged alphabetically by surname. These printouts list the AD/ED of the voter. With the AD/ED information, a researcher can locate the current records which are arranged in binders by AD/ED and then alphabetically by surname. Pre-1983 records are organized by year, Assembly/Election District (AD/ED) and the first initial of the surname. To locate cancelled records, both the name and address are needed.

Description of Facility:

This NYC government office is on the Grand Concourse level of the building. A receptionist is available to take inquiries. Staff conduct the search of records.

Fees/Copies:

Mail requests are accepted for a $3 fee (certified check or money order payable to the Board of Elections, City of New York). This covers a search for one name and one year. Each additional name and/or year is $3. No refund is made if the record is not found. Photocopies can be made of buff cards for the years available. Transcripts are made from the microfilm. Provide the full name at registration, address where residing at the time of registration, and date of birth or age. Use the address in a Presidential election year when the individual was more likely to have voted.

Restrictions on Use:

Unlike the Board of Elections Borough Offices in Manhattan, Queens and Staten Island, researchers visiting this office cannot view old records directly. Only current registrations can be viewed by the public. Staff will conduct the search and provide a copy for the $3 fee.

THE BRONX COUNTY HISTORICAL SOCIETY
THEODORE KAZIMIROFF RESEARCH LIBRARY AND ARCHIVES

Facility Director: Dr. Gary Hermalyn, Executive Director

Address: 3309 Bainbridge Avenue
Bronx, NY 10467

(Cross Streets: East 208th and East 210th Streets)

Phone Number: (212) 881-8900

Hours of Operation:

Monday to Friday: 9:00 am to 5:00 pm (by appointment only)
Closed Saturday, Sunday and legal holidays.

Closest Public Transportation:

Subway: D to 205th Street
4 to Mosholu Parkway

Bus: Bx10, Bx16, Bx28, Bx30 or Bx34 to Bainbridge Avenue and East 208th or 210th Street
Westchester #20 to Jerome Avenue and 210th Street

Directions:

Take the D train to the 205th Street station (last stop). Exit at the <u>south</u> end of the station. Go up the escalator (<u>not</u> the ramp). Turn right at the turnstile and go up the stairs to the street. Walk straight ahead for 2 1/2 blocks (same side of the street) until you see the 2-story brick building with a green awning marked "The Bronx County Historical Society."

Description of Resources:

The Society, founded in 1968, has a collection of books, photographs, manuscripts, newspapers and pamphlets about the Bronx. The following are some of the items of interest to genealogists:

1.   <u>Photographs</u>: over 15,000 photographs showing a chronological progression of the Bronx from the 1860s to the present; and over 1,500 different post cards of Bronx scenes. Photographs of buildings are arranged in a catalog by street and corner.

2.   <u>Newspaper Clippings</u>: vertical files containing news clippings from local Bronx newspapers. Clippings are about Bronx neighborhoods as well as people from the Bronx.

3.   <u>Bronx Newspapers</u>: The following local papers are available. One year is retained by the Library, and the remainder is in the Archives:

Bronx Beat, 1982 to the present (selected issues)
Bronx Chronicle, 1975-1976 (selected issues)
Bronx Home News, 1909-1948
Bronx News, 1975-1986, 1988
Bronx Press Review, 1955 to the present (selected issues)
City Island News (now *Island Current*), 1953 to the present
Co-op City Times, 1970 to the present (selected issues)
Fordham News Express, 1985 to the present (selected issues)
Journal News, 1964-1976 (selected issues)
Mosholu Parkway Press, 1976-1977 (selected issues)
Parkchester News, 1973-1978 (selected issues)
Parkchester Press Review, 1948-1949 (selected issues)

Parkway News, 1973-1975 (selected issues), 1976-1978
Riverdale Press, 1950-1981

4. Books: approximately 1,000 books about the Bronx and its people as well as information on other parts of New York City. Examples are:

    Brown, Martin B. *The Brown Book: A Biographical Record of Public Officials of the City of New York for 1898-1899.* 1899. [Contains biographical sketches and photos of city officials].

    Wells, James L., Louis F. Haffen and Josiah A. Briggs. *The Bronx and Its People.* 4 vols., 1927.

5. Audio and Video Tapes: videotapes of the Society's lectures, forums and walking tours since 1985. In addition, films for the Bronx history shows aired on Channel 25, "Bronx Faces and Places," and tapes of the oral history radio program "Out of the Past."

6. *Trow's New York City Directories* (include Manhattan and part or all of the Bronx), 1850-1913, 1917 and 1918; and the 1907 Business Directory. These original volumes are in poor condition (brittle pages).

7. Fire and Police Department Records: Fire Department blotters (early 1900s); Police Department records (1866-1912) showing arrests each day.

Finding Aids:

The Library has a catalog which is not open to the public. Materials under subject headings such as "Personalities," "Communities" and "Bronx Business" may be useful to genealogists.

Description of Facility:

The Reading Room is open to the public. Four researchers can be accommodated at a time at one table. There is one microfilm reader/printer available to the public for viewing the *Bronx Home News.*

Fees/Copies:

The staff will photocopy materials at $.25 per page. Copies from the microfilm reader/printer are $.35 per page. Fees for duplicating photographs range from $5 for a slide to $25 for photographs without negatives. In addition, publications of the Society are for sale, such as:

    Hermalyn, Gary, Janet Butler and Laura Tosi. *Genealogy of The Bronx: An Annotated Guide to Sources of Information.* 1986. ($5)

    Di Brino, Nicholas. *History of the Morris Park Racecourse and the Morris Family.* 1977. ($10)

    McNamara, John. *History in Asphalt: The Origin of Bronx Street and Place Names.* 1984. ($34)

Annual membership dues start at $15 for students and senior citizens, $20 for an individual, and $25 for a family. Members receive a subscription to the semi-annual *The Bronx County Historical Society Journal,* *The Bronx Historian* newsletter and invitations to historical tours, lectures and educational programs.

Restrictions on Use:

Some of the material listed above, including newspapers more than one year old, are stored in another building and are not readily accessible. Call at least 2 days in advance to order them.

Materials do not circulate.

CITY CLERK'S OFFICE - BRONX
MARRIAGE LICENSE BUREAU

Facility Director: Walter Curtis, Borough Administrator

Address: 1780 Grand Concourse, 2nd floor
Bronx, NY 10457

(Cross Street: Eastburn Avenue)

Mail Address: Add "Attention: Marriage Record Unit" to lower left corner of the envelope.

Phone Number: (212) 731-2277

Hours of Operation:

Monday to Friday: 9:00 am to 4:00 pm
Closed Saturday, Sunday and legal holidays.

Closest Public Transportation and Directions:

See "BOARD OF ELECTIONS - BRONX."

Description of Resources:

Bronx City Clerk's Office marriage records are available from 1914.

The City Clerk's Office records for the Bronx, 1908-1913, are located in the CITY CLERK'S OFFICE - MANHATTAN. (In 1898, the Bronx became a separate Borough, and in 1914 it became a separate County.) See "CITY CLERK'S OFFICE - MANHATTAN" for a more detailed description of these records.

NOTE: The Bronx Office currently has marriage records from 1898 to the present. Three independent sets of records exist for the period 1914-1937, when the City Clerk's Office, the NYC Health Department and the County Clerk's Office maintained marriage records. The Health Department records, 1898-1937, and County Clerk's records, 1914-1937, are being accessioned by the MUNICIPAL ARCHIVES. See "NEW YORK CITY DEPARTMENT OF RECORDS AND INFORMATION SERVICES - MUNICIPAL ARCHIVES" for these and earlier Bronx marriage records.

Original marriage records for eastern Bronx (then part of Westchester County), 1880-1895, are also on file at the NEW YORK STATE HEALTH DEPARTMENT in Albany.

Finding Aids:

The bride/groom indexes for records maintained by the City Clerk from 1914 to the present are in the same format as in the Manhattan Office. See "CITY CLERK'S OFFICE - MANHATTAN."

Description of Facility:

The Office is on the second floor, i.e. one flight up from the Grand Concourse level. Seating is available for 2 people. There are six staff persons who assist the public.

Fees/Copies and Restrictions on Use:

See "CITY CLERK'S OFFICE - MANHATTAN."

CITY REGISTER'S OFFICE
BRONX

Facility Director: Patricia Siciliano, Deputy City Register

Address: 1932 Arthur Avenue
Bronx, NY 10457

(Cross Street: East Tremont Avenue)

Phone Number: (212) 579-6821 (Room 301)
(212) 579-6830 (Room 201)

Hours of Operation:

Monday to Friday: 9:00 am to 4:00 pm
Closed Saturday, Sunday and legal holidays.

Closest Public Transportation:

Subway: D to Tremont Avenue
          4 to 161st Street/Yankee Stadium

          <u>and</u>

Bus: Bx40 to Arthur and East Tremont Avenues
          Bx15 or Bx55 to 3rd and East Tremont Avenues

Directions:

Take the D train to the Tremont Avenue station. Exit at the <u>north</u> end of the platform. Exit to the <u>east</u> side of the Grand Concourse (to the right when facing the token booth). Walk one short block north to Burnside Avenue and the Grand Concourse. (Do not cross Burnside Avenue.) The Bx40 bus stop is on the corner of Burnside Avenue on the east side of the Concourse. Take the Bx40 bus to Arthur and East Tremont Avenues.

Description of Resources:

This office has real property records (deeds, mortgages, maps) for Bronx County, 1914 to the present, and copies of all records pertaining to land now in Bronx County that was formerly part of New York County, 1874-1914, and formerly part of Westchester County, 1680-1895.

See "CITY REGISTER'S OFFICE, MANHATTAN" for a description of records and block/lot microfiche jackets.

Finding Aids:

This office has indexes for grantors/grantees and mortgagors/mortgagees. Grantor/grantee indexes are arranged alphabetically by the first letter of the surname and chronologically.

For pre-1891 records, researchers can use the grantor/grantee microfilm indexes in the CITY REGISTER'S OFFICE, MANHATTAN or the original indexes in the WESTCHESTER COUNTY ARCHIVES which include Bronx properties.

To trace the ownership of a particular piece of property, the street address or location is needed. Tax block and lot numbers must then be determined. There are several ways to obtain these numbers:

1.   If the building still exists, use the computer index. See "CITY REGISTER'S OFFICE, MANHATTAN" for a description; or,

2.   Use the Real Estate Data Inc. (REDI) directory for the Bronx included in *New York Boroughs* which is available in the NEW YORK PUBLIC LIBRARY, MAP DIVISION. See "CITY REGISTER'S OFFICE, MANHATTAN" for a description of this directory; or,

3. The clerk in Room 300 can provide the block and lot number; or,

4. The researcher can check the maps in Room 201.

Once the block and lot numbers are known, go to the index arranged by block and lot numbers to get the liber and page numbers (or reel and page numbers after 1968) of the instruments filed. The liber and page number is necessary in order to find instruments recorded before 1968. Reel and page numbers are not needed for instruments filed after 1968 if the block/lot jacket is used. See "CITY REGISTER'S OFFICE, MANHATTAN" for a description of block/lot jackets.

To locate Bronx records, 1945 to the present, researchers will soon be able to use one of the four computer terminals in Room 201. The computer can already access information for all NYC boroughs (except Staten Island) from 1982 to the present. See "CITY REGISTER'S OFFICE, MANHATTAN" for more information on this system.

NOTE: There are about 580 Torrens properties in the Bronx. Torrens properties are not included in the computer system. The ledger for these properties, arranged in order of the date of filing, is in the Deputy City Register's office. Torrens files are arranged by block and lot numbers. See "CITY REGISTER'S OFFICE, MANHATTAN" for a description of Torrens properties.

Description of Facility:

This is a New York City government office. Room 201 contains property information, 1930 to the present, as well as 22 microfiche and 8 microfilm readers. The Office has one microfilm reader/printer and one microfiche reader/printer. Room 300 has the older libers. Employees are very busy and cannot help researchers for more than a short time.

The grantor/grantee ledger indexes are stored in different locations around the office (second and third floor) and in the basement. Microfilms are in Room 201.

Fees/Copies and Restrictions on Use:

See "CITY REGISTER'S OFFICE, MANHATTAN." Certified copies of documents can be obtained in Room 301. There is a minimum wait of 24 hours to receive certified copies or copies can be mailed.

CIVIL COURT OF THE CITY OF NEW YORK
BRONX COUNTY

Facility Director: Gerard Duer, Clerk of the County

Address: 851 Grand Concourse
Bronx, NY 10451

(Cross Streets: East 161st Street and Walton Avenue)

Phone Number: (212) 590-3574, 3597

Hours of Operation:

Monday to Friday: 9:00 am to 5:00 pm
Closed Saturday, Sunday and legal holidays.

Closest Public Transportation and Directions:

See "COUNTY CLERK'S OFFICE - STATE SUPREME COURT, BRONX COUNTY."

Description of Resources:

The Civil Court has name change records filed in the Bronx from 1927 to the present.

See also "COUNTY CLERK'S OFFICE - STATE SUPREME COURT, BRONX COUNTY" for name changes recorded in State Supreme Court.

Finding Aids:

The records, 1927-1938, are indexed in ledgers in groups of years by the first letter of the original surname. From 1938 to the present, the index is arranged by both old and new name. Fill out a yellow card to request a file.

Description of Facility:

The indexes are located at Window 6 of the Record Room on the ground level (also known as the basement). The case files are located in a back room of the basement and are retrieved by the staff. See "Restrictions on Use." There is one staff person available to pull files.

Fees/Copies:

Two photocopy machines are available at $.10 per copy. Certified copies of records cost $4 per page.

Restrictions on Use:

Index books, 1927-1984, are available one at a time.

Individual files are difficult to retrieve because the space in which they are stored belongs to the Department of Housing Preservation and Development. Since desks and tables block access to the file cabinets, one or two days notice is required. There is no problem of access to files from 1985 to the present.

COUNTY CLERK'S OFFICE - STATE SUPREME COURT
BRONX COUNTY

Facility Director: Leo Levy, County Clerk

Address: 851 Grand Concourse, Room 118
Bronx, NY 10451

(Cross Streets: East 161st Street and Walton Avenue)

Phone Number: (212) 590-3635 (Naturalizations, Census)
(212) 590-3629 (Name Changes, Business Records)
(212) 590-3637 (Military Discharge Records, Microfilm)
(212) 590-3638 (Court Cases, Matrimonials, Incompetencies)

Hours of Operation:

Monday to Friday: 9:00 am to 4:45 pm
Closed Saturday, Sunday and legal holidays.

Closest Public Transportation:

Subway: C or D to 161st Street/Yankee Stadium
          4 to 161st Street/Yankee Stadium

Bus: Bx1 to Grand Concourse and East 161 Street
      Bx55 (to "Yankee Stadium" only) to 161st Street and River Avenue (last stop)

Directions:

Take the D train to 161st Street-Yankee Stadium station. Exit to <u>Walton Avenue</u> at the <u>north</u> end of the platform. You will emerge diagonally opposite the Court House. Cross East 161st Street and enter the Bronx Supreme Court building through the Walton Avenue entrance. Take the elevator to the first floor.

NOTE: The #4 train can also be used but the station is 2-3 blocks away. Exit at the <u>south</u> end of the platform. Descend the steps to exit at 161st Street and River Avenue. Cross to the south side of 161st Street, and walk uphill (eastward) on 161st Street (passing Gerard Avenue) to Walton Avenue. Turn right to reach the side entrance of the Court House.

Description of Resources:

Bronx County was created in 1914. For earlier records see "COUNTY CLERK'S OFFICE - NEW YORK COUNTY (MANHATTAN)."

1.   <u>New York State Census, 1915 and 1925</u>: original copies of the NYS Census books for the Bronx.

    NOTE: The 1915 and 1925 Census is available also at the NEW YORK STATE EDUCATION DEPARTMENT, OFFICE OF CULTURAL EDUCATION, NEW YORK STATE LIBRARY where copies can be made from microfilm.

2.   <u>Naturalizations</u> filed in State Supreme Court, Bronx County, 1914 to January 1934; and Declarations of Intention, 1914-1952. After January 1934, Bronx residents had to go to U.S. DISTRICT COURT, SOUTHERN DISTRICT to be naturalized.

3.   <u>Court Cases</u> brought against an individual or corporation or actions filed by an individual or corporation, 1914 to the present. Civil cases, 1953-1957, and criminal cases, 1914-1978, are on microfilm. (Microfilming of 1952 and earlier civil cases, and 1979 and later criminal cases, is underway.)

4.   <u>Business Records</u>

    Businesses (Trade Names) and Partnerships, 1914 to the present

Certificates of Incorporation, 1914 to the present. (These include incorporations of synagogues and landsmanshaftn.)
Limited Partnerships, 1920 to the present

5. <u>Military Discharge Records</u>: 1917 to the present, for veterans who filed a copy of their DD 214 form (discharge papers) in this Office. See "Restrictions on Use."

6. <u>Matrimonial Records</u>: 1914 to the present for divorce, separations and annulments brought in State Supreme Court, Bronx County. See "Restrictions on Use."

7. <u>Name Changes</u>: filed by an individual or a business in Supreme Court, Bronx County, 1914 to the present.

8. <u>Incompetency Records and Conservatorships</u>: Incompetency Records involving persons who could not handle their own affairs or persons committed, 1914 to the present; and Conservatorships, 1977 to the present.

9. <u>Surrenders of Children</u>: filed with the County Clerk, 1914 to the present. See "Restrictions on Use."

Finding Aids:

1. <u>Census</u>: Street address is needed to find information. Street maps of the Bronx detailing Assembly/Election Districts (AD/ED) are available for 1915 and 1925. Once the address is located on the map and the AD/ED numbers are found, the AD/ED must be located in the census volumes. Then look for the page with the address and family.

2. <u>Naturalizations</u>: An alphabetical card file for Naturalization Petitions covering all years provides the name, petition number or liber and page numbers.

   Declarations are indexed in a separate alphabetical card file, 1914-1927 and 1927-1952. There is also an index card file labeled "Certificates 1926 to present." These names do not necessarily appear in the index to petitions and should be checked also.

3. <u>Court Cases</u> (including <u>Matrimonials</u>) are indexed in ledgers, <u>Index to Clerk's Minutes</u>, by year and arranged alphabetically by the first two letters of the surname and the first letter of the given name of the plaintiff.

   There are also index cards arranged in groups of years covering Court Cases for the period 1914-1975/76. These cards are arranged alphabetically by name of plaintiff. While the cards are easier to use than the ledgers, the card system is less reliable because some cards are missing.

4. <u>Business Records</u> (except Limited Partnerships) are indexed in card files by type of record and arranged in groups of years and alphabetically by the name of the business. Separate card indexes are available for <u>Businesses and Partnerships</u>, <u>Incorporations</u> and <u>Dissolution of Incorporations</u>. In addition, the Office has a cross reference card index, <u>Persons Conducting Business</u>, for 1938 to the present, which is an index arranged alphabetically by surname of owners of businesses and partnerships on file.

   There is a two-volume ledger index for <u>Limited Partnerships</u>, arranged by year and the first letter of the name of the business.

5. <u>Military Discharge Records</u> are arranged alphabetically in a file by the surname of the veteran. There is no separate index. See "Restrictions on Use."

6. <u>Name Changes</u> for individuals and businesses are indexed together in two card files. A separate index exists for new and old names. Both card files are arranged alphabetically by name.

7. <u>Incompetency Records and Conservatorships</u>: The two-volume ledger index covering both Incompetency Records and Conservatorships is arranged by year and alphabetically by the first letter of the surname. Conservatorships have case numbers beginning with 19000.

Description of Facility:

Naturalization and Census records are located in Room 118M on the mezzanine floor. From Room 118 on the first floor, ascend the right staircase to the mezzanine. The records and indexes (except the card file index to Declarations of Intention, 1927-1952) are in the room behind the counter (opposite the stairs). The card file index to Declarations of Intention, 1927-1952, is located outside the room. Researchers are permitted behind the counter but must identify themselves first to the clerk on duty. There are one or two staff persons available who have other duties but may be able to assist if not busy. There is no seating available. Two researchers can work at the counter at a time.

Incompetency and Conservatorship indexes are located behind the counter in the Law Department, Room 118. Request the index at Window 13.

The indexes to Court Cases (including Matrimonials) are located on the first floor in Room 118 and on the mezzanine, Room 118M. The ledger indexes, 1968 to the present, and card file index, 1928-1975/76 are on the first floor, Room 118, in the entrance area. The card file indexes are in cabinets. Signs on top of each cabinet indicate the years covered. The ledgers are on open shelves. The 1914-1967 ledgers and 1914-1927 card file are on the mezzanine. The cabinet for the 1914-1921 card file is opposite the (right) staircase and the 1922-1927 card file is against the wall behind the (right) staircase. Pre-1968 ledger indexes line the corridor on the mezzanine from the (right) staircase to the Bindery and Microfilm Rooms.

Case files for civil records, 1978 to the present, are located in the Record Room on the mezzanine (straight ahead from the left staircase). Microfilmed civil records, currently 1953-1957, can be found in the Microfilm Room (straight ahead from the right staircase). Pre-1978 civil records not yet microfilmed are not on-site. These must be requisitioned from the clerk at the Record Room. See "Restrictions on Use." Seating is available at several tables. However, researchers must compete for space in this area with attorneys taking depositions.

Criminal case records, 1914-1978, can be viewed in the Microfilm Room. For later case files, go to Room 123 on the first floor.

There are 4 microfilm readers available, one of which is a reader/printer. Two are in the Microfilm Room and 2 are in the Bindery Room (next door to the Microfilm Room).

Military Discharge Records are located in the Microfilm Room, on the mezzanine, Room 118M.

Name Change and Business Records and indexes are located in the Miscellaneous Records Department on the mezzanine, Room 118M (opposite the right staircase). Seating is available at three tables for 10 researchers. One staff person is available to help researchers.

Fees/Copies:

Only copying by hand is allowed for Census records. A certified copy (extract) of the census data is $1 per address. Staff assistance in the search for census data also costs $1 per address.

Copies of Naturalizations are made by staff at $8 for a Petition and $4 for a Declaration (or $12 for both). Researchers can photocopy these records themselves on-site.

For other Court records, there are photocopy machines available at $.10 per page. Copies of microfilmed records can be made at $.25 per page.

Restrictions on Use:

Court Cases pre-1978 that are not on microfilm must be ordered a day or two in advance. Check with the Microfilm Room directly to determine if the record you are seeking has been filmed. Staff in the Record Room may not know the current status of filming.

Matrimonial records are closed except to a party of the action or his/her attorney.

Military Discharge Records and indexes are closed. These records are open to the veteran or his representative only.

Records of Surrenders of Children and indexes to these records are closed.

SURROGATE'S COURT - BRONX COUNTY
RECORD ROOM

Facility Director:	Michael Prisco, Chief Clerk
Address:	851 Grand Concourse, Room 317
	Bronx, NY 10451
	(Cross Street: East 161st Street and Walton Avenue)
Phone Number:	(212) 590-3616, 3931

Hours of Operation:

Monday to Friday: 9:00 am to 5:00 pm
Closed Saturday, Sunday and legal holidays.

Closest Public Transportation and Directions:

See "COUNTY CLERK'S OFFICE - STATE SUPREME COURT, BRONX COUNTY." Take the elevator to the third floor.

Description of Resources:

Probate, administration, adoption and guardianship records are located here. The oldest records date back to 1914.

See "SURROGATE'S COURT - NEW YORK COUNTY (MANHATTAN)" for more detail on the content of these files and pre-1914 records of Bronx residents.

Finding Aids:

The office has blue bound ledgers (photocopies of the original vertically-mounted indexes), arranged alphabetically by surname. The ledgers cover the 1914-1980 period. The date of death and case number is noted next to each name for probate, administration and guardianship records.

For records since 1980 and for all surnames "A" through "Gr" for all years, there is a card file in a card-conveyor cabinet which can be accessed by pushing the "up" or "down" button until the shelf with the desired letter comes up. This card file is arranged alphabetically by name. (The index to future records will be computerized.)

Description of Facility:

The Record Room is located on the third floor in Room 317. The room has tables which can seat 10-12 persons. There are two staff persons available to assist researchers.

Files for administration cases after 1946 and probate cases after 1958 are located on this floor and can be retrieved immediately. Older files are located in the basement. See "Restrictions on Use."

Fees/Copies:

There is a photocopy machine in the room at $.15 per page. Certified copies or copies by mail are $4 per page for wills and $3 per page for letters testamentary, letters of administration and guardianship. Requests by mail which require a search (i.e. case number is not provided) cost $20 if the case is under 25 years old and $53 if the case over 25 years, plus the $4 per page fee for copies. Cash or money orders are accepted -- no personal checks.

Restrictions on Use:

There is a three-day wait for pre-1959 probate records and pre-1947 administration records. Files on adoptions and certain guardianship records are confidential and are closed to the public.

BROOKLYN

BOARD OF EDUCATION
SCHOOL RECORDS

Facility Director: Robert Terte, Director

Address: Public Affairs Office
Board of Education
110 Livingston Street
Brooklyn, NY 11201
Attention: School Records

Or, write directly to the local Elementary or High School:

Attention: Record Secretary
Re: Old Pupil Records

Phone Number: (718) 935-4320

Hours of Operation, Closest Public Transportation, Directions and Description of Facility:

Not applicable. Inquiries to determine the possible location of records of schools that closed are handled by mail only.

Description of Resources:

Every New York City school prepares and retains an Office Record Card on each of its students. This card includes a parent or guardian's name, address of student (sometimes changes of address), proof of age (possibly birth certificate number), birth date, birth place and schools attended.

Academic records are transferred from school to school with the child until graduation from high school. These records remain in the high school.

Records are maintained for 50 years. However, it is not uncommon for records to be kept much longer. The availability of records can be decreased by vandalism, fire, flood or loss during transfer from one school to another.

Finding Aids:

To find a record, identify the local school in the neighborhood where the child lived. If you know the school number and it still exists, write to that school first. When a school closes permanently, its records are transferred to the school with which it merged, usually the nearest school. To determine which school this is, send a written request to the Public Affairs Office of the Board of Education (address above).

Written requests to a local school should have the student's name, when he/she attended, date of birth, parents' names and any other identifying information. State that your request is for genealogical research and specify the information you wish.

Restrictions on Use:

Requests should be made by a direct relative closest to the person in question. The principal of the school is the custodian of these records and has the right to deny the release of information. A record may be denied if the person making the request does not have a reasonable interest in it.

BOARD OF ELECTIONS
BROOKLYN BOROUGH OFFICE

Facility Director: Mariette Liguori, Acting Chief Clerk

Address: 345 Adams Street, 4th floor
                          Brooklyn, NY 11201

                          (Cross Streets: Willoughby and Pearl Streets)

Phone Number: (718) 330-2250

Hours of Operation:

Monday to Friday: 9:00 am to 5:00 pm
Closed Saturday, Sunday and legal holidays.

Closest Public Transportation:

Subway: 2, 3, 4 or 5 to Borough Hall
         M, N or R to Court Street/Borough Hall
         A, C or F to Jay Street/Borough Hall

Bus: B41, B45 or B51 to Joralemon and Court Streets
         B25, B26, B37, B38 or B52 to Fulton and Adams Streets
         B67 or B75 to Fulton and Jay Streets

Directions:

Take the Lexington Avenue #4 or #5 (express) train to the Borough Hall station. After exiting the turnstile, go up the stairway to your left (under the Municipal Building). Cross the street and turn right. Adams Street will be straight ahead. Cross Adams to reach the building.

Description of Resources:

The Office has voter registration records from 1890 to the present. In many cases, the registration form provides the date of naturalization and the court in which naturalized. Records, 1957-1979, are on microfilm. Records from 1980 to the present are on "buff" cards. The Office maintains the hard copy ("cancelled buff" and "active buff") records from 1957 to the present.

Finding Aids:

To locate pre-1957 and 1972-1986 records, the address of the voter is needed. The address is then converted into ward or Assembly/Election District in order to find the record. The Office has Assembly/Election District maps from the late 1800s. Records, 1957-1972, are alphabetized by surname.

Records from 1987 to the present can be located by name. Active records are arranged by Assembly/Election District. However, a computer printout arranged alphabetically is available. It lists name, address, affiliation and Assembly/Election District.

Description of Facility:

This is a NYC government office. Staff conduct the search of pre-1980 records. Records, 1890-1956, are located in the vault in the basement. Records from 1957 to the present are located on the 4th floor.

Fees/Copies:

Mail requests are accepted for a $3 fee (certified check or money order payable to the Board of Elections, City of New York). Personal checks are not accepted. This covers a search for one name and one year. Each additional name and/or year is $3. No refund is made if the record is not found. Provide the full name at registration, the year(s) of voting and the address where the voter lived at the time of registration. Use the address in a Presidential election year when the individual was more likely to have voted.

Ask for a copy of the "cancelled buff" rather than a transcribed copy of the data. For a copy of a current record (an "active buff"), the request must be approved by the Chief Clerk.

There is no charge for viewing the computer printout or for an in-person search of the post-1979 records.

Restrictions on Use:

Unlike the Board of Elections Borough Offices in Manhattan, Queens and Staten Island, researchers visiting this office cannot view the pre-1980 records directly. Staff will conduct the search and provide the copy for the $3 fee.

Pre-1957 records that are in the vault may take 2-3 days to locate.

BROOKLYN HISTORICAL SOCIETY
LIBRARY

Facility Director:	Irene Tichenor, Head Librarian
	Claire M. Lamers, Assistant Head Librarian
Address:	128 Pierrepont Street
	Brooklyn, NY 11201
	(Cross Street: Corner of Clinton Street)
Phone Number:	(718) 624-0890

Hours of Operation:

Tuesday to Saturday: 10:00 am to 4:45 pm
Closed Sunday, Monday and legal holidays.

NOTE: Facility may close in high temperatures. Also, the Library may close on Saturday if the next Monday is a legal holiday. Call in advance.

Closest Public Transportation:

Subway: M, N or R to Court Street/Borough Hall
           2 or 3 to Clark Street or Borough Hall
           4 or 5 to Borough Hall

Bus: B25, B41 or B51 to Montague Street and Cadman Plaza West
        B38 or B52 to Tillary Street and Cadman Plaza West

Directions:

Take the M, N or R train to the Court Street/Borough Hall station. Exit to Clinton Street (back of the train if coming from Manhattan). Walk one block _north_ to Pierrepont Street. The Society is on the corner.

Description of Resources:

(The following is adapted from the "Guide to Genealogical Research in the Brooklyn Historical Society" prepared by Claire M. Lamers.)

The Library has an extensive collection of research materials including 155,000 volumes, 750 maps and atlases, 350 local and regional newspapers, 700 periodicals and serials and over 2000 feet of manuscripts and archival materials. The following is a detailed description of the collections of interest to genealogists:

1. Stiles-Toedteberg Family History Collection contains over 14,000 family histories and charts, both published and unpublished. The collection includes the Society's Family Bible Records (both transcript and originals); and the Collective Genealogy Collection, which contains material on early families of Long Island, New York County and New England.

2. Genealogical Reference Collection consists of research guides, genealogical records surveys, catalogs of genealogy collections in other libraries, indexes to genealogical periodicals and histories of various ethnic groups who emigrated to the United States. This collection also includes bibliographies of ship passenger lists as well as published passenger lists, such as:

   Filby, P. William, ed. _Passenger and Immigration Lists Index: A Guide to Published Archival Records of about 500,000 Passengers Who Came to the United States and Canada in the Seventeenth, Eighteenth and Nineteenth Centuries._ Detroit: Gale Research Co., 1981-

   National Archives. _Index to Passenger Lists of Vessels Arriving at New York, 1820-1846._ (microfilm)

3. Vital Records Collection consists mainly of typescript material on births, marriages and deaths abstracted from church records (no synagogues), newspapers, cemetery records, court records and

manuscripts. Most of the material (mainly 17th to 19th century) relates to Kings, Queens, Nassau and Suffolk Counties but material from New York County, New York State and other states is included. Of particular interest are:

Abstracts of Vital Records from Newspapers (see listing below).

Abstracts of Wills
Kings County, 1787-1842; indexes 1650-1850, 1850-1890.
Queens County, 1787-1850; indexes, Jamaica 1680-1781, 1787-1835.
New York County, 17th, 18th and part of 19th centuries; and indexes.

Hennenlotter Collection relates mostly to families in Flatbush, Flatlands and Gravesend and was compiled during the latter part of 19th and early 20th centuries. The index cards are arranged by surname and vital records pertaining to each individual are included.

Robbins Collection of Suffolk County wills and letters of administration, 1787-1880 (index cards).

Census Records. In addition to indexes to U.S. Census records of New York State, 1790-1850, and scattered volumes of other states, the Library has typescript copies of census records for various towns and counties in New York State. On microfilm, U.S. Census records are available for:

Kings, New York and surrounding counties, 1800-1880
Kings, Queens, Richmond and Suffolk counties, 1890 Union veterans
Kings County, 1900
New York State, 1910

Military Records include published histories and pension lists from the Colonial Wars to the late 19th century, with particular emphasis on regiments and people who served in the Civil War.

4. Local History Collection includes material on county, town and church histories of Kings, Queens, Nassau and Suffolk counties. The collection includes some material on other parts of New York City, New York State, the New England states and the southeast as well as material on Europe (particularly England and Holland).

Of particular interest to Jewish genealogists is the material on Brooklyn neighborhoods such as Williamsburg, Boro Park and Coney Island.

5. Manuscripts and Archives Collection includes histories, genealogies, official records and church records (no synagogue records) that contain genealogical information. Included here is the collection of abstracts of wills and letters of administration of New York Counties from the 17th to the mid-19th century compiled by William A. Eardeley. The Library has a card file index for this collection arranged by surname. Each card contains the name of the individual, date of the will or letters of administration, county seat and location of the material in Eardeley's files.

6. Newspaper Collection includes 350 local and regional newspapers, the majority of which are from Kings, Queens, Nassau and Suffolk Counties covering the 18th-20th centuries. See "Restrictions on Use." Other newspaper-related materials of interest to genealogists include:

The Brooklyn and Long Island Scrapbooks compiled from c.1870 to 1970. These 160 volumes (on microfiche) include articles, obituaries, pictures, brochures and programs relating to the history, families and residents of Kings, Queens, Nassau and Suffolk counties. Most of the articles are from Brooklyn and Long Island newspapers, particularly the *Brooklyn Daily Eagle*.

Brooklyn Daily Eagle - abstracts of marriages and deaths, 1841-1880, 1907, 1909 (indexed); index to obituaries, 1891-1902; abstracts of vital statistics (excluding marriages and deaths), 1841-1846 (indexed).

Brooklyn newspapers - abstracts of marriages and deaths, 1791-1886 (indexed).

Long Island Democrat (Jamaica) - abstracts of births, marriages and deaths, 1835-1856 (indexed); scrapbook of clippings of vital records, 1861-1885 (indexed).

Long Island Star (Brooklyn) - card file index to vital records, 1807-1846.

Long Islander (Huntington) - index, 1839-1857; abstracts of marriages and deaths, 1839-1881; scrapbooks of clippings of vital records, 1847-1879 **(indexed)**.

Newtown Register (Queens) - scrapbook of clippings of vital records, 1877-1882 (indexed).

New York Evening Post - abstracts of marriages and deaths, 1801-1890 (indexed).

The Christian Intelligencer of the Reformed Dutch Church (New York City) - abstracts of marriages and deaths, 1830-1871 (indexed).

In addition, the Library has the Genealogy Query Columns from the *Boston Evening Transcript,* 1896-1941, and the *Hartford Times,* 1957-1961 (microcards).

7. Periodicals and Serials Collections: The Library has over 700 periodical titles on a variety of subjects. Local history periodicals relate mainly to Kings, Queens, Nassau, Suffolk and New York counties. The Library also has periodicals from other state historical societies as well as national and foreign publications. This collection includes *The New York Genealogical and Biographical Society Record, National Genealogical Society Quarterly,* and the *New England Historic and Genealogical Register* as well as family newsletters.

8. Maps and Atlases Collection of 750 maps and atlases includes ward maps for use with census materials.

9. City Directories for Brooklyn, 1796, 1802/3, 1811/12, 1822-1926, 1829-1910, 1912/13 and 1933/4 and New York/Bronx, 1786-1933/4.

Finding Aids:

The Library's Main Card Catalog is arranged by author, title and subject. Typical subject headings are "Genealogy," "Immigration" and "Passenger Lists." Geographic place names are interfiled alphabetically in the Main Card Catalog.

The Library also has a Genealogy Catalog by family name. This indexes published and manuscript materials.

There is a card file index for the Brooklyn and Long Island Scrapbooks. Entries are for persons, places and subjects. The index has two sections: one for Brooklyn clippings and the other for Long Island (including Queens) clippings.

The Society published a catalog of genealogies in its collection in 1935, *Catalogue of American Genealogies in the Library of the Long Island Historical Society.* This may be helpful to researchers who are unable to visit the Library, although it is not as up-to-date as the card catalog.

Of note, not all genealogical materials have been assigned call numbers (although all are included in the card catalog). These are arranged alphabetically by family name on the shelves.

The Library's Manuscript Catalog indexes its manuscript material. Entries are usually by the name of the individual or location. There is limited subject access. A catalog of the Brooklyn manuscripts was published by Brooklyn Rediscovery in 1980 as *A Guide to Brooklyn Manuscripts in the Long Island Historical Society.*

Another source which may help researchers utilize the Library's Long Island material is *Long Island Genealogical Source Material* (a Bibliography), Washington, DC: National Genealogical Society, 1962, by Herbert F. Seversmith and Kenn Stryker-Rodda.

The Library's Periodicals Catalog indexes all but the most current publications. Current publication are indexed in a file maintained by the Reference Librarian and in the Main Catalog.

The Maps and Atlases Catalog indexes these materials by subject (usually location), author and title. A selected list of atlases of Kings, Queens, Nassau and Suffolk counties is in the "Library Manual," a loose-leaf binder on the librarian's desk. Ward maps are kept with the census material.

Description of Facility:

The Society was formerly known as the Long Island Historical Society. The Library has a seating capacity of 24. This includes space for 16 non-members. Two to five staff persons are available to assist researchers.

There are 2 microfilm and 2 microfiche readers available. Materials on two floors -- the Main floor and Gallery -- are on open shelves for members only. (See "Restrictions on Use").

The Brooklyn Historical Society Genealogy Workshop meets the first Saturday of every month from October to June.

Fees/Copies:

Non-members must pay a fee of $2 per day (students $1 per day). Membership starts at $25 for individuals. Student and senior citizen membership is $15.

Copies of materials at $.30 per page are made by the staff. Copies can be made within 15 minutes. See "Restrictions on Use."

For a prepaid fee of $15 with mail requests, the Library will check two sources for a specific name and specific year. The fee includes 3 photocopies. Additional photocopies are $.30 per page. Up to 10 pages of a specific genealogy will be photocopied. The Library cannot guarantee a positive answer but makes every effort to secure the information. The fee is for the search. Mail requests take about 4 weeks. Enclose a self-addressed stamped envelope.

Restrictions on Use:

Non-members do not have access to the open shelves and can request no more than three books at a time. Library staff retrieve materials for non-members.

Only one manuscript can be viewed at a time. In cases where a document is kept in the vault, special approval is needed to obtain it.

If material is too fragile, the staff will not photocopy it. No manuscripts or typescripts will be photocopied.

Due to age, condition and storage problems, the only newspapers that are available to the general public are the ones that have been microfilmed and the issues of local papers for the current year. A list of "Newspapers on Microfilm" is available from the staff.

Researchers must use pencils only.

BROOKLYN PUBLIC LIBRARY
BUSINESS LIBRARY

Facility Director: Joan Canning, Business Librarian

Address: 280 Cadman Plaza West
Brooklyn, NY 11201

(Cross Streets: Tillary and Clinton Streets)

Phone Number: (718) 780-7800

Hours of Operation:

Monday to Wednesday: 10:00 am to 8:00 pm
Thursday: 10:00 am to 6:00 pm
Friday: 12:00 noon to 6:00 pm
Saturday: 11:00 am to 3:00 pm (closed June, July and August)

Closed Sunday and legal holidays.

Closest Public Transportation:

Subway: M, N or R to Court Street/Borough Hall
2 or 3 to Clark Street or Borough Hall
4 or 5 to Borough Hall

Bus: B25, B38, B41, B51 or B52 to Tillary and Cadman Plaza West

Directions:

Take the M, N or R train to the Court Street/Borough Hall station. Exit to Montague Street and Cadman Plaza West. Walk north two blocks to the entrance of the Library.

or,

Take the #2 or #3 train to the Clark Street station. Exit the station and take the elevator to the lobby of the St. George Hotel. Exit the Hotel to Clark Street and walk east toward the park. Turn south on Cadman Plaza West and walk one block to the Library.

Description of Resources:

The Business Library, founded in 1943, has an extensive collection of materials of interest to genealogists including:

1. Newspapers and Periodicals: 20 daily business newspapers and over 1,800 business and financial periodicals, as well as local newspapers such as the *Brooklyn Daily Eagle,* 1841-1963. Years available for each periodical vary.

2. City Directories: most of the available City Directories for Brooklyn and New York, 1786-1934:

    NYC Directories (Manhattan and parts of the Bronx) 1786-1933/4.
    Brooklyn, 1796, 1822-1826, 1829-1910, 1912/13, 1933/4.

3. Biographical Directories: an extensive collection of Who's Who of various countries and directories of specific professions. Examples of the latter include:

    Who's Who in Insurance. 1952- . [Orange label, Insurance]
    Who's Who in Finance and Industry. 1936- . [Orange label, Executives]
    Who's Who in American Law. 1977- . [Orange label, Lawyers]
    Who's Who in Canadian Business. 1980/81- . [Orange Label, Executives]

The Library also has *D-U-N-S Business Identification Service* which includes names of 7-8 million corporations, many of which are the names of people; and the *Biography and Genealogy Master Index*, 1980 and updates.

4. Telephone Directories: over 1,500 current residential (White Pages) and classified (Yellow Pages) telephone books including five NYC boroughs and suburban counties. The collection includes all U.S. cities with a population of 20,000 or more, many small U.S. cities and most major foreign cities. For the New York metropolitan area, the Library has the following directories on microfilm or microfiche:

	White Pages	Yellow Pages
Bronx	1929-1973/74, 1976/77-	same
Brooklyn, Queens, Staten Island	1924-1929	same
Brooklyn	1929-1973/74, 1976/77-	1944-1973/74, 1976/77-
Manhattan	1878-1973/74, 1976/77-	1828-1973/74, 1976/77-
Queens	1927-1973/74, 1976/77-	same
Staten Island	1927-1973, 1976-77-	same
Rockaways (Queens)	1928-1934, 1949-1973/74	
Nassau	1913-1973/74, 1977-	same
Suffolk	1928-1973/74, 1976/77-	1962/63-1973/74, 1976/77-
Rockland	1910-1973/74	same
Westchester	1906-1973/74, 1978-	
Westchester, Putnam, NY, Greenwich, CT	1915-1973/74	
Greenwich, CT	1961/62-1967/68, 1970/71-1973	

In addition, the Library has *Cole Directory* (earlier editions called *Cole's Cross Reference Directory*) for Brooklyn and Manhattan, from 1971 to the present. These are reverse directories listing names by address and by phone number for listed numbers only.

5. Maps and Property Ownership: 21 volumes of the latest Sanborn maps for all land and properties in Brooklyn. In addition, the Library has the current Real Estate Data, Inc. (REDI), *Real Estate Directory of Brooklyn* (on microfiche) and *Manhattan* (hard copy). See "CITY REGISTER - MANHATTAN" for a description of the content of these directories.

6. Passenger Ships: *Morton Allan Directory of European Passenger Steamship Arrivals*, for the years 1890-1930 for the Port of New York, and 1904-1926 for the Ports of Philadelphia, Boston and Baltimore. [R656-M88]

Finding Aids:

The Library has a card catalog for books, arranged by author, title and subject. Biographical Dictionaries can be found under "Who's Who."

In addition, the Library has the following indexes:

The Business Index, from 1979 to the present. This indexes such periodicals as *Barron's*, *Wall Street Journal* and the financial pages of the *New York Times*.

Business Periodicals Index, from 1958 to the present.

The New York Times Index, from 1851 to the present.

The Newspaper Index, from 1979 to the present, includes, the *Christian Science Monitor*, *Los Angeles Times*, *New York Times*, *Wall Street Journal* and *Washington Post*.

The Library has a free walking tour of the Business Library (main floor) on tape which lasts about a half hour. Tapes are also available describing the periodicals collection and the business-related U.S. Government documents collection. The Library will provide the cassette player. Users must provide identification which will be held until the cassette player is returned.

Description of Facility:

The Business Library is on the first floor to the left of the entrance. It can accommodate up to 100 people. Most materials on the first floor are in self-service cabinets or on open shelves. There are 10 librarians on duty who can provide assistance. The Library has 13 microfilm readers -- most of which are reader/printers. There are also 6 microfiche readers (4 of which are reader/printers) and one microcard reader.

At least two-thirds of the collection is located in the basement (including the *Morton Allan Directory*). These materials can be retrieved by filling out a call slip. Service is very quick, i.e. less than 5 minutes.

Circulating books may be borrowed using a Brooklyn Public Library card. Books borrowed may be returned to any branch of the Brooklyn Public Library.

Most directories are located around the room and have color-coded labels, i.e. orange - Who's Who; yellow - products; red - state manuals; blue - foreign manuals; and green - services.

The REDI volume and microfiche, and the *D-U-N-S Business Identification Service* microfiche can be obtained at the Reference Desk.

City Directories and telephone directories (microfilm) are in the self-service file cabinets to the left of the entrance to the Business Library. Telephone directories (microfiche) may be obtained at the Reference Desk.

Cole Directory, 1971 to the present, can be found in the file cabinets in the middle of the room to the far right of the entrance. The most recent is located at the Reference Desk.

Fees/Copies:

The Library has 5 photocopy machines available. Copies can be made by the researcher at $.15 per page. Copies of microfilm/microfiche are $.10 per page.

Restrictions on Use:

Sanborn maps may not be photocopied. Researchers should bring identification for use of materials located at the Reference Desk.

BROOKLYN PUBLIC LIBRARY - CENTRAL LIBRARY
HISTORY/BIOGRAPHY/RELIGION DIVISION AND
PERIODICAL AND MICROMATERIALS DIVISION

Facility Director: Vernon Jordan, Chief, History/Biography/Religion Division
                            Robert Hayes, Chief, Periodical and Micromaterials Division
                            Elizabeth White, Local History Librarian, Brooklyn Collection

Address: Grand Army Plaza
                            Brooklyn, NY 11238

                            (Cross Streets: Flatbush Avenue and Eastern Parkway)

Phone Number: (718) 780-7794 (History/Biography/Religion)
                            (718) 780-7729 (Periodical and Micromaterials)

Hours of Operation:

Monday to Thursday: 9:00 am to 8:00 pm
Friday and Saturday: 10:00 am to 6:00 pm
Sunday: 1:00 pm to 5:00 pm (closed on Sunday during the summer)

Closed all legal holidays. NOTE: Winter and summer periods vary from year to year. Generally, winter hours begin the third week in September and end the first week in June. Check with the Library before a Sunday visit.

Researchers planning to use the Brooklyn Collection should call in advance for an appointment. While the Collection can be accessed on Sundays, the assistance of the Local History Librarian is not available.

Closest Public Transportation:

Subway: 2 or 3 to Eastern Parkway/Brooklyn Museum
          D or Q to 7th Avenue/Flatbush Avenue

Bus: B41, B69 or B71 to Prospect Park and Grand Army Plaza

Directions:

Take the #2 or #3 train to the Eastern Parkway/Brooklyn Museum station. From Manhattan, exit at the <u>rear</u> of the station. Go up the stairs and turn left when you reach the street. Walk along the Park (on Eastern Parkway) to the end of the block. The main entrance to the Library is at the corner.

Description of Resources:

A.   The History/Biography/Religion Division has the following collections of interest to genealogists:

1.   <u>Brooklyn Collection</u> contains books, newspaper clippings, photographs, maps and other material about historic and present-day Brooklyn. Newspaper clippings include items on Brooklyn neighborhoods, schools, libraries, churches and synagogues. Clippings on people are limited to notable individuals or persons who were featured in newspaper articles.

The Collection includes <u>maps</u> of current Brooklyn (contiguous with Kings County) as well as historic maps showing Brooklyn in colonial and Revolutionary times. Street maps of the City of Brooklyn are available from 1834.

<u>Town records</u> which were formerly part of the St. Francis College Collection are available here on microfilm. (These towns, later absorbed into the City of Brooklyn, became part of the City of New York in 1898 when the City of Brooklyn became one of New York City's boroughs.) The original records are in the MUNICIPAL ARCHIVES. See "NEW YORK CITY DEPARTMENT OF RECORDS AND INFORMATION SERVICES, MUNICIPAL ARCHIVES" for additional information on the these records.

Brooklyn Daily Eagle index, July 1891-1902, original newspaper clipping files (morgue), 1904-1954, and photo collection belonging to the now-defunct _Brooklyn Daily Eagle_ newspaper can be accessed here. The photo collection has been extensively "weeded"; many of the general scenes of Brooklyn (buildings, parks, etc.) have been incorporated into the Brooklyn Collection. The Brooklyn Collection also includes copies of the _Brooklyn Eagle Almanac, 1886-1929_. These volumes include a section on "Necrology of Important Personages," listing people who died during the year by date of death. (See also "Periodical and Micromaterials Division" and "Restrictions on Use.")

Photograph Collections include the Daniel Berry Austin collection, c.1900-1906, with photos of residential and public buildings, street scenes, and cemeteries in Brooklyn; the Ben Attas collection, 1960-1967, with photos of people in Prospect Park and photos of Sheepshead Bay; the Bob Arnold collection with views of cemeteries (mostly non-Jewish) and the Sephardic Jewish Center; the George Bradford Brainard collection, c.1879-1887, with photos of people (by occupation), Brooklyn residences, schools, churches and parks; and the _Brooklyn Daily Eagle_ baseball photographs (portraits and action scenes) and miscellaneous negatives of street scenes and news events. There are additional views of Brooklyn subjects from the _Brooklyn Daily Eagle_ and other sources, as well as the Irving Herzberg collection, which includes photos of Hasidic Jews in Brooklyn's Williamsburg section, 1962-1976, Jewish life on Ocean Parkway, 1960s-1970s, and photos of people at Coney Island, 1957-1977.

2. Yizkor Books: The History/Biography/Religion Division has a number of Yizkor books in its collection. Most are in Hebrew or Yiddish. (See Appendix A for a list of Yizkor books available in other libraries in New York City.)

3. Biographies: The Division has a large number of biographies and collected biographies on open shelves. Check the card catalog for other biographies available in the stacks.

4. Maps and Atlases: The Library has U.S. Geographical Survey maps (topographical) covering all states and Defense Mapping Agency maps of the world. In addition, it has historical and contemporary maps of New York City and New York State, including Sanborn fire insurance maps for New York State, 1886-1915.

B. The Periodical and Micromaterials Division has the following materials of interest:

1. Newspapers: This Division has a unique collection of Brooklyn newspapers on microfilm. The following is a complete listing:

Brooklyn Citizen, Jan. 1887 - Mar. 1947
Brooklyn Daily Eagle, Oct. 1841 - Jan. 1955
Brooklyn Daily Times (BDT), Jan. 1855 - Dec. 1932
BDT Home Edition, Jan. 1927, Dec. 1933
BDT Long Island Edition, Jan. 1927 - Dec. 1932
BDT Noon Edition, Jan. 1927 - Dec. 1928
BDT Wall Street Edition, Jan. 1926 - Dec. 1934
Brooklyn Eagle, Nov. 1955; Oct. 1960 - June 1963
Brooklyn Heights Press, Nov. 1939 - Dec. 1959
Brooklyn Standard Union (aka Standard Union), Sept. 1863 - Jan. 1932
Standard Union Pictorial Edition, Jan. 1920 - Dec. 1924
Brooklyn Sunday Review, Mar. 1873 - Dec. 1874
Brooklyn Sunday Star, Sept. 1927 - Mar. 1928
Brooklyn Sunday Sun, Nov. 1873 - Nov. 1876
Brooklyn Tablet, Apr. 1908 - Mar. 1985
Brooklyn Times Union, Jan. 1935 - Dec. 1936
Brooklyn Times Union City Edition, July 1932 - June 1937
Brooklyn Union, Mar. 1868 - Mar. 1869
Brooklyn Weekly Eagle, Mar. 1842 - Feb. 1845
Brooklyn Weekly News, May 1914 - Apr. 1915
Churchman, Mar. 1954 - Feb. 1955
Daily Long Island Democrat Greater Brooklyn, Apr. 1895 - Nov. 1895
Flatbush Kings & County, July 1927 - Dec. 1927

Home Talk, June 1901 - Dec. 1929
Home Talk Star, July 1928 - June 1931
Home Talk Star and Item, Jan. 1932 - Dec. 1938
Junior Eagle, Feb. 1907 - Dec. 1910
Kings County Inspector, Apr. 1892 - Aug. 1893
Kings County Rural & Brighton Gazette, Jan. 1880 - Dec. 1885
Long Islander, July 1839 - Dec. 1936
The Voice, Jan. 1885 - Dec. 1888
Weekly Chat, Feb. 1903 - Oct. 1929
Williamsburg Daily Times, Feb. 1848 - June 1854
Williamsburg Gazette, Nov. 1835 - Dec. 1850

The Library also has the *New York Times* from 1851 to the present, the *New York Times Index* and the *Personal Name Index to the New York Times Index*, 1851-1974 and 1975-1984.

2.   Brooklyn City Directories on microfilm are available for 1796, 1822-1826, 1829-1910, 1912/1913, 1933/1934.

Finding Aids:

1.   Brooklyn Collection: Materials are indexed by subject, name of individual or organization in a card index accessible to the Local History Librarian only. Consult with the librarian to locate materials.

2.   Town Records: The Local History Librarian has a folder listing the contents of each of the 52 microfilm reels that make up this collection. These are broad general headings only, e.g. "Roll 16 Gravesend Board of Health Minutes, Book 323, 1887-89."

3.   *Brooklyn Daily Eagle:* Only July 1891 to 1902 are indexed in volumes. These indexes have headings such as "marriages," "obituaries," "murders and suicides," which list individual names. The clipping file, 1904-1954, serves as the only "index" for this period. Clippings are arranged by subject and name of individual or organization. See "Restrictions on Use".

4.   Photographs: Most of the photograph collections include negative numbers, dates and identification of the subject. The *Brooklyn Eagle* collection generally identifies a photo by subject or name and the date the photo was used in the newspaper.

5.   Yizkor Books: Check the card catalog under "Jews in..."

6.   Biographies: These are indexed in the card catalog under subject, author and title of the book. Collected biographies can be located on open shelves under call numbers beginning with 920.

Description of Facility:

The History/Biography/Religion Division is located on the 2nd floor. Take the left escalator or stairs to reach it. This Division can seat about 70 people. The Brooklyn Collection is in a separate room inside this Division and is not accessible to researchers. The librarian brings the material requested. The *Brooklyn Daily Eagle* clipping file is stored in the basement. See "Restrictions on Use." There are no microfilm readers available in this room but arrangements can be made to use the Town Records microfilms in the Periodical Room. See "Restrictions on Use."

The Periodical and Micromaterials Room is located on the 1st floor opposite the information desk. It can seat about 120 people. There are two librarians on duty to assist researchers. Seventeen microfilm readers/printer are available. In addition, there are 3 microfiche readers and one microcard reader.

Fees/Copies:

The Library has 3 photocopy machines and copies can be made at $.15 per page. Copies from microfilm cost $.10 per page.

Restrictions on Use:

The librarian makes one trip weekly to the basement for materials stored there. Requests for *Brooklyn Daily Eagle* clippings must be made by Wednesday noon at the latest for viewing on Friday or during the following week.

Researchers are requested to handle everything with care. Much of the Brooklyn Collection is already extremely fragile. Use only pencils, not ink, for note taking. Tracing of materials is not allowed.

Researchers must bring a library card or other identification showing name and address to use materials not on open shelves in this Library.

Use of the microfilm and microfiche readers may be limited to one hour per person if all machines are being used. A sign-in log is used during busy periods.

CENTER FOR HOLOCAUST STUDIES, DOCUMENTATION AND RESEARCH

Facility Director: Dr. Yaffa Eliach, Director
Bonnie Gurewitsch, Librarian/Archivist

Address: 1610 Avenue J
Brooklyn, NY 11230

(Cross Streets: East 16th and 17th Streets)

Phone Number: (718) 338-6494

Hours of Operation:

Monday to Friday: 9:00 am to 5:00 pm

Closed Friday during the month of July.
Closed Saturday, Sunday, Jewish and legal holidays.

Closest Public Transportation:

Subway: D to Avenue J
Bus: B6 or B11 to Avenue J and East 16th Street

Directions:

Take the D train to the Avenue J station. After exiting the station, walk east one block on Avenue J and cross East 16th Street. The Center is located across the street from the Yeshiva of Flatbush High School building.

Description of Resources:

The Center for Holocaust Studies was the first Holocaust research center established in the USA. It opened in 1974 and includes an archives and reference library of over 2,500 books, periodicals, journals and pamphlets. The following are of particular interest to genealogists:

1.   Yizkor Books: The library has 93 Yizkor books and its collection is constantly growing. (See Appendix A for a list of Yizkor books available in other libraries in New York City.)

2.   Autograph File Collection (1933-1945): Includes letters from displaced persons in Europe to relatives in North America, and a list of Jewish deportees from Eisenach, Germany. 16 items.

3.   Jacob Kestenbaum Papers (1938-1956): Includes correspondence, affidavits and other documents concerning Kestenbaum's efforts to assist Jewish refugees in Europe to emigrate to the USA.

4.   Personal Histories and Personal Documents: The Center has the largest collection of personal Holocaust histories in the USA with over 1,800 oral and written histories of Holocaust survivors, former American soldiers and liberators. Personal documents including letters, memoirs, diaries, Kennkarten (identification cards), passports, ration cards, affidavits, photos and other material covering the 1933-1946 period, are sometimes available.

The following is a partial list of surnames included in the Center's collection. For additional names, consult with the Center's staff. Place of origin or places described in the testimony are in parentheses:

Adamski (Oppeln, Germany)
Aisenshtin (Babi Yar)
Auerbacher (Theresienstadt)
Baharlias (Volos, Greece)
Baigelman (Lodz, Poland)
Benjamini (Czernowitz, Romania)
Bernstein (Grodno, Poland)
Biegeleisen (Kracow, Poland)
Billys/Bialystok (Lodz, Poland)
Birponz (Gersfeld, Germany)
Bisgaier (Sedziszow, Poland)
Blonder (Oswiecim, Poland)
Blum (Saratov, Russia)
Brafman (Vienna, Austria)
Bram (Breslau, Germany)
Brandstatter (Poland)
Briks (Koprzywnica, Poland)
Brodman (Dachau/Ohrdruf)
Bronspiegel (Deblin, Poland)
Calka (Lodz, Poland)
Eisenman/Aizenman (Wierzbnik, Poland)
Engel (Hungary)
Fisch (Budapest, Hungary)
Fishkin (Rubiezewicz, Poland)
Fluek
Fox (Lodz, Poland)
Fuchs (Theresienstadt)
Gastwirth (Vilna, Poland)
Glazar (Treblinka/Theresienstadt)
Glicksman (Belchatow, Poland)
Glicksman (Szczercow, Poland)
Goetz (Schwabenheim, Germany)
Goldberg (Lubomel/Fahrenwald)
Goldberger (Hlohovec, Czechoslovakia)
Goldberger (Vienna, Austria)
Golombek (Poland)
Gorin (Berlin, Germany)
Gruber (Poland)
Gruenhut (Linnsbruck)
Grun (Gorond, Czechoslovakia)
Grunbaum (Rotterdam, Netherlands)
Grussgott (Bardejov, Czechoslovakia)
Gutfreund (Sanok, Poland)

Halpern (Biecz, Poland)
Hardy (France)
Hennenberg (Oswiecim, Poland)
Heuman (Berlin, Germany)
Hirsch (Nowy Wisnicz, Poland)
Hollander (Tacavo, Czechoslovakia)
Honig (Chust, Hungary)
Hunter (Jozefow, Poland)
Jacin (Wielun, Poland)
Juravel (Szamotuly, Poland)
Kaner (Lodz, Poland)
Kohn (Satu Mare, Romania)
Kolodny (Amsterdam, Netherlands)
Labret (Danzig/Gdansk)
Lachman (Duesseldorf, Germany)
Laufer (Lodz, Poland)
Leesha (Amsterdam, Netherlands)
Leib (Lodz, Poland)
Lenger (Hannover, Germany)
Lenz (Amsterdam, Netherlands)
Lewis (Kracow, Poland)
Maas (Mutterstadt, Germany)
Mann (Budapest, Hungary)
Mayer (Sanok, Poland)
Menzel (Cluj, Romania)
Mermelstein (Munkas, Cz.)
Minsky/Rotkeliechen (Warsaw, Poland)
Mitastein (Warsaw, Poland)
Nachstern (Norway)
Nass (Bobrka, Poland)
Noyovitz (Kirjard, Czechoslovakia)
Oppenheimer (Tarnow, Poland)
Pach (Duesseldorf, Germany)
Posner (Berlin, Germany)
Potock (Auschwitz)
Rawicki (Plock, Poland)
Rigler (Siauliai, Lithuania)
Roer (Untermaubach, Germany)
Rosenberg (Minsk)
Rosenblatt/Diament (Czestochowa, Poland)
Rosenstein (Srodawka, Poland)
Rosenzweig (Cracow, Poland)

Rosenzweig (Szydlowiec, Poland)
Ross (Halle, Germany)
Rothkopf (Lubraniec, Poland)
Salzberg (Zawiercie, Poland)
Sandowski/Zylberminc (Piotrkow, Poland)
Scheinbrum (Vienna, Austria)
Schley (Warsaw, Poland)
Schreier (Mielec, Poland)
Segalowitz (Klaipeda, Lithuania)
Silber (Szalok, Hungary; Michalovce, Czechoslovakia)
Sloan/Weisner (Druzkieniki/ Druskininkai, Poland)
Spiegel/Hochszpiegel (Bergen-Belsen)
Spira (Cracow, Poland)
Steel/Koeppel (Germany)
Stein (Vienna, Austria)
Streim (Mielec, Poland)
Svarc (Uzhorod, Czechoslovakia)
Tabris (Siauliai, Lithuania)
Taylor/Tuchsznaider (Warsaw, Poland)
Tenenbaum (Tomaszow Mazowiecki, Poland)
Tepper (Hannover, Germany)
Terna/Taussig/Horner
Tessler (Ruscova, Romania)
Tessler (Visuel-de-Sus, Romania)
Walbrom (Gera, Germany)
Wieder (Duvhe, Czechoslovakia)
Weinberg (Orlova, Cz.)
Weinberger (Warsaw, Poland)
Weiner (Cluj, Romania)
Weingarten (Cracow, Poland)
Wertheim (Eisleben, Germany)
Wisnicki (Lodz, Poland)
Wiss (Warsaw, Poland)
Wittenberg (Vilna, Poland)
Yaary (Lodz, Poland)
Yablon (Czestochowa, Poland)
Zeiri (Italy)

Finding Aids:

1. <u>Yizkor Books</u> are indexed by locality name, author and title.

2. <u>Jacob Kestenbaum Papers</u> are indexed by the name of the refugee being assisted.

3. <u>Personal Histories and Personal Documents</u> are indexed by personal name and town, shtetl, ghetto or concentration camp.

A published description of these and other collections of the Center is available in *Guide to Historical Resources in Kings County (Brooklyn) New York Repositories,* vol. I, 1987, by New York Historical Resources Center.

Description of Facility:

The Center is located in a house across the street from the Yeshiva of Flatbush High School building. The Center can accommodate 4 researchers at a table. There are three staff members available to provide assistance. Researchers wishing to listen to oral histories are advised to bring their own cassette players.

Fees/Copies:

The Center will respond to written requests for specific information by informing the researcher of materials in its collection useful to the subject being researched. There is no cost for this service. Photocopies of materials can be made at $.10 per page. Copies of photographs can be made upon request. Costs vary according to the size of the photo.

Membership dues start at $25 for a regular member and $15 for a student.

Restrictions on Use:

The research library is open to the public for on-site use of materials only. No materials may be removed from the Center. Some materials are restricted and permission from the Archivist is required for viewing.

CITY CLERK'S OFFICE - BROOKLYN
MARRIAGE LICENSE BUREAU

Facility Director:	Johnnie Mae Johnson, Deputy City Clerk

Address: Municipal Building, Room 205
210 Joralemon Street
Brooklyn, NY 11201

(Cross Streets: Court and Adams Streets)

Mail Address: Add "Attention - Marriage Records Unit" to lower left corner of the envelope.

Phone Number: (718) 802-3581

Hours of Operation:

Monday to Friday: 9:00 am to 12:00 noon; 1:00 pm to 4:00 pm
Closed Saturday, Sunday and legal holidays.

Closest Public Transportation:

Subway: 2, 3, 4 or 5 to Borough Hall
M, N or R to Court Street/Borough Hall

Bus: B41, B45 or B51 to Joralemon and Court Streets
B25, B26, B37, B38 or B52 to Fulton and Adams Streets
B67 or B75 to Fulton and Jay Streets

Directions:

Take the #4 or #5 (express) train to the Borough Hall station. The exit is directly under the Municipal Building.

Description of Resources:

Brooklyn City Clerk's Office marriage records are available from 1908.

NOTE: Two independent sets of records exist for the period 1908-1937, when both the Department of Health and the City Clerk's Office maintained marriage records. The Health Department records, 1866-1937, are being accessioned by the MUNICIPAL ARCHIVES. See "NEW YORK CITY DEPARTMENT OF RECORDS AND INFORMATION SERVICES - MUNICIPAL ARCHIVES" and "CITY CLERK'S OFFICE - MANHATTAN" for a more detailed description of these records.

Finding Aids:

The bride/groom indexes for records maintained by the City Clerk from 1908 to the present are in the same format as in the Manhattan office. See "CITY CLERK'S OFFICE - MANHATTAN."

Description of Facility:

This government office is staffed by one or two persons. Records can be obtained immediately if staff are not busy.

Fees/Copies and Restrictions on Use:

See "CITY CLERK'S OFFICE - MANHATTAN." The Brooklyn Office does not accept personal checks.

CITY REGISTER'S OFFICE
BROOKLYN

Facility Director: Ronald Douglas, Deputy City Register

Address: Municipal Building
210 Joralemon Street
Brooklyn, NY 11201

(Cross Streets: Court and Adams Streets)

Phone Number: (718) 802-3590

Hours of Operation:

Monday to Friday: 9:00 am to 4:00 pm
Closed Saturday, Sunday and legal holidays.

Closest Public Transportation and Directions:

See "CITY CLERK'S OFFICE - BROOKLYN, MARRIAGE LICENSE BUREAU."

Description of Resources:

This office has real property records (deeds, mortgages, maps) for Brooklyn (Kings County) from 1689 to the present.

See "CITY REGISTER'S OFFICE, MANHATTAN" for a description of these records and block/lot microfiche jackets.

Finding Aids:

This office has indexes for grantor/grantee and mortgagor/mortgagee as well as block and lot number. Grantor/grantee indexes, arranged alphabetically by the first two letters of the surname and chronologically by date of recording, are difficult to use. Records can be located by using either these name indexes or block and lot indexes. Lot numbers were assigned in Kings County beginning in 1900. Prior to that date, records are indexed by block and metes and bounds.

To locate records on a particular piece of property by address only, use one of the following:

1.   If the building still exists, use the computer in Room 2 to determine the block and lot numbers. See "CITY REGISTER'S OFFICE, MANHATTAN" for a description of the computer index; or,

2.   The Office has the *Brooklyn Real Estate Register,* published yearly. Locating block and lot number is very easy if this volume is used. Unfortunately the book is accessible only to clerks of the City Register's Office and representatives of title search firms. It is not available for use by the general public in this office. However, the BROOKLYN BUSINESS LIBRARY, Reference Desk, has a copy of the *Real Estate Directory of Brooklyn* and the NEW YORK PUBLIC LIBRARY, MAP DIVISION has *New York Boroughs* (both similar to the *Brooklyn Real Estate Register,* but on microfiche) issued by Real Estate Data Incorporated (REDI). These directories list properties by address and provide block and lot numbers, as well as other information such as name, address and telephone number of the current owner of each parcel; or,

3.   Start in Room 200, the Real Property Assessment Division, to check the block index books for the block and lot numbers. Clerks in this office will assist researchers in identifying block and lot numbers; or,

4.   Go to Room 2 on the ground floor. In the right rear are lot history indexes for each block with maps showing lot number for each house number. These also give ownership history to approximately the 1930s.

Once the block and lot numbers are known, consult the block and lot indexes in Room 2 (red books) to obtain the liber and page numbers (or reel and page numbers after 1968) for deeds, mortgages and other instruments on file on a particular property. These list all conveyances by block and lot in chronological order.

NOTE: More than 1,800 properties in Brooklyn (mostly Canarsie) are filed under the Torrens Land Title Registration System using Memorial Certificates rather than deeds. See "CITY REGISTER'S OFFICE, MANHATTAN" for a description of Torrens properties. The office has a card index for these properties arranged three ways: grantor/grantee, block/lot numbers and certificate number. Each of these is further subdivided into "active" and cancelled."

From 1982 to the present, indexes except for Torrens properties have been computerized. See "CITY REGISTER'S OFFICE, MANHATTAN"for a complete description of the computer system. Instructions for use of the computer are posted near the terminals.

To see the deed, mortgage or other conveyance, use the 1950-1967 libers (hard copy) in Room 2 or go upstairs to Room 203 and get the block/lot microfilm jacket (1968 or later) or microfilm reel (all years) by filling out the appropriate form with the land section number, liber (or reel) and page numbers and year. Be sure to indicate whether the instrument is a mortgage or deed.

Description of Facility:

This is a NYC government office. There are three staff members on duty in Room 203 who can help researchers. Records can be obtained in 5-10 minutes. Liber indexes to 1981 and records, 1950-1967, are located on open shelves in Room 2. Indexes and records on microfilm are located in Room 203.

There are 3 computer terminals in Room 2 on the first floor. About 25 microfiche and 10 microfilm readers are available in Room 203 on the second floor. There are 6 microfilm/microfiche reader/printers.

Fees/Copies and Restrictions on Use:

See "CITY REGISTER'S OFFICE - MANHATTAN." For a certified copy, apply at the main floor service desk. Copies will be ready by noon of the next day.

CIVIL COURT OF THE CITY OF NEW YORK
BROOKLYN (KINGS COUNTY)

Facility Director: Stewart A. Feigel, Clerk of the County
Patricia Gonzalez, Record Room Clerk

Address: 141 Livingston Street
Brooklyn, NY 11201

(Cross Streets: Smith Street and Boerum Place)

Phone Number: (718) 643-8125 (Room 304)
(718) 643-8133 (Room 301)
(718) 643-8123 (Room 303)

Hours of Operation:

Monday to Friday: 9:00 am to 5:00 pm
Closed Saturday, Sunday and legal holidays.

Closest Public Transportation:

Subway: A, C or F to Jay Street/Borough Hall
M, N or R to Court Street/Borough Hall
2, 3, 4 or 5 to Borough Hall

Bus: B41, B45, B61, B67 or B75 to Livingston and Smith Streets

Directions:

Take the A, C or F train to the Jay Street/Borough Hall station. From Manhattan, exit at the front of the station to Jay Street (Borough Hall exit). Walk south on Jay Street (Jay becomes Smith Street) to Livingston Street. The building is on the corner.

Description of Resources:

The Civil Court has name change records filed in Brooklyn from 1927 to the present.

See also "COUNTY CLERK'S OFFICE - STATE SUPREME COURT, KINGS COUNTY (BROOKLYN)." Name changes also were recorded in State Supreme Court.

Finding Aids:

There are annual bound ledgers that list name changes. These ledgers are arranged by the first letter of the surname and then chronologically. Information in the ledgers includes name changed from, name changed to, order file date and file number. Once the researcher identifies the file number, the original name change document can be requested.

Description of Facility:

The Record Room (Room 304) has the annual bound ledgers listing name changes, 1962-1984. A more complete index (1934 to the present) can be found in Room 301. These are annual typed lists. Ledgers, 1927-1961, can be found in the sub-basement.

The actual documents, 1986 to present, are located next door to the Record Room in Room 303. Old records, pre-1986, are in the sub-basement. Researchers have to go down to the sub-basement to view old files. Records, 1927-1938, are in bundles. Records from 1939 to the present are in file folders.

There is no seating available in the Record Room (Room 304). Counter space is available for 2 researchers. Desk space is available for 4 researchers in the sub-basement.

The clerks on duty in each of the rooms described above will provide assistance if they are not busy. This is a working office.

Fees/Copies:

Information may be copied by hand. The photocopy machine in the sub-basement belongs to the Process Server. Copies can be made at $.25 per page.

Restrictions on Use:

Researchers must show valid identification with a photo before being permitted to go down to the sub-basement.

COUNTY CLERK'S OFFICE - STATE SUPREME COURT
KINGS COUNTY (BROOKLYN)

Facility Director: Anthony N. Durso, County Clerk
                           Dorothy Laub, Administrator

Address: 360 Adams Street, Room 189
                           Brooklyn, NY 11201

                           (Cross Streets: Johnson, Court and Joralemon Streets)

Phone Number: (718) 643-5790 (Census and Incompetency records)
                           (718) 643-5894 (Naturalizations and all other records)

Hours of Operation:

Monday to Friday: 9:00 am to 4:45 pm
Closed Saturday, Sunday and legal holidays.

Closest Public Transportation:

Subway: 2, 3, 4 or 5 to Borough Hall
         M, N or R to Court Street/Borough Hall
         A, C or F to Jay Street/Borough Hall

Bus: B41, B45 or B51 to Joralemon and Court Streets
         B25, B26, B37, B38 or B52 to Fulton and Adams Streets

Directions:

Take the #2, #3, #4 or #5 (express) train to the Borough Hall station or the M, N or R train to the Court Street/Borough Hall station. Exit the #4 or #5 train and go up the staircase at the center of the platform. Walk east a half block toward Adams Street. Go past the little park. The Supreme Court Building is the large, modern structure on your left. Enter the building through the <u>south</u> entrance.

From the #2, #3, M, N or R train, follow the signs to the Supreme Court Building when exiting the station.

Description of Resources:

1. <u>Naturalizations</u> and <u>Declarations of Intention</u> filed in State Supreme Court, Kings County, 1856-1924. See "Restrictions on Use." After 1924, Brooklyn residents were naturalized in the U.S. DISTRICT COURT of either the Eastern or Southern District.

2. <u>Census Records</u> for Kings County (Brooklyn) include the New York State Census for 1855, 1865, 1875, 1892, 1905, 1915 and 1925; and the U.S. Census for 1850, 1860, 1870 and 1880.

    NOTE: The 1915 and 1925 Census is available also at the NEW YORK STATE EDUCATION DEPARTMENT, OFFICE OF CULTURAL EDUCATION, NEW YORK STATE LIBRARY.

3. <u>Matrimonial Records</u> from c.1850 to the present for divorces, separations or annulments brought in State Supreme Court, Kings County (Brooklyn). See "Restrictions on Use."

4. <u>Court Cases</u>: brought against an individual or corporation or actions filed by an individual or corporation from 1923 to the present.

5. <u>Business Records</u> including:

    Certificates of Incorporation, c.1850 to the present
    Limited Partnerships, 1829 to the present
    Trade Names, "Doing business as...," 1895 to the present
    Religious Corporations, 1785 to the present

6. <u>Incompetencies and Conservatorships</u>

Incompetency cases, 1918 to the present
Conservatorships, 1973 to the present

7. <u>Military Discharge Records</u>: filed on a voluntary basis by veterans after the first and second World Wars. See "Restrictions on Use."

8. <u>Name Changes</u>: for individuals and organization from 1848 to the present.

9. <u>Surrenders of Children and Adoptions</u>: See "Restrictions on Use."

Finding Aids:

1. <u>Naturalizations</u>: Index libers are arranged by groups of years and then alphabetically by the first letter of the surname. See "Restrictions on Use."

2. <u>Census Records</u>: A specific address is needed to locate data. With the address, the Assembly/Election District (AD/ED) can be located on the AD/ED maps. Census volumes are arranged by AD/ED and then address.

3. <u>Matrimonial Records</u>, <u>Business Records</u>, <u>Incompetency Records</u> and other <u>Court Cases</u>: Each has index libers by groups of years and alphabetically by the first two letters of the surname.

4. <u>Military Discharge Records</u>: There is no index. The records are arranged in alphabetical order of name. See "Restrictions on Use."

5. <u>Name Changes</u>: Liber indexes are arranged by groups of years and alphabetically by the first letter of the new and old names.

Description of Facility:

Naturalizations, Matrimonial Records, Business Records, Military Discharges, Name Changes, Surrenders of Children, Adoptions and other Court Cases are located in the basement. Take the elevator down to the "C" level, Room 079. The Naturalization indexes are located to the far left under the counter (on the clerk's side of the counter).

Index libers to Matrimonial Records, Business Records, Name Changes and other Court Cases are located on the first floor (ground level) in Room 189.

Census records, Conservatorships and Incompetency index libers and records are located in Room 105.

Room 079 can accommodate 27 people at tables and more at the counters. Rooms 105 and 189 have ample counter space for researchers but no seats.

Fees/Copies:

1. <u>Naturalizations</u>: For mail requests, the County Clerk's Office charges $5 for a 2-year search of the index libers and $4 per page (or per half page, for oversize pages) for photocopies. There may be no charge if you come in person (and get a helpful clerk).

    NOTE: The NATIONAL ARCHIVES, NORTHEAST REGION has copies of all Naturalization records pre-1906 and charges $.35 per page with a minimum order of $5.

2. <u>Census</u>: The fee is $5 per address search conducted by staff. The staff will only conduct searches of the 1892-1925 Censuses. There is no refund if the name/address is not found. There is no charge for a search conducted by the researcher. All records may be searched in person.

3. <u>Other records</u>: There are three photocopy machines available in Room 079 and one in Room 105. Copies cost $.10 per page in Room 079 and $.15 in Room 105. Certified copies of records costs $4 per page.

Restrictions on Use:

<u>Naturalizations</u>: There is no staff at the present time assigned to handle Naturalization records. As a result, access to these records may be limited. Be charming and you may have success. The State Supreme Court in Brooklyn is noted for its inconsistent policies as they relate to charges and access to Naturalization records. The "Fees/Copies" section above is believed to be the latest policy.

<u>Matrimonial Records</u> may only be viewed by the parties or their attorneys. The index libers are open to the public.

<u>Military Discharge Records</u> may only be viewed by the concerned individual, a duly authorized agent, or a representative of the veteran.

<u>Surrenders of Children and Adoption</u>: Both indexes and cases files are closed to the public and may not be viewed without a court order.

SEPHARDIC COMMUNITY CENTER
SEPHARDIC ARCHIVES

Facility Director: David Shasha, Director, Sephardic Archives

Address: 1901 Ocean Parkway
Brooklyn, NY 11223

(Cross Street: Corner of Avenue S)

Phone Number: (718) 627-4300

Hours of Operation:

Monday to Friday: 8:30 am to 5:00 pm (an appointment is recommended)
Closes two hours before sundown on Friday.
Closed Saturday, Jewish and legal holidays.

Closest Public Transportation:

Subway: F to Kings Highway (and McDonald Avenue)
          D to Kings Highway (and East 16th Street)

Bus: B5 to Kings Highway and Ocean Parkway
       B68 to Coney Island Avenue and Avenue S

Directions:

Take the F train to the Kings Highway station. Walk five short blocks east to Ocean Parkway. Cross Ocean Parkway and walk two blocks south on Ocean Parkway to Avenue S. The Center is on the southeast corner.

Description of Resources:

The Archives collects documents, memorabilia and artifacts from the Sephardic community with emphasis on, but not restricted to, the Syrian Jewish community of Brooklyn. The collection contains items relating to the history of this community in Syria as well as its years in the New York area. These include:

1. Magen David Congregation: Records of this first Syrian synagogue established in Brooklyn and its associated charities such as annual reports, 1921-1951, financial records, records of contributions, attendance record book, other school records, 1937-1953, and miscellaneous papers. Some records are in Hebrew and Spanish.

2. *Victory Bulletins* (1942-1945): A complete set of this newspaper published by the Girls Junior League, a community social organization. The newspaper included letters from and articles about soldiers, and photographs taken overseas and in Brooklyn about war-related activities. A reprinted volume, *Victory Bulletins, July 1942-September 1945: Wartime Newspapers of the Syrian Jewish Community in Brooklyn,* is available for sale.

3. Photographs and Slides: A small collection of photos, 1923-1946, including the Great Synagogue of Aleppo, Syria; group photos in front of the school in Aleppo and Damascus, 1923, 1928 and 1939; group photos of banquets of the Mapleton Lodge No. 452 at the Imperial Manor, 1930 and of the Magen David Community Center, 1946; and seven photos of the Sultan family, 1914-1983. There is also a slide collection, 1943-1983, including photos of Syrian Jews in service overseas during WWII and portraits of soldiers.

4. Legal Documents: Includes five ketubot in Hebrew, 1910-1920; one NYC marriage record, 1927; the passport of Selim Chammah, born in Aleppo, Syria, 1921; and the certificate of Naturalization of Raymond Zalta, 1926.

5. <u>Oral Histories</u>: There are c.110 oral histories (in English), part of an on-going effort to record the story of how those who came from Syria transplanted themselves in New York. Sixty oral histories have been transcribed and are available in a book by Joseph Sutton, *Aleppo Chronicles,* 1987.

Finding Aids:

There is no central catalog. Oral histories and photographs are not arranged at this time. However, material can be located by the Director.

A published description of the holdings of the Archives is available in *Guide to Historical Resources in Kings County (Brooklyn) New York Repositories,* vol. I, 1987, by New York Historical Resources Center.

Description of Facility:

The Archives is housed in the Library of the Community Center. There is one full-time staff person. The Archives office is on the 2nd floor of the Center. Space is available for one researcher to work in the Library located on the first floor.

Fees/Copies:

The Library has a photocopy machine which can be used without a fee to copy a reasonable amount of material. Copies of *Aleppo Chronicles* can be purchased through the Center at $26 and *Victory Bulletins, July 1942-September 1945* at $10.

Restrictions on Use:

The materials are located in a closet and are retrieved by staff on request.

SURROGATE'S COURT - KINGS COUNTY (BROOKLYN)
RECORD ROOM

Facility Director: Horace Neysmith, Supervisor

Address: 2 Johnson Street (Supreme Court Building)
Room 109
Brooklyn, NY 11201

(Cross Streets: Adams Street and Cadman Plaza)

Phone Number: (718) 643-8016

Hours of Operation:

Monday to Friday: 9:00 am to 5:00 pm
Closed Saturday, Sunday and legal holidays.

Closest Public Transportation and Directions:

See "COUNTY CLERK'S OFFICE - STATE SUPREME COURT, KINGS COUNTY (BROOKLYN)." Go to Room 109 at the <u>north</u> end of the ground floor.

Description of Resources:

Surrogate's Court records, c.1785 to the present, include files of proceedings in probate, administration, guardianship and adoptions. In addition there are libers with copies of the recorded wills dating back to the 1700s.

See "SURROGATE'S COURT - NEW YORK COUNTY (MANHATTAN)" for more detail on the content of these files.

Finding Aids:

Index card files located in this room are in alphabetical order of name. Persons with aliases are often listed under both names (maiden name may be listed on the card). Each card includes name of individual, file number, year filed and notations "P" (Probate), "LA" (Letters of Administration), "G" (Guardianship) or "SDB" (Safety Deposit Box).

Index cards for cases filed between 1936/37 and 1951 also include date of death. Index cards for cases filed after 1951 include date of death and address of deceased. Index cards for guardianship files show date of birth.

If there is a probate liber number on the card, the will can be found in the indicated volume. A copy of the will may also be in the probate file.

Description of Facility:

This is a government office. Table/counter top space is provided with seating for 4 people. To order a file, fill out a request form found on the counter. Be sure to include the file number and the year of filing. There are two clerks available to pull files.

Drawers of card files are centrally located in the Record Room and are available to the public. Will libers through 1924 are located on open shelves under the card files. Case files after 1970 are located behind the counter in this room. Earlier files are maintained in the basement and must be accessed by the staff. Requests for these earlier files should be batched so that the clerks can retrieve them in one trip.

Fees/Copies:

Photocopies can be made in this room at $.15 per page. For mail requests (even when the file number is provided by the researcher), the fee is $20 if the record is less than 25 years old, and $53 if it is more than 25 years, plus $4 per page.

Restrictions on Use:

Adoption records are closed and may be opened only by decision of the judge.

Clerks may object to pulling large numbers of files from the basement. Be reasonable. A posted sign says that files will be retrieved from the basement at set times, i.e. 10:00 am and 2:00 pm. Clerks will usually go down at other times as needed.

Bring pencils to take notes. A sign on the desk indicates ink/pens may not be used.

U.S. DISTRICT COURT - EASTERN DISTRICT OF NEW YORK
NATURALIZATION DIVISION

Facility Director: Argentina Solorzana, Acting Naturalization Supervisor

Address: 225 Cadman Plaza East, Room 208
Brooklyn, NY 11201

(Cross Streets: Adams and Tillary Streets)

Phone Number: (718) 330-7264, 2107

Hours of Operation:

Monday, Wednesday, Thursday:	8:30 am to 5:00 pm
Tuesday, Friday:	1:00 pm to 4:30 pm

Closed Saturday, Sunday and legal holidays except Election Day.

Closest Public Transportation:

Subway: 4 or 5 to Borough Hall
M, N or R to Court Street/Borough Hall
2 or 3 to Clark Street
A, C or F to Jay Street/Borough Hall

Bus: B37, B67 or B75 to Tillary and Adams Street

Directions:

Take the #4 or #5 (express) train to the Borough Hall station. After exiting the turnstile, go up the left stairway. Walk east to Adams Street. Turn north on Adams and walk 2 long blocks to Tillary Street. The building is on the northwest corner of Tillary and Adams Streets.

Description of Resources:

This office has Petitions for Naturalization filed in U.S. District Court, Eastern District of New York, from 1986 to the present and Declarations of Intention filed from February 1, 1979 to the present. In addition, the Court has the index to Petitions from 1978 to the present.

Naturalization petitions and indexes prior to 1958, Declarations prior to 1959, and Declaration indexes prior to 1950 are located in the NATIONAL ARCHIVES, NORTHEAST REGION. Naturalization petitions, 1958-1985 (index, 1958-1977) and Declarations, 1960-January 31, 1979, are located in the Federal Records Center of the NATIONAL ARCHIVES AND RECORDS ADMINISTRATION (not in the NATIONAL ARCHIVES, NORTHEAST REGION).

NOTE: The Eastern District covers Kings, Queens, Richmond, Nassau and Suffolk Counties. However, residents of counties outside Brooklyn were more likely to file for Naturalization at the local STATE SUPREME COURT in their county. Few of the residents of Queens, Staten Island, Nassau or Suffolk were naturalized through the Eastern District Court when the local Supreme Court performed this function. (The last Naturalizations in Brooklyn State Supreme Court took place in 1924, Queens in 1941, Staten Island in 1960 and Nassau in 1986.) Residency was not a requirement for filing. Many Brooklyn residents who worked in Manhattan filed papers through the U.S. DISTRICT COURT - SOUTHERN DISTRICT OF NEW YORK.

Finding Aids:

This office has index stubs of Petitions for Naturalization from 1978-1983, arranged alphabetically by surname; and from 1984 to the present, arranged alphabetically by surname for each year. These stubs include the petition number.

There is no alphabetical index to Declarations of Intention. However, the staff can locate records if the year is known.

Description of Facility:

This is a government office. There are one or two staff persons at the counter to respond to inquiries.

Fees/Copies:

A photocopy machine is available in the clerk's office. There is no charge for copies of records located in this office.

Restrictions on Use:

Researchers wishing to view Petitions for Naturalization filed 1978-1985, which are now in the custody of the Federal Records Center (FRC) of the NATIONAL ARCHIVES AND RECORDS ADMINISTRATION, must know the Petition number, box number, accession number and FRC shelf location number. Obtain these numbers from this office before visiting the FRC. Petition numbers, 1978-1985, can be obtained from the index stubs located in this office. Box, accession and FRC shelf location numbers are on the Federal Record Center's Records Transmittal and Receipt form (SF 135) also available in this office.

QUEENS

BOARD OF ELECTIONS
QUEENS BOROUGH OFFICE

Facility Director: Gloria D'Amico, Chief Clerk

Address: 42-16 West Street, 5th floor
Long Island City, NY 11101

(Cross Streets: Jackson Avenue and Queens Boulevard)

Phone Number: (718) 392-8989

Hours of Operation:

Monday to Friday: 9:00 am to 5:00 pm
Closed Saturday, Sunday and legal holidays.

Closest Public Transportation:

Subway: E, F, G or R to Queens Plaza
7 or N to Queensboro Plaza

Bus: M32, Q39, Q60, Q67, Q101, Q102 to Queens Boulevard and Jackson Avenue

Directions:

Take the E, F, G or R train to the Queens Plaza station. Exit to "Bridge Plaza South" or "Jackson Avenue." The building is southeast of the intersection of Queens Boulevard and Jackson Avenue. (The entrance to this building complex is marked "QP Market Place." There are big signs on the fence of the parking lot.) The entrance is on West Street (which looks more like a driveway than a street). Take the elevator to the 5th floor.

Description of Resources:

The office has voter registration information from 1949 to the present. Records, 1957-1978, are on microfilm. Records, 1978 to the present, are on "buff" cards. Registration records may provide the date of naturalization and the court in which naturalized. Records, 1949-1956, are signature cards which do not have as much information as later records. For example, pre-1957 the cards include only year of birth. Later records include date of birth.

For records, 1898-1948, see "NEW YORK CITY DEPARTMENT OF RECORDS AND INFORMATION SERVICES - MUNICIPAL ARCHIVES." The Queens Board of Elections has the Queens Assembly/Election District maps from 1919 to the present.

Finding Aids:

An alphabetical printout of voters who are registered currently is available. Current records are arranged by Assembly/Election District and alphabetically by name. Inactive records ("cancellations") are stored by year of cancellation and alphabetically by name.

Description of Facility:

This is a NYC government office. Computer printouts listing active voters are located opposite the information desk on the 5th floor. Records of inactive voters, as well as microfilm and paper records of active voters, are located on the 4th floor. Go to the 5th floor for permission to use the records. There are 4 microfilm readers available.

Fees/Copies:

There is no cost for examining these records and copying information in person. Photocopies can be made by staff at $.20 per page.

Mail requests are accepted for a $3 fee (certified check or money order payable to the Board of Elections, City of New York). This covers a search for one name and one year. Each additional name and/or year is $3. No refund is made if the record is not found. Provide the full name at registration, address where residing at time of registration, and date of birth or age. Use the address in a Presidential election year when the individual was more likely to have voted.

Restrictions on Use:

Only paper and microfilm records can be viewed directly by researchers. Researchers cannot access the computer.

Inactive records, 1978-1986, may be difficult to use since they are in cardboard boxes stacked on top of each other. These boxes are heavy and fragile.

CITY CLERK'S OFFICE - QUEENS
MARRIAGE LICENSE BUREAU

Facility Director:	Dora Young, Deputy City Clerk
Address:	Queens Borough Hall 120-55 Queens Boulevard Kew Gardens, NY 11424 (Cross Streets: 82nd and 83rd Avenues)
Mail Address:	Add "Attention - Marriage Records Unit" to lower left corner of the envelope.
Phone Number:	(718) 520-3665

Hours of Operation:

Monday to Friday: 9:00 am to 4:00 pm
Closed Saturday, Sunday and legal holidays.

NOTE: Records can be obtained immediately except between 11:00 am and 2:00 pm.

Closest Public Transportation and Directions:

See "CIVIL COURT OF THE CITY OF NEW YORK, QUEENS COUNTY." Walk along Queens Boulevard toward 83rd Avenue. Follow the signs to the Marriage License Bureau which can be entered from the rear of the Queens Borough Hall building.

Description of Resources:

Queens City Clerk's Office has marriage records from 1881 to the present.

NOTE: Two independent sets of records exist for the period 1908-1937 when both the NYC Department of Health and the City Clerk's Office maintained marriage records. Both sets of records are available in this office. The Health Department records are for 1898-1937 and the City Clerk's records are from 1908 to the present. In addition, the Office has marriage records of the Town Clerk of Newtown, 1881-1898, and the City Registrar of Long Island City, 1881-1897; and a register of marriages for College Point, Far Rockaway, Flushing, Jamaica, Richmond Hill, Rockaway and Whitestone, 1881-1898. All but the records created by the City Clerk's Office are being accessioned by the MUNICIPAL ARCHIVES. See "NEW YORK CITY DEPARTMENT OF RECORDS AND INFORMATION SERVICES - MUNICIPAL ARCHIVES" and "CITY CLERK'S OFFICE - MANHATTAN" for a more detailed description of these records.

Original marriage records for Queens County, 1880-1898, are also available at the NEW YORK STATE HEALTH DEPARTMENT in Albany. During this period, all of present-day Nassau County was part of Queens County.

Finding Aids:

The bride/groom indexes for records maintained by the City Clerk's Office, 1908 to the present, are in the same format as in the Manhattan office. See "CITY CLERK'S OFFICE - MANHATTAN."

Description of Facility:

This is a NYC government office staffed by six persons who assist the public.

Fees/Copies and Restrictions on Use:

See "CITY CLERK'S OFFICE - MANHATTAN." The Queens Office does not accept personal checks.

CITY REGISTER'S OFFICE
QUEENS

Facility Director: Ann Levinson, Deputy City Register

Address: 90-27 Sutphin Boulevard, 2nd floor
Jamaica, NY 11435

(Cross Streets: 90th and Jamaica Avenues)

Phone Number: (718) 658-4600

Hours of Operation:

Monday to Friday: 9:00 am to 4:00 pm
Closed Saturday, Sunday and legal holidays.

Closest Public Transportation:

Subway: E, J or Z to Sutphin Boulevard (and Archer Avenue)
          R to Sutphin Boulevard (and Hillside Avenue)

Train: Long Island Railroad to Jamaica

Bus: Q6, Q8, Q9, Q24, Q30, Q31, Q40, Q41, Q43, Q44, Q54 or Q56 to Jamaica Avenue and Sutphin
          Boulevard

Directions:

Take the E train to the Sutphin Boulevard station or take the Long Island Railroad to Jamaica. Exit the train and walk one and a half blocks north on Sutphin Boulevard. The building is on the right.

Description of Resources:

All real property recorded instruments (deeds, mortgages, maps) for Queens County are located here. Records are available from the 1670s to the present. Pre-1899 records for present-day Nassau County are located here also.

See "CITY REGISTER'S OFFICE, MANHATTAN" for a description of these records and the block/lot microfiche jackets.

Finding Aids:

Records in this office may be searched by property location after 1914 or by name of property owner. Records filed pre-1914 are indexed only in grantor/grantee indexes arranged alphabetically. Block and lot numbers were not used in Queens until 1914. After 1914, the researcher can also locate records by address of the property. With the address,

1. Use the computer to determine block and lot numbers if the building still exists. See "CITY REGISTER'S OFFICE, MANHATTAN" for a description of the computer index; or,

2. Go to the Real Property Assessment Bureau, Room 304 (3rd floor) to get the Tax block and lot numbers. This information can be obtained instantly if an operator is available at the computer terminal near the door; or,

3. The Office has copies of the *Real Estate Directory of Queens* issued by Real Estate Data Incorporated (REDI). Locating block and lot numbers is very easy if this volume is used. See the "CITY REGISTER'S OFFICE, MANHATTAN" for a description of the REDI volume. The QUEENS BOROUGH PUBLIC LIBRARY, Social Science reference desk and the NEW YORK PUBLIC LIBRARY, MAP DIVISION have similar information issued by REDI on microfiche; or,

4. Researchers can get the numbers manually by locating the block on the map opposite the door in Room 304. Get the Section (blue) and Volume (red) numbers for the area in which the property is located. Then find the Section/Volume ledger with these numbers. These ledgers are in narrow blue binders under the counters. On the first page of each ledger is a map of the area with Tax block numbers. Locate the particular block and turn to that page in the ledger to find the lot number. If the boundary is unclear, look in the printout, Tentative Assessment Roll, in the brown binder next to blue ones. Find the Tax block number and locate the address next to the current owner's name. The lot number appears directly above the address. Copy both the Tax block and lot numbers.

For deeds or mortgages recorded between 1914 and June 1964, the researcher must first convert the Tax block number to the original Land block number. This can be done by consulting the Tax Block to Land Block, Queens County, oversized volume on the counter at the entrance (2nd floor).

To find a record of all transactions involving a parcel from:

1. 1914 to June 1964, consult the blue Land block index (for deeds) or the orange (for mortgages). This deed index includes the name of the grantor, grantee, date, liber and page numbers (where the actual deed is recorded) and a map of the block showing the location and dimensions of the property.

2. July 1964 to December 1981, go to the far side of the 2nd floor (opposite the counters) to find the large blue Tax block ledgers. Use these to obtain the liber and page numbers (or reel and page numbers if after 1968). NOTE: For records since 1968, researchers can go directly to the block/lot jackets for copies of recorded instruments. However, the Office staff caution that block/lot jackets may not include all recorded instruments.

3. January 1982 to the present, use the computer. The computer can access information for all NYC boroughs except Staten Island. See also "CITY REGISTER'S OFFICE, MANHATTAN" for more information on this system.

NOTE: Researchers should be aware that some 290 properties are not filed by block and lot number and are not included in the computer index. These are recorded under the Torrens Land Title Registration System. See "CITY CLERK'S OFFICE, MANHATTAN" for a description. There is no index to Torrens properties in Queens.

To view a deed or mortgage, go to the counter behind the microfilm readers in the Main Room (2nd floor). The documents are either on microfilm (all years) or in block/lot microfilm jackets (1968 to the present). The latter look like microfiche. Fill out a slip with the Tax block and lot numbers to obtain the block/lot microfilm jacket; or provide the liber and page numbers to obtain the microfilm. Paper copies of deeds and mortgages recorded 1914-1968 are also available in libers in the Main Room. Use the liber number to locate the volume. Volume numbers are listed at the end of each counter. The document begins on the page indicated.

Description of Facility:

This is a NYC government office. All Queens County real estate records are now located in the Main Room on the 2nd floor, except pre-1914 records (originals) in the basement (left of the elevator). The staff-operated computer terminals and ledgers for determining Tax block and lot numbers are located in the Real Property Assessment Bureau, Room 304 on the 3rd floor. Researchers can use one of the 4 computer terminals located in the City Register's Office, in the back of the Main Room on the 2nd floor (left of the entrance). There are 38 microfiche and 24 microfilm readers on the 2nd floor at the far end of the room. The Office has 4 microfiche and 6 microfilm/microfiche reader/printers.

Fees/Copies and Restrictions on Use:

See "CITY REGISTER'S OFFICE, MANHATTAN." This office discourages use of the computer terminals to locate records other than those for Queens County.

CIVIL COURT OF THE CITY OF NEW YORK
QUEENS COUNTY

Facility Director: Bernard J. Daly, Clerk of the County
                              Edward Quinn, Supervisor, Record Room

Address: Queens Borough Hall, Room G-9
                              120-55 Queens Boulevard
                              Kew Gardens, NY 11424

                              (Cross Streets: 82nd and 83rd Avenues)

Phone Number: (718) 520-3621, 3622 (Record Room)

Hours of Operation:

Monday to Friday: 9:00 am to 5:00 pm
Closed Saturday, Sunday and legal holidays.

Closest Public Transportation:

Subway: E, F or R to Union Turnpike
Bus: Q10, Q37, Q44, Q44VP or Q60 to Queens Boulevard and Union Turnpike

Directions:

Take the E or F (express) train or R (local) train to the Union Turnpike station. From Manhattan, exit at the front of the station. Exit to the north side of Queens Boulevard. Enter Queens Borough Hall through the main entrance. Go down one flight. Turn left to Room G-9 on the ground floor.

Description of Resources:

The Civil Court has name change records filed in Queens from 1927 to the present.

See also "COUNTY CLERK'S OFFICE - STATE SUPREME COURT, QUEENS COUNTY." Name changes also were recorded in State Supreme Court.

Finding Aids:

The Record Room has annual ledger books that are arranged alphabetically by the first letter of the surname. The ledgers provide index numbers for each case file.

Description of Facility:

The index ledgers to name change records, and files from 1982 to the present, are located in Room G-9. Files, 1927-1981, are located in the Civil Court Jury room. Requests for these files should be directed to the clerks in Room G-9. There are three to four staff persons working in this office. One is always at the front desk to assist researchers. About 10 researchers can be accommodated at one time.

Fees/Copies:

A photocopy machine is available next door in Room G-8. Copies cost $.15 per page.

Restrictions on Use:

None. All records are open to the public.

COUNTY CLERK'S OFFICE - STATE SUPREME COURT
QUEENS COUNTY

Facility Director: John J. Durante, County Clerk

Address: 88-11 Sutphin Boulevard, Room 105
     Jamaica, NY 11435

     (Cross Streets: 88th and 89th Avenues)

Phone Number: (718) 520-3137

Hours of Operation:

Monday to Friday: 9:00 am to 4:00 pm
Closed Saturday, Sunday and legal holidays.

Closest Public Transportation:

Subway: R to Sutphin Boulevard (and Hillside Avenue)
           E, J or Z to Sutphin Boulevard (and Archer Avenue)

Train: Long Island Railroad to Jamaica

Bus: Q40, Q43 or Q44 to 88th or 89th Avenue and Sutphin Boulevard

Directions:

From Manhattan, take the R (local) train to the Sutphin Boulevard station; or take the E or F (express) train to the Union Turnpike station and change on the same platform for the R (local). Get off at the front of the station. Go up the stairs to the right, "To Court." Walk one block south on Sutphin Boulevard. The court building is on the left.

Description of Resources:

1. Naturalizations: filed in State Supreme Court, Queens County, 1794-1941. After 1941, Queens residents had to go to U.S. DISTRICT COURT to be naturalized. The NATIONAL ARCHIVES, NORTHEAST REGION has copies of the pre-September 1906 naturalizations filed in this Court.

    This office also has Declarations of Intention, 1895-1953.

2. New York State Census: for Queens County for 1892, 1915 and 1925. The 1892 Census for Queens includes present-day Nassau County.

    NOTE: The QUEENS BOROUGH PUBLIC LIBRARY and the NEW YORK STATE LIBRARY in Albany have microfilm copies of the 1915 and 1925 Censuses for Queens County (but not the indexes).

3. Matrimonial Records: from 1847 to the present for divorces, separations and annulments brought in State Supreme Court, Queens County. See "Restrictions on Use."

4. Military Discharge Records: from 1917 to the present, for veterans who filed a copy of their DD 214 form (discharge papers) in this Office. See "Restrictions on Use."

5. Court Cases: cases brought against an individual or corporation or actions filed by an individual or corporation in the Courts of Common Rule, Chancery or Common Pleas, 1861-1876; and in the State Supreme Court, Queens County, 1869 to the present.

6. Business Records

    Business Certificates (aka Trade Names, "Doing Business As..." and Assumed Business Names), 1900 to the present
    Certificates of Incorporation, 1851 to the present
    Limited Partnerships, 1943 to the present

7. <u>Incompetency and Conservatorship Records</u>

Infants, Lunatics and Drunkards, 1860-1909
Incompetency cases, 1880 to the present
Conservatorships, 1973 to the present

8. <u>Name Changes</u>

Name Change records are available from 1847 to the present.

9. <u>Town Records</u>

The Office has one volume of Town records for the Town of Jamaica, 1656-1692.

10. <u>Adoptions and Surrenders of Children</u>

Adoptions (index only), 1928-1938 and Surrenders of Children, 1962 to the present, are available here. See "Restrictions on Use."

Finding Aids:

1. <u>Naturalizations</u>: There is an alphabetical card index to Petitions, 1794-1941, as well as liber indexes. Researchers wishing to view the card index (which is easier to use than the libers) should request access from the staff in Room 105.

   For <u>Declarations of Intention</u>, 1895-1905, only the index at the front of each volume is available. These volumes cover groups of years. The indexes are arranged alphabetically by the first letter of the surname. For 1906-1953, there are two liber indexes, arranged by the first letter of the surname and the first letter of the first name.

2. <u>Census</u> records are searched by staff. For the 1892 Census, the name alone is sufficient. This office has a card index arranged by surname for most of the 1892 Census. Some communities are not included in this index. (NOTE: The 1892 Census did not include street addresses.) For the 1915 and 1925 Census, provide the name/address. This office has a master index for 1915 and 1925 arranged by community which shows the volume numbers corresponding to each community. A second card index arranged by volume number and street name lists the pages within each book that include that street name. These indexes were created by the County Clerk's Office and are only available here.

3. <u>Matrimonial Records</u>, 1847-1929, can be located by looking in the Common Rule ledgers found against the wall in Room 106. These records are indexed in groups of years and then by first letter of the surname. For records, 1929-1946, use the alphabetical <u>Index to Matrimonial Actions</u> (libers) located under the counter between Sections F and G. For later years, matrimonial records are in the same index libers as other cases. These libers include the names of the parties and the date of the action.

4. <u>Military Discharge Records</u>: Behind Counter 4 are index cards filed by name. The clerk can advise if a record exists for a particular person. Military Discharge libers are organized by year and then alphabetically. These give the name of the veteran, the date the papers were filed, and the file number. (These libers are useful for those who want to look up many names.)

5. <u>Court Cases</u> are indexed by year or groups of years and alphabetically by the first two letters of the surname.

6. <u>Business Records</u>: Business Certificates and Limited Partnerships are arranged by groups of years and alphabetically by the first letter of the name. Certificates of Incorporation and Limited Partnerships, 1983 to the present, are arranged in a similar manner but use the first <u>two</u> letters of the name. Separate indexes are available for Incorporation of Churches (including Synagogues) and Incorporation of Cemeteries, 1849-1865 and 1878-1912.

7. <u>Incompetency and Conservatorship</u> cases are indexed alphabetically by the first letter of the surname.

8. <u>Name Changes</u>: There are indexes to Common Rule, 1847-1928, and Chancery and Common Pleas, 1861-1876, arranged alphabetically. Records, 1929-1960, are indexed in groups of years and then alphabetically by the first letter of the original surname. After 1960, these cases are indexed together with other court cases.

9.   Town Records are in one volume. (Not indexed).

Description of Facility:

Make a left turn after passing the guards to reach Room 106. This is a large room with libers lining the walls and under the counters. Many people can work at the counters at a time. However, there are no seats. Room 106 has the index libers for Court Cases, 1929 to the present, Matrimonial Records, Name Changes (1927 to the present) and Business Records on open shelves. Indexes for Court Cases pre-1929 and Assumed Business Names, pre-1950, are stored in the Record Room in the basement.

The actual files for all cases and Name Change indexes pre-1927 are in the basement Record Room. Once the file number has been determined, go down the stairs on the left side of Room 106. The basement Record Room can seat 15-20 people.

The indexes for Incompetency cases and Conservatorships are behind counter 6. The latter indexes are open to the public and may be requested from the clerk.

Naturalization, Census and Town Record inquiries should be made to the two staff persons in Room 105 (enter this Administrative Office through Room 104 or 106). This is a working office. Space can be made for one researcher.

Declarations of Intention and Naturalization records and liber indexes, and Military Discharge libers, are in the Executive Lobby. i.e. the hallway between Room 105 and 106. (Census records are located here also but these may not be handled by the researcher directly.)

Fees/Copies:

Mail requests for Census record searches cost $1 for each address and $5 per name for Naturalization searches. All other records cost $.15 per page if the researcher makes the copy. There are 3 photocopy machines located in the basement Record Room and 2 in Room 106. For mail requests or certified copies, the charge is $4 per page.

Payment must be made by certified check, money order or cash. No personal or corporate checks are accepted.

Restrictions on Use:

Researchers generally cannot search Census records themselves. In limited situations, when the office is not busy, these records may be searched in person.

Matrimonial Records are restricted to the parties or their attorneys. Matrimonial indexes, however, are open to researchers.

Military Discharge records are restricted to the concerned individuals.

Records and indexes of Surrenders of Children and the index for Adoptions are sealed. These records may not be opened without a court order.

QUEENS BOROUGH PUBLIC LIBRARY
LONG ISLAND DIVISION

Facility Director: Charles Young, Curator

Address: 89-11 Merrick Boulevard
                          Jamaica, NY 11432

                          (Cross Streets: 89th and 90th Avenues)

Phone Number: (718) 990-0770

Hours of Operation:

Monday and Friday: 10:00 am to 9:00 pm
Tuesday to Thursday: 10:00 am to 6:00 pm
Saturday: 10:00 am to 5:30 pm
Sunday: 12:00 am to 5:00 pm (except June, July and August)

Closed legal holidays and Sunday during the summer.

Closest Public Transportation:

Subway: R to 169th Street
         F to 169th Street (Saturday, Sunday and weekday evenings only)

Bus: Q1, Q2, Q3, Q17, Q36, Q75, N1, N2, N3, N6, N22, N22A or N24 to Jamaica Bus Terminal

Directions:

From Manhattan, take the R (local) train to the 169th Street station; or, take the F (express) train to the Parsons Boulevard station and change on the same platform for the R (local) to 169th Street. Exit at the back of the train to 168th Street. After exiting the turnstiles, go up the last stairway to the left. Walk one block west to Merrick Boulevard (166th Street) and turn left. Walk two blocks south on Merrick Boulevard to the Library. The Library is across the street from the Bus Terminal.

Description of Resources:

The Long Island Division of the Queens Borough Public Library, established in 1912, is a reference and research center devoted to the study of the four counties of Long Island -- Queens, Brooklyn, Nassau and Suffolk. Materials include books, maps, photographs, manuscripts, census records and clipping files with emphasis on the history and genealogy of the area. Specific collections which may be of interest to genealogists include:

1. Picture Collections: Includes pictures covering different localities in Queens and Long Island, from the early part of the 20th century to the present. In addition, there is a postcard collection arranged by locality from approximately 1890 to 1940.

   The Long Island Division has a copy of the microfiche collection, *Photographic Views of New York City 1870's to 1970's*. See "NEW YORK PUBLIC LIBRARY - U.S. HISTORY, LOCAL HISTORY AND GENEALOGY DIVISION AND MICROFORMS DIVISION" for a detailed description of this collection and finding aids.

2. Census: While the Long Island Division focuses on the four counties of Long Island, it has microfilm reels for some other New York State counties. The following New York metropolitan area census records are available:

New York State Census:
Queens, 1915 and 1925

<u>Federal Census</u>:
Kings, Queens, Suffolk, 1800-1880, 1890 (Suffolk-Brookhaven Township only) and Veteran's schedules for the three counties. NOTE: Pre-1899, Queens County included present-day Nassau County.
Kings, Queens, Nassau, Suffolk, 1900, 1910
New York County, 1800, 1820 (part)
Richmond, 1800, 1810, 1890 (Veteran's schedules)
Rockland, 1800, 1820, 1830
Westchester, 1800, 1830, 1850
New York State (12 of 14 reels), U.S. Mortality Census, 1850-1880
New York State (entire State) Soundex, 1880, 1900
U.S. (entire) Index to the surviving 1890 schedules

New York State and New Jersey, U.S. Census Enumeration District Descriptions, 1900. (Also for 1900: NE, NV, NH, NM, NC, ND and OH.)
New York State, U.S. Census Enumeration District Descriptions, 1910

3. <u>City Directories</u> (on microfilm, some in paper copies)

Brooklyn, 1796, 1802/3, 1811/12, 1822-1909/10, 1912, 1913, 1933/34
Brooklyn and Long Island (Business), 1878/79, 1899
New York City (generally includes Manhattan and parts of the Bronx), 1786-1924/25, 1933/34
Queens (Business and Residential) 1898-1902, 1904, 1906-1909/10, 1912, 1933
Flushing, 1887/88
Great Neck, 1937/38, 1946/47-1955
Hempstead/Freeport, 1897, 1901/2-1911/12
Long Island, 1864/65, 1872/73-1878/79, 1888/89
Long Island City, 1888/89
Montauk (Business), 1915-1917
Patchogue (Business and Residential), 1904

4. <u>Telephone Directories</u> (on microfilm)

Brooklyn, 1929-1973/74
Brooklyn classified, 1928, 1944-1973/74
Brooklyn, Queens and Staten Island, 1924-1928/29
Manhattan, 1932/33-1973/74
Queens, 1927-1973/74
Queens classified, 1927/28-1930, 1957-1973/74
Suffolk/Nassau/Queens supplement, 1908-1927

5. <u>Newspapers</u>

Herald Tribune clipping and picture file (complete morgue). About one-third of this collection, including surname files, is on microfiche and is directly accessible to researchers in the Long Island Division. NOTE: The files on microfiche were in danger of spoilage (mold or water damage). See "Restrictions on Use" for remainder of this collection.

Brooklyn Daily Eagle, October 1841-January 1955.

Newsday, 1973 to present (includes for various times the Nassau, Nassau/Queens, Suffolk and NYC editions).   In addition, there is an annual index to *Newsday,* 1977-1983, that includes an alphabetical listing of obituaries.

The Library has an extensive collection of Queens newspapers on microfilm. A sample list follows:

Queens - Borough-wide
Long Island Democrat, 1835-1912
Long Island Farmer, 1821-1920
Long Island Press, 1922-1977
Long Island Star-Journal, 1882-1968
Newtown Register, 1873-1935
Queens Chronicle, 1984-
Queens Post, 1950-1961
Queens Review, 1935-1951
Queens Tribune, 1975-
Queens Voice, 1965-1970
Queens Week, 1983-

Astoria & Long Island City
Western Queens Gazette, 1982-

Bayside
Bayside Times, 1936-

College Point
College Point News, 1947

Flushing
Flushing Daily Times, 1866-1925
Home Town News, 1955-1960
Long Island Herald, 1948-1974
North Shore News, 1938-1966

Forest Hills
Long Island Post, 1950-1970

Glen Oaks
Glen Oaks News, 1952-1976

Glendale
Glendale Register, 1968-

Jackson Heights
Jackson Heights News, 1918-1970

Jamaica
Community Chatter, 1970-1971
Community News, 1947
Community Voice, 1973-1974
Jamaica Herald, 1927
New York Voice, 1971-
Queens Evening News, 1927-1939

Kew Gardens Hills
Kew Hills News, 1953-1976

Little Neck
Little Neck Ledger, 1951-

Long Island City
Daily Star, 1881-1933
Long Island Graphic, 1952-1957

Maspeth
Queens Ledger, 1941-

Queens Village
Queens County Times, 1960-1975
Queens Illustrated News, 1973-

Richmond Hill
Long Island News, 1944-1946
Richmond Hill Courier, 1927-1928

Ridgewood
Ridgewood Times, 1941-

Rockaway Beach
Argus, 1934-1939
Rockaway Journal, 1935-
Rockaway News, 1910-1941
Rockaway Point News, 1961-1971
Rockaway Record, 1964-1981
Wave, 1896-

St. Albans
St. Albans Life, 1946-1952

South Jamaica
Inside Rochdale News, 1965-1978

South Queens
Forum of South Queens, 1968-

Whitestone
Whitestone Herald, 1871-1949

Woodhaven
Leader-Observer, 1927-

Woodside
Woodside Herald, 1975-

6.   Community Files: Vertical files on neighborhoods in Queens and communities on Long Island, including thousands of newspaper clippings and pictures.

7.   Property Records (on microfilm)

Queens County Conveyances, 1683-1806
Queens County Mortgages, 1754-1815

8. <u>Wills</u> (on microfilm)

New York County wills, 1680-1877
New York County Surrogate Court wills, 1662-1761, 1815-1829

9. <u>Town Records</u>: Records (on microfilm) include land transactions, wills and town meetings:

Flushing, 1790-1892
Hempstead, 1644-1874
Jamaica, 1855-1897

Newtown, 1653-1874
Oyster Bay, 1684-1874
Westchester, late 1600s to 1800s

Brookhaven Town archives, Suffolk County, 1845-1924 (bulk 1880-1890), include fragmentary material from daily school registers, 1878-1921; registers of electors, election poll list and registration list, c.1893-1924; tax assessment roll book and extracts of lists, 1872-1885.

Flushing Village and Town archives, 1786-1881 (bulk 1817-1876), include roll book of public school, 1848-1853; minute book, Board of Education, District 5, 1841-1876; assessment roll (Town) 1817-1821 and (Village) 1857; Justice's Court docket book, c.1877-1881; account book for census of Flushing inhabitants, 1786.

10. <u>Coroner's Office Inquests of Deaths</u> (on microfilm): Copies of records for 1862-1864, 1868-1877 are located at the end of the "New York County Surrogate Court Wills" microfilm.

11. <u>Maps</u>: An extensive collection of maps including:

Queens Assembly District, 1945-1948, 1957, 1965 and 1977
Real Estate atlases of Queens, various years from 1890 to 1970

12. <u>Genealogies/Family Histories</u>: Approximately 3,500 genealogies and family histories including early Long Island settlers.

13. <u>Passenger Records</u> (on microfilm): Passenger lists of vessels arriving at New York harbor, 1820-1897. Arranged in order of arrival.

Surname index to passenger lists of vessels arriving at New York, 1820-1846. NOTE: There is no name index between 1846 and June 16, 1897.

14. <u>Blue Label Card File</u>: Index cards with genealogical information about Long Island personalities abstracted from newspapers and records. The card file includes information from the 1700s and appears to run to the 1930s.

15. <u>Revolutionary War Soldiers</u>: U.S. Adjutant General's Office general index of Revolutionary War soldiers and sailors showing rank and regiment.

16. <u>William A. Eardeley Collection</u>, c.1920-1929, includes notes on Long Island families including birth, marriage and death dates; notebooks listing tombstone inscriptions from Brooklyn, Queens and Manhattan; listings of deaths from fevers in Manhattan between 1798 and 1822.

17. <u>Exempt Firemen's Association of Queens</u> and <u>Flushing</u>: Queens Collection includes notices of deaths of members, 1944-1947. Flushing Collection includes membership cards, c.1916-1924.

18. <u>Historical Documents Collection</u>: Some of the paper materials of the QUEENS COLLEGE, HISTORICAL DOCUMENTS COLLECTION have been transferred to this Library and may be viewed here. See "Restrictions on Use."

19. <u>Other Materials</u>: Although the emphasis of this collection is on the counties of Long Island, the Library has an extensive collection of materials from other states in the Northeast. Example: The Connecticut State Library, Vital Records, c.1750-c.1850 (on microfilm).

20. <u>Real Estate Directory</u>: Latest microfiche edition of the Real Estate Data Inc. (REDI) directory for Queens. Although the microfiche is located at the Social Science reference desk (not in the Long Island Division), it is of interest to genealogists. The directory is arranged by address and provides block and lot number, name of current owner and other information about a piece of property.

Finding Aids:

The card catalog provides a separate index for the community file, periodicals, manuscripts, genealogies and other books. All are indexed alphabetically.

The Library also has finding aids in binders organized by state and local communities. These are located inside the glass-enclosed area and must be requested from the librarian.

Description of Facility:

The Long Island Division is on the main floor of the Library towards the rear of the building. There is an information table at the entrance to the building. The Division is located in a room that seats 23 people. There are 2 microfilm and one microfiche readers available. If the machines in this Division are occupied, researchers may use the 14 microfilm and one microfiche readers in the Magazine and Documents room. A librarian is available to assist researchers.

Microfilm and microfiche records are in open self-service cabinets providing easy access to researchers. However, half of the manuscript collection is located in the basement and must be requested from the librarian. See "Restrictions on Use."

Fees/Copies:

There is one photocopy machine in the Long Island Division and 4 more outside the room. Copies are made by the staff of the Division and are $.15 per page. There are 4-6 microfilm reader/printers and one microfiche reader/printer in the Magazine and Documents room. Copies cost $.15 per page and can be made by the researcher.

Restrictions on Use:

Materials located in the basement, e.g. original Town records, telephone directories (paper copies) and some biographies, cannot be retrieved on Sunday. However, telephone arrangements can be made at least 2 days in advance to view these materials (but not newspaper clippings).

Herald Tribune clippings are stored off-site and must be requested in writing at least one week in advance.

Researchers wishing to view materials in the Historical Documents Collection should contact the Director at Queens College for permission and for information on the materials located at the Library. See "QUEENS COLLEGE, HISTORICAL DOCUMENTS COLLECTION."

No material except microfilms may be taken out of the room.

Researchers are requested to ask the librarian for assistance when using the vertical files.

QUEENS COLLEGE
HISTORICAL DOCUMENTS COLLECTION

Facility Director: Dr. Leo Hershkowitz, Director

Address: Queens College
History Department, Room 217
Powdermaker Hall
Flushing, NY 11367

(Cross Streets: Melbourne Avenue and 150th Street)

Phone Number: (718) 520-7910
(718) 520-7366 (History Department)

Hours of Operation:

Monday to Friday: by appointment only
Closed Saturday, Sunday and legal holidays.

Closest Public Transportation:

Subway: E, F, G or R to Continental Avenue/Forest Hills or Union Turnpike
        7 to Main Street
Train: LIRR to Main Street

      <u>and</u>

Bus: Q44VP to Melbourne Avenue and 150th Street (Gate 2)
       Q25 or Q25-34 to Kissena Boulevard and Melbourne Avenue (Gate 1)
       Q17 to Kissena Boulevard and Long Island (Horace Harding) Expressway,
       Q65A to Kissena Boulevard and Jewel Avenue

Directions:

Take the E or F train to the Continental-Forest Hills station. Exit the station at the <u>north</u> side of Queens Boulevard. The Q65A bus stops in front of the Ridgewood Bank on Queens Boulevard near 70th Road. Take the bus to Jewel Avenue and 150th Street. Cross Jewel and walk two blocks on 150th Street to Melbourne Avenue (Gate 2 of the campus). Walk straight ahead to reach Powdermaker Hall. The History Department is on the 2nd floor.

Description of Resources:

The Historical Documents Collection (HDC) includes over 800,000 original New York City documents dating from the Dutch administration of New Amsterdam to the beginning of the 20th century. The collection is a valuable source of information on New York history of the 17th to 19th centuries and is especially rich in social history. Many colonial and early national newspapers (on microfilm and microcard) are included.

The following records in the collection may be of interest to genealogists:

1. <u>Court Records, New York County</u> include Surrogate's Court inventories of estates, 1783-1844, and wills, 1658-1879; Supreme Court insolvency assignments, 1754-c.1850; Supreme Court, common orders, c.1850-1909; Chancery Court minutes, 1683-1956 (microfilm); Mayor's Court minutes, 1706-1945 (microfilm).

2. <u>Property Records, Queens County</u> (microfilm) include conveyances, 1683-1806, and mortgages, 1754-1815. (NOTE: Queens County included present-day Nassau County during this period.)

3. <u>Property Records, New York County</u> (microfilm) include conveyances, 1754-1860, and mortgages, 1754-1860.

4. Tax Assessment Rolls, New York County, 1699-1840 (most from 1790-1840) in paper copy and 1699-1829 on microfilm. The tax records for 1816 and 1819 include a census of the County.

5. Coroner's Office, New York County (microfilm) records, 1752-1918.

6. Town Records (microfilm) include Flushing, 1790-1889; Newtown, 1653-1872; Jamaica, 1814-1895; Westchester, 1796-1897; Richmond and Ulster Counties.

7. Revolutionary War Petitions, c.1790-1829, presented to the New York Mayor's Court by insolvent Revolutionary War veterans, describe their activities during the war.

8. Albany Records (microfilm) include administration of estates, 1700-1825; inventories of estates, c.1600-1826; wills, 1629-1802; custom records, 1704-1766; Chancery Court records, 1701-1870.

9. New Amsterdam Records (microfilm) include Dutch Council minutes, 1638-1664, and Dutch records, 1638-1671.

Finding Aids:

1. Court Records: A complete alphabetical listing of names of persons whose wills are on file in the Historical Documents Collection was published in *National Genealogical Society Quarterly,* Vol. 51 (June 1963) 90-99; Vol. 51 (Sept. 1963) 174-178, 185; Vol. 54 (June 1966) 98-124.

   Liber indexes are available at the SURROGATE'S COURT - NEW YORK COUNTY (MANHATTAN) for the records of that court. Supreme Court, New York County, insolvency assignments are indexed alphabetically by surname.

2. Tax Assessment Rolls are not indexed.

3. Property Records: Grantor/grantee and mortgagor indexes are available for New York County records at the CITY REGISTER'S OFFICE, MANHATTAN and for Queens County at the CITY REGISTER'S OFFICE, QUEENS.

A published description of the collections of the Center is available in *Guide to Historical Resources in Queens County, New York Repositories,* 1987, New York Historical Resources Center, Cornell University.

A partial listing of the collection can be found in the *National Union Catalog of Manuscript Collections* (nos. 74-924 to 74-935).

Description of Facility:

There is a microfilm reader/printer which can be made available to users of this Collection.

Fees/Copies:

Copies are made by staff at $2 per page.

Restrictions on Use:

Records (except microfilm) are currently not open to the public at the College. However, mail inquiries for copies of records are accepted. Some of the paper records have been transferred to the QUEENS BOROUGH PUBLIC LIBRARY where they can be made available to researchers. Contact the HDC Director for access.

SURROGATE'S COURT - QUEENS COUNTY
RECORD ROOM

Facility Director: Leonard Pryor, Record Clerk

Address: Supreme Court Building, 7th floor
88-11 Sutphin Boulevard
Jamaica, NY 11435

(Cross Streets: 88th and 89th Avenues)

Phone Number: (718) 520-3128

Hours of Operation:

Monday to Friday: 9:00 am to 4:45 pm
Closed Saturday, Sunday and legal holidays.

Closest Public Transportation and Directions:

See "COUNTY CLERK'S OFFICE - STATE SUPREME COURT - QUEENS." Take the elevator to the 7th floor.

Description of Resources:

The Record Room has all probate, administration and guardianship records from 1830 to the present; and scattered records pre-1830. The records for 1964-1972 are on microfiche. (The filming of records will continue. Earlier years will be filmed next, i.e. 1963, 1962, etc.) Will libers from 1787 to the present are on open shelves around the room and under the index card file cabinets. See "SURROGATE'S COURT - NEW YORK COUNTY (MANHATTAN)" for a detailed description of these records.

NOTE: Through 1898, Queens County included what is now Nassau County.

Finding Aids:

The Record Room has one alphabetical name index for records, 1787-1986, located in 6 file cabinets. The index from January 1987 to the present is on computer. The card file index, c.1940-1986, and computer index include name and last address of individual, date of death, type of proceeding filed and file number. Earlier index cards include name, file number and type of proceeding.

Description of Facility:

The Record Room is located on the 7th floor. To order a file, fill out a request form; be sure to include the file number and the year of filing. There are 2-3 staff persons who can locate records immediately. The work table can seat 8 people. There are two computer monitors and two microfiche reader/printers.

Fees/Copies:

Two photocopy machines are available in the room at $.15 per page. Copies from the microfiche reader/printers cost $.25 per page.

Mail requests cost $53 for the search of a record by full name (not surname) over 25 years old and $20 for records under 25 years, plus the cost of copying the record, i.e. $4 per page for a certified copy or $.25 for uncertified copies. The search fee is not charged if the file number is provided by the researcher. For a pre-1900 record that is fragile, the document will not be photocopied but will be typed, at a charge of $4 per page.

Restrictions on Use:

Files on adoptions and certain guardianship records are closed to the public.

STATEN ISLAND

BOARD OF ELECTIONS
STATEN ISLAND BOROUGH OFFICE

Facility Director: Barbara Kett, Chief Clerk

Address: 25 Hyatt Street, 4th floor
Staten Island, NY 10301

(Cross Streets: Central Avenue and St. Marks Place)

NOTE: The office is planning to move within the next year. Call in advance.

Phone Number: (718) 727-4300

Hours of Operation:

Monday to Friday: 9:00 am to 5:00 pm. Researchers should arrive by 4:00 pm.
Closed Saturday, Sunday and legal holidays.

Closest Public Transportation:

Ferry: Staten Island Ferry from South Ferry Terminal (Manhattan)

Directions:

Take the Staten Island Ferry from the South Ferry Terminal in Manhattan (near the South Ferry station of the #1 train; the Whitehall Street station of the N or R train; and the Bowling Green station of the #4 or #5 train). Hyatt Street is one block behind the Borough Hall building -- opposite the municipal parking lot.

Description of Resources:

The Staten Island office has voter registration records from 1957 to the present. For records, 1898-1956, see "NEW YORK CITY DEPARTMENT OF RECORDS AND INFORMATION SERVICES, MUNICIPAL ARCHIVES."

Finding Aids:

Records, 1957-1981, are on microfilm and are arranged alphabetically. Original copies, "buff" cards, 1957 to the present are also available. Active "buffs" are arranged by Assembly/Election District (AD/ED) and then alphabetized by name. Cancelled "buffs" are arranged alphabetically. For active voters, there is a computer printout arranged alphabetically by name which lists the AD/ED of the voter.

Description of Facility:

This is a NYC government office. From 5 to 6 researchers can work at one time. Prior arrangements should be made. The office has one microfilm reader.

Fees/Copies:

See "BOARD OF ELECTIONS, BRONX BOROUGH OFFICE." There is no charge for viewing active files (1982 or later) in person. The office will charge the $3 search fee for use of the microfilm reader. Photocopies of records are $.20 per page.

Restrictions on Use:

None.

CITY CLERK'S OFFICE - STATEN ISLAND (RICHMOND)
MARRIAGE LICENSE BUREAU

Facility Director:	Joanne O. Zerilli, Borough Administrator
Address:	Borough Hall 10 Richmond Terrace, Room 311 Staten Island, NY 10301 (Cross Street: Opposite the Ferry Terminal)
Mail Address:	Add "Attention - Marriage Records Unit" to lower left corner of the envelope.
Phone Number:	(718) 390-5175 or 5176

Hours of Operation:

Monday to Friday: 9:00 am to 4:00 pm
Closed Saturday, Sunday and legal holidays.

Closest Public Transportation and Directions:

See "BOARD OF ELECTIONS, STATEN ISLAND BOROUGH OFFICE." Borough Hall is the building with the clock across from the Ferry Terminal in Staten Island. Use the Stuyvesant Place entrance to the building after 9:30 am.

Description of Resources:

City Clerk's marriage records for Staten Island (Richmond County) are available from 1908 to the present.

NOTE: Two independent sets of records exist for the period 1908-1937 when both the City Clerk's Office and the NYC Department of Health maintained marriage records. The Health Department records are for 1898-1937 and the City Clerk's Office records are from 1908 to the present. The Health Department records are being accessioned by the MUNICIPAL ARCHIVES. See "NEW YORK CITY DEPARTMENT OF RECORDS AND INFORMATION SERVICES, MUNICIPAL ARCHIVES" and "CITY CLERK'S OFFICE - MANHATTAN" for a more detailed description of these records. The MUNICIPAL ARCHIVES also has pre-1898 marriage records for localities on Staten Island.

Original marriage records (certificates) for Staten Island, 1880-1898, are also available at the NEW YORK STATE HEALTH DEPARTMENT in Albany.

Finding Aids:

The City Clerk's liber indexes for brides and grooms are available from 1908 to the present and are in the same format as those in the Manhattan office. See "CITY CLERK'S OFFICE - MANHATTAN."

Description of Facility:

This NYC government office is staffed by two persons who assist the public.

Fees/Copies and Restrictions on Use:

See "CITY CLERK'S OFFICE - MANHATTAN." The Staten Island Office does not accept personal checks.

CIVIL COURT OF THE CITY OF NEW YORK
STATEN ISLAND (RICHMOND COUNTY)

Facility Director: Joseph DiBrienza, Clerk of the County

Address: 927 Castleton Avenue
Staten Island, NY 10310

(Cross Streets: Bement and Oakland Avenues)

Phone Number: (718) 390-5422

Hours of Operation:

Monday to Friday: 9:00 am to 5:00 pm
Closed Saturday, Sunday and legal holidays.

Closest Public Transportation:

Ferry: Staten Island Ferry from South Ferry Terminal (Manhattan) <u>and</u>
Bus: S3 or S102 to Castleton and Bement Avenues

Directions:

Take the Staten Island Ferry from the South Ferry Terminal in Manhattan (near the South Ferry station of the #1 train; the Whitehall Street station of the N or R train; and the Bowling Green station of the #4 or #5 train). At the Ferry Terminal in Staten Island, go up Bus Ramp C for the S3 (Castleton Avenue) or S102 (Henderson Avenue) bus to Castleton and Bement Avenues.

Description of Resources:

The Court has name change records for individuals who legally changed their names in Staten Island from 1927 to the present.

See also "COUNTY CLERK'S OFFICE - STATE SUPREME COURT, RICHMOND COUNTY" for name changes recorded in State Supreme Court.

Finding Aids:

The indexes to name change records are in ledgers in groups of years and alphabetized by both old and new names. The actual records are in case files.

Description of Facility:

The indexes and records are located in the basement in the General Clerk's Office. The clerks on duty can assist researchers.

Fees/Copies:

A photocopy machine is located in the General Clerk's Office. Copies cost $.15 per page. Certified copies of records cost $4 per page.

Restrictions on Use:

None. All records are located on-site.

COUNTY CLERK'S OFFICE - STATE SUPREME COURT
RICHMOND COUNTY (STATEN ISLAND)

Facility Director: Mario J. Esposito, County Clerk
Carol Fietkau, Deputy County Clerk

Address: County Court House
18 Richmond Terrace
Staten Island, NY 10301

(Cross Street: Schuyler Street. Opposite the Ferry Terminal.)

Phone Number: (718) 390-5389 (Court desk)
(718) 390-5390 (Real Property records)
(718) 390-5393 (All other records)

Hours of Operation:

Monday to Friday: 9:00 am to 5:00 pm
Closed Saturday, Sunday and legal holidays.

Closest Public Transportation and Directions:

See "BOARD OF ELECTIONS, STATEN ISLAND BOROUGH OFFICE." The County Court House is across from the Ferry Terminal in Staten Island and next to Borough Hall.

Description of Resources:

The County Clerk's Office in Staten Island also performs the functions of the City Register's Office in recording real property instruments. The Office has deposited many of its old records with the NEW YORK CITY DEPARTMENT OF RECORDS AND INFORMATION SERVICES, MUNICIPAL ARCHIVES. Where this is the case, it is so noted. Some County records are also at the STATEN ISLAND HISTORICAL SOCIETY and the STATEN ISLAND INSTITUTE OF ARTS AND SCIENCES. The following records are at the County Clerk's Office:

1.   <u>Naturalizations</u> filed in State Supreme Court, Richmond County, 1820-1960 (1820-1924, on microfilm) and Declarations of Intention, c.1884-1929 (may be some gaps). See "Restrictions on Use."

    After 1960, Staten Island residents were naturalized in U.S. DISTRICT COURT of either the Southern or Eastern Districts. The NATIONAL ARCHIVES, NORTHEAST REGION has copies of pre-September 1906 Naturalizations. See also "NEW YORK CITY DEPARTMENT OF RECORDS AND INFORMATION SERVICES, MUNICIPAL ARCHIVES" for Naturalization records from this office.

2.   <u>Census Records</u> for Richmond County include the U.S. Census, 1860 and 1870 (incomplete), and 1880; and the New York State Census, Richmond County, 1855 and 1865 (incomplete), 1875, 1915 and 1925.

    These original records are in poor condition. Census records, 1860, 1865, 1870 and 1880, are also on microfilm.

    NOTE: The 1915 and 1925 Census is available also at the NEW YORK STATE EDUCATION DEPARTMENT, OFFICE OF CULTURAL EDUCATION, NEW YORK STATE LIBRARY where copies can be made from microfilm.

3.   <u>Court Cases</u> brought against an individual or actions filed by an individual, 1947 to the present. Cases filed 1947-1976 are on microfilm. The Office also has the records of the Court of Common Pleas, 1711-1833, on microfilm. For other Court records, 1706-1947, see "NEW YORK CITY DEPARTMENT OF RECORDS AND INFORMATION SERVICES, MUNICIPAL ARCHIVES."

4.   <u>Real Property Records</u> (deeds, mortgages, maps) recorded in Richmond County (Staten Island), 1681 to the present.

5. <u>Matrimonial Records</u>: Divorces, separations and annulments, 1934 to the present. See "Restrictions on Use."

   For earlier records, 1861-1933, see the "NEW YORK CITY DEPARTMENT OF RECORDS AND INFORMATION SERVICES, MUNICIPAL ARCHIVES."

6. <u>Military Discharge Records</u>, 1917 to the present, for veterans who filed a copy of a DD 214 form (discharge papers) in this Office.

7. <u>Business Records</u> including:

   Certificates of Incorporation, 1930 to the present
   Assumed Names (Trade Names and Limited Partnerships), 1930 to the present

   See "NEW YORK CITY DEPARTMENT OF RECORDS AND INFORMATION SERVICES, MUNICIPAL ARCHIVES" for Certificates of Incorporation, 1848-1929.

8. <u>Surrenders of Children</u>: Duplicate orders issued by the Surrogate's Court for Surrenders of Children are filed in the County Clerk's Office. See "Restrictions on Use."

9. <u>Name Changes</u> for individuals whose names were legally changed in State Supreme Court, Richmond County, 1930 to the present.

   For earlier records, 1840-1929, see "NEW YORK CITY DEPARTMENT OF RECORDS AND INFORMATION SERVICES, MUNICIPAL ARCHIVES."

10. <u>Incompetency Records</u> and <u>Conservatorship Records</u>, 1930 to the present.

    See "NEW YORK CITY DEPARTMENT OF RECORDS AND INFORMATION SERVICES, MUNICIPAL ARCHIVES" for earlier records, 1840-1929.

Finding Aids:

1. <u>Naturalizations</u>: The Office has a card index, 1820-1906, arranged alphabetically by surname. This index is located at the entrance to Room 100. A microfilm copy of this index is on the balcony above Room 103. Liber indexes (2 volumes), arranged alphabetically by the first two letters of the surname and the first letter of the first name, are available for 1907-1931 and 1932-1960. These are located in Room 104. NOTE: For most entries in this index, only the first letter of the first name (not the full first name) is listed.

   Naturalization records are in libers on the 4th floor of Borough Hall. A microfilm copy of records, 1820-1924, is located on the balcony above Room 103.

   <u>Declarations of Intention</u>, 1884-1906, are indexed alphabetically by the first letter of the surname. The index is at the front of each volume. These records are on the 4th floor of Borough Hall. No index is available for later years. See "Restrictions on Use."

2. <u>Census Records</u> were enumerated by Wards or AD/ED for NYS 20th century censuses. This office does not have copies of the Ward maps but staff can assist in locating streets in the Census volumes. The Census volumes are located in Room 104 of the Court House. Microfilm copies are on the balcony above Room 103.

3. <u>Court Cases</u> and <u>Matrimonial Records</u>: Divorces and annulments were indexed together with other court cases until 1974. Since 1974 separate Matrimonial ledgers are arranged in groups of years and alphabetically by the first letter of the surname. Separations were indexed separately, 1966-1974. Since 1974 they are indexed with other Matrimonial records. These separate indexes are located in Room 103. For 1930-1974, liber indexes (<u>Index to Rule Book</u>) are available for <u>Court Cases</u> (including <u>Matrimonial</u> cases) in Room 104. No index can be found for earlier records. See "Restrictions on Use."

4. <u>Real Property Records</u>: Deeds recorded from 1683 to October 1973 and from July 1986 to the present are indexed in libers by both grantor and grantee. These libers are arranged by groups of years and alphabetically by surname. The grantor/grantee indexes for deeds recorded between October 1981 and

July 1986 are on microfiche. There is no grantor/grantee index for the period October 1973 to September 1981.

Liber indexes for mortgagor/mortgagee from 1683 to September 1975 and from July 1986 to the present are arranged alphabetically by surname. Mortgagor/mortgagee indexes for mortgages recorded October 1981-July 1986 are on microfiche. There is no mortgagor/mortgagee index for the period September 1975 to September 1981.

These alphabetical indexes are the only indexes available for instruments filed pre-1923.

Deeds and mortgages filed from 1923 to September 1981 are indexed also by Land Map Block and lot number. These numbers can be obtained by consulting a map in this office.

Deeds and mortgages filed from October 1, 1981 to October 16, 1986 are filed by Tax Block and lot numbers. These records are on microfiche.

Deeds and mortgages filed after October 16, 1986 are in a computer index. Reel and page numbers of records can be obtained by entering Tax Block and lot numbers, address or name. See the staff behind the counter in Room 103 for information from the computer.

Records from 1681 to 1902 (microfilm), 1906 to 1981 (paper copy), 1981 to 1986 (microfiche) and 1986 to the present (paper copy) are in Room 103. Records from 1902 to April 1906 are on the 4th floor of the Borough Hall building. Index libers and all other Property records are located in Room 103 of the Court building.

5. Military Discharge Records: The first volume, which includes the pre-1945 records, has an index in the front of the volume arranged alphabetically by the first letter of the surname. This volume is located in a cabinet opposite the entrance to Room 103. The liber indexes for records filed from 1945 to 1968 and 1968 to the present are located under the table at the front of Room 103. These are arranged also by the first letter of the surname. The actual records are located in Room 104 of the Court House. However, some volumes (#26, 34, 45, 50, 63 and 77) are on the 4th floor of the Borough Hall building.

6. Business Records: The Office has the index libers for Assumed Names from 1900 to the present. These indexes are located in Room 103. Certificates of Incorporation index libers, 1891-1930, are on the 4th floor of the Borough Hall building. Indexes, 1931 to the present, are in Room 103. These indexes are arranged alphabetically by the first letter of the company's name. There are no indexes for 1848-1890 records.

7. Surrenders of Children: See "Restrictions on Use."

8. Name Changes, Incompetency Records and Conservatorship Records are indexed with Special Proceedings. Special Proceedings indexes are available for 1913-1927 (2 vols.), and 1930 to the present. The 1913-1927 indexes are on the 4th floor of the Borough Hall building. The indexes for 1930 and later are in Room 104. These indexes are arranged by groups of years and the first letter of the surname. The pre-1913 indexes and the 1928-1929 index cannot be located.

Description of Facility:

Most records and indexes are in Rooms 103, 104 or on the 4th floor of the Borough Hall building next door. (See "Finding Aids" for specific locations.) This office has minimal seating space for researchers. Staff have other responsibilities but will try to help. Stop in Room 100 for assistance. There are four microfiche reader/printers in Room 103 and one microfilm reader/printer on the balcony of Room 103. To get to the balcony, use the stairs inside Room 103.

See "Restrictions on Use" for records located on the 4th floor of Borough Hall.

Fees/Copies:

A photocopy machine at $.25 per page is available. Microfilm and microfiche copies cost $.25 per page. Copies of Naturalization or Census records (not on microfilm) can be mailed to the researcher after an in-person search. There may be a 1-2 day wait for Naturalizations. Certified copies cost $4 per page. The

Office will respond to mail requests for records from non-City residents only. Copies cost $5 for a two-year search.

The Office will respond to mail requests for Real Property records from out-of-towners if the liber and page numbers are provided.

Restrictions on Use:

Researchers interested in using records located on the 4th floor of the Borough Hall building should call in advance to assure that staff is available to escort researchers to that building. The room is locked. Materials are in disarray and staff assistance is needed to locate a particular volume.

Many older records have been moved to the NEW YORK CITY DEPARTMENT OF RECORDS AND INFORMATION SERVICES, MUNICIPAL ARCHIVES. Go to Room 100 for the inventory list of the records in the MUNICIPAL ARCHIVES. The ARCHIVES does not have indexes to the records deposited with them. The only indexes available are those located in the County Clerk's Office.

There are gaps in both the records and indexes available in this office. Some have been discarded. Pre-1930 indexes for Court Cases (including Matrimonials) and indexes for Special Proceedings (including Name Changes, Incompetency Records and Conservatorships), pre-1913 and 1928-1929, cannot be located.

Matrimonial Records are closed to the public for 100 years. These records may be viewed by the parties or their representatives. Available indexes are open to the public. Surrenders of Children records are also closed to the public and may not be examined without a court order. The actual case files and indexes are in the Surrogate's Court. These too are closed to the public.

City residents must do searches in-person. The Office does not have sufficient staff to respond to mail inquiries.

STATEN ISLAND HISTORICAL SOCIETY

Facility Director:	Stephen Barto, Archivist
Address:	St. Patrick's Place and Center Street Staten Island, NY (Cross Street: Clarke Avenue)
Mail Address:	441 Clarke Avenue Staten Island, NY 10306
Phone Number:	(718) 351-1611, 1617

Hours of Operation:

Monday to Friday: 10:00 am to 5:00 pm (by appointment only)
The Library/Archives is closed Saturday, Sunday and legal holidays.

Closest Public Transportation:

Ferry: Staten Island Ferry from South Ferry Terminal (Manhattan), <u>and</u>
Bus: S113 to Court Place and Richmond Road

Directions:

Take the Staten Island Ferry from the South Ferry Terminal in Manhattan (near the South Ferry station of the #1 train; the Whitehall Street station of the N or R train; and the Bowling Green station of the #4 or #5 train). At the Ferry Terminal in Staten Island, go up Bus Ramp B for the S113 bus to Court Place and Richmond Road (Richmondtown Restoration). Walk one block up the hill to the Court House. Contact the Library from the reception desk in the Court House.

Description of Resources:

The Society's collections include:

1. <u>Photographs</u>: Staten Island scenes, buildings, portraits of Staten Island residents and personnel of the Volunteer Fire Departments.

2. <u>Biographical and Genealogical File</u>: Genealogical records on Staten Island families since the 17th century.

   The Society has the papers of numerous Staten Island families, mostly non-Jewish. The exceptions are the Carl Isaacs papers (1908-1978), which include the papers of Askel Isaacs, first vice president of B'nai Jeshurun Synagogue, and the papers of the Alter Mord family.

3. <u>County Clerk's Office</u>: Property maps (c.1815-1934) filed in the office of the Richmond County Clerk.

4. <u>Hessian Revolutionary War Diaries</u> (1776-1784): Microfilm copies of daybooks of Hessian regiments stationed on Staten Island. Typescript translations are available for some of these. The originals of the diaries are in the Marburg State Archive in Germany.

5. <u>Maps</u>: Printed, photocopied and manuscript maps of Staten Island from 1648.

6. <u>Military Records</u>: Register of all men from Staten Island who served in World War I; and pension claim forms for survivors and families from the Revolution to World War I.

7. <u>Nursery School Records</u>: Records and photographs from the Port Richmond Day Nursery (1906-1948), the Cradle Roll Nursery (1920-1938) and the West Brighton Day Nursery (1940).

8. <u>Real Estate Records</u> (1844-1984): Maps, title abstracts and other listings relating to realtors and real estate on Staten Island.

9. <u>Staten Island Data File</u> (1935-1951): Card file index documenting vital statistics for thousands of people, as well as events in newspapers, occupations, place names, road records and Black history on Staten Island. This card file was begun by the WPA.

10. <u>Staten Island Records</u> (1609-1967): Microfilms of various Staten Island records including deeds, wills, marriage and death records, Surrogate Court decrees, patents and military records from various sources including the State Supreme Court.

11. <u>Church and Funeral Home Records</u>: Records of the Connell Funeral Home (1907-1936) and many churches on Staten Island.

Finding Aids:

In addition to the card file index described above (#9), the Society has preliminary inventories for its manuscript and archival collections and some subject indexing. Indexing of manuscripts and archival collections by proper names is limited (usually by a single individual or family name per collection).

Description of Facility:

The Society is housed in the former PS 28 school building and is located on the grounds of Richmondtown Restoration. The Library/Archives Room is on the ground floor. Seating is available for 2 researchers.

Fees/Copies:

There is a $2 fee for use of this facility by non-members. One microfilm reader/printer and two photocopy machines are available at $.20 per page. Membership starts at $15 per year for an individual and $30 for a family. Members receive the quarterly journal, *Staten Island Historian,* free general admission to Richmondtown Restoration, discounts on most programs and a 10% discount on Museum Store purchases.

Restrictions on Use:

None. In very few instances the Archivist may determine that records cannot be viewed for reasons of confidentiality.

STATEN ISLAND INSTITUTE OF ARTS AND SCIENCES

Facility Director: John Paul Richiuso, Archivist/Librarian

Address: 75 Stuyvesant Place
Staten Island, NY 10301

(Cross Streets: Wall Street and Hamilton Avenue)

Phone Number: (718) 727-1135

Hours of Operation:

Tuesday to Friday: 10:00 am to 5:00 pm (by appointment only)
Closed Saturday, Sunday, Monday and legal holidays.

Closest Public Transportation and Directions:

See "BOARD OF ELECTIONS, STATEN ISLAND BOROUGH OFFICE." From the Borough Hall building, walk two blocks on Richmond Terrace to Wall Street. Turn left on Wall one block to Stuyvesant Place. Turn right on Stuyvesant to #75.

Description of Resources:

The Institute has the following materials in its collections:

1. <u>Newspapers</u> (on microfilm)

    Newsletter, 1897
    Richmond Argus, 1902-1904
    Richmond County Free Press, 1834-1835
    Richmond County Gazette, 1860-1891
    Richmond County Mirror, 1837-1839
    Richmond County Sentinel, 1876-1879, 1886-1889
    Richmond County Standard, 1882-1895, 1901
    Richmond Republican, 1827-1834
    Staten Island Gazette, 1903-1904
    Staten Island Independent, 1894-1896, 1898-1900
    Staten Island World, 1902-1904
    The Sepoy, 1859-1860
    The Staaten Islander, 1856-1857
    The Staten Islander, 1886-1927, 1934
    Times-Transcript, 1927-1941

    In addition, the Institute has a news clipping file arranged by name from 1910 to the present.

2. <u>Architectural Survey Collection</u>: Photographs and maps of Staten Island.

3. <u>Biographies Collection</u>: Letters, clippings, photographs and other biographical data on Staten Islanders compiled by William T. Davis and Charles Leng for their book, *Staten Island and its People.*

    In addition, the Institute has numerous collections of family papers, photographs and genealogies of Staten Island families. While mostly non-Jewish, the collection includes information on Isaac Abraham Almstaedt (Almstead).

4. <u>Military Records Collection</u>: Muster rolls of the Revolutionary War, 1776-1779; muster rolls of the Staten Island Militia, 1800-1814 and 1848; and Civil War enlistment records.

5. <u>Photograph Collection</u>: Photographs of people, Staten Island scenes, buildings, churches and cemeteries.

6. <u>Richmond County Records</u>: Includes photocopies of the Supervisors* Book, 1766-1823; proceedings of the Board of Supervisors, 1877-1897; Justice of the Peace dockets, 1706-1896; and County Coroner papers, 1787 and 1879. Also included is an inventory of County and borough archives, 1940 and 1942.

   *Until 1898, the County was governed by a Board of Supervisors.

7. <u>Maps and Atlases</u>: Includes insurance atlases for Staten Island, 1874, 1878 and 1917-1935. Printed and photocopied maps are also available here.

8. <u>City Directories</u> (Business and Residential)

   Richmond County Directory, 1862
   Handbook of the Staten Island Railroad, 1870
   Webb's Consolidated Directory of the North and South Shore of Staten Island, 1882/83, 1884
   Standard Directory of Richmond County, 1893/94
   Standard Directory of Richmond Borough, 1897/98
   Industries of Staten Island Before Consolidation, 1898
   Trow's Business and Residential Directory of the Borough of Richmond, 1899, 1900
   Richmond Borough Directory, 1912
   Staten Island Advance Business and Telephone Directory, 1921/22, 1922/23
   Polk's Directory of Staten Island, 1933/34

Finding Aids:

The Institute has a typewritten guide to its collections.

Indexes are available for the following newspapers: *Richmond County Gazette, Richmond County Mirror, Richmond County Sentinel, Richmond Republican, The Sepoy* and *The Staaten Islander*. Indexes are available for some years for the *Richmond Standard* (1887-1894), *Staten Island Independent* (1898-1900), *The Staten Islander* (1934) and the *Staten Island World*.

Description of Facility:

The Institute is at 75 Stuyvesant Place. The Archives is not in the main building but is located next door, at 51 Stuyvesant Place, in the basement of the District Health Center. Researchers must go first to 75 Stuyvesant Place. There are two staff persons to assist researchers. Space is available for 2 researchers at one time. There is one microfilm reader but no reader/printer.

Fees/Copies:

There is a $1 research fee for non-members. A photocopy machine is available at $.10 per page. Membership starts at $10 for students and senior citizens, $20 for an individual, and $30 for a family. Members receive a bi-monthly newsletter, discounts on lectures and films and a 20% discount on purchases in the gift shop.

Restrictions on Use:

Researchers must call 2 or 3 days in advance to make an appointment.
Space is limited and the appointment calendar fills up quickly.

SURROGATE'S COURT - RICHMOND COUNTY (STATEN ISLAND) RECORD ROOM

Facility Director: Matteo L. Lumetta, Chief Clerk

Address: County Court House
18 Richmond Terrace, Room 201
Staten Island, NY 10301

(Cross Street: Schuyler Street. Opposite the Ferry Terminal.)

Phone Number: (718) 390-5400

Hours of Operation:

Monday to Friday: 9:00 am to 5:00 pm
Closed Saturday, Sunday and legal holidays.

Closest Public Transportation and Directions:

See "BOARD OF ELECTIONS, STATEN ISLAND BOROUGH OFFICE." The County Court House is across from the Ferry Terminal in Staten Island and next to Borough Hall.

Description of Resources:

The Surrogate's Court in Staten Island (Richmond County) has files, 1787 to the present for probate and administration; and records of surrenders of children and adoptions from 1927. Guardianship files start c.1930. All closed guardianship files and probate files pre-1943 are on microfiche. See "SURROGATE'S COURT - NEW YORK COUNTY (MANHATTAN)" for a detailed description of these records.

Finding Aids:

The office has an index card file arranged alphabetically by surname, 1960 to the present. Earlier records are indexed in libers by the first 2 letters of the surname.

Description of Facility:

This is a small government office with seating capacity for four researchers. There are three clerks who pull files.

Fees/Copies:

A photocopy machine is available in the Clerk's office at $.15 per page. A microfiche reader/printer is available and costs $.25 per page. Certified copies or copies by mail are $4 per page. Requests by mail which require a search (i.e. case number is not provided) cost $20 if the case is under 25 years old and $53 if the case is over 25 years, plus the $4 per page fee for copies. Personal checks are not accepted.

Restrictions on Use:

Files are retrieved only once per day at 11:00 am. Requests after 11:00 am are pulled the following day. Files on adoptions, surrenders of children and certain guardianship records are closed to the public.

ALBANY

NEW YORK STATE EDUCATION DEPARTMENT
OFFICE OF CULTURAL EDUCATION
NEW YORK STATE ARCHIVES AND RECORDS ADMINISTRATION

Facility Director: Larry J. Hackman, State Archivist and Records Administrator
Christine W. Ward, Principal Archivist, Bureau of State Archival Services

Address: Cultural Education Center, 11th floor
Empire State Plaza
Albany, NY 12230

(Cross Street: Madison Avenue)

Phone Number: (518) 474-8955

Hours of Operation:

Monday to Friday: 9:00 am to 5:00 pm
Closed Saturday, Sunday and legal holidays.

Closest Public Transportation:

Train: Amtrak to Albany (station in Rensselaer)
Bus: Greyhound or Trailways to Albany

Directions:

Take the Amtrak train to Albany. The station is across the Hudson River in Rensselaer. From the train station, take bus #30 or a taxi to the Empire State Plaza. (The train ride takes 2 1/2 hours from Manhattan. Ask for the round trip excursion fare.)

Description of Resources:

The State Archives was created in 1971. At present, the Archives maintains approximately 50,000 cubic feet of Colonial and State government records including legislative and judicial records. The following records are of interest to genealogists. (Use of items noted with an "(R)" are restricted. Researchers who wish to view these records should contact the Archives in advance.)

1. <u>Census Records</u>: The Archives has the original copy (complete for all New York State Counties) of the 1915 and 1925 State census; Assembly/Election District maps for the Bronx, Brooklyn and Manhattan; and a card file index for Albany County, 1925 State census. See "Restrictions on Use."

2. <u>Military Records</u> include Revolutionary War manuscripts; Civil War records including abstracts of muster rolls, c.1870-1880s (arranged by regiment), bounty claims (New York City), 1866-1868, and other records listing officers and enlisted men; claim records for the War of 1812 (published index); a card file for New York State men who served with the U.S. volunteer organizations in the Spanish-American War; muster rolls of New York National Guard units dating from the post-Civil War era up to World War I; and records of the Adjutant General including World War I Veteran's Bonus Cards, 1914-1919.

3. <u>Court Records</u>: All pre-1847 records of defunct courts, including the Court of Chancery, 1684-1847; Supreme Court of Judicature (Albany, Geneva and Utica), 1797-1847; Court of Probates (and its predecessor, the Prerogative Court), 1664-1823; and Court for the Trial of Impeachments and Correction of Errors, 1777-1847 (except those records deposited with the COUNTY CLERK'S OFFICE, STATE SUPREME COURT, NEW YORK COUNTY (MANHATTAN), DIVISION OF OLD RECORDS).

NOTE: Prior to 1788, the jurisdiction of the Court of Probates included all matters in New York, Kings, Orange, Rockland and Westchester Counties and estates valued over fifty pounds elsewhere.

After 1788, the Court's jurisdiction was limited to estates of New York residents who died out of State and to deceased non-residents who owned property in New York. Records include:

> Probated wills, 1671-1815 (also available through the FAMILY HISTORY CENTERS (LDS))
> Administration papers, c.1700-1823, and letters of administration, 1795-1823
> Estate inventories and accounts, 1666-1823

Jurisdiction of the Court of Chancery, New York's highest court of equity, 1683-1847, included business partnerships, land partitions and mortgage foreclosures, the appointment of guardians for minors, lunatics and drunkards, and, after 1787, divorces. A few Naturalizations were also filed in the Court of Chancery (see below). The Archives has all the papers filed in this Court, except the records of the 1st Circuit (New York City and vicinity) which can be found in the COUNTY CLERK'S OFFICE - STATE SUPREME COURT - NEW YORK COUNTY (MANHATTAN), DIVISION OF OLD RECORDS. A name index for Chancery Decrees, 1800-1847, is available (on microfilm).

4. Naturalization Records: The Court of Chancery records described above also include Naturalization papers (indexed), c.1800-1847, for the 5th, 6th and 8th circuits. These circuits covered central and western New York State. In addition, Naturalization papers for Albany, 1799-1812, Utica, 1822 and 1838-1839, filed in the Supreme Court of Judicature are available here.

5. Land Records involving property transactions in which the government was a primary party include applications for land grants, 1642-1898, land patents, 1664-1979, and Surveyor General maps, c.1775-1900.

6. Governor's Office records include:

> Applications for executive clemency and pardon, c.1860-1926; and executive pardons, 1799-1925 (executive clemency records) (R)
> Application for restoration of citizenship rights, 1911-1918 (R)
> Journal of pardons, proclamations and nomination for office, 1859-1916
> Register of applications for appointment, 1864-1905 (indexed)
> Requisitions and mandates for extradition, 1857-1938

7. State Board of Charities records (arranged mostly by county) include:

> Annual reports of incorporated charities, 1871-1872
> Census of inmates in almshouses, 1875-1921
> Census of non-institutionalized insane and idiots, 1871-1872
> List of officers of incorporated charities, 1870
> Register of children removed from poor houses, 1873-1874
> Register of insane in county poor houses, 1871
> Reports on institutionalized and non-institutionalized epileptics receiving poor relief, 1895
> Register of tramps applying for relief to overseer of the poor, 1875-1876

8. Division of Youth: State Agricultural and Industrial School at Industry (Western House of Refuge) records include:

> Records of admission, attendance and discharge, 1896-1911
> Registers of school attendance and student progress, 1873-1893
> Case files of male inmates, 1849-1911 (indexed) (R)
> Case files of female inmates, 1876-1904 (indexed) (R)

9. Department of Correctional Services holdings include the following:

> Albion Correctional Facility, inmate admission ledgers (indexed) and case files, 1893-1971 (R)
> Auburn Correctional Facility, inmate case files, 1919-1952 (R); register of male inmates received, 1817-1953; register of deaths, 1888-1937; discharged by death, 1933-1959 (R); register of female inmates discharged, 1893-1919
> Bedford Hills Correctional Facility, inmate case files, 1924-1957 (R)
> Clinton Correctional Facility (Dannemora Prison), inmate admission ledgers, 1846-1866, 1926-1948; medical and psychiatric reports of inmates, 1934-1967 (R)

Elmira Correctional Facility, inmate biographical ledger, 1879-1957; biographical register of returned men, 1913-1937 (R)

New York House of Refuge, inmate case files, 1824-1935 (indexed); admission registers, 1888-1932; register of inmates admitted and discharged, 1859-1982; parole register, 1892-1933 (R); register of deferred applications for parole, 1806-1891 (R)

Ossining Correctional Facility (Sing Sing Prison), inmate admission registers, 1865-1960; case files of inmates sentenced to electrocution, 1939-1963 (R)

11. State Education Department records include:

Inventory of church records, 1936-1942
Inventory of State and local government records, 1936-1941

12. Department of Health records (most arranged alphabetically by surname) include:

Deceased and released typhoid carrier case files, 1920-1975 (R)
Polio confidential case report cards, 1921-1975 (R)
Raybrook State Tuberculosis Hospital, application book of patients, 1932-1942 (R)
Tuberculosis reporting cards, 1939-1975 (R)
Typhoid fever reporting cards, 1921-1954; and supplementary records, 1959-1971 (R)
Veteran's Home at Oxford, admission case files, 1897-1963 (arranged chronologically by year of discharge or death and then alphabetically by surname) (R)

13. Department of Social Services records include:

Indian census and annuity rolls, 1881-1950 (arranged by Tribe)

14. Department of State records include documents from the Dutch Colonial period including land patents, 1630-1664, and deeds, 1652-1653. British Colonial records include marriage bonds issued by the Provincial Secretary, 1753-1784. Other holdings include appointment records, 1777-1973; affidavits of restoration to citizenship, 1869-1898; executive restorations of citizenship rights, 1889-1931; and incorporation certificates, 1811-1825; wills of out-of-State residents, 1823-1940; and alien depositions of intent to become citizens, 1825-1913. These depositions were filed with the Secretary of State by aliens before they could acquire title to real property. The depositions contain the name of the individual and the county in which the deposition was made, and sometimes the country of origin and occupation.

15. Legislature: The following are records from the sample survey of the Factory Investigating Commission. Most of the sample was taken in New York City factories. NOTE: These records are arranged by establishment. They are not indexed by name and as a result are not easily accessed. See also "Restrictions on Use."

Employee background cards, 1913-1914 (6,700 cards)
Establishment profile cards, 1912-1913 (3,800 cards)
Employment history cards, 1913-1914 (2,050 cards)
Individual annual earnings cards, 1912 (2,400 cards)
Personal financial history cards, 1913-1914 (2,050 cards)

Finding Aids:

There are four types of finding aids available in the Archives. Some are available also in other libraries and researchers are encouraged to consult them before visiting the Archives.

1. A published *Guide to Records in the New York State Archives,* 1981 (out-of-print), contains brief histories of major State agencies and lists of archival record series that originated in each agency. Histories of agencies for which the Archives holds no records are also included.

2. Descriptive inventories of the records of individual State government agencies are also available. These inventories contain more detailed information on the history and functions of an agency and narrative descriptions of the scope and content of information found in each record series. Copies of these inventories may be available at other libraries.

3. Detailed lists of the records in individual boxes, or the contents of specific volumes or individual microfilm reels within a particular record series, are available only in the Archives Research Room.

4. Specialized finding aids, which are usually detailed indexes or item descriptions of the contents of a single or several related series pertaining to a given topic are available. Some have been published but others, especially card indexes, are available only in the Research Room. Several of the these indexes are noted under "Description of Resources."

The published finding aids (free) include:

From the New York State Archives: Information Concerning Records of Genealogical Interest, September 1983.
From the New York State Archives: Civil War Records in the New York State Archives.
From the New York State Archives: Selected Records in the State Archives Relating to Women, A Descriptive List, March 1985.
From the New York State Archives: List of Pre-1847 Court Records in the State Archives, December 1984.
For the Record, a newsletter published several times during the year.

Description of Facility:

The Archives is located on the 11th floor of the Cultural Education Center in Albany's Empire State Plaza. Records may be viewed in the Research Room only. The Archives Research Room facilities are shared with the Manuscripts and Special Collections Unit of the NEW YORK STATE LIBRARY. A reference archivist is on duty at all times to provide assistance to researchers.

There are 2 microfilm readers in the Research Room and one microfilm reader/printer. A separate enclosed area is available in the Research Room where researchers may use their own typing or tape recording equipment. Arrangements should be made in advance to reserve space.

Fees/Copies:

A variety of photoduplication services are available. Copies are made by staff at $.25 per page for paper records and $.75 per page for copies of microfilmed material. Microfilm may be purchased at $20 per roll or borrowed through the New York State Interlibrary Loan network. (Contact your local library for information.)

A fee schedule for photoduplication services is available from the Archives. Staff will respond to mail and telephone requests for information about holdings and copies but cannot search records for specific information about an individual.

Restrictions on Use:

Because of their condition, some records including Census Records, are closed to researchers. Researchers are required to use microfilm copies when they are available. Researchers can view microfilm copies of the Census records in the NEW YORK STATE EDUCATION DEPARTMENT, NEW YORK STATE LIBRARY on the 7th floor of the Cultural Education Center in Albany or through any of the FAMILY HISTORY CENTERS (LDS). Researchers can use the Assembly/Election District maps or card file index in the Archives as finding aids before going to the STATE LIBRARY.

The Factory Investigating Commission records of the Legislature (index cards) are fragile and access is limited.

Coats, briefcases and other containers must be checked in lockers outside the Research Room. Only pencils may be used. Smoking and eating are prohibited.

Researchers must sign the annual registration form that includes an agreement to abide by the rules governing use of the Archives holdings. Researchers must sign in and out in the Research Room log book each day.

Only Archives staff may copy records. The Archives reserves the right to approve copying and to determine the method of photoduplication based upon the condition of the records. Some records are too fragile to be handled.

NEW YORK STATE EDUCATION DEPARTMENT
OFFICE OF CULTURAL EDUCATION
NEW YORK STATE LIBRARY

Facility Director:	Jerome Yavarkovsky, Director
Address:	Cultural Education Center, 7th Floor
	Empire State Plaza
	Albany, NY 12230
	(Cross Street: Madison Avenue)
Phone Number:	(518) 474-5161 (Humanities Reference Service)
	(518) 474-4461, 6282 (Manuscripts)
	(518) 474-3092 (Microforms)

Hours of Operation:

Monday to Friday: 9:00 am to 5:00 pm
Closed Saturday, Sunday and legal holidays.

Closest Public Transportation and Directions:

See "NEW YORK STATE EDUCATION DEPARTMENT, OFFICE OF CULTURAL EDUCATION, NEW YORK STATE ARCHIVES AND RECORDS ADMINISTRATION."

Description of Resources:

The New York State Library was established in 1818 to serve the government and the people of New York State. Its collection includes the following items of interest to genealogists:

1. <u>Census Records</u> (on microfilm)

   U.S. Census:

   > Population schedules for New York State: 1790 (printed), 1800-1910
   >
   > Special schedules for New York State:
   > Agriculture, 1850-1880
   > Industry/Manufactures, 1820-1860, 1870 (Essex-Yates), 1880 Social Statistics, 1850, 1860 (Monroe-Yates), 1870
   > Mortality schedules, 1850-1880
   > Defective, Dependent and Delinquent Classes, 1880

   New York State Census for the following counties and years (records underlined are incomplete):

   > Entire State (62 counties), 1915 and 1925
   > Albany, 1855, 1865, 1875, 1892, 1905
   > Chautauqua, <u>1825</u>, <u>1835</u>, 1855, 1865, 1875, <u>1892</u>, 1905
   > Columbia, <u>1845</u>, 1855, 1865, <u>1875</u>, 1905
   > Fulton, 1875, 1905
   > Greene, 1855, 1865, 1875, 1892, 1905
   > Hamilton, 1892, 1905
   > Madison, 1855, 1865, 1875, 1892, 1905
   > Monroe (only Rochester), 1855
   > Montgomery, 1865, 1875, 1892, 1905
   > Niagara, <u>1855</u>, 1865, 1875
   > Rensselaer, 1855, 1865, 1875, <u>1905</u>
   > St. Lawrence, <u>1845</u>, <u>1865</u>
   > Steuben, 1825, 1835, <u>1845</u>, 1855, 1865, 1875, 1892, 1905

Warren, 1855
Washington, 1825, 1835, 1855, 1865, 1875, 1892, 1905

2. <u>City Directories</u>: The Library has one of the most complete collections of City Directories of New York State communities in both books and microfilm. It has all of the existing NYC Directories as well as some for suburban NYC counties.

3. <u>Church and Cemetery Records</u>: NYS church (Protestant denominations only) and cemetery records include published records, registers deposited in the State Library, and others compiled by New York State chapters of the Daughters of the American Revolution.

   The collection also includes published records of many churches and cemeteries in the Northeast; and English parish registers, primarily volumes published by county record societies.

4. <u>Wills</u>: Printed or microfilm copies of wills, administrative papers, abstracts, indexes and court calendars include:

   Fernow, Berthold. *Calendar of Wills on file and recorded in the Offices of the Clerk of the Court of Appeals, of the County Clerk at Albany, and the Secretary of State, 1626-1836.* 1967. [H974.7 F36a]
   Sawyer, Ray C., editor. *Index of New York State Wills, 1662-1850, on file at the Office of the Surrogate for New York County in the Hall of Records, New York City.* 1932. [H974.71 qS27]
   New-York Historical Society. *Collections: Abstracts of Wills 1665-1800, on file in the Surrogate's Office, County of New York.* 1892-1973. [H974.7 N552 v. 25-41]
   Pelletreau, William Smith, editor. *Early Wills of Westchester County, New York, 1664-1784.* 1898. [H974.727 P38]
   Pelletreau, William Smith, editor. *Early Long Island Wills of Suffolk County, 1691-1703* [An unabridged manuscript known as "The Lester Will Book", a record of the Prerogative Court of Suffolk County, with genealogical and historical notes]. 1897. [H974.725 P38]

5. <u>Daughters of the American Revolution (DAR) Records</u>: The Library is a depository for the following record series compiled by the New York State Chapters of the Daughters of the American Revolution: Bible records; Cemetery, Church and Town records; Family Histories; New Project, Genealogical Data (grandparents forms); Graves of Revolutionary Soldiers in New York; and Lineage Books, 1890-1921.

6. <u>Maps and Atlases</u> (Cartographic Collection): Geographic and historical printed maps of the Colony and State of New York from the mid-17th century to the present; manuscript maps, c.1780-1870; and maps from the 19th and 20th centuries of towns, villages, land patents and, in some cases, individual farm lots.

   The Library has over 1,000 atlases, including a nearly complete set of 19th-century NYS and county atlases; and Sanborn insurance atlases (on microfilm) for most of New York State. Atlases of the State begin in 1829 with the publication of David H. Burr's *Atlas of the State of New York.* County atlases, c.1860-1880, often include names of persons.

7. <u>Print Collection</u>: Includes views of New York State and portraits of its citizens, past and present. The collection includes portrait volumes of the State Legislature, 1858-1879.

8. <u>County Histories</u>: A majority of the county histories in the collection were published in the late 19th and early 20th centuries. These histories contain descriptions of the principal settlements within the county and genealogies or biographical sketches of early settlers and prominent citizens.

   NOTE: *New York County and Regional Histories and Atlases,* a 116-reel microfilm set containing 481 items from the collection at the State Library, is available on interlibrary loan.

9. <u>Military Records</u>: Include lists (not always complete) of New Yorkers who served in the Colonial and State militia, War of 1812, Revolutionary War and Civil War. These are printed compilations, not actual records. In addition, the collection includes histories of New York regiments in the Civil War.

10. <u>Genealogies</u>: The collection includes about 12,500 family histories, national in scope, but with an emphasis on New York State families. In addition, the Manuscripts Collection includes family bibles, diaries, notebooks and correspondence.

11. <u>Passenger Records</u>: The collection includes:

National Archives and Record Service. *Index to Passenger Lists of Vessels Arriving at New York, 1820-1846* [on 103 rolls of microfilm]. [MA-FM 929.37471 I38]

Filby, P. William with Mary K. Meyer, eds. *Passenger and Immigration Lists Index.* 3 vol., 1981. [H929.373 qP287]

Filby, P. William, ed. *Passenger and Immigration Lists Bibliography, 1538-1900.* 1975. [HR325.73025 N338]

12. <u>Newspapers</u> (all on microfilm)

Albany (extensive collection)
Boston Globe, 1980-
Chicago Tribune, 1849-1921, 1960-
Los Angeles Times, 1960-
Newsday, 1964-
New York Daily News, 1970-
New York Times, 1852-
Wall Street Journal, 1889-
Washington Post, 1900-

Finding Aids:

The Library has two public catalogs: an automated catalog arranged by author/title and subject; and a microfiche catalog of its holdings (Dictionary Catalog). Also, there are several card files or indexes of local history and genealogy materials. Entries in the microfiche catalog of interest to genealogists are: "Biography," "Deeds," "Family records," "Registries of birth," "Wills," etc. In addition, the Library has:

1. <u>Surnames Card File</u> which identifies books, articles, pamphlets and manuscripts in the State Library alphabetically by surname.

2. <u>Vital Records Card File</u> arranged by County: This card file indexes sources of county and other local birth, baptism and death records (<u>not</u> surnames or ethnic/religious groups). Cities, towns and communities are filed alphabetically within the county.

3. <u>Census Records</u>: The Library has the published indexes, 1800-1860, to the U.S. censuses for all of New York State. In addition, it has the Soundex index for New York State, 1880 and 1900, and the 1910 street index for 37 U.S. cities.

No comprehensive indexes are available for State Census records. The NEW YORK STATE ARCHIVES has a card index for Albany County, 1925. In addition, the ARCHIVES has Assembly/Election District maps for the 1915 and 1925 censuses for the Bronx, Brooklyn and Manhattan.

4. <u>City Directories</u>: Check both the card catalog, under "City Directories (United States)", and the microforms catalog. Researchers should also check *City Directories of the United States, 1860-1901 Guide to the Microfilm Collection* [MA 917.3 qC581 84-24010] for City Directories on microfilm.

5. <u>Church and Cemetery Records</u>: These New York State records are accessed through the Vital Records Card File (see above). Out-of-state records can be located through the microfiche catalog. For church records, search by place, then by church name. To locate English parish registers, researchers should consult *A Guide to English Parish Registers in the New York State Library* [HO16.942 N532].

6. <u>Wills</u>: For additional titles, check the microfiche catalog and the automated catalog under the subject "Wills."

7. <u>Daughters of the American Revolution Records</u> are indexed in the *Master Index, New York State DAR Genealogical Records* [H929 qD23m] and *Master Index, Supplement 1972-1978, Records and Corrections* [H929 qD23m 1972b]. Bible records and Family Histories are also listed in the Surnames Card File; and Cemetery, Church and Town Records are listed in the Vital Records Card File. Genealogical Data is indexed in the New Project Genealogical Data card index. Graves of Revolutionary War soldiers in New York are indexed in the Revolutionary War Soldiers Card Index. There is an *Index*

to the Rolls of Honor (Ancestor Index) in the Lineage Books of the NSDAR [369.135 A] for Lineage Books.

8. <u>Maps and Atlases</u> are accessed by a card catalog with entries filed by geographic location.

9. <u>Print Collection.</u> This collection is indexed by name and subject.

Description of Facility:

The 7th floor of the Cultural Education Center is the principal public service floor of the Library. An information desk is at the left when entering from the elevators. The Local History and Genealogy Reference Center is to the right. Manuscripts and Special Collections are on the 11th floor, where the Research Room is shared with the NEW YORK STATE ARCHIVES.

Printed books are cataloged by height into octavos (books under 10" tall), quartos (10" to 14") and folios (over 14"). Quartos have a "q" prefix in the call number and folios have an "f" prefix. Signs at the end of the stacks indicate locations. (The octavo and quarto books are filed together on the shelves, but the folios have a separate location.)

"H" in the call number indicates that the book is located in the Local History and Genealogy area; "R" indicates it is in the Reference Collection on the 7th floor; and "A" indicates it is located on the 11th floor in the Manuscripts and Special Collections area.

Most genealogies are shelved in the Genealogy area (call numbers 929.2). Local histories are adjacent to the reading area. Histories of all localities in any one county are grouped together on the shelves. All histories begin with the call number 974. Localities in NYS start with H974.7 and New Jersey with H974.9.

Some materials are in closed stacks and must be paged while you wait (e.g. book form City Directories and telephone books).

The DAR Surnames Card File, Vital Records Card File, New Project Genealogical Data Card Index, Revolutionary War Soldiers Card Index and Index to the Rolls of Honor (Ancestor Index) in the Lineage Books of the NSDAR can be found in the Local History and Genealogy Area.

Federal and State Census Records (population schedules) are located on the 7th floor. Federal special schedules are on microfilm on the 11th floor in the Manuscripts and Special Collections area.

The Library has 19 microfilm readers, 5 reader/printers, 13 microfiche readers and 3 microfiche reader/printers on the 7th floor. It shares 2 microfilm readers and one reader/printer on the 11th floor with the Archives.

Fees/Copies:

The photocopy machine is located near the Local History and Genealogy area. Copies can be made by researchers at $.10 a page. If copies are made by the staff, the fee is $.15 per page. Paper copies of microfilm or microfiche are also $.10 per page (self-service) and $.15 (if made by staff). Film/fiche copiers take dimes only. There is a dollar bill changer near the film/fiche readers (available 9 am to 4 pm). However, researchers are advised to bring dimes and not depend on the bill changer, since it often runs out of dimes in the course of the day. There is a minimum charge of $1 for billing and handling of mail requests. Prints and maps can be duplicated at $2.50. (Ask for the Library's most recent "Photoduplication Rates for Work Done by Photoduplication staff.")

The following publications are available from the Library:

Gateway to America: Genealogical Research in the New York State Library. 1981. ($3)
New York State Census Records, 1790-1925 [Lists federal and state census manuscripts in repositories throughout NYS, including the State Library and Archives]. Bibliography Bulletin #88, 64p., October 1981. ($3)
Adoptees. January 1985, 2p. (free)
Cartographic Resources and Services of the New York State Library. 1980, 7p. (free)
DAR Records. January 1985, 2p. (free)
Loyalist Records. April 1986, 2p. (free)

Local History and Genealogy: A Guide to Collections and Services. pamphlet (free)
Manuscripts and Special Collections: A Guide to Collections and Services. pamphlet (free)
New York State Census Records. February 1986, 2p. (free)
New York State Library Holocaust Resource Collection. January 1986, 17p. (free)
New York State Military Records. February 1986, 2p. (free)
New York State Wills. April 1986, 2p. (free)
Tracing Your Immigrant Ancestors. April 1986, 2p. (free)
Vital Records. April 1986, 2p. (free)

Restrictions on Use:

Some of the materials in the Manuscript and Special Collections are fragile. Determination of availability for and type of photoduplication is made by the Library staff.

Prior to publication of original materials, researchers should inquire about possible restrictions. Publication of any original materials from the collections of the Library should credit the New York State Library as the source of the material.   See "NEW YORK STATE EDUCATION DEPARTMENT, OFFICE OF CULTURAL EDUCATION, NEW YORK STATE ARCHIVES AND RECORDS ADMINISTRATION" for other restrictions in using the Research Room on the 11th floor.

NEW YORK STATE HEALTH DEPARTMENT
VITAL RECORDS SECTION, GENEALOGY UNIT

Facility Director: Peter Carrucci, Director, Vital Records

Address: Corning Tower Building
Room 244 (2nd Floor)
Empire State Plaza
Albany, NY 12237

(Cross Street: Madison Avenue)

Phone Number: (518) 486-1308
(518) 473-8814

Hours of Operation:

Monday to Friday: 8:30 am to 4:30 pm

Call in advance for an appointment to view indexes. These are scheduled at 2-hour intervals.
Closed Saturday, Sunday and legal holidays.

Closest Public Transportation and Directions:

See "NEW YORK STATE EDUCATION DEPARTMENT, OFFICE OF CULTURAL EDUCATION, NEW YORK STATE ARCHIVES AND RECORDS ADMINISTRATION."

Description of Resources:

1. Birth Records from 1881 and Death Records from 1880 for the entire State except records filed in Albany, Buffalo, Yonkers and New York City (and City of Brooklyn). For these cities, the Department has the following:

    Albany, Buffalo and Yonkers: Records from 1914 to the present.
    New York City: Only records for Queens and Richmond Counties, 1880-1898, the eastern portion of the Bronx (part of Westchester County), 1880-1895, and towns in Kings County before annexation to the City of Brooklyn.

    For pre-1914 birth and death records in Albany, Buffalo and Yonkers, contact the City Clerk's Office in these cities. For New York City birth records, 1898 to the present, and death records, 1930 to the present, see "NEW YORK CITY DEPARTMENT OF HEALTH, BUREAU OF VITAL RECORDS." For earlier New York City records, see "NEW YORK CITY DEPARTMENT OF RECORDS AND INFORMATION SERVICES, MUNICIPAL ARCHIVES."

2. Marriage Records for the entire State from 1880 except licenses issued in Albany, Buffalo, Yonkers and New York City (and City of Brooklyn). For these cities, the Department has the following:

    Albany and Buffalo: Records from 1908 to the present.
    New York City: Only records for Queens and Richmond Counties, 1880-1898, the eastern portion of the Bronx (part of Westchester County), 1880-1895 and towns in Kings County before annexation to the City of Brooklyn.
    Yonkers: Records from 1914 to the present.

    For marriage records in New York City, see "CITY CLERK'S OFFICE, MARRIAGE LICENSE BUREAU" of the appropriate borough or "NEW YORK CITY DEPARTMENT OF RECORDS AND INFORMATION SERVICES, MUNICIPAL ARCHIVES." For pre-1908 records in Albany and Buffalo or pre-1914 records in Yonkers, contact the City Clerk's Office in these cities.

    See also "COUNTY CLERK'S OFFICE, WESTCHESTER COUNTY ARCHIVES" for marriages in Westchester County, 1908-1915; "COUNTY CLERK'S OFFICE, NASSAU COUNTY" and "COUNTY CLERK'S OFFICE, SUFFOLK COUNTY" for marriage records, 1908-1935.

Finding Aids:

State-wide indexes for births, marriages and deaths (on microfiche) are arranged by year and then alphabetically by name except marriage indexes, 1908-1914. These 1908-1914 indexes are arranged by the New York State Health Department's Soundex system (see Appendix C). Marriage indexes are available by both the bride's and groom's names. These indexes are open to the public for the same years that records can be ordered. See "Restrictions on Use."

Description of Facility:

The Vital Records Section is on the second floor (Room 244) of the Corning Tower Building at the Empire State Plaza. The office has two microfiche readers available for researchers.

Fees/Copies:

For a copy of a birth, marriage or death record, complete the appropriate box on the application form (see Appendix B-7). There is a $6 fee (per one spelling of the name) for a copy of a birth, marriage or death record. This includes a 3-year search if the certificate number is not provided. For additional years, the fee is as follows:

> 4 to 10 years, $11
> 11 to 20 years, $16
> 21 to 30 years, $21
> 31 to 40 years, $26
> 41 to 50 years, $31
> 51 to 60 years, $36

There is no refund if the record is not found.

Restrictions on Use:

Many local registrars were not filing every record before 1914. It is advisable to consult local city or town clerks if the State cannot locate a pre-1914 birth, marriage or death record.

The Health Commissioner's Administrative Rules and Regulations, Part 35.5, Vital Records (based on the Public Health Law, Section 4173, 4174) permits the release of records as follows: birth records on file at least 75 years and the person to whom the record relates is deceased; death records on file at least 50 years; and marriage records on file at least 50 years and the parties to the marriage named in the record are deceased. This ruling was adopted in March, 1979.

Researchers may not search the records directly. However, the indexes for the years released, may be viewed. Call at least one day in advance for an appointment. Researchers are required to show some form of identification for in-person searches of indexes.

NASSAU COUNTY

COUNTY CLERK'S OFFICE
NASSAU COUNTY, NEW YORK

Facility Director: Harold W. McConnell, County Clerk

Address: 240 Old Country Road, Room 109
Mineola, NY 11501

(Cross Street: East of Franklin Avenue)

Phone Number: (516) 535-2663
(516) 535-2272 (Census)
(516) 535-2270 (Business)
(516) 535-3245 (Basement Vault)
(516) 535-2279 (Name Changes)
(516) 535-2772, 2773 (Naturalizations, Military)
(516) 535-3228 (Property Records)

Hours of Operation:

Monday to Friday: 9:00 am to 4:00 pm
Closed Saturday, Sunday and legal holidays.

Closest Public Transportation:

Train: Long Island Rail Road (LIRR) to Mineola
Bus: N15, N22, N24 or N79 to Old Country Road and County Seat Drive

Directions:

From Manhattan, take the LIRR at Pennsylvania Station (32nd Street and 7th Avenue) to the Mineola station. Walk two blocks south on Mineola Boulevard (becomes Franklin Avenue) to Old Country Road. Cross Old Country Road and turn east two blocks to the County Office Building.

Description of Resources:

Nassau County was created in 1899, one year after the consolidation of the five New York City counties. Prior to 1899, Nassau County was part of Queens County. The County Clerk's Office has the following records:

1. Census

   New York State Census, Nassau County, 1915 and 1925

2. Naturalizations

   Petitions for Naturalization, 1899 to September 12, 1986
   Declarations of Intention, 1900-1980

   There are also Naturalization Petitions for soldiers stationed at Camp Mills (at Mitchell Field) during World War I, 1918-1919.

   After 1986, petitions had to be filed in U.S. DISTRICT COURT in Manhattan or Brooklyn.

3. Marriage Records

   Certificates issued by the County Clerk's Office, January 9, 1908 to April 29, 1935.

   See also "NEW YORK STATE HEALTH DEPARTMENT, VITAL RECORDS SECTION, GENEALOGY UNIT."

4. Court Cases

Cases filed in Supreme Court and County Court from 1899 to the present. Pre-1968 records are on microfilm. Later records are in file folders.

5. Matrimonial Cases

Divorces, annulments and separations from 1899 to the present. See "Restrictions on Use."

6. Name Changes

Records of individuals who legally changed their names in Nassau County (Supreme Court) from 1899 to the present. Records, 1899-1965, are in Miscellaneous Libers. From 1966 to the present, records are on microfilm.

7. Business Records

Business Names, "Doing business as...," 1900 to the present
Certificates of Incorporation, 1899 to the present
Limited Partnerships, 1899 to the present

Records, 1899-1986, are on microfilm. Later records are originals.

8. Military Discharges

Veteran's Discharge papers, from World War I to the present (filed on a voluntary basis). See "Restrictions on Use."

9. Surrenders of Children

Surrenders of Children were filed from 1936 to the present. See "Restrictions on Use."

10. Commitments, Conservatorships and Incompetencies

Commitments, 1938 to the present
Conservatorships, 1938 to the present
Incompetency Records, 1938 to the present

See "Restrictions on Use."

11. Property Records

Deeds, mortgages and maps from the late 17th century to the present. Records, pre-1899 are on microfilm and 1967-1987, are on microfiche. Records, 1899-1986 and April 1, 1987 to the present, are in ledgers.

NOTE: Pre-1899 records are not considered "official" records. They are copies of records in the CITY REGISTER'S OFFICE - QUEENS. The quality of the microfilm is poor.

Finding Aids:

1. Census: There are no finding aids or Assembly/Election District maps available here.

2. Naturalizations: The Office has certificate stubs filed alphabetically by name of petitioner for Naturalizations. Both Naturalization and Declaration records are in bound ledgers in groups of years. Each ledger also has an index at the beginning of the book. There is a one volume index, 1918-1919, for petitions filed at Camp Mills. These indexes are arranged alphabetically by the first letter of the surname.

3. Marriage Records: The indexes are in ledgers arranged alphabetically by the first two letters of the brides' and grooms' surnames.

4. Court Cases: Supreme Court (civil) and County Court proceedings are indexed together. From 1899-1937, indexes are in ledgers arranged alphabetically by the first two letters of the surname. From 1938 to the present, there is a card index arranged alphabetically by the surname of the plaintiff. There are separate card indexes for business plaintiffs and for individual plaintiffs.

Supreme Court (criminal) proceedings are indexed separately in a card file also arranged alphabetically by surname.

5. <u>Matrimonial Records</u>: Divorces and annulments from 1899 to the present are indexed with all other court cases. From 1899-1937, indexes are in ledgers. From 1938 to the present, these records are indexed on cards arranged alphabetically. Separations are included with all other court cases, 1899-1965. From 1966 to the present they are indexed separately.

6. <u>Name Changes</u> are indexed in a card file arranged alphabetically by new and old names.

7. <u>Business Records</u>: There are two card indexes--one for Incorporations and one for Limited Partnerships and Business Names. Both are arranged alphabetically by the name of the business.

8. <u>Military Discharges</u>: A card index, arranged alphabetically by name, includes the liber and page number of the record.

9. <u>Surrenders of Children</u>, <u>Commitments</u>, <u>Conservatorships</u> and <u>Incompetency Records</u>: See "Restrictions on Use."

10. <u>Property Records</u>

Records can be located by name of owner or by street address. The Office has grantor/grantee and mortgagor/mortgagee indexes, 1899 to the present. See "CITY REGISTER'S OFFICE - QUEENS" for pre-1899 grantor/grantee indexes.

To trace the history of a particular piece of property, street address must be converted to Section, block and lot numbers. Check the map to the right of the entrance of Room 111 for the current section number. Next, look at the map in the appropriate Section ledger for block and lot numbers.

Once the Section, block and lot numbers are known, check the property card (index card) for a listing of all transactions from 1946 to the present. This card will provide liber and page numbers for deeds and mortgages recorded. A separate property card is available for each block and lot number. Pre-1946, there are ledger indexes by Section and block. Researchers must search through the listing of all transactions in a particular block for the appropriate lot number. Go to Room 2 for the deed and mortgage records in libers or on microfiche.

Description of Facility:

The County Clerk's Office is in the County Office Building (blue and white building) on the south side of Old Country Road (across from the Court House). There is a small cafeteria in the basement.

<u>Census</u> records are in the Documents Room, Room 106. Go to the Requisition Department in this room to request these volumes.

<u>Court Cases</u> (all), <u>Matrimonial</u> records (all) and <u>Name Change</u> records (microfilm only) are also in the Documents Room, Room 106. There is one microfilm reader/printer in this room. <u>Name Change</u> libers are in the Mortgage and Deeds Room in the basement.

<u>Business Records</u> are in Room 104. There are 2 microfilm readers and 2 reader/printers.

<u>Marriage Records</u> and <u>Military Discharges</u> are in Room 5, a storage room known as the basement vault. Marriage records are located to the right of the entrance, on the bottom shelf. The room is locked and opened only between 3:00 pm and 3:45 pm. See the supervisor in the Documents Room, Room 108 before 3:00 pm. There is no photocopy machine in this room. Researchers can use the one located in Room 2.

The <u>Military Discharges</u> card index and <u>Naturalization Records</u> and indexes are on the third floor in Room 310. There is a table with 3-4 chairs for researchers in a small room entered from Room 310. Three staff persons are available to assist the public. There is no photocopy machine in Room 310. Researchers can use the one located next door in Room 307.

<u>Property Records</u> are in the basement in Room 2. Mortgage libers are to the left of the entrance and deed libers are to the right. There are 25 microfiche readers, 6 reader/printers and 4 photocopy machines in this room. Liber indexes and property cards are in Room 111. Property cards are behind the counter.

<u>Commitments</u>, <u>Conservatorships</u> and <u>Incompetency Records</u> are in the Documents Room. See "Restrictions on Use."

Fees/Copies:

There are 10 photocopy machines available to the public. These are in Room 2, Room 104, Room 105, Room 106 and Room 307. Copies cost $.25 per page.

The cost of certified copies varies from $.50 per page to $1 per page based upon the type of record.

Restrictions on Use:

Surrenders of Children records and indexes are sealed and may not be opened without a Court order.

Matrimonial, Commitment and Incompetency records are closed. Matrimonial records are open only to the parties involved and their attorneys, however, the indexes are open to the public.

Military Discharge records are open only to the individual involved or his representative.

Supreme Court case files are not on-site and must be ordered one day in advance.

SURROGATE'S COURT
NASSAU COUNTY, NEW YORK

Facility Director:	Vincent P. Mallamo, Deputy Chief Clerk
Address:	262 Old Country Road, 3rd Floor Mineola, NY 11501
	(Cross Streets: Country Seat Drive and Washington Avenue)
Phone Number:	(516) 535-2086

Hours of Operation:

Monday to Friday: 9:00 am to 5:00 pm
Closed Saturday, Sunday and legal holidays.

Closest Public Transportation and Directions:

See "COUNTY CLERK'S OFFICE, NASSAU COUNTY." Walk one block east on Old Country Road to reach the County Court House (middle building on the next block).

Description of Resources:

The Records Department maintains case records for all proceedings pertaining to decedents' estates (probate, administration, estate taxes, accountings and miscellaneous claims and actions) and guardianships for Nassau County from 1899 to the present. Records from 1957 to the present are on microfiche. (Eventually all records will be on microfiche.)

Records of Surrenders of Children and Adoptions exist from 1924 and Conservatorships from 1985 to the present. See "Restrictions on Use."

NOTE: Prior to 1899, Nassau County was part of Queens County. For estate records pre-1899, see "SURROGATE'S COURT, QUEENS COUNTY."

Finding Aids:

The Records Department has a computer printout in alphabetical order of surname for all records (except Adoptions and Surrenders of Children) from 1899 to the present.

Description of Facility:

The Records Department is on the 3rd floor of the County Court House. There are two clerks on duty. A long narrow table against the wall outside the office can seat 8 researchers. There are 2 microfiche readers and one reader/printer on this table. The computer printouts are also here.

Fees/Copies:

There is one photocopy machine available at $.25 per page. Copies from the microfiche reader/printer are also $.25 per page. Requests by mail which require a search (i.e. case number is not provided) cost $20 if the case is under 25 years old and $53 if the case over 25 years, plus the $4 per page fee for certified copies or $1 per page for uncertified copies. If the writer requests information from the file (i.e. name and address of executors, heirs or size of the estate) but no photocopies, only the search fee is charged.

Restrictions on Use:

Records pre-1957 are stored in the basement. Requests for these records must be made before 11:00 am or 2:00 pm, when they are retrieved.

Surrenders of Children and Adoption records are sealed and may be examined only after obtaining a court order.

SUFFOLK COUNTY

COUNTY CLERK'S OFFICE
SUFFOLK COUNTY, NEW YORK

Facility Director: Juliette A. Kinsella, County Clerk
                           Edward R. Hines, Chief Deputy County Clerk

Address: County Center
                           Riverhead, NY 11901

                           (Cross Streets: Center Drive and Center Drive South)

Phone Number: (516) 548-3400
                           (516) 548-3115 (Documents Room/Civil Actions)
                           (516) 548-3032 (Naturalizations)
                           (516) 548-3424 (Business)
                           (516) 548-3417 (Property)
                           (516) 548-3700 (Property Tax Delinquencies)

Hours of Operation:

Monday to Friday: 9:00 am to 5:00 pm
Closed Saturday, Sunday and legal holidays.

Closest Public Transportation:

Train: Long Island Rail Road (LIRR) to Riverhead
Bus: Suffolk Transit S62, S92, 8A to County Center

Directions:

From Manhattan, take the LIRR at Pennsylvania Station (32nd Street and 7th Avenue) to the Riverhead station. Take the #8A bus or a taxi from the station to County Center.

If driving, take the Long Island Expressway to Exit 71. Follow the signs to County Center.

Description of Resources:

Suffolk County was formed in 1683. The following records are available in the County Clerk's Office:

1.   Naturalizations

     Petition for Naturalization, 1864 to the present
     Declarations of Intention, 1864-1977

2.   Marriage Records

     Certificates issued by the County Clerk's Office, 1908-1929 (bound ledgers) and 1929-c.1935 (files).

     See also "NEW YORK STATE HEALTH DEPARTMENT, VITAL RECORDS SECTION, GENEALOGY UNIT."

3.   Matrimonial Records

     Divorces, separations and annulments, 1724 to the present

     NOTE: Prior to 1973, Matrimonial cases of Suffolk County residents were filed in Suffolk County Supreme Court but were heard in Nassau County Supreme Court. After the case was completed, the file was returned to the County Clerk's Office in Suffolk. See "Restrictions on Use."

4.   Court Cases

     Includes all cases filed in the Supreme Court and County Court in Suffolk County, 1724 to the present.

     NOTE: There are branches of the Suffolk County Supreme Court in Hauppauge, Bay Shore and Riverhead. Once a case is closed, the file is sent to the County Clerk's Office in Riverhead.

5. Business Names

Assumed Names (Trade Names), 1900 to the present
Certificates of Incorporation (on microfilm), 1875 to the present
Limited Partnerships, c.1900 to the present

6. Military Discharges

Veteran's Discharge papers, World War I and II veterans, filed on a voluntary basis. See "Restrictions on Use."

7. Conservatorships, Incompetencies and Commitments

Conservatorships, 1956 to the present
Incompetencies and Commitments (filed with other Court cases)

Conservatorships, Incompetencies and Commitments of Suffolk County residents are filed in Suffolk County Supreme Court but are heard in Nassau County. The papers are stored in Riverhead and sent to the Court as requested.

8. Name Changes

Name Change records for individuals who legally changed their names in Suffolk County (filed with other Court cases).

9. Property Records

Deeds, 1650 to the present
Mortgages, 1755 to the present
Filed maps, 1850s to the present (microfilm)

Records of Property Tax Delinquencies, 1952-1977, are on microfilm. From 1978 to November 1984, records are in ledger books; from December 1984 to the present, records are computerized. Tax sale books, 1901-1983/84, are also available.

Finding Aids:

1. Naturalizations

Indexes for Naturalizations are in libers, arranged alphabetically by the first letter of the surname and then alphabetically by the first name. There is no index for Declarations of Intention.

2. Marriage Records

Marriage certificates are indexed by the both the brides' and the grooms' names and are arranged alphabetically by the first letter of the surname and the first letter of the first name.

3. Matrimonial Cases, Incompetencies, Commitments, Name Changes and other Court Cases are indexed together in ledgers from 1724 to April 1984. The ledgers are arranged by groups of years, then alphabetically by the first two letters of the surname. These records were indexed by the name of the plaintiff only. Name change records are indexed by the original name only. From May 1984 to the present, the index is computerized and case files can be located by the name of the plaintiff or defendant.

4. Business Names

Assumed Names and Limited Partnerships are indexed in one card file. Certificates of Incorporation are in a separate card file. The indexes are arranged alphabetically by the name of the business.

5. Military Discharges

Indexes are in ledgers arranged by groups of years, by the first letter of the surname and then alphabetically by the first name.

6. Conservatorships are indexed in a separate ledger from 1956 to April 1984. From May 1984 to the present, they are included in the computerized index.

7. Property Records

Mortgagor indexes, 1755-1950, and deed grantor/grantee indexes, 1650-1950, are in bound books arranged alphabetically by the first letter of the surname and then first name. The whole county is in one alphabetical series. Mortgagor indexes and grantor/grantee indexes, 1951-1976, are in bound books arranged by township, and then alphabetically as above. After 1976, indexes are again county-wide but on microfilm, arranged alphabetically by surname. Microfilming is current up to the last three months. As of January 1988, the index is also computerized. The Office will maintain up to five years of the index on computer.

The Office also has indexes by district (township/village), section and block and lot number, 1977 to the present. However, these are not considered official indexes.

Filed maps are indexed by township and then alphabetically by the name of the filed map, i.e. name of subdivision or property owner.

Property Tax Delinquencies are arranged by town and item or tax map number.

Description of Facility:

The County Clerk's Office is in the County Center. There is a cafeteria on the first floor.

Naturalization Records are on the first floor near the Surrogate's Court. There are three staff persons who can assist researchers. Seating is not available for researchers in this room.

Marriage Records and Military Discharges are behind the counter in Room E18A, the Documents Room for Criminal Cases. See the clerk in Room E24A, the Documents Room for Civil Actions, if you wish to view these records.

Business Records: The index is in 10 file cabinets against the wall of Room E4 on the first floor. The records are on microfilm in the Print Room. The Print Room has 2 microfilm reader/printers.

Court Cases: Civil case indexes and files are in Room E24B and Criminal cases in Room E18A. No seating is available in these rooms. There are five staff persons who can assist the public.

Matrimonial Records, Name Changes, Conservatorships, Incompetencies and Commitments are in Room E24B.

Property Records (except Property Tax Delinquencies) are in the Record Room. There are 55 microfilm readers available in this room and 2 reader/printers.

Property Tax Delinquencies are on the 2nd floor. There are 15 staff persons available to assist researchers. No seating is available in this room.

Fees/Copies:

There are 6 photocopy machines available for public use. Photocopies and microfilm copies cost $.25 per page.

Certified copies of mortgages or deeds cost $1 per page. A search for a property record by the Title Division costs $15. The name and approximate date of the transaction should be provided. Certified copies of Business records are $4.

Restrictions on Use:

Files from mid-1986 and earlier are not on-site. Records requested in the morning can be retrieved by 1:00 pm. Those requested in the afternoon can be retrieved by 4:30 pm.

Matrimonial records can be viewed only by the parties involved or their attorneys. These records can be viewed if a notarized letter is obtained from one of the parties.

Permission must be granted by the veteran or his representative to view Military Discharge papers.

SURROGATE'S COURT
SUFFOLK COUNTY, NEW YORK

Facility Director: Michael Cipollino, Chief Clerk
Elva Adams, Records Clerk

Address: County Center
Riverhead, NY 11901

(Cross Streets: Center Drive and Center Drive South)

Phone Number: (516) 548-3664, 3666

Hours of Operation:

Monday to Friday: 9:00 am to 5:00 pm
Closed Saturday, Sunday and legal holidays.

Closest Public Transportation and Directions:

See "COUNTY CLERK'S OFFICE, SUFFOLK COUNTY."

Description of Resources:

The Records Department has wills, probate files and letters of administration from June, 1787 to the present. The Department also has records of guardianships, adoptions and estate taxes. Records pre-1958 and some later records are on microfiche.

Finding Aids:

Index cards, filed alphabetically by surname, indicate the town, date of death, file number and, if there is a will, the date it was filed. In 1931, letters were added to the index card indicating the type of action: P = probate, A = administration, T = transfer tax, G = guardianship.

Description of Facility:

The Records Department is located on the first floor of the County Center. One staff person is on duty to assist researchers. There are 5 microfiche readers and one reader/printer.

Fees/Copies:

Two photocopy machines are available. Copies can be made at $.25 per page. Copies from the microfiche reader/printer are also $.25 per page. Certified copies are $4 per page. Requests by mail which require a search (i.e. case number is not provided) cost $20 if the case is under 25 years old and $53 if the case is over 25 years, plus the $4 per page fee for copies.

Restrictions on Use:

Paper records pre-1958 are not on-site. These files are retrieved every Friday, and only if a determination has been made by the Records Clerk that the microfiche is illegible.

Adoption records are sealed and may be examined only after obtaining a court order.

WESTCHESTER COUNTY

COUNTY CLERK'S OFFICE
WESTCHESTER COUNTY, NEW YORK

Facility Director: Andrew J. Spano, County Clerk

Address: 110 Grove Street
White Plains, NY 10601

(Cross Streets: Martine Avenue and Quarropas Street)

Phone Number: (914) 285-3080
(914) 285-3093 (Land Records)

Hours of Operation:

Monday to Friday: 9:00 am to 5:00 pm
Closed Saturday, Sunday and legal holidays.

NOTE: Land Records office opens 8:00 am. Staff assistance is available only after 9:00 am.

Closest Public Transportation:

Train: Metro North Railroad to White Plains
Bus: Westchester Bus 1B, 3 (express), 5, 13, 14 or 20 to Martine Avenue and Grove Street

Metered (1-, 2- and 12-hour) parking is available below the Public Library and inside the Galleria shopping mall across the street.

Directions:

From Manhattan, take the Metro North Railroad from Grand Central Terminal to White Plains. Exit at the south end of the platform and turn left at the street level. Walk 2 blocks south on Ferris Avenue to Martine Avenue. Turn east on Martine (pass the Library) to Grove Street. The County Clerk's Office is in the building across the street from the Galleria mall.

Description of Resources:

1. Naturalizations

   Petitions for Naturalization, 1980 to the present, and naturalization index, 1927 to the present. For pre-1979 records, see "COUNTY CLERK'S OFFICE - WESTCHESTER COUNTY ARCHIVES."

2. Court Cases

   Supreme Court and County Court (includes Matrimonial, Incompetency, Conservatorships, Name Changes and all other court cases), 1895 to the present. The Office also has indexes to cases dating back to 1847. For pre-1895 cases, see "COUNTY CLERK'S OFFICE - WESTCHESTER COUNTY ARCHIVES."

3. Business Names

   Incorporation Records, 1927 to the present, and all indexes for Incorporations 1843 to the present
   Assumed Business Names, 1900 to the present
   Limited Partnerships, 1942 to the present

4. Military Discharges

   Veteran's Discharges, 1986 to the present, and indexes, WWI to the present. Discharges prior to 1986 are at the WESTCHESTER COUNTY ARCHIVES but requests for them must be made through this Office.

5. <u>Property Records</u>

    Deeds and Mortgages, 1826 to the present
    Mortgage Tax Records, 1967 to the present

    Indexes to property records, 1680 to the present

6. <u>District Attorney's Records</u>

    Indictments, 1949 to the present

7. <u>Maps</u>

    Current county maps and atlases (land records). See also "Finding Aids" below.

Finding Aids:

1. <u>Naturalizations</u>: The Office has certificate "stubs" filed alphabetically by name of petitioner for Naturalizations, 1927 to the present. See "Restrictions on Use."

2. <u>Court Cases</u>: Supreme Court and County Court cases are indexed separately. The indexes for cases, 1847-1977, are in libers arranged by groups of years or by year, and alphabetically by the first three letters of the plaintiff's surname. From 1978 to 1985, the index is on cards arranged by year and then alphabetically by surname.

    From 1986 to the present, a computer index is available. Names can be accessed by directing the computer to provide only names with an exact spelling or all names that "sound like" the name entered. The computer can access cases by name of defendant as well as name of plaintiff.

3. <u>Business Names</u>: The following indexes are available:

    Assumed Business Names, 1900-1975, are indexed on cards arranged alphabetically by name. From 1976 to the present, records are indexed in the computer system that indexes court cases.
    Certificates of Incorporation, 1843-1960, are indexed in ledgers arranged by groups of years and by the first three letters of the name. From 1960-1985, there are index cards arranged alphabetically by name. After 1985, the index is computerized.
    Limited Partnerships, 1942-1985, are indexed in libers arranged by the first letter of the name. After 1985, the index is computerized.

4. <u>Military Discharges</u>: The Office has a card file index arranged alphabetically by name.

5. <u>Property Records</u>: Records can be accessed by name of grantor/grantee and mortgagor/mortgagee for all years. Indexes, 1680-1983, are in libers. NOTE: The original copies of the 1680-1898 indexes are in the WESTCHESTER COUNTY ARCHIVES. This office has a typewritten copy of the indexes, 1680-1898, arranged alphabetically. Records, 1898-1931, are arranged by town or city, groups of years and then alphabetically. Indexes, 1931-1966, are arranged by town or city, groups of years and alphabetically by the first letter of the surname and the first vowel in the first name. Indexes, 1967-1983, are consolidated (bound printouts) for the entire County, arranged in groups of years and alphabetically by name. From 1981 to the present the index has been computerized. See description under "Court Cases" above. There is an overlap beginning in 1981 when the index was computerized.

6. <u>Maps</u>: Map locations can be found if the address is known. Maps are indexed by sector and block number. Every map ever filed is listed in this index. If the address of a current owner is not known, the Westchester County Property Tax Department, 110 Grove Street, L-222, White Plains, New York 10601, telephone (914) 285-4325, has an index by name of owner. See also "COUNTY CLERK'S OFFICE - WESTCHESTER COUNTY ARCHIVES."

Description of Facility:

All record rooms are on the third floor of the building. Rooms 330 and 345 have computer terminals located on counters.

<u>Naturalization</u> records and stubs are in Room 340. There are four staff persons available to assist researchers, one of whom is at the counter. The waiting area includes seating for 24 persons (6 at a table).

Court Cases and Business Records are in Room 330. There are two to three staff persons at the counter to assist researchers. Seating is available for 6 persons at a table. There are 4 computer terminals (no printers) at which indexes can be accessed.

Libers for Court Cases are under the counter facing the table in Room 330. Index cards, 1978-1985, are in cabinets to the left of the information counter. The computer terminals are against the wall to the right of the entrance.

Libers for Business Names are under the information counter in Room 330. Index cards for Assumed Business Names are in cabinet #1 to the left of the entrance. Index cards for Certificates of Incorporation are in cabinets #4 and #5 to the left of the information counter.

Property Records are in Room 345. There are two to three staff persons to assist researchers, one of whom is at the counter. Limited seating is available for researchers but there is plenty of counter space. There are 4 computer terminals in this room. There is generally no wait for a terminal.

Maps and atlases (land records) of the County can be found in Room 345.

Fees/Copies:

Photocopying of Naturalization records or stubs is done by the staff at $.25 per page. Copies of other records can be made by the public at $.25 per page at the photocopy machines in Rooms 330 and 345. There are 2 machines in Room 330 and one in Room 345. Certified copies of records cost $4 per page.

Restrictions on Use:

Naturalization indexes are searched by the staff and cannot be accessed directly by the researcher in this office. However, researchers can use the index at the WESTCHESTER COUNTY ARCHIVES.

Not all records are immediately available. Court Cases, 1895-1980, and Business Name records pre-1970s are stored in the Westchester County Records Center. Records are transferred to the Records Center and WESTCHESTER COUNTY ARCHIVES as space is needed. Call in advance to determine the location of records. Files must be ordered before 11:00 am on Monday, Wednesday or Friday. Records are delivered to the Office in White Plains by 3:00 pm the same day. Deliveries are not made from the Records Center on Tuesday or Thursday.

COUNTY CLERK'S OFFICE - WESTCHESTER COUNTY ARCHIVES
WESTCHESTER COUNTY, NEW YORK

Facility Director: David W. Carmicheal, County Archivist

Address: 2199 Saw Mill River Road (Route 9A)
Elmsford, NY 10523

(Cross Street: South of Route 119)

Phone Number: (914) 592-1925

Hours of Operation:

Tuesday & Wednesday: 9:00 am to 4:00 pm
Closed Monday, Thursday, Friday, Saturday, Sunday and legal holidays.

NOTE: Researchers should call for hours before planning a visit. The Archives is open each week but the days and hours may change.

Closest Public Transportation:

Train: Metro North to White Plains, and
Bus: Westchester Bus #5 (to Yonkers) to 2199 Saw Mill River Road.

Directions:

From Manhattan, take the Metro North train from Grand Central Terminal to White Plains. Exit the train and walk (less than one block) to the Bus Terminal under the train station. Take the #5 bus (to Yonkers). The bus stop is directly in front of the Archives.

Description of Resources:

The Westchester County Archives was established in 1985 to preserve County records of historical value and make these available to researchers.

NOTE: Parts of Westchester County were annexed by New York County in the late 19th century. These areas ultimately became the Bronx. Researchers should check Westchester County records for residents of the western area of the Bronx (Kingsbridge, West Farms and Morrisania, pre-1874) and the eastern area of the Bronx (pre-1895).

The Archives has the following records of interest to genealogists. Where separate index volumes are available, these are noted below.

1. Board of Elections

   Voter enrollments, 1929-1971

2. Surrogate's Court Records

   Estate inventories (probate files), 1775, 1787-1865
   Wills, 1777-1942

3. Commissioner of Jurors

   Exempt (from juries) firemen and fire companies, 1895-1901
   Jurors exemption affidavits, 1892-1925
   Jurors exemption lists, 1892-c.1925
   Jurors record book, 1892-1955

4. County Clerk - Property Records

   Deeds, 1667-1825 (also original grantor and grantee indexes, 1680-1898)
   Homestead exemption records, c.1850-1978 (gaps), also indexes c.1850-1978

Mortgage tax records, 1906-1966
Mortgages, 1755-1825 (also original mortgagor index, 1680-1898)
Proceedings of the Commissioners of Forfeiture, 1784-1786

5. <u>County Clerk - Court Records</u>

Court of Common Pleas, minutes, 1710-1846
Court of Sessions, minutes, 1778-1895
Judgments, decrees and executions, 1813-1932 (also index 1813-1911)

6. <u>County Clerk - Incorporations and Certifications</u>

Architects' registration, 1919-1951
Assumed Business Names, index only, 1900-1933
Dental hygienists' affidavits, 1947-1950
Dentists' register and affidavits, 1941-1950
Farm names registered, 1912-1949
Foreign notaries, 1883-1944
Horseshoers' register, 1899-1904
Incorporation Records, 1876-1926
Insurance agents' certificates, index only, 1912-1922
Osteopaths' register and affidavits, 1941-1943
Podiatrists' register, 1895-1951
Practical nurses' register, 1938-1946
Professional engineers' register, 1947-1951
Religious societies' register, 1784-1909

7. <u>County Clerk - Legal Records (General)</u>

Appointments to Office, 1883-1892
Coroner's inquests, index only, 1886-1925
Oaths of Office, 1789-1829 (gaps), 1875-1968 (also index c.1845-1886)
Register of agents and principals, 1894-1899
Roll of Officers, 1857-1869
Veterans Discharges, c.1920-1985 (see "Restrictions on Use")

Volumes of "Miscellaneous Records," 1840-1916. These appear to include all kinds of records--deeds, Naturalizations, Incorporations--entered by the County Clerk. These volumes may have been used when other ledgers were missing or misplaced.

8. <u>County Clerk - Naturalizations</u>

Naturalizations were filed in several courts in the County before 1927. In 1927, the records were centralized at the County Clerk's Office. The following record groups can now be found at the Archives:

Declarations of Intention, county-wide, 1927-1979 (also index) and
    Mount Vernon, 1892-1895
    White Plains, 1857-1930
    White Plains/Discharged Soldiers, 1864-1883
    Yonkers, 1874-1895, 1916-1926
Final Applications to Become Citizen (Law of 1895), 1895-1896
Military Petitions, 1918-1919
Naturalization Petitions, county-wide, 1927-1979 (also liber index) and
Miscellaneous records, 1808-1906
    Mt. Vernon/Discharged Soldiers, 1892-1894
    Mt. Vernon/Full Age, 1892-1895
    Mt. Vernon/Minors, 1892-1895
    White Plains/Discharged Soldiers, 1884-1895
    White Plains/Full Age, 1872-1979
    White Plains/Minors, 1872-1906

Yonkers/Discharged Soldiers, 1889-1892
Yonkers/Full Age, 1888-1895, 1916-1942
Yonkers/Minors, 1888-1895
Rejected Petitions, 1898-1906
Surrogate's Naturalizations: First and Final Papers, 1879-1894

In addition to the above petitions, the Archives has the following "Records of Naturalization" and "Records of Petition" which appear to be summaries of the Naturalization Petitions prepared by the Clerk of the Court. These "Records" include name, address, town and names of witnesses only. The summaries may be useful for those years in which the actual petitions are not available:

Records of Naturalization, 1844-1857, 1864-1870
Record of Petition:
    Mt. Vernon/Discharged Soldiers, 1886-1894
    Mt. Vernon/Full Age, 1892-1895
    Mt. Vernon/Minors, 1892-1895
    White Plains/Full Age, 1857-1871, 1884-1906
    White Plains/Minors, 1884-1906
    Yonkers/Discharged Soldiers, 1889-1893
    Yonkers/Full Age, 1880-1895
    Yonkers/Minors, 1888-1895

The Archives also has a file, "Naturalization Background Materials, 1910, 1916," which includes information on the laws in effect and whether a spouse or children had to file separately.

9.   <u>County Clerk - Marriage Records</u>

Marriage licenses were issued by the County Clerk's Office, 1908-1916 only. These records are now in the Archives. The "Register of Marriages" is a summary of the marriage licenses. Sometimes these "summaries" include more detailed information than the affidavits or licenses:

Affidavits to obtain marriage license, 1908-1913
Marriage affidavits and licenses, 1913-1914
Register of Marriages, 1908-1916 (also index 1908-1910, 1914-1916)

See also "NEW YORK STATE HEALTH DEPARTMENT, VITAL RECORDS SECTION, GENEALOGY UNIT."

10.   <u>Selected Maps and Atlases</u>

The Archives houses some 30,000 maps, including filed maps pertaining to specific parcels of land. Municipality maps, 1896-1961; Westchester County atlases, 1867-1931; and block maps, 1935, are available. In addition, the Archives has the County Clerk's Office, Land Records Division maps and atlases listed below:

New York City, 23rd Ward, c.1900
New York City, 24th Ward, 1888, 1890
New York City - lands annexed (23rd/24th Wards), 1888

Hudson River Valley, 1891
Mount Vernon and Town of Pelham, 1899, 1908
Yonkers, 1896, 1907, 1920
Westchester, 1867, 1872, 1881, 1893, 1901, 1910, 1910-1911, 1929-1931
Westchester - Block Maps, 1935 (also index)
White Plains, c.1950, and insurance map, 1931-1961

Maps of municipalities, 1920-1967
Westchester County Register's Office maps, 1792-1888 (also indexes 1766-1868). These maps and
    indexes include parts of the Bronx.

The Archives also has historical maps (1858-1974) from the County Planning Department.

11. Census

   New York State Census, Westchester County, 1905, 1915, 1925

12. Other

   Ledger of the Wood, Wire, and Metal Lather's Union
   New York State Governor's Office - Appointments to Office, 1795-1840
   Policemen's Benevolent Association - Yearbook, 1928

Finding Aids:

A published *Guide to the Collections* lists each of the record groups and series as well as indexes (summarized above). In addition, researchers should be aware of the following:

1. Board of Elections: Voter enrollment records are arranged by Assembly District (AD) and Election District (ED). The Archives does not have a set of the AD/ED maps for each year.

2. Surrogate's Court Records: Estate inventories are arranged by year and then by surname. Wills are indexed in each volume. It is recommended that researchers interested in these records consult the master index (alphabetized by surname) in the Surrogate's Court Record Room in White Plains.

3. Commissioner of Jurors: These records are not indexed. They are arranged chronologically.

4. County Clerk - Property Records: Indexes are available for deeds (grantee and grantor, 1680-1898); homestead exemptions, c.1850-1978; and mortgages (mortgagor, 1680-1898). Mortgage tax records are not indexed and are difficult to access. An index to the Proceedings of the Commissioners of Forfeiture has been published by the Westchester County Historical Society and is available in the Archives.

5. County Clerk - Court Records: Transcripts of Judgments, Decrees and Executions are indexed by surname, 1813-1911. Minutes of the Courts of Common Pleas and Sessions are arranged chronologically. There is no index.

6. County Clerk - Incorporations and Certifications: These records are generally indexed by surname at the front of each volume.

7. County Clerk - Legal Records (General): These records, including the "Miscellaneous Records," are generally indexed by surname at the front of the volume. Of note, the Archives has a cross-index of surnames for the years 1898-1931, which lists variations of spellings for surnames filed in County Clerk's Office records during these years.

   There is no index to Veteran's Discharge records at the Archives. The card index to these records is in the COUNTY CLERK'S OFFICE in White Plains.

8. County Clerk - Naturalizations: County-wide indexes are available for Declarations of Intention, 1927-1976, and Naturalization Petitions, 1927-1956. Local Declarations and Naturalization Petitions are indexed by first letter of the surname within each volume.

   A computerized name index to all Naturalizations in the Archives collection is currently being created by the Archives staff and will be completed in 1989.

9. County Clerk - Vital Records: There is a name index of both brides and grooms to the Register of Marriages, 1908-1910 and 1914-1916.

10. Maps and Atlases: The Archives has an index to block maps of Westchester County, 1935, and an index to the Register's Office maps, c.1766-1869. The latter are arranged by town.

   The Archives is in the process of placing some 35,000 maps (those located here and at the COUNTY CLERK'S OFFICE, WESTCHESTER COUNTY) on aperture cards which will be available at both locations. A subject index being prepared will include names of persons appearing on the maps. The index will be completed by 1990.

Description of Facility:

The Archives is in a one-story brick building set back from the road. Enter through the main entrance. Seating is available for 8-12 researchers. There are 3 microfilm/microfiche readers. One is also a reader/printer. The Archives has one photocopy machine which is operated by staff. There are three staff persons available to assist researchers.

Fees/Copies:

A copy of the *Guide to the Collections* may be purchased for $2. All photocopying is done by the Archives staff. Copies are $.50 per page. Certified copies cost $4 per page for the first 8 pages and $.50 for each additional page. Maps can be photocopied at $4 each.

The Archives will respond to mail requests. The cost of a search is $5 for each name searched for a 5-year period in each record group plus $.50 per page. In addition, there is a fee of $.25 for 1-10 pages, $.50 for 11-100 pages and $1 for over 100 pages. Postage for maps is $.60 per map.

Restrictions on Use:

Requests for copies of Veteran's Discharge records must be made to the COUNTY CLERK'S OFFICE, WESTCHESTER COUNTY in White Plains.

SURROGATE'S COURT
WESTCHESTER COUNTY, NEW YORK

Facility Director: Philip E. Pugsley, Chief Clerk

Address: 111 Grove Street, Room 702
White Plains, NY 10601

(Cross Streets: Maple Street, opposite Galleria)

Phone Number: (914) 285-3734

Hours of Operation:

Monday to Friday: 9:00 am to 5:00 pm
Closed Saturday, Sunday and legal holidays.

Closest Public Transportation and Directions:

See "COUNTY CLERK'S OFFICE, WESTCHESTER COUNTY." Although the Court has a different address from the County Clerk's Office, the buildings are connected by an inside corridor.

Description of Resources:

The Westchester Surrogate's Court has records of probate, letters of administration, guardianships, adoptions and various miscellaneous files (trustee, wrongful deaths, intervivos trusts, etc.) for Westchester County. The Court has wills from 1942 to the present, letters of administration from 1787 and guardianships from 1839. Records pre-1954 are not on site. See "Restrictions on Use."

See "COUNTY CLERK'S OFFICE - WESTCHESTER COUNTY ARCHIVES" for estate inventories (1777, 1782-1865) and wills (1777-1942).

NOTE: Parts of Westchester County were annexed by New York County in the late 19th century. These areas ultimately became the Bronx. Researchers should check Westchester County records for residents of the western area of the Bronx (Kingsbridge, West Farms and Morrisania, pre-1874) and the eastern area of the Bronx (pre-1895).

Finding Aids:

The Record Room has index cards arranged in a Soundex system (same as the National Archives Soundex system described in Appendix C). Each card includes name, date of death, address and file number.

Description of Facility:

The Record Room is in the Court Tower, 7th floor, Room 702. There are four staff persons available to assist researchers.

Fees/Copies:

Certified copies of wills and letters of administration are available at $4 per page. One photocopy machine is available for public use at $.25 per page. The search fee for mail requests is $53 for records over 25 years old and $20 for records under 25 years if the file number is not known and no copies are requested. If the file number is provided, or if unknown but copies of all pages in the file are ordered, mail requests cost $.25 per page for uncertified copies or $4 per page for certified copies.

Restrictions on Use:

Files pre-1954 are not on site and must be ordered before 11:00 am on Monday, Wednesday or Friday. Deliveries are made by 3:00 pm. Deliveries are not made from the Records Center on Tuesday or Thursday. Adoption records cannot be unsealed without an order of the Court.

TRENTON

NEW JERSEY STATE DEPARTMENT OF HEALTH
BUREAU OF VITAL STATISTICS

Facility Director: Charles A. Karkut, State Registrar

Address: South Warren and Market Streets
Trenton, NJ

Mail Address: State Registrar - Search Unit, CN 360
Trenton, NJ 08625-0360

Phone Number: (609) 292-4087
(609) 633-2860 (Rapid Response Telephone Ordering)

Hours of Operation, Closest Public Transportation, Directions and Description of Facility:

Not applicable. See "Restrictions on Use."

Description of Resources:

Birth, marriage and death records from June 1878 to the present are maintained by the New Jersey Department of Health.

Birth, marriage and death records were centralized at the State level in May 1848. County records, 1795-1848, and pre-1901 State records can be found in the NEW JERSEY STATE ARCHIVES. See "Restrictions on Use".

Finding Aids:

Birth and Marriage Records: Pre-1901 indexes are arranged by year and county and then alphabetically. From 1901 to the present, statewide indexes are arranged alphabetically.

Death Records: There are no indexes for records pre-1901. Pre-1901 records are arranged chronologically by year and county. From 1901 to the present, statewide indexes are arranged alphabetically.

Fees/Copies:

Complete the appropriate box of the application (see Appendix B-8) to obtain a birth, death or marriage record. There is a $4 fee for each name searched. Searches for more than one year cost $1 for each additional year per name. If found, a certified copy is forwarded at no additional cost. If not found, the fee is not refunded. Additional copies ordered at the same time cost $2 per copy. Only checks or money orders are accepted. Checks should be made payable to the State Registrar. Expect a 4 to 6 week wait for records.

For a more rapid response, the Health Department has a telephone request service (8:00 am to 3:00 pm). For an additional fee of $5 per call, the record or records can be searched within one or two days. The fee must be charged to a credit card (VISA, Mastercard, etc.). This rapid service is intended for emergency cases only, e.g. passports.

Restrictions on Use:

Researchers cannot examine the indexes or records in this office directly. However, the NEW JERSEY STATE ARCHIVES has a microfilm copy of birth and marriage indexes, 1878-1900, and all birth, marriage and death records for this period. These are available at the ARCHIVES for in-person searches only.

NEW JERSEY DEPARTMENT OF STATE
DIVISION OF ARCHIVES AND RECORDS MANAGEMENT
NEW JERSEY STATE ARCHIVES

Facility Director: Karl Niederer, Chief

Address: 185 West State Street, CN 307
Trenton, NJ 08625-0307

(Cross Streets: Calhoun and Willow Streets)

Phone Number: (609) 292-6260, 6261

Hours of Operation:

Monday to Friday:	8:30 am to 4:30 pm
Saturday:	9:00 am to 5:00 pm

Closed Sunday, major holidays and Saturdays of 3-day holiday weekends. May be open on minor holidays such as Columbus Day, Veteran's Day and Election Day. These vary from year to year. Check in advance.

Closest Public Transportation:

Train: NJ Transit or Amtrak to Trenton (from NYC); or
Philadelphia SEPTA train or Amtrak to Trenton (from Philadelphia);

and

Bus: NJ Transit P, S or G to West State and Calhoun Streets.

Directions:

If coming from New York City, take the NJ Transit train from Pennsylvania Station (32nd Street and 7th Avenue) to Trenton. If coming from Philadelphia, take the SEPTA train to Trenton. (Ask for the excursion fare which is available on most round-trip tickets). From the train station in Trenton, take the P, S or G bus to West State Street and Calhoun Street. The Archives is located in the basement of the State Library building.

Description of Resources:

The State Archives serves as the official repository for all colonial and State government records of historical value. Its holdings date from the 17th century to the present, and include the records of the legislative, judicial and executive branches of New Jersey State government. It has records from some of the State's counties and municipalities; from non-governmental sources; and holds some records about New Jersey residents compiled by federal agencies.

All New Jersey county records microfilmed by the Genealogical Society of Utah are available here and through the FAMILY HISTORY CENTERS (LDS). County records prior to 1900 have been filmed and plans have been announced to extend filming in New Jersey to 1930.

The following are of interest to genealogists:

1. Vital Records

    Colonial Marriage Bonds, 1711-1795, filed with the Secretary of State, include names of the parties married, county of residence and date of the marriage bond. Parents were named in marriage bonds when parental consent was required, i.e. when one of the parties was a minor.

    County Marriages, 1795-1848, recorded by County Clerks, include names of the bride and groom, date of marriage and name of the person who married them. These records rarely include parents' names. Each of the County Clerk's Offices retained the original copy of these records with the exception of Atlantic, Somerset and Middlesex Counties. The original records of Atlantic (part) and Somerset

Counties are held by the Archives. The original Middlesex records are held at Rutgers University, Alexander Library, Department of Special Collections and Archives.

The Archives has microfilm copies of the records of the following counties:

Burlington	Hunterdon	Passaic (1837-1878)
Cape May	Mercer	Salem
Cumberland	Middlesex	Sussex
Essex (1795-1875)	Monmouth (1795-1843)	Union (1857-1878)
Gloucester	Morris	Warren

NOTE: County marriage records have been published for Atlantic, Bergen, Burlington, Camden, Cape May, Cumberland, Essex, Gloucester, Hunterdon, Mercer, Middlesex, Monmouth, Morris, Salem and Somerset. Copies of these published sources are available in the NEW JERSEY STATE LIBRARY.

State of New Jersey vital records began May 1, 1848. The State Archives has the original birth, marriage and death records for the period May 1, 1848 to May 31, 1878. These records are accessible to the public on microfilm in the Archives Search Room.

NOTE: There was an overlap in the recording of marriages after 1848 when some counties continued to record marriages. Researchers should examine both sets of records when searching for a marriage that occurred after 1848.

A microfilm copy of the indexes to birth and marriage records from June 1, 1878 to December 31, 1900 is available. The Archives also has a microfilm copy of all birth, marriage and death records for this period. These records are open to the public for in-person searches only. See "Restrictions on Use" concerning mail requests.

For birth, marriage and death records from 1900 to the present, see "NEW JERSEY STATE DEPARTMENT OF HEALTH, BUREAU OF VITAL STATISTICS."

2. Matrimonial Records include divorce records generally spanning the period 1743-1850. During this time, divorces were granted only by decree of the Chancery Court or by legislative act. The Archives holds all Chancery Court records prior to 1850. For later records, see "SUPERIOR COURT OF NEW JERSEY, TRENTON."

3. Wills and Other Probate Records: Original copies of all New Jersey wills and inventories filed from 1670 to 1900. Some 18th-century administration bonds, guardianship papers and probate accounts also are filed with this group. See "Restrictions on Use."

The Archives has the following Surrogate's Court records on microfilm for the five counties closest to NYC:

Bergen County - Surrogate's dockets, 1783-1962 (index 1783-1962); wills, 1804-1905; letters of administration, 1804-1900.

Essex County - Surrogate's dockets, 1783-1900 (index 1783-1972); wills, 1804-1900; guardianships, 1871-1900; letters of administration, 1804-1901.

Hudson County - Surrogate's dockets, 1804-1902 (index 1804-1953); letters of administration and guardianships, 1840-1900 (index 1868-1906); wills, 1840-1901.

Passaic County - wills and proceedings, 1835-1911 (index 1838-1919); letters of administration and guardianships, 1837-1903.

Union County - Surrogate's dockets, 1854-1900 (index, 1857-1949); letters of administration, 1857-1894; guardianships 1857-1925; wills, 1854-1911.

See "SUPERIOR COURT OF NEW JERSEY, TRENTON" for copies of wills, letters of administration and guardianships filed in County Surrogate's Courts from 1901 to the present.

4. Census: The following census records are available here for New Jersey counties:

U.S. Census, 1800 (published information, Cumberland County only), 1830-1880, 1890 (incomplete - only part of Jersey City), 1900 and 1910; and the special census schedules for New Jersey: Agriculture, Industry and Mortality, 1850-1880; Civil War Veterans and their Widows, 1890; Social Statistics, 1850 and 1860.

NOTE: There are no extant copies of the federal census for New Jersey for 1790, 1800, 1810 or 1820 (except for Cumberland County, 1800).

New Jersey Census, 1855 and 1865 (incomplete); 1875 (Essex and Sussex Counties only), 1885, 1895, 1905 and 1915. (The Archives has both the originals and microfilm copies. See "Restrictions on Use.")

5. New Jersey Tax Ratables: The State Archives has municipal tax ratables for the period 1773-1822. Each book covers a specific township or municipal ward for a specific year and lists all landowners, household heads and single adult males. Their taxable assets such as land, livestock, mills, slaves and carriages are enumerated.

6. Property Records: Until 1785, conveyances of land were recorded in the Secretary of State's Office. These Secretary of State deeds, 1664-1800s (most date prior to 1785), are now housed in the Archives. Conveyances between private individuals predominate in this series, but some proprietary deeds are also included.

The County Clerk's Office (in some counties, County Register's Office) maintained all recorded deeds after 1785 and some include records from earlier in the 18th century. The State Archives has microfilm copies of the deeds on file in 19 of the 21 New Jersey counties. The indexes only, not the actual records, are available for Union and Morris Counties. The years available vary for each county. For example, copies of property records of the five counties closest to NYC available here include:

Bergen County - Deeds, 1785-1901 (no index available here; see "COUNTY CLERK'S OFFICE, BERGEN COUNTY"); mortgages, 1766-1870 (index, 1766-1912).
Essex County - Deeds, 1785-1900 (index, 1785-1909); mortgages, 1777-1861 (index, 1765-1909).
Hudson County - Deeds, 1840-1900 (index, 1840-1922); mortgages, 1840-1866 (index, 1840-1905).
Passaic County - Deeds, 1837-1900 (index, 1837-1916); mortgages, 1837-1866 (index, 1837-1902).
Union County - Index to deeds only (1857-1909); mortgages, 1857-1870 (index, 1857-1914).

7. Military Records for New Jersey from the colonial period up to World War I. While the Archives has no federal records of soldiers who served in World War I, it does have unofficial service records (on microfilm) from the New Jersey Department of Defense. See "Restrictions on Use." State militia and National Guard records are available but are not indexed.

Of note, Veteran's Burial records, 1863-1923, and Veteran's Grave Registration records, c.1776-1980, are available for Essex County; and Veteran's Individual Grave Field Report Sheets (on microfilm) arranged by cemetery are available for Essex County and part of Middlesex County (cemeteries "A" to "George's Road" only). These latter records include many listed in Jewish cemeteries.

8. Tavern Licenses (original records) are located here for:

Bergen County, 1790-1866
Camden County, 1828-1875 (indexed)
Essex County, 1726-1871 (indexed)
Hunterdon County, 1738-1870 (indexed)
Mercer County, 1840-1881 (indexed)
Middlesex County, 1757-1801 (indexed)
Ocean County, 1850-1895
Somerset County, 1784-1876 (indexed)
Sussex County, 1753-1860 (indexed)

In order to obtain a tavern license, the approval of householders living in the area of the proposed tavern had to be obtained. These signatures were filed as part of the license record.

9. Justice of the Peace docket books for some counties (including Essex County, 1785-1911, on microfilm). These often list marriages conducted by the judge which he may or may not have filed with the county. The records are arranged by the judge's name and groups of years.

10. Naturalization Records for the colonial period and for part of the 19th century in the following record series:

Chancery Court Declarations and Naturalizations, 1832-1862

Supreme Court Naturalizations:
    Bound volumes, 1851-1873
    Numbered files, 1761, 1790-1860
    Index to Supreme Court Minutes, 1681-1837
Petitions to the Legislature for Naturalization, 1749-1810

The County Clerk's Offices maintained Naturalization records also. Microfilm copies of some of these records are available at the Archives. Specifically, for four counties close to NYC the Archives has the following records:

Essex County - Declarations of Intention, 1849-1906 (index 1849-1906); Petitions for Naturalization/ Naturalization Papers, 1779-1906 (index 1830-1906).

Hudson County - Declarations of Intention and Petitions for Naturalization, 1840-1906 (index to Petitions, 1840-1906).

Passaic County - Declarations of Intention, 1844-1870, 1873-1906; Naturalization records, 1837-1906 (index to Naturalizations, 1837-1906).

Union County - Declarations of Intention, 1857-1928 (index 1857-1894); Petitions for Naturalization/ Naturalization Papers, 1857-1930 (index 1857-1987).

For later records in Essex and Hudson Counties, see "COUNTY CLERK'S OFFICE, ESSEX COUNTY" and "COUNTY CLERK'S OFFICE, HUDSON COUNTY."

11. Newspapers: The Archives has extensive holdings of New Jersey newspapers on microfilm, numbering over 5,000 reels. These can be requested on interlibrary loan.

The Archives also has an alphabetical card index to marriages and deaths reported in Trenton newspapers from December 1777 to 1900.

12. Court Records: Civil court records are available for both county and State levels of government. These records provide information concerning heirs to estates, debts, divorces, loyalists in the revolutionary period and many other matters. The State Archives has the following State court records:

    Chancery Court, 1743-1850
    Court of Errors and Appeals, dockets, 1869-1949 (incomplete files prior to 1869)
    Prerogative Court, Administrative Bonds, 1716-1775
    Prerogative Court, case files and bound volumes, c.pre-1900
    Supreme Court, case files and index, prior to 1844
    Supreme Court, minute books, 1681-1873
    Supreme Court, judgment books, 1681-1866

The Archives also has microfilm records of some county courts such as the Essex County Court of Common Pleas, 1709-1849; and Orphan Court records for Bergen County, 1785-1902, Essex County, 1793-1902, Hudson County, 1840-1902, Passaic County, 1837-1900, and Union County, 1857-1900.

Later State court records (including those filed at the county level) are filed with the Clerk of the SUPERIOR COURT OF NEW JERSEY, TRENTON.

13. Slave Records (on microfilm) such as births of Black children, Essex County, 1804-1843; slave receipts, Essex County, c.1787-1805; certificates and deeds of manumission, Essex County, 1805-1853 (index 1805-1817).

14. Road Returns are available for some counties (microfilm) including Essex County, 1698-1930 (indexed). These records may include the names of householders living along the road.

Finding Aids:

In addition to the indexes noted above, the Archives has typed listings of all of its holdings on a particular county. The Archives has a published *Guide to Family History Sources in the New Jersey State Archives,* 1987, a 32-page volume, which is available at $5. Individual record groups are indexed as follows:

1. Vital Records: Alphabetical indexes are available for county marriage records, 1795-1848. Marriages, May 1848-May 1864, are arranged by county and the first letter of the surname of the groom.

Marriages, June 1864-May 1878, have an alphabetical index by groom. Marriages, June 1878-1900, have an alphabetical index by bride and groom.

Birth records, May 1848-1900, and death records, May 1848-May 1878, have alphabetical indexes. There are no indexes for death records, June 1878-1900, but the yearly registers for deaths are arranged geographically.

2. Matrimonial Records: Divorces granted by the legislature through actual divorce acts can be accessed by using printed session laws available in the NEW JERSEY STATE LIBRARY. The best index for pre-20th-century laws is:

Hood, John. *Index of Colonial and State Laws of New Jersey Between the Years 1663-1903 Inclusive.* 1905.

For finding aids to Chancery Court decrees, see Court Cases (below).

3. Wills and Other Probate Records: There are two published indexes to wills:

New Jersey, Secretary of State. *Index of Wills, Inventories, etc...Prior to 1901.* (Reprinted as *New Jersey Index of Wills,* 1969). The set is arranged by county and then alphabetically by testator's name.

Smeal, Lee and Ronald Vern Jackson. *Index to New Jersey Wills 1689-1890, the Testators,* 1979. The index is arranged alphabetically by testator's name and covers the entire State.

Surrogate's Court records are arranged by county and chronologically by date. Indexes are arranged differently for each county. All have some alphabetical arrangement. Some are by the first three letters of the surname only.

4. Census: For federal censuses, the Archives has the published indexes for 1800 (Cumberland County only) and 1830-1860, and the Soundex for 1880 and 1900. No indexes are available for the State censuses. However, the NEW JERSEY STATE LIBRARY has atlases of ward maps for some localities.

5. New Jersey Tax Ratables: Two publications function as partial indexes to this collection:

Stryker-Rodda, Kenn. *Revolutionary Census of New Jersey,* 1986. (Indexes tax ratables for 1773-1774, 1778-1780 and 1784-1786).

Jackson, Ronald Vern. *New Jersey Tax Lists, 1772-1822,* 1981. (Does not include Hunterdon County or scattered townships elsewhere in the State).

6. Property Records: The principal index to the Secretary of State's Deeds is *Colonial Conveyances of East and West New Jersey, 1664-1794,* 1974. Property records of the County Clerks or County Registers are arranged by county and chronologically by date. Indexes are arranged differently for each county. All have some alphabetical arrangement. Some are by the first three letters of the surname only.

7. Military Records: In addition to published indexes for Revolutionary War and Civil War records, the Archives has an alphabetical card index to manuscript records of New Jersey residents who were involved in the Revolutionary War on the patriot side; and an alphabetical card index to records of the New Jersey Volunteers, a loyalist regiment. Other indexed collections include the Spanish American War, 1898-1899; Mexican Border Service, 1916; and the Unofficial Service records for World War I.

8. Naturalization Records are arranged by county and chronologically by date. Indexes, arranged alphabetically by the first letter(s) of the surname, are available for each county.

9. Court Records for Chancery Court pre-1850 and Supreme Court actions-at-law, c.1740s-1844, are indexed by complainant. The name of the plaintiff/complainant and defendant, approximate date and name of the court are needed to locate a specific record.

Often, the court records lack comprehensive indexes making them difficult and time consuming to use.

NOTE: Researchers should be aware of the following changes in county boundaries for the five counties in New Jersey that are closest to New York City: Bergen and Essex Counties were established in 1682 as two of the original counties in the State. Passaic County was split off from Bergen in 1837, and Hudson County was split off from Bergen in 1840. Portions of Essex went to Somerset County in 1741, Passaic

County in 1837 and Union County in 1857. For a more detailed description and information on other boundary changes in the State, see:

Snyder, John P. *The Story of New Jersey's Civil Boundaries, 1606-1968.* 1969.

Description of Facility:

The State Archives is located on the "B" (basement) level of the State Library building. There are two staff persons available to assist researchers in the Search Room. Seating is available for 20 researchers. The Archives has 5 microfilm/microfiche readers and 5 reader/printers.

Fees/Copies:

The fee for photocopies is $.50 per sheet for manuscripts and $.10 for published materials. Manuscript copies are made by the staff.

Reader/printer copies produced from microfilm cost $.50 each for Search Room patrons, and $1 each for copies sent by mail. A self-addressed stamped envelope should be included with each request.

A search for birth, marriage or death records, May 1848-May 1878, may be requested through the mail for a fee of $4 per record. Complete the appropriate box of the application (see Appendix B-9) to obtain a birth, death or marriage record. If the record is found, a typed transcript will be mailed at no additional charge. Payment should be by check or money order, made payable to "New Jersey General Treasury." See "Restrictions on Use."

Restrictions on Use:

Vital Statistics: The Archives will not do searches or make copies of birth, marriage and death records after May 1878. These are available for in-person searches or can be requested by mail from the NEW JERSEY STATE DEPARTMENT OF HEALTH, State Registrar - Search Unit, CN 360, Trenton, NJ 08625-0360.

Wills and Other Probate Records: In order to preserve original manuscript wills prior to 1817, photocopies can only be provided from the microfilm copy.

Census Records: In order to preserve the originals of the State censuses, only the microfilm copy is open to the public.

Military Records: The Archives will not do searches or make copies of the unofficial service records for World War I. Researchers can view these records in person.

Other: Pens, food, drinks and smoking are prohibited in the Archives Search Room. Secure lockers are provided for personal belongings and briefcases.

Where manuscripts have been microfilmed, researchers are asked to make copies from the microfilm.

The Archives reserves the right to restrict the use of certain collections when necessary for preservation.

NEW JERSEY STATE LIBRARY
NEW JERSEY REFERENCE SERVICES

Facility Director: Barbara F. Weaver, Assistant Commissioner of Education and State Librarian

Address: 185 State Street, CN 520
Trenton, NJ 08625-0520

(Cross Streets: Calhoun Street and Willow Street)

Phone Number: (609) 292-6294

Hours of Operation:

Monday to Thursday:	8:30 am to 8:30 pm
Friday:	8:30 am to 5:00 pm
Saturday:	9:00 am to 5:00 pm

Closed Sunday and major holidays. Open on Martin Luther King Day, Columbus Day, Election Day and Veteran's Day.

Closest Public Transportation and Directions:

See "NEW JERSEY DEPARTMENT OF STATE, DIVISION OF ARCHIVES AND RECORDS MANAGEMENT, NEW JERSEY STATE ARCHIVES."

Description of Resources:

The following are of interest to genealogists:

1. Jerseyana: Materials on all aspects of New Jersey -- its history, culture, people, geography, politics -- make up this collection.

2. Genealogy: County and local histories, genealogical guide books, published genealogies, passenger lists, published vital records and census records on microfilm are all part of this collection. The focus is on New Jersey, but the collection also includes other states, especially those representing the main patterns of population migration to and from New Jersey. Most of this collection does not circulate.

    U.S. Census: The collection includes the following on microfilm:

    Delaware - 1790-1880; indexes 1790-1850
    Maryland - 1790-1880; indexes 1790-1850
    Pennsylvania - 1790-1850 (indexed); 1860-1880 (counties bordering New Jersey including Philadelphia)
    New Jersey - 1830-1880, 1900-1910; indexes 1830-1850, 1880, 1900
    New York - 1790-1850 (indexed); 1860-1880 (counties bordering New Jersey including New York City)
    Other extant states - 1790-1820 (indexed)

    NJ Census (microfilm): 1855 and 1865 (incomplete), 1895-1915 (not indexed)

3. Maps and Pictures: Several hundred maps and atlases from the 17th century to the present are located here. Postcard and picture collections supplement these materials.

    Ward maps are available for the following cities:

Camden, 1850-1915	Passaic City, 1880-1915
Jersey City, 1870-1910	Paterson, 1880-1915
Newark, 1850-1901	Trenton, 1850-1915

4. Newspaper Clippings: An extensive file of newspaper articles serves as a primary source of information on New Jersey. These clippings are arranged by subject and year and go back to the mid-1960s. In addition, a periodical index provides access to magazine articles on New Jersey.

5.   City Directories: The Library has over 500 New Jersey City Directories dating back to the 1850s (on microfilm, microfiche and books).

6.   Documents: As the official repository of New Jersey State government publications, the New Jersey Reference Services maintains a retrospective collection of materials on New Jersey published by State agencies.

Finding Aids:

In addition to a general card catalog, there are specialized card catalogs including a Family Name Index (arranged by surname).

Description of Facility:

The Library Reading Room is on Level 3 (street level) of the building.   Seating is available for 30 researchers.   Five librarians are available to assist researchers.   The Library has 4 microfilm and 3 microfiche readers.   One of each of these is a reader/printer.

Fees/Copies:

One photocopy machine at $.10 per page is available in the Reading Room.   Microfilm and microfiche copies cost $.25 per page.   In response to written requests, staff will check indexes, directories, bibliographies and other appropriate sources and will provide a limited amount of photocopy.   There is a $3 charge for up to 6 pages and $.15 per page thereafter for mail requests.

Restrictions on Use:

None.

SUPERIOR COURT OF NEW JERSEY
TRENTON, NEW JERSEY

Facility Director: John M. Mayson, Clerk
                                Robert C. Wagner, Deputy Clerk

Address: R.J. Hughes Justice Complex, CN 971
                                Trenton, NJ 08625-0971

                                (Cross Streets: Warren and Market Streets)

Phone Number: (609) 292-4987
                                (609) 292-4988 (Index, 1982+)
                                (609) 292-4814 (Index, pre-1982)

Hours of Operation:

Monday to Friday: 9:00 am to 5:00 pm
Closed Saturday, Sunday and legal holidays.

Closest Public Transportation:

Train: NJ Transit or Amtrak to Trenton (from NYC); or
          Philadelphia SEPTA train or Amtrak to Trenton (from Philadelphia);

          <u>and</u>

Bus: NJ Transit L to the Justice Complex

Directions:

See "NEW JERSEY STATE ARCHIVES" for directions to Trenton. From the train station, take the NJ Transit L bus to the Justice Complex. The bus stops in front of the building.

Description of Resources:

The following court records for <u>all</u> 21 counties in the State of New Jersey are available:

1.   <u>Court Cases</u>

    Defunct Courts:

    Old Chancery Court, 1850-1947 (index 1825-1847)
    Errors and Appeals Court, 1869-1947
    Prerogative Court (Opinions), 1890-1928
    Supreme Court (Certiorari docket books), 1892-1948
    Supreme Court (Certiorari index books), 1892-1948
    Old Supreme Court (Corporation index to judgments), 1906-1946
    Old Supreme Court (Docket index), 1850-1941

    Superior Court: Civil Cases, 1948 to the present

    NOTE: Superior Court Criminal Cases are located in the county of venue.

2.   <u>Name Change Records</u>

    The Court has copies of Name Change cases filed in the 21 New Jersey counties, 1920 to the present. Case files include the complaint explaining why the individual or family requested the change.

    NOTE: Pre-1982 records may not include all Name Changes filed in the State. The County Clerk's Offices have the most complete set of records for this period. For 1982 to the present, the Court has all records (on microfiche) except cases still open in "direct filing" counties. These include Camden,

Mercer, Monmouth, Morris, Ocean, Union, and after November 1, 1988, Cumberland, Gloucester and Salem Counties.

Copies of Name Change judgments, 1877 to the present, are also on file in the Secretary of State's Office in Trenton.

3. Matrimonial Records: divorces, separations and annulments filed in:

Old Chancery Court, 1850-1947
Superior Court, 1948 to the present

4. Adoption Records

Superior Court Clerk's Office, 1953-1978

NOTE: Records from 1979 to the present are located in the county of record.

5. Incompetency Records

Old Chancery Court, 1850-1947
Superior Court Clerk's Office, 1948 to the present

6. Probate Records

Wills, letters of administration and guardianships, 1901 to the present

Finding Aids:

Ledger indexes are available for pre-1979 Matrimonial records, pre-1980 Probate records and pre-1982 for most other types of cases noted above. These indexes are arranged by the first letter of the surname and the first two key consonants (L,M,N,R,T).

The index for later cases, for all counties except "direct filing" counties is in a computer and is arranged alphabetically by the name of the plaintiff/defendant. This index is in one alphabetical series. Indexes for "direct filing" counties are maintained in the County Clerk's Office of the county of venue.

Name Changes, 1982 to the present, are indexed by old and new names. Pre-1982 indexes are arranged by the old name only. All 21 counties are included in the pre-1982 ledger indexes. The computer index, 1982 to the present, does not include cases from "direct filing" counties as noted above.

Description of Facility:

Records and indexes are located in several different rooms in the Justice Complex. Researchers should begin in the Vault Section on the P-1 level of the Justice Complex. Indexes to pre-1979 Matrimonial records and other case files pre-1982 are located here. Current records are located on the 6th floor, except Probate records which are on the 4th floor.

Fees/Copies:

Copies of wills can be made by staff at $1 per page. Copies of judgments are $2 per page for the first 4 pages; $.50 per page for pages 5-14; $.25 per page for pages 15-24 and $.10 per page thereafter.

Copies of other case records are $.50 per page for the first 10 pages; $.25 per pages 11-20 and $.10 per page thereafter.

Certified copies cost $2 per page for the first 4 pages and $.50 for each added page.

Restrictions on Use:

Records pre-1900 are generally located in the Records Center and take one to two days to retrieve. The Clerk's office will respond to telephone inquires to determine if a file is available and will order it from the Records Center on request.

The Court does not have an index for Court Cases, including Name Change cases, of "direct filing" counties, 1982 to the present.

BERGEN COUNTY

COUNTY CLERK'S OFFICE
BERGEN COUNTY, NEW JERSEY

Facility Director: Kathleen Donovan, County Clerk

Address: Bergen County Justice Center
Main Street
Hackensack, NJ 07601-7691

(Cross Streets: Essex and Hudson Streets)

Phone Number: (201) 646-2033 (Naturalizations)
(201) 646-3011 (Name Changes)
(201) 646-2095 (Matrimonial Records)
(201) 646-2092 (Property Records)
(201) 646-2106 (Other)

Hours of Operation:

Monday: 9:00 am to 7:45 pm
Tuesday to Friday: 9:00 am to 4:30 pm

Closed Saturday, Sunday and legal holidays.

Closest Public Transportation:

Bus: NJ Transit 165 to Main/Hudson and Essex Streets, Hackensack

Directions:

From Manhattan, take the NJ Transit Bus #165 from Port Authority Bus Terminal, 42nd Street and 8th Avenue, to Main/Hudson and Essex Streets, Hackensack.

Description of Resources:

Bergen County was established in 1682. Passaic County was split off from Bergen in 1837, and Hudson County in 1840. The County Clerk's Office has the following records:

1.   Naturalizations

Petitions for Naturalization and Declarations of Intention, 1804 to the present.

There are also Naturalization Petitions and Declarations for soldiers who were stationed at Camp Merritt during World War I.

2.   Name Changes: Records of persons or families who filed name changes in,

Bergen County Court, 1916-1978
Superior Court, 1979 to the present

See "Restrictions on Use." See also "SUPERIOR COURT OF NEW JERSEY, TRENTON."

3.   Court Cases

Court of Common Pleas, 1799-1866 (microfilm)
Circuit Court, 1898-1900 (microfilm)
County Court, 1942-1978 (microfilm)
Superior Court criminal cases, 1978 to the present

Superior Court civil cases are maintained in the County Clerk's Office for one year after the case is closed and then case files are transferred to SUPERIOR COURT OF NEW JERSEY, TRENTON. The original Court of Common Pleas and Circuit Court records were transferred to the County's HISTORICAL ARCHIVES.

4. Matrimonial Records: Divorce cases are maintained in the County Clerk's Office for 5 years and then transferred to SUPERIOR COURT OF NEW JERSEY, TRENTON.

5. Business Records

Trade Names, 1906 to the present
Incorporations, 1787-1968. Incorporation of churches and synagogues are filed in the County Clerk's Office, 1787 to the present.

After 1968, Incorporations are filed with the Secretary of State in Trenton.

6. Property Records: Include deeds and mortgages, dating back to 1714.

7. Military Discharge Records: Voluntarily filed by veterans. Records dating back to World War I are open to the public.

Finding Aids:

1. Naturalizations: These records are indexed in ledgers by year and the first two letters of the surname.

2. Name Changes: Cases filed in County Court, 1916-1978, are indexed in ledgers by year and the first three letters of the old and new surnames.

   All Superior Court cases filed after 1981 and still open (and some filed in 1979 and 1980) and cases closed within the previous 4-5 years, are on a computer index together with the index for all other Court cases. Cases are indexed by both the new and old names. This index is periodically purged to eliminate closed cases. See "Restrictions on Use."

3. Court Cases: For County Court cases, the Office has ledger indexes arranged by year and then by the first three letters of the surname.

   For Superior Court cases (criminal and civil) filed after 1981, see above description of the computer index. Cases are indexed alphabetically by names of both plaintiff and defendant.

4. Matrimonial Records: Divorce cases are indexed by computer from 1981 to the present. This is the same computer system as that used for all Court cases. Most matrimonial cases can be identified easily (surnames of plaintiff and defendant are the same). Pre-1981 indexes are in docket books arranged by the first three letters of the defendant's surname.

5. Business Records: For Trade Names, there are ledger indexes, 1906-1986 (5 books), arranged by groups of years and by the first three letters and first vowel of the surname. From 1987 to the present, there is a separate computerized index for Trade Names. For Incorporations, there are ledger indexes arranged by the first three letters of the name of the corporation.

6. Property Records: These records are indexed alphabetically in ledgers in groups of years for both deeds and mortgages.

7. Military Discharge Records: The ledger index is arranged alphabetically by the surname of the veteran.

Description of Facility:

Naturalization records and index ledgers are in Room 113. There is one staff person available to assist researchers. This room has seating for 2 researchers.

Name Changes, Court Cases, Matrimonial, Business Records (Trade Names), and indexes for these records are in Room 119. There are 3 microfilm readers available in Room 119. The Office has one microfilm reader/printer for staff use only. Three staff persons are available to assist researchers. Seating is available for 2 researchers.

Business Records (Corporations), Military Records and Property Records and indexes are part of the Registry Division and are located in the Search Room, Room 214. There are three staff persons available to assist the public and seating for 2 researchers.

Fees/Copies:

One photocopy machine is available in each room. Copies cost $.25 per page for the first 10 pages, $.15 per page for the next 10 pages and $.10 per page for additional pages over 20. Copies made by staff and mail requests cost $1 per page. Copies from the reader/printer cost $.25 per page.

Restrictions on Use:

Matrimonial Records are generally open to the public. However, case files may be closed if the judge impounds the records.

Many records are centralized in SUPERIOR COURT OF NEW JERSEY, TRENTON. These include Court Cases that are more than one year old and Matrimonial Records that are more than 5 years old.

The computerized index that covers Court cases does not include closed cases more than 4-5 years old. As a result, docket and case file numbers for Court Cases including Name Changes located in this office, cannot be determined here for all cases filed after 1978. Researchers should contact the SUPERIOR COURT OF NEW JERSEY, TRENTON for docket and case file numbers of cases closed after 1978.

DEPARTMENT OF PARKS, DIVISION OF CULTURAL AND HISTORIC AFFAIRS
HISTORICAL ARCHIVES, BERGEN COUNTY

Facility Director: Ruth Van Wagner, Director

Address: Court Plaza South
21 Main Street, Room 203W
Hackensack, NJ 07601-7000

(Cross Streets: Essex and Sussex Streets)

Phone Number: (201) 646-2780

Hours of Operation:

Monday to Friday: 9:00 am to 4:30 pm (by appointment only)
Closed Saturday, Sunday and legal holidays.

Closest Public Transportation and Directions:

See "COUNTY CLERK'S OFFICE, BERGEN COUNTY."

Description of Resources:

The Archives was established in 1988 to maintain and preserve historical County records. The following records, previously in the County Clerk's Office, have been transferred to the Archives:

1.   Marriage Records, two volumes, 1795-1866 and 1863-1873.

2.   Slave Records include births, 1804-1843, and manumission of slaves, 1805-1841.

3.   Road Returns (originals): These are surveys of highways, 1762 to the present. For early records, the names of householders are shown on diagrams. Ledgers are arranged by year and alphabetically. NOTE: The first volume, 1715-1761 Bergen County Road Returns, is part of the Budke Collection of the New York Public Library, Rare Book and Manuscripts Division (Room 324). [B.C. 11]

4.   Bergen County Freeholder Minutes: 1712 to the present.

5.   Voter Registrations: 1860s-1870s, and census of voters.

6.   Court Records (originals) include Court of Common Pleas, 1799-1866; Circuit Court, 1898-1900; and County Court, 1942-1978; Justice of the Peace dockets, mid-19th century.

7.   Property Record (originals) include deeds 1714-1825; and Tax Records, early 1900s.

8.   Military Records include a census of Bergen County males, 18-45 years old, in 1860/1861 for military service in the Civil War.

Finding Aids:

The Archives has a list of records received from the County Clerk's Office. An inventory is being prepared.

Description of Facility:

The Archives is located on the second floor, in Room 203W. Seating is available for 8 researchers. There are two staff persons available to assist researchers.

Fees/Copies:

Photocopies can be made at $.10 per page.

Restrictions on Use:

The Archives does not accept mail requests for research.

SURROGATE'S COURT
BERGEN COUNTY, NEW JERSEY

Facility Director: Georgia Jineiro, Supervisor, Record Room

Address: Bergen County Justice Center, Room 211
Main Street
Hackensack, NJ 07601-7691

(Cross Streets: Essex and Hudson Streets)

Phone Number: (201) 646-2287, 2261

Hours of Operation:

Monday to Friday: 9:00 am to 4:15 pm
Closed Saturday, Sunday and legal holidays.

Closest Public Transportation and Directions:

See "COUNTY CLERK'S OFFICE, BERGEN COUNTY."

Description of Resources:

The Bergen County Surrogate's Court has records of probate, administration, guardianship and adoption from 1714 to the present. Records, 1714-1962, are in ledger books. Records from 1963 to the present are on microfilm.

Finding Aids:

The indexes for records are in bound ledgers arranged by year and alphabetized by the first two letters of the surname and the first letter of the first name.

Description of Facility:

Records and indexes are located in the Record Room on the second floor. There are 3 microfilm readers for use by the public.

Fees/Copies:

Copies of records can be ordered in Room 211 at $2 per page. Copies will be mailed or can be picked up at a later time. There is no cost for hand copying information.

Restrictions on Use:

Researchers may not see the complete case file.

Adoption records after 1930 are not open to the public.

ESSEX COUNTY

COUNTY CLERK'S OFFICE
ESSEX COUNTY, NEW JERSEY

Facility Director:	Nicholas V. Caputo, County Clerk
	Pat Drake, Deputy Clerk
Address:	Hall of Records, Room 240
	465 Martin Luther King Boulevard
	Newark, NJ 07102
	(Cross Streets: 13th Avenue and West Market Street)
Phone Number:	(201) 621-4921

Hours of Operation:

Monday to Friday: 8:30 am to 4:00 pm
Closed Saturday, Sunday and legal holidays.

Closest Public Transportation:

Train: NJ Transit, Amtrak or PATH trains to Newark; and
Bus: NJ Transit 21 or 34 to Martin Luther King Boulevard and West Market Street.

Directions:

(Fastest) From Manhattan, take either the NJ Transit or Amtrak train to Newark station. Exit the station through the waiting room (Market Street exit). From Newark station (Raymond Plaza West and Market Street), take either bus #21 or #34 to Martin Luther King Boulevard and West Market Street. Or,

(Slower) Take the PATH train to Newark station. Remaining directions from Newark station are as above.

Description of Resources:

Essex County was established in 1682. Union County was split off from Essex in 1857. The County Clerk's Office has the following records:

1. Naturalizations

    Naturalization records and Petitions for Naturalization, 1779-1930
    Declarations of Intention, 1849-1931

    After 1931, residents of Essex County were naturalized in the U.S. DISTRICT COURT in Newark.

2. Name Changes: For persons or families who filed in Essex County Superior Court from 1881 to the present.

    See also "SUPERIOR COURT OF NEW JERSEY, TRENTON."

3. Court Cases: Superior Court civil case files are maintained in the County Clerk's Office for three years after the case is closed and then the case files are transferred to SUPERIOR COURT OF NEW JERSEY, TRENTON. The indexes for earlier cases (from 1948), as well as Superior Court criminal cases, are also available here.

    The County Clerk's Office has the records of defunct courts which operated in Essex County from 1709. These Courts included Common Pleas, General Sessions, Quarter Sessions, Circuit, Oyer and Terminer and County Court.

4. Matrimonial Records: Divorce cases are maintained in the Clerk's Office for 5 years and then transferred to the SUPERIOR COURT OF NEW JERSEY, TRENTON. Indexes for older Essex County cases (from 1948) are located here.

5. Marriage Records: in ledgers, 1795-1849 (very poor condition) and in files, 1850-1910.

6. Business Records include:

   Trade Names (Firm Names), 1906 to the present
   Incorporated Businesses, 1880-1968/69. After 1968, incorporations are filed with the Secretary of State in Trenton. Only non-profit religious corporations (e.g. synagogues and churches), banking or insurance corporations file in the County Clerk's Office at present.
   Certificates of Incorporation, 1819-1899
   Co-partnerships, 1846 to the present
   Miscellaneous Corporations (including religious organizations and social clubs), 1802 to the present

7. Road Records: These are Freeholder resolutions concerning surveys of roads, 1698 to the present. The old records (to about 1880) describe the property adjacent to the road by the names of householders living there, or may indicate the name of a former householder and note "deceased."

8. Registries of Slave Births or Contracts: Include five receipts for the sale of slaves, 1787-1805; and the certificates of birth of children born to slaves, 1804-1843 (filed by the owner).

9. Veteran's Licenses and Lists of Soldiers: Include stubs of peddlers' licenses issued to soldiers and sailors from 1904 to the present. These stubs include the name, address, date of discharge and branch of the armed forces (or unit) in which the individual served, as well as the date of the license.

10. Adoptions: There is one bound volume of adoptions of children, 1880-1924.

11. Census: The County Clerk's Office has original copies of the:

    U.S. Census, Essex County, 1850 and 1880
    New Jersey Census, Essex County, 1855, 1865 and 1875.

    NOTE: The 1850 and 1855 Census of Essex County included all of what is now Union County.

12. Gun Permits (including denials), 1926 to the present. The permit application often indicates the individual's occupation since it is usually the basis for requiring a weapon.

13. Lunacy Papers: Records of individuals committed to mental hospitals, 1951 to the present.

Many of the records described above have been microfilmed by the Mormons. Copies of these films are available through the FAMILY HISTORY CENTERS (LDS) and a set is also available in Trenton. See "NEW JERSEY DEPARTMENT OF STATE - DIVISION OF ARCHIVES AND RECORDS MANAGEMENT, NEW JERSEY STATE ARCHIVES."

Researchers should check the inventory of records in the Vault for additional materials of interest. This inventory, prepared in 1980, includes such additional items as:

   Commissioners of Deeds, 1879-1900 (Item 142)
   Firemen's Register, 1857-1894 (Item 158)
   Home Life Cases (Child Support), 1925-1935 (Item 173)
   Index to Firemen's Certificates, 1918-1925 (Item 240)
   Index of Registered Nurses, 1903-1945 (Items 131, 132)
   Index to Insolvent Debtors, 1880-1895 (Item 113)
   Justices of the Peace, 1878-1897, 1879-1920 (Items 137, 141)
   List of Common Pleas Judges and dates served, 1930-1947 (Item 161)
   Osteopath Register, 1913-1944 (Item 129)
   Physician's Certificates, 1841 to present; and Register, 1829-1931 (Item 128)
   Widows' Pension Docket, 1913-1936 (Item 175)

Finding Aids:

1. Naturalization records, 1830-1931 and Declarations, 1849-1931, are indexed in groups of years arranged alphabetically by the first letter of the surname, the next key consonant (L,M,N,R,T) and the first letter of the first name. Check also the "Miscellaneous Index" which has many entries for Declarations of Intention.

2. Name Change records are indexed in three bound volumes by the first letter of the surname and the next key consonant (L,M,N,R,T). Both old and new names are indexed.

3. Court Cases: Superior Court civil cases pre-1982 are indexed in ledgers in groups of years and alphabetically by the first letter of the surname and the next key consonant (L,M,N,R,T). After 1982, the index is on microfiche. The index is arranged alphabetically by the defendant's/plaintiff's name and the case docket number.

   Some indexes are available for cases of defunct courts. Check the inventory available at the Supervising Clerk's desk in the County Clerk's Vault to determine what is available for a particular court.

4. Matrimonial Records: Indexes, 1948-1979, are in ledgers arranged by the first letter of the surname and the next 2 key consonants (L,M,N,R,T). After 1980, the index is on microfiche arranged alphabetically.

5. Marriage Records: There is an index to Marriage records in bound volumes, arranged alphabetically by the first letter of the groom's surname for the period 1795-1879.

6. Business Records: The indexes to Trade Names (Firm Names), Incorporated Businesses and Co-Partnerships are in ledgers arranged by the first letter of the company's name and the next key consonant (L,M,N,R,T).

   The index to Religious Societies is in ledgers arranged alphabetically by the first letter of the name of the organization.

7. Road Records: Indexes, 1690 to the present, are in four bound volumes arranged alphabetically by the first letter of the street name and the next key consonant (L,M,N,R,T). Records are arranged chronologically by the date the road was put through.

8. Veteran's Licenses: These records are indexed in the front of each volume by the first letter of the surname. Ledger indexes are also available and are arranged by the first letter of the surname and the next key consonant (L,M,N,R,T).

9. Census: The 1880 Census is arranged by town.

10. Gun Permits: The index is arranged alphabetically by the surname of the applicant.

11. Lunacy Papers: There is a ledger index to these records arranged by the first letter of the surname of the patient, then the first key consonant (L,M,N,R,T) and the first letter of the first name.

Description of Facility:

Most records are in the County Clerk's Office Vault, Room 240. There are five to six staff persons available to help researchers in this office. One or 2 stools are available at each of the tables in the room (entrance level). There is one microfiche reader available. The following are the locations of specific record groups:

Naturalization records and indexes, Court Cases of defunct courts, Adoption records and Census volumes are in the County Clerk's Vault, Room 240 on the third floor balcony. Naturalization records, 1779-1906, are in file cabinets. Petitions, 1906-1930, and Declarations, 1850-1931, are in bound volumes.

Ledger indexes and microfiche indexes for Court Cases of the Superior Court are in Room 240 (entrance level). Case files for cases closed in the last 3 years are here also. All earlier cases are on file in the SUPERIOR COURT OF NEW JERSEY, TRENTON.

Name Change indexes, 1881-1967, and records, 1881 to the present, are in the County Clerk's Vault, Room 240 (entrance level). One ledger index, 1967 to the present, is on the counter across the hall in Room 239.

Matrimonial Records and indexes are in Room 238.

Marriage Records and indexes, 1795-1849, are in the Clerk's Vault, Room 240 on the entrance level. Later marriage certificates are in boxes on the second floor of the Vault.

Business Records, Road Records, Gun Permits, Veteran's Permits and Lunacy indexes are in the County Clerk's Vault, Room 240 (entrance level).

<u>Registries of Slave Births and Contracts</u> are in the County Clerk's Vault, Room 240. See the Supervising Clerk for permission to view these records.

Fees/Copies:

Photocopies can be made by staff at $1.50 per page. Certified copies cost $3 extra per document.

Restrictions on Use:

There is no seating on the third floor balcony where many of the old records are kept. The records are difficult to find and covered by a thick brown dust. Researchers are advised to dress accordingly.

The New Jersey Census (1855-1875) are loose sheets and bound rolls. It may be easier to use the microfilmed copies in the NEWARK PUBLIC LIBRARY or in the NEW JERSEY STATE ARCHIVES in Trenton.

COUNTY REGISTER'S OFFICE
ESSEX COUNTY, NEW JERSEY

Facility Director: Ms. Larrie West Stalks, County Register

Address: Hall of Records, Room 130
465 Martin Luther King Boulevard
Newark, NJ 07102

(Cross Streets: 13th Avenue and West Market Street)

Phone Number: (201) 621-4960
(201) 621-4718 (Vault)

Hours of Operation:

Monday to Friday: 8:30 am to 4:00 pm
Closed Saturday, Sunday and legal holidays.

Closest Public Transportation and Directions:

See "COUNTY CLERK'S OFFICE, ESSEX COUNTY."

Description of Resources:

The Register's Office has the following records of interest to genealogists:

1. Property Records include deeds and mortgages dating back to 1688.

2. Military Discharge Records (known in this office as "Service Discharge" records) are voluntarily filed by veterans. Records dating back to World War I are open to the public.

3. Maps: The Office has bound atlases with detailed street maps (showing individual buildings) for Essex County 1881, 1890 and 1906; the City of Newark 1911, 1926 and 1927; and other communities in the County.

Finding Aids:

1. Property Records: Records are indexed in groups of years by the first two or three letters of the surname and the first letter of the first name of the grantor or grantee and mortgagor or mortgagee.

    Researchers wishing to trace the history of a particular property can check the address in the atlas on the counter to the left of the entrance to Room 130. The atlas is arranged by street name and house number and provides the name of the current owner, lot size and block and lot number. Use the current owner's name to begin the search in the grantor/grantee indexes.

2. Military Discharge Records: A card index arranged alphabetically is available. See "Restrictions on Use."

Description of Facility:

Property Records are in the Register's Vault, Room 108 and Room 125 (two entrances). Go up the short staircase to the left of the entrance of the building, enter Room 130, the City Register's Office, continue across the room and exit through the door marked "128" to the corridor to the Vault. Room 125 is on the right.

Military Discharge Records are in Room 125. These records are open to the public. The index, however, is behind the counter in Room 128/130 (two entrances).

Maps are in Room 125 inside the "cage."

Fees/Copies:

There are 6 photocopy machines available in Room 125. Copies cost $.25 per page. NOTE: The machines accept only quarters.

Restrictions on Use:

The index to the Military Discharge records is not directly accessible to researchers. Staff will only look up a specific name.

NEW JERSEY HISTORICAL SOCIETY
LIBRARY

Facility Director: Sarah Collins, Library Director

Address: 230 Broadway
Newark, NJ 07104

(Cross Streets: Taylor Street and 3rd Avenue)

Phone Number: (201) 483-3939

Hours of Operation:

Wednesday to Friday: 10:00 am to 4:00 pm
Closed Saturday, Sunday, Monday, Tuesday and legal holidays.

NOTE: Hours can vary. Call in advance for an appointment to use the manuscript collection and to check the hours of the library.

Closest Public Transportation:

Train: NJ Transit, Amtrak or PATH train to Newark; <u>and</u>
Bus: NJ Transit 13 to Broadway and 3rd Avenue.

Directions:

See "COUNTY CLERK'S OFFICE, ESSEX COUNTY" for directions to Newark station. From the station, take the #13 bus or a taxi to Broadway and Taylor Street. The entrance to the building is through the <u>back</u> door facing the parking lot. Enter through Taylor Street. (The main entrance on Broadway is closed.)

Description of Resources:

(The following is adapted from "A Guide to Family History and Genealogical Resources in the New Jersey Historical Society Library" prepared in September 1985 by the Library.)

1. <u>Weyel Index</u> to birth and family records, Centerville and Bayonne, New Jersey, 1884-1917. This is an index to the records of Annie Specert Weyel, a midwife. The approximately 4,000 cards identify the child's name, parents' names, place of birth, mother's maiden name, street address and number of children in each family.

2. <u>New Jersey Biographical Card Index</u>: This collection of 75,000 cards is a name index of births, marriages and deaths compiled as a WPA project primarily from central and northern New Jersey newspapers in the Society's collection (c.1790-1900). Some additional cards largely derived from Trinity Church, Newark, burial records and from the genealogical compilations of Elmer T. Hutchinson were added in 1958.

3. <u>New Jersey Federal Census</u> microfilms for New Jersey, 1830-1880, 1890 (part of Jersey City) and 1900.

4. <u>New Jersey Education Tax Ratables</u> (1778-1832): These microfilm records include the value of property, holdings, cattle, etc., used to compute taxes of property owners. NOTE: The originals are at the NEW JERSEY STATE LIBRARY in Trenton.

5. <u>Genealogical Collections</u>: Include the Elias Boudinot Stockton Genealogical Collection (pre-1920), which includes information on New Jersey families and some out-of-state families, principally New York (c.75,000 cards and 1,500 file folders); the Freeman Worth Gardner Genealogical Card Index (c.35,000 cards) containing information on descendants of early families of Woodbridge, New Jersey and vicinity (pre-1945); the Charles Carroll Gardner Genealogical Collection (c.30,000 cards and notebooks, manuscripts and folders) which include data (pre-1912) on northern New Jersey families. These collections include information mostly from the 1700s to 1900.

6. American Genealogical Foundation Card Index: This is an alphabetical bibliography of 10,000 printed genealogies. The books listed are not necessarily in the Library's collection.

7. Index to Civil War Soldier's Graves in New Jersey: This is an index to *New Jersey Regiment Infantry Volunteers - U.S. Civil War: Burial Records by County of the Veterans Who are Buried in the State of New Jersey.*

8. Genealogical Manuscript Collections: A surname index to 20 of these manuscript collections has been prepared by the Library. See "Restrictions on Use."

9. Family Files and Charts: Approximately 1,200 files of unpublished materials and 60 genealogical charts on New Jersey and related families.

   NOTE: The Library welcomes donations of family papers, originals or copies. A Family File including typescripts of research in progress will be started for any family with a New Jersey connection.

10. Family Bible Records: Photocopies and typescripts of approximately 400 family bible records are on file.

11. New Jersey State Society, Daughters of the American Revolution Library: Includes typescripts, contributed by DAR chapters, of Bible records, vital statistics, church records, family genealogies and other sources. Also includes 300 printed histories and genealogies.

12. Maps: Include maps of Essex County, c.1900-1910, showing wards. NOTE: These can be used as finding aids for the Federal census. In addition, the Library has 19th-century maps for various communities in New Jersey.

13. Other Genealogical Materials: The Library also collects family newsletters, genealogical journals and materials on other states. Among its holdings are: *The American Genealogist, National Genealogical Society Quarterly, New England Historical & Genealogical Register, New York Genealogical and Biographical Record, Maryland and Delaware Genealogist, Pennsylvania Genealogical Magazine* and *South Carolina Historical and Genealogical Magazine.*

Finding Aids:

In addition to the indexes described above, the Library has:

1. New Jersey Federal Census: Printed indexes for the 1830-1860 Censuses.

2. New Jersey Education Tax Ratables are arranged by county. The index is on the first reel.

3. New Jersey State Society, Daughters of the American Revolution Library: This collection can be accessed by the DAR Subject Index, arranged by surname. There are also some DAR chapter/church name headings.

4. Manuscript Collections: The Library has a Manuscript Card Catalog in the Manuscript Room and a published *Guide to the Manuscript Collections of the New Jersey Historical Society,* 1985. Entries in the card catalog are primarily names of individuals, families and institutions.

5. Family Charts: The Library has a published *Guide to the Genealogy Chart Collection in NJHS,* a 7-page pamphlet that identifies 60 charts and lists 170 allied lines. See "Fees/Copies."

Description of Facility:

The Historical Society is housed in a 4-story building covering the full length of the block. The Library, which is located on the first floor, can seat up to 30 people. Seating is available for an additional 12 people in the Maps and Manuscript Room. There is one librarian on duty in each room to assist researchers. The Library has 3 microfilm readers, one of which is a reader/printer.

The Library has a Genealogy Club (free to members) that meets on the third Saturday of each month.

Fees/Copies:

There is a $1 fee per day for use of the Library by non-members. The annual membership fee is $25. Staff will make photocopies at $.35 per page with a maximum limit of 25 pages. Copies made by researchers from microfilm cost $.25 per page.

Copies of the *Guide to the Genealogy Chart Collection in NJHS* cost $3 (or $4 postpaid). The *Guide* includes an application for chart searches by staff and the charges for a search. Staff will search a specific chart selected by a patron for one or two individuals.

Restrictions on Use:

Concurrent with the opening of the surname index to the Genealogical Manuscript Collections, the Library removed these collections from the public area. However, access may be obtained by requesting a particular manuscript from the librarian.

NEWARK PUBLIC LIBRARY
NEW JERSEY REFERENCE DIVISION

Facility Director: Dr. Alex Boyd, Director, Newark Public Library

George Hawley, Supervising Librarian, New Jersey Reference Division

Address: 5 Washington Street

Newark, NJ

(Cross Street: Broad Street. North end of Washington Park)

Mail Address: P.O. Box 630

Newark, NJ 07101-0630

Phone Number: (201) 733-7775, 7776

Hours of Operation:

Monday, Tuesday, Thursday, Friday:	9:00 am to 5:30 pm
Wednesday:	9:00 am to 9:00 pm
Saturday:	9:00 am to 5:00 pm (to 1:00 pm in the summer)

Closed Sunday and legal holidays.

Closest Public Transportation:

Train: NJ Transit, Amtrak or PATH train to Newark; <u>and</u>

Bus: NJ Transit 72 or 76

Directions:

See "COUNTY CLERK'S OFFICE, ESSEX COUNTY" for directions to Newark station. From the station, take bus #72 or bus #76 to Washington and Broad Streets. Or take a cab from the station to the Museum/Library Block.

Description of Resources:

1. <u>City Directories</u>

    Newark City Directories, 1835-1902 (on microfilm) and 1903-1964/65 (originals).

    NOTE: The Newark Business Library, 34 Commerce Street, Newark, New Jersey, 07102, telephone (201) 733-7779, has a collection of more than 2,000 New Jersey City Directories.

2. <u>Census</u> (on microfilm)

    U.S. Census for New Jersey, 1830-1910
    New Jersey State Census, 1855 and 1865 (incomplete); 1875 (Essex and Sussex Counties only), 1885, 1895, 1905 and 1915. NOTE: These are all the extant NJ State Census records.

3. <u>Newspapers</u> (microfilm)

    Newark Evening News, 1883-1972, and *Sunday News,* 1872-1972 (known as the *Newark Sunday Call,* 1872-1946). Includes the newspaper and morgue, a clipping file with 3,000,000+ clips, 1888-1972, as well as a collection of 700,000+ photos, c.1900-1972. See "Restrictions on Use."

    Newark Daily Advertiser and *Sentinel of Freedom,* c.19th and first half of 20th century.

    Jewish Chronicle, 1921-1943 and *Jewish News,* March 1946 to the present (mostly social news). Both papers are in English and were published in Newark.

4. New Jersey Illustrations Index and Picture Collection

This index of pictures of people and buildings covers the period 1840 to the present. The index includes 200,000 cards covering individual black and white photos in the Library's picture collection, all pictures published in the 30,000 books in the New Jersey Reference Division, articles in scholarly magazines, lithographs in 19th-century periodicals (e.g. *Harpers, Godeys, New York Illustrated*), broadsides, drawings in atlases, and postcards. Photos are added daily as prints are purchased. The collection includes the <u>Dr. Sam Berg Collection</u>, 8,000 photos of ethnic areas (mostly Jewish) and building-by-building photographs of Newark, c.1940-1960. (The index does not cover the 700,000+ photos from the newspaper collection described above.)

The index is arranged by subject, country and surname. Most names of individuals are indexed under the subject heading "Portraits and Settings."

5. Fire Insurance Atlases (for Essex County and the northern tier of the State, i.e. Hudson, Bergen and parts of Passaic Counties)

These Atlases include property lines and building descriptions and are available from 1868 to about 1960 for Essex County. Atlases for the northern tier counties are available only for the 20th century. Real estate atlases showing lots but not buildings are available up to the present.

6. Information on Notable Persons

This is a card file index of biographical information arranged by name.

7. NJ Reference Books

Includes such volumes as the *Jewish Community Blue Book,* 1924.

Finding Aids:

In addition to those outlined above:

1. Census

U.S. Census - The Library has published indexes by name for 1830, 1840, 1850.

NJ State Census - There is a crossover address/ward book for Newark (late 1800s) and ward maps for Jersey City.

2. Newspapers: There is a handwritten index, 1918-1972, for the *Newark Evening News* by name, geographic area and topic. No index exists for other papers. The newspaper picture collection is indexed by geographic location, topic and first three letters of the surname.

3. NJ Reference Books are cataloged by author, title and subject.

Description of Facility:

The Reference Room is on the third floor. It can accommodate 20-25 persons. There are six professional librarians and four clerks available to assist researchers. The room has 8 microfilm readers of which 2 are reader/printers.

Fees/Copies:

A photocopy machine is available in the Reference Room at $.10 per page. The photo lab can make copies of black and white prints (8x10 glossy positive) of non-copyright library-owned material at $6.50 per print for non-profit (personal) use or $10 per print for commercial use.

For mail requests, copies of obituaries can be made for $6 (up to 6 pages) and subject requests for $8 (up to 20 pages) from any source within the Library.

Restrictions on Use:

To obtain material, the user must show some form of identification, e.g. local library card, driver's license.

Material marked "Do not photocopy" is restricted. In addition, specific collections may have restrictions, depending upon the wishes of the donors.

The Newspaper photo collection is stored in a warehouse and requests must be made 1-2 days in advance for a search to be made. The *Newark Evening News* and *Sunday News* morgue is being microfilmed and is not accessible at the present time. Call in advance to determine availability.

SURROGATE'S COURT
ESSEX COUNTY, NEW JERSEY

Facility Director: Herbert Gladstone, Chief Clerk

Address: Hall of Records, Room 213
465 Martin Luther King Boulevard
Newark, NJ 07102

(Cross Streets: 13th Avenue and West Market Street)

Phone Number: (201) 621-4900

Hours of Operation:

Monday to Friday: 8:30 am to 4:00 pm
Closed Saturday, Sunday and legal holidays.

Closest Public Transportation and Directions:

See "COUNTY CLERK'S OFFICE, ESSEX COUNTY."

Description of Resources:

The Court has wills, letters of administration, guardianships of minors and incompetents, adoptions of children, adult adoptions, trusteeships, deeds of assignment, trust agreements and conservatorships from 1795 to the present. Documents are in libers, in individual case files or on microfilm. Records (except will books and administration books) after 1972 are on microfilm. All records from 1983 to the present have been microfilmed. The Court plans to microfilm everything after 1972.

Every estate file from 1946 to the present includes a copy of the death certificate. Earlier records may or may not include this document.

Finding Aids:

Indexes are arranged by the first 3 letters of the surname. The "Lusk system" is used for all Surrogate's records that are open to the public. Directions describing how to use the index are on the inside cover of each index book. Adoptions are included in these indexes to 1941.

Description of Facility:

The Surrogate's Vault is on the second floor of the Hall of Records in Room 213. All indexes and pre-1972 records are located here. There is one staff person available to assist researchers. Nine stools are scattered around the room at the tables at which researchers work. Microfilmed records are available in the Microfilm Room, Room 204. There are 5 microfilm readers available for use by the public. Two staff persons are on duty who can assist researchers.

Fees/Copies:

Copies of records can be made by staff at $2 per page. The search of a name by staff costs an additional $2.50 per name searched.

Restrictions on Use:

The records and index for adoptions of children from 1941 to the present are sealed. (Adult adoptions are open records.)

U.S. DISTRICT COURT, NEW JERSEY - NATURALIZATION SECTION
NEWARK, NEW JERSEY

Facility Director: Jean Cherubini, Deputy Clerk
Ana Villavicencio, Deputy Clerk

Address: Main Post Office Building
Federal Square, Room 309C
Newark, NJ 07102

(Cross Streets: Walnut and Franklin Streets)

Phone Number: (201) 645-2527, 2578

Hours of Operation:

Monday to Friday: 8:00 am to 4:00 pm
Closed Saturday, Sunday and legal holidays.

Closest Public Transportation:

Train: NJ Transit, Amtrak or PATH train to Newark, and
Bus: NJ Transit 13, 27, 39, 62 or 70 to Broad and Walnut Streets.

Directions:

From Manhattan, take the NJ Transit train to Newark station. Leave through the rear of the station (Raymond Plaza East exit). Turn right when exiting the station for the bus stop. Take the #39, #62 or #70 bus to Broad and Walnut Streets. Cross Broad Street and walk one block on Walnut to Federal Square. The Main Post Office Building is located between City Hall and the Federal Court House (behind the church).

Description of Resources:

The U.S. District Court of New Jersey sits in Newark, Trenton and Camden. The Newark office was opened in 1911 and proceedings began in 1913. Any person who was a resident of the State of New Jersey for at least 6 months could file a Petition for Naturalization in any of these offices.

The Newark office has Petitions for Naturalization, November 1982 to the present, and Declarations of Intention, July 1982 to the present, for persons who filed in the Newark section of the U.S. District Court.

In addition, the office has indexes for Petitions and Naturalizations from 1914 to the present. See "Finding Aids."

For Petitions and Declarations, 1914-1982, filed in U.S. District Court of New Jersey, Newark office, see "NATIONAL ARCHIVES, NORTHEAST REGION." The NATIONAL ARCHIVES also has petitions filed in Camp Fort Dix, Camden and Trenton. See "COUNTY CLERK'S OFFICE, ESSEX COUNTY, NEW JERSEY" for Petitions filed in Superior Court, Essex County, 1779-1930 and for Declarations filed 1849-1931.

Finding Aids:

The office has separate indexes for Petitions for Naturalization and Declarations of Intention. From 1915 to March 1985, both indexes are microfiche copies of the stubs or index cards, arranged alphabetically by the name of the petitioner. From April 1985 to the present, the indexes are the actual stubs arranged alphabetically.

Description of Facility:

The indexes are located on the third floor of the Main Post Office building in Room 309C. The records are stored in Room 347 but must be requested from the staff in Room 309C. Staff will retrieve the appropriate volumes. See "Restrictions on Use." There are two staff persons behind the counter available to assist researchers. Seating is available for two researchers.

Fees/Copies:

Records can be hand copied by the researcher or photocopies can be made by the staff at $.50 per page.

Restrictions on Use:

Researchers who come in person may have direct access to the indexes but may not be able to view the records the same day. Call at least one day in advance to request records so that the volumes can be retrieved. Staff will respond to telephone requests and look up names. Researchers can then make an appointment to view the records or order copies by telephone or mail at $.50 per page.

NOTE: The office plans to transfer records more than 5 years old to the NATIONAL ARCHIVES, NORTHEAST REGION every year. Check if records have been moved before visiting this facility.

HUDSON COUNTY

CHANCERY COURT
HUDSON COUNTY, NEW JERSEY

Facility Director: Hon. Stephen J. Schaeffer, Judge, Chancery Court

Address: Hudson County Administration Building
595 Newark Avenue, Room 204
Jersey City, NJ 07306

(Cross Streets: Central, Baldwin and Pavonia Avenues)

Phone Number: (201) 795-6635

Hours of Operation:

Monday to Friday: 9:00 am to 4:00 pm
Closed Saturday, Sunday and legal holidays.

Closest Public Transportation:

Train: PATH train to Journal Square (Jersey City)
Bus: NJ Transit 9 or 84 to Newark and Baldwin Avenues

Directions:

From Manhattan, take the PATH train to the Journal Square Station. Go up the stairs/escalator, exit the turnstiles and go up one more escalator. Go through the doors to "One Path Plaza, Buses, Parking and Kiss'n Ride" and turn right immediately. Walk straight ahead to exit the terminal. Cross a small plaza and go up the stairs. Walk straight ahead (on Magnolia Avenue) passing the NJ Bell building and cross Summit Avenue. Turn left on Summit and walk one block to Pavonia Avenue. Turn right on Pavonia Avenue and walk one-half block. Pass the prison and enter the Administration Building through the back entrance (parking area). This is the G-level of the building. Take the elevator to the second floor.

Description of Resources:

This Court hears matrimonial cases of Hudson County residents. Divorce and separation records are maintained in this office for 6-7 years. The case files are then transferred to SUPERIOR COURT OF NEW JERSEY, TRENTON. Indexes for Hudson County cases since 1971 are located here.

Finding Aids:

The indexes for matrimonial records, 1971 to the present, are in libers arranged in groups of years and then alphabetically by the first 3 letters of the surname.

Description of Facility:

Matrimonial records and indexes are located in Room 204. Indexes are in a side room to the right of the entrance to this room. There is one staff person available at the desk to assist researchers. The office has one photocopy machine.

Fees/Copies:

Copies of Matrimonial records can be made at no cost.

Restrictions on Use:

None

COUNTY CLERK'S OFFICE
HUDSON COUNTY, NEW JERSEY

Facility Director:	Frank E. Rodgers, County Clerk Pat Cummings, Record Center
Address:	Hudson County Administration Building 595 Newark Avenue, Room 101 Jersey City, NJ 07306 and Old Court House 583 Newark Avenue Jersey City, NJ 07306 (Cross Streets: Central, Baldwin and Pavonia Avenues)
Phone Number:	(201) 795-6112, 6113 (201) 795-6130 (Naturalizations) (201) 795-6618 (Record Center)

Hours of Operation:

Monday to Friday: 9:00 am to 4:00 pm
Closed Saturday, Sunday and legal holidays.

Closest Public Transportation and Directions:

See "CHANCERY COURT, HUDSON COUNTY." Take the elevator to the first floor for the County Clerk's Office.

Description of Resources:

Hudson County was formed in 1840. Prior to that, it was part of Bergen County. See "COUNTY CLERK'S OFFICE, BERGEN COUNTY" and "SUPERIOR COURT OF NEW JERSEY, TRENTON" for earlier records.

1. Naturalizations

    Petitions for Naturalization, 1840 to the present
    Declarations of Intention, 1893-c.1981

    Naturalization records, 1840-1906, are folded court orders filed in vertical drawers and arranged by year and sometimes alphabetically. Declarations and Petitions, 1907 to the present, are in libers arranged chronologically.

2. Name Changes: Filed by persons or families in Hudson County from 1875 to the present.

    See also "SUPERIOR COURT OF NEW JERSEY, TRENTON."

3. Court Cases: Superior Court civil case files are maintained in the County Clerk's Office for 5 years after the case is closed and then the case files are transferred to SUPERIOR COURT OF NEW JERSEY, TRENTON. Superior Court criminal cases from 1924 to the present are available here.

    The County Clerk's Office has the records of defunct courts which operated in Hudson County from as early as 1844. These included General Sessions, Common Pleas, Circuit and County Courts.

4. Business Records include:

    Business Names (Firm Names), 1910 to the present
    Incorporations, 1875-1968. Non-profit corporations are filed in the County, 1875 to the present.
    Partnerships, 1960-1985/86

    Incorporations after 1968, and Partnerships after 1985, are filed with the Secretary of State in Trenton.

Finding Aids:

Naturalizations: The Office has liber indexes for Petitions for Naturalizations, 1840 to the present, and for Declarations of Intention, 1900-1901, 1916-1924 and 1930-1981. Pre-1916, each Declaration liber has an index at the front of the volume, are arranged by groups of years and alphabetically by the first letter of the surname.

Name Changes and Business Records: Separate liber indexes are available for each type of record and are arranged in groups of years and then alphabetically by the Lusk system (first 3 letters of the surname). There are separate indexes for Business Names (1922 to the present), Partnerships and Incorporations. Name Changes are indexed by the old name only.

Court Records: Only the index for open civil cases is available here. The index is on microfiche and is arranged alphabetically. The indexes for criminal cases, 1924 to the present, are in libers arranged by groups of years and then alphabetically by the first letter of the surname of the plaintiff.

Description of Facility:

ADMINISTRATION BUILDING:

Naturalization Records, Court Cases (criminal cases only), Name Change indexes and Business Records are located in the Hudson County Administration Building.

Naturalization Records are in Room 125, entered through Room 104 (County Register's Office). Most of the records are in the room (door marked "Private") behind the office taking passport and naturalization applications. Space is available for 1-2 researchers in this room. Declarations of Intention and early Declaration indexes are in bookcases in the hallway behind the double doors (actually part of Room 104).

Petitions for Naturalization, 1840-1906, are in metal cabinets near the windows. Some of the indexes to Naturalizations (1890-present) are on a table in front of the shelves holding the records. The earlier Naturalization indexes (pre-1890), the last two volumes (1930-c.1981) of the Declaration index and recent Naturalization records are in Examiner's Room #1, located near the entrance to this room.

Court Cases (criminal cases only), Name Change indexes and indexes to Business Records (except Business names, 1910-1921) are in the Record Room of the County Clerk's Office, which can be entered from Room 101 on the first floor. This is a large room where most researchers work standing at tables. Some stools are available. The indexes are along the wall near the staff desks. There are four to six staff persons available in this area to assist researchers. Seating can be made available for one researcher at a desk.

Name Change index libers are under the second long table on the aisle. Liber indexes to Business Names, 1922-1943, are in shelves behind the Name Change indexes. The indexes after 1943 are on a table in the Record Room. One to two staff persons are available to assist researchers.

OLD COURT HOUSE:

The County has recently renovated the Old Court House next door and many older records (defunct Court Cases, Name Changes, Business Names, 1910-1921, etc.) are now in the basement Record Center (also known as the Archives). There is one staff person available to assist researchers. No seating is available for researchers.

Files of open Court Cases (civil cases including current Name Changes) are on the first floor in the Record Room to the right of the entrance of the Old Court House. There is one microfiche reader in this room. There are one to two staff persons available who can assist researchers.

Fees/Copies:

Copies of Naturalization records can be made by researchers at the photocopy machines in the adjacent County Register's Office copy room at $.25 per page. All other records are made by staff at $1.50 per page.

Restrictions on Use:

Researchers planning to use the records in the Old Court House, basement Record Center (Archives) are advised to make an appointment in advance.

COUNTY REGISTER'S OFFICE
HUDSON COUNTY, NEW JERSEY

Facility Director: Kenneth C. Chmielewski, Register of Deeds and Mortgages
John Hampton, Deputy Register

Address: Hudson County Administration Building
595 Newark Avenue, Room 104
Jersey City, NJ 07306

(Cross Streets: Central, Baldwin and Pavonia Avenues)

Phone Number: (201) 795-6577

Hours of Operation:

Monday to Friday: 9:00 am to 4:00 pm
Closed Saturday, Sunday and legal holidays.

Closest Public Transportation and Directions:

See "CHANCERY COURT, HUDSON COUNTY." Take the elevator to the first floor for the County Register's Office.

Description of Resources:

1. <u>Property Records</u> include deeds and mortgages from 1805 to the present. These include records that were filed originally in Bergen County. Hudson County was formed in 1840. Prior to that it was part of Bergen County.

2. <u>Military Discharge Records</u> (known in this office as "Veteran's Discharge Records") voluntarily filed by veterans. Records were filed beginning in 1931 but include discharge records of veterans from World War I. The records are open to the public.

3. <u>Maps:</u> The Office has bound atlases or tax maps with detailed street maps for Hudson County (1881, 1894, 1909, 1923, 1934) and the following communities:

Bayonne, 1919, 1923, 1937	Greenville, 1881, 1894	North Bergen, 1908, 1964
Bergen, 1894	Guttenberg, 1959	Secaucus, 1916, 1982
East Newark, 1921	Jersey City, 1873, 1887, 1894,	Weehawken Township, 1899
Harrison, 1916, 1920	1908, 1919, 1927, 1928, 1960	West Hoboken, 1906, 1916
Hoboken, 1982	Kearny, 1909, 1920, 1922	West New York, 1922, 1958

Finding Aids:

1. <u>Property Records</u> from 1805 to October 31, 1985 are indexed in libers by grantor/grantee for deeds; and mortgagor/mortgagee for mortgages. These indexes are further separated into "individuals" and "corporations." The indexes are arranged in groups of years and then alphabetically by the first three letters of the surname and the first letter of the first name.

   The indexes from November 1, 1985 to the present are computer printouts arranged by groups of years and alphabetically. These indexes are further separated into "humans" and "corporations."

2. <u>Military Discharge Records:</u> The indexes are in libers arranged by the first three letters of the surname and the first letter of the first name.

Description of Facility:

This is a large government office with long tables at which researchers can stand. There are a few stools around the room. The 11 staff persons who sit opposite the supervisor's desk, are available to assist researchers.

The grantor/grantee and mortgagor/mortgagee liber indexes are on open shelves in the aisle opposite the telephone booths and behind the staff area. The actual records are on open shelves around the room.

Military Discharge records and indexes are located to the left of the entrance in the shelves behind the staircase.

Maps and atlases of Hudson County are in the Copy Room to the right of the supervisor's desk. There are 3 photocopy machines in the Copy Room.

Fees/Copies:

Photocopies can be made at $.25 per page.

Restrictions on Use:

None.

SURROGATE'S COURT
HUDSON COUNTY, NEW JERSEY

Facility Director:	Donald W. DeLeo, Surrogate Rita M. Rosenberg, Supervising Clerk
Address:	Hudson County Administration Building 595 Newark Avenue, Room 107 Jersey City, NJ 07306
	(Cross Streets: Central, Baldwin and Pavonia Avenues)
Phone Number:	(201) 795-6377

Hours of Operation:

Monday to Friday: 9:00 am to 4:00 pm
Closed Saturday, Sunday and legal holidays.

Closest Public Transportation and Directions:

See "CHANCERY COURT, HUDSON COUNTY." This office can be reached by taking the elevator to the first floor. The records are in Room 106, which can be entered directly from the corridor or through Room 107.

Description of Resources:

The Hudson County Surrogate's Court has wills, letters of administration, guardianships and adoptions from 1800 to the present.

Finding Aids:

Liber indexes are grouped by years (1800-1953, 1954-1979 and 1980 to the present) and then arranged alphabetically by the first 3 letters of the surname and the first letter of the first name. These indexes provide the liber and page number where wills, letters of administration and guardianship papers can be found. Pre-1940 indexes include adoptions. The index also provides a docket number. Researchers should look up the case in the appropriate docket liber in order to determine if any other papers exist in the case file. If additional records exist, staff can bring the case file from the vault.

Description of Facility:

This is a large government office with tables at which researchers can stand. The index libers line the shelves near the staff office. Two staff persons are available who can assist researchers.

Fees/Copies:

Photocopies are made by staff and cost $2 per page.

Restrictions on Use:

Adoptions after 1940 are sealed and cannot be viewed by the public.

NATIONAL ARCHIVES AND RECORDS ADMINISTRATION
NATIONAL ARCHIVES, NORTHEAST REGION

Facility Director: Dr. Robert C. Morris, Director
Anthony J. Fantozzi, Assistant Director

Address: Building 22
Military Ocean Terminal
Bayonne, NJ 07002-5388

NOTE: The Archives is planning to relocate to Manhattan in 1989. Call in advance.

Phone Number: (201) 823-7252

Hours of Operation:

Monday to Friday: 8:00 am to 4:30 pm
Third Saturday
  each month: 8:30 am to 4:00 pm (for microfilm research only, not Naturalization Records)

Closed remaining Saturdays, Sunday and legal holidays (except Election Day).

Closest Public Transportation:

Bus: Bayonne Bus to 32nd Street and Kennedy Boulevard.

Directions:

From Manhattan, take the Bayonne Bus from Port Authority Bus Terminal. Get off at 32nd Street and Kennedy Boulevard. Cross the Boulevard and walk east (or take a taxi) on 32nd Street. This is a 10-minute walk. Cross the railroad tracks to the main gate of the Military Ocean Terminal. Sign in at the visitor's center. Board the Military Bus (free) for the ride to Building 22.

Description of Resources:

Although the National Archives was not established until 1934, its major holdings date back to 1775. The National Archives, Northeast Region, is one of 11 regional repositories for historically valuable records of the federal government. These records represent only 2% or 3% of those generated by federal agencies. The holdings of this branch of the National Archives are chiefly of regional interest but also include microfilm copies of many of the most important records in the National Archives, Washington. The Federal Records Center (FRC), a sister agency which is part of the National Archives and Records Administration, stores current records of federal agencies. After a period of time, the FRC transfers records designated for permanent keeping to the National Archives. The following describes the records of the National Archives, Northeast Region. Related record groups in the FRC are noted.

1.   <u>Census Records</u> (microfilm): All existing population schedules are available for the following years: 1790, 1800, 1810, 1820, 1830, 1840, 1850, 1860, 1870, 1880, 1900 and 1910. The 1890 Census was destroyed by fire for most states. The only surviving fragments covering the New York metropolitan area are Jersey City, New Jersey; Eastchester, New York (in Westchester County); and Brookhaven Township, New York (in Suffolk County).

   Special schedules available include all existing Mortality schedules, 1850, 1860, 1870 and 1880.

2.   <u>Immigrant and Passenger Arrivals</u> (microfilm) include passenger lists of vessels arriving at:

   New York harbor, 1820-August 14, 1905 (indexes 1820-1846, June 16, 1897-June 30, 1902), 1943-1952 (Soundex index 1944-1948). There are <u>no</u> lists for the 1905-1942 period in the Archives.
   Atlantic and Gulf Coasts and ports on the Great Lakes, 1820-1873
   Canadian Pacific port entries, 1929-1949 (Soundex index 1924-1952 for Canadian Pacific port <u>and</u> Atlantic port entries)

Canadian border entries through small ports in Vermont, index, 1895-1929
Galveston, Texas, 1896-1948 (index 1896-1951)

The Archives also has (on microfilm) registers of vessels arriving at the port of New York from foreign ports, 1789-1919; and a subject index to correspondence and case files of the Immigration and Naturalization Service, 1903-1952.

3. Military Records (microfilm) include Veterans Administration, War Department and Adjutant General's Office records as follows:

Civil War Union Veterans and Widows of Union Veterans, enumeration schedules, 1890
Civil War, index to compiled service records of volunteer Union Soldiers who served in organizations from the States of New Jersey and New York
Revolutionary War rolls, 1775-1783
Revolutionary War, compiled service records of soldiers who served in the American Army, Navy, and members of the Departments of Quartermaster General and the Commissary General of military stores
Revolutionary War pension and bounty-land-warrant applications files, 1800-1900
War of 1812, index to service records of volunteer soldiers

4. Naturalization Records are available for the following Courts in Federal Region 2 (New York, New Jersey and Puerto Rico):

i. "Old Law" Naturalization Records for New York City: Photocopies of Naturalization Records filed in Federal, State and local courts in New York City, 1792-1906. Any naturalization completed prior to October 1906 in any NYC court should be found in this group of records. These courts include:

Federal Courts:

U.S. Circuit Court, Southern District, New York, 1846-1876
U.S. District Court, Southern District, New York, 1824-1906
U.S. District Court, Eastern District, New York, 1865-1906

State and Local Courts:

Court of Common Pleas for the City and County of NY, 1792-1895
Marine Court of the City of New York, 1806-1849
Superior Court of the City of New York, 1828-1895
Supreme Court, 1st Judicial District, formerly Supreme Court, City and County of NY, 1868-1906
City Court of Brooklyn, 1836-1894
County Court, Kings County, 1856-1906
County Court, Queens County, 1799-1906
Surrogate's Court, Queens County, 1888-1898
County Court, Richmond County, 1869-1906

ii. U.S. District Court for the Eastern District of New York (covers Kings, Queens, Richmond, Nassau and Suffolk Counties)

Naturalization Records, 1865-1957
Declarations of Intention, 1865-1959

NOTE: Naturalizations, 1958-1985, and Declarations, 1960-1979, are in the custody of the Federal Records Center in Bayonne (not the Archives). See "U.S. DISTRICT COURT - EASTERN DISTRICT OF NEW YORK" for later records.

iii. U.S. District Court for the Southern District of New York (covers Manhattan, Bronx, Westchester, Putnam, Rockland, Orange, Dutchess and Sullivan Counties. However, most records are for residents of Manhattan and the Bronx. Residents of other jurisdictions, e.g. Brooklyn, may also have been naturalized in this Court.)

Naturalization Records, 1824-1929
Declarations of Intention, 1842-1940

NOTE: Naturalizations, 1929-1940, and Declarations, 1967-1976, are in the custody of the Federal Records Center in Bayonne (not the Archives). Declarations, 1941-1966, are missing and presumed to have been destroyed. See "U.S. DISTRICT COURT - SOUTHERN DISTRICT OF NEW YORK" for later records.

iv. U.S. Circuit Court for the Southern District of New York (now defunct)

Naturalization Records, 1906-1911
Declarations of Intention, 1845-1911

v. U.S. District Court for the District of New Jersey

Camden Office - Naturalizations and Declarations of Intention, 1932-1981
Camp Fort Dix - Naturalizations filed by soldiers, May 1918-September 1919 and May 1942-December 1946
Newark Office - Naturalizations, 1914-October 1982, and Declarations of Intention, 1914-June 1982
Trenton Office - Naturalizations, 1838-September 1906

NOTE: Newark Office records, 1982 to the present, are in the U.S. DISTRICT COURT - NATURALIZATION SECTION, NEWARK, NEW JERSEY. For Trenton Office records, 1930 to the present, go to 402 East State Street, Room 301, Trenton, NJ (Mail address: Clerk, U.S. District Court, P.O. Box 575, Trenton, NJ 08603). The records are in the basement. Camden Office records, 1982 to the present, are at 401 Market Street, Room 304, Camden, NJ (Mail address: Clerk, U.S. District Court, P.O. Box 2797, Camden, NJ 08101). There were no Naturalizations filed in the Trenton Office, 1906-1929. The Newark Office was opened in 1911 and began Naturalizations in 1913. The Camden Office opened in 1926.

vi. U.S. District Court for Puerto Rico

Naturalization Petitions and related records, 1917-1929

5. Other Court Records: Court cases filed, 1789-1967 (RG 21) in the U.S. District Courts in New York State, New Jersey and Puerto Rico; the Court of Appeals-Second Circuit (cases appealed from New York State, Connecticut and Vermont); and all Circuit Courts in New York State and New Jersey. Dates vary for each court. (NOTE: The functions of the Circuit Courts were absorbed by the U.S. District Courts in 1911.)

The cases filed in these courts include legal proceedings in bankruptcy, and criminal, admiralty and civil actions.

6. Income Tax Records: Post-Civil War income tax records relating to business and corporate taxes for the following district offices are available: Albany, 1910-1917; Buffalo, 1862-1917; Lower Manhattan (Second Collection District), 1910-1917; Lower Manhattan (Third District), 1913-1917; Newark, 1917; Syracuse, 1883-1917. In addition, the Archives has Assessment Lists for New York State, 1862-1873, and New Jersey, 1868-1873.

7. Internal Revenue Service (IRS) Employees: Registers of individuals employed by the IRS in Brooklyn, 1885-1919, and Buffalo, NY, 1875-1919, are available. These include employee name, position title, compensation, date of appointment, date and reason for termination of service, place and year of birth and information concerning the employee's prior civil and military service.

8. Chinese Re-entry Permits: Case files (RG 85), 1880s-1944, of some 30,000 Chinese immigrants who applied for re-entry permits under the Chinese Exclusion Acts of 1882 and 1902 are located here. The case files include correspondence, reports, transcripts of interrogations and testimony, as well as the original identification forms issued by the Immigration and Naturalization Service.

Finding Aids:

1. Census Records: Name indexes to the 1880, 1900 and 1910 Censuses are arranged according to the National Archives Soundex system. The name index to the 1890 Census is arranged alphabetically. (See Appendix C for a description of this system.)

   The 1880 index covers only households with children 10 and under. The 1910 index (for only 21 states) is not available for New York, New Jersey and Connecticut. However, the Archives has a microfiche copy of the 1910 Census Street Index for 39 cities including New York City (Manhattan, Bronx, Brooklyn, Staten Island -- but not Queens) and Elizabeth, Newark and Paterson, NJ.

2. Immigrant and Passenger Arrivals: Indexes included under "Description of Resources" are arranged alphabetically, except the 1944-1948 index to New York arrivals and the 1924-1952 Canadian border entries. These are arranged according to the National Archives Soundex system.

3. Military Records: In addition to the War of 1812 index and the index to Civil War compiled service records of volunteer Union soldiers, there is a general index to compiled service records of Revolutionary War soldiers; and an index to compiled service records of American Naval personnel who served during the Revolutionary War.

4. Naturalization Records: Indexes to most Naturalization records (except where noted) must be requested from the staff on duty. The following are available:

   i. "Old Law" Naturalization Records for New York City (1792-1906)

      Federal, State and local records are combined in one Soundex index.

   ii. U.S. District Court for the Eastern District of New York

      Naturalizations, 1865-1906, may be accessed via the Soundex index listed above ("Old Law"). Naturalizations, 1906-1977, are indexed alphabetically by name and in groups of years, i.e. 1906-1957 and 1958-1977.

      The index to records, 1958-1977, is in the custody of the Federal Records Center (not the Archives). This card index ("stubs") is arranged alphabetically in one series. The stubs include Petition number. In order to locate records, the box number, accession number and Federal Records Center (FRC) shelf location numbers must be obtained in addition to Petition number. These numbers are on the Records Transmittal and Receipt form (SF 135) available in the FRC. The indexes to 1978-1985 records are at the U.S. DISTRICT COURT - EASTERN DISTRICT OF NEW YORK. See "Restrictions on Use."

      Declarations of Intention, 1865-1916, are indexed alphabetically by surname in each individual volume. The Archives has 17 volumes of indexes covering the period 1909-1949. These are organized by year and then first letter of the surname. There is no alphabetical index to Declarations of Intention filed in 1950 or later.

      NOTE: Very few Declarations were filed after 1951. Since 1952, Declarations of Intention are no longer required. Immigrants can file a Petition for Naturalization directly, after living in the U.S. for 5 years. Declarations are filed only if the immigrant elects to do so, e.g. documentation needed for employment, etc.

   iii. U.S. District Court for the Southern District of New York

      Naturalizations, 1824-1906, may be accessed via the Soundex index listed above ("Old Law"). Naturalizations, 1906-1940, are indexed alphabetically by name in a card index.

      Declarations of Intention, 1842-1916, are indexed alphabetically by surname in each individual volume. Declarations, 1917-1954, are indexed alphabetically by name in a card index.

   iv. U.S. Circuit Court for the Southern District of New York

      Naturalizations, 1846-1876, may be accessed via the Soundex index listed above ("Old Law"). Naturalizations, 1906-1911, are indexed alphabetically by name.
      Declarations of Intention, 1845-1911, are indexed by name in each volume.

 v.   <u>U.S. District Court for New Jersey</u>

     Camden office - There is a microfiche index, 1932-1981, arranged alphabetically by name.

     Camp Fort Dix - Naturalizations are indexed alphabetically in a loose-leaf binder.

     Newark office - There are separate indexes, 1915-March 1985, for Petitions for Naturalization and Declarations of Intention. The indexes are microfiche copies of the Naturalization stubs and Declaration index cards. Both are arranged alphabetically by name.

     Trenton office - There is a card index to Naturalization records arranged alphabetically by name.

 vi.   <u>U.S. District Court for Puerto Rico</u>

     There is a one-volume index arranged alphabetically by first letter of the surname.

5.   <u>Other Court Records</u> are only partially indexed. For the U.S. District Courts or Court of Appeals-Second Circuit, the researcher is advised to contact the Court directly for the case or docket number. The Archives has few defendant/plaintiff indexes for Circuit Court records.

6.   <u>Income Tax Records</u> of individual businesses are not easily accessed. These records are arranged by year, District or Collection Office, and type of tax. Further, the only index to this collection is a list arranged by year and box number.

7.   <u>Internal Revenue Service Employees</u> records are not indexed. However, there are only three thin volumes of records which can be scanned quickly by the researcher.

8.   <u>Chinese Re-entry Permits</u>: Case files are arranged numerically by case number. The Archives has created a computerized alphabetical name index. Names were indexed as filed and may not be surnames. Researchers using this index should search under the first name of an individual as well as the surname.

Description of Facility:

Two to three staff persons are available to assist researchers. There are 18 microfilm readers and seats for 18 at the research tables.

Microfilm reels (Census records and passenger lists) are in self-service file cabinets located around the room. There is a 10-20 minute wait for paper records (Naturalizations).

Fees/Copies:

The cost of copying one page of microfilm is $.30 or $.80, depending upon the size of the page, when researchers make their own copies. Fees are substantially greater if copies are made by a staff member. Copies of paper records are $.35 per page. Copies can be obtained immediately. Mail requests are charged a minimum of $5. This can include more than one record, e.g. 14 pages at $.35 per page. It takes about one week to receive a response to mail requests. Personal checks are accepted.

Restrictions on Use:

Eastern District Court Naturalizations, 1978-1985, cannot be easily accessed since the index is located at the U.S. DISTRICT COURT - EASTERN DISTRICT OF NEW YORK. Researchers must obtain also the box, accession and FRC shelf location numbers to locate the Petition at the FRC. Researchers wishing to view these records should contact the U.S. DISTRICT COURT OFFICE - EASTERN DISTRICT first to obtain these numbers.

All briefcases must be left in lockers adjacent to the Research Room. There is no charge for the lockers.

NOTE: The Federal Records Center will remain in Bayonne, NJ when the Archives moves to Manhattan. Southern District Court Naturalizations, 1929-1940, and Declarations, 1967-1976, and Eastern District Court Naturalizations, 1958-1985, Declarations, 1960-1979 and Naturalization index, 1958-1977, are currently in the custody of the Federal Records Center. The Archives may accession these records if sufficient space is available at the new facility. Researchers planning to use these records should call in advance.

FAMILY HISTORY CENTERS (LDS)

FAMILY HISTORY CENTERS (LDS)

The Family History Center in Manhattan, which has been closed since June 1987, will reopen in Spring 1989. It is located at 125 Columbus Ave., New York, NY 10023 (corner of West 65th Street). For information on reopening, hours of operation and services available at this facility, call (212) 580-1919.

The following are other Centers in the New York metropolitan area:

	PLAINVIEW	YORKTOWN HEIGHTS	EAST BRUNSWICK	MORRISTOWN
Facility Director:	Jean Eide	Geraldine Greenlese	Helen J. Rogers	Alfred R. Mott
Address:	160 Washington Ave. Plainview, NY	Route 134 Yorktown Heights, NY	303 Dunham's Corner Rd. East Brunswick, NJ	283 James Street Room 15 Morristown, NJ
Mail Address:	c/o Jean Eide 47 Westwood Road N. Massapequa Park, NY 11762	c/o G. Greenlese 3726 Meadow Lane Shrub Oak, NY 10588	c/o Helen J. Rogers 1907 Midfield Road Feasterville, PA 19047	c/o Alfred R. Mott 103 Klinger Road East Hanover, NJ 07936
Phone Number:	(516) 433-0122	(914) 941-9754	(201) 254-1480	(201) 539-5362
Hours of Operation:				
Tuesday:	10:00 am to 4:00 pm 7:30 pm to 9:30 pm	7:00 pm to 9:00 pm	7:00 pm to 10:00 pm	10:00 am to 4:00 pm 7:00 pm to 10:00 pm
Wednesday:	Closed	9:30 am to 12:00 noon 7:00 pm to 9:00 pm	10:00 am to 2:00 pm 7:00 pm to 10:00 pm	10:00 am to 4:00 pm 7:00 pm to 10:00 pm
Thursday:	10:00 am to 4:00 pm 7:30 pm to 9:30 pm	9:00 am to 12:00 noon	10:00 am to 10:00 pm	Closed
Saturday:	Closed	Closed	10:00 am to 3:00 pm	Closed
Sunday:	Closed a/	12:30 pm to 2:00 pm a/	Closed b/	Closed c/

a/Closed July and August, Christmas and Easter weeks.
b/Closed first week in August, first week in September; the week of Thanksgiving and two weeks at Christmas.
c/Closed the month of August and three weeks at Christmas.

NOTE: All Centers are closed Monday, Friday and legal holidays. Call in advance. Hours are subject to change.

Description of Resources:

The Church of Jesus Christ of Latter-day Saints (LDS), also known as the Mormon Church, operates the Family History Library in Salt Lake City and Family History Centers worldwide. The Family History Library has the most extensive collection in the world of materials and records of interest to genealogists. Records on microfilm can be loaned to any of its local Centers.

The Library in Salt Lake City has an extensive collection of Jewish records from all over the world. For a list of 1,735 microfilms of Polish-Jewish records, see *Avotaynu* vol. II, No. 1, January 1986; for 2,100 microfilms of German-Jewish records, see vol. III, No. 1, Winter 1987; for Hungarian-Jewish records, see vol. IV, No. 1, Winter 1988.

Finding Aids:

Each local Family History Center has a complete set of microfiche listing the LDS holdings in Salt Lake City. These include:

1. *Family History Library Catalog* (FHLC), formerly known as the Genealogical Library Catalog (GLC). This microfiche copy of the catalog of the Library in Salt Lake City includes books, manuscripts and microforms in the Library's collection as of March 1988. The index is arranged by surname, subject, author/title and locality.

2. *International Genealogical Index* (IGI), an index to 121 million names of deceased persons for whom LDS Temple ordinances have been performed. It includes birth, marriage and christening dates and places in the computerized files of the LDS.

3. *Family Registry,* an alphabetical list, updated quarterly, of surnames being researched, and the names and addresses of individuals or family organizations who have registered these names.

Each local Family History Center also has the *Accelerated Indexing System* (AIS), an index by name primarily from the U.S. Census to 1850 (in some states, to 1860). Some other record sources from 1608 to 1885 are included. The error and omission rate is about 20%. (Researchers should check the actual census microfilm if unable to find a name.)

Some local Family History Centers maintain a listing at the librarian's desk of all films currently on loan from Salt Lake City. These films are usually available to any researcher. Check with the librarian.

See also "NEW YORK PUBLIC LIBRARY, U.S. HISTORY, LOCAL HISTORY AND GENEALOGY DIVISION AND MICROFORMS DIVISION" for the *International Genealogical Index,* 1988, and *Family Registry,* 1984.

Description of Facility:

The Centers have the following equipment:

	PLAINVIEW	YORKTOWN HEIGHTS	EAST BRUNSWICK	MORRISTOWN
Microfilm				
Readers:	7	3	5	6
Printers:	1	-	1	-
Microfiche				
Readers:	5	5	6	3
Printers:	*	-	*	-

*Printer copies both film and fiche.

Fees/Copies:

Microfilms are available on loan from Salt Lake City by ordering through a local Family History Center. The basic charges are the same at each Center. To retain a film for: 3 weeks, $2.50; 6 months, $4; permanent loan, $6. To change an order from 3 weeks to 6 months, there is an added charge of $1.50; from 3 weeks to permanent loan, $3.50; and from 6 months to permanent loan, $2. The additional postage charge for each film ordered varies between Centers: $.30 per film (Plainview and Morristown), $.50 per film (Yorktown), $1 per film (East Brunswick).

NOTE: The approval of the Director is needed to place films on permanent loan in Plainview. The Center in Morristown will not place films on permanent loan.

Copies of microfilm pages are $.25 per page in Plainview and $.40 per page in East Brunswick.

Restrictions on Use:

All microfilms and microfiche must be used in the local Family History Center. The typical wait is 4-6 weeks from the date ordered.

No books are sent through the mail.

APPENDIX A

BIBLIOGRAPHY OF EASTERN EUROPEAN MEMORIAL (YIZKOR) BOOKS
COMPILED BY ZACHARY M. BAKER

WITH CALL NUMBERS FOR FIVE JUDAICA LIBRARIES IN NEW YORK

Memorial (or yizkor) books are among the most frequently consulted published sources on individual Eastern European Jewish communities. The narrative sections that comprise the bulk of a memorial book treat the history, culture and institutions of the town's Jewish community with particular emphasis on the period between the two world wars and the Holocaust. Many memorial books also include articles on prominent local rabbinical families and lists of Holocaust martyrs, which can be of particular value to the genealogist.

Most memorial books are in Hebrew and/or Yiddish, though some also have sections in English or other languages. While some memorial books are written by individual authors, most represent the collective editorial efforts of organizations of former townspeople (also known as *landsmanshaft* societies), which serve as the publishers of the overwhelming majority of these works.

What follows is a revised and expanded version of Zachary M. Baker's "Appendix I: Bibliography of Eastern European Memorial Books" that was published in *From a Ruined Garden: The Memorial Books of Polish Jewry*, translated and edited by Jack Kugelmass and Jonathan Boyarin (New York: Schocken Books, 1983; paperback edition, [1985]. That bibliography updated Baker's "Bibliography of Eastern European Memorial Books" that appeared in the Fall 1979-Winter 1980 issue of *Toledot: The Journal of Jewish Genealogy*, which, in turn, was substantially based on the "Bibliographical List of Memorial Books Published in the Years 1943-1972," compiled by David Bass (*Yad Vashem Studies* 9, 1973).

Copies of virtually all memorial books can be located in New York City, with its unequaled Judaica library resources. In addition to updating earlier versions of this bibliography, five New York City libraries have been surveyed for their holdings of memorial books. Call numbers at these libraries are listed after each citation:

YIVO:	YIVO Institute for Jewish Research Library
NYPL:	New York Public Library, Jewish Division
JTS:	Jewish Theological Seminary Library
YU:	Yeshiva University Library
BUND:	Bund Archives of the Jewish Labor Movement

The notation "nc" indicates an uncataloged book. A number alone (no preceding letters) at NYPL also indicates an uncataloged book.

This bibliography is arranged in three sections: General Reference Works, Countries and Regions, Localities. The last two sections are arranged alphabetically by place name.

Official forms of place names are given, with an indication in parentheses of the countries to which the localities belonged before World War I. The following abbreviations are used: (AH) Austria-Hungary, (R) Russian Empire. This conforms to the style of the 1979-80 version of the bibliography. (The bibliography in *From a Ruined Garden* indicates the country to which the locality belonged between the two world wars.)

Book titles are given in transliteration from the Hebrew or Yiddish originals. Place names that appear within book titles are, however, not systematically transliterated but are instead given in their official forms. English titles are supplied in brackets after the Hebrew or Yiddish titles. An asterisk (*) after an English title indicates that the translated title was supplied in the work itself. Otherwise the titles have been translated by the compiler.

The languages in which the book is written are noted at the end of each citation as follows: (H) Hebrew, (Y) Yiddish, (E) English, (F) French, (G) German, (Hu) Hungarian, (J) Judezmo, (P) Polish, (R) Russian, (Ro) Romanian, (S) Spanish, (SC) Serbo-Croatian.

The following cross-references are used:

a) A "see" reference sends the reader from an alternate spelling of a place name to the official form.

b) A "see under" reference sends the reader from the name of a locality discussed in a special chapter of a book on another locality to the full citation for the latter book.

c) A "see also" reference sends the reader to other books that include chapters on a locality.

GENERAL REFERENCE WORKS

Arim ve-imahot be-yisrael; matsevet kodesh le-kehilot yisrael she-nehrevu bi-yedei aritsim u-tmeim be-milhemet ha-olam ha-aharona [Towns and mother-cities in Israel; memorial of the Jewish communities which perished...]. Ed.: Y. L. Fishman (Maimon). Jerusalem, The Rav Kuk Institute (H)

vol. 1, 1947. 371 p., ports.

vol. 2, 1948. 354 p., ports.

vol. 3, *Warsaw.* [By] D. Flinker. 1948. 308 p., ports.

vol. 4, 1950. 313 p., ports.

vol. 5, *Stanislawow.* Eds.: D. Sadan, M. Gelerter. 1952. Ports., music.

vol. 6, *Brody.* [By] N. Gelber. 1956. 347 p., ports., map.

vol. 7, *Bratislava (Pressburg).* [By] Sh. Weingarten-Hakohen. 1960. 184 p., ports.

YIVO: 3/36951 (vols. 1-6)   NYPL: *PXK Fishman

JTS: DS135 E8 M3

BUND: 666 (vol. 3), 946170 (vol. 4)

Pinkas ha-kehilot; entsiklopediya shel ha-yishuvim le-min hivasdam ve-ad le-aher shoat milhemet ha-olam ha-sheniya [Pinkas hakehillot: encyclopedia of Jewish communities*]. Jerusalem, Yad Vashem Martyrs' and Heroes' Remembrance Authority, 1969- . [An index to the communities included in these volumes appeared in the Fall 1988 issue of *Search: International Quarterly for Researchers of Jewish Genealogy.*]

Romania. vol. 1: Eds.: Theodore Lavi, Aviva Broshni. 1969. 224, 552 p., illus. (H); vol. 2: Eds.: Jan Ancel, Theodore Lavi. 1980. 5, 568 p., illus., maps (H)

Germany: Bavaria. Ed.: Baruch Zvi Ophir. 1972. 12, 683, 40 p., illus. (H,E); *Wuerttemberg, Hohenzollern and Baden.* Ed.: Joseph Walk. 1986. 13, 549 p., illus., maps, ports. (H)

Hungary. Ed.: Theodore Lavi. 1975. 8, 557 p., illus. (H)

Poland. vol. 1: *The communities of Lodz and its region.* Eds.: Danuta Dabrowska, Abraham Wein. 1976. 15, 285, 15 p., illus. (H,E); vol. 2: *Eastern Galicia.* Eds.: Danuta Dabrowska, Abraham Wein, Aharon Weiss. 1980. 31, 563 p., illus., maps (H,E); vol. 3: *Western Galicia and Silesia.* 1984. 23, 392 p., illus., maps (H)

The Netherlands. Authors: Joseph Michman, Hartog Beem, Dan Michman. 1985. 10, 434 p., illus., maps, ports. (H)

Latvia and Estonia. Ed.: Dov Levin. 1988. 11, 396 p., illus., maps, ports. (H)

YIVO: Ref DS135   NYPL: *PXK

JTS: Ref DS135 E83 P5   YU: Ref DS135 E83 P5

COUNTRIES AND REGIONS

Bessarabia (R). *Al admat Bessarabia; divrei mehkar, zikhronot, reshimot, teudot ve-divrei safrut le-kviat ha-dmut shel yahaduta* [Upon the land of Bessarabia; studies, memoirs, articles, documents and essays depicting its image]. Ed: K. A. Bertini. Tel Aviv, United Assoc. of Former Residents of Bessarabia, 1959. 2 vols.: 266, 213 p., ports. (H)

YIVO: 3/60880   NYPL: *PXW(Bessarabia)

JTS: DS135 R93 B455 A4

Bessarabia (R). *Bessarabia ha-yehudit be-ma'aroteha; ben shtei milhamot ha-olam 1914-1940* [The Jews in Bessarabia; between the world wars 1914-1940*]. [By] David Vinitzky. Jerusalem-Tel Aviv, The Zionist Library, Gvilei Bessarabia, 1973. 2 vols.: 719 p., illus. (H)

YIVO: 3/72229   NYPL: *PXW(Bessarabia) 75-2345

JTS: DS135 R93 B455 V5

Bessarabia (R). *Pirkei Bessarabia; measef le-avara shel yahadut Bessarabia* [Chapters from the history of Bessarabian Jewry]. Eds.: L. Kupferstein, Y. Koren. Tel Aviv, "Netiv," 1952. 140 p., ports. (H)

YIVO: 15/7742   NYPL: *PXW

Bessarabia (R). *Yahadut Bessarabia* [The Jewry of Bessarabia]. Eds.: K.A. Bertini et al. Jerusalem, The Encyclopaedia of the Jewish Diaspora, 1971. 986 columns, ports., maps (H)

YIVO: 3/70457   NYPL: *PX+

JTS: Ref +DS135 E8 E55 v.11

Bulgaria. *Yahadut Bulgaria* [Bulgaria*]. Eds.: A. Romano et al. Jerusalem, The Encyclopaedia of the Jewish Diaspora, 1967. 1018 columns, ports., maps, facsims. (H)

YIVO: 3/70573   NYPL: *PX+

JTS: Ref +DS135 E8 E55 v.10

Carpatho-Ruthenia (AH) see Karpatalja

Crimea (R). *Yahadut Krim me-kadmuta ve-ad ha-shoa* [The Jews of Crimea from their beginnings until the Holocaust]. Ed.: Yehezkel Keren. Jerusalem, Reuben Mass, 1981. 337 p., illus. (H)
NYPL: JAY H-716   JTS: DS135 R93 C7 K4
YU: DS135 R93 K768

Galicia (AH). *Gedenkbukh Galicia* [Memorial book of Galicia]. Ed.: N. Zucker. Buenos Aires, "Zychronot" Publ., 1964. 334 p., ports., facsims. (Y)
YIVO: 3/63928   NYPL: *PXV(Galicia)
JTS: DS135 P62 G3 Z8   BUND: 946153

Galicia (AH). *Pinkes Galicia* [Memorial book of Galicia]. Ed.: N. Zucker. Buenos Aires, Former Residents of Galicia in Argentina, 1945. 638 p., ports. (Y)
YIVO: DS135 G2 P5   NYPL: *PXV(Galicia) 84-438
BUND: 94656

Greece. *In memoriam; hommage aux victimes juives des Nazis en Grèce,* 2nd ed. Ed.: Michael Molho. Thessalonique, Communauté Israélite de Thessalonique, 1973. 469 p., illus. (F)
[Greek ed., 1974: 502 p.]
NYPL: *PXM 80-3229 (Greek ed.)
JTS: DS135 G7 M59 (3 vols., 1948-1953)
YU: D810 J4 M58

Karpatalja (region) (AH). *Karpatorus* [Karpatorus*]. Ed.: Y. Erez. Jerusalem, The Encyclopaedia of the Jewish Diaspora, 1959. 590 columns, ports., facsims. (H)
YIVO: 3/47248   NYPL: *PX+
JTS: Ref +DS135 E8 E55 v.7

Karpatalja (region) (AH). *Sefer zikhron kedoshim le-yehudei Karpatorus-Marmarosh* [Memorial book of the martyrs of Karpatorus-Marmarosh]. [By] Sh. Rosman. Rehovot, 1969. 643 p., ports. (Y)
YIVO: 3/69934   NYPL: *PXW(Trans Carpathian)
JTS: DS135 R93 C26 R6   YU: 933.5 C998K

Latvia. *The Jews in Latvia.* Ed.: M. Bobe et al. Tel Aviv, Association of Latvian and Estonian Jews in Israel, 1971. 384 p., illus. (E)
YIVO: 3/71082   NYPL: *PXW 76-5880
JTS: DS135 R93 L25 J4

Latvia. *Yahadut Latvia; sefer zikaron* [The Jews of Latvia; a memorial book]. Eds.: B. Eliyav, M. Bobe, A. Kramer. Tel Aviv, Former Residents of Latvia and Estonia in Israel, 1953. 458 p., ports., map (H)
YIVO: 3/40893   NYPL: *PXW
JTS: DS135 R93 L3 E4   YU: 933.547.5 L929
BUND: 946116

Latvia. *Yidn in Letland* [Latvian Jewry*]. Ed.: Mendel Bobe. Tel Aviv, Reshafim, 1972. 368 p., illus. (Y)
YIVO: 3/70486   JTS: DS135 R93 L25 B62

Lithuania. *Bleter fun yidish Lite* [Lithuanian Jews; a memorial book*]. Ed.: Jacob Rabinovitch. Tel Aviv, Hamenora, 1974. 289 p., illus. (Y,H,E)
YIVO: 3/72603   NYPL: *PXV(Lithuania)75-5641
JTS: DS135 L5 R27

Lithuania. *Lite* [Lithuania], vol. 1. Eds.: M. Sudarsky, U. Katzenelenbogen, J. Kissin. New York, Jewish-Lithuanian Cultural Society, 1951. 2070 columns, viii p., ports., maps, facsims. (Y); [Lithuania], vol. 2. Ed.: Ch. Leikowicz. Tel Aviv, I. L. Peretz, 1965. 894 columns, ports., facsims. (Y)
YIVO: DS135 L5 L5   NYPL: *PXV+
JTS: +DS135 L5 L5 (vol. 1)
YU: 933.547.5 L776

Lithuania. *Yahadut Lita* [Lithuanian Jewry*], vol. 1. Eds.: N. Goren, L. Garfinkel et al. Tel Aviv, Am-Hasefer, 1959. 648 p., ports., maps, facsims., music (H); vol. 2, 1972 (H); vol. 3. Eds.: R. Hasman, D. Lipec et al. Tel Aviv, Association for Mutual Help of Former Residents of Lithuania in Israel, 1967. 396 p., ports., maps (H); vol. 4: The Holocaust, 1941-1945. Ed.: Leib Garfunkel. Tel Aviv, 1984 (H)
YIVO: DS135 L5 Y3   NYPL: *PXV(Lithuania)+
JTS: +DS135 R93 L5 Y3

Maramures (region) (AH). *Sefer Marmarosh; mea ve-shishim kehilot kedoshot be-yishuvan u-ve-hurbanan* [The Marmaros book; in memory of a hundred and sixty Jewish communities*]. Eds.: S. Y. Gross, Y.Yosef Cohen. Tel Aviv, Beit Marmaros, 1983. 58, 436, 151 p., illus., map, ports. (H,Y,E)
YIVO: nc   NYPL: *PXR+ 84-457
JTS: +DS135 R72 M3 S4 1983

Poland. *Megilat Polin* [The scroll of Poland]. Part 5: Holocaust, vol. I. Jerusalem, Society of Religious Jews from Poland, 1961. 351 p., ports., facsims. (H,Y)
YIVO: 3/65502   NYPL: *PXV+

Transcarpathian Ruthenia (AH) see Karpatalja

Transylvania (AH). *Toldot ha-kehilot be-Transylvania; perakim mi-sevalot ha-yehudim ve-nitsane ha-gevura bi-tekufat ha-shoa be-Hungaria* [History of the communities of Transylvania]. [By] Yehuda Shvartz. Hadera, Ha-Aguda Yad le-Kehilot Transylvania, [1976]. 293 p., illus. (H)
YIVO: nc   NYPL: *PXR 78-506
JTS: DS135 R72 T77 S32   YU: DS135 R72 T77

Ukraine (R). *Shtet un shtetlekh in Ukraine un in andere teyln fun Rusland; Forshungen in yidisher geshikhte un yidishn lebnsshteyger* [Cities and towns in the history of the Jews in Russia and the Ukraine*]. By M. Osherowitch. New York, The M. Osherowitch Jubillee [sic] Committee, 1948. 2 vols. (305, 306 p.) (Y)
YIVO: 3/26473-4   NYPL: *PXW
JTS: DS135 R9 O8

Ukraine (R). *Yidn in Ukraine* [Jews in the Ukraine*]. Eds.: M. Osherowitch, J. Lestschinsky et al. New York, Association for the Commemoration of the Ukrainian Jews, 1961-1967. 2 vols. (342 p.), ports., maps, facsims. (Y)
YIVO: 3/63992   NYPL: *PXW(Ukraine)+

Zaglebie (AH). *Pinkes Zaglembye; memorial book.* Ed.: J. Rapoport. Melbourne, Zaglembie Society and Zaglembie Committee in Melbourne; Tel Aviv, Hamenorah, 1972. 82, 613 p., illus. (Y,E)
YIVO: 9/75920   NYPL: *PXV(Zaglebie) 75-5593
BUND: 505/09

Zakarpatskaya Oblast (AH) see Karpatalja

LOCALITIES

Akkerman (R). *Akkerman ve-ayarot ha-mehoz; sefer edut ve-zikaron* [Akkerman and the towns of its district; memorial book]. Chairman of the editorial board: Nisan Amitai Stambul. Tel Aviv, Society of Emigrants from Akkerman and Vicinity, 1983. 511 p., illus., map (H)

Aleksandria (R). *Pinkas ha-kehila Aleksandria (Wolyn); sefer yizkor* [Memorial book of the community of Aleksandria (Wolyn)]. Comp.: Shmuel Yizreeli; ed.: Natan Livneh. Tel Aviv, Aleksandria Society, 1972. 314 p., illus. (H)
NYPL: *PXW(Aleksandriya) 79-2894
JTS: DS135 R93 A54 P5

Aleksandrow (R). *Aleksander* [Aleksandrow - near Lodz]. Ed.: N. Blumenthal. Tel Aviv, Association of Former Residents of Aleksandrow in Israel, 1968. 391 p., ports., facsims. (H,Y)
YIVO: 3/68118   NYPL: *PXV(Aleksandrow)
JTS: DS135 P62 A53   BUND: 521

Alt Lesle (R) see Wloclawek

Amdur (R) see Indura

Amshinov (Mszczonow) (R) see under Zyrardow

Andrychow (AH) see Wadowice

Annopol (R). *Rachov-Annopol; pirkei edut ve-zikaron* [Rachov-Annopol; testimony and remembrance*]. Ed.: Shmuel Nitzan. Israel, Rachov/Annopol and Surrounding Region Society, 1978. 80, 544 p., illus. (H,Y,E)
YIVO: 9/77821   NYPL: 10900
JTS: DS135 P62 R25 N5

Antopol (R). *Antopol (Antepolie); sefer yizkor* [Antopol (Antepolie) yizkor book*]. Ed.: Benzion H. Ayalon. Tel Aviv, Antopol Societies in Israel and America, 1972. 11, 754, 170 p., illus. (H,Y,E)
YIVO: 3/70467   NYPL: *PXW(Antopol)+83-373
JTS: +DS135 R93 A6 A92

Antopol (R). *Antopol (5400-5702); mi-toldoteha shel kehila ahat be-Polesie* [Antopol, 1648-1942; from the history of one Jewish community in Polesie]. Ed.: Yosef. Tel Aviv, 5727 [1966/67]. 164 p., illus. (H)
NYPL: *PXW(Antopol) Yosef
JTS: DS135 R93 A6 Y6

Apt (R) see Opatow

Augustow (R). *Sefer yizkor le-kehilat Augustow ve-ha-seviva* [Memorial book of the community of Augustow and vicinity]. Ed.: J. Alexandroni. Tel Aviv, Association of Former Residents of Augustow and Vicinity, 1966. 549 p., ports. (H,Y)
YIVO: 3/67679   NYPL: *PXV(Augustow)
JTS: DS135 P62 A8   YU: 933.5 P762A

Auschwitz (AH) see Oswiecim

Babi Yar (R). *Yisker-bukh fun di umgekumene yidn in Babi-Yar* [The Babi Yar book of remembrance*]. Eds.: Yoseph Vinokurov, Shimon Kipnis, Nora Levin. Philadelphia, Publishing House of Peace, 1982. 202, 82 p., illus., ports. (Y,R,E)
YIVO: nc   JTS: DS135 R93 K48 K65 1983

Baia Mare (AH) see Nagybanya

Baklerove (Bakalarzewo) (R) see under Suwalki

Balin (R) see under Kamenets-Podolskiy

Balmazujvaros (AH) see under Debrecen

Baranovka (R) see Novograd-Volynskiy

Baranow (AH). *Sefer yizkor Baranow* [A memorial to the Jewish community of Baranow*]. Ed.: N. Blumenthal. Jerusalem, Yad Vashem, 1964. xvi, 236 p., ports., tabs., facsims. (H,Y,E)
YIVO: 3/66603   NYPL: *PXV(Baranow)
YU: 933.5 P762 B225

Baranowicze (R). *Baranovits; sefer zikaron* [Baranovits, memorial book]. Tel Aviv, Association of Former Residents of Baranovits in Israel, 1953. vi, 668 p., ports., map, facsims. (H,Y)
YIVO: 3/43807   NYPL: *PXW(Baranovichi)+
BUND: 94659

Barylow (AH) see under Radziechow

Baytsh (AH) see Biecz

Beclean (Betlen) (AH) see under Des

Bedzin (R). *Pinkas Bendin* [Pinkas Bendin; a memorial to the Jewish community of Bendin*]. Ed.: A. Sh. Stein. Tel Aviv, Association of Former Residents of Bedzin in Israel, 1959. 431 p., ports. (H,Y)
YIVO: 3/59886   NYPL: *PXV(Bedzin)+
JTS: +DS135 P62 B385   BUND: 946132

Bedzin (R) see also under Piotrkow Trybunalski

Belchatow (R). *Belchatow yisker-bukh* [Belchatow memorial book]. Buenos Aires, Association of Polish Jews in Argentine, 1951. 511 p., ports., map (Y)
YIVO: 3/29124   NYPL: *PXV(Belchatow)
JTS: DS135 P62 B45 Y4   BUND: 94668

Belgorod-Dnestrovski (R) see Akkerman

Beligrod (AH) see under Lesko

Belz (AH). *Belz; sefer zikaron* [Belz memorial book]. Ed.: Yosef Rubin. Tel Aviv, Belz Societies in Israel and America, 1974. 559 p., illus. (H,Y)
YIVO: 3/73122   NYPL: *PXV(Belzec) 75-5700
JTS: DS135 P62 B458 S4   YU: DS135 P62 B415

Bendery (R). *Kehilat Bendery; sefer zikaron* [Yizkor book of our birthplace Bendery*]. Ed.: M. Tamari. Tel Aviv, Bendery Societies in Israel and the United States, 1975. 446, 42 p., illus. (H,Y,E)
YIVO: 9/75286   NYPL: *PXW(Bendery) 77-3793
JTS: DS135 R93 B364 K43

Bendin (R) see Bedzin

Beresteczko (R). *Hayeta ayara...sefer zikaron le-kehilat Beresteczko ve-ha-seviva* [There was a town...memorial book of Beresteczko...and vicinity]. Ed.: M. Singer. Haifa, Association of Former Residents of Beresteczko in Israel, 1961. 555 p., ports., map, facsims. (H,Y)
YIVO: 3/66093   NYPL: *PXW(Berestechko)
JTS: DS135 R93 B38 S5

Bereza-Kartuska (R) see under Pruzana

Berezno (R). *Mayn shtetele Berezne* [My town Berezne]. [By] G. Bigil. Tel Aviv, Berezner Society in Israel, 1954. 182 p., ports., map (H,Y)
YIVO: 3/45420   NYPL: 2862
YU: DS135 P62 B3853

Berezo (AH) see under Postyen

Bershad (R). *Be-tsel ayara* [Bershad*]. [By] Nahman Huberman. Jerusalem, The Encyclopaedia of the Jewish Diaspora, 1956. 247 p., port. (H)
YIVO: 3/47490   NYPL: *PXW(Bershad)
JTS: DS135 R93 B42 H8   BUND: 946113

Berzhan (AH) see Brzezany

Betlen (AH) see under Des

Biala Podlaska (R). *Podlyashe in natsi-klem; notitsn fun khurbn* [Podlasie en las garras del nazismo*]. [By] M. I. Faignboim [Feigenbaum]. Buenos Aires, Committee of Friends, 1953. 241 p., illus. (Y)
YIVO: 3/40963
NYPL: *PXV(Biala Podlaska) 74-4931
JTS: DS135 P62 B5 F3

Biala Podlaska (R). *Sefer Biala Podlaska* [Book of Biala Podlaska]. Ed.: M. J. Feigenbaum. Tel Aviv, Kupat Gmilut Hesed of the Community of Biala Podlaska, 1961. 501 p., ports., facsims. (H,Y)
YIVO: 3/64729   NYPL: *PXV(Biala Podlaska)+
JTS: DS135 P62 B5 F32   BUND: 946140

Biala Rawska (R). *Sefer yizkor le-kedoshei Biala Rawska* [Memorial book to the martyrs of Biala Rawska]. Eds.: Eliyahu Freudenreich, Arye Yaakobovits. Tel Aviv, Biala Rawska Societies in Israel and the Diaspora, 1972. 255 p., illus. (H,Y)
YIVO: 9/73463
NYPL: *PXV(Biala Rawska) 75-1503

Bialystok (R). *Bialystok; bilder album...* [Bialystok; photo album...*]. Ed.: D. Sohn. New York, Bialystoker Album Committee, 1951. 386 p. (Y,E)
YIVO: 3/29266   NYPL: *PXV+
JTS: +DS135 P62 B54 S6   YU: 933.543.85682
BUND: 9466

Bialystok (R). *Der Bialystoker yisker-bukh* [The Bialystoker memorial book*]. Ed.: I. Shmulewitz. New York, Bialystoker Center, 1982. xi, 396, 205, x p., ports., illus. (Y,E)
YIVO: 9/78713   NYPL: *PXV(Bialystock) 82-2354
JTS: +DS135 P62 B54 B5   YU: DS135 P62 B52

Bialystok (R). *Pinkes Bialystok; grunt-materyaln tsu der geshikhte fun di yidn in Bialystok biz nokh der ershter velt-milkhome* [Pinkos Bialystok (the chronicle of Bialystok); basic material for the history of the Jews in Bialystok until the period after the First World War*]. Ed.: Yudl Mark. New York, Bialystok Jewish Historical Association, 1949-1950. 2 vols. (Y)

YIVO: 3/26404　　　NYPL: *PXV
JTS: DS135 P62 B54　　　BUND: 94612

Biecz (AH). *Sefer zikaron le-kedoshei ayaratenu Biecz* [Memorial book of the martyrs of Biecz]. Ed.: P. Wagshal. Ramat Gan, Association of Former Residents of Biecz and Vicinity in Israel, 1960. 243 p., ports. (H,Y)

YIVO: 9/75544　　　NYPL: *PXV(Biecz)
JTS: DS135 P62 B5496 S4

Bielica (R). *Pinkas Bielica* [Book of Belitzah-Bielica*]. Ed.: L. Losh. Tel Aviv, Former Residents of Bielica in Israel and the USA, 1968. 511 p., ports., map, facsims. (H,Y,E)

YIVO: 9/77508　　　NYPL: *PXV(Belitsa)
JTS: DS135 R93 B346　　　YU: DS135 R93 B346

Bielitz-Biala (AH) see Bielsko-Biala

Bielsk-Podlaski (R). *Bielsk-Podlaski; sefer yizkor...* [Bielsk-Podliask; book in the holy memory of the Bielsk-Podliask Jews*]. Ed.: H. Rabin. Tel Aviv, Bielsk Societies in Israel and the United States, 1975. 554, 44 p., illus. (H,Y,E)

YIVO: nc　　　NYPL: *PXV(Bielsk) 80-3058
YU: nc 81-1012

Bielsko-Biala (AH). *Bielitz-Biala (Bielsko-Biala); pirkei avar* [chapters from the past]. [By] Elijahu Miron. Israel, 1973. 182 p., illus. (H,G)

NYPL: *PXV(Bielsko-Biala) 88-466

Biezun (R). *Sefer ha-zikaron le-kedoshei Biezun* [Memorial book of the martyrs of Biezun]. Tel Aviv, Former Residents of Biezun, 1956. 186 p., ports. (H,Y)

YIVO: 3/51725　　　NYPL: *PXV(Biezun) 76-5564

Bikovsk (Bukowsko) (AH) see under Sanok

Bilgoraj (R). *Bilgoraj yisker-bukh* [Bilgoraj memorial book]. [By] Moshe Teitlboym. Jerusalem, 1955. 243 p., illus. (Y)

YIVO: 3/66894　　　BUND: 518

Bilgoraj (R). *Khurbn Bilgoraj* [Destruction of Bilgoraj]. Ed.: A. Kronenberg. Tel Aviv, 1956. x, 365 p., ports. (Y)

YIVO: 3/51702

Bisk (AH) see Busk

Bitolj (Turkey) see Monastir

Bitshutsh (AH) see Buczacz

Bivolari (Romania). *Ayaratenu Bivolari* [Our town Bivolari]. Eds.: Moscu Abramovici et al. Haifa, Bivolari Immigrants Organization in Israel, 1981. 160, 37 p., illus. (H,Ro,E)

YIVO: nc　　　NYPL: *PXM(Bivolari) 87-4211
JTS: DS135 R72 B5 A95

Bledow (R) see under Mogielnica

Bobrka (AH). *Le-zekher kehilat Bobrka u-benoteha* [Boiberke memorial book*]. Ed.: Sh. Kallay. Jerusalem, Association of Former Residents of Bobrka and Vicinity, 1964. 218, 38 p., ports., facsims. (H,Y,E)

YIVO: 3/66604　　　NYPL: *PXW(Bobrka)+
JTS: +DS135 R93 B588 K3
YU: +DS135 R93 B64

Bobruisk (R). *Bobruisk; sefer zikaron le-kehilat Bobruisk u-benoteha* [Memorial book of the community of Bobruisk and its surroundings]. Ed.: Y. Slutski. Tel Aviv, Former Residents of Bobruisk in Israel and the USA, 1967. 2 vols.: 871 p., ports., map, facsims. (H,Y)

YIVO: 3/68094　　　NYPL: *PXW(Bobruisk)
JTS: +DS135 R93 B59　　　YU: DS135 R93 B59
BUND: 946164

Boiberik (AH) see Bobrka

Bolechow (AH). *Sefer ha-zikaron le-kedoshei Bolechow* [Memorial book of the martyrs of Bolechow]. Ed.: Y. Eshel. Association of Former Residents of Bolechow in Israel, 1957. 352 p., ports. (H,Y)

YIVO: 3/50532　　　NYPL: *PXW(Bolekhov)
JTS: DS135 P62 B65 E8　　　YU: 933.5 P762B

Bolimow (R) see under Lowicz

Boremel (R) see under Beresteczko

Borsa (AH). *Sefer zikaron Borsha, o: ayarat-ahavim be-yarketei ha-karpatim* [Memorial book of Borsha, or: The beloved village by the foot of the Carpat[h]ians*]. Written and edited by Gedaliahu Stein. Kiryat Motzkin, 1985. 655 p., illus., maps, ports. (H)

YU: nc 87-1369　　　NYPL: 20240

Borszczow (AH). *Sefer Borszczow* [The book of Borstchoff*]. Ed.: N. Blumenthal. Tel Aviv, Association of Former Residents of Borszczow in Israel, 1960. 341 p., ports., facsims. (H,Y)
YIVO: 3/62322   NYPL: *PXW(Borschchev)
JTS: DS135 R93 B6 B4   BUND: 946145

Boryslaw (AH) see under Drohobycz

Bransk (R). *Braynsk; sefer ha-zikaron* [Brainsk; book of memories*]. [By] A. Trus and J. Cohen. New York, Brainsker Relief Committee of New York, 1948. 440 p., ports., facsims. (Y)
YIVO: 3/26526   NYPL: *PXV(Bransk)
JTS: DS135 P62 B66   BUND: 94636

Bratislava (Pozsony) (AH) see under *Arim ve-imahot*, vol. 7

Braslaw (R). *Emesh shoa; yad le-kehilot / gevidmet di kehiles Braslaw...* [Darkness and desolation; in memory of the communities of Braslaw, Dubene, Jaisi, Jod, Kislowszczizna, Okmienic, Opsa, Plusy, Rimszan, Slobodka, Zamosz, Zaracz*]. Eds.: Machnes Ariel, Klinov Rina. [Israel], Association of Braslaw and Surroundings in Israel and America; Ghetto Fighters' House and Hakibbutz Hameuchad Publishing House, 1986. 636 p., illus., maps, ports. (H,Y,E)
YIVO: nc   NYPL: 20069

Braynsk (R) see Bransk

Brest Litovsk (R) see Brzesc nad Bugiem

Breziv (AH) see Brzozow

Brezova nad Bradlom (Berezo) (AH) see under Postyen

Briceni (R) see Brichany

Brichany (R). *Britshan; Britsheni ha-yehudit be-mahatsit ha-mea ha-aharona* [Brichany; its Jewry in the first half of our century]. Eds.: Y. Amizur et al. Tel Aviv, Former Residents of Brichany, 1964. 296 p., ports., map (H)
YIVO: 3/66877   NYPL: *PXW(Brichany)
JTS: DS135 R93 B77

Brichevo (R). *Pinkas Brichevo* [Memorial book of Brichevo]. Ed.: K. A. Bertini. Tel Aviv, Former Residents of Brichevo (Bessarabia) in Israel, 1970. 531 p., ports., map, facsims. (H,Y)
YIVO: 3/70219   NYPL: *PXW(Bricheva)
JTS: DS135 R93 B75 P5

Briegel (AH) see Brzesko

Brisk (R) see Brzesc nad Bugiem

Brisk Kuyavsk (Brzesc Kujawski) (R) see under Wloclawek

Brody (AH) see under *Arim ve-imahot*, vol. 6

Broslev (R) see Bratslav

Broszniow (AH) see under Rozniatow

Brzesc Kujawski (R) see under Wloclawek

Brzesc nad Bugiem (R). *Brisk de-Lita* [Brest Lit.(owsk) Volume*]. Ed.: E. Steinman. Jerusalem, The Encyclopaedia of the Jewish Diaspora, 1954-1955. 2 vols., ports., map (H,Y)
YIVO: 3/47248   NYPL: *PXV(Brest Litovsk)+
JTS: Ref +DS135 E8 E55 v.2
BUND: 946125

Brzesko (AH). *Sefer yizkor shel kehilat Briegel-Brzesko ve-ha-seviva* [Memorial book of Briegel-Brzesko and vicinity]. Eds.: Hayim Teller, Liber Brenner (Yiddish). Ramat-Gan, 1980. 267 p., illus. (H,Y)

Brzezany (AH). *Brzezany, Narajow ve-ha-seviva; toldot kehilot she-nehrevu* [Brzezany memorial book*]. Ed.: Menachem Katz. Haifa, Brzezany-Narajow Societies in Israel and the United States, 1978. 28, 473 p., illus. (H,Y,E)
YIVO: 9/78596   JTS: DS135 R93 B4 B4
YU: DS135 R93 B3843

Brzeziny (R). *Bzhezhin yisker-bukh* [Brzeziny memorial book*]. Eds.: A. Alperin, N. Summer. New York, Brzeziner Book Committee, 1961. 288 p., ports. (Y)
YIVO: 3/64730   NYPL: *PXV(Breziny)+
JTS: DS135 P62 B7   BUND: 946137

Brzeznica (R) see under Radomsko

Brzozow (AH). *Sefer zikaron kehilat Breziv (Brzozow)* [A memorial to the Brzozow community*]. Ed.: Avraham Levite. [Israel], The Survivors of Brzozow, 1984. 348, [16], 195 p., illus., maps, ports. (H,Y,E)
NYPL: 18562

Buchach (AH) see Buczacz

Buczacz (AH). *Sefer Buczacz; matsevet zikaron le-kehila kedosha* [Book of Buczacz; in memory of a martyred community]. Ed.: I. Kahan. Tel Aviv, Am Oved, 1956. 302 p., ports., facsims. (H)
YIVO: 3/47812   NYPL: *PXW(Buchach)

Budapest (AH) see under *Arim ve-imahot*, vol. 1

Budzanow (AH). *Sefer Budzanow* [Book of Budzanow*]. Ed.: J. Siegelman. Haifa, Former Residents of Budzanow in Israel, 1968. 319 p., ports., maps, facsims. (H,Y,E)

YIVO: 3/70333   NYPL: *PXW(Budanow)
JTS: DS135 R93 B815   YU: 933.5 U35B

Bukaczowce (AH) see under Rohatyn

Bukowsko (AH) see under Sanok

Bursztyn (AH). *Sefer Bursztyn* [Book of Bursztyn]. Ed.: S. Kanc. Jerusalem, The Encyclopaedia of the Jewish Diaspora, 1960. 426 columns, ports., facsims. (H,Y)

YIVO: 3/62314   NYPL: *PXW(Burshtyn)
JTS: DS135 R93 B83 K3   BUND: 946150

Busk (AH). *Sefer Busk; le-zekher ha-kehila she-harva* [Busk; in memory of our community*]. Ed.: A. Shayari. Haifa, Busker Organization in Israel, 1965. 293 p., ports., facsims. (H,Y,E,P)

YIVO: 3/67329   NYPL: *PXV(Busko Zdroj)
JTS: DS135 R93 B87 S5

Bychawa (R). *Bychawa; sefer zikaron* [Bychawa; a memorial to the Jewish community of Bychawa Lubelska*]. Ed.: J. Adini. Bychawa Organization in Israel, 1968. 636 p., ports., map, facsims. (H,Y)

YIVO: 3/70383   NYPL: *PXV(Bychawa)
JTS: DS135 P62 B93 B5

Byten (R). *Pinkas Byten* [Memorial book of Byten]. Ed.: D. Abramowich, M. W. Bernstein. Buenos Aires, Former Residents of Byten in Argentina, 1954. 605 p., map, facsims. (Y)

YIVO: 3/60482A   NYPL: *PXV(Byten)
JTS: DS135 R93 B98 A3   YU: DS135 R93 B9
BUND: 94663

Cakovec (AH). *Megilat ha-shoa shel kehilat kodesh Cakovec* [Holocaust scroll of the holy community of Cakovec]. [By] Moshe Etz-Hayyim (Tibor Grunwald). Tel Aviv, 1977. 182, 12 p., illus. (H,SC)

YIVO: 9/76502   NYPL: 8760
JTS: DS135 Y82 C3 E8   YU: DS135 Y82 C343

Calarasi (R) see Kalarash

Capresti (R) see Kapreshty

Cernauti (Czernowitz) (AH) see under *Arim ve-imahot*, vol. 4

Cetatea-Alba (R) see Akkerman

Charsznica (R) see under Miechow

Chelm (R). *Sefer ha-zikaron le-kehilat Chelm; 40 shana le-hurbana* [Yizkor book in memory of Chelm*]. Ed.: Sh. Kanc. Tel Aviv, Chelm Society in Israel and the U.S., [1980/81]. 828 columns, illus. (H,Y)

YIVO: nc   NYPL: *PXV(Chelm) 88-469
JTS: DS135 P62 C5   YU: nc 82-0601

Chelm (R). *Yisker-bukh Chelm* [Commemoration book Chelm*]. Ed.: M. Bakalczuk-Felin. Johannesburg, Former Residents of Chelm, 1954. 731 p., ports., facsims. (Y)

YIVO: 3/45639   NYPL: *PXV(Chelm)+
JTS: DS135 P62 C5 B3 YU: K5 P762K
BUND: 94626

Chernovtsy (Czernowitz) (AH) see under *Arim ve-imahot*, vol. 4

Chervonoarmeisk (R) see Radziwillow

Chmielnik (R). *Pinkas Chmielnik* [Memorial book of Chmielnik]. Tel Aviv, Former Residents of Chmielnik in Israel, 1960. 1299 columns, ports., facsims. (H,Y)

YIVO: 3/63200   NYPL: *PXV(Chmielnik)+
JTS: +DS135 P62 C52 P5
YU: DS135 P62 C52

Chodecz (R) see under Wloclawek

Cholojow (AH) see under Radziechow

Chorostkow (AH). *Sefer Chorostkow* [Chorostkow book*]. Ed.: D. Shtokfish. Tel Aviv, Committee of Former Residents of Chorostkow in Israel, 1968. 418 p., ports., facsims. (H,Y)

YIVO: 3/68074   NYPL: *PXW(Khorostkov)
JTS: DS135 R93 K42   YU: DS135 R93 K42

Chorzele (R). *Sefer zikaron le-kehilat Chorzel* [Memorial book of the community of Chorzel]. Ed.: L. Losh. Tel Aviv, Association of Former Residents of Chorzele in Israel, 1967. 272 p., ports., facsims. (H,Y)

YIVO: 3/67680   NYPL: *PXV(Chorzele)
JTS: DS135 P62 C537   YU: 933.5 P762C L879

Chrzanow (AH). *Sefer Chrzanow* [The book of Chrzanow]. [By] Mordecai Bokhner. Regensburg, 1948. xiii, 377 p. (Y)

YIVO: 3/29422   NYPL: *PXV
BUND: 94679

Ciechanow (R). *Yisker-bukh fun der Tshekhanover yidisher kehile; sefer yizkor le-kehilat Ciechanow* [Memorial book of the community of Ciechanow]. Ed.: A. W. Yassni. Tel Aviv, Former Residents of Ciechanow in Israel and in the Diaspora, 1962. 535 p., ports. (H,Y)
YIVO: 3/66114   NYPL: *PXV(Ciechanow) 78-5220

Ciechanowiec (R). *Ciechanowiec; mehoz Bialystok, sefer edut ve-zikaron* [Ciechanoviec-Bialystok district; memorial and records*]. Ed.: E. Leoni. Tel Aviv, The Ciechanovitzer Immigrant Assoc. in Israel and the USA, 1964. 936, 78 p., ports., facsims. (H,Y,E)
YIVO: 3/66752   NYPL: *PXV(Ciechanowiec)
JTS: DS135 P62 C54 L4

Ciechocinek (R) see under Wloclawek

Cieszanow (AH). *Sefer zikaron le-kehila kedosha Cieszanow* [Memorial book of the martyred community Cieszanow]. Ed.: D. Ravid. Tel Aviv, Former Residents of Cieszanow in Israel, 1970. 331 p., ports. (H,Y)
YIVO: 3/69275   NYPL: *PXV(Cieszanow)+
JTS: +DS135 P62 C56

Cluj (AH) see Kolozsvar

Cmielow (R) see under Ostrowiec

Cracow (AH) see Krakow

Csaktornya (AH) see Cakovec

Csenger (AH). *Sefer yizkor le-kedoshei Csenger, Porcsalma ve-ha-seviva* [Memorial book of the martyrs of Csenger, Porcsalma and vicinity]. [By] Sh. Friedmann. Tel Aviv, 1966. 108, 60 p., ports., facsims. (H,Hu)
NYPL: 6289

Czarny Dunajec (AH) see under Nowy Targ

Czerbin (R) see under Ostroleka

Czernowitz (AH) see under *Arim ve-imahot*, vol. 4

Czestochowa (R). *Churban Czenstochow - The destruction of Czenstokov - Khurbn Tshenstokhov.* [By] Benjamin Orenstein. [Western Germany], Central Farwaltung fun der Czenstochower Landsmanszaft in der Amerikaner Zone in Dajczland, 1948. 463 p., illus., ports. (Y in Latin characters)
YIVO: 3/26398   NYPL: *PXV
JTS: Restr DS135 P62 C92 O72

Czestochowa (R). *Sefer Tshenstokhov* [Memorial book of Czestochow]. Ed.: M. Schutzman. Jerusalem, The Encyclopaedia of the Jewish Diaspora, 1967-1968. 2 vols., ports. (H,Y)
YIVO: 3/68393   NYPL: *PXV(Czestochowa)+
JTS: Ref +DS135 E8 E55 v.8
YU: DS135 P62 C89

Czestochowa (R). *Tshenstokhover landsmanshaft in Montreal* [Czenstochover landsmanschaft in Montreal*]. Ed.: B. Orenstein. Montreal, The Czenstochover Society in Montreal, 1966. 349, [28] p., ports. (Y)
YIVO: 3/67337   NYPL: *PXV(Czestochowa)1966

Czestochowa (R). *Tshenstokhov; nayer tsugob-material tsum bukh "Tshenstokhover yidn"* [Czenstochov; a new supplement to the book "Czenstochover Yidn"*]. Ed.: S. D. Singer. New York, United Relief Committee in New York, 1958. 336, iv p., ports. (Y)
YIVO: 3/56492   NYPL: *PXV(Czestochowa)+
JTS: +DS135 P62 C92 U5
BUND: 946104

Czestochowa (R). *Tshenstokhover yidn* [The Jews of Czestochowa]. Ed.: R. Mahler. New York, United Czestochower Relief Committee and Ladies Auxiliary, 1947. cxliv, 404 p., ports., facsims. (Y)
YIVO: 3/50153   NYPL: *PXV(Czestochowa)+
JTS: +DS135 P62 C9 U5   BUND: 94611

Czortkow (AH). *Sefer yizkor le-hantsahat kedoshei kehilat Czortkow* [Memorial book of Czortkow*]. Ed.: Y. Austri-Dunn. Tel Aviv, Haifa, Former Residents of Czortkow in Israel, 1967. 435, 36 p., ports., map, facsims. (H,Y,E)
YIVO: 3/68048   NYPL: *PXV(Chortkov)
JTS: DS135 R93 C5 S4   YU: 933.5 R969C A941

Czyzewo (R). *Sefer zikaron Czyzewo* [Memorial book Tshijewo*]. Ed.: Sh. Kanc. Tel Aviv, Former Residents of Czyzewo in Israel and the USA, 1961. 1206 columns, ports., facsims. (H,Y)
YIVO: 3/66171   NYPL: *PXV(Czyzew) 77-3791

Dabrowa Gornicza (R). *Sefer kehilat yehudei Dabrowa Gornicza ve-hurbana* [Memorial book of Dombrawa Gornitza]. Eds.: N. Gelbart et al. Tel Aviv, Former Residents of Dombrowa Gornitza, 1971. 696 p., ports., facsims. (H,Y)
YIVO: 3/70082
NYPL: *PXV(Dabrowa Gornicza)+
JTS: +DS135 P62 D28 S4   YU: 933.47(438) D116G

Dabrowica (R). *Sefer Dombrovitsa* [Book of Dabrowica]. Ed.: L. Losh. Tel Aviv, Association of Former Residents of Dabrowica in Israel, 1964. 928 p., ports., maps, facsims. (H,Y)
YIVO: 9/73406   NYPL: 2861

Daugavpils (R). *Le-zekher kehilat Dvinsk* [In memory of the community of Dvinsk]. Haifa, [1975]. 63 p., illus. (H)
NYPL: *PXW(Daugavpils) 77-3787
YU: DS135 R93 D3184

Daugieliszki (R) see under Swieciany

David Horodok (R) see Dawidgrodek

Dawidgrodek (R). *Sefer zikaron Dawidgrodek* [Memorial book of Davidgrodek]. Eds.: Y. Idan et al. Tel Aviv, Former Residents of Dawidgrodek in Israel, [195-]. 487 p., ports. (H,Y)
YIVO: 3/54661   NYPL: nc
JTS: DS135 R93 D32 S4   BUND: 946110

Debica (AH). *Sefer Dembits* [Book of Debica]. Ed.: D. Leibl. Tel Aviv, Association of Former Residents of Debica, 1960. 204 p., ports. (H,Y)
YIVO: 3/63059   NYPL: *PXV(Debica) 88-465

Deblin (R). *Sefer Deblin-Modrzyc* [Demblin-Modrzyc book*]. Ed.: D. Shtokfish. Tel Aviv, Association of Former Residents of Demblin-Modrzyc, 1969. 694 p., ports., facsims. (H,Y)
YIVO: 3/69321   NYPL: *PXV(Deblin)
JTS: DS135 P62 D38

Debrecen (AH). *Mea shana le-yehudei Debrecen; le-zekher kedoshei ha-kehila ve-yishuvei ha-seviva* [Hundred years of Debrecen Jewry; in memory of the martyrs of Debrecen and vicinity]. [By] M. E. Gonda. Tel Aviv, Committee for Commemoration of the Debrecen Jewry, 1970. 264, 409 p., ports., facsims. (H,Hu)
YIVO: 9/77966   NYPL: *PXT 76-6740
JTS: DS135 H92 D4 G6

Dej (AH) see Des

Delatycze (R) see under Lubcza

Dembits (AH) see Debica

Demblin (R) see Deblin

Derecske (AH). *Sefer zikaron le-yehudei Derecske ve-geliloteha* [Emlékkönyv Derecske és vidéke zsidósága* - Memorial book to the Jews of Derecske and its environs]. [By] Arje Moskovits. Tel Aviv, Society of Derecske Emigrants in Israel, 1984. 186, [93], 185 p., illus., facsims., ports. (H,Hu)
NYPL: 17968   YU: DS135 H92 D475

Derecske (AH) see also under Debrecen

Dereczyn (R). *Sefer Dereczyn* [Deretchin memorial book*]. Tel Aviv, Deretchiners Societies in Israel and USA, [196-]. 494 p., ports., facsims. (H,Y)
YIVO: 3/71005   NYPL: *PXW(Derechin) 78-685
JTS: DS135 R93 D47 S4

Derewno (R) see under Rubiezewicze; Stolpce

Des (AH). *Des..., Bethlen, Magyarlapos, Retteg, Nagyilonda és kornyeke* [...and vicinity]. Ed.: Z. Singer. Tel Aviv, Former Residents of Des, [197-]. 2 vols. (683 p.), ports., facsims. (Hu)
YIVO: nc   NYPL: *PXM 75-6975
JTS: DS135 R72 D45 S5   YU: 933.5 H936D

Devenishki (R) see Dziewieniszki

Dibetsk (Dubiecko) (AH) see under Dynow (*Khurbn Dynow*)

Dieveniskes (R) see Dziewieniszki

Dinov (AH) see Dynow

Disna (R) see Dzisna

Divenishok (R) see Dziewieniszki

Dmytrow (AH) see under Radziechow

Dnepropetrovsk (R) see Yekaterinoslav

Dobromil (AH). *Sefer zikaron le-zekher Dobromil* [Memorial book Dobromil*]. Ed.: M. Gelbart. Tel Aviv, The Dobromiler Society in New York and the Dobromiler Organization in Israel, 1964. 389, 138 p., ports., facsims. (H,Y,E)
YIVO: 3/66864   NYPL: *PXW(Dobromil)
JTS: DS135 R93 D6 G4   YU: 933.5 R969 D634

Dobryn (R) see under Wloclawek

Dobrzyn (R). *Ayarati; sefer zikaron le-ayarot Dobrzyn-Golub* [My town; in memory of the communities Dobrzyn-Gollob*]. Ed.: M. Harpaz. [Tel Aviv], Association of Former Residents of Dobrzyn-Golub, 1969. 459, 29 p., ports., facsims. (H,Y,E)
NYPL: *PXV(Golub)   JTS: DS135 P62 G58

Dobrzyn (R). *Yisker bletlekh* [Our village*]. [By] Shmuel Russak. Tel Aviv, 1972. 6, 90 p., illus. (Y,E)
YIVO: 3/70283, 3/72117
NYPL: *PXV(Golub-Dobrzyn) 75-1498

Dokszyce (R). *Sefer yizkor Dokszyce-Parafianow* [Dokszyc-Parafianow book*]. Ed.: D. Shtokfish. Tel Aviv, Assoc. of Former Residents of Dokszyce-Parafianow in Israel, 1970. 350 p., ports., facsims. (H,Y)

YIVO: nc   NYPL: *PXW(Dokshitsy)
JTS: DS135 R93 D648   YU: K5 R969D

Dolhinow (R). *Esh tamid - yizkor le-Dolhinow; sefer zikaron le-kehilat Dolhinow ve-ha-seviva* [Eternal flame; in memory of Dolhinow]. Eds.: Josef Chrust, Matityahu Bar-Razon. Tel Aviv, Society of Dolhinow Emigrants in Israel, [198-]. 718 p., illus., maps, ports. (H,Y,E)

NYPL: *PXW(Dolginovo) 87-2640

Dombrava Gornitsha (R) see Dabrowa Gornicza

Dombrovitsa (R) see Dabrowica

Drodzyn (R) see under Stolin

Drohiczyn nad Bugiem (R). *Sefer Drohiczyn* [Drohiczyn book]. Ed.: D. Shtokfish. Tel Aviv, 1969. 576, 67 p., illus. (H,Y,E)

YIVO: 3/69273A   JTS: DS135 P62 D76

Drohiczyn Poleski (R). *Drohiczyn; finf hundert yor yidish lebn* [Memorial book Drohichyn*]. Ed.: D. B. Warshawsky. Chicago, Book-Committee Drohichyn, 1958. viii, 424 p., ports., map, facsims. (Y)

YIVO: 3/53177   NYPL: *PXV(Drogichin)
JTS: DS135 P62 D759   BUND: 946105

Drohobycz (AH). *Sefer zikaron le-Drohobycz, Boryslaw ve-ha-seviva* [Memorial to the Jews of Drohobycz, Boryslaw and surroundings*]. Ed.: N. M. Gelber. Tel Aviv, Assoc. of Former Residents of Drohobycz, Boryslaw and Surroundings, 1959. 224 p., ports. (H,Y)

YIVO: 3/71400
NYPL: *PXW(Drogobych)+ 80-446
YU: 933.5 R969D   BUND: 241

Droshkopol (R) see Druzkopol

Druja (R). *Sefer Druja ve-kehilot Miory, Drujsk, ve-Leonpol* [The book of Druya and the communities of Miory, Druysk and Leonpol*]. Ed.: Mordekhai Neishtat. Tel Aviv, Druja and Surrounding Region Society, 1973. 255 p., illus. (H,Y)

YIVO: nc   NYPL: *PXW(Druia) 82-1573

Druja (R) see also under Glebokie

Drujsk (R) see under Druja (*Sefer Druja*)

Druzkopol (R). *Ayaratenu Druzkopol* [Our town Droshkopol]. Eds.: Y. Shiloni et al. [Haifa], Former Residents of Droshkopol in Israel, 1957. 108 p., ports. (H), mimeo.

YIVO: 3/51887

Druzkopol (R). *Di geshikhte fun mayn shtetele Druzkopol* [The story of my "stetele Droshkopol"*]. [By] A. Boxer (Ben-Arjeh). Ed.: S. Eisenberg. Haifa,1962. 108 p., ports (Y), mimeo.

Dubene (Dubinowo) (R) see under Braslaw

Dubiecko (AH) see under Dynow (*Khurbn Dynow*)

Dubno (R). *Dubno; sefer zikaron* [Dubno; a memorial to the Jewish community of Dubno, Wolyn*]. Ed.: Y. Adini. Tel Aviv, Dubno Organization in Israel, 1956. 752 columns, ports., maps, facsims. (H,Y)

YIVO: 3/67514   NYPL: *PXW(Dubno)
JTS: DS135 R93 D8 A3   YU: 933.5R

Dubossary (R). *Dubossary; sefer zikaron* [Dubossary memorial book]. Ed.: Y. Rubin. Tel Aviv, Association of Former Residents of Dubossary in America, Argentina and Israel, 1965. 377 p., ports., maps, music (H,Y)

YIVO: 3/67326   NYPL: *PXW(Dubossary)
JTS: DS135 R93 D82   YU: 933.5 R969D R896

Dubrovitsa (R) see Dabrowica

Dukszty (R) see under Swieciany

Dumbraveny (R). *Sefer Dombroven; ner-zikaron le-moshava ha-haklait ha-yehudit ha-rishonah be-Bessarabia* [Dombroven book; memorial to the first Jewish agricultural colony in Bessarabia]. Ed.: Haim Toren. Jerusalem, Dombroven Societies in Israel and The Diaspora, 1974. 8, 252 p., illus. (H,Y)

YIVO: 9/75283   NYPL: *PXT 76-5563
JTS: DS135 R72 D87 T68

Dunajska Streda (AH) see Dunaszerdahely

Dunaszerdahely (AH). *Sefer zikaron le-kehilat Dunaszerdahely* [A memorial to the Jewish community of Dunaszerdahely (Dunajska Streda)*]. [By] Abraham (Alfred) Engel. Israel, Committee of Dunaszerdahely Emigrants, 1975. 429, 157 p., illus. (H,Hu)

YIVO: nc   JTS: DS135 C96 D863 E55
YU: nc 76-1279

Dunilowicze (R) see under Glebokie

Dvart (R) see Warta

Dvinsk (R) see Daugavpils

Dyatlovo (R) see Zdzieciol

Dynow (AH). *Khurbn Dynow, Sonik, Dibetsk* [The destruction of Dynow, Sanok, Dubiecko]. [By] David Moritz. New York, [1949/50]. 156 p., illus. (Y)
YIVO: 3/29446 NYPL: *PXV
JTS: DS135 P62 D88 M67 BUND: 945112

Dynow (AH). *Sefer Dynow; sefer zikaron le-kedoshei kehilat Dynow she-nispu ba-shoa ha-natsit* [The memorial book of Jewish Dinov*]. Eds.: Yitzhak Kose, Moshe Rinat. Tel Aviv, Dynow Society, 1979. 324 p., illus., map (H,Y)
YIVO: 9/78959 NYPL: *PXV(Dinow) 88-468
YU: DS135 P62 D927

Dzerzhinsk (R) see Koidanovo

Dzialoszyce (R). *Sefer yizkor shel kehilat Dzialoszyce ve-ha-seviva* [Yizkor book of the Jewish community in Dzialoszyce and surroundings*]. Tel Aviv, Hamenora, 1973. 44, 423 p., illus. (H,Y,E)
YIVO: 9/77483 NYPL: *PXV(Dzialoszyce) 75-1500
JTS: DS135 P62 D9 S4 YU: 933.5(438) D999

Dziewieniszki (R). *Sefer Divenishok; yad vashem le-ayara yehudit* [Devenishki book; memorial book*]. Ed.: David Shtokfish. Israel, Divenishok Societies in Israel and the United States, 1977. 536 p., illus. (H,Y)
YIVO: 9/77658 NYPL: 8680
JTS: DS135 P62 D53 S4 YU: DS135 R93 D59

Dzikow (AH) see Tarnobrzeg

Dzisna (R). *Disna; sefer zikaron le-kehila* [Disna; memorial book of the community]. Eds.: A. Beilin et al. Tel Aviv, Former Residents of Disna in Israel and the USA, 1969. 277 p., ports., facsims. (H,Y)
YIVO: 3/70386 NYPL: *PXV(Disna)
JTS: DS135 R93 D533 B4 YU: 933.5 R969D

Edineti (R) see Yedintsy

Eger (AH). *Yehudei Erlau* [The Jews of Eger]. Eds.: Arthur Abraham Ehrenfeld-Elkay, Tibor Meir Klein-Z'ira. Jerusalem, Eger Commemorative Committee, 1975. 64, 36, 100 p., illus. (H,Hu)
YIVO: nc NYPL: 8024
JTS: DS135 H92 E353 E32
YU: DS135 H92 E353

Ejszyszki (R). *Eishishok, koroteha ve-hurbana* [Ejszyszki, its history and destruction]. Ed.: Sh. Barkeli. Jerusalem, Committee of the Survivors of Ejszyszki in Israel, 1960. 136 p., ports. (H,Y)
YIVO: 3/36953 NYPL: *PXW(Eisiskes)

Ekaterinoslav (R) see Yekaterinoslav

Erlau (AH) see Eger

Falenica (R). *Sefer Falenica* [Falenica book*]. Ed.: D. Shtokfish. Tel Aviv, Former Residents of Falenica in Israel, 1967. 478 p., ports., facsims. (H,Y)
YIVO: 3/70387 NYPL: *PXV(Falenica) 79-320
JTS: DS135 P62 F34 S8

Falenica (R) see also under Otwock

Fehergyarmat (AH). *Ayaratenu le-she-avar Fehergyarmat* [Our former city Fehergyarmat]. [By] J. Blasz. Bnei Brak, 1965. 44, 52 p., ports., music, facsims. (H,Hu)
YIVO: 3/67530 NYPL: *ZP-*PBM p.v. 1041
JTS: DS135 H92 F4

Felshtin (R). *Felshtin; zamlbukh lekoved tsum ondenk fun di Felshtiner kdoyshim* [Felshtin; collection in memory of the martyrs of Felshtin]. New York, First Felshtiner Progressive Benevolent Association, 1937. 670 p., illus. (Y,E)
YIVO: 15/340
NYPL: *PXW(First Feltshtener Benevolent Assn)
JTS: DS135 R93 F4 BUND: 94623

Filipow (R) see under Suwalki

Frampol (Lublin) (R). *Sefer Frampol* [Frampol book*]. Ed.: D. Shtokfish. Tel Aviv, [Book Committee], 1966. 414 p., ports. (H,Y)
YIVO: 3/67513 NYPL: *PXV(Frampol)
JTS: DS135 P62 F7 S8

Frampol (Podolia) (R) see under Kamenets-Podolskiy

Gabin (R). *Gombin; dos lebn un umkum fun a yidish shtetl in Poyln* [Gombin; the life and destruction of a Jewish town in Poland*]. Eds.: Jack Zicklin et al. New York, Gombin Society in America, 1969. 228, 162 p., illus. (Y,E)
YIVO: nc NYPL: *PXV(Gabin) 1969
JTS: DS135 P62 G2 G6 BUND: 946167

Gargzdai (R). *Sefer Gorzd (Lita); ayara be-hayeha u-be-hilayona* [Gorzd book; a memorial to the Jewish community of Gorzd*]. Ed.: Yitzhak Alperovitz. Tel Aviv, The Gorzd Society, 1980. 79, 417 p., illus. (H,Y,E)
YIVO: nc NYPL: *PXV(Gargzdai) 88-463
JTS: DS135 L52 G3 A4

Garwolin (R). *Garwolin yisker-bukh* [Garwolin memorial book]. Eds.: Moshe Zaltsman, Baruch Shein. Tel Aviv, New York, Garwolin Societies, 1972. 304 p., illus. (H,Y)
YIVO: 3/71395   NYPL: *PXV(Garwolin)+76-272
JTS: +DS135 P62 G394 N3
YU: 933.47(438) G244N

Ger (R) see Gora Kalwaria

Gherla (AH) see Szamosujvar

Glebokie (R). *Khurbn Glubok...Koziany* [The destruction of Glebokie...Koziany]. [By] M. and Z. Rajak. Buenos Aires, Former Residents' Association in Argentina, 1956. 426 p., ports. (Y)
YIVO: 3/52478   NYPL: *PXV(Glubokoye) 78-5719
JTS: DS135 R93 G55 R35   BUND: 946146

Glebokie (R) see also under Vilna (*Vilner zamlbukh...*)

Glina (AH) see Gliniany

Gliniany (AH). *Kehilat Glina 1473-1943; toldoteha ve-hurbana* [The community of Glina 1473-1943; its history and destruction]. [By] Asher Korech. Jerusalem, 1950. 138 p., illus. (H)
YIVO: 3/39933   NYPL: *PXV(Gliniany)
JTS: DS135 R93 G53 K6

Gliniany (AH). *Khurbn Glinyane* [The tragic end of our Gliniany*]. New York, Emergency Relief Committee for Gliniany and Vicinity, 1946. [52] p. (Y,E)
YIVO: 3/48972   NYPL: *PXV(Gliniany) 84-414
BUND: 946169

Gliniany (AH). *Megiles Gline* [The book of Gline*]. Ed.: H. Halpern. New York, Former Residents of Gline, 1950. 307 p. (Y)
YIVO: 3/29358   NYPL: *PXV
JTS: DS135 R93 G53 H3   BUND: 94628

Glinojeck (R). *Mayn shtetele Glinovyetsk; un di vayterdike vandlungen Plotsk-Wierzbnik, zikhroynes* [My town Glinojeck...]. [By] Shlomo Moshkovich. Paris, 1976. 335 p., illus. (Y)
YIVO: 8/78549   NYPL: *PXV(Glinojeck) 87-536
JTS: DS135 P62 G52

Glubok (R) see Glebokie

Glusk (R) see under Bobruisk; Slutsk

Gniewaszow (R). *Sefer Gniewaszow* [Memorial book Gniewashow*]. Ed.: D. Shtokfish. Tel Aviv, Association of Gniewashow in Israel and the Diaspora, 1971. 533, 19 p., ports. (H,Y,E)
YIVO: 3/70106   NYPL: *PXV(Gniewoszow)
JTS: DS135 P62 G52 S75   YU: 933.5 P762G
BUND: 523

Golub (R) see under Dobrzyn (*Ayarati*)

Gombin (R) see Gabin

Gomel (R) see under *Arim ve-imahot*, vol. 2

Goniadz (R). *Sefer yizkor Goniadz* [Our hometown Goniondz*]. Eds.: J. Ben-Meir (Treshansky), A. L. Fayans. Tel Aviv, The Committee of Goniondz Association in the USA and in Israel, 1960. 808, xix p., ports., maps (H,Y,E)
YIVO: 3/61637   NYPL: *PXV(Goniadz)
JTS: DS135 P62 G6 S4   YU: 933.47(438) G638
BUND: 497

Gora Kalwaria (R). *Megiles Ger*. Ed.: Gregorio Sapoznikow. Buenos Aires, Ger Societies in Argentina, Israel and the United States, 1975. 512 p., illus. (Y)
YIVO: 9/77640   NYPL: 6485
JTS: DS135 P62 S36

Gorlice (AH). *Sefer Gorlice; ha-kehila be-vinyana u-be-hurbana* [Gorlice book; the community at rise and fall*]. Ed.: M. Y. Bar-On. [Association of Former Residents of Gorlice and Vicinity in Israel], 1962. 338 p., ports., map, facsims. (H,Y)
YIVO: 3/65802   NYPL: *PXV(Gorlice)+
JTS: DS135 P62 G63 B3

Gorodnitsa (R) see under Novograd-Volynskiy

Gorzd (R) see Gargzdai

Gostynin (R). *Pinkes Gostynin; yisker-bukh* [Pinkas Gostynin; book of Gostynin*]. Ed.: J. M. Biderman. New York, Gostynin Memorial Book Committees, 1960. 358 p., ports. (Y)
YIVO: 3/61290   NYPL: *PXV(Gostynin)
JTS: DS135 P62 G66 B5   YU: DS135 P62 G66
BUND: 946133

Goworowo (R). *Goworowo; sefer zikaron* [Govorowo memorial book*]. Eds.: A. Burstin, D. Kossovsky. Tel Aviv, The Govorover Societies in Israel, the USA and Canada, 1966. 496, xvi p., ports., facsims. (H,Y,E)
YIVO: 3/67747   NYPL: *PXV(Goworowo)
JTS: DS135 P62 G67   BUND: 511

Grabowiec (R). *Sefer zikaron le-kehilat Grabowiec* [Memorial book Grabowitz*]. Ed.: Shimon Kanc. Tel Aviv, Grabowiec Society, 1975. 432, 5, 26 p., illus. (H,Y,E)
NYPL: *PXV(Grabowiec) 77-3821
JTS: DS135 P62 G693 S4

Grajewo (R). *Grayeve yisker-bukh* [Grayewo memorial book]. Ed.: Dr. G. Gorin. New York, United Grayever Relief Committee, 1950. 51, [38], 311 p., illus. (Y,E)
YIVO: 3/29355   NYPL: *PXV(Grajewo)
JTS: DS135 P62 G7   BUND: 9467

Greiding (AH) see Grodek Jagiellonski

Gritsa (R) see Grojec

Grodek (near Bialystok) (R). *Sefer zikaron le-kehilat Horodok* [Horodok; in memory of the Jewish community*]. Ed.: M. Simon (Shemen). Tel Aviv, Associations of Former Residents of Grodek in Israel and Argentina, 1963. 142 p., ports., facsims. (H,Y)
YIVO: 3/66584   NYPL: 5114

Grodek Jagiellonski (AH). *Sefer Greiding* [Greiding book]. Ed.: Yehuda Margel. Tel Aviv, 1981 (H)

Grodno (R). *Grodno* [Grodno*]. Ed.: Dov Rabin. Jerusalem, Grodno Society; The Encyclopaedia of the Jewish Diaspora, 1973. 744 columns, illus. (H,Y)
YIVO: 3/47248   NYPL: *PX+
JTS: Ref +DS135 E8 E55 v.9
BUND: 503

Grodno (R). *Kovets Grodna - Zaml-heft Grodne* [Grodno collection]. Ed.: Yitzhak Yelin. Tel Aviv, Grodner Association of Israel, Dec. 1958. no. 1: 50 p., illus. (H,Y)
YIVO: 15/7979

Grojec (R). *Megilat Gritse* [Megilat Gritze*]. Ed.: I. B. Alterman. Tel Aviv, Gritzer Association in Israel, 1955. iv, 408 p., ports. (H,Y)
YIVO: 3/50306   NYPL: *PXV(Grojec)
BUND: 94687

Gross Magendorf (Nagymagyar) (AH) see under Dunaszerdahely

Grosswardein (AH) see Oradea

Grozovo (R) see under Slutsk

Gusiatyn (R) see Husiatyn (R)

Gyor (AH). *Le-zekher kedoshei Gyor* [In memory of the martyrs of Gyor]. Ed.: Hana Spiegel. Haifa, [197-/8-]. 36 p., illus., maps (H)

Hajdunanas (AH) see under Debrecen

Hajdusamson (AH) see under Debrecen

Halmi (AH). *Zikhron netsah le-kehilot ha-kedoshot Halmin-Turcz ve-ha-seviva asher nehrevu ba-shoa* [In memory of the communities of Halmin-Turcz and vicinity]. Ed.: Yehuda Shvartz. Tel Aviv, Halmin-Turcz and Vicinity Society, [1968]. 138 p., illus. (H)
YIVO: nc   NYPL: *PXM
JTS: DS135 R72 H338

Haydutsishok (Hoduciszki) (R) see under Swieciany

Hivniv (AH) see Uhnow

Hlusk (Glusk) (R) see under Slutsk

Hoduciszki (R) see under Swieciany

Holojow (Cholojow) (AH) see under Radziechow

Holszany (R). *Lebn um umkum fun Olshan* [The life and destruction of Olshan]. Tel Aviv, Former Residents of Olshan in Israel, 1965. 431, 136 p., ports., facsims. (H,Y)
YIVO: 3/67089   NYPL: *PXW(Ol'Shany)
JTS: DS135 R93 O5 L4

Holynka (R) see under Dereczyn

Homel (Gomel) (R) see under *Arim ve-imahot*, vol. 2

Horochow (R). *Sefer Horochow* [Horchiv memorial book*]. Ed.: Y. Kariv. Tel Aviv, Horchiv Committee in Israel, 1966. 357, 79 p., ports., map, facsims. (H,Y,E)
YIVO: 3/67751   NYPL: *PXW(Gorokhov)
JTS: DS135 R93 G69 D3   YU: 933.5 R969G

Horodec (R). *Horodets; a geshikhte fun a shtetl, 1142-1942* [Horodec; history of a town, 1142-1942]. Ed.: A. Ben-Ezra. "Horodetz" Book Committee, 1949. 238 p., ports., map, facsims. (Y)
YIVO: 3/29357   NYPL: *PXV+
JTS: +DS135 R93 G67 B4
YU: 933.547 G672B   BUND: 94616

Horodenka (AH). *Sefer Horodenka* [The book of Horodenka]. Ed.: Sh. Meltzer. Tel Aviv, Former Residents of Horodenka and Vicinity in Israel and the USA, 1963. 425, vii p., ports., map, facsims. (H,Y)
YIVO: 3/66585   NYPL: *PXW(Gorodenka)
JTS: DS135 R93 G66 M44
YU: DS135 R93 G65   BUND: 946154

Horodlo (R). *Di kehile fun Horodlo; yisker-bukh...* [The community of Horodlo; memorial book...]. Ed.: Y. Ch. Zawidowitch. Tel Aviv, Former Residents of Horodlo in Israel, 1962. 324 p., ports., facsims. (Y)

YIVO: 3/67745   NYPL: *PXV(Horodlo)
JTS: DS135 P62 H659   YU: 933.5 P762H

Horodlo (R). *Kehilat Horodlo; sefer zikaron le-kedoshei Horodlo (Polin) ve-li-kedoshei ha-kefarim ha-semukhim* [The community of Horodlo; memorial book...]. Ed.: Y. Ch. Zawidowitch. Tel Aviv, Former Residents of Horodlo in Israel, 1959. 260 p., ports., facsims. (H)

YIVO: 3/64384   NYPL: *PXV(Horodlo) 84-370
JTS: DS135 P62 H658   YU: DS135 P62 H65

Horodno (R) see under Stolin

Horodok (R) see Grodek (near Bialystok)

Horyngrod (R) see under Tuczyn

Hoszcza (R). *Hoshtsh; sefer zikaron* [Hoshtch-Wolyn; in memory of the Jewish community*]. Eds.: B. H. Ayalon-Baranicka, A. Yaron-Kritzmar. Tel Aviv, Former Residents of Hoshtch in Israel, 1957. 269 p., ports., facsims. (H)

Hoszcza (R). *Sefer Hoshtsh; yisker-bukh* [The book of Hosht--in memoriam*]. Ed.: R. Fink. New York and Tel Aviv, Society of Hosht, 1957. xvi, 294 p., ports., facsims. (Y)

YIVO: 3/50505   NYPL: *PXW(Goscho)
JTS: DS135 R93 G65 F5 BUND: 94680

Hotin (R) see Khotin

Hrubieszow (R). *Pinkas Hrubieszow* [Memorial book of Hrubieshov*]. Ed.: B. Kaplinsky. Tel Aviv, Hrubieshov Associations in Israel and the USA, 1962. 811, xviii columns, ports. (H,Y,E,P)

YIVO: 3/65801   NYPL: *PXV(Hrubieszow)+

Husiatyn (R). *Husiatyn; Podoler Gubernye* [Husiatyn; Podolia-Ukraine*]. Ed.: B. Diamond. New York, Former Residents of Husiatyn in America, 1968. 146, [40], 123 p., ports. (Y,E)

YIVO: 3/68206   NYPL: *PXW(Gusyatin) 83-379
YU: nc 75-0600

Husiatyn (AH). *Kehilatiyim: Husiatyn ve-Kopyczynce* [Two communities: Husiatyn and Kopyczynce*]. [By] Abraham Backer. Tel Aviv, Husiatyn Society, 1977. 286 p., illus. (H,Y)

YIVO: 9/77792   NYPL: *PXW(Gusyatin) 81-906
YU: DS135 R93 G852

Husiatyn (AH). *Mibet aba; pirkei zikhronot mi-yemei yaldut be-ayarat moladeti Husiatyn* [From my parents' home; memorial chapter...]. [By] A. Y. Avitov (Birnbojm). Tel Aviv, The author, 1965, 155 p., ports. (H)

YIVO: 4/67593   NYPL: *PWZ

Husiatyn (AH). *Sefer zikaron Husiatyn ve-ha-seviva* [Memorial book of Husiatyn and the surrounding region]. Ed.: Abraham Backer. Tel Aviv, Husiatyn-Galicia Society, 1976. 499 p., illus. (H,Y)

JTS: DS135 R93 G88 B33

Iklad (AH) see under Szamosujvar

Ileanda (Nagyilonda) (AH) see under Des

Ilja (R). *Kehilat Ilja; pirkei hayim ve-hashmada* [The community of Ilja; chapters of life and destruction]. Ed.: A. Kopilevitz. [Tel Aviv], Association of Former Residents of Ilja in Israel, 1962. 466 p., ports., facsims. (H,Y)

YIVO: 9/77583   NYPL: *PXW(Il'ia) 88-464
JTS: DS135 R93 I49 K6

Indura (R). *Amdur, mayn geboyrn-shtetl* [Amdur, my hometown]. [By] Iedidio Efron. Buenos Aires, 1973. 252, 33 p., illus. (Y,S)

YIVO: 1/71661   NYPL: *PXW(Indura) 77-3818
JTS: DS135 R93 I54 E42

Istrik (Ustrzyki Dolne) (AH) see under Lesko

Ivano-Frankovsk (Stanislawow) (AH) see under *Arim ve-imahot*, vol. 5

Iwacewicze (R) see under Byten

Iwie (R). *Sefer zikaron le-kehilat Iwie* [Ivie; in memory of the Jewish community*]. Ed.: M. Kaganovich. Tel Aviv, Association of Former Residents of Ivie in Israel and "United Ivier Relief" in America, 1968. 738 p., ports., map (H,Y)

YIVO: 3/77980   NYPL: *PXW(Iv'ye)
JTS: DS135 R93 I9   YU: DS135 R93 I927
BUND: 505/96

Iwieniec (R). *Sefer Iwieniec, Kamien ve-ha-seviva; sefer zikaron* [The memorial book of Iwieniec, Kamien, and the surrounding region]. Tel Aviv, Iwieniec Societies in Israel and the Diaspora, 1973. 484 p., illus. (H,Y)

YIVO: 3/71088   NYPL: *PXW(Ivenets) 74-2700
JTS: DS135 R93 I89 S4 BUND: 522

Jablonka (AH) see under Nowy Targ

Jadow (R). *Sefer Jadow* [The book of Jadow*]. Ed.: A. W. Jassni. Jerusalem, The Encyclopaedia of the Jewish Diaspora, 1966. 472, xxiii p., ports. (H,Y,E)

YIVO: 3/67706   NYPL: *PXV(Jadow)
JTS: DS135 P62 J275   YU: DS135 P62 J275

Jaisi (Jejsa) (R) see under Braslaw

Janova (R) see Jonava

Janow (near Pinsk) (R). *Janow al yad Pinsk; sefer zikaron* [Janow near Pinsk; memorial book*]. Ed.: M. Nadav (Katzikowski). Jerusalem, Assoc. of Former Residents of Janow near Pinsk in Israel, 1969. 420 p., ports. (H,Y)

YIVO: 3/70089   NYPL: *PXW(Ivanovo)
JTS: DS135 R93 I88   YU: 933.5 R969Y

Janow (near Trembowla) (AH) see under Budzanow; Trembowla

Jaroslaw (AH). *Sefer Jaroslaw* [Jaroslav book*]. Ed.: Yitzhak Alperowitz. Tel Aviv, Jaroslaw Society, 1978. 371, 28 p., illus. (H,Y,E)

YIVO: 3/77676   NYPL: *PXV(Jaroslaw) 80-4339
JTS: DS135 P62 J29 S3   YU: DS135 P62 J297

Jaryczow Nowy (AH). *Khurbn Jaryczow bay Lemberg; sefer zikaron le-kedoshei Jaryczow u-sevivoteha* [Destruction of Jaryczow; memorial book to the martyrs of Jaryczow and surroundings]. [By] Mordekhai Gerstl. New York, A. Boym, 1948. 78 p., ports. (Y)

YIVO: 3/50076   NYPL: *PXW(Novy Yarychev)
JTS: DS135 P62 J325 G4

Jaslo (AH). *Toldot yehudei Jaslo; me-reshit hityashvutam be-tokh ha-ir ad yemei ha-hurban al yedei ha-natsim...* [History of the Jews of Jaslo...]. [By] Moshe Natan Even-Hayim. Tel Aviv, Jaslo Society, 1953. 360 p., map, ports., illus. (H)

YIVO: 3/69206   JTS: DS135 P62 J3 R3

Jaworow (AH). *"Judenstadt Jaworow;" der umkum fun Yavorover idn* [Swastika over Jaworow*]. [By] S. Druck. New York, First Jaworower Indep. Ass'n, 1950. 69, iv, 35 p., ports. (Y,E)

YIVO: 3/40105   NYPL: *PXW(Yavorov)
JTS: DS135 P62 J37 D7   BUND: 275

Jaworow (AH). *Matsevet zikaron le-kehilat Jaworow ve-ha-seviva* [Monument to the community of Jaworow and the surrounding region]. Ed.: Michael Bar-Lev. Haifa, Jaworow Societies in Israel and the United States, 1979. 252 p., illus. (H,Y)

YIVO: 9/77662   NYPL: *PXW(Yavarov) 81-1019
JTS: DS135 P62 J37 B3   YU: DS135 B93 Y385

Jedrzejow (R). *Sefer ha-zikaron le-yehudei Jedrzejow* [Memorial book of the Jews of Jedrzejow]. Ed.: Sh. D. Yerushalmi. Tel Aviv, Former Residents of Jedrzejow in Israel, 1965. 490 p., ports., facsims. (H,Y)

YIVO: 3/67090   NYPL: *PXV(Jedrzejow) 1965
JTS: DS135 P62 J43 Y4   YU: 933.47(438) Y47J

Jedwabne (R). *Sefer Jedwabne; historiya ve-zikaron* [Yedwabne; history and memorial book*]. Eds.: Julius L. Baker, Jacob L. Baker; assisted by Moshe Tzinovitz. Jerusalem-New York, The Yedwabner Societies in Israel and in the United States of America, 1980. 121, 110 p., illus. (H,Y,E)

YIVO: nc   NYPL: 12061
YU: nc 82-0725

Jeremicze (R) see under Turzec

Jezierna (AH) *Sefer Jezierna* [Memorial book of Jezierna*]. Ed.: J. Sigelman. Haifa, Committee of Former Residents of Jezierna in Israel, 1971. 354 p., ports. (H,Y)

NYPL: *PXW(Ozernyany)
JTS: DS135 R93 D958 S4
YU: K5 P762Y

Jezierzany (AH). *Sefer Ozieran ve-ha-seviva* [Memorial book; Jezierzany and surroundings*]. Ed.: M. A. Tenenblatt. Jerusalem, The Encyclopaedia of the Jewish Diaspora, 1959. 498 columns, ports. (H,Y)

YIVO: 3/59996   NYPL: *PXW(Ozeryany)
JTS: DS135 R93 O97 T4   YU: DS135 R93 O97

Jeznas (R). *Le-zikhram shel kedoshei kehilat Jezna she-nispu bi-shnat 1941* [Memorial book of the martyrs of Jeznas who perished in 1941]. Ed.: D. Aloni. Jerusalem, Former Residents of Jeznas in Israel, 1967. 105 p., ports., maps, facsims. (H), mimeo.

YIVO: nc

Jod (Jody) (R) see under Braslaw

Jonava (R). *Yanove oyf di breges fun Vilye; tsum ondenk fun di khorev-gevorene yidishe kehile in Yanove* [Yizkor book in memory of the Jewish community of Yanova*]. Ed.: Shimeon Noy. Tel Aviv, Jonava Society, 1972. 35, 429 p., illus. (Y,E)

YIVO: 9/73396   NYPL: *PXW(Jonava) 75-1483

Jordanow (AH) see under Nowy Targ

Jozefow (R). *Sefer zikaron le-kehilat Jozefow ve-le-kedosheha* [Memorial book to the community of Jozefow and its martyrs]. Ed.: Azriel Omer-Lemer. Tel Aviv, Jozefow Societies in Israel and the U.S.A., 1975. 462 p., illus. (H,Y)
YIVO: 9/77521   NYPL: *PXV(Jozefow) 81-145
JTS: DS135 P62 J68 S4   YU: DS135 P62 J697

Kadzidlo (R) see under Ostroleka

Kalarash (R). *Sefer Kalarash; le-hantsahat zikhram shel yehudei ha-ayara she-nehreva bi-yemei ha-shoa* [The book of Kalarash in memory of the town's Jews, which was destroyed in the Holocaust]. Eds.: N. Tamir et al. Tel Aviv, 1966. 533 p., ports., facsims. (H,Y)
YIVO: 3/68116   NYPL: *PXW(Kalarash)
JTS: DS135 R93 K23   YU: 933.5 R969 Z78E

Kalisz (R). *The Kalish book.* Ed.: I. M. Lask. Tel Aviv, The Societies of Former Residents of Kalish and the Vicinity in Israel and the USA, 1968. 327 p. (E)
YIVO: 3/67749A   NYPL: *PXV(Kalisz) 73-1576
JTS: +DS135 P62 K291

Kalisz (R). *Kalisz she-hayeta; ir ve-em be-yisrael be-medinat "Polin-Gadol"* [The Kalisz that was...]. Haifa, Bet ha-sefer ha-reali ha-ivri and The Kalisz Society, [1979/80]. 136 p., illus., ports., maps (H)
YIVO: 3/78435

Kalisz (R). *Sefer Kalish* [The Kalish book *]. Tel Aviv, The Israel-American Book Committee, 1964-1968. 2 vols. (624, 598 p.), ports., facsims. (H,Y)
YIVO: 3/67749   NYPL: *PXV(Kalisz)+
JTS: +DS135 P62 K29   YU: 933.5 P762 K14
BUND: 946171 (vol. 1)

Kalov (AH) see Nagykallo

Kalusz (AH). *Kalusz; hayeha ve-hurbana shel ha-kehila* [Kalusz; the life and destruction of the community]. Eds.: Shabtai Unger, Moshe Ettinger. Tel Aviv, Kalusz Society, 1980. 325, 330, 15 p., illus. (H,Y,E)
YIVO: 3/78435   NYPL: *PXW(Kalush) 82-1681

Kaluszyn (R). *Kehilat Kaluszyn* [The community of Kaluszyn]. Translated from Yiddish: Yitzhak Shoshani. Tel Aviv, I.L. Peretz and Society of Kaluszyn Emigrants in Israel, 1977-1978. 2 vols. (H)
YIVO: 9/76009

Kaluszyn (R). *Sefer Kaluszyn; geheylikt der khorev gevorener kehile* [Memorial book of Kaluszyn]. Eds.: A. Shamir, Sh. Soroka. Tel Aviv, Former Residents of Kaluszyn in Israel, 1961. 545, [15] p., ports., facsims. (Y)
YIVO: 3/65310   NYPL: *PXV(Kaluszyn)+
JTS: Restr +DS135 P62 K3 S5
BUND: 946199

Kalwaria (AH) see under Wadowice

Kamenets-Litovsk (R) see Kamieniec Litewski

Kamenets-Podolskiy (R). *Kamenets-Podolsk u-sevivata* [Kamenets-Podolsk and its surroundings]. Eds.: A. Rosen, Ch. Sharig, Y. Bernstein. Tel Aviv, Association of Former Residents of Kamenets-Podolsk and Its Surroundings in Israel, 1965. 263 p., ports., facsims. (H)
YIVO: 3/67325   NYPL: *PXW(Kamenets-Podolski)
JTS: DS135 R93 K25   YU: 933.5 R969K R813

Kamenets-Podolskiy (R). *Kamenetz-Podolsk; a memorial to a city annihilated by the Nazis.* Ed.: Leon S. Blatman. New York, published by the Sponsors of the Kamenetz-Podolsk Memorial Book, 1966. 133 p., illus., ports. (E)
YIVO: 3/67723
NYPL: *PXW(Kamenets-Podolski) 86-1459

Kamien (R) see under Iwieniec

Kamien Koszyrski (R). *Sefer ha-zikaron le-kehilat Kamien Koszyrski ve-ha-seviva...* [Kamin Koshirsky book; in memory of the Jewish community*]. Eds.: A. A. Stein et al. Tel Aviv, Former Residents of Kamin Koshirsky and Surroundings in Israel, 1965. 974 columns, ports. (H,Y)
YIVO: 3/67607   NYPL: *PXW(Kamen-Kashirskiy)
JTS: +DS135 P62 K325   YU: 933.52 762K S819

Kamieniec Litewski (R). *Sefer yizkor le-kehilot Kamenits de-Lita, Zastavye ve-ha-koloniyot* [Kamenetz Litovsk, Zastavye, and colonies memorial book*]. Eds.: Shmuel Eisenstadt, Mordechai Gelbart. Tel Aviv, Kamieniec and Zastavye Committees in Israel and the United States, 1970. 626, 185 p., illus., map (H,Y,E)
YIVO: 9/73403   NYPL: 4842

Kamiensk (R) see under Radomsko

Kammeny Brod (R) see under Novograd-Volynskiy

Kapreshty (R). *Kapresht ayaratenu--undzer shtetele Kapresht; sefer zikaron le-kehila yehudit be-Bessarabia* [Kapresht, our village; memorial book for the Jewish community of Kapresht, Bessarabia*]. Eds.: M. Rishpy, Av. B. Yanowitz. Haifa, Kapresht Society in Israel, 1980. 496 p., map, illus. (H,Y)
YIVO: nc   NYPL: 13801

Kapsukas (R) see Marijampole

Kapulye (Kopyl) (R) see under Slutsk

Karcag (AH). *Toldot kehilat Karcag ve-kehilot mehoz Nagykunsag* [History of the community of Karcag and the communities of the district of Nagykunsag]. [By] Moshe Hershko. Jerusalem, Karcag Society, 1977. 53, 219 p., illus. (H,Hu)
JTS: DS135 H92 K37 H47

Karczew (R) see under Otwock

Kartuz-Bereze (Bereza Kartuska) (R) see under Pruzana

Kaszony (AH) see Kosyno

Kazimierz (R). *Pinkas Kuzmir* [Kazimierz--memorial book*]. Ed.: D. Shtokfish. Tel Aviv, Former Residents of Kazimierz in Israel and the Diaspora, 1970. 655 p., ports., facsims. (H,Y)
YIVO: 3/69771   NYPL: *PXV(Kazimierz)
JTS: DS135 P62 K38 P5   YU: K5 P762K

Kedainiai (R). *Keydan; sefer zikaron* [Keidan memorial book*]. Ed.: Josef Chrust. Tel Aviv, Keidan Societies in Israel, South America, and the United States, 1977. 39, 313 p., illus. (H,Y,E)
YIVO: 9/77437   NYPL: *PXW(Kedainiai) 81-94
JTS: DS135 L5 K4 S4   YU: DS135 R93 L555

Kelts (R) see Kielce

Keydan (R) see Kedainiai

Khmelnitskii (R) see Proskurov

Kholm (R) see Chelm

Khotin (R). *Sefer kehilat Khotin (Bessarabia)* [The book of the community of Khotin (Bessarabia)]. Ed.: Shlomo Shitnovitzer. Tel Aviv, Khotin (Bessarabia) Society, 1974. 333 p., illus. (Y)
YIVO: 9/73389   NYPL: *PXW(Hotin) 75-3355
JTS: DS135 R93 K44 S4   YU: DS135 R72 H677

Khozhel (R) see Chorzele

Kibart (R) see Kybartai

Kielce (R). *Al betenu she-harav - Fun der khorever heym* [About our house which was devastated*]. Ed.: David Shtokfish. Tel Aviv, Kielce Societies in Israel and in the Diaspora, 1981. 246 p., illus., ports. (H,Y,P,E)
YIVO: nc

Kielce (R). *Sefer Kielce; toldot kehilat Kielce* [The history of the community of Kielce]. [By] P. Zitron. Tel Aviv, Former Residents of Kielce in Israel, 1957. 328 p., ports. (H,Y)
YIVO: 3/52843   NYPL: *PXV(Kielce)

Kiemieliszki (R) see under Swieciany

Kiernozia (R) see under Lowicz

Kislowszczyzna (R) see under Braslaw

Kisvarda (AH). *Sefer yizkor le-kehilat Kleinwardein ve-ha-seviva* [Memorial book of Kleinwardein and vicinity]. Tel Aviv, Kleinwardein Society, 1980. 79, 190 p., illus. (H,Hu,E)
NYPL: *PXT 87-3579   JTS: DS135 H92 K5 J6
YU: nc 81-1115

Kitai-Gorod (R) see under Kamenets-Podolskiy

Kitev (AH) see Kuty

Klausenburg (AH) see Kolozsvar

Kleck (R). *Pinkas Kletsk* [Pinkas Klezk; a memorial to the Jewish community of Klezk-Poland*]. Ed.: E. S. Stein. Tel Aviv, Former Residents of Klezk in Israel, 1959. 385 p., ports., map, facsims. (H,Y)
YIVO: 3/59997   NYPL: *PXV(Kleck)+
JTS: DS135 R93 K65 S73   YU: 933.47 K64 SC2

Kleinwardein (AH) see Kisvarda

Klobucko (R). *Sefer Klobutsk; mazkeret kavod le-kehila ha-kedosha she-hushmeda* [The book of Klobucko; in memory of a martyred community which was destroyed]. Tel Aviv, Former Residents of Klobucko in Israel, 1960. 439 p., ports., facsims. (Y)
YIVO: 3/65429   NYPL: 2858

Klosowa (R). *Sefer Klosowa; kibuts hotsvei avanim a(l) sh(em) Yosef Trumpeldor be-Klosowa u-flugotav, measef* [The story of Kibbutz Klosova*]. Ed.: Haim Dan. Beit Lohamei Hagetaot, Ghetto Fighters House, 1978. 405 p., illus. (H)

Knenitsh (Knihynicze) (AH) see under Rohatyn

Knihynicze (AH) see under Rohatyn

Kobryn (R). *Kobryn; zamlbukh (an iberblik ibern yidishn Kobryn)* [Kobryn; collection (an overview of Jewish Kobryn)]. Ed.: Melech Glotzer. Buenos Aires, Kobryn Book Committee, 1951. 310 p., illus. (Y)
YIVO: 3/47046   NYPL: *PXW(Kobrin) 88-8508

Kobryn (R). *Sefer Kobryn; megilat hayim ve-hurban* [Book of Kobryn; the scroll of life and destruction]. Eds.: B. Schwartz, Y. H. Biletzky. Tel Aviv, 1951. 347 p., ports. (H)
YIVO: 3/46792   NYPL: *PXW(Kobrin)
JTS: DS135 P62 K66   BUND: 94583

Kobylnik (R). *Sefer Kobylnik* [Memorial book of Kobilnik*]. Ed.: I. Siegelman. Haifa, Committee of Former Residents of Kobilnik in Israel, 1967. 292 p., ports., map (H,Y)
YIVO: 3/68046   NYPL: *PXW(Kobyl'nik)
JTS: DS135 P62 K6614

Kock (R). *Sefer Kotsk* [Memorial book of Kotsk]. Ed.: E. Porat. Tel Aviv, Former Residents of Kotsk in Israel..., 1961. 424 p., ports., map, facsims. (H,Y)
YIVO: 9/77581   NYPL: *PXV(Kock) 77-3769
JTS: DS135 P62 K662 P6

Koidanovo (R). *Koydenov; zamlbukh tsum ondenk fun di Koydenover kdoyshim* [Koidanov; memorial volume of the martyrs of Koidanov]. Ed.: A. Reisin. New York, United Koidanover Assn., 1955. 216, [41], 207 p., ports., facsims. (Y)
YIVO: 3/47038
NYPL: *ZP-*PBM p.v.1180, no. 1
JTS: DS135 R93 K652 R4
YU: DS135 R93 D97   BUND: 946126

Kolarovgrad (Bulgaria) see Shumla

Kolbuszowa (AH). *Pinkas Kolbishov (Kolbasov)* [Kolbuszowa memorial book*]. Ed.: I. M. Biderman. New York, United Kolbushover, 1971. 793, 88 p., ports. (H,Y,E)
YIVO: 3/70317   NYPL: *PXV(Kolbuszowa)
JTS: DS135 P62 K663 B5

Kolki (R). *Fun ash aroysgerufn* [Summoned from the ashes]. [By] Daniel Kac. Warsaw, Czytelnik, Zydowski Instytut Historyczny w Polsce, 1983. 399 p., illus., map, ports. (Y)

Kolno (R). *Sefer zikaron le-kehilat Kolno* [Kolno memorial book*]. Eds.: A. Remba, B. Halevy. Tel Aviv, The Kolner Organization and Sifriat Poalim, 1971. 680, 70 p., ports., facsims. (H,Y,E)
YIVO: 3/70381   NYPL: *PXV(Kolno)
JTS: DS135 P62 K664 R4   YU: DS135 P62 K6645

Kolo (R). *Azoy zenen zey umgekumen - Kakh hem nispu* [This is how they perished*]. [By] A. M. Harap. Israel, Memorial Book Committee and the Author, 1974. 169, 8 p., illus. (Y,H,E)
YIVO: nc

Kolo (R). *Sefer Kolo* [Memorial book of Kolo]. Ed.: M. Halter. Tel Aviv, Former Residents of Kolo in Israel and the USA, 1958. 408 p., ports. (H,Y)
YIVO: 3/57487   NYPL: *PXV(Kolo)
JTS: DS135 P62 K665 H34
YU: 933.5 P762K   BUND: 946139

Kolomyja (AH). *Pinkes Kolomey* [Memorial book of Kolomey]. Ed.: Sh. Bickel. New York, 1957. 448 p., ports. (Y)
YIVO: 3/51895   NYPL: *PXW(Kolomea)
JTS: DS135 R93 K654 B5   BUND: 94690

Kolomyja (AH). *Sefer zikaron le-kehilat Kolomey ve-ha-seviva* [Kolomeyer memorial book*]. Eds.: D. Noy, M. Schutzman. [Tel Aviv], Former Residents of Kolomey and Surroundings in Israel, [1972]. 395 p., ports., facsims. (H)
YIVO: nc   NYPL: *PXW(Kolomea)75-2279
JTS: DS135 R93 K654 S4

Kolonia Synajska (R) see under Dereczyn

Kolozsborsa (AH) see Borsa

Kolozsvar (AH). *Sefer zikaron le-yahadut Kluzh-Kolozsvar* [Memorial volume of the Jews of Cluj-Kolozsvar*]. Ed.: M. Carmilly-Weinberger. New York, 1970. 156, 313 p., ports., facsims. (H,E,Hu)
YIVO: 3/69999   NYPL: *PXM(Cluj)
JTS: DS135 R72 C59 C37
YU: 933.47(498) C649C   BUND: 512

Kolozsvar (AH). *Zikaron netsah le-kehila ha-kedosha Kolozhvar-Klauzenburg asher nehreva ba-shoa* [Everlasting memorial of the martyred community Kolozsvar-Klausenburg which perished in the Holocaust]. [Eds.]: Sh. Zimroni, Y. Schwartz. Tel Aviv, Former Residents of Kolozsvar in Israel, 1968. 118 p. (H,Hu), mimeo.
YIVO: 3/68161   NYPL: *PXM
JTS: DS135 R72 C59

Koltyniany (R) see under Swieciany

Konin (R). *Kehilat Konin be-ferihata u-ve-hurbana* [Memorial book Konin*]. Ed.: M. Gelbart. Tel Aviv, Assoc. of Konin Jews in Israel, 1968. 772, 24 p., map, facsims. (H,Y,E)
YIVO: 3/68204   NYPL: *PXV(Konin)
JTS: DS135 P62 K67 G4   YU: K5 P762K
BUND: 505/110

Konyar (AH) see under Debrecen

Kopin (R) see under Kamenets-Podolskiy

Koprzywnica (R). *Sefer Pokshivnitsa* [Memorial book of Koprzywnica]. Ed.: E. Erlich. Tel Aviv, Former Residents of Koprzywnica in Israel, 1971. 351 p., ports., facsims. (H,Y)
YIVO: 3/71003   NYPL: *PXV(Koprzywnica)
JTS: DS135 P62 K671 S4   YU: 933.47(438) K83E

Kopyczynce (AH) see under Husiatyn (*Kehilatiyim*)

Kopyl (R) see under Slutsk

Korczyna (AH). *Korczyna; sefer zikaron* [Korczyna memorial book*]. New York, Committee of the Korczyna Memorial Book, 1967. 495 p., ports. (H,Y)
YIVO: 3/67975   NYPL: *PXV(Korczyn)
JTS: DS135 P62 K672   YU: DS135 P62 K6735
BUND: 946166

Korelicze (R). *Korelits; hayeha ve-hurbana shel kehila yehudit* [Korelitz; the life and destruction of a Jewish community*]. Ed.: Michael Walzer-Fass. Tel Aviv, Korelicze Societies in Israel and the U.S.A., 1973. 61, 357 p., illus. (H,Y,E)
YIVO: 9/73402   NYPL: *PXW(Korolichi) 76-2164
YU: nc 75-0286

Korelicze (R) see also under Nowogrodek

Korets (R) see Korzec

Koriv (R) see Kurow

Korzec (R). *Korets (Wolyn); sefer zikaron le-kehilatenu she-ala aleha ha-koret* [The Korets book; in memory of our community that is no more*]. Ed.: E. Leoni. Tel Aviv, Former Residents of Korets in Israel, 1959. 791 p., ports., facsims. (H,Y)
YIVO: 3/65792   NYPL: *PXW(Korets) 75-5610
JTS: DS135 R93 K67 L4

Kosow (East Galicia) (AH). *Sefer Kosow-Galicia ha-mizrahit* [Memorial book of Kosow--Kosow Huculski*]. Eds.: G. Kressel, L. Oliczky. Tel Aviv, Former Residents of Kosow and Vicinity in Israel, 1964. 430 p., ports., facsims. (H,Y)
YIVO: 3/67404   NYPL: *PXW(Kosov)
JTS: DS135 R93 K68 K7   YU: 933.5 R969K
BUND: 506

Kosow (East Galicia) (AH). *Megiles Kosow* [The scroll of Kosow]. [By] Yehoshua Gertner. Tel Aviv, Amkho, 1981. 156 p. (Y)
YIVO: 8/79147   NYPL: *PXW(Kosow)

Kosow (Polesie) (R). *Pinkas kehilat Kosow Poleski* [Memorial book of Kosow Poleski]. Jerusalem, Relief Org. of Former Residents of Kosow Poleski in Israel, 1956. 81 p., ports. (H)
YIVO: 3/42403

Kostopol (R). *Sefer Kostopol; hayeha u-mota shel kehila* [Kostopol; the life and death of a community*]. Ed.: A. Lerner. Tel Aviv, Former Residents of Kostopol in Israel, 1967. 386 p., ports. (H)
YIVO: 9/77487   NYPL: *PXW(Kostopol)+
JTS: +DS135 P62 K675

Kosyno (AH). *The Jews of Kaszony, Subcarpathia.* By Joseph Eden (Einczig). New York, 1988. v, 131 p., illus., map, ports. (E,H,Hu)
YIVO: nc   NYPL: nc
JTS: DS135 R93 K678 E3

Kotsk (R) see Kock

Kowal (R) see under Wloclawek

Kowel (R). *Kowel; sefer edut ve-zikaron le-kehilatenu she-ala aleha ha-koret* [Kowel; testimony and memorial book of our destroyed community]. Ed.: E. Leoni-Zopperfin. Tel Aviv, Former Residents of Kowel in Israel, 1959. 539 p., ports. (H,Y)
NYPL: 21921

Kowel (R). *Pinkes Kowel* [Memorial book of Kowel]. Ed.: B. Baler. Buenos Aires, Former Residents of Kowel and Surroundings in Argentina, 1951. 511 p., ports., facsims. (Y)
YIVO: 3/38814   YU: DS135 R93 K6846
BUND: 94695

Kozangrodek (R) see under Luniniec

Koziany (R) see under Glebokie; Swieciany

Kozieniec (R). *The book of Kozienice.* Ed.: B. Kaplinsky. Tel Aviv-New York, The Kozienice Organization, 1985. xxxvi, 677 p., illus. (E)
JTS: +DS135 P62 K679

Kozieniec (R). *Sefer zikaron le-kehilat Kozieniec* [Memorial book of the community of Kozieniec]. Ed.: B. Kaplinsky. Tel Aviv, Former Residents of Kozieniec in Israel..., 1969. 516 p., ports., map, music, facsims. (H,Y)
YIVO: 3/70328   NYPL: *PXV(Kozience)+
JTS: +DS135 P62 K678   YU: 933.47(438) K88K

Krakow (AH). *Sefer Kroke, ir va-em be-yisrael* [Memorial book of Krakow, mother and town in Israel]. Eds.: A. Bauminger et al. Jerusalem, The Rav Kuk Inst. and Former Residents of Krakow in Israel, 1959. 429 p., ports., facsims. (H)
YIVO: 3/59998   NYPL: *PXV(Cracow)+ 84-306
JTS: DS135 P62 K6815   YU: 933.5 P762K
BUND: 495

Krakow (AH) see also under *Arim ve-imahot,* vol. 2

Krakowiec (AH) see under Jaworow (*Matsevet zikaron le-kehilat Jaworow...*)

Krasnik (R). *Sefer Krasnik.* Ed.: David Shtokfish. Tel Aviv, Krasnik Societies in Israel and the Diaspora, 1973. 673 p., illus. (H,Y)
YIVO: 9/77427   NYPL: *PXV(Krasnik) 75-8552
JTS: DS135 P62 K693 S4

Krasnobrod (R). *Krasnobrod; sefer zikaron* [Krasnobrod; a memorial to the Jewish community*]. Ed.: M. Kushnir. Tel Aviv, Former Residents of Krasnobrod in Israel, 1956. 526 p., ports., facsims. (H,Y)
YIVO: 3/47840, 3/52479   NYPL: *PXV(Krasnobrod) 76-5703

Krasnystaw (R). *Yisker tsum ondenk fun kdoyshey Krasnystaw* [Memorial book of the martyrs of Krasnystaw]. Ed.: A. Stunzeiger. Munich, Publ. "Bafrayung"--Poalei Zion, 1948. 150 p., ports. (Y)
YIVO: 3/26200   NYPL: *PXV(Krasnystaw)83-381

Krememits (R) see Krzemieniec

Kripa (Horyngrod) (R) see under Tuczyn

Krivitsh (R) see Krzywicze

Kroscienko (AH) see under Nowy Targ

Kroshnik (R) see Krasnik

Krosniewiec (R) see under Kutno

Krynki (R). *Krinik in khurbn: memuarn* [Krinki en ruines*]. [By] Alex Sofer. Montevideo, Los Comites de Ayuda a los Residentes de Krinki de Montevideo y Buenos Aires, 1948. 269, [27] p., illus., map, ports. (Y)
YIVO: 4/41713

Krynki (R). *Pinkas Krynki* [Memorial book of Krynki]. Ed.: D. Rabin. Tel Aviv, Former Residents of Krynki in Israel and in the Diaspora, 1970. 373 p., ports., map, facsims. (H,Y)
YIVO: 3/69359   NYPL: *PXV(Krynki)
JTS: DS135 P62 K7 P5   YU: 933.5 R969K
BUND: 316

Krzemienica (R) see under Wolkowysk (*Volkovisker yisker-bukh*)

Krzemieniec (R). *Kremenits, Vishgorodek un Pitshayev; yisker-bukh* [Memorial book of Krzemieniec]. Ed.: P. Lerner. Buenos Aires, Former Residents of Kremenits and Vicinity in Argentina, 1965. 468 p., ports., facsims. (Y)
YIVO: 3/67512   NYPL: nc

Krzemieniec (R). *Pinkas Kremenits; sefer zikaron* [Memorial book of Krzemieniec]. Ed.: A. S. Stein. Tel Aviv, Former Residents of Krzemieniec in Israel, 1954. 450 p., ports., facsims. (H,Y)
YIVO: 3/45322   NYPL: *PXV(Krzemieniec)
JTS: DS135 R93 K7   BUND: 94694

Krzywicze (R). *Ner tamid; yizkor le-Krivitsh* [Kryvitsh yizkor book*]. Ed.: Matityahu Bar-Ratzon. Tel Aviv, Krivitsh Societies in Israel and the Diaspora, 1977. 724 p., illus. (H,Y)
YIVO: 9/77451   NYPL: *PXW(Krivichi) 78-5704
JTS: DS135 R93 K746 N47
YU: DS135 R93 K746

Kshoynzh (Ksiaz Wielki) (R) see under Miechow

Ksiaz Wielki (R) see under Miechow

Kunow (R) see under Ostrowiec

Kurow (R). *Yisker-bukh Koriv; sefer yizkor, matsevet zikaron la-ayaratenu Koriv* [Yizkor book in memoriam of our hometown Kurow*]. Ed.: M. Grossman. Tel Aviv, Former Residents of Kurow in Israel, 1955. 1148 columns, ports., facsims. (Y)
YIVO: 3/46492   NYPL: *PXV(Kurow)+
JTS: +DS135 P62 K8   YU: DS135 P62 K83
BUND: 94625

Kurzeniec (R). *Megilat Kurenits; ayara be-hayeha u-ve-mota* [The scroll of Kurzeniec; the town living and dead]. Ed.: A. Meyerowitz. Tel Aviv, Former Residents of Kurzeniec in Israel and in the USA, 1956. 335 p., ports. (H)
YIVO: 3/50506   YU: 933.547 K96M

Kutno (R). *Kutno ve-ha-seviva* [Kutno and surroundings book*]. Ed.: D. Shtokfish. Tel Aviv, Former Residents of Kutno and Surroundings in Israel and the Diaspora, 1968. 591 p., ports., facsims. (H,Y)
YIVO: 3/71184A   NYPL: *PXV(Kutno)+
JTS: +DS135 P62 K86 S9
YU: Folio 933.5 P762

Kuty (AH). *Kitever yisker-bukh* [Kitever memorial book]. Ed.: E. Husen. New York, Kitever Sick and Benevolent Society in New York, 1958. 240 p., ports. (Y)

YIVO: 3/58655   NYPL: *PXW(Kuty)
JTS: DS135 R93 K85 H8   BUND: 946122

Kuzmir (R) see Kazimierz

Kybartai (R). *Kibart (Lita)*. By Yosef Rosin. Haifa, Executive Committee of the Society of Former Residents of Kibart, 1988. 2, 62, [20] p., illus., map, ports., facsims. (H)

YIVO: nc

Lachowicze (R). *Lachowicze; sefer zikaron* [Memorial book of Lachowicze]. Ed.: J. Rubin. Tel Aviv, Assoc. of Former Residents of Lachowicze, [1948/49]. 395 p., ports. (H,Y)

YIVO: 3/28864   NYPL: *PXW(Lyakhovice)
JTS: DS135 R93 L95 R5   YU: 933.5 R969L

Lachwa (R). *Rishonim la-mered; Lachwa* [First ghetto revolt, Lachwa*]. Eds.: H. A. Malachi et al. Jerusalem, The Encyclopaedia of the Jewish Diaspora, 1957. 500 columns, ports., facsims. (H,Y)

YIVO: 3/58987   NYPL: *PXW(Lakhva)
YU: DS135 R93 L23

Lancut (AH). *Lancut; hayeha ve-hurbana shel kehila yehudit* [Lancut; the life and destruction of a Jewish community*]. Eds.: M. Waltzer, N. Kudish. Tel Aviv, Associations of Former Residents of Lancut in Israel and USA, 1963. 465, lix p., ports., facsims. (H,Y,E)

YIVO: 3/66579   NYPL: *PXV(Lancut)
JTS: DS135 P62 L34   YU: 933.5 P7626 W242
BUND: 946160

Lanovits (R) see Lanowce

Lanowce (R). *Lanovits; sefer zikaron le-kedoshei Lanovits she-nispu be-shoat ha-natsim* [Lanowce; memorial book of the martyrs of Lanowce who perished during the Holocaust]. Ed.: H. Rabin. Tel Aviv, Association of Former Residents of Lanowce, 1970. 440 p., ports. (H,Y)

NYPL: *PXW(Lanovtsy)   JTS: DS135 R93 L24
YU: 933.5 R969L

Lapichi (R) see under Bobruisk

Lask (R). *Lask; sefer zikaron* [Memorial book of Lask]. Ed.: Z. Tzurnamal. Tel Aviv, Assoc. of Former Residents of Lask in Israel, 1968. 737, 164 p., ports., facsims. (H,Y,E)

YIVO: 3/68208   NYPL: *PXV(Lask)
JTS: DS135 P62 L37   YU: 933.5 P762L

Lask (R) see also under Pabianice

Laskarzew (R). *Sefer Laskarzew-Sobolew* [Laskarzew-Sobolew*]. Ed.: Moshe Levani. Paris, La Société de Laskarzew-Sobolew en France, [197-/8-]. 708 p., illus., map, ports. (Y)

Leczyca (R). *Sefer Linshits* [Memorial book of Leczyca]. Ed.: J. Frenkel. Tel Aviv, Former Residents of Leczyca in Israel, 1953. 223 p., ports. (H)

YIVO: 3/46791   NYPL: *PXV(Leczya)
JTS: DS135 P62 L42 S4

Lemberg (AH) see Lwow

Lenin (R). *Kehilat Lenin; sefer zikaron* [The community of Lenin; memorial book]. Ed.: M. Tamari. Tel Aviv, Former Residents of Lenin in Israel and in the USA, 1957. 407 p., ports. (H,Y)

YIVO: 3/51726   NYPL: *PXW(Lenin)
JTS: DS135 R93 L4 T3   YU: 933.5 R969L
BUND: 946109

Leonpol (R) see under Druja (*Sefer Druja*)

Lesko (AH). *Sefer yizkor; mukdash le-yehudei ha-ayarot she-nispu ba-shoa be-shanim 1939-44, Linsk, Istrik...ve-ha-seviva* [Memorial book; dedicated to the Jews of Linsk, Istrik...and vicinity who perished in the Holocaust in the years 1939-44]. Eds.: N. Mark, Sh. Friedlander. [Tel Aviv], Book Committee of the "Libai" Organization, [1965]. 516 p., ports. (H,Y)

YIVO: 3/67260   NYPL: *PXV(Lesko)
JTS: DS135 P62 L47

Levertev (R) see Lubartow

Lezajsk (AH). *Lizhensk; sefer zikaron le-kedoshei Lizhensk she-nispu be-shoat ha-natsim* [Memorial book of the martyrs of Lezajsk who perished in the Holocaust]. Ed.: H. Rabin. Tel Aviv, Former Residents of Lezajsk in Israel, [1970]. 495 p., ports., facsims. (H,Y)

YIVO: 3/70088   NYPL: *PXV(Lezajsk)
JTS: DS135 P62 L49   YU: DS135 P62 L49

Libovne (R) see Luboml

Lida (R). *Sefer Lida* [The book of Lida*]. Eds.: A. Manor et al. Tel Aviv, Former Residents of Lida in Israel and the Relief Committee of the Lida Jews in USA, 1970. 438, xvii p., ports., maps, facsims. (H,Y,E)

YIVO: 3/70329   NYPL: *PXV(Lida)+
JTS: +DS135 R93 L48   YU: DS135 R93 L48
BUND: 94621A

Likeva (R) see Lukow

Linshits (R) see Leczyca

Linsk (AH) see Lesko

Lipkany (R). *Kehilat Lipkany; sefer zikaron* [The community of Lipkany; memorial book]. Tel Aviv, Former Residents of Lipkany in Israel, 1963. 407 p., ports. (H,Y)
YIVO: 3/66009   NYPL: *PXW(Lipkany)
JTS: DS135 R93 L57 S5   YU: nc 75-0957

Lipkany (R). *Lipkan fun amol* [Lipcan of old*]. By Aaron Shuster. Montreal, Author, 1957. 217 p., illus., ports. (Y)
YIVO: 4/51872   NYPL: 14966
JTS: DS135 R93 L57

Lipniszki (R). *Sefer zikaron shel kehilat Lipnishok* [Memorial book of the community of Lipniszki]. Ed.: A. Levin. Tel Aviv, Former Residents of Lipniszki in Israel, 1968. 206 p., ports., map (H,Y)
YIVO: 3/70231   NYPL: *PXW(Lipnishki)
JTS: DS135 R93 L58   YU: DS135 R93 L494

Litevisk (Lutowiska) (AH) see under Lesko

Lizhensk (AH) see Lezajsk

Lodz (R). *Kehilat Lodz; ir ve-em be-yisrael* [The community of Lodz; a Jewish mother-city]. [By] Aaron Ze'ev Aescoly. Jerusalem, Ha-Mahlakah le-inyanei ha-no'ar shel ha-Histadrut ha-Tsiyonit [Youth Section of the Zionist Organization], [1947/48]. 238 p. (H)
YIVO: 3/35045   NYPL: *PXV
JTS: DS135 P62 L675 A4   YU: DS135 P62 L62

Lodz (R). *Lodzer yisker-bukh* [Lodzer yiskor book*]. New York, United Emergency Relief Committee for the City of Lodz, 1943. Various pagings, ports. (Y)
YIVO: 4/14893   NYPL: *PXV
JTS: DS135 P62 L675 U58
BUND: 9469

Lodz (R). *Yiddish Lodz; a yiskor book.* Melbourne, Lodzer Center, 1974. 13, 243 p., illus. (Y,E)
YIVO: nc   NYPL: *PXV(Lodz) 78-2866
JTS: +DS135 P62 L675 Y5

Lomza (R). *Lomzhe; ir oyfkum un untergang* [The rise and fall of Lomza]. Ed.: H. Sabatka. New York, American Committee for the Book of Lomza, 1957. 371 p., ports., facsims. (Y)
YIVO: 3/51701   NYPL: *PXV(Lomza)+ 79-1103
BUND: 94692

Lomza (R). *Sefer zikaron le-kehilat Lomza* [Lomza--In memory of the Jewish community*]. Ed.: Y. T. Lewinski. Tel Aviv, Former Residents of Lomza in Israel, 1952. 337 p., ports., facsims. (H)
YIVO: 9/76912   NYPL: *PXV(Lomza)+ 77-169
JTS: +DS135 P62 L678 L4
YU: 933.5 P762 L864L   BUND: 9461

Lopatyn (AH) see under Radziechow

Losice (R). *Loshits; lezeykher an umgebrakhte kehile* [Losice; in memory of a Jewish community, exterminaed by Nazi murderers*]. Ed.: M. Shener. Tel Aviv, Former Residents of Losice in Israel, 1963. 459 p., ports., facsims. (H,Y)
YIVO: 3/66334   NYPL: *PXV(Losice) 76-5778
JTS: DS135 P62 L679 L6

Lowicz (R). *Lowicz; ir be-Mazovia u-seviva, sefer zikaron* [Lowicz; a town in Mazovia, memorial book*]. Ed.: G. Shaiak. [Tel Aviv], Former Residents of Lowicz in Melbourne and Sydney, Australia, 1966. 395, xxii p., ports., facsims. (H,Y,E)
YIVO: 3/67750   JTS: +DS135 P62 L68 S5

Lubartow (R). *Khurbn Levartov* [The destruction of Lubartow]. Ed.: B. Tshubinski. Paris, Association of Lubartow, 1947. 117 p., ports., facsims. (Y)
YIVO: 3/24332   NYPL: *PXV(Lubartow)+
JTS: +DS135 P62 L82 C45
BUND: 94631

Lubcza (R). *Lubtsh ve-Delatitsh; sefer zikaron* [Lubtch ve-Delatich; in memory of the Jewish community*]. Ed.: K. Hilel. Haifa, Former Residents of Lubtsh-Delatitsh in Israel, 1971. 480 p., ports., map, facsims. (H,Y)
YIVO: 3/70090   NYPL: *PXW(Lyubcha)
JTS: DS135 R93 L99 L8

Lubenichi (R) see under Bobruisk

Lublin (R). *Dos bukh fun Lublin* [The memorial book of Lublin]. Paris, Former Residents of Lublin in Paris, 1952. 685 p., ports., facsims. (Y)
YIVO: 3/40292   NYPL: *PXV(Lublin)+
BUND: 94630

Lublin (R). *Lublin* [Lublin volume*]. Eds.: N. Blumenthal, M. Korzen. Jerusalem, The Encyclopaedia of the Jewish Diaspora, 1957. 816 columns, ports., map, facsims. (H,Y)
YIVO: 3/47248   NYPL: *PX+
JTS: Ref +DS135 E8 E55 v.5
BUND: 436

Luboml (R). *Sefer yizkor le-kehilat Luboml* [Yizkor book of Luboml*]. Ed.: Berl Kagan. Tel Aviv, 1974. 390, 18 p., illus. (H,Y,E)
YIVO: 9/75285   NYPL: *PXW(Lyuboml) 79-2913
JTS: DS135 R93 L995 S4

Lubraniec (R) see under Wloclawek

Luck (R). *Sefer Lutsk* [Memorial book of Lutsk]. Ed.: N. Sharon. Tel Aviv, Former Residents of Lutsk in Israel, 1961. 608 p., ports., facsims. (H,Y)
YIVO: 3/64383   NYPL: *PXW(Lutsk)+
JTS: DS135 R93 L83   BUND: 946138

Ludmir (R) see Wlodzimierz

Ludwipol (R). *Sefer zikaron le-kehilat Ludwipol* [Ludvipol-Wolyn; in memory of the Jewish community*]. Ed.: N. Ayalon. Tel Aviv, Ludvipol Relief Society of Israel, 1965. 335 p., ports., map, facsims. (H,Y)
YIVO: 3/68115   NYPL: *PXW(Sosnovoye)+
JTS: +DS135 R93 S68 A9
YU: 933.5 R969L

Lukow (R). *Sefer Lukow; geheylikt der khorev gevorener kehile* [The book of Lukow; dedicated to a destroyed community]. Ed.: B. Heller. Tel Aviv, Former Residents of Lukow in Israel and the USA, 1968. 652 p., ports., facsims. (H,Y)
YIVO: 9/77582   NYPL: *PXV(Lukow)
JTS: DS135 P62 L85 H4   BUND: 499

Luniniec (R). *Yizkor kehilot Luniniec/Kozhanhorodok* [Memorial book of the communities of Luniniec/Kozhanhorodok]. Eds.: Y. Zeevi (Wilk) et al. Tel Aviv, Assoc. of Former Residents of Luniniec/Kozhanhorodok in Israel, 1952. 268 p., ports. (H,Y)
YIVO: 3/41035   NYPL: *PXW(Luninets) 76-5565
BUND: 94697

Lutowiska (AH) see under Lesko

Lutsk (R) see Luck

Lvov (AH) see Lwow

Lwow (AH). *Lwow* [Lwow volume*], part I. Ed.: N. M. Gelber. Jerusalem, The Encyclopaedia of the Jewish Diaspora, 1956. 772 columns, ports., facsims. (H)
YIVO: 3/47248   NYPL: *PX+
JTS: Ref +DS135 E8 E55 v.4

Lwow (AH) see also *Arim ve-imahot*, vol. 1

Lyngmiany (R) see under Stolin

Lynki (R) see under Stolin

Lyntupy (R) see under Swieciany

Lyskow (R) see under Wolkowysk (*Volkovisker yisker-bukh*)

Lyszkowice (R) see under Lowicz

Lyuban (R) see under Slutsk

Mad (AH). *Ha-kehilah ha-yehudit shel Mad, Hungaria* [The Jewish community of Maad, Hungary*]. Ed.: Arieh Lewy. Jerusalem, Mad Commemorative Committee, 1974. 154, 31 p., illus. (H,E,Hu)
YIVO: 3/72630   NYPL: *PXT 76-5639
JTS: DS135 H92 M28 L485
YU: DS135 H92 M424

Magyarlapos (AH) see under Des

Makow-Mazowiecki (R). *Sefer zikaron le-kehilat Makow-Mazowiecki* [Memorial book of the community of Makow-Mazowiecki]. Ed.: J. Brat. Tel Aviv, Former Residents of Makow-Mazowiecki in Israel, 1969. 505 p., ports., facsims. (H,Y)
YIVO: 3/69272   NYPL: *PXV(Makow-Mazowiecki)
JTS: DS135 P62 M28 S4   YU: 933.5 P762M

Makow Podhalanski (AH) see under Nowy Targ

Malecz (R) see under Pruzana

Margareten (AH) see Margita

Margita (AH). *Sefer yizkor le-kehilat Margareten ve-ha-seviva* [Memorial book of the community of Margareten and the surrounding region]. Ed.: Aharon Kleinmann. Jerusalem, Hayim Frank, 1979. 200, 275 p. (H,Hu)
YIVO: nc   NYPL: 14004
YU: nc 83-1073

Marijampole (R). *Marijampole al gedot ha-nahar Sheshupe (Lita)* [Marijampole on the river Sheshupe (Lithuania)*]. Ed.: Avraham Tory-Golub. Tel Aviv, Committee of Survivors from Marijampole in Israel, 1983. 74, 245 p., illus., map, ports. (H,Y,E)
YIVO: nc   NYPL: 20460
JTS: +DS135 L5 M3 M3

Markuleshty (R). *Markuleshty; yad le-moshava yehudit be-Bessarabia* [Markuleshty; memorial to a Jewish colony in Bessarabia]. Eds.: Leib Kuperstein, Meir Kotik. Tel Aviv, Markuleshty Society, 1977. 272 p., illus. (H,Y)
YIVO: 9/77060
NYPL: *PXW(Markuleshty) 79-1033
JTS: DS135 R93 M335   YU: DS135 R93 M335

Markuszow (R). *Hurbana u-gevurata shel ha-ayara Markuszow* [The destruction and heroism of the town of Markuszow]. Ed.: D. Shtokfish. Tel Aviv, Former Residents of Markuszow in Israel, 1955. 436 p., ports. (Y)
YIVO: 3/47950   NYPL: *PXV(Markuszow)

Marosvasarhely (AH). *Korot yehudei Marosvasarhely ve-ha-seviva* [History of the Jews in Marosvasarhely]. [By] Yitzhak Perri (Friedmann). Tel Aviv, Ghetto Fighters House, Ha-Kibbutz ha-Meuhad, 1977. (H)
YIVO: nc   JTS: DS135 R72 T5 P4
YU: DS135 R72 T576

Marvits (Murawica) (R) see under Mlynow

Medenice (AH) see under Drohobycz

Melits (AH) see Mielec

Meretsh (R) see Merkine

Merkine (R). *Meretsh;   ayara   yehudit   be-Lita* [Merkine*]. Ed.: Uri Shefer. Tel Aviv, [Society of Meretsh Immigrants in Israel], 1988. 195 p., illus., map, ports. (H)
YIVO: nc

Meytshet (R) see Molczadz

Mezhirechye (R) see Miedzyrzec-Wolyn

Mezritsh (R) see Miedzyrzec

Miava (AH) see under Postyen

Michalovce (AH) see Nagymihaly

Michow (R). *Michow (Lubelski); sefer zikaron le-kedoshei Michow she-nispu be-shoat ha-natsim ba-shanim 1939-1942* [Memorial book to the martyrs of Michow who perished in the Holocaust...]. Ed.: Hayim Rabin. [Israel], Former Residents of Michow, 1987. 343 p., illus., map, ports. (H,Y)
YIVO: nc

Miechow (R). *Sefer yizkor Miechow, Charsznica, Ks iaz* [Miechov memorial book, Charshnitza and Kshoynge*]. Eds.: N. Blumenthal, A. Ben-Azar (Broshy). Tel Aviv, Former Residents of Miechov, Charshnitza and Kshoynzh, 1971. 314, [4] p., ports., facsims. (H,Y)
YIVO: 9/73462   NYPL: *PXV(Miechow) 82-2352
YU: DS135 P62 M4877

Miedzyrzec (R). *Mezritsh; zamlbukh* [The Mezritsh volume]. Ed.: Y. Horn. Buenos Aires, Assoc. of Former Residents of Mezritsh in Argentina, 1952. 635 p., ports., facsims. (Y)
YIVO: 3/40563   NYPL: *PXV(Miedzyrecz)
BUND: 9460

Miedzyrzec (R). *Sefer Mezritsh; lezeykher di kdoyshim fun undzer shtot* [Mezritsh book, in memory of the martyrs of our city]. Eds.: Binem Heller, Yitzhak Ronkin. Israel, Mezritsh Societies in Israel and the Diaspora, 1978. 821 p., illus. (H,Y)
YIVO: nc   NYPL: *PXV(Miedzyrecz) 85-2013

Miedzyrzec (R). *Di yidn-shtot Mezritsh; fun ir breyshis biz erev der velt-milkhome* [Historia de Mezritch (Mezritch Podlasie); su población judía*]. [By] Meir Edelboim. Buenos Aires, Sociedad de Residentes de Mezritch en la Argentina, 1957. 424 p., facsims. (Y)
YIVO: 3/52953   NYPL: *PXV(Miedzyrecz)
JTS: DS135 P62 M38 E3   BUND: 94686

Miedzyrzec-Wolyn (R). *Mezeritsh gadol be-vinyana u-be-hurbana* [Mezhiritch-Wolyn; in memory of the Jewish community*]. Ed.: B. H. Ayalon-Baranick. Tel Aviv, Former Residents of Mezhiritch, 1955. 442 columns, ports., facsims. (H,Y)
YIVO: 3/57416   JTS: +DS135 R93 M4 A85

Miedzyrzec-Wolyn (R). *Pinkas ha-kehila Mezhirits* [Memorial book of Mezhirits]. Ed.: Natan Livneh. Tel Aviv, Committee of Former Residents of Mezhirits in Israel, 1973. 71 p., illus. (H,Y)
NYPL: *PXW(Mezhirech'ye) 75-3249
JTS: +DS135 R93 M4 P45

Mielec (AH). *Melitser yidn* [Mielec Jews]. [By] Shlomo Klagsbrun. Tel Aviv, Nay-Lebn, 1979. 288 p., illus. (Y)
YIVO: 9/77793   NYPL: *PXV(Mielec) 82-1666
JTS: DS135 P62 M45 K54

Mielec (AH). *Sefer zikaron le-kehilat Mielec; sipur hashmadat ha-kehila ha-yehudit* [Remembering Mielec; the destruction of the Jewish community*]. [New York], Mielec Yiskor-Book Committee, 1979. 84, 122 p., illus., ports. (H,Y,E)

Mielnica (R) see under Kowel (*Pinkes Kowel*)

Mikepercs (AH) see under Debrecen

Mikolajow (AH) see under Radziechow

Mikulince (AH). *Mikulince; sefer yizkor* [Mikulince yizkor book*]. Ed.: Haim Preshel. [Israel], The Organisation of Mikulincean Survivors in Israel and in the United States of America, 1985. 356, 266 p., illus., ports. (H,E)
YIVO: nc

Mikulov (Nikolsburg) (AH) see under *Arim ve-imahot*, vol. 4

Milosna (R) see under Rembertow

Minkovtsy (R) see under Kamenets-Podolskiy

Minsk (R). *Albom Minsk* [The Minsk album; selected pictures collected by David Cohen from the two volumes of the book "The Jewish Mother-City Minsk"*]. Eds.: Shlomo Even-Shoshan, Nehemiya Maccabee. [Israel], Association of Olim from Minsk and its Surroundings in Israel, Hakibbutz Hameuchad Publishing House, 1988. 71 p., illus., maps, ports. (H,E)
YIVO: nc

Minsk (R). *Minsk ir ve-em* [Minsk; Jewish mother city: a memorial anthology*]. Ed.: Shlomo Even-Shushan. Jerusalem, Association of Olim from Minsk and its Surroundings in Israel; Ghetto Fighters' House; Kiryat Sefer, 1975-1985. 2 vols., illus., ports. (H)
YIVO: 9/78645   NYPL: *PXW(Minsk) 83-311
JTS: DS135 R93 M59 M55
YU: DS135 R93 M555   BUND: 50111 (vol. 1)

Minsk-Mazowiecki (R). *Sefer Minsk-Mazowiecki* [Minsk-Mazowiecki memorial book*]. Ed.: Ephraim Shedletzky. Jerusalem, Minsk-Mazowiecki Societies in Israel and Abroad, 1977. 6, 633 p., illus. (H,Y,E)
YIVO: 9/77369
NYPL: *PXV(Minsk-Mazowiecki) 87-6485
JTS: DS135 P62 M5 S5   YU: DS135 P62 M537

Miory (R) see under Druja (*Sefer Druja*)

Mir (R). *Sefer Mir* [Memorial book of Mir]. Ed.: N. Blumenthal. Jerusalem, The Encyclopaedia of the Jewish Diaspora, 1962. 768, 62 columns, ports. (H,Y,E)
YIVO: 3/66140   NYPL: *PXW(Mir)

Miskolc (AH). *Kedoshei Miskolc ve-ha-seviva; ha-kehilot me-Hidasnemeti ad Mezokovesd u-me-Ozd ad Szerencs* [The martyrs of Miskolc and vicinity; the communities from Hidasnemeti to Mezokovesd and from Ozd to Szerencs]. [By] Slomo Paszternak. Bnei Brak, 1970. 14, 38, 277 p., illus., ports. (Hu,E,H)

Mizocz (R). *Mizocz; sefer zikaron* [Memorial book of Mizocz]. Ed.: A. Ben-Oni. Tel Aviv, Former Residents of Mizocz in Israel, 1961. 293, [24] p., ports., facsims. (H)
YIVO: 3/64390   NYPL: *PXW(Mizoch)
JTS: DS135 R93 M62

Mlawa (R). *Mlawa ha-yehudit; koroteha, hitpathuta, kilayona - Di yidishe Mlave; geshikhte, oyfshtand, umkum* [Jewish Mlawa; its history, development, destruction*]. Ed.: David Shtokfish. [Israel], Mlawa Societies in Israel and in the Diaspora, 1984. 2 vols. (536, 584 p.), illus., maps, ports. (H,Y,E)
YIVO: nc   NYPL: *PXV(Mlawa) 87-6488
YU: nc 86-0215

Mlawa (R). *Pinkes Mlave* [Memorial book of Mlawa]. New York, World Assoc. of Former Residents of Mlawa, 1950. 483, 63 p., ports. (Y)
YIVO: 3/29356   NYPL: *PXV(Mlawa)
JTS: DS135 P62 M6 P5   BUND: 94618

Mlynow (R). *Sefer Mlynow-Marvits* [Mlynov-Muravica memorial book*]. Ed.: J. Sigelman. Haifa, Former Residents of Mlynov-Muravica in Israel, 1970. 511 p., ports. (Y,H)
YIVO: 7/71185A   NYPL: *PXW(Mlinov)
JTS: DS135 R93 M637   YU: 933.5 R969M

Modrzyc (R) see Deblin

Mogielnica (R) *Sefer yizkor Mogielnica-Bledow* [Memorial book of Mogielnica-Bledow]. Ed.: Yisrael Zonder. Tel Aviv, Mogielnica and Bledow Society, 1972. 808 p., illus., map, ports. (H,Y)
JTS: +DS135 P62 M65 S4

Molczadz (R). *Sefer-zikaron le-kehilat Meytshet* [Memorial book of the community of Meytshet]. Ed.: Benzion H. Ayalon. Tel Aviv, Meytshet Societies in Israel and Abroad, 1973. 460, 12 p., illus. (H,Y)
YIVO: 3/71301   NYPL: *PXW(Molchad) 75-866
JTS: DS135 R93 M647 S4   YU: DS135 R93 M647

Monasterzyska (AH). *Sefer Monastrishtz* [Monasterzyska; a memorial book*]. Ed.: M. Segal. Tel Aviv, Monasterzyska Association, 1974. 126 p., illus. (H,Y,E)
YIVO: 9/75623

Monastir (Turkey). *Ir u-shema Monastir* [A city called Monastir]. [By] Uri Oren. Tel Aviv, Naor, 1972. 167 p., illus. (H)
NYPL: 12951   JTS: DS135 Y82 B5 O74

Monastir (Turkey). *A town called Monastir*. [By] Uri Oren; translated from the Hebrew by Mark Segal. Tel Aviv, Dror Publications, 1971. 240 p., illus., ports. (E)
YIVO: 3/72396   JTS: DS135 Y82 B5 O4713

Mosty (R) see under Piaski

Mosty-Wielkie (AH). *Mosty-Wielkie--Most Rabati, sefer zikaron* [Mosty-Wielkie memorial book*]. Eds.: Moshe Shtarkman, Abraham Ackner, A.L. Binot. Tel Aviv, Mosty Wielkie Societies in Israel and the United States, 1975-1977. 2 vols., illus. (H,Y,E)
YIVO: 9/75289
NYPL: *PXW(Velikiye-Mosty) 82-2367
JTS: DS135 R93 V375 M67
YU: DS135 R93 V375

Motele (R) see Motol

Motol (R). *Hurban Motele* [The destruction of Motele]. [By] A. L. Poliak. Jerusalem, Council of Motele Immigrants, 1957. 87 p. (H)

Mszczonow (R) see under Zyrardow

Mukacevo (Munkacs) (AH) see under *Arim ve-imahot*, vol. 1

Munkacs (AH) see under *Arim ve-imahot*, vol. 1

Murawica (R) see under Mlynow

Myjava (Miava) (AH) see under Postyen

Mysleniec (R) see under Wadowice

Myszyniec (R) see under Ostroleka

Nadarzyn (R) see under Pruszkow

Nadworna (AH). *Nadworna; sefer edut ve-zikaron* [Nadworna, Stanislav district; memorial and records*]. Ed.: Israel Carmi (Otto Kramer). Tel Aviv, Nadworna Societies in Israel and the United States, 1975. 281, 67 p., illus. (H,Y,E)
YIVO: 9/76560
NYPL: *PXW(Nadvornaya) 88-498
YU: DS135 R93 N326

Nadzin (Nadarzyn) (R) see under Pruszkow

Nagybanya (AH). *Nagybanya ve-ha-seviva* [Nagybanya and the surrounding region]. Ed.: Naftali Stern. Bne Brak, 1976. 245, 175 p., illus. (H,Hu)
YIVO: nc

Nagyilonda (AH) see under Des

Nagykallo (AH). *Ha-tsadik me-Kalov ve-kehilato; tsiyun le-nefesh hayeha zts"l ve-le-kehila nihahedet...* [The tsadik of Kalov and his community...]. [By] Tuvia (Laszlo) Szilágyi-Windt; translated from Hungarian and edited: Yehuda Edelshtein. Haifa, [1970?]. 208 p., facsims., illus., ports. (H)
YIVO: nc   NYPL: *PQV
JTS: BM755 T23 S916

Nagymagyar (AH) see under Dunaszerdahely

Nagymihaly (AH). *Sefer Michalovce ve-ha-seviva* [The book of Michalovce*]. Ed.: M. Ben-Zeev (M. Farkas). Tel Aviv, Committee of Former Residents of Michalovce in Israel, 1969. 240, 64, 103 p., ports., facsims. (H,E,Hu)
YIVO: 9/73423   NYPL: *PXT(Michalovce)
JTS: DS135 C96 M537   YU: 933.5(437) M999B

Nagyszollos (AH). *Sefer zikaron le-kehilat Selish ve-ha-seviva* [A memorial to the Jewish community of Sevlus (Nagyszollos) District*]. Ed.: Shmuel ha-Kohen Weingarten. Israel, Selish Society, 1976. 326 p., illus. (H)
YIVO: 9/78961
NYPL: *PXW(Vinogradov) 87-6493

Nagyszollos (AH). *Sefer zikaron...* [Memorial book*] - Musaf [Addenda]. Eds.: J. H. Klein, J. M. Hollander. Israel, The Committee of Olei Nagyszollos and Vicinity in Israel, 1981. 94 p., ports. (H,E)

Nagytapolcsany (AH) see Topolcany

Nagyvarad (AH) see Oradea

Naliboki (R). *Ayaratenu Nalibok, hayeha ve-hurbana* [Our town Nalibok, its existence and destruction*]. Tel Aviv, Former Residents of Nalibok, 1967. 239 p., ports., map (H,Y)
YIVO: 3/68045   BUND: 946207

Naliboki (R) see also under Stolpce

Narajow (AH) see under Brzezany

Navaredok (R) see Nowogrodek

Naymark (AH) see Nowy Targ

Nemirov (R) see under *Arim ve-imahot*, vol. 2

Nestilye (R) see Uscilug

Neumarkt (AH) see Nowy Targ

Nevel (R) see under Vitebsk (*Sefer Vitebsk*)

Nieswiez (R). *Sefer Nieswiez*. Ed.: David Shtokfish. Tel Aviv, Nieswiez Societies in Israel and the Diaspora, 1976. 531 p., illus. (H,Y)
YIVO: 9/78648   NYPL: *PXW+(Nesvizh) 86-2667

Nieszawa (R) see under Wloclawek

Nikolsburg (AH) see under *Arim ve-imahot*, vol. 4

Novograd-Volynskiy (R). *Zvhil-Novogradvolinsk.* Eds.: A. Ori, M. Bone. Tel Aviv, Association of Former Residents of Zvhil and the Environment, 1962. 354, 232, 16 p., ports. (H,Y,E)

YIVO: 3/65426   NYPL: *PXW(Novagrad Volynsky)
JTS: DS135 R93 N63 Z8   YU: 933.5 R969N

Novo Minsk (R) see Minsk Mazowiecki

Novyi Vitkov (Witkow Nowy) (AH) see under Radziechow

Novyi Yarichev (AH) see Jaryczow Nowy

Nowe Miasto (R) see under Plonsk

Nowogrod (R) see under Lomza (*Lomzhe; ir oyfkum un untergang*)

Nowogrodek (R). *Pinkas Navaredok* [Navaredok memorial book*]. Eds.: E. Yerushalmi et al. Tel Aviv, Alexander Harkavy Navaredker Relief Committee in the USA and...in Israel, 1963. 419 p., ports., maps, facsims. (H,Y)

YIVO: 3/66578   NYPL: *PXW(Novogrudok)
JTS: DS135 R93 N69 P5   YU: nc 75-1107

Nowo-Swieciany (R) see under Swieciany

Nowy Dwor (near Warszawa) (R). *Pinkas Nowy Dwor* [Memorial book of Nowy-Dwor]. Eds.: A. Shamri, D. First. Tel Aviv, Former Residents of Nowy-Dwor in Israel, USA, Argentina..., 1965. 556, xix p., ports., map, facsims. (H,Y,E)

YIVO: 3/67088   NYPL: *PXV(Nowy Dwor)
JTS: DS135 P62 N643 S5   YU: DS135 P62 N6
BUND: 946163

Nowy Dwor (R). *Ondenk bukh fun Nowy Dwor* [Memorial book of Nowy Dwor]. Los Angeles, Nowy Dwor Relief Committee, [1947]. 60 p., illus., ports. (Y)

YIVO: 15/4178   BUND: 94614

Nowy Dwor (R) see also under Szczuczyn (*Sefer zikaron le-kehilot Szczuczyn, Wasiliszki...*)

Nowy Sacz (AH). *Le-zekher kehilat Tsants* [In memory of the community of Tsants]. Ed.: Ya'akovi Tefuhah. Jerusalem, Bet ha-sefer ha-tikhon ha-dati la-banot Oylinah di Rotshild, [1967/68]. 174 p., illus., facsims., music, ports. (H)

Nowy Sacz (AH). *Sefer Sants* [The book of the Jewish community of Nowy Sacz*]. Ed.: R. Mahler. New York, Former Residents of Sants in New York, 1970. 886 p., ports., facsims. (H,Y)

YIVO: 3/69678   NYPL: *PXV(Nowy Sacz)
JTS: DS135 P62 N648 M3
YU: 933.5 P762S   BUND: 501

Nowy Targ (AH). *Sefer Nowy Targ ve-ha-seviva* [Remembrance book Nowy Targ and vicinity*]. Ed.: Michael Walzer-Fass. Tel Aviv, Townspeople Association of Nowy Targ and Vicinity, 1979. 301 p., illus. (H,Y,E)

YIVO: nc   NYPL: 14972

Nowy Zagorz (AH) see under Sanok

Odessa (R) see under *Arim ve-imahot,* vol. 2

Okmieniec (R) see under Braslaw

Okuniew (R) see under Rembertow

Olkeniki(R). *Ha-ayara be-lehavot; sefer zikaron le-kehilat Olkenik pelekh Vilna* [Olkeniki in flames; a memorial book*]. Ed.: Sh. Farber. Tel Aviv, Association of Former Residents of Olkeniki and Surroundings, 1962. 287, [4] p., ports. (H,Y)

YIVO: 3/66961

Olkusz (AH). *Olkusz (Elkish); sefer zikaron le-kehila she-huhehada ba-shoa* [Olkusz; memorial book to a community that was exterminated during the Holocaust]. Ed.: Zvi Yashiv. Tel Aviv, Olkusz Society, [1971/72]. 280 p., map, illus. (H,Y)

Olshan (R) see Holszany

Olyka (R). *Pinkas ha-kehila Olyka; sefer yizkor* [Memorial book of the community of Olyka]. Ed.: Natan Livneh. Tel Aviv, Olyka Society, 1972. 397 p., illus. (H,Y)

YIVO: 9/73386   NYPL: *PXW(Olyka) 75-3326
JTS: DS135 R93 O536 L55
YU: nc 75-1108

Opatow (R). *Apt (Opatow); sefer zikaron le-ir va-em be-yisrael* [Apt; a town which does not exist any more*]. Ed.: Z. Yasheev. Tel Aviv, The Apt Organization in Israel, USA, Canada and Brazil, 1966. 441, [3], 20 p., ports. (H,Y,E)

YIVO: 3/67748   NYPL: *PXV(Opatow)+
JTS: +DS135 P62 O63 Y3

Opatow (R) see also under Ostrowiec (*Ostrovtse; geheylikt dem ondenk...*)

Opole (R). *Sefer Opole-Lubelski* [Memorial book of Opole-Lubelski*]. Ed.: David Shtokfish. Tel Aviv, Opole Societies in Israel and the Diaspora, 1977. 467 p., illus. (H,Y)

YIVO: 9/79197

Opsa (R) see under Braslaw

Oradea (AH). *A tegnap városa; a nagyváradi zsidóság emlékkönyve* [Ir ve-etmol; sefer zikaron le-yehudei Grosswardein* = A city and yesterday; memorial book to the Jews of Grosswardein]. Eds.: Schön Dezsö et al. Tel Aviv, 1981. 446 p., illus., maps, ports. (Hu)

NYPL: *PXR+ 86-3819   JTS: +DS135 R72 O7 T4

Oradea (AH). *Sefer zikaron le-yahadut Grosswardein-Oradea-Nagyvarad ve-ha-seviva, mishnat yisoda ve-ad-hurbana* [Memorial book to the Jews of Grosswardein-Oradea-Nagyvarad and vicinity...]. Ed.: Zvi Grossman. Tel Aviv, Grosswardein Society in Israel, 1984. 451, 67 p., illus., maps, ports. (H)

NYPL: *PXR+ 88-562   JTS: +DS135 R72 O716 G7 1984

Orgeyev (R). *Orheyev be-vinyana u-be-hurbana* [Orheyev alive and destroyed]. Eds.: Y. Spivak et al. Tel Aviv, Committee of Former Residents of Orheyev, 1959. 216 p., ports. (H,Y)

YIVO: 9/77885   NYPL: *PXM(Orgeyev)
JTS: +DS135 R93 O7 S6   YU: DS135 R72 O7

Orhei (R) see Orgeyev

Orlowa (R) see under Zoludek

Oshmena (R) see Oszmiana

Oshpitsin (AH) see Oswiecim

Osiek (R) see under Staszow

Osipovichi (R) see under Bobruisk

Ostra (R) see Ostrog

Ostrog (R). *Ostrog.* [By] Judah Loeb Levin. Jerusalem-Tel Aviv, Yad Yahadut Polin, 1966. 111 p., map, ports., illus. (H)

NYPL: *PXW(Ostrog)   JTS: DS135 R93 O88 L4

Ostrog (R). *Pinkas Ostra; sefer zikaron...* [Ostrog-Wolyn; in memory of the Jewish community*]. Ed.: H. Ayalon-Baranick. Tel Aviv, Association of Former Residents of Ostrog, 1960. 640 columns, ports., maps, facsims. (H,Y)

YIVO: 3/67331   NYPL: *PXW(Ostrog)
JTS: DS135 R93 O88 A9

Ostrog (R). *Sefer Ostrog (Vohlin); matsevet zikaron le-kehila kedosha* [Ostrog book; a memorial to the Ostrog holy community*]. Ed.: Yitzhak Alperowitz; Chief Coordinator: Chaim Finkel. Tel Aviv, The Ostrog Society in Israel, 1987. 402, 34 p., illus., ports., map (H,Y,E,P)

YIVO: nc   NYPL: 22642
JTS: DS135 R93 O88 S4

Ostrog (R). *Ven dos lebn hot geblit* [When life was blooming]. [By] M. Grines. Buenos Aires, 1954. 471 p., ports. (Y)

YIVO: 3/41891   NYPL: *PXW

Ostrog (R) see also under *Arim ve-imahot,* vol. 1

Ostroleka (R). *Sefer kehilat Ostrolenka* [Book of kehilat Ostrolenka*]. Ed.: Y. Ivri. Tel Aviv, Association of Former Residents of Ostrolenka, 1963. 579 p., ports. (H,Y)

YIVO: 3/66413   NYPL: *PXV(Ostroleka)+
JTS: +DS135 P62 O7 S4

Ostrowiec (R). *Ostrovtse; geheylikt dem ondenk...fun Ostrovtse, Apt...* [Ostrovtse; dedicated to the memory of Ostrovtse, Apt...]. Buenos Aires, Former Residents of Ostrovtse...in Argentina, 1949. 217, [3] p., ports. (Y)

YIVO: 3/29102   NYPL: *PXV(Ostrowiec) 84-351
JTS: DS135 P62 O8   YU: 933.5 P7628
BUND: 94613

Ostrowiec (R). *Ostrovtse; a denkmol oyf di khurves fun a farnikhtete yidishe kehile* [Ostrowiec; a monument on the ruins of an annihilated Jewish community*]. Eds.: Gershon Silberberg, M. S. Geshuri. Tel Aviv, Society of Ostrovtser Jews in Israel, with the cooperation of the Ostrovtser Societies in New York and Toronto, [197-/8-]. 560, [106], 134 p., illus., maps, ports. (Y,H,E)

NYPL: *PXV(Ostrowiec)   JTS: DS135 P62 O8 S4

Ostrow-Mazowiecka (R). *Ostrow Mazowiecka.* [By] Judah Loeb Levin. Jerusalem-Tel Aviv, Yad Yahadut Polin, 1966. 164 p., ports., illus. (H)

NYPL: *PXV(Ostrow)   JTS: DS135 P62 O78 L4

Ostrow-Mazowiecka (R). *Sefer ha-zikaron le-kehilat Ostrov-Mazovyetsk* [Memorial book of the community of Ostrow-Mazowiecka]. Ed.: A. Margalit. Tel Aviv, Association of Former Residents of Ostrow-Mazowieck, 1960. 653 p., ports. (H,Y)

YIVO: 3/61638   NYPL: *PXV(Ostrow)
JTS: DS135 P62 O78 G6   BUND: 657

Ostryna (R) see under Szczuczyn (*Sefer zikaron le-kehilot Szczuczyn, Wasiliszki...*)

Oswiecim (AH). *Sefer Oshpitsin* [Oswiecim-Auschwitz memorial book*]. Eds.: Ch. Wolnerman, A. Burstin, M. S. Geshuri. Jerusalem, Oshpitsin Society, 1977. 622 p., illus. (H,Y)

YIVO: nc

Oszmiana (R). *Sefer zikaron le-kehilat Oshmana* [Oshmana memorial book*]. Ed.: M. Gelbart. Tel Aviv, Oshmaner Organization in Israel and the Oshmaner Society in the USA, 1969. 659, 109 p., ports. (H,Y,E)

YIVO: 3/69278   NYPL: *PXW(Oshmyany)

JTS: DS135 R93 O67   YU: 933.5 L776O

Otvotsk (R) see Otwock

Otwock (R). *Khurbn Otvotsk, Falenits, Kartshev* [The destruction of Otvotsk, Falenits, Kartshev]. [By] B. Orenstein. [Bamberg], Former Residents of Otvotsk, Falenits and Kartshev in the American Zone in Germany, 1948. 87 p., ports. (Y)

YIVO: 3/26553   NYPL: *PXV

JTS: DS135 P62 O86 O72   BUND: 94530

Otwock (R). *Yisker-bukh; Otvotsk-Kartshev* [Memorial book of Otvotsk and Kartshev*]. Ed.: Sh. Kanc. Tel Aviv, Former Residents of Otvotsk-Kartshev, 1968. 1086 columns, ports. (H,Y)

YIVO: 3/68210   NYPL: *PXV(Otwock)

JTS: DS135 P62 O86 Y5

Ozarow (R) see under Ostrowiec

Ozieran (AH) see Jezierzany

Ozorkow (R). *Ozorkow.* [By] Judah Loeb Levin. Jerusalem, Yad Yahadut Polin, 1966. 128 p., illus. (H)

YIVO: 9/77484   NYPL: *PXV(Ozorkow)

JTS: DS135 P62 O9

Pabianice (R). *Sefer Pabianice* [Memorial book of Pabianice]. Ed.: A. W. Yassni. Tel Aviv, Former Residents of Pabianice in Israel, 1956. 419 p., ports., facsims. (H,Y)

YIVO: 3/50754   NYPL: *PXV(Pabianice)

Paks (AH). *Mazkeret Paks* [Paks memorial book]. Ed.: D. Sofer. Jerusalem, 1962-[1972/73]. 3 vols., ports., facsims. (H)

YIVO: nc (vols. 2-3)   NYPL: *PXT(Paks) 83-468

JTS: DS135 H92 P3

Papa (AH). *Sefer zikaron Papa; le-zekher kedoshei ha-kehila ve-yishuvei ha-seviva* [Memorial book of Papa...]. [By] Jehuda-Gyula Lang. Israel, Papa Memorial Committee, [197-]. 28, 188 p., illus., ports. (H,Hu)

YIVO: nc   NYPL: *PXT(Papa) 84-505

Parafianowo (R) see under Dokszyce

Parczew (R). *Parczew - sefer zikaron le-kedoshei Parczew ve-ha-seviva* [Parczew - memorial book of the martyrs of Parczew and vicinity]. Eds.: Sh. Zonnenshein et al. Haifa, Association of Former Residents of Parczew in Israel, 1977. 328 p., ports. (H,Y)

Parichi (R) see under Bobruisk

Parysow (R). *Sefer Porisov* [Parysow; a memorial to the Jewish community of Parysow, Poland*]. Ed.: Y. Granatstein. Tel Aviv, Former Residents of Parysow in Israel, 1971. 625 p., ports. (H,Y)

YIVO: 3/70382   NYPL: *PXV(Parysow)

JTS: DS135 P62 P376 S4   YU: K5 P762P

Perehinsko (AH) see under Rozniatow

Petrikov (R) see Piotrkow Trybunalski

Piaski (R). *Pyesk ve-Most; sefer yizkor* [Piesk and Most, a memorial book*]. Tel Aviv, Piesk and Most Societies in Israel and the Disapora, 1975. 657, 17, 52 p., illus. (H,Y,E)

YIVO: 9/77892   NYPL: *PXW(Peski) 77-3794

JTS: DS135 R93 P4 S4   YU: nc 80-0877

Piatnica (R) see under Lomza (*Lomzhe, ir oyfkum un untergang*)

Piesk (R) see Piaski

Piestany (AH) see Postyen

Pilev (R) see Pulawy

Pinczow (R). *Sefer zikaron le-kehilat Pintshev; in Pintshev togt shoyn nisht* [A book of memory of the Jewish community of Pinczow, Poland*]. Ed.: M. Shener. Tel Aviv, Former Residents of Pinczow in Israel and in the Diaspora, 1970. 480 p., ports. (H,Y)

YIVO: 3/69790   NYPL: *PXV(Pinczow)

JTS: DS135 P62 P495   YU: 933.5 P762P

Pinsk (R). *Pinsk sefer edut ve-zikaron le-kehilat Pinsk-Karlin* [Pinsk*]. Ed.: N. Tamir (Mirski). Tel Aviv, Former Residents of Pinsk-Karlin in Israel, 1966-1977. 3 vols., ports., facsims. (H,Y)

YIVO: 9/73394   NYPL: *PXW(Pinsk) 76-279

JTS: +DS135 R93 P5 P5   YU: DS135 R93 P54

BUND: 946175

Pinsk (R). *Toyznt yor Pinsk; geshikhte fun der shtot, der yidisher yishev, institutsyes, sotsyale bavegungen, perzenlekhkeytn, gezelshaftlekhe tuer, Pinsk iber der velt* [A thousand years of Pinsk; history of the city, its Jewish community, institutions, social movements, personalities, community leaders, Pinsk around the world]. Ed.: B. Hoffman. New York, Pinsker Branch 210, Workmen's Circle, 1941. 15, 500 p., illus. (Y)

YIVO: 15/1368   NYPL: *PXV+ Hoffman
JTS: +DS135 R93 P5 H6   BUND: 94624

Piotrkow Trybunalski (R). *Piotrkow Trybunalski ve-ha-seviva* [Piotrkow Trybunalski and vicinity*]. Eds.: Y. Melz, N. (Lavy) Lau. Tel Aviv, Former Residents of Piotrkow Tryb. in Israel, [1965]. 1192 columns, lxiv p., ports., facsims. (H,Y,E)

YIVO: 3/67628A   NYPL: *PXV(Piotrkow)+
JTS: +DS135 P62 P5   YU: DS135 P62 P5

Pitshayev (R) see Poczajow

Plantsh (Polaniec) (R) see under Staszow

Plawno (R) see under Radomsko

Plintsk (R) see Plonsk

Plock (R). *Plotsk; bletlekh geshikhte fun idishn lebn in der alter heym* [Plock; páginas de historia de la vida judía de Allende el Mar*]. Ed.: Yosef Horn. Buenos Aires, Sociedad de Residentes de Plock en la Argentina, 1945. 255 p., illus., ports. (Y)

YIVO: 3/17980   NYPL: *PXV
JTS: DS135 P62 P57 S6   BUND: 94664

Plock (R). *Plotsk; toldot kehila atikat yomin be-Polin* [Plotzk; a history of an ancient Jewish community in Poland*]. Ed.: E. Eisenberg. Tel Aviv, World Committee for the Plotzk Memorial Book, 1967. 684, 96 p., ports., maps, facsims. (H,Y,E)

YIVO: 3/68068   NYPL: *PXV(Plock)+
JTS: DS135 P62 P566   YU: DS135 P62 P566
BUND: 946165

Plock (R). *Yidn in Plotsk* [Jews in Plotzk*]. [By] S. Greenspan. New York, 1960. 325 p., ports. (Y)

YIVO: 3/61317   NYPL: *PXV(Plock)
JTS: DS135 P62 P56 G74   YU: 933.5 P762 P729E
BUND: 101, 946130

Plonsk (R). *Sefer Plonsk ve-ha-seviva* [Memorial book of Plonsk and vicinity]. Ed.: Sh. Zemah. Tel Aviv, Former Residents of Plonsk in Israel, 1963. 775 p., ports., map, facsims. (H,Y)

YIVO: 9/76756   NYPL: *PXV(Plonsk) 76-5726

Plotsk (R) see Plock

Plusy (R) see under Braslaw

Poczajow (R). *Pitshayever yisker-bukh* [Memorial book dedicated to the Jews of Pitchayev-Wohlyn executed by the Germans*]. Ed.: H. Gelernt. Philadelphia, The Pitchayever Wohliner Aid Society, 1960. 311 p., ports. (Y)

YIVO: 3/62172   NYPL: nc
JTS: DS135 R93 P58 G4   BUND: 946136

Poczajow (R) see also under Krzemieniec

Podbrodzie (R) see under Swieciany

Podhajce (AH). *Sefer Podhajce.* Ed.: M. S. Geshuri. Tel Aviv, Podhajce Society, 1972. 295, 17 p., illus. (H,Y,E)

YIVO: 9/73392
NYPL: *PXW(Podgaytsy) 74-2705

Pogost (R) see under Slutsk

Pohost (Pogost) (R) see under Slutsk

Pokshivnitsa (R) see Koprzywnica

Polaniec (R) see under Staszow

Poligon (R) see under Swieciany

Polonnoye (R) see under Novograd-Volynskiy

Porcsalma (AH) see under Csenger

Porisov (R) see Parysow

Porozow (R) see under Wolkowysk (*Volkovisker yisker-bukh*)

Postawy (R) see under Glebokie

Postyen (AH). *Gedenkbuch der Gemeinden Piestany und Umgebung.* [By] Sh. Grunwald. Jerusalem, 1969. 111, [10] p., ports. (G)

JTS: DS135 C96 P52 G78   YU: 933.5 C998P

Pozsony (AH) see *Arim ve-imahot*, vol. 7

Praga (R). *Sefer Praga; mukdash le-zekher kedoshei irenu* [Praga book; dedicated to the memory of the martyrs of our town]. Ed.: Gabriel Weisman. Tel Aviv, Praga Society, 1974. 563 p., illus. (H,Y)

YIVO: 9/73399   NYPL: *PXV(Praga) 77-3783
JTS: DS135 P62 P66 S4

Premisle (AH) see Przemysl

Pressburg (Pozsony) (AH) see under *Arim ve-imahot*, vol. 7

Proshnits (R) see Przasnysz

Proskurov (R). *Khurbn Proskurov; tsum ondenken fun di heylige neshomes vos zaynen umgekumen in der shreklikher shkhite, vos iz ongefirt gevoren durkh di haydamakes* [The destruction of Proskurov; in memory of the sacred souls who perished during the terrible slaughter of the Haidamaks]. New York, 1924. 111 p., illus. (Y,H)

YIVO: 15/1163   NYPL: *PXW(Proskurov)
JTS: DS135 R93 P76 H 7   BUND: 94693

Pruszkow (R). *Sefer Pruszkow, Nadzin ve-ha-seviva* [Memorial book of Pruszkow, Nadzin and vicinity]. Ed.: D. Brodsky. Tel Aviv, Former Residents of Pruszkow in Israel, 1967. 334 p., ports., facsims. (H,Y)

YIVO: 3/67744   NYPL: *PXV(Pruszkow)
JTS: DS135 P62 P7

Pruzana (R). *Pinkas me-hamesh kehilot harevot...* [Memorial book of five destroyed communities...]. Ed.: M. W. Bernstein. Buenos Aires, Former Residents of Pruzana..., 1958. 972 p., ports., facsims. (Y)

YIVO: 3/57408   NYPL: *PXW Bernstein
JTS: DS135 R93 W43 B4   BUND: 946103

Pruzana (R). *Pinkas Pruzhany ve-ha-seviva; edut ve-zikaron le-kehilot she-hushmedu ba-shoa* [Pinkas Pruz'any and its vicinity (Bereze, Malch, Shershev, Seltz and Lineve); chronicle of six communities perished in the Holocaust*]. Ed.: Joseph Friedlaender. Tel Aviv, United Pruziner and Vicinity Relief Committee in New York and in Philadelphia and the Pruz'ana Landshaft Association in Israel, 1983. 542, 169 p., illus., maps, ports. (H,E)

NYPL: *PXW(Pruzhany) 85-1938

Przasnysz (R). *Sefer zikaron kehilat Proshnits* [Memorial book to the community of Proshnitz*]. Ed.: Shlomo Bachrach. Tel Aviv, Proshnitz Society, 1974. 273 p., illus. (H,Y,E)

YIVO: 3/71704   NYPL: *PXV(Przasnysz) 75-762
JTS: DS135 P62 P73 S4   BUND: 519

Przeclaw (AH) see under Radomysl Wielki

Przedborz (R). *Przedborz--33 shanim le-hurbana* [Przedborz memorial book*]. Ed.: Shimon Kanc. Tel Aviv, Przedborz Societies in Israel and America, 1977. 84, 548 p., illus. (H,Y,E)

YIVO: 9/77249   NYPL: 7967
JTS: DS135 P62 P737 P7   YU: nc 78-1486

Przedborz (R) see also under Radomsko

Przedecz (R). *Sefer yizkor le-kedoshei ir Pshaytsh korbanot ha-shoa* [Memorial book to the Holocaust victims of the city of Pshaytsh]. Eds.: Moshe Bilavsky et al. Tel Aviv, Przedecz Societies in Israel and the Diaspora, 1974. 400 p., illus. (H,Y)

YIVO: 9/75392   NYPL: *PXV(Przedecz) 87-532
JTS: DS135 P62 P7377 S4
YU: DS135 P62 P7377

Przemysl (AH). *Sefer Przemysl* [Przemysl memorial book*]. Ed.: A. Menczer. Tel Aviv, Former Residents of Przemysl in Israel, 1964. 522 p., ports., facsims. (H,Y)

YIVO: 3/66756   NYPL: *PXV(Przemysl)
JTS: DS135 P62 P75 M4

Przytyk (R). *Sefer Przytyk.* Ed.: David Shtokfish. Tel Aviv, Przytyk Societies in Israel, France and the USA, 1973. 7, 461 p., illus. (H,Y)

YIVO: 3/71004   NYPL: *PXV(Przytyk) 75-5589
JTS: DS135 P62 P787 S4   YU: DS135 P62 P787

Pshaytsh (R) see Przedecz

Pshedbozh (R) see Przedborz

Pshemishl (AH) see Przemysl

Pshetslav (Przeclaw) (AH) see under Radomysl Wielki

Pshitik (R) see Przytyk

Pulawy (R). *Yisker-bukh Pulawy* [In memoriam--the city of Pulawy*]. Ed.: M. W. Bernstein. New York, Pulawer Yiskor Book Committee, 1964. 494 p., ports., maps, facsims. (Y)

YIVO: 3/67051   NYPL: *PXV(Pulawy)
JTS: DS135 P62 P84 B4   YU: nc 75-1165
BUND: 946162

Pultusk (R). *Pultusk; sefer zikaron* [Pultusk memorial book]. Ed.: Yitzhak Ivri. Tel Aviv, Pultusk Society, 1971. 683 p., illus. (H,Y)

YIVO: 3/70385   NYPL: *PXV(Pultusk)
JTS: DS135 P62 P86 I85   BUND: 496

Punsk (R) see under Suwalki

Raab (AH) see Gyor

Rabka (AH) see under Nowy Targ

Rachev (R) see under Novograd-Volynskiy

Raciaz (R). *Galed le-kehilat Raciaz* [Memorial book of the community of Racionz*]. Ed.: E. Tsoref. Tel Aviv, Former Residents of Raciaz, 1965. 446, 47 p., ports., facsims. (H,Y,E)

YIVO: 3/67244   NYPL: *PXV(Raciaz)
JTS: DS135 P62 R27 Z6

Raczki (R) see under Suwalki

Radikhov (AH) see Radziechow

Radom (R). *Dos yidishe Radom in khurves; ondenkbukh* [The havoc of Jewish Radom*]. Stuttgart, The Committee of Radom Jews in Stuttgart, 1948. 1 vol., illus. (Y)
YIVO: 3/26515   JTS: DS135 P62 R32
YU: 933.47(438)   BUND: 94661

Radom (R). *Radom* [Radom; a memorial to the Jewish community of Radom, Poland*]. Ed.: A. Sh. Stein. Tel Aviv, Former Residents of Radom in Israel and in the Diaspora, 1961. 346, [20] p., ports., facsims. (H)
YIVO: 9/77981   NYPL: *PXV(Radom)+

Radom (R). *Sefer Radom* [The book of Radom; the story of a Jewish community in Poland destroyed by the Nazis*]. Ed.: Y. Perlow; [English section]: Alfred Lipson. Tel Aviv, Former Residents of Radom in Israel and the USA, 1961. 451, [23], lxxviii, 120 p., illus., ports. (Y,E)
YIVO: 3/66110   NYPL: *PXV(Radom)+
JTS: +DS135 P62 R32 P4   YU: 933.5 P762R
BUND: 946155

Radomsko (R). *Sefer yizkor le-kehilat Radomsk ve-ha-seviva* [Memorial book of the community of Radomsk and vicinity]. Ed.: L. Losh. Tel Aviv, Former Residents of Radomsk..., 1967. 603 p., ports., music, facsims. (H,Y)
YIVO: 3/68358   NYPL: *PXV(Radomsko)+
JTS: +DS135 P62 R34 L6   YU: 933.5 P762R
BUND: 946176

Radomysl Wielki (AH). *Radomysl Rabati ve-ha-seviva; sefer yizkor* [Radomysl Wielki and neighbourhood; memorial book*]. Eds.: H. Harshoshanim et al. Tel Aviv, Former Residents of Radomysl and Surroundings in Israel, 1965. 1065, liii p., ports., map, facsims. (H,Y,E)
YIVO: 3/70295   NYPL: *PXV(Radomysl)+
JTS: DS135 P62 R3267

Radoszkowice (R). *Radoshkovits; sefer zikaron* [Radoshkowitz; a memorial to the Jewish community*]. Eds.: M. Robinson et al. Tel Aviv, Former Residents of Radoshkowitz in Israel, 1953. 222 p., ports. (H)
YIVO: 3/43756   NYPL: *PXW(Radoshkovichi)
JTS: DS135 R93 R3   YU: DS135 R93 R3

Radzanow (R) see under Szransk

Radziechow (AH). *Sefer zikaron le-kehilot Radikhov, Lopatyn, Witkow Nowy, Cholojow, Toporow, Stanislawcyzk, Stremiltsh, Shtruvits, ve-ha-kefarim Ubin, Barylow, Wolica-Wygoda, Skrilow, Zawidcze, Mikolajow, Dmytrow, Sienkow, ve-od* [Memorial book of Radikhov, Lopatyn, Witkow Nowy, Cholojow, Toporow, Stanislawcyzk, Stremiltsh, Shtruvits, and the villages Ubin, Barylow, Wolica-Wygoda, Skrilow (i.e., Sknilow?), Zawidcze, Mikolajow, Dmytrow, Sienkow, etc.]. Ed.: G. Kressel. Tel Aviv, Society of Radikhov, Lopatyn and Vicinity, 1976. 656 p., illus. (H,Y)
YIVO: nc   NYPL: 11368
YU: nc 81-0185

Radzin (R). *Radzin 1939-1943*. Ed.: Y. Rosenkrantz. Tel Aviv, Committee of Former Residents of Radzin and Pudel in Israel. 17 p. (H), mimeo.
YIVO: 3/42420

Radzin (R). *Sefer Radzin* [The book of Radzin]. Ed.: I. Siegelman. Tel Aviv, Council of Former Residents of Radzin (Podolsky) in Israel, 1957. 358 p. (H,Y)
YIVO: 3/51724   JTS: DS135 P62 R33 S55

Radziwillow (R). *Radziwillow; sefer zikaron* [A memorial to the Jewish community of Radziwillow, Wolyn*]. Ed.: Y. Adini. Tel Aviv, The Radziwillow Organization in Israel, 1966. 438, [15] p., ports., map, facsims. (H,Y)
YIVO: 9/77486   NYPL: *PXW(Cherwonoarmeisk)
JTS: DS135 R93 R32 R3   YU: 933.5 R969 R133 A235

Radzymin (R). *Sefer zikaron le-kehilat Radzymin* [Le livre du souvenir de la communauté juive de Radzymin*]. Ed.: Gershon Hel. Tel Aviv, The Encyclopaedia of the Jewish Diaspora, 1975. 389 p., illus. (H,Y,F)
YIVO: 9/75284
NYPL: *PXV(Radzymin)+ 77-3792
JTS: +DS135 P62 R342 S4
YU: DS135 P62 R3287

Rakhov (R) see Annopol

Rakishok (R) see Rokiskis

Rakospalota (AH). *Toldot kehilat Rakospalota* [History of the Rakospalota community]. [By] Rachel Aharoni. Tel Aviv, 1978. 52, 204 p., illus. (H,Hu)

Rakow (R). *Sefer zikaron le-kehilat Rakow* [Memorial book of the community of Rakow]. Ed.: H. Abramson. Tel Aviv, Former Residents of Rakow in Israel and the USA, 1959. 184, [13] p., ports., facsims. (H,Y)

YIVO: 3/64347   YU: nc 75-1176
BUND: 946168

Ratno (R). *Ratne; sipura shel kehila yehudit she-hushmeda* [Ratne; the story of a Jewish community that was destroyed]. Ed.: Nahman Tamir. Tel Aviv, Ratno Society in Israel, 1983. 331 p., illus., map, ports. (H)

NYPL: 17628

Ratno (R). *Yisker-bukh Ratne; dos lebn un umkum fun a yidish shtetl in Volin* [Memorial book of Ratno; the life and destruction of a Jewish town in Wolyn]. Eds.: Y. Botoshansky, Y. Yanasovitsh. Buenos Aires, Former Residents of Ratno in Argentina and the USA, 1954. 806 p., ports., map (Y)

YIVO: 3/45636   NYPL: *PXW(Ratno)
YU: DS135 R93 R33   BUND: 94629

Rawa Ruska (AH). *Sefer zikaron le-kehilat Rawa Ruska ve-ha-seviva* [Rawa Ruska memorial book*]. Eds.: A. M. Ringel, I. Z. Rubin. Tel Aviv, Rawa Ruska Society, 1973. 468 p., illus. (H,Y,E)

YIVO: 9/73393
NYPL: *PXW(Rawa Ruska)+ 76-2181
JTS: +DS135 R93 R377 S4
YU: +DS135 R93 R377

Raysha (AH) see Rzeszow

Rayvits (R) see Rejowiec

Rejowiec (R). *"Shtil vi in Rayvits..."; oyfn khurbn fun mayn heym* ["As silent as in Rayvits..."; on the destruction of my home]. [By] Shmuel Drelikhman. Bergen-Belsen, 1947. 46 p., ports. (Y)

YIVO: 3/36899

Rembertow (R). *Sefer zikaron le-kehilot Rembertow, Okuniew, Milosna* [Yizkor book in memory of Rembertov, Okuniev, Milosna*]. Ed.: Shimon Kanc. Tel Aviv, Rembertow, Okuniew and Milosna Societies in Israel, the USA, France, Mexico City, Canada, Chile and Brazil, 1974. 16, 465 p., illus. (H,Y)

YIVO: 9/73405   NYPL: *PXV(Rembertow) 75-3319
JTS: DS135 P62 R456 Y59
YU: DS135 P62 R456

Retteg (AH) see under Des

Rietavas (R). *Sefer Ritova; gal-ed le-zekher ayaratenu* [Memorial book: the Ritavas Community; a tribute to the memory of our town*]. Ed.: Alter Levite. Tel Aviv, Ritova Societies in Israel and the Diaspora, 1977. 37, 223 p., illus. (H,Y,E)

YIVO: 9/78958

Rimszan (Rymszany) (R) see under Braslaw

Riskeva (R) see Ruscova

Rohatyn (AH). *Kehilat Rohatyn ve-ha-seviva* [Rohatyn; the history of a Jewish community*]. Ed.: M. Amihai. Tel Aviv, Former Residents of Rohatyn in Israel, 1962. 362, [15], 62 p., ports., facsims. (H,Y,E)

YIVO: 3/65794, 3/66846   NYPL: *PXV(Rohatyn)

Rokiskis (R). *Yisker-bukh fun Rakishok un umgegnt* [Yizkor book of Rakishok and environs*]. Ed.: M. Bakalczuk-Felin. Johannesburg, The Rakishker Landsmanshaft of Johannesburg, 1952. 626 p., ports., facsim. (Y)

YIVO: 3/41767   NYPL: *PXW(Rokishkis)
JTS: DS135 L5 R3 R34   YU: DS135 R93 R63
BUND: 9465

Rokitno (R). *Rokitno (Volin) ve-ha-seviva; sefer edut ve-zikaron* [Rokitno-Wolyn and surroundings; memorial book and testimony]. Ed.: E. Leoni. Tel Aviv, Former Residents of Rokitno in Israel, 1967. 459 p., ports., maps (H,Y)

YIVO: nc   NYPL: *PXW(Rokitno)

Romanova (R) see under Slutsk

Rotin (AH) see Rohatyn

Rovno (R) see Rowne

Rowne (R). *A zikorn far Rowne* [In memory of Rowne]. Eds.: Y. Margulyets, Z. Finkelshteyn, Y. Shvartsapel. [Munich], Rowne Landsmanshaft in Germany, [1947?]. 43 p., ports. (Y), mimeo.

YIVO: 3/59880

Rowne (R). *Rowne; sefer zikaron* [Rowno; a memorial to the Jewish community of Rowno, Wolyn*]. Ed.: A. Avitachi. Tel Aviv, "Yalkut Wolyn"--Former Residents of Rowno in Israel, 1956. 591 p., ports., map, facsims. (H)

YIVO: 3/49957   NYPL: *PXV(Rovno)
JTS: DS135 R93 R6 A9   YU: DS135 R93 R6

Rozan (R). *Sefer zikaron le-kehilat Rozan (al ha-Narew)* [Rozhan memorial book*]. Ed.: Benjamin Halevy. Tel Aviv, Rozhan Societies in Israel and the USA, 1977. 518, 96 p., illus. (H,Y,E)
YIVO: nc NYPL: *PXV(Rozan) 82-1627
JTS: DS135 P62 R6 S4 YU: nc 78-0238
BUND: 438

Rozana (R). *Rozhinoy; sefer zikaron le-kehilat Rozhinoy ve-ha-seviva* [Rozana; a memorial to the Jewish community*]. Ed.: M. Sokolowsky. Tel Aviv, Former Residents of Rozhinoy in Israel, 1957. 232 p., ports. (H,Y)
YIVO: 3/51689 NYPL: *PXW(Ruzhany)
JTS: DS135 R93 R65 S4 BUND: 946143

Rozanka (R) see under Szczuczyn (*Sefer zikaron le-kehilot Szczuczyn, Wasiliszki...*)

Rozhan (R) see Rozan

Rozhinoy (R) see Rozana

Rozniatow (AH). *Sefer zikaron le-kehilat Rozniatow, Perehinsko, Broszniow, Swaryczow ve-ha-seviva* [Yizkor-book in memory of Rozniatow, Perehinsko, Broszniow, Swaryczow and environs*]. Ed.: Shimon Kanc. Tel Aviv, Rozniatow, Perehinsko, Broszniow and Environs Societies in Israel and the USA, 1974. 58, 537 p., illus. (H,Y,E)
YIVO: nc

Rozprza (R) see under Piotrkow Trybunalski

Rozwadow (AH). *Sefer yizkor Rozwadow ve-ha-seviva* [Rozwadow memorial book*]. Ed.: N. Blumental. Jerusalem, Former Residents of Rozwadow in Israel..., 1968. 349 p., ports. (H,Y,E)
YIVO: 3/68092, 9/73391 NYPL: *PXV(Rozwado)+
JTS: +DS135 P62 R65 S4 YU: DS135 P62 R65

Rozyszcze (R). *Rozyszcze ayarati* [Rozyszcze my old home*]. Ed.: Gershon Zik. Tel Aviv, Rozyszcze Societies in Israel, the United States, Canada, Brazil, and Argentina, 1976. 482, 76 p., illus. (H,Y,E)
YIVO: nc

Rubeshov (R) see Hrubieszow

Rubiezewicze (R). *Sefer Rubizhevitsh, Derevne ve-ha-seviva* [Rubiezewicze and surroundings book*]. Ed.: D. Shtokfish. Tel Aviv, 1968. 422 p., illus. (Y,H)
YIVO: 3/68352 NYPL: *PXW(Rubezhevichi)
JTS: DS135 R93 R77

Rubiezewicze (R) see also under Stolpce

Rudki (AH). *Rudki; sefer yizkor le-yehudei Rudki ve-ha-seviva* [Rudki memorial book; of the Jews of Rudki and vicinity*]. Ed.: Joseph Chrust. Israel, Rudki Society, 1978. 374 p., illus. (H,Y,E)
YIVO: nc NYPL: *PXW(Rudki) 84-303

Ruscova (AH). *Sefer le-zikaron kedoshei Ruskova ve-Soblas, mehoz Marmarosh* [Memorial book of the martyrs of Ruskova and Soblas, Marmarosh District]. Ed.: Y. Z. Moskowits. Tel Aviv, Former Residents of Ruskova and Soblas in Israel and in the Diaspora, 1969. 126 p., ports., facsims. (H,Y)
YIVO: 3/70380 NYPL: *PXM(Ruskova) 77-1765
JTS: DS135 R72 R85 S4 YU: DS135 R72 R877

Ryki (R). *Yisker-bukh tsum fareybikn dem ondenk fun der khorev-gevorener yidisher kehile Ryki* [Ryki; a memorial to the community of Ryki, Poland*]. Ed.: Shimon Kanc. Tel Aviv, Ryki Societies in Israel, Canada, Los Angeles, France, and Brazil, 1973. 611 p., illus. (H,Y)
YIVO: 3/71650 NYPL: *PXV(Ryki) 76-2058
JTS: DS135 P62 R93 Y59

Rypin (R). *Sefer Rypin* [Ripin; a memorial to the Jewish community of Ripin--Poland*]. Ed.: Sh. Kanc. Tel Aviv, Former Residents of Ripin in Israel and in the Diaspora, 1962. 942, 15 p., ports., facsims. (H,Y,E)
YIVO: 3/66154 NYPL: *PXV(Rypin)+
JTS: DS135 P62 R82 S4 BUND: 504

Rytwiany (R) see under Staszow

Rzeszow (AH). *Kehilat Raysha; sefer zikaron* [Rzeszow Jews; memorial book*]. Ed.: M. Yari-Wold. Tel Aviv, Former Residents of Rzeszow in Israel and the USA, 1967. 620, 142 p., ports., maps, facsims. (H,Y,E)
YIVO: 3/68095 NYPL: *PXV(Rzeszow)+
JTS: +DS135 P62 R95 YU: DS135 P62 R95

Saloniki (Turkey). *Saloniki; ir va-em be-yisrael* [Salonique, ville-mère en Israël*]. Jerusalem-Tel Aviv, Centre de recherches sur le Judaisme de Salonique, Union des Juifs de Grèce, 1967. 358, xviii p., ports., maps, facsims. (H,F)
YIVO: 3/71703 NYPL: *PXM+
JTS: +DS135 G72 S2

Saloniki (Turkey). *Zikhron Saloniki; gedulata ve-hurbana shel Yerushalayim de-Balkan* [Zikhron Saloniki; grandeza i destruyicion de Yeruchalayim del Balkan*]. Tel Aviv, Committee for the Publication of the Saloniki Book, [1971/72-1985/86]. 2 vols., illus., facsims., ports. (H,J)
NYPL: *PXM 76-2119   JTS: +DS135 G72 S2 Z5
YU: DS135 G72 T59

Sambor (AH). *Sefer Sambor-Stary Sambor; pirkei edut ve-zikaron le-kehilot Sambor-Stary Sambor mi-reshitan ve-ad hurbanan* [The book of Sambor and Stari Sambor; a memorial to the Jewish communities of Sambor and Stari Sambor, the story of the two Jewish communities from their beginnings to their end*]. Ed.: Alexander Manor. Tel Aviv, Sambor/Stary Sambor Society, 1980. xlvi, 323 p., illus. (H,Y,E)
YIVO: 9/79198   NYPL: *PXV(Sambor) 82-2353
JTS: DS135 P62 S15 M3   YU: DS135 R93 S147

Sammerein (Somorja) (AH) see under Dunaszerdahely

Samorin (Somorja) (AH) see under Dunaszerdahely

Sanok (AH). *Sefer zikaron le-kehilat Sanok ve-ha-seviva* [Memorial book of Sanok and vicinity]. Ed.: E. Sharvit. Jerusalem, Former Residents of Sanok and Vicinity in Israel, 1970. 686 p., ports., facsims. (H,Y)
YIVO: 3/69257   NYPL: *PXV(Sanok)
JTS: DS135 P62 S16   YU: 933.5 P762 S228

Sanok (AH) see also under Dynow (*Khurbn Dynow*)

Sants (AH) see Nowy Sacz

Sarkeystsene (Szarkowszczyna) (R) see under Glebokie

Sarnaki (R). *Sefer yizkor le-kehilat Sarnaki* [Memorial book of the community of Sarnaki]. Ed.: D. Shuval. Haifa, Former Residents of Sarnaki in Israel, 1968. 415 p., ports. (H,Y)
YIVO: 3/68205   NYPL: *PXV(Sarnaki)
JTS: DS135 P62 S2 S4   YU: 933.47(438) S246S

Sarny (R). *Sefer yizkor le-kehilat Sarny* [Memorial book of the community of Sarny]. Ed.: Y. Kariv. Tel Aviv, Former Residents of Sarny and Vicinity in Israel, 1961. 508, 32 p., ports., facsims. (H,Y)
YIVO: 3/65716   NYPL: *PXW(Sarny)
JTS: DS135 R93 S3   YU: DS135 R93 S3

Sasow (AH). *Mayn shtetl Sasow* [My town Sasow]. [By] Moshe Rafael. Jerusalem, 1979. (Y)

Satmar (AH) see Satu Mare

Satorujhely (AH) see under Zemplenmegye

Satu Mare (AH). *Zekhor et Satmar; sefer ha-zikaron shel yehudei Satmar* [Remember Satmar; the memorial book of the Jews of Satmar]. Ed.: Naftali Stern. Bnei Brak, 1984. 160, 240 p., illus., maps, ports. (H,Hu)
NYPL: 19783

Schodnica (AH) see under Drohobycz

Schutt Szerdahely (AH) see Dunaszerdahely

Secureni (R) see Sekiryany

Sedziszow (R) see under Wodzislaw

Sekiryani (R). *Sekurian (Bessarabia) be-vinyana u-be-hurbana* [Sekiryani, Bessarabia--alive and destroyed]. Ed.: Z. Igrat. Tel Aviv, [Committee of Former Residents of Sekiryani], 1954. 260 p., ports. (H)
YIVO: nc   NYPL: *PXW(Sekiryany)

Selib (Wsielub) (R) see under Nowogrodek

Selish (AH) see Nagyszollos

Selts (Sielec) (R) see under Pruzana

Semyatichi (R) see Siemiatycze

Sendishev (Sedziszow) (R) see under Wodzislaw

Serock (R). *Sefer Serotsk* [The book of Serock]. Ed.: M. Gelbart. Former Residents of Serock in Israel, 1971. 736 p., ports. (H,Y)
YIVO: 3/71564   NYPL: *PXV(Serock) 75-3340
JTS: DS135 P62 S4 S4   YU: 933.47(438) S486G

Sevlus (AH) see Nagyszollos

Shchedrin (R) see under Bobruisk

Shebreshin (R) see Szczebrzeszyn

Shedlets (R) see Siedlce

Shelib (Wsielub) (R) see under Nowogrodek

Sherpts (R) see Sierpc

Shidlovtse (R) see Szydlowiec

Shimsk (R) see Szumsk

Shkud (R) see Skuodas

Shpola (R). *Shpola; masekhet hayei yehudim ba-ayara* [Shpola; a picture of Jewish life in the town]. [By] David Cohen. [Haifa], Association of Former Residents of Shpola (Ukraine) in Israel, 1965. 307 p., ports. (H)
YIVO: 3/67592   NYPL: *PXW(Shpola)
JTS: DS135 R93 S47   YU: 933.47 S559C

Shransk (R) see Szransk

Shtruvits (Szczurowice) (AH) see under Radziechow

Shumen (Bulgaria) see Shumla

Shumla (Bulgaria). *Yehudei Bulgaria--Kehilat Shumla* [The Jews in Bulgaria--The community in Shumla*]. [By] Benjamin J. Arditti. Tel Aviv, Community Council, 1968. 179 p., ports. (H)
JTS: DS135 B83 S53   YU: nc 75-950846

Siedlce (R). *Oyf di khurves fun mayn heym (khurbn Shedlets)* [On the ruins of my home; the destruction of Siedlce]. [By] M. Fainzilber. Tel Aviv, Committee of Townspeople, 1952. 260 p., illus., map, ports. (Y)
YIVO: 3/39932

Siedlce (R). *Sefer yizkor le-kehilat Shedlets* [Memorial book of the community of Siedlce]. Ed.: A. W. Yassni. Buenos Aires, Former Residents of Siedlce in Israel and Argentina, 1956. xvi, 813 p., ports., facsims. (H,Y)
YIVO: 3/50697   NYPL: *PXV(Siedlce)
YU: 933.5 P762S   BUND: 94685

Siedliszcze (R). *Sefer zikaron le-kehilat Siedliszcze ve-ha-seviva* [Memorial book of the community of Siedliszcze and vicinity]. Ed.: B. Haruvi. Tel Aviv, Former Residents of Siedliszcze in Israel, 1970. 360 p., ports., facsims. (H,Y)
YIVO: 3/71322   NYPL: *PXV(Siedlce) 75-1502
JTS: DS135 P62 S544 S4

Sielec (R) see under Pruzana

Siemiatycze (R). *Kehilat Semiatycze* [The community of Semiatich*]. Ed.: E. Tash (Tur-Shalom). Tel Aviv, Assoc. of Former Residents of Semiatich in Israel and the Diaspora, 1965. 449 p., ports., map, facsims. (H,Y,E)
YIVO: 3/67042   NYPL: *PXV(Siemiatycze)
JTS: DS135 P62 S555 T3   BUND: 491 shelf

Sienkow (AH) see under Radziechow

Sierpc (R). *Kehilat Sierpc; sefer zikaron* [The community of Sierpc; memorial book]. Ed.: E. Talmi (Wloka). Tel Aviv, Former Residents of Sierpc in Israel and Abroad, 1959. 603 p., ports., map, facsims. (H,Y)
YIVO: 3/59900   NYPL: *PXV(Sierpc)+
JTS: DS135 P62 S557 T3   BUND: 946196

Sierpc (R). *Khurbn Sierpc 1939-1945; zikhroynes fun di ibergeblibene landslayt vos gefinen zikh in der Amerikaner Zone in Daytshland* [The destruction of Sierpc 1939-1945; memories of the remnants of the community of Sierpc in the American Zone in Germany]. Eds.: A. Meirantz, H. Nemlich. Munich, Committee of the Former Residents of Sierpc in the American Zone in Germany, 1947. 55 p., ports. (Y)
BUND: 94526

Sierpc (R). *Zaml-bukh fun Sherptser sheyres ha-khurbn, 1939-1945* [Collection of Sierpc Holocaust survivors, 1939-1945]. [Germany], Sherpcer Jewish Committee (U.S. Zone, Germany), 1948. 93 p., illus., ports. (Y)
YIVO: 3/48016   BUND: 94451

Siniawka (R) see under Kleck

Sislevitsh (R) see Swislocz

Skala (AH). *Sefer Skala*. Ed.: Max Mermelstein (Weidenfeld). New York-Tel Aviv, Skala Benevolent Society, 1978. 98, 261 p., illus. (H,Y,E)
YIVO: 9/77607
NYPL: *PXW(Skala Podolskaya) 78-4402
JTS: DS135 R93 S5 S4

Skalat (AH). *Es shtarbt a shtetl; megiles Skalat* [Skalat destroyed*]. [By] Abraham Weissbrod. Ed.: I. Kaplan. Munich, Central Historical Commission of the Central Committee of Liberated Jews in the U.S. Zone of Germany, 1948. 184 p., maps, ports. (Y)
YIVO: 3/26383   NYPL: *ZP-515
JTS: DS135 R93 S537 W4
YU: 933.47 W342   BUND: 945186

Skalat (AH). *Skalat; kovets zikaron le-kehila she-harva ba-shoa* [Skalat; memorial volume of the community which perished in the Holocaust]. Ed.: H. Bronstein. Tel Aviv, The Yaacov Krol School in Petah-Tikva and Former Residents of Skalat in Israel, 1971. 160 p., ports., facsims. (H)
YIVO: 3/71321   NYPL: *PXW(Skalat)
JTS: DS135 R93 S537 S55
YU: DS135 R93 S537

Skarzysko-Kamienna (R). *Skarzysko-Kamienna sefer zikaron* [The "yischor" book in memoriam of the Jewish community of Skarzysko and its surroundings*]. Tel Aviv, Skarzysko Society, 1973. 260 p., illus. (H,Y)
YIVO: 3/71671
NYPL: *PXV(Skarzysko)+ 78-5229

Skierniewice (R). *Sefer Skierniewice* [The book of Skierniewice]. Ed.: J. Perlow. Tel Aviv, Former Residents of Skierniewice in Israel, 1955. 722 p., ports., facsims. (Y)
YIVO: 3/61318A
NYPL: *PXV(Skierniewice) 75-5640
JTS: DS135 P62 S57 P4   BUND: 94689

Sknilow (AH) see under Radziechow

Skole (AH) see under Galicia (*Gedenkbukh Galicia*)

Skuodas (R). *Kehilat Shkud; kovets zikaron* [Memorial book of Skuodas]. Tel Aviv, Former Residents of Skuodas, 1948. 68 p., ports., facsims. (H,Y)
YIVO: 3/57525   NYPL: *PXV(Skuodas) 84-448

Slobodka (R) see under Braslaw

Slonim (R). *Pinkas Slonim* [Memorial book of Slonim]. Ed.: K. Lichtenstein. Tel Aviv, Former Residents of Slonim in Israel, [1962-1979]. 4 vols., illus., ports. (H,Y,E)
YIVO: 3/65725   NYPL: *PXW(Slonim)+
JTS: DS135 P62 S54 L5   YU: 933.5 R969S
BUND: 515 (vols. 1-2)

Slupia (R) see under Ostrowiec

Slutsk (R). *Pinkas Slutsk u-benoteha* [Slutsk and vicinity memorial book*]. Eds.: N. Chinitz, Sh. Nachmani. Tel Aviv, Yizkor-Book Committee, 1962. 450 p., ports., maps, facsims. (H,Y,E)
YIVO: 3/65803   NYPL: *PXW(Slutsk)
JTS: DS135 R93 S56 P55   YU: DS135 R93 S57
BUND: 946156

Sluzewo (R) see under Wloclawek

Smorgonie (R). *Smorgon mehoz Vilno; sefer edut ve-zikaron* [Smorgonie, District Vilna; memorial book and testimony]. Ed.: E. Tash (Tur-Shalom). [Tel Aviv], Assoc. of Former Residents of Smorgonie in Israel and USA, 1965. 584 p., ports., facsims. (H,Y)
YIVO: 3/67808   NYPL: *PXW(Smorgon)
JTS: DS135 R93 S58   YU: 933.5 L7765

Smotrich (R) see under Kamenets-Podolskiy

Soblas (AH) see under Ruscova

Sobolew (R) see under Laskarzew

Sobota (R) see under Lowicz

Sochaczew (R). *Pinkas Sochaczew* [Memorial book of Sochaczew]. Eds.: A. Sh. Stein, G. Weissman. Jerusalem, Former Residents of Sochaczew in Israel, 1962. 843 p., ports. (H,Y)
YIVO: 3/65715   NYPL: *PXV(Sochaczew)
BUND: 517, 946157

Sokal (AH). *Sefer Sokal, Tartakow...ve-ha-seviva* [Memorial book of Sokal, Tartakow...and surroundings]. Ed.: A. Chomel. Tel Aviv, Former Residents of Sokal and Surroundings, 1968. 576 p., ports., facsims. (H,Y)
YIVO: 3/68373   NYPL: *PXW(Sokal)
JTS: DS135 R93 S59 S4

Sokolka (R). *Sefer Sokolka* [Memorial book of Sokolka]. Jerusalem, The Encyclopaedia of the Jewish Diaspora, 1968. 768 columns, ports., facsims. (H,Y)
YIVO: 3/69382   NYPL: *PXV(Sokolka)+
JTS: +DS135 P62 S63   YU: DS135 P62 S63

Sokolovka (Yustingrad) (R) see Yustingrad

Sokolow (R). *In shotn fun Treblinka (khurbn Sokolow-Podlaski)* [In the shadow of Treblinka*]. [By] Symcha Polakiewicz. Tel Aviv, Sokolow-Podlaski Society, 1957. 167 p. (Y)
YIVO: 3/51898   NYPL: *PXV
JTS: DS135 P62 S65 P6

Sokolow (R). *Mayn khorev shtetl Sokolow; shilderungen, bilder un portretn fun a shtot umgekumene yidn* [My destroyed town of Sokolow]. [By] Peretz Granatstein. Buenos Aires, Union Central Israelita Polaca en la Argentina, 1946. 188 p., illus. (Y)
YIVO: 3/26818   NYPL: *PXV(Sokolow)
JTS: DS135 P62 S65 G7   BUND: 94480

Sokolow (R). *Sefer ha-zikaron; Sokolow-Podlask* [Memorial book Sokolow-Podlask]. Ed.: M. Gelbart. Tel Aviv, Former Residents of Sokolow-Podlask in Israel and...in the USA, 1962. 758, [55] p., ports. (Y,H)
YIVO: 3/66264
NYPL: *PXV(Sokolow-Podlaski) 75-5625
YU: 933.5 P762S G314   BUND: 946172

Sokoly (R). *Sefer zikaron le-kedoshei Sokoly* [Memorial book of the martyrs of Sokoly]. Ed.: M. Grossman. Tel Aviv, Former Residents of Sokoly, 1962. 625 p., ports. (Y)
YIVO: 3/65784   NYPL: *PXV(Sokoly) 75-3422
JTS: DS135 P62 S64 G76

Sokoly (R). *Sokoly--be-ma'avak le-hayim* [Sokoly--in a struggle for survival]. Trans. and ed.: Shmuel Klisher. Tel Aviv, Sokoly Society, 1975. 438 p., illus. (H)
NYPL: *PXV(Sokoly) 84-375

Sombor (AH) see Zombor

Somorja (AH) see under Dunaszerdahely

Sompolno (R). *Dapei ed shel sarid ha-ayara Sompolno* [Pages of witness of the remnants of the town Sompolno]. [By] Yitzhak Kominkovski. Tel Aviv, Alef, 1981. 103 p., illus., ports. (H)
NYPL: 12155   JTS: DS135 P62 S67
YU: DS135 P62 S64

Sonik (AH) see Sanok

Sopockinie (R). *Korot ayara ahat; megilat ha-shigshug ve-ha-hurban shel kehilat Sopotkin* [Sopotkin; in memory of the Jewish community*]. [By] Alexander Manor (Menchinsky). [Tel Aviv], Sopotkin Society, 1960. 124 p., illus. (H)
YIVO: 9/77907

Sopotkin (R) see Sopockinie

Sosnovoye (R) see Ludwipol

Sosnowiec (AH). *Sefer Sosnowiec ve-ha-seviva be-Zaglembie* [Book of Sosnowiec and the surrounding region in Zaglebie]. Ed.: Meir Shimon Geshuri (Bruckner). Tel Aviv, Sosnowiec Societies in Israel, the United States, France, and other countries, 1973-1974. 2 vols., illus. (H,Y)
YIVO: 3/71651   NYPL: *PXV(Sosnowiec)85-2020
JTS: DS135 P62 S69 S4   YU: DS135 P62 S657

Stanislawczyk (AH) see under Radziechow

Stanislawow (AH). *Al horvotayikh Stanislawow; divrei edut le-kilayon kehilat Stanislawow ve-sevivata mipi adei-riah ve-al-pi teudot* [On the ruins of Stanislawow; concerning the annihilation of the community of Stanislawow and vicinity...]. [By] Ami Weitz. Tel Aviv, 1947. 113 p. (H)
YIVO: 3/42604   NYPL: *PXV(Stanislawow)

Stanislawow (AH) see also under *Arim ve-imahot*, vol. 5

Starachowice (R) see under Wierzbnik

Starobin (R) see under Slutsk

Stary Sambor (AH) see under Sambor

Starye Dorogi (R) see under Slutsk

Staszow (R). *Sefer Staszow* [The Staszow book*]. Ed.: E. Erlich. Tel Aviv, Former Residents of Staszow in Israel...and in the Diaspora, 1962. 690 p., ports., facsims. (H,Y,E)
YIVO: 3/66333   NYPL: *PXV(Staszow)
JTS: DS135 P62 S72 E4

Stavische (R). *Stavisht.* Ed.: A. Weissman. Tel Aviv, The Stavisht Society, New York, 1961. 252 columns, ports. (H,Y)
YIVO: 3/65258   NYPL: 5200

Stawiski (R). *Stawiski; sefer yizkor* [Stawiski memorial book]. Ed.: I. Rubin. Tel Aviv, Stavisk Society, 1973. 379, 5 p., illus. (H,Y,E)
YIVO: 3/71563   NYPL: *PXV(Stawiski) 76-2105
JTS: DS135 P62 S737 R8

Stepan (R). *Ayaratenu Stepan* [The Stepan Story; excerpts*]. Ed.: Yitzchak Ganuz. Tel Aviv, Stepan Society, 1977. 4, 364 p., illus. (H,E)
YIVO: 9/77385   NYPL: 8926
JTS: DS135 P62 S7385 G3
YU: DS135 R93 S663

Steybts (R) see Stolpce

Stiyanev (Stojanow) (AH) see under Sokal

Stoczek-Wegrowski (R). *Pinkes Stok (bay Vengrov); matsevet netsah* [Memorial book of Stok, near Wegrow]. Ed.: I. Zudicker. Buenos Aires, Stok Societies in Israel, North America and Argentina, 1974. 654 p., illus. (H,Y)
YIVO: 9/73580   NYPL: *PXV(Stok) 79-1032
JTS: DS135 P62 S74 P55   BUND: 429

Stojaciszki (R) see under Swieciany

Stojanow (AH) see under Sokal

Stok (R) see Stoczek-Wegrowski

Stolin (R). *Albom Stolin* [Stolin album]. Eds.: Phinehas Doron, Z. Blizovski. Jerusalem, 1960. 88 p., illus., ports. (H,Y)
YIVO: 3/63996

Stolin (R). *Stolin; sefer zikaron le-kehilat Stolin ve-ha-seviva* [Stolin; a memorial to the Jewish communities of Stolin and vicinity*]. Eds.: A. Avatichi, Y. Ben-Zakkai. Tel Aviv, Former Residents of Stolin and Vicinity in Israel, 1952. 263 p., ports. (H)
YIVO: 3/29601   NYPL: *PXW(Stolin)

Stolpce (R). *Sefer zikaron; Steibts-Sverzhnye ve-ha-ayarot ha-semukhot...* [Memorial volume of Steibtz-Swerznie and the neighbouring villages...*]. Ed.: N. Hinitz. Tel Aviv, Former Residents of Steibtz in Israel, 1964. 537, xxiii p., ports., map, facsims. (H,Y,E)
YIVO: 3/66777   NYPL: *PXW(Stolbtsy)
JTS: DS135 R93 S86 H5   YU: DS135 R93 S68

Stramtura (AH). *Agadot Strimtera; sipura shel kehilat yehudit me-reshita ve-ad ahrita* [Tales of Strimtera; the story of a Jewish community from beginning to end]. [By] Sh. Avni. Tel Aviv, Reshafim, [1985/86]. 270 p. (H)
NYPL: 20717   YU: nc 88-0942

Stremiltsh (Strzemilcze) (AH) see under Radziechow

Strimtera (AH) see Stramtura

Strusow (AH) see under Trembowla

Stryj (AH). *Sefer Stryj* [Memorial book of Stryj]. Eds.: N. Kudish et al. Tel Aviv, Former Residents of Stryj in Israel, 1962. 260, 68 p., ports., facsims. (H,Y,E)
YIVO: 3/65799   NYPL: *PXW(Stryj)
JTS: DS135 R93 S87   YU: DS135 R93 S83
BUND: 502

Strzegowo (R). *Strzegowo yisker-bukh* [Memorial book of Strzegowo]. New York, United Strzegower Relief Committee, 1951. 135, [18] p., ports., facsims. (H,Y,E)
YIVO: 3/29168   NYPL: *PXV(Strzegowo)
JTS: DS135 P62 S75 U5   BUND: 94655

Strzemilcze (AH) see under Radziechow

Strzyzow (AH). *Sefer Strizhuv ve-ha-seviva* [Memorial book of Strzyzow and vicinity]. Eds.: J. Berglas, Sh. Yahalomi (Diamant). Tel Aviv, Former Residents of Strzyzow in Israel and Diaspora, 1969. 480 p., ports., facsims. (H,Y)
YIVO: 3/70008   NYPL: *PXV(Strzyzow)+
JTS: DS135 P62 S77   YU: 933.5 P762S

Stutshin (R) see Szczuczyn

Sucha (AH) see under Wadowice

Suchocin (R) see under Plonsk

Suchowola (R). *Khurbn Sukhovolye; lezikorn fun a yidish shtetl tsvishn Bialystok un Grodne* [The Holocaust in Suchowola; in memory of a Jewish shtetl between Bialystok and Grodno]. Description by Lazar Simhah; ed. by Sh. Zabludovski. Mexico, published by a group of Suchowola Landslayt in Mexico, 1947. 72 p., illus., ports. (Y)
YIVO: 3/23410   BUND: 94646

Suchowola (R). *Sefer Suchowola* [Memorial book of Suchowola]. Eds.: H. Steinberg et al. Jerusalem, The Encyclopaedia of the Jewish Diaspora, 1957. 616 columns, [2] p., ports., map, facsims. (H,Y)
YIVO: 3/58988   NYPL: *PXV(Suchowola)
YU: DS135 P62 S8

Suwalki (R). *Yisker-bukh Suvalk* [Memorial book of Suvalk]. Ed.: B. Kahan [Kagan]. New York, The Suvalk and Vicinity Relief Committee of New York, 1961. 825 columns, ports., facsims. (Y)
YIVO: 3/62721   NYPL: *PXV(Suwalki) 84-229
JTS: DS135 P62 S8 K3   YU: DS135 P62 S858

Swaryczow (AH) see under Rozniatow

Swieciany (R). *Sefer zikaron le-esrim ve-shalosh kehilot she-nehrevu be-ezor Svintsian* [Svintzian Region; memorial book of twenty-three Jewish communities*]. Ed.: Sh. Kanc. Tel Aviv, Former Residents of the Svintzian District in Israel, 1965. 1954 columns, ports., maps, music, facsims. (H,Y)
YIVO: 3/67270   NYPL: *PXW(Shvenchonis)+
JTS: +DS135 L5 S85 K3

Swierzen (R) see under Stolpce

Swir (R). *Ayaratenu Swir* [Our townlet Swir*]. Ed.: Ch. Swironi (Drutz). Tel Aviv, Former Residents of Swir in Israel and...in the United States, 1959. 240 p., ports., map (H,Y)
YIVO: 3/62186, 3/73069   NYPL: *PXW(Swir) 76-2191
JTS: DS135 R93 S94 S9

Swir (R). *Haya hayeta ayarat Swir; ben shtei milhamot ha-olam* [There once was a town Swir; between the two world wars]. [By] Herzl Vayner. [Israel], Swir Society, 1975. 227 p., illus. (H,Y)
YIVO: 9/73619   NYPL: *PXV(Svir) 77-3730
JTS: DS135 R93 S944 V35

Swislocz (R). *Kehilat Swisiocz pelekh Grodno* [The community of Swisocz, Grodno District]. Ed.: H. Rabin. Tel Aviv, Former Residents of Swislocz in Israel, 1961. 159 p., ports. (H,Y)
YIVO: 3/66297   NYPL: *PXW(Svisloch) 88-467

Swislocz (R). *Sefer Swislocz* [Swislocz book], [vol.] 2. Ed.: Yerahmiel Lifshits. Netanya, Former Residents of Swislocz in Israel, 1984. 289 p., illus., facsims., maps, ports. (H)
NYPL: *PXW(Svisloch) 88-467

Swislocz (R) see also under Wolkowysk (*Volkovisker yisker-bukh*)

Szamosujvar (AH). *Sefer zikaron shel kedoshei ayaratenu Számosujvar-Iklad ve-ha-seviva...* [Memorial book of the martyrs of our town Szamosujvar-Iklad and surroundings]. Eds.: M. Bar-On, B. Herskovits. Tel Aviv, Former Residents of Szamosujvar-Iklad and Surroundings in Israel, 1971. 190, 90 p., ports., facsims. (H,Hu)
NYPL: *PXM   JTS: DS135 R72 G46 S4
YU: DS135 R72 G457

Szarkowszczyzna (R) see under Glebokie

Szatmarnemeti (AH) see Satu Mare

Szczawnica (AH) see under Nowy Targ

362

Szczebrzeszyn (R). *Sefer zikaron le-kehilat Shebreshin* [Book of memory to the Jewish community of Shebreshin*]. Ed.: Dov Shuval. Haifa, Association of Former Inhabitants of Shebreshin in Israel and the Diaspora, 1984. xiv, 518 p., illus., maps, ports. (Y,H,E)
YIVO: nc   NYPL: 20649

Szczekociny (R). *Pinkas Szczekociny* [A memorial book to the Jewish community of Szczekociny*]. Ed.: J. Schweizer. Tel Aviv, Former Residents of Szczekociny in Israel, 1959. 276 p., ports., facsims. (H,Y)
YIVO: 3/65428

Szczuczyn (District Bialystok) (R). *Hurban kehilat Szczuczyn* [The destruction of the community of Szczuczyn]. Tel Aviv, Former Residents of Szczuczyn in Israel and..., 1954. 151 p., ports. (Y)
YIVO: 3/44816   NYPL: *PXW(Shchuchin) 77-3675

Szczuczyn (R). *Sefer zikaron le-kehilot Szczuczyn, Wasiliszki...* [Memorial book of the communities Szczuczyn, Wasiliszki...]. Ed.: L. Losh. Tel Aviv, Former Residents of Szczuczyn, Wasiliszki..., 1966. 456 p., ports., map, facsims. (H,Y)
YIVO: 3/68047   NYPL: *PXW(Shchuchin)

Szczurowice (AH) see under Radziechow

Szereszow (R) see under Pruzana

Szikszo (AH). *Nitsutsot--mi-kehilat Szikszo ve-mehoz Abauj-Turna she-nidmu; toldot hayehem ve-ad hurbanam* [Sparks; from the community of Szikszo and the region of Abauj Turna]. [By] Israel Fleishman. Bnei Brak, 1972. 96, 374 p., illus. (H,Hu)
YIVO: nc   JTS: DS135 H92 S93 F5
YU: nc 81-0460

Szkudy (R) see Skuodas

Szransk (R). *Kehilat Szransk ve-ha-seviva; sefer zikaron* [The Jewish community of Szrensk and the vicinity; a memorial volume*]. Ed.: Y. Rimon (Granat). Jerusalem, [Former Residents of Szrensk in Israel], 1960. 518, 70 p., ports., maps, facsims. (H,Y,E)
YIVO: 3/65785   NYPL: *PXV(Szrensk) 82-1598

Szumsk (R). *Szumsk...sefer zikaron le-kedoshei Szumsk...* [Szumsk...memorial book of the martyrs of Szumsk...]. Ed.: H. Rabin. [Tel Aviv, Former Residents of Szumsk in Israel, 1968]. 477 p., ports., map, facsims. (H,Y)
YIVO: 3/68356   NYPL: *PXW(Shumskoye)
JTS: DS135 R93 S495   YU: 933.5 R9695

Szurdok (AH) see Stramtura

Szydlow (R) see under Staszow

Szydlowiec (R). *Shidlovtser yisker-bukh* [Yizkor book Szydlowiec*]. Ed.: Berl Kagan. New York, 1974. 7, 912, 22 p., illus. (Y,E)
YIVO: 9/73398   NYPL: *PXV(Szydlowiec) 76-5553
JTS: DS135 P62 S957 K34   BUND: 494

Targowica (R). *Sefer Trovits* [Memorial book of Targovica*]. Ed.: I. Siegelman. Haifa, Former Residents of Targovica in Israel, 1967. 452 p., ports., map, facsims. (H,Y)
NYPL: *PXW(Torgovitsa)
JTS: DS135 R93 T64   YU: 933.5 R969T

Targu-Lapus (Magyarlapos) (AH) see under Des

Targu-Mures (AH) see Marosvasarhely

Tarnobrzeg (AH). *Kehilat Tarnobrzeg-Dzikow (Galicia ha-ma'aravit)* [The community of Tarnobrzeg-Dzikow (Western Galicia)]. Ed.: Yaakov Yehoshua Fleisher. Tel Aviv, Tarnobrzeg-Dzikow Society, 1973. 379 p., illus. (H,Y)
YIVO: 9/73390
NYPL: *PXV(Tarnobrzeg)+ 77-3795
JTS: +DS135 P62 T37 K44

Tarnogrod (R). *Sefer Tarnogrod; le-zikaron ha-kehila ha-yehudit she-nehreva* [Book of Tarnogrod; in memory of the destroyed Jewish community]. Ed.: Sh. Kanc. Tel Aviv, Organization of Former Residents of Tarnogrod and Vicinity in Israel, United States and England, 1966. 592 p., ports. (H,Y)
YIVO: 3/69374

Tarnopol (AH). *Tarnopol* [Tarnopol volume*]. Ed.: Ph. Korngruen. Jerusalem, The Encyclopaedia of the Jewish Diaspora, 1955. 474 columns, ports., facsims. (H,Y,E)
YIVO: 3/47248   NYPL: *PX+
JTS: Ref +DS135 E8 E55 v.3
BUND: 94622

Tarnow (AH). *Tarnow; kiyuma ve-hurbana shel ir yehudit* [The life and decline of a Jewish city]. Ed.: A. Chomet. Tel Aviv, Association of Former Residents of Tarnow, 1954-1968. 2 vols. (xx, 928; 433 p.), ports., facsims., map (H,Y)
YIVO: 3/45637   NYPL: *PXV(Tarnow)
JTS: DS135 P62 T34   YU: 933.5 P762T V.2
BUND: 94638 (vol. 1), 498 (vol. 2)

Tartakow (AH) see under Sokal

Tasnad (AH). *Tasnad; tei'ur le-zekher kehilat Tasnad (Transylvania) ve-ha-seviva ve-yeshivat Maharam Brisk, me-reshitan ve-ad le-aher y'mei ha-shoah* [Tasnad; description, in memory of the community of Tasnad (Transylvania) and the surrounding region, and the Brisk Yeshiva, from their beginnings until after the Holocaust]. [By] Avraham Fuks. Jerusalem, 1973. 276 p., illus. (H)
YIVO: 3/72308   NYPL: *PXR 75-2347
JTS: DS135 R72 T373 F8   YU: DS135 R72 T378

Teglas (AH) see under Debrecen

Telechany (R). *Telekhan* [Telekhan memorial book*]. Ed.: Sh. Sokoler. Los Angeles, Telekhan Memorial Book Committee, 1963. 189, 15 p., ports., map (H,Y,E)
YIVO: 3/66278   NYPL: *PXW(Telekhany)
YU: DS135 R93 T45

Telenesti-Targ (R). *Ha-ayara ha-ketana she-be-Bessarabia; le-zekher Telenesti - ayaratenu* [A small town in Bessarabia; in memory of our town Telenesti]. Ed.: Rachel Fels. Kefar Habad, Bet ha-sefer li-defus "Yad ha-Hamisha," 1981. 127, [25] p., illus., map, ports. (H,Y)

Telsiai (R). *Sefer Telz (Lita); matsevet zikaron le-kehila kedosha* [Telsiai book*]. Ed.: Yitzhak Alperovitz. Tel Aviv, Telz Society in Israel, 1984. 505 p., illus., map, ports. (H,Y)
YIVO: nc   NYPL: *PXV(Telsiai) 88-518
JTS: +DS135 L52 T4 A4

Telz (R) see Telsiai

Teplik (R). *Teplik, mayn shtetele; kapitlen fun fuftsik yor lebn* [My town Teplik; chapters from fifty years of life]. [By] Valentin Chernovetzky. Buenos Aires, El Magazine Argentino, 1946-1950. 2 vols., illus. (Y)
YIVO: 4/47278   NYPL: 16841
JTS: DS135 R93 T46 C45

Terebovlya (AH) see Trembowla

Ternovka (R). *Ayaratenu Ternovka; pirkei zikaron ve-matseva* [Our town Ternovka; chapters of remembrance and a monument]. [By] G. Bar-Zvi. Tel Aviv, Ternovka Society, 1972. 103 p., illus. (H)
YIVO: 3/70071   NYPL: *PXW(Ternovka)76-5552
JTS: DS135 R93 T47   YU: DS135 R93 T47

Thessaloniki (Turkey) see Saloniki

Tighina (R) see Bendery

Tiktin (R) see Tykocin

Timkovichi (R) see under Slutsk

Tishevits (R) see Tyszowce

Tlumacz (AH). *Tlumacz-Tolmitsh; sefer edut ve-zikaron* [Memorial book of Tlumacz*]. Eds.: Shlomo Blond et al. Tel Aviv, Tlumacz Society, 1976. 187, 533 p., illus. (H,Y,E)
YIVO: 9/76373   NYPL: *PXW(Tlumach)77-3790
JTS: DS135 R93 T55 B55   YU: DS135 R93 T577

Tluste (AH). *Sefer Tluste* [Memorial book of Tluste]. Ed.: G. Lindenberg. Tel Aviv, Association of Former Residents of Tluste and Vicinity in Israel and USA, 1965. 289 p., ports., map, facsims. (H,Y)
YIVO: 3/70163   NYPL: *PXW(Tolstoye)
JTS: DS135 R93 T6   YU: 933.5 R969 T654L

Tluszcz (R). *Sefer zikaron le-kehilat Tluszcz* [Memorial book of the community of Tluszcz]. Ed.: M. Gelbart. Tel Aviv, Association of Former Residents of Tluszcz in Israel, 1971. 340 p. (H,Y)
YIVO: 3/71300   NYPL: *PXV(Tluszcz)
JTS: DS135 P62 T55   YU: 933.5 P762T

Tolmitsh (AH) see Tlumacz

Tolstoye (AH) see Tluste

Tomaszow-Lubelski (R). *Sefer zikaron shel Tomaszow-Lub.* [Memorial book of Tomaszow-Lubelski]. Ed.: Moshe Gordon. Jerusalem, 1972. 28, 549 p., illus. (H)
YIVO: 9/77965   NYPL: *PXV(Tomaszow) 76-5720
JTS: DS135 P62 T654

Tomaszow Lubelski (R). *Tomashover (Lubelski) yisker-bukh* [Memorial book of Tomaszow Lubelski]. New York, Tomashover Relief Committee, 1965. 912 p., ports., facsims. (Y)
YIVO: 3/67327   NYPL: *PXV(Tomaszow Lubelski)
JTS: DS135 P62 T6 T64   YU: DS135 P62 T65
BUND: nc

Tomaszow Mazowiecki (R). *Sefer zikaron le-kehilat Tomaszow Mazowiecki* [Tomashow-Mazowieck; a memorial to the Jewish community of Tomashow-Mazovieck*]. Ed.: M. Wajsberg. Tel Aviv, Tomashow Organization in Israel, 1969. 648 p., ports., map, facsims. (H,Y,E,F)
YIVO: 3/69276
NYPL: *PXV(Tomaszow Mazowiecki)+
JTS: +DS135 P62 T67   YU: 933.5 P762T
BUND: 500

Topolcany (AH). *Korot mekorot le-kehila yehudit-Topolcany* [The story and source of the Jewish community of Topoltchany*]. [By] Yehoshua Robert Buchler. Lahavot Haviva, Topolcany Book Committee, 1976. 74, 64, 174 p., illus. (H,E,G)
YIVO: 9/76450   NYPL: *PXT(Topolcany) 83-380
JTS: DS135 C96 T6 B8   YU: DS135 C96 T663

Toporow (AH) see under Radziechow

Torna (Galicia) (AH) see Tarnow

Torna (Turna nad Bodvou) (AH) see Turna

Trembowla (R). *Sefer yizkor le-kehilot Trembowla, Strusow ve-Janow ve-ha-seviva* [Memorial book for the Jewish communities of Trembowla, Strusow, Janow and vicinity*]. Bnai Brak, Trembowla Society, [1981?]. li, 379 p., illus., maps (H,E)
YIVO: nc
NYPL: *PXW(Terebovlia) 87-6491
YU: DS135 R93 T467

Trisk (R) see Turzysk

Troki (R). *Troki.* Tel Aviv, [1954]. 79 p., map (H)
YIVO: 3/76839

Trovits (R) see Targowica

Trzebinia (AH). *Kehilat Tshebin* [The community of Trzebinia*]. Eds.: P. Goldwasser et al. Haifa, Committee of Trzebinians in Israel, 1969. 21, 435, 35 p., ports., map, facsims. (H,E)

Tshebin (AH) see Trzebinia

Tshekhanov (R) see Ciechanow

Tshekhanovets (R) see Ciechanowiec

Tshenstokhov (R) see Czestochowa

Tsheshanov (AH) see Cieszanow

Tshizheva (R) see Czyzewo

Tshmelev (Cmielow) (R) see under Ostrowiec

Tuczyn (R). *Sefer zikaron le-kehilat Tuczyn-Kripe* [Tutchin-Krippe, Wolyn; in memory of the Jewish community*]. Ed.: B. H. Ayalon. Tel Aviv, Tutchin and Krippe Relief Society of Israel..., 1967. 383 p., ports., map, facsims. (H,Y)
YIVO: 9/77509   NYPL: *PXW(Tuchin)
JTS: +DS135 R93 T75 A9
YU: 933.5 R969T

Turbin (R) see Turobin

Turcz (AH) see Halmi

Turets (R) see Turzec

Turka (AH). *Sefer zikaron le-kehilat Turka al nehar Stryj ve-ha-seviva* [Memorial book of the community of Turka on the Stryj River and vicinity]. Ed.: J. Siegelman. Haifa, Former Residents of Turka (Stryj) in Israel, 1966. 472 p., ports., map, facsims. (H,Y)
YIVO: 9/77485   NYPL: *PXW(Turka)
JTS: DS135 R93 T8   YU: 933.5 R969T S571

Turna (AH). *Torna - Turna n/Bodvou; zsidósága* [The Jews of Torna]. Ed.: Chaviva Gassner-Guttmann. [Israel, 197-/8-]. 321-384 p., illus., ports. (Hu)

Turobin (R). *Sefer Turobin; pinkas zikaron* [The Turobin book; in memory of the Jewish community*]. Ed.: M. S. Geshuri. Tel Aviv, Former Residents of Turobin in Israel, 1967. 397 p., ports., map, facsims. (H,Y)
YIVO: 3/68816   NYPL: *PXV(Turobin)
JTS: DS135 P62 T86

Turzec (R). *Kehilot Turzec ve-Jeremicze; sefer zikaron* [Book of remembrance--Tooretz-Yeremitz*]. Eds.: Michael Walzer-Fass, Moshe Kaplan. Israel, Turzec and Jeremicze Societies in Israel and America, 1978. 114, 421 p., illus. (H,Y,E)
YIVO: 9/77992B   NYPL: 8651
JTS: DS135 R93 T88 K4   YU: DS135 R93 T784

Turzysk (R). *Pinkas ha-kehila Trisk; sefer yizkor* [Memorial book of Trisk]. Ed.: Natan Livneh. Tel Aviv, Trisk Society, 1975. 376 p., illus. (H,Y)
YIVO: 9/77633   NYPL: *PXW(Turiysk) 78-463
JTS: DS135 R93 T785 P55

Tykocin (R). *Sefer Tiktin* [Memorial book of Tiktin]. Eds.: M. Bar-Yuda, Z. Ben-Nahum. Tel Aviv, Former Residents of Tiktin in Israel, 1959. 606 p., ports., facsims. (H)
YIVO: 3/68159   NYPL: *PXV(Tykocin)
JTS: DS135 P62 T92

Tysmienica (AH). *Tismenits; a matseyve oyf di khurves fun a farnikhteter yidisher kehile* [Tysmienica; a memorial book*]. Ed.: Shlomo Blond. Tel Aviv, Hamenora, 1974. 262 p., illus. (H,Y)
YIVO: 9/73404   NYPL: *PXW(Tysmonitsa) 78-491
JTS: DS135 R93 T933 B55

Tyszowce (R). *Pinkas Tishovits* [Tiszowic book*]. Ed.: Y. Zipper. Tel Aviv, Assoc. of Former Residents of Tiszowic in Israel, 1970. 324 p., ports., facsims. (H,Y)
YIVO: 3/70091   NYPL: *PXV(Tyszowce)
JTS: DS135 P62 T98   BUND: 505/315

Ubinie (AH) see under Radziechow

Uhnow (AH). *Hivniv (Uhnow); sefer zikaron le-kehila* [Hivniv (Uhnow); memorial book to a community]. Tel Aviv, Uhnow Society, 1981. 298, 83 p., illus. (H)
YIVO: nc   NYPL: *PXW(Ugnev) 84-304
YU: DS135 R93 U286

Ujhely (Satorujhely) (AH) see under Zemplenmegye

Ujpest (AH). *Sefer zikhronot shel k(ehila) k(edosha) Ujpest* [Memorial book of the community of Ujpest]. [By] Laszlo Szilagy-Windt; Hebrew translation: Menahem Miron. Tel Aviv, 1975. 27, 325 p., illus. (H,Hu)
JTS: DS135 H92 U52 S9

Ungvar (AH). *Shoat yehudei rusiah ha-karpatit-- Uzhorod* [The Holocaust in Carpatho-Ruthenia-- Uzhorod]. [By] Dov Dinur. Jerusalem, Section for Holocaust Research, Institute of Contemporary Jewry, Hebrew University of Jerusalem; World Union of Carpatho-Ruthenian Jews; and Hebrew Schools, [1983]. 6, 123, 15 p., facsims. (H)
NYPL: 20587   JTS: DS135 R93 C26 D53
YU: nc 87-1345

Ungvar (AH) see also *Arim ve-imahot*, vol. 4

Urechye (R) see under Slutsk

Uscilug (R). *Kehilat Ustila be-vinyana u-be-hurbana* [The growth and destruction of the community of Uscilug]. Ed.: A. Avinadav. Tel Aviv, Association of Former Residents of Uscilug, [1961]. 334 p., ports. (H,Y)
YIVO: 3/71814   NYPL: *PXV(Ustila)

Ustila (R) see Uscilug

Ustrzyki Dolne (AH) see under Lesko

Utena (R). *Yisker-bukh Utyan un umgegnt* [Memorial book of Utyan and vicinity]. Tel Aviv, Nay Lebn, 1979. 296 p., illus., ports. (Y)

Utyan (R) see Utena

Uzhorod (Ungvar) (AH) see under *Arim ve-imahot*, vol. 4

Uzlovoye (Cholojow) (AH) see under Radziechow

Vamospercs (AH) see under Debrecen

Vas (AH). *Sefer zikaron mehoz Vas* [Memorial book of the region of Vas]. Ed.: Avraham Levinger. Israel, Vas Commemorative Committee, 1974. 214 p., illus. (H)
YIVO: 9/73441   NYPL: *PXT 77-3365

Vashniev (Wasniow) (R) see under Ostrowiec

Vasilishok (R) see Wasiliszki

Vayslits (R) see Wislica

Velky Mager (Nagymagyar) (AH) see under Dunaszerdahely

Vengrov (R) see Wegrow

Venice (Italy) see under *Arim ve-imahot*, vol. 4

Verbo (AH) see under Postyen

Verzhbnik (R) see Wierzbnik

Vidz (R) see Widze

Vilna (R). *Bleter vegn Vilne; zamlbukh* [Pages about Vilna; a compilation]. Eds.: L. Ran, L. Koriski. Lodz, Association of Jews from Vilna in Poland, 1947. xvii, 77 p., ports., music, facsims. (Y)
YIVO: 15/3150   NYPL: *PXV(Vilna)
JTS: DS135 R93 V5 R35   BUND: 94491

Vilna (R). *Vilner zamlbukh - measef Vilna* [Vilna collection*]. Ed.: Yisrael Rudnicki. Tel Aviv, World Federation of Jews from Vilna and Vicinity in Israel, 1974. 140 p., illus., facsims. (Y,H)
YIVO: 9/73620   NYPL: 4203
BUND: 634

Vilna (R). *Yerusholayim de-Lita* [Jerusalem of Lithuania, illustrated and documented*]. Collected and arranged by Leyzer Ran. New York, Vilna Album Committee, 1974. 3 vols., illus. (H,Y,E,R)
YIVO: N7417.6 R3   NYPL: *PXW(Vilna)+ 76-2170
JTS: DS135 R93 V5 Y47   BUND: 505/100

Vilna (R) see also under Lithuania and under *Arim ve-imahot*, vol. 1

Vilnius (R) see Vilna

Vinogradov (AH) see Nagyszollos

Vishneva (AH) see Wiszniew

Vishnevets (R) see Wisniowiec Nowy

Vishogrod (R) see Wyszogrod

Viskit (Wiskitki) (R) see under Zyrardow

Visooroszi (AH) see Ruscova

Visotsk (R) see Wysock

Vitebsk (R). *Sefer Vitebsk* [Memorial book of Vitebsk]. Ed.: B. Karu. Tel Aviv, Former Residents of Vitebsk and Surroundings in Israel, 1957. 508 columns, ports., facsims. (H)
YIVO: 3/51700   NYPL: *PXW(Vitebsk)
YU: 933.547 V838K   BUND: 946114

Vitebsk (R). *Vitebsk amol; geshikhte, zikhroynes, khurbn* [Vitebsk in the past; history, memoirs, destruction]. Eds.: G. Aronson, J. Lestschinsky, A. Kihn. New York, 1956. 644 p., ports. (Y)
YIVO: 3/48102   NYPL: *PXW(Vitebsk)
JTS: DS135 R93 V6   YU: DS135 R93 V6
BUND: 94688

Vitkov (Novyy) (Witkow Nowy) (AH) see under Radziechow

Vizna (R) see under Slutsk

Vladimir Volynskiy (R) see Wlodzimierz

Vladimirets (R) see Wlodzimierzec

Vloyn (R) see Wielun

Voislavitsa (R) see Wojslawice

Volozhin (R) see Wolozyn

Voronovo (R) see Werenow

Voydislav (R) see Wodzislaw

Vrbove (Verbo) (AH) see under Postyen

Vurka (R) see Warka

Wadowice (AH). *Sefer zikaron le-kehilot Wadowice, Andrychow, Kalwarja, Myslenice, Sucha* [Memorial book of the communities Wadowice...] Ed.: D. Jakubowicz. Ramat Gan, Former Residents of Wadowice... and Masada, 1967. 454 p., ports., facsims. (H,Y)
YIVO: 3/69274   NYPL: *PXV(Wadowice)
JTS: DS135 P62 W353

Warez (AH) see under Sokal

Warka (R). *Vurka; sefer zikaron* [Vurka memorial book]. Tel Aviv, Vurka Societies in Israel, France, Argentina, England and the United States, 1976. 407 p., illus. (H,Y)
YIVO: nc   NYPL: 15173
BUND: 287

Warsaw (R). *Dos amolike yidishe Varshe, biz der shvel fun dritn khurbn; yisker-bletlekh nokh tayere noente umgekumene* [Jewish Warsaw that was; a Yiddish literary anthology*]. Montreal, Farband of Warsaw Jews in Montreal, 1967. 848, 56 p., facsims., illus., ports. (Y)
YIVO: 1/67671   NYPL: *PXV(Warsaw)
JTS: PJ5125 A5   BUND: 630

Warsaw (R). *Pinkes Varshe* [Book of Warsaw]. Eds.: P. Katz et al. Buenos Aires, Former Residents of Warsaw and Surroundings in Argentina, 1955. 1351 columns, lvi p., ports., music, maps (Y)
YIVO: 3/47855   NYPL: *PXV+(Warsaw)
JTS: +DS135 P62 W3 P5   YU: 933.503 E61W V.1
BUND: 94698

Warsaw (R). *Warsaw* [Warsaw volume*]. Ed.: J. Gruenbaum. Jerusalem, The Encyclopaedia of the Jewish Diaspora, 1953-1973. 3 vols., ports., maps, facsims. (H,Y)
YIVO: 3/47248   NYPL: *PX+
JTS: Ref +DS135 E8 E55 v.1, 6, 12
BUND: 545 (1953), 330 (1973)

Warsaw (R) see also under *Arim ve-imahot,* vol. 3

Warszawa (R) see Warsaw

Warta (R). *Sefer D'Vart.* Ed.: Eliezer Estrin. Tel Aviv, D'Vart Society, 1974. 567 p., illus. (H,Y)
YIVO: 9/77666   NYPL: *PXV(Bardo) 79-205
JTS: DS135 P62 W325 S4   YU: DS135 P62 B346

Wasiliszki (R). *Tahat shilton ha-germani ha-shanim 1941-1945* [Under German rule in the years 1941-1945]. Tel Aviv, Former Residents of Wasiliszki in Israel, [1986/87]. 1 vol., illus. (H)

Wasiliszki (R) see also under Szczuczyn (*Sefer zikaron le-kehilot Szczuczyn, Wasiliszki*)

Wasniow (R) see under Ostrowiec

Wegrow (R). *Kehilat Wegrow; sefer zikaron* [Community of Wegrow; memorial book]. Ed.: M. Tamari. Tel Aviv, Former Residents of Wegrow in Israel, 1961. 418 p., ports., facsims. (H,Y)
YIVO: 2/65427   NYPL: *PXV(Wegrow)
BUND: 493

Werenow (R). *Voronova; sefer zikaron le-kedoshei Voronova she-nispu ba-shoat ha-natsim* [Voronova; memorial book to the martyrs of Voronova who died during the Nazi Holocaust]. Ed.: H. Rabin. Israel, Voronova Societies in Israel and the United States, 1971. 440 p., illus. (H,Y)
YIVO: 3/70230   NYPL: *PXW(Voronovo)
JTS: DS135 R93 V73 R3

Widze (R). *Fertsik yor nokhn umkum fun di Vidzer Yidn z"l* [Forty years after the annihilation of the Jews of Widze]. [By] Yaakov Parmunt. Kefar Giladi, The Council of the Society of Widze Jews in the Land of Israel, [1982/83]. 8 leaves. (Y)

Widze (R) see also under Swieciany

Wieliczka (AH). *Kehilat Wieliczka; sefer zikaron* [The Jewish community of Wieliczka; a memorial book*]. Ed.: Shmuel Meiri. Tel Aviv, The Wieliczka Association in Israel, 1980. 160, [9], 93 p., illus. (H,Y,E,P)

YIVO: 9/78960   NYPL: 12072
JTS: DS135 P62 W365 K44
YU: DS135 P62 W624

Wielun (R). *Sefer zikaron le-kehilat Wielun* [Wielun memorial book*]. Tel Aviv, Wielun Organization in Israel and the Memorial Book Committee in USA, 1971. 534, 24 p., ports. (H,Y,E)

YIVO: 3/70388   NYPL: *PXV(Wielun)+
JTS: +DS135 P62 W37 S4
YU: DS135 P62 W638

Wieruszow (R). *Wieruszow; sefer yizkor* [Wieruszow; memorial book]. Tel Aviv, Former Residents of Wieruszow Book Committee, 1970. 907 p., ports., maps, facsims. (H,Y)

YIVO: 3/69759   NYPL: *PXV(Wieruszow)
JTS: DS135 P62 W64

Wierzbnik (R). *Sefer Wierzbnik-Starachowice* [Wierzbnik-Starachowitz; a memorial book*]. Ed.: Mark Schutzman. Tel Aviv, Wierzbnik-Starachowitz Societies in Israel and the Diaspora, 1973. 29, 399, 100, 83 p., illus. (H,Y,E)

YIVO: nc   NYPL: *PXV(Wierzbnik)76-5651
JTS: DS135 P62 W376 S4

Wilejka (R). *Sefer zikaron kehilat Wilejka ha-mehozit, plakh Vilna* [Memorial book of the community of Vileika*]. Eds.: Kalman Farber, Joseph Se'evi. Tel Aviv, Wilejka Society, 1972. 12, 326 p., illus. (H,Y,E)

YIVO: 9/73388   NYPL: 1973
JTS: DS135 R93 V4 S4   YU: nc 75-0583
BUND: 242

Wilno (R) see Vilna

Wiskitki (R) see under Zyrardow

Wislica (R). *Sefer Vayslits; dos Vayslitser yisker-bukh...* [Book of Wislica]. Tel Aviv, Association of Former Residents of Wislica, 1971. 299 p., ports., map (H,Y,P)

YIVO: 3/71002   NYPL: *PXV(Wislica)
JTS: DS135 P62 W38 S4   YU: 933.5 P762W

Wisniowiec Nowy (R). *Wisniowiec; sefer zikaron le-kedoshei Wisniowiec she-nispu be-shoat ha-natsim* [Wisniowiec; memorial book of the martyrs of Wisniowiec who perished in the Nazi holocaust]. Ed.: H. Rabin. [Tel Aviv], Former Residents of Wisniowiec. 540 p., ports. (H,Y)

YIVO: 9/77584   NYPL: *PXW(Vishnevets)
JTS: DS135 R93 V59   YU: 933.5 U35V

Wiszniew (AH). *Vishneva, ke-fi she-hayeta ve-enena od; sefer zikaron* [Wiszniew; as it was and is no more; memorial book]. Ed.: Hayyim Abramson. Tel Aviv, Wiszniew Society in Israel, 1972. 216 p., illus. (H,Y)

YIVO: 9/77893   NYPL: *PXV(Vishnevo) 75-1443
JTS: DS135 R93 V598 V5   YU: DS135 R93 V598

Witkow Nowy (AH) see under Radziechow

Wloclawek (R). *Wloclawek ve-ha-seviva; sefer zikaron* [Wloclawek and vicinity; memorial book*]. Eds.: K. F. Thursh, M. Korzen. [Israel], Assoc. of Former Residents of Wloclawek in Israel and the USA, 1967. 1032 columns, ports., facsims. (H,Y)

YIVO: 3/68114   NYPL: *PXV(Wloclawek)+
JTS: +DS135 P62 W4   YU: DS135 P62 W76
BUND: 513

Wlodawa (R). *Wlodawa; ner zikaron* [In memory of Wlodawa]. Ed.: D. Rovner. Haifa, 1968. 211 p., ports., facsims. (H,Y,E,P), mimeo.

Wlodawa (R). *Yisker-bukh tsu Vlodave* [Yizkor book in memory of Vlodava and region Sobibor*]. Ed.: Shimon Kanc. Tel Aviv, Wlodawa Societies in Israel and North and South America, 1974. 1290, 128 columns, illus. (H,Y,E)

YIVO: 9/73395   NYPL: *PXV(Wlodawa) 75-8553
JTS: +DS135 P62 W43 S4

Wlodzimierz (R). *Pinkas Ludmir; sefer zikaron le-kehilat Ludmir* [Wladimir Wolynsk; in memory of the Jewish community*]. Tel Aviv, Former Residents of Wladimir in Israel, 1962. 624 columns, ports., facsims. (H,Y)

YIVO: 3/66884   NYPL: 15170

Wlodzimierzec (R). *Sefer Vladimerets* [The book of Vladimerets]. Ed.: A. Meyerowitz. Tel Aviv, Former Residents of Vladimerets in Israel, [196-]. 515 p., ports., map (H,Y,E)

YIVO: 3/66583   NYPL: *PXW(Vladimirets) 79-198

Wodzislaw (R). *Sefer Wodzislaw-Sedziszow.* Ed.: M. Schutzman. Israel, Community Council of Wodzislaw-Sedziszow Emigrants in Israel, 1979. 437 p., illus. (H,Y)

YIVO: nc

Wojslawice (R). *Sefer zikaron Voislavitse* [Yizkor book in memory of Voislavize*]. Ed.: Sh. Kanc. Tel Aviv, Former Residents of Voislavize, 1970. 515 p., ports., facsims. (H,Y)
YIVO: 3/70384   NYPL: *PXV(Wislowiec)
JTS: DS135 P62 W65 Y5

Wolborz (R) see under Piotrkow Trybunalski

Wolbrom (R). *Wolbrom irenu* [Our town Wolbrom]. Ed.: M. Geshuri (Bruckner). Tel Aviv, Association of Former Residents of Wolbrom in Israel, 1962. 909 p., ports., map (H,Y)
YIVO: 3/65810   NYPL: *PXV(Wolbrom)
JTS: DS135 P62 W73 G4   BUND: 946148

Wolica-Wygoda (AH) see under Radziechow

Wolkowysk (R). *Hurban Wolkowysk be-milhemet ha-olam ha-sheniya 1939-1945* [The destruction of Wolkowysk during the Second World War 1939-1945]. Tel Aviv, Committee of Former Residents of Wolkowysk in Eretz-Israel, 1946. 96 p., ports. (H)
YIVO: 3/23489   NYPL: *PXW(Volkovysk)
JTS: DS135 R93 V64 H8

Wolkowysk (R). *Volkovisker yisker-bukh* [Wolkovisker yizkor book*]. Ed.: M. Einhorn. New York, 1949. 2 vols. (990 p.), ports. (Y,E)
YIVO: 3/29353   NYPL: *PXW(Volkovysk)
JTS: DS135 R93 V64   YU: 933.5 R969V
BUND: 524 (vol. 1), 94637 (vol. 2)

Wolma (R) see under Rubiezewicze

Wolomin (R). *Sefer zikaron kehilat Wolomin* [Volomin; a memorial to the Jewish community of Volomin (Poland)*]. Ed.: Shimon Kanc. Tel Aviv, Wolomin Society, 1971. 600 p., illus. (H,Y)
YIVO: 3/71565   NYPL: *PXV(Wolomin)
JTS: DS135 P62 W67 S4   YU: 933.5 P762V

Wolozyn (R). *Wolozyn; sefer shel ha-ir ve-shel yeshivat "Ets Hayim"* [Wolozin; the book of the city and of the Etz Hayyim Yeshiva*]. Ed.: E. Leoni. Tel Aviv, Former Residents of Wolozin in Israel and the USA, 1970. 679, 35 p., ports., map, facsims. (H,Y,E)
YIVO: 3/69358   NYPL: *PXW(Volozhin)
JTS: DS135 R93 V67   YU: DS135 R93 V67

Wolpa (R) see under Wolkowysk (*Volkovisker yisker-bukh*)

Wsielub (R) see under Nowogrodek

Wysock (near Rowne) (R). *Ayaratenu Visotsk; sefer zikaron* [Our town Visotsk; memorial book]. Haifa, Association of Former Residents of Visotsk in Israel, 1963. 231 p., ports., maps (H,Y)
YIVO: 3/66602   NYPL: *PXW(Vysotsk)
JTS: DS135 R93 V56 A9

Wysokie-Mazowieckie (R). *Wysokie-Mazowieckie; sefer zikaron* [Visoka-Mazovietsk*]. Ed.: I. Rubin. Tel Aviv, Wysokie-Mazowieckie Society, 1975. 280 p., illus. (H,Y,E)
YIVO: 9/75288
NYPL: *PXV(Wysokie-Mazowieckie) 80-600
JTS: DS135 P62 W888 V57

Wyszkow (R). *Sefer Wyszkow* [Wishkow book*]. Ed.: D. Shtokfish. Tel Aviv, Association of Former Residents of Wishkow in Israel and Abroad, 1964. 351 p., ports., facsims. (H,Y)
YIVO: 3/66751   NYPL: *PXV(Wyszkow)+
JTS: +DS135 P62 W9   BUND: 946220

Wyszogrod (R). *Wyszogrod; sefer zikaron* [Vishogrod; dedicated to the memory...*]. Ed.: H. Rabin. [Tel Aviv], Former Residents of Vishogrod and..., [1971]. 316, 48 p., ports., facsims. (H,Y,E)
YIVO: 3/70019   NYPL: *PXV(Wyszogrod)+
JTS: +DS135 P62 W958

Wyzgrodek (R) see under Krzemieniec

Yagistov (R) see Augustow

Yampol (R). *Ayara be-lehavot; pinkas Yampola, pelekh Volyn* [Town in flames; book of Yampola, district Wolyn]. Ed.: L. Gelman. Jerusalem, Commemoration Committee for the Town with the Assistance of Yad Vashem and the World Jewish Congress, 1963. [154] p. (H,Y)
YIVO: 3/66582   NYPL: 2856

Yanova (R) see Jonava

Yanovichi (R) see under Vitebsk (*Vitebsk amol*)

Yartshev (AH) see Jaryczow Nowy

Yavoriv (AH) see Jaworow

Yedintsy (R). *Yad le-Yedinits; sefer zikaron le-yehudei Yedinits-Bessarabia* [Yad l'Yedinitz; memorial book for the Jewish community of Yedintzi, Bessarabia*]. Eds.: Mordekhai Reicher, Yosef Magen-Shitz. Tel Aviv, Yedinitz Society, 1973. 1022 p., illus. (H,Y)
YIVO: 9/73397   NYPL: *PXM(Edinitz) 75-1514
JTS: +DS135 R93 Y42 Y3

Yedvabne (R) see Jedwabne

Yekaterinoslav (R). *Sefer Yekaterinoslav-Dnepropetrovsk.* Eds.: Zvi Harkavi, Yaakov Goldburt. Jerusalem-Tel Aviv, Yekaterinoslav-Dnepropetrovsk Society, 1973. 167 p., illus. (H)
YIVO: 9/77203
NYPL: *PXW(Dnepropetrovsk) 78-666
YU: DS135 R93 D597

Yendrikhov (Andrychow) (AH) see under Wadowice

Yendzheva (R) see Jedrzejow

Yustingrad (R). *Sokolievka / Justingrad; a century of struggle and suffering in a Ukrainian shtetl, as recounted by survivors to its scattered descendants.* Eds.: Leo Miller, Diana F. Miller. New York, A Logvin Book, Loewenthal Press, 1983. 202 p., facsims., illus., maps, ports. (E,H,Y) Incl. facsim. and tr. of 1972 Mashabei Sadeh booklet.
YIVO: 9/80813   NYPL: *PXW(Sokolievka) 85-2337
JTS: DS135 R93 Y87 S66

Yustingrad (R). *Yustingrad-Sokolivka; ayara she-nihreva* [Yustingrad-Sokolivka; a town that was destroyed]. Kibbutz Mashabei Sadeh, 1972. 63, [17] p., ports., map, illus. (H)
YIVO: 3/71320   JTS: DS135 R93 Y87 Y86
YU: DS135 R93 Y87

Zablotow (AH). *Ir u-metim; Zablotow ha-melea ve-ha-hareva* [A city and the dead; Zablotow alive and destroyed]. Tel Aviv, Former Residents of Zablotow in Israel and the USA, 1949. 218 p., ports. (H,Y)
YIVO: 3/73089   NYPL: *PXW(Zablotov)+88-502

Zabludow (R). *Zabludow; dapim mi-tokh "yisker-bukh"* [Pages from the memorial book]. Eds.: Nehama Shavli-Shimush et al. Tel Aviv, Former Residents of Zabludow in Israel, [1986/87]. 170, 23 p., illus., map (H)

Zabludow (R). *Zabludow yisker-bukh* [Zabludowo; in memoriam*]. Eds.: Sh. Tsesler et al. Buenos Aires, Zabludowo Book Committee, 1961. 507 p., ports., map, facsims. (Y)
YIVO: 3/66414   NYPL: *PXV(Zabludow)

Zagaipol (R) see Yustingrad

Zakopane (AH) see under Nowy Targ

Zaloshits (R) see Dzialoszyce

Zambrow (R). *Sefer Zambrow; Zambrove* [The book of Zambrov*]. Ed.: Y. T. Lewinsky. Tel Aviv, The Zambrover Societies in USA, Argentina and Israel, 1963. 627, 69 p., ports., facsims. (H,Y,E)
YIVO: 3/66549   NYPL: *PXV(Zambrow)
JTS: DS135 P62 Z27   YU: 933.5 P762Z

Zamekhov (R) see under Kamenets-Podolskiy

Zamosc (R). *Pinkes Zamosc; yizker-bukh* [Pinkas Zamosc; in memoriam*]. Ed.: M. W. Bernstein. Buenos Aires, Committee of the Zamosc Memorial Book, 1957. 1265 p., ports., facsims. (Y)
YIVO: 3/53182   NYPL: *PXV(Zamosc)
BUND: 946102

Zamosc (R). *Zamosc be-genona u-be-shivra* [The rise and fall of Zamosc]. Ed.: M. Tamari. Tel Aviv, Former Residents of Zamosc in Israel, 1953. 327 p., ports., facsims. (H,P)
YIVO: 3/43512   NYPL: *PXV(Zamosc) 83-381
JTS: DS135 P62 Z3   YU: 933.5 P7627 T153
BUND: 946111

Zamosze (R) see under Braslaw

Zaracze (R) see under Braslaw

Zareby Kowcielne (R). *Le-zikhron olam; di Zaromber yidn vos zaynen umgekumen al kidesh-hashem* [For eternal remembrance; the Jews of Zaromb...]. [New York], United Zaromber Relief, 1947. 68 p., ports., map, facsims. (Y)
YIVO: 15/3036

Zarki (R). *Kehilat Zarki; ayara be-hayeha u-ve-khilyona* [The community of Zarki; life and destruction of a town]. Ed.: Y. Lador. Tel Aviv, Former Residents of Zarki in Israel, 1959. 324 p., ports. (H,Y)
YIVO: 3/63105A   NYPL: *PXV(Zarki)
JTS: DS135 P62 Z35 L3

Zaromb (R) see Zareby Koscielne

Zarszyn (AH) see under Sanok

Zassow (AH) see under Radomysl

Zastawie (R) see under Kamieniec Litewski

Zawidcze (AH) see under Radziechow

Zawiercie (R). *Sefer zikaron; kedoshei Zawiercie ve-ha-seviva* [Memorial book of the martyrs of Zawiercie and vicinity]. Ed.: Sh. Spivak. Tel Aviv, Former Residents of Zawiercie and Vicinity, 1948. 570 p., ports. (H,Y)
YIVO: 3/62326   NYPL: *PXV(Zawierce)

Zbaraz (AH). *Sefer Zbaraz* [Zbaraz: the Zbaraz memorial book*]. Ed.: Moshe Sommerstein. Tel Aviv, The Organization of Former Zbaraz Residents, 1983. 45, 128 p., illus., ports. (H,Y,E)
YIVO: nc

Zborow (AH). *Sefer zikaron le-kehilat Zborow* [Memorial book of the community of Zborow]. Ed.: Eliyahu (Adik) Zilberman. Haifa, Zborow Society, 1975. 477 p., illus. (H,Y)
YIVO: nc   NYPL: 15172

Zdunska Wola (R). *Zdunska Wola* [The Zdunska-Wola book*]. Ed.: E. Erlich. Tel Aviv, Zdunska-Wola Associations in Israel and in the Diaspora, 1968. 718, 8, 55 p., ports., facsims. (H,Y,E)
YIVO: 3/69277   NYPL: *PXV(Zdunska Wola)+
JTS: DS135 P62 Z38   BUND: 514

Zdzieciol (R). *Pinkas Zhetl* [Pinkas Zetel; a memorial to the Jewish community of Zetel*]. Ed.: B. Kaplinski. Tel Aviv, Zetel Association in Israel, 1957. 482 p., ports., facsims. (H,Y)
YIVO: 3/55855   NYPL: *PXW(Dyatlovo)
JTS: +DS135 R93 D95 K36
YU: 933.5 R696 D994 K17   BUND: 946124

Zelechow (R). *Yisker-bukh fun der Zhelekhover yidisher kehile* [Memorial book of the community of Zelechow]. Ed.: W. Yassni. Chicago, Former Residents of Zelechow in Chicago, 1953. 398, xxiv p., facsims. (Y)
YIVO: 3/45072   JTS: +DS135 P62 Z39 J3
YU: 933.47(438) Z49J   BUND: 94627

Zelow (R). *Sefer zikaron le-kehilat Zelow* [Memorial book of the community of Zelow]. Ed.: Avraham Kalushiner. Tel Aviv, Zelow Society, 1976. 447 p., illus. (H,Y)
YIVO: 9/77520   NYPL: *PXV(Zelow) 80-605
JTS: DS135 P62 Z4 K3

Zemplen (AH) see Zemplenmegye

Zemplenmegye (AH). *Mah tovu uhelekha Yaakov; korot yehudei mehoz Zemplen* [Vanished communities in Hungary; the history and tragic fate of the Jews in Ujhely and Zemplen County*]. By Meir Sas [Szasz]; translated from Hebrew by Carl Alpert. Toronto, Memorial Book Committee, 1986. 141, [56], 170, 214 p., illus., ports., maps, facsims. (H,Hu,E)
NYPL: nc

Zetel (R) see Zdzieciol

Zgierz (R). *Sefer Zgierz, mazkeret netsah le-kehila yehudit be-Polin* [Memorial book Zgierz*], vol. 1: Ed.: David Shtokfish; vol. 2: Eds: Sh. Kanc, Z. Fisher. Tel Aviv, Zgierz Society, 1975-1986. 2 vols., illus. (H,Y)
YIVO: 9/75287   NYPL: *PXV(Zgierz) 76-389
BUND: 270 (vol. 1)

Zhelekhov (R) see Zelechow

Zhetl (R) see Zdzieciol

Zholkva (AH) see Zolkiew

Zinkov (R). *Pinkas Zinkov* [Zinkover memorial book*]. Tel Aviv-New York, Joint Committee of Zinkover Landsleit in the United States and Israel, 1966. 239, 16 p., ports. (H,Y,E)
YIVO: 3/67746   NYPL: *PXW(Zinkov)
JTS: DS135 R93 Z5   YU: 933.5 R969 Z78E

Zloczew (Lodz) (R). *Sefer Zloczew* [Book of Zloczew]. Tel Aviv, Committee of the Association of Former Residents of Zloczew, [1971]. 432, [21] p., ports., facsims. (H,Y)
YIVO: 3/70294   NYPL: *PXV(Zloczew)
JTS: +DS135 P62 Z557 S4
YU: +DS135 P62 Z557

Zloczow (AH). *Der untergang fun Zloczów* [The destruction of Zloczów]. [By] Szlojme Mayer. Munich, Ibergang, 1947. 45 p., illus., ports. (Y in Latin characters)
YIVO: 3/26330, 3/26823

Zloczow (AH). *Sefer kehilat Zloczow* [The city of Zloczow*]. Ed.: Baruch Karu (Krupnik). Tel Aviv, Zloczow Society, 1967. 540, 208 columns, illus. (H,E)
YIVO: 3/68093   NYPL: *PXW(Zolochev)
JTS: +DS135 R93 Z48   YU: 933.5 R969 Z86K

Zolkiew (AH). *Sefer Zolkiew (kirya nisegava)* [Memorial book of Zolkiew]. Eds.: N. M. Gelber, Y. Ben-Shem. Jerusalem, The Encyclopaedia of the Jewish Diaspora, 1969. 844 columns, ports., map, facsims. (H)
YIVO: 3/69383   NYPL: *PXV(Zholkva)
JTS: +DS135 R93 Z48

Zolochev (AH) see Zloczow

Zoludek (R). *Sefer Zoludek ve-Orlowa; galed le-zikaron* [The book of Zoludek and Orlowa; a living memorial*]. Ed.: A. Meyerowitz. Tel Aviv, Former Residents of Zoludek in Israel and the USA, [n.d.]. 329, [5] p., ports., map (H,Y,E)
YIVO: 3/67644   NYPL: *PXW(Zheludok)
JTS: DS135 R93 Z47   YU: 933.5 R969Z
BUND: 538

Zoludzk (R). *Ner tamid le-zekher kehilat Zoludzk* [Memorial book of the community of Zoludzk]. Ed.: A. Avinadav. Tel Aviv, Association of Former Residents of Zoludzk in Israel, 1970. 185, 3 p., ports., map (H,Y)
NYPL: *PXW(Zhelutsk) 85-1927

Zombor (AH). *Kehilat Sombor be-hurbana; dapei zikaron le-kedoshei ha-kehila* [The Sombor community in its destruction; pages of commemoration to the martyrs of the community]. [By] E. H. Spitzer. Jerusalem, 1970. 29 p., ports. (H)
NYPL: 2863

Zvihil (R) see Novograd-Volynskiy

Zwiahel (R) see Novograd-Volynskiy

Zwolen (R). *Zvoliner yisker-bukh* [Zwolen memorial book]. New York, Zwolen Society, 1982. 564, 112 p., illus. (Y,E)
YIVO: nc
NYPL: *PXV(Zwolen) 87-4199
JTS: DS135 P62 Z97 Z95

Zychlin (R). *Sefer Zychlin* [The memorial book of Zychlin*]. Ed.: Ammi Shamir. Tel Aviv, Zychliner Organization of Israel and America, 1974. 4, 350 p., illus. (H,Y,E,)
YIVO: nc
NYPL: *PXV(Zychlin) 76-2190
JTS: DS135 P62 Z878 S4

Zyrardow (R). *Pinkas Zyrardow, Amshinov un Viskit* [Memorial book of Zyrardow, Amshinov and Viskit]. Ed.: M. W. Bernstein. Buenos Aires, Association of Former Residents in the USA, Israel, France and Argentina, 1961. 699 p., ports., facsims. (Y)
YIVO: 3/65786A   NYPL: *PXV(Zyrardow)
JTS: DS135 P62 Z98 B4   BUND: 946197

THE CITY OF NEW YORK - OFFICE OF THE CITY CLERK
MARRIAGE LICENSE BUREAU

REQUEST FOR A SEARCH OF A MARRIAGE LICENSE ISSUED IN ONE OF THE FIVE BOROUGHS OF THE
CITY OF NEW YORK AND A TRANSCRIPT OF SUCH MARRIAGE LICENSE

Today's Date: _____

Date of Marriage Ceremony: MONTH- DAY- YEAR-	Borough where the license was issued	
If uncertain, specify other years you want searched:		
GROOM (man) Full name:		
BRIDE (woman) Full MAIDEN name:		
If woman was previously married, give LAST NAME of former husband(s):		
Reason search & copy are needed:	How Many	
Name of person requesting search:	Your relationship to Bride & Groom:	
Your Address City	State	Zip

DO NOT WRITE BELOW - THIS SPACE FOR OFFICE USE

License
Number:_____/_____   Microfilm Cart No. _____/_____/_____

Searched by:_____   Type of Cert_____

Receipt No._____   Amount-$_____   Typist_____

Date Mailed_____   Cert No.(s) _____

Date Request was received_____   Amount of Money Received - $_____

NO RECORD ( ) Amount Refunded-$_____   Receipt No._____Mailed_____

This is to certify that_____

residing at_____ Born_____

at_____AND _____

Residing at_____ Born_____

at_____Were married on _____

at_____By _____

Groom's Parents_____

Bride's Parents_____

Witnesses_____

Previous Marriages_____

REMARKS_____

APPENDIX B-1

BUREAU OF VITAL RECORDS
125 Worth Street
New York, N.Y. 10013

APPLICATION FOR A BIRTH RECORD

(Print All Items Clearly)

LAST NAME ON BIRTH RECORD	FIRST NAME	☐ FEMALE ☐ MALE

DATE OF BIRTH Month Day Year	PLACE OF BIRTH (NAME OF HOSPITAL, OR IF AT HOME, NO. AND STREET	BOROUGH OF BIRTH

MOTHER'S MAIDEN NAME (Name Before Marriage) FIRST LAST	CERTIFICATE NUMBER IF KNOWN

FATHER'S NAME FIRST LAST	
NO. OF COPIES	YOUR RELATIONSHIP TO PERSON NAMED ON BIRTH RECORD, IF SELF, STATE "SELF"	*For Office Only*
FOR WHAT PURPOSE ARE YOU GOING TO USE THIS BIRTH RECORD	

NOTE: Copy of a birth record can be issued only to persons to whom the record of birth relates, if of age, or a parent or other lawful representative.
IF THIS REQUEST IS NOT FOR YOUR OWN BIRTH RECORD OR THAT OF YOUR CHILD, NOTARIZED AUTHORIZATION FROM THE PARENT OR THE PERSON NAMED ON THE CERTIFICATE MUST BE PRESENTED WITH THIS APPLICATION.

Section 3.19, New York City Health Code provides, in part:". . . no person shall make a false, untrue or misleading statement or forge the signature of another on a certificate, application, registration, report or other document required to be prepared pursuant to this Code."
Section 558 (d) of the New York City Charter provides that any violation of the Health Code shall be treated and punished as a misdemeanor.

SIGN YOUR NAME AND ADDRESS BELOW

NAME	
ADDRESS	
CITY	STATE	ZIP CODE

NOTE: PLEASE ATTACH A STAMPED SELF-ADDRESSED ENVELOPE

FEES

SEARCH FOR TWO CONSECUTIVE YEARS AND ONE COPY   OR A CERTIFIED "NOT FOUND STATEMENT" 5.00
EACH ADDITIONAL COPY REQUESTED... 5.00
EACH EXTRA YEAR SEARCHED (WITH THIS APPLICATION)... 1.00

1. Make check or money order payable to: Department of Health, N.Y.C.
2. If from a foreign country, send an international money order or a check drawn on a U.S. bank.
3. Stamps or foreign currency will not be accepted. CASH NOT ACCEPTED BY MAIL.

FOR OFFICE USE ONLY

SEARCH RESULTS ➤	REPORTED BY ☐ CRT ☐ MANUAL INITIAL ➤	CERTIFICATE NUMBER	LAST NAME - 4 LETTERS	DATE OF BIRTH		
				Month	Day	Year
READING DATE		DATE ISSUED: BY MAIL		DATE ISSUED: IN PERSON		

VR-67 (REV. 7/86)

THE CITY OF NEW YORK—DEPARTMENT OF HEALTH
BUREAU OF VITAL RECORDS
125 WORTH STREET
NEW YORK, NEW YORK 10013

APPLICATION FOR A COPY OF A DEATH RECORD

PRINT ALL ITEMS CLEARLY

1. LAST NAME AT TIME OF DEATH		2. FIRST NAME	2A. ☐ FEMALE ☐ MALE
3. DATE OF DEATH Month Day Year	4. PLACE OF DEATH	5. BOROUGH	6. AGE
7. NO. OF COPIES	8. SPOUSE'S NAME	9. OCCUPATION OF THE DECEASED	
10. FATHER'S NAME		11. SOCIAL SECURITY NUMBER	
12. MOTHER'S NAME (Name Before Marriage)		13. BURIAL PERMIT NUMBER (IF KNOWN)	
14. FOR WHAT PURPOSE ARE YOU GOING TO USE THIS CERTIFICATE		15. YOUR RELATIONSHIP TO DECEDENT	

NOTE: Section 205.07 of the Health Code provides, in part:" . . . The confidential medical report of death shall not be subject to subpoena or to inspection." Therefore, copies of the medical report of death cannot be issued.

SIGN YOUR NAME AND ADDRESS BELOW

NAME

ADDRESS

CITY   STATE   ZIP CODE

INFORMATION: APPLICATION SHOULD BE MADE IN PERSON OR BY MAIL TO ABOVE BUREAU.

NOTE: 1. CASH NOT ACCEPTED BY MAIL 2. PLEASE ATTACH A STAMPED SELF-ADDRESSED ENVELOPE.	(FOR OFFICE USE ONLY)

FEES

SEARCH FOR TWO CONSECUTIVE YEARS AND ONE COPY.................................$5.00
EACH ADDITIONAL COPY REQUESTED $5.00
EACH EXTRA YEAR SEARCHED (WITH THIS APPLICATION) $1.00
IF RECORD IS NOT ON FILE, A CERTIFIED "NOT FOUND STATEMENT" WILL BE ISSUED.
  1. Make check or money order payable to: Department of Health, N.Y.C.
  2. If from a foreign country, send an international money order or a check drawn on a U.S. bank.
  3. Stamps or foreign currency will not be accepted.

APPENDIX B-3

MUNICIPAL ARCHIVES
Department of Records and Information Services

31 Chambers Street
New York, N.Y. 10007
(212) 566-5292
IDILIO GRACIA PENA, *Director*

APPLICATION FOR A COPY OF A BIRTH RECORD

-Enclose stamped, self-addressed envelope.

-Make check or money order payable to:
     NYC Dep't. of Records.

FEES

$5.00   Search of birth records in one year and one
         City/Borough for one name and issuance of
         one certified copy or "not found statement."
$1.00   Per additional year to be searched in one
         City/Borough for same name.
$1.00   Per additional City/Borough to be searched
         in one year for same name.
$1.00   Per additional copy of record.

PLEASE PRINT OR TYPE:

Last name on birth record	First name	Female/Male
Date of birth Month Day Year	Certificate number, if known	
Place of birth--if at home, house number and street	City/Borough	
Father's name, if known	Mother's name, if known	
Your relationship to person listed above	Number of copies requested	
Purpose for which this record will be used	Total fee enclosed	
Your name, please print	Signature	
Address		
City	State	Zip Code

MUNICIPAL ARCHIVES
Department of Records and Information Services

31 Chambers Street
New York, N.Y. 10007

(212) 566-5292
IDILIO GRACIA PENA, *Director*

APPLICATION FOR A COPY OF A DEATH RECORD

-Enclose stamped, self-addressed envelope.

-Make check or money order payable to:
     NYC Dep't. of Records.

FEES

$5.00   Search of death records in one year and one
        City/Borough for one name and issuance of
        one certified copy or "not found" statement.
$1.00   Per additional year to be searched in one
        City/Borough for same name.
$1.00   Per additional City/Borough to be searched
        in one year for same name.
$1.00   Per additional copy of record.

PLEASE PRINT OR TYPE:

Last name at time of death	First name	Female/Male
Date of death Month Day Year	Occupation	
Place of death	City/Borough	Age
Father's name, if known	Mother's name, if known	
Your relationship to decedent	Certificate no. if known	
Purpose for which this record will be used	Number of copies requested	
Your name, please print	Signature	
Address		
City	State	Zip Code

MUNICIPAL ARCHIVES
Department of Records and Information Services

31 Chambers Street
New York, N.Y. 10007

(212) 566-5292
IDILIO GRACIA PENA, *Director*

APPLICATION FOR A COPY OF A MARRIAGE RECORD

-Enclose stamped, self-addressed envelope.

-Make check or money order payable to:
    NYC Dep't. of Records.

FEES

$5.00   Search of marriage records in one year and
        one City/Borough for one Groom and/or Bride
        and issuance of one certified copy or
        "not found" statement.
$1.00   Per additional year to be searched in one
        City/Borough for same names.
$1.00   Per additional City/Borough to be searched
        in one year for same names.
$1.00   Per additional copy of record.

PLEASE PRINT OR TYPE:

Last name of Groom	First name of Groom
Last name of Bride (Maiden name)	First name of Bride

Date of marriage

Month	Day	Year(s)	
Place of marriage		City/Borough	

Your relationship to people named above	Certificate no. if known
Purpose for which this record will be used	Number of copies requested

Your name, please print	Signature

Address

City	State	Zip Code

General Information and Application for Genealogical Services

If the requested record is needed to settle an estate, a letter of authorization is required from the executor, public administrator or attorney for the estate. The relationship of the person of record to the estate must be provided.

VITAL RECORDS COPIES CANNOT BE PROVIDED FOR COMMERCIAL PURPOSES.

1. FEE - $6.00 per search and copy or $6.00 per search and notification of no-record for EACH record requested.
2. Original records of births, deaths and marriages for the entire state begin with 1880, EXCEPT for records filed in Albany, Buffalo and Yonkers prior to 1914. Applications for these cities should be made directly to the local office.
3. We do not have ANY records for the city of New York, except for Queens and Richmond Counties between 1880 and 1898.
4. Please read Administrative Rule 35.5 on the reverse side of this sheet which specifies years available for genealogical research.

To insure a complete search, provide as much information as possible. Please complete for type of record requested, birth, death OR marriage.

Birth

Name at Birth _____

Date of Birth _____

Place of Birth _____

Father's Name _____

Mother's Maiden Name _____

Birth

Name at Birth _____

Date of Birth _____

Place of Birth _____

Father's Name _____

Mother's Maiden Name _____

Marriage

Name of Bride _____

Name of Groom _____

Date of Marriage _____

Place of Marriage and/or License _____

Marriage

Name of Bride _____

Name of Groom _____

Date of Marriage _____

Place of Marriage and/or License _____

Death

Name at Death _____

Date of Death _____ Age at Death _____

Place of Death _____

Names of Parents _____

Name of Spouse _____

Death

Name at Death _____

Date of Death _____ Age at Death _____

Place of Death _____

Names of Parents _____

Name of Spouse _____

For what purpose is information required? _____

What is your relationship to person whose record is requested? _____

In what capacity are you acting? _____

SIGNATURE OF APPLICANT _____ DATE _____

ADDRESS _____

Send record to: (please print)

Name _____

Address _____

City _____ State _____ Zip Code _____

If requesting birth and marriage records, please sign the following statement:

To the best of my knowledge, the person(s) named in the application are deceased.

_____
SIGNATURE OF APPLICANT

APPENDIX B-7

REG-3
[illegible] **New Jersey State Department of Health**   APPLICATION FOR CERTIFIED COPY
                                                              OF VITAL RECORD

1 *VITAL RECORDS - JUNE, 1878 TO PRESENT*
    When the correct year of the event is supplied, the total fee (payable in advance) for a search is four dollars for each name for which a search must be made.
    Searches for more than one year cost one dollar for each additional year per name. If found, a certified copy will be forwarded at no additional cost. If not found,
    the fee will not be refunded. Additional copies may be ordered at this time at a charge of two dollars per copy. Specify the total number of copies requested.
2 *VITAL RECORDS - MAY, 1848 THROUGH MAY, 1878*
    These records have been transferred to the Archives Section, Division of Archives and Records Management, Department of State, CN 307, Trenton, NJ
    08625. Information as to fee schedules and how to obtain records from the Archives can be obtained from that Section.

Name of Applicant	Date of Application	**FOR STATE USE ONLY**
Street Address	Telephone No.	
City State	Zip Code	Certified Copy Completed

MAKE CHECK OR MONEY ORDER PAYABLE TO "STATE REGISTRAR."
DO NOT MAIL CASH OR STAMPS. PLEASE PRINT OR TYPE.

Amount Received

Why is a Certified Copy being requested?

- ☐ School/Sports
- ☐ Social Security ID Card
- ☐ Passport
- ☐ Driver License
- ☐ Genealogy
- ☐ Welfare
- ☐ Soc. Sec. Disability
- ☐ Other Soc. Sec. Benefits
- ☐ Medicare
- ☐ Veteran Benefits
- ☐ Other (specify) _____

Method of Payment
- ☐ Check
- ☐ Money Order
- ☐ Cash

Fee Due

▼ **FILL IN ONLY IF YOU WANT A BIRTH RECORD** ▼	No. Copies Requested	Amount Refunded	Date Refunded
Full Name of Child at Time of Birth		Received By	

Place of Birth (City, Town or Township)	County	Enclosures
Date of Birth	Name of Hospital, If Any	☐ REG-34 ☐ REG-36 ☐ REG-37 ☐ REG-38 ☐ X ☐ REG-30 ☐ REG-40 ☐ REG-41 ☐ C

Father's Name

SEARCH UNIT

Mother's Maiden Name

First Search

If Child's Name was Changed, Indicate New Name and How it was changed

REG-30

Alphabetical Second Check

▼ **FILL IN IF YOU WANT A MARRIAGE RECORD** ▼	No. Copies Requested	File Date on Record
Name of Husband		**PROCESSING UNIT**
Maiden Name of Wife		Places
Place of Marriage (City, Township)	County	W.W.
Date of Marriage or Close Approximation		Late Months

FOR ANY DEATH RECORD BEFORE 1901, A SEARCH CANNOT
BE MADE UNLESS YOU CAN NAME THE COUNTY WHERE THE
EVENT TOOK PLACE.

Second Check

CORRESPONDENCE/RECEPTION UNIT

▼ **FILL IN ONLY IF YOU WANT A DEATH RECORD** ▼	No. Copies Requested	REG-L7
Name of Deceased	Date of Death	Hospital Records
Place of Death (City, Town, Township, County)	Age at Death	REG-28
Residence if Different from Place of Death		Comments
Father's Name		
Mother's Maiden Name		

Address your envelope to:

   STATE REGISTRAR — SEARCH UNIT
   NEW JERSEY STATE DEPARTMENT OF HEALTH
   CN 360, TRENTON, NJ 08625-0360
   COMPLETE SECTION BELOW - TYPE OR PRINT CLEARLY!
   This will be used as a mailing label when we send the results of the search.

Name

Street Address

City   State   Zip Code

Dear Applicant:

The fee you paid is correct unless either block below is
checked.

☐ An additional fee of $_____ is due,
   since either additional years or another name was
   involved. Send it with this form.

☐ You are entitled to a refund check of $_____
   which will be forwarded within 45 days of _____
   If you have occasion to write about this matter, return
   this form with your letter.
                                    —STATE REGISTRAR

H-3460

VITAL RECORDS REQUEST
NEW JERSEY STATE ARCHIVES – DEPARTMENT OF STATE
185 West State Street CN 307, Trenton, New Jersey   08625
Telephone: (609) 292-6260

THE STATE ARCHIVES MAINTAINS ALL BIRTH, MARRIAGE AND DEATH RECORDS FROM MAY 1848 THROUGH MAY 1878. All requests for vital records information after May 1878 should be directed to: State Registrar - Search Unit, New Jersey State Department of Health, CN 360, Trenton, New Jersey 08625

THE ADVANCE FEE FOR EACH SEARCH TYPE (i.e. BIRTH, DEATH or MARRIAGE) IS FOUR DOLLARS ($4.00) PER NAME. IF BIRTH, DEATH, AND MARRIAGE RECORDS ARE REQUESTED FOR ONE PERSON, THE TOTAL ADVANCE FEE WILL BE TWELVE DOLLARS (3 search types X $4.00 = $12.00). IF FOUND, A TYPED TRANSCRIPT WILL BE MAILED AT NO ADDITIONAL CHARGE. ALL FEES ARE NONREFUNDABLE, WHETHER OR NOT THE REQUESTED RECORDS ARE FOUND.

ADVANCE PAYMENT SHOULD BE IN THE FORM OF CHECK OR MONEY ORDER ONLY, PAYABLE TO: NEW JERSEY GENERAL TREASURY.

PLEASE PRINT OR TYPE

REQUESTOR NAME	TELEPHONE NUMBER	REQUEST DATE	
REQUESTOR ADDRESS (No. and Street)	CITY	STATE	ZIP CODE

COMPLETE FOR BIRTH RECORD ONLY

FULL NAME OF CHILD AT TIME OF BIRTH	BIRTH DATE
PLACE OF BIRTH (City, Town, Township)	COUNTY
FATHER'S NAME	MOTHER'S MAIDEN NAME

STATE USE ONLY

DATE RECEIVED

DATE RESEARCHED

AMOUNT RECEIVED

NOTES

COMPLETE FOR MARRIAGE RECORD ONLY

NAME OF HUSBAND	MAIDEN NAME OF WIFE
PLACE OF MARRIAGE (City, Township)	
COUNTY OF MARRIAGE (Searches between 1848-1864)	MARRIAGE DATE

COMPLETE FOR DEATH RECORD ONLY

DECEASED'S NAME	DATE OF DEATH
PLACE OF DEATH (City, Town, Township or County)	AGE AT DEATH
FATHERS NAME	
MOTHERS MAIDEN NAME	

APPENDIX C

SOUNDEX CODE SYSTEMS

		National Archives	HIAS	NYC Health Dept.	NYS Health Dept
1.	First letter of family name	Each code begins with the first letter of the surname.	Same as National Archives, except consonants that are similarly pronounced are underlined in this system: C, K filed under C E, I filed under E J, Y filed under J S, Z filed under S V, W filed under V	Same as HIAS.	Same as National Archives.
2.	Code next 3 consonants (do not include first letter of the surname.)	**Code** **Key letter or equivalent** 1 B, F, P, V 2 C, G, J, K, Q, S, X, Z 3 D, T 4 L 5 M, N 6 R	**Code** **Key Letter or equivalent** 1 B, F, P, V, W Remainder same as National Archives.	Same as National Archives.	Same as National Archives.
3.	Exceptions	A, E, I, O, U, Y, H, W are not coded.	A, E, I, O, U, Y, H are not coded. W is coded (See rule #2.)	Same as National Archives.	Same as National Archives.
		When double consonants or two key letters or equivalent appear together, the two are coded as one letter.	Same as National Archives. Also, if two such consonants are separated by an H, the second consonant is ignored. Three family names are arbitrarily assigned a coded number, regardless of spelling: Moskowitz M-212 Schwartz S-162 Horowitz H-613	Same as National Archives.	Same as HIAS but also if separated by W, ignore the second consonant.
		Names with prefixes such as *van, Von, de, le, Di, D', dela, or du,* may be coded both with or without the title or prefix.	Same as National Archives.	Same as National Archives.	Same as National Archives.
4.	Arrangement	Within each surname code, names are arranged alphabetically by the first name.	Same as National Archives.	Arranged by date of birth.	Same as National Archives.

The Soundex system used by the National Archives was patented by Robert C. Russell, April 2, 1918 (#1,261,167).

NEW YORK PUBLIC LIBRARY ANNEX - FOREIGN TELEPHONE DIRECTORIES

This is a copy of the "Foreign Telephone Book List" at the Annex. It is not complete; check at the information desk in the north hall (315) at the NYPL (42nd Street) for additional countries and years.

Note: all holdings are paper except as noted below.
*   microfilm and paper
**   only microfilm

COUNTRY	CITY	HOLDINGS
ARGENTINA	Buenos Aires	1918, 1921-1933, 1938, 1942, 1946-1952, 1955, 1957/58
AUSTRALIA	Adelaide	1931-1937
	Brisbane	1932-1938, 1947-1949, 1952-1954, 1956, 1957, 1959, 1960
	Melbourne	1931-1939, 1946-1961
	Perth	1936, 1939, 1947
	Sidney	1931, 1935, 1937-1939, 1946-1961
AUSTRIA	Vienna	1928-1930, 1932-1934, 1936-1937, 1938*, 1948-1961
BELGIUM	Brussels	1947-1962
BOLIVIA		Scattered years
BRAZIL	Rio de Janeiro	1918, 1920, 1931, 1935, 1939, 1942-1943, 1947-1949, 1951-1961
	Sao Paulo	1930, 1933-1934, 1939, 1943, 1945, 1947
CANADA	Calgary	1918-1921, 1923-1938, 1945, 1947, 1951, 1953-1956, 1960-1962
	Edmonton	1919-1921, 1923-1938, 1940, 1947-1955, 1961-1962
	Montreal	1911, 1913, 1915-1939, 1943-1962
	Ottawa	1919, 1927, 1929, 1938, 1940-1959
	Quebec	1913-1915, 1917, 1921, 1923-1937, 1943, 1948-1959, 1961
	Toronto	1912-1921, 1923-1930, 1932-1933, 1935-1962
	Winnipeg	1912, 1917-1938, 1940, 1943-1962
CHILE	Santiago	1924, 1927, 1932-1937, 1939, 1946-1948, 1952, 1954, 1959, 1961-1962
CHINA	Hong Kong	1938, 1947-1950, 1954-1962
	Shanghai	1928, 1930, 1932-1939
COLUMBIA	Bogota	1961-1962
COSTA RICA	San Jose	1960-1961
CUBA	Havana	1920, 1923-1933, 1935-1938, 1940, 1945, 1947-1949, 1951-1957, 1959
CYPRUS	Nicosia	1960
CZECHOSLOVAKIA	Prague	1932-1938, 1940, 1947, 1950, 1952, 1954
	Bohemia	1934-1935, 1935-1936, 1936-1937, 1937-1938
	Moravia/Silesia	1932, 1933, 1936
	Slovakia/Russian Lower Carpathia	1934-1935
DENMARK	Copenhagen	1911, 1917-1919, 1928-1938, 1940-1947, 1949-1963
EGYPT	Cairo	1935-1937, 1957
	Port Said	1932-1935
FINLAND	Helsingfors	1948, 1952-1954, 1956
	Helsinki	1957-1959, 1961-1962
FRANCE	Paris	1914, 1923-1924, 1926-1938, 1946-1961
GERMANY	Berlin	1913, 1926-1935*, 1937-1938*, 1952-1963
	Dusseldorf	1931-1936, 1959-1960
	Frankfurt	1928-1937
	Hamburg	1927, 1930-1935
	Leipzig	1932-1934, 1936
	Munchen	1932-1937
	Stuttgart	1936
GREAT BRITAIN	London	1927-1962 (also Northern Ireland, Scotland, South Wales)

COUNTRY	CITY	HOLDINGS
HUNGARY	Budapest	1913, 1928-1933, 1934*, 1936*, 1937, 1938*, 1940*, 1947-1950, 1954
INDIA	Bombay	1923, 1934-1939, 1946, 1948-1949, 1951, 1953-1956, 1960-1961
	Calcutta	1934-1939, 1941, 1952-1953, 1956, 1960-1961
INDONESIA	Bandung	1959
IRAQ	Baghdad	1948
IRELAND	Dublin	1929-1938, 1945-1948, 1952-1961
ITALY	Lazia	1953-1960
	Milano	1931-1934, 1948-1962
	Rome	1932, 1945-1951, 1959-1960
JAMAICA		1961-1962
KENYA		1961-1962
LITHUANIA	Kaunas	1937**
	Various places	1932-1937**
MALAYA		1961-1962
MEXICO	Mexico City	1928-1936, 1942-1961
NETHERLANDS	Amsterdam	1929-1939, 1947-1961
	Hague	1947-1948, 1950, 1953-1960
	Rotterdam	1953-1961
NETHERLANDS WEST INDIES	Aruba	1960
	Curacao	1960
NEW GUINEA		1960
NEW ZEALAND	Wellington	1946, 1948, 1950, 1952-1954, 1956, 1961
NORTHERN RHODESIA		1961-1962
NORWAY	Oslo	1928, 1937, 1946, 1949
NYASALAND		1961-1962
PAKISTAN	Karachi	1951, 1955, 1957
PANAMA	Panamy Y Colon	1960-1961
PARAGUAY		1958
PERU	Lima	1921, 1932-1938, 1946-1949, 1953, 1961-1962
PHILLIPINES	Cebu	1933, 1935-1938, 1960
	Luzon	1933, 1935-1938
	Manila	1929-1950
POLAND	Warsaw	1931-1935*, 1935-1936, 1936-1937*, 1934-1940
	All Districts except Warsaw	1936*-1937
PORTUGAL	Lisbon	1933, 1935-1937, 1947-1949, 1951-1962
PUERTO RICO	San Juan	1934, 1961-1962
SOUTH AFRICA	Johannesburg	1928
SOUTHERN RHODESIA		1961-1962
SPAIN	Barcelona	1926-1962
	Madrid	1932-1935, 1947-1960
SWEDEN	Stockholm	1923, 1928-1937, 1941-1961
UGANDA		1961-1962
URUGUAY		1920, 1932-1933, 1947-1948, 1958
VENEZUELA	Caracas	1953-1954, 1955
YUGOSLAVIA	Belgrade	1934, 1955

NEW YORK PUBLIC LIBRARY MICROFORMS DIVISION
CITY DIRECTORIES (OTHER THAN NYC)

City	Years	City	Years	City	Years
Akron, OH	1859-1901	Galena, IL	1854-1860	Mobile, AL	1837-1901,
Albany, NY	1813-1901	Galveston, TX	1856-1902		1906-1935
Alton, IL	1858	Geneva, NY	1857-1858	Moline, IL	1855-1859
Atchinson, KS	1859-1861	Georgia, Regional	1850	Monongahela, PA	1859
Atlanta, GA	1859-1935	Gloucester, MA	1860	Montana Terr	1868-1879
Auburn, NY	1857-1860	Grand Rapids, MI	1859-1901	Morrisania, NY	1853
Augusta, GA	1841-1859	Great Falls, NH	1848	Mt. Vernon, OH	1858-1859
Austin, TX	1857	Greene Co., AL	1855-1856	Muscatine, IA	1856-1860
Baltimore, MD	1752-1935	Greenpoint, NY	1854	Nashua, NH	1841-1858
Bangor, ME	1834-1860	Hamilton, OH	1858-1859	Nashville, TN	1853-1935
Belleville, IL	1860	Harrisburg, PA	1839-1901	Nevada City, CA	1856
Beloit, WS	1858	Hartford, CT	1799-1935	Nevada Territory	1862-1882
Biddeford, ME	1856-1857	Haverhill, MA	1853-1860	New Albany, IN	1856-1860[k]
Binghamton, NY	1857-1860	Henry Co., IA	1859-1860	Newark, NJ	1835-1934[dl]
Boston, MA	1789-1935	Hudson, NY	1851-1857[b]	New Bedford, MA	1836-1859
Bridgeport, CT	1855-1858	Illinois	1847-1860	New Brunswick, NJ	1855
Brighton, MA	1850	Indiana	1858-1861	Newburgh, NY	1856-1861
Buffalo, NY	1828-1935	Indianapolis, IN	1855-1901	Newburyport, MA	1849-1860
Bureau Co., IL	1858-1859	Iowa	1846-1857	New England	1849-1860[m]
Burlington, IA	1856-1859	Iowa City, IA	1857	New Hampshire	1849
Burlington, VT	1865-1901	Jackson, MS	1860	New Haven, CT	1840-1931
Cambridge, MA	1847-1860	Janesville, WI	1858-1860[c]	New Ipswich, NH	1858
Camden, NJ	1860	Jefferson Co., IN	1859	New Jersey, Region	1850-1851[n]
Camden, SC	1816-1824	Jersey City, NJ	1852-1901[d]	New London, CT	1855-1860
Charleston, SC	1785-1901	Joliet, IL	1872-1902[e]	New Orleans, LA	1805-1901[h]
Charlestown, MA	1831-1860	Kansas City, MO	1849-1901	Newport, RI	1856-1858
Chattanooga, TN	1871-1881	Keene, NH	1827-1830	New York State	1842-1859
Chelsea, MA	1847-1860	Kenosha, WI	1858	Norfolk, VA	1801-1901
Chester, PA	1859-1860	Kentucky	1859-1860	Norristown, PA	1860-1861
Chicago, IL	1839-1929	Keokuk, IA	1854	Norwich, PA	1846-1860
Chillicothe, OH	1855-1859	Kingston, NY	1857-1858	Oakland, CA	1869-1881
Cincinnati, OH	1819-1935	Lafayette, IN	1858-1859	Ogdensburg, NY	1857
Circleville, OH	1859	Lancaster, PA	1843-1857	Ohio, Regional	1853-1861
Clarksville, TN	1859-1860	Lancaster Co., PA	1859-1860	Omaha, NE	1866-1935
Cleveland, OH	1837-1935	Lawrence, MA	1848	Oshkosh, WI	1857
Clinton, MA	1856	Lawrenceburgh, IN	1859-1860	Oswego, NY	1852-1859[b]
Columbia, SC	1859-1860	Leavenworth, KS	1860-1861	Paterson, NJ	1855-1935
Columbus, GA	1859-1860	Lexington, KY	1806,1818,	Pawtucket, RI	1857-1858[ao]
Columbus, OH	1843-1935		1864-1939	Pennsylvania	1844-1860
Concord, NH	1830-1860	Little Rock, AR	1871-1902	Peoria, IL	1844-1920
Connecticut	1849-1859	Logansport, IN	1859-1860	Peterborough, NH	1830
Dallas, TX	1875-1901	Los Angeles, CA	1872-1901	Petersburg, VA	1859[lp]
Davenport, IA	1855-1881	Louisville, KY	1832-1901	Philadelphia, PA	1785-1901[lqr]
Dayton, OH	1850-1902	Lowell, MA	1832-1901	Pittsburgh, PA	1760-1901[fh]
Delaware, OH	1859	Luneburgh, MA	1834	Pittsfield, MA	1859-1860
Denver, CO	1859-1928	Lynn, MA	1832-1858	Plymouth, MA	1846-1860
Des Moines	1866-1901	Madison, IN	1859-1860[fg]	Portland, ME	1823-1935
Detroit, MI	1857-1902	Madison, WI	1855-1859	Portland, OR	1863-1935
Dorchester, MA	1850	Maine	1849-1856	Portsmouth, NH	1821-1861
Dover, NH	1830-1859	Manchester, NH	1844-1901	Portsmouth, OH	1858-1859[fh]
Dubuque, IA	1858-1859	Mansfield, OH	1858-1859	Poughkeepsie, NY	1843-1860
East, The	1846	Marietta, OH	1860-1861	Providence, RI	1824-1902
East Boston, MA	1848-1852	Marysville, CA	1853-1858	Quincy, IL	1855-1860
Elmira, NY	1857-1860	Massachusetts	1850-1859	Racine, WI	1850-1859
Erie, PA	1853-1902	Medford, MS	1849	Randolph, IL	1859
Erie Co, PA	1859-1860	Memphis, TN	1849-1901[h]	Reading, PA	1806-1901[s]
Essex Co, NJ	1859-1860	Michigan, Regional	1856-1860	Rhode Island	1849
Evansville, IN	1858-1901	Middletown, NY	1857-1858	Richmond, IN	1857-1861
Fall River, MA	1853-1901[a]	Milford, MA	1856-1859	Richmond, VA	1819-1935
Fitchburg, MA	1847-1860	Milwaukee, WI	1847-1935	Rochester, NY	1827-1901[b]
Fond du Lac, WI	1857-1858	Mineral Point, WI	1859	Rock County, WS	1857-1858
Fort Wayne, IN	1858-1879	Minneapolis, MN	1865-1935[fi]	Rockford, IL	1857-1860
Fort Worth, TX	1877-1878	Mississippi Valley	1844	Rock Island, IL	1855-1859[t]
Frederick, MD	1859-1860	Missouri, Regional	1860[j]	Rome, NY	1857-1860

Roxbury, MA	1847-1860	Southbridge, MA	1854	Washington, DC	1822-1926
Saco, ME	1849[u]	Springfield, IL	1855-1860	Watertown, NY	1840-1855
Sacramento, CA	1851-1881[v]	Springfield, MA	1845-1861	Waukesha, WI	1858
St. Anthony, MN	1859-1860	Springfield, OH	1852-1860	Westchester, NY	1861
St. Louis, MO	1821-1935[fhj]	Steubenville, OH	1856-1857	West, The	1837
St. Paul, MN	1856-1901	Stockton, CA	1852-1856	Westchester, PA	1857
Salem, MA	1837-1859	Syracuse, NY	1851-1901	Western Reserve	1852
Salt Lake City, UT	1867-1901	Taunton, MA	1850-1859	Wheeling, WV	1839-1851[fhp]
San Antonio, TX	1877-1902	Tennessee	1860[w]	Whitewater, WI	1858
Sandusky, OH	1855-1858	Terre Haute, IN	1858-1860	Will County, IL	1859
San Francisco, CA	1850-1935	Toledo, OH	1858-1902	Williamburgh, NY	1847-1854
Savannah, GA	1848-1901	Topeka, KS	1868-1880	Wilmington, DE	1814, 1845-1901
Schenectady, NY	1841-1861	Trenton, NJ	1844-1859	Wisconsin	1857-1859
Scranton, PA	1861-1901	Troy, NY	1829-1902[b]	Worcester, MA	1828-1901
Seattle, WA	1872-1901	Utica, NY	1817-1901[b]	Wythe County, VA	1857
Shelbyville, IN	1860-1861	Vermont	1849-1860[sx]	Yonkers, NY	1859-1860
Somerville, MA	1851	Vicksburg, MS	1860[hy]	Zanesville, OH	1851-1861[f],
South, The	1854	Vincennes, IN	1891-1892[z]		1864-1865[z]
South Boston, MA	1852	Virginia	1852[l]		

a) For 1844-1845, see Providence, RI
b) For 1842-1843, see New York State
c) For 1857-1858, see Rock County, WI
d) For 1859, see Essex County, NJ
e) For 1859-1860, see Will County, Il
f) For 1837, see The West
g) For 1841, see Pittsburgh, PA
h) For 1844, see Mississippi Valley
i) For 1859-1860, see St. Anthony, MN
j) For 1854-1855, see Illinois
k) For 1836, 1845-1846, 1848, see Louisville, KY
l) For 1851, see Delaware
m) For 1835, see Massachusetts
n) For 1860, see Newark, NJ
o) For 1855-1856, see Providence, RI
p) For 1852, see Virginia
q) For 1845, see New York, NY
r) For 1853, see Lancaster, PA
s) For 1856, see New England Business Directory
t) For 1856, 1858, 1860, see Davenport, IA
u) For 1856, 1857, see Biddeford, ME
v) For 1850, 1859, see San Francisco, CA
w) For 1854, see The South
x) For 1860, see New England Business Directory
y) For 1858, see New Orleans, LA
z) *ZAN-G207

APPENDIX F

NEW YORK PUBLIC LIBRARY ANNEX
SELECTED U.S. AND FOREIGN NEWSPAPERS

This is a selected list of Annex holdings. The years listed do not necessarily represent a complete year's worth of the paper. Researchers should call to verify titles and dates before going to the Annex.

*   Gaps exist
**   Located in the Schomburg Center

STATE/COUNTRY	CITY	NEWSPAPER	HOLDINGS
U.S. NEWSPAPERS:			
Alabama	Birmingham	*Birmingham News*	1966-
Alaska	Anchorage	*Anchorage Times*	1962-
Alaska	Juneau	*Southeast Alaska Empire*	1958-
Alaska	Fairbanks	*Tundra Times*	1962-1974
Arizona	Phoenix	*Arizona Republic*	1968-
Arkansas	Little Rock	*Arkansas Gazette*	1968-
California	Los Angeles	*Los Angeles Times*	1958-
California	San Francisco	*San Francisco Chronicle*	1865-
Colorado	Denver	*Denver Post*	1969-1973
Colorado	Denver	*Rocky Mountain News*	1958-1968
Connecticut	Hartford	*Hartford Courant*	1967-1976
D.C.	Washington	*Evening Star*	1852-1981
D.C.	Washington	*Washington Post*	1958-
Florida	Miami	*Miami Herald*	1957-
Georgia	Atlanta	*Atlanta Constitution*	1945-
Hawaii	Honolulu	*Honolulu Star Bulletin*	1959-
Illinois	Chicago	*Chicago Tribune*	1947-
Indiana	Indianapolis	*Indianapolis Star*	1967-
Iowa	Des Moines	*Des Moines Register*	1968-
Kansas	Witchita	*Witchita Eagle Beacon*	1969-
Kentucky	Louisville	*Courier-Journal*	1967-
Louisiana	New Orleans	*Times-Picayune*	1958-
Maine	Portland	*Portland Press Herald*	1969-
Maryland	Baltimore	*Sun*	1837-
Maryland	Silver Spring	*National Observer*	1962-1977
Massachusetts	Boston	*Christian Science Monitor*	1908-
Massachusetts	Boston	*Boston Globe*	1873-1878, 1972-
Massachusetts	Boston	*Boston Herald*	1894-1905, 1952-1967
Massachusetts	Boston	*Boston Herald Traveler*	1967-1972
Michigan	Detroit	*Detroit News*	1945-
Minnesota	Minneapolis	*Minneapolis Star Tribune*	1967-
Mississippi	Jackson	*Clarion Ledger*	1967-
Missouri	St. Louis	*St. Louis Post Dispatch*	1939-
Montana	Great Falls	*Great Falls Tribune*	1969- *
Nebraska	Omaha	*Omaha World Herald*	1969-
New Hampshire	Manchester	*Manchester Union Leader*	1971-
New Jersey	Newark	*Star Ledger*	1972-
New Jersey	Newark	*Evening News*	1958-1972 *
New Mexico	Albuquerque	*Albuquerque Journal*	1969- *
New York	Albany	*Albany Times Union*	1968-
New York	Rochester	*Democrat and Chronicle*	1969-
North Carolina	Charlotte	*Charlotte Observer*	1969-
North Dakota	Fargo	*Forum*	1971-
Ohio	Cincinnati	*Cincinnati Enquirer*	1968-
Ohio	Cleveland	*Plain Dealer*	1965-
Oklahoma	Oklahoma City	*Daily Oklahoman*	1969-
Oregon	Portland	*Oregonian*	1958-
Pennsylvania	Philadelphia	*Philadelphia Inquirer*	1860-1876, 1942-
Pennsylvania	Pittsburgh	*Pittsburgh Press*	1967- *
Puerto Rico	San Juan	*El Mundo* (Spanish)	1962-1982
Puerto Rico	San Juan	*El Imparcial*	1962-1973
Rhode Island	Providence	*Providence Journal*	1969-

STATE/COUNTRY	CITY	NEWSPAPER	HOLDINGS
Rhode Island	Providence	*Providence Journal*	1969-
South Carolina	Charleston	*News & Courier*	1968- *
South Dakota	Sioux Falls	*Argus Leader*	1971-
Tennessee	Nashville	*Tennessean*	1968-
Texas	Dallas	*Dallas Morning News*	1958-
Texas	Houston	*Houston Post*	1969-
Utah	Salt Lake City	*Deseret News*	1968- *
Vermont	Burlington	*Burlington Free Press*	1971-
Virginia	Richmond	*Times-Dispatch*	1966-
Washington	Seattle	*Seattle Times*	1966-
West Virginia	Charleston	*Charleston Gazette*	1969-
Wisconsin	Milwaukee	*Milwaukee Journal*	1966-1973

FOREIGN NEWSPAPERS:

STATE/COUNTRY	CITY	NEWSPAPER	HOLDINGS
Albania	Tirana	*Bashkimi*	1956-1976
Argentina	Buenos Aires	*La Prensa*	1869-1950, 1956-
Argentina	Buenos Aires	*Herald*	1941-1973 (inc)
Australia	Sydney	*Sydney Morning Herald*	1940-
Australia	Canberra	*Australian*	1964-1975
Austria	Vienna	*Arbeiter Zeitung*	1907-1934, 1969-
Belgium	Brussels	*Le Soir*	1949-
Brazil	Sao Paulo	*O Estado De Sao Paulo*	1875-1939, 1968-
Canada	Vancouver	*The Sun*	1966- *
Canada	Montreal	*Montreal Star*	1940-1979
Canada	Saskatoon	*Western Producer*	1937-1973
Canada	Toronto	*Globe and Mail*	1966-1976
Ceylon	Colombo	*Ceylon Daily News*	1966-1972
Chile	Santiago	*El Mercurio*	1915-1917, 1944-1947, 1969-1972
Columbia	Bogota	*El Tiempo*	1968-
Costa Rica	San Jose	*La Prensa Libre*	1969-1981, 1987-
Cuba	Havana	*Granma* (formerly *Revolucion*)	1959-
Denmark	Copenhagen	*Berlingske Tidende*	1935-1941, 1949-
Dominican Republic	Santo Domingo	*El Caribe*	1969-1973
Egypt	Cairo	*Egyptian Gazette & Mail*	1968-
England	Leeds	*Yorkshire Eve Post*	1971- *
England	London	*The Observer*	1923- *
England	London	*The Observer* (Sunday Supplement)	1964-
England	London	*Sunday Times*	1822-
England	London	*Times*	1785-
England	London	*Daily Worker*	1942-1966
England	London	*Morning Star*	1967- *
England	Manchester	*The Guardian*	1929-
Ethiopia	Addis Ababa	*Ethiopian Herald*	1971-
Finland	Helsinki	*Helsingin Sanomat*	1956-
France	Paris	*Le Figaro*	1880-1940, 1944-
France	Paris	*Le Monde*	1944- *
France	Paris	*International Herald Tribune*	1887-
France	Paris	*Le Combat*	1944-1974
France	Paris	*L'Humanité*	1906, 1912-1940*, 1944-1948,1968-
France	Paris	*Le Peuple*	1921-1940, 1944-1977 1980-1986
Germany	East Berlin	*Neues Deutschland*	1969-
Germany	West Berlin	*Der Tagesspiegel*	1949- *
Germany	Frankfurt	*Allgemeine Zeitung*	1900-1943, 1967- *
Germany	Hamburg	*Die Welt*	1969-
Greece	Athens	*Io Vema*	1969-
Guatemala	Guatemala City	*Diario de Centro America*	1947-1972, 1980-
India	Calcutta	*Amrita Bazar Patrika*	1962- *
India	Calcutta	*Statesman*	1926- *
India	Bombay	*Times of India*	1919-1950
India	New Delhi	*Times of India*	1973-
Indonesia	Jakarta	*Indonesian Observer*	1965-
Iran	Tehran	*Tehran Journal*	1971-1979
Iraq	Baghdad	*Baghdad Observer*	1964-1974
Ireland	Dublin	*Irish Times*	1924-
Italy	Turin	*La Stampa*	1976-
Italy	Milan	*Corriere Della Sera*	1917-1920, 1922-1933, 1938-1975

STATE/COUNTRY	CITY	NEWSPAPER	HOLDINGS
Japan	Tokyo	*Manichi Daily News*	1956-1962
Kenya	Nairobi	*Daily Nation*	1969-1973
Korea	Seoul	*Korea Times*	1964-
Mexico	Mexico City	*El Universal*	1933- *
Netherlands	Rotterdam	*NRC Handelsblad*	1938-1973
New Zealand	Auckland	*New Zealand Herald*	1966- *
Northern Ireland	Belfast	*Belfast Telegraph*	1970- *
Norway	Oslo	*Aftenposten*	1915-1941* 1949-1983
Pakistan	Karachi	*Dawn*	1943-1947, 1951-1973
Panama	Panama City	*Estrella de Panama*	1858-1909, 1971-1972
Peru	Lima	*El Comercio*	1969-1973
Philippines	Manila	*Bulletin Today*	1973-
Portugal	Lisbon	*O Seculo*	1969-1977
Rhodesia	Salisbury	*Rhodesia Herald***	1969-
Scotland	Edinburgh	*Scotsman*	1933-
Singapore	Singapore	*Straits Times*	1956-
South Africa	Cape Town	*Cape Times*	1913- *
Spain	Madrid	*El Pais*	1976-
Spain	Madrid	*ABC Madrid*	1956-1978
Sweden	Stockholm	*Svenska Dagblandet*	1969-
Switzerland	Geneva	*Journal de Geneve*	1976- *
Switzerland	Zurich	*Neue Zuercher Zeitung*	1900-1909, 1914-1950, 1954-
Thailand	Bangkok	*Bangkok Post*	1953- *
U.S.S.R.	Moscow	*Moscow News*	1930-1949, 1956-
Vatican	Vatican City	*L'Osservatore Romano*	1930-
Venezuela	Caracas	*El Nacional*	1968-
Vietnam, North	Hanoi	*Vietnam Courier*	1964-
Vietnam, South	Saigon	*Saigon Post*	1964-1975

This is not a complete list of Jewish cemeteries in the New York metropolitan area. There are numerous Jewish cemeteries in the Newark and Elizabeth, NJ area, as well as other Jewish cemeteries in Long Island, Staten Island, New Jersey, Westchester and southern Connecticut. Cong. Shearith Israel's first three cemeteries (pre-1850) are located in Manhattan.

Brooklyn (B), Queens (Q), Nassau (N) and Suffolk (S) - New York

Map #	
20	Acacia - 83-84 Liberty Ave., Ozone Park 11417 (Q)
19	Bayside - 80-35 Pitkin Ave., Ozone Park 11417 (Q)
24	Beth David - Elmont Rd., Elmont 11003 (N)
7	Beth El (New Union Field) - 80 Ave. & Cypress Hills St., Glendale 11385 (Q)
28	Beth Moses - Wellwood Ave., Pinelawn 11735 (S)
11	Beth Olom - Cypress Hills St., Brooklyn 11208 (B)
5	Hungarian - Cypress Ave. & Cypress Hills St., Ridgewood 11385 (Q)
33	Huntington - Old Country Rd., Huntington 11743 (S)
10	Knollwood - Cooper Ave. & Cypress Ave., Ridgewood 11385 (Q)
15	Linden Hill (Ahavath Chesed/Central Synagogue) - 52-22 Metropolitan Ave., Ridgewood 11385 (Q)
6	Machpelah - 82-30 Cypress Hills St., Glendale 11385 (Q)
21	Maimonides - 895 Jamaica Ave., Brooklyn (B) [Records at Maimonides, Elmont]
24	Maimonides - Elmont Rd., P.O. Box 125, Elmont 11003 (N)
19	Mokom Sholom - 80-07 Pitkin Ave., Ozone Park 11417 (Q)
23	Montefiore - 121-83 Springfield Blvd., St. Albans 11413 (Q)
25	Mt. Ararat - Babylon Rd., Farmingdale 11735 (S)
4	Mt. Carmel - Cypress Hills St., Glendale 11385 (Q)
2	Mt. Carmel (New) - Cypress Hills St. & Cooper Ave., Glendale 11385 (Q)
34	Mt. Golda - 500 Old Country Rd., Huntington 11743 (S)
17	Mt. Hebron - College Point Blvd. & Horace Harding Expwy., Flushing 11367 (Q)
22	Mt. Hope - 895 Jamaica Ave., Brooklyn (B) [Records at Maimonides, Elmont]
9	Mt. Judah - Cypress Ave., Ridgewood 11385 (Q)
14	Mt. Lebanon - 78-00 Myrtle Ave., Glendale 11385 (Q)
3	Mt. Neboh - 82-07 Cypress Hills St., Glendale 11385 (Q)
16	Mt. Zion - 59-63 54 Ave., Maspeth 11378 (Q)
26	New Montefiore - Wellwood Ave., Pinelawn 11735 (S)
12	Salem Field (Temple Emanu-El), 775 Jamaica Ave., Brooklyn 11208 (B)
11	Shearith Israel - Cypress Hills St., Brooklyn (B) [Records at 8 W. 70 St., New York 10023]
8	Union Field - Cypress Ave., Ridgewood 11385 (Q)
18	Washington - Bay Pkwy. & McDonald Ave., Brooklyn 11230 (B)
27	Wellwood - Wellwood Ave., Pinelawn 11735 (S)

Staten Island - New York

Map #	
29	Baron Hirsch - 1126 Richmond Ave. 10314
31	Mt. Richmond - 420 Clark Ave. 10306
30	Silver Lake - 926 Victory Blvd. 10301
32	United Hebrew - 122 Arthur Kill Rd. 10306

New Jersey (each is followed by name of county)

A	Arlington Jewish - North Arlington 07032 (Bergen)
B	Beth Abraham - East Brunswick 08816 (Middlesex)
D	Beth El - Forest Ave., Paramus (P.O. Box 329, Westwood 07675) (Bergen)
C	Beth Israel Mem. Park - U.S. Hwy. 1, Woodbridge 07095 (Middlesex)
D	Cedar Park - same as Beth El, Paramus
E	East Ridgelawn - Clifton 07012 (Passaic)
F	Floral Park - Rt. 130, Deans (Middlesex)
G	King Solomon Mem. Park - Dwasline Rd. & Allwood Rd., Clifton 07012 (Passaic)
H	Mt. Moriah - 685 Fairview Ave., Fairview 07022 (Bergen)
J	New Mt. Lebanon - Iselin 08830 (Middlesex)
K	New Mt. Zion - Lyndhurst 07071 (Bergen)
F	New Washington - Deans (Middlesex)
L	Riverside - Saddle Brook (P.O. Box 177, Rochelle Park 07662) (Bergen)

Westchester (W) and Putnam (P) Counties - New York

M	Kensico - Valhalla 10595 (W)
N	King David - Adams Corners 10579 (P)
O	Mt. Eden - 20 Commerce St., Valhalla 10595 (W)
P	Mt. Hope - Saw Mill River Rd., Hastings 10706 (W)
Q	Mt. Pleasant - 80 Commerce St., Hawthorne 10532 (W)
M	Sharon Gardens - same as Kensico
R	Temple Israel - Mt. Hope, Hastings 10706 (W)
S	Westchester Hills (Free Synagogue) - Saw Mill River Rd., Hastings 10706 (W)

NEW YORK AREA JEWISH CEMETERIES

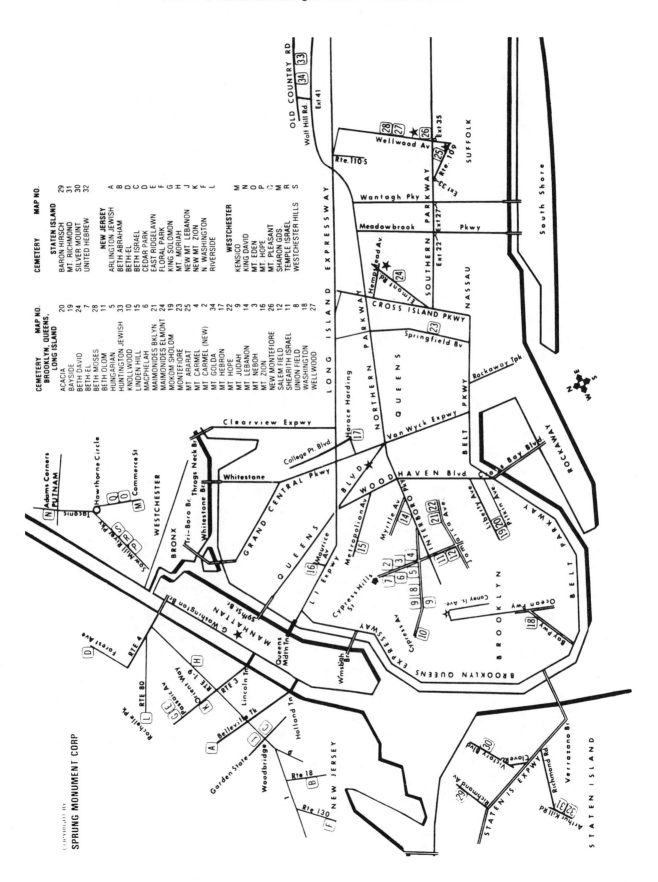

CEMETERY	MAP NO.
BROOKLYN, QUEENS,	
LONG ISLAND	
ACACIA	20
BAYSIDE	19
BETH DAVID	24
BETH-EL	7
BETH MOSES	28
BETH OLOM	11
HUNGARIAN	5
HUNTINGTON JEWISH	33
KNOLLWOOD	10
LINDEN HILL	15
MACPHELAH	6
MAIMONIDES BKLYN	21
MAIMONIDES ELMONT	24
MOKOM SHOLOM	19
MONTEFIORE	23
MT ARARAT	25
MT CARMEL	4
MT CARMEL (NEW)	2
MT GOLDA	34
MT HEBRON	17
MT HOPE	22
MT JUDAH	9
MT LEBANON	14
MT NEBOH	3
MT ZION	16
NEW MONTEFIORE	26
SALEM FIELD	12
SHEARITH ISRAEL	11
UNION FIELD	8
WASHINGTON	18
WELLWOOD	27

CEMETERY	MAP NO.
STATEN ISLAND	
BARON HIRSCH	29
MT. RICHMOND	31
SILVER MOUNT	30
UNITED HEBREW	32
NEW JERSEY	
ARLINGTON JEWISH	A
BETH ABRAHAM	B
BETH-EL	C
BETH ISRAEL	D
CEDAR PARK	D
EAST RIDGELAWN	E
FLORAL PARK	F
KING SOLOMON	G
MT. MORIAH	H
NEW MT LEBANON	J
NEW MT ZION	K
N. WASHINGTON	F
RIVERSIDE	L
WESTCHESTER	
KENSICO	M
KING DAVID	N
MT. EDEN	O
MT. HOPE	P
MT. PLEASANT	C
SHARON GDS.	M
TEMPLE ISRAEL	R
WESTCHESTER HILLS	S

391

NAME INDEX

Includes authors, editors, names in collections and names in titles of collections.

PLACE INDEX

Does not include places mentioned in Appendixes A, D, E and F.

SUBJECT INDEX

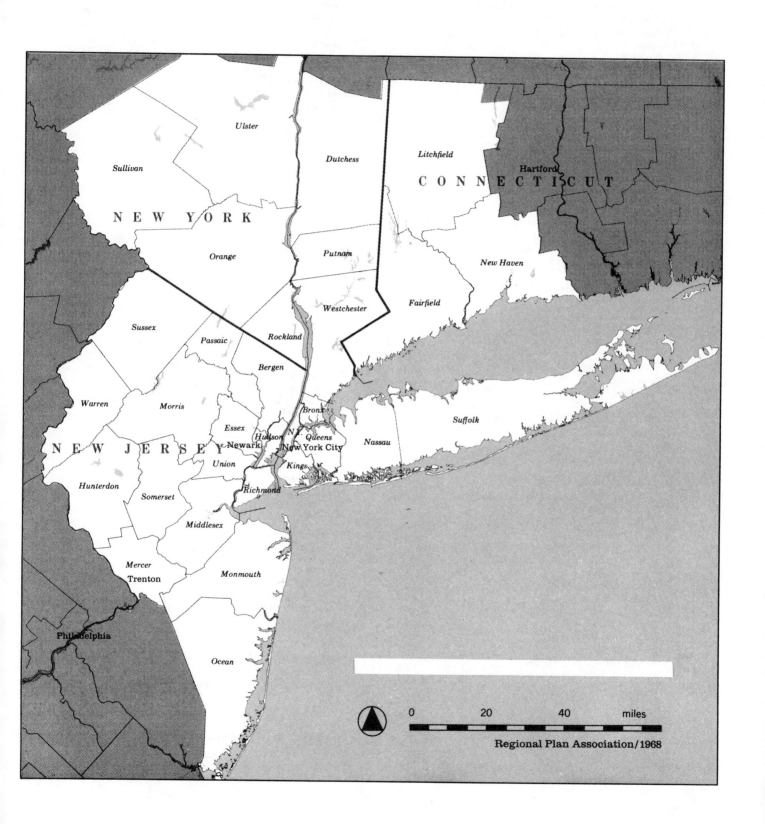

Sullivan

Ulster

NEW YORK

Dutchess

Litchfield

Hartford

CONNECTICUT

Orange

Putnam

New Haven

Sussex

Passaic

Westchester

Fairfield

Rockland

Warren

Morris

Bergen

Bronx

Suffolk

Essex

Hudson   N.

Queens

Nassau

NEW JERSEY   Newark

New York City

Hunterdon

Union

Kings

Somerset

Richmond

Middlesex

Mercer

Monmouth

Trenton

Philadelphia

Ocean

0   20   40   miles

Regional Plan Association / 1968